HISTORY
OF
LOUISIANA.

HISTORY

OF

LOUISIANA.

THE SPANISH DOMINATION.

BY

CHARLES GAYARRÉ.

WITH CITY AND TOPOGRAPHICAL MAPS OF THE
STATE, ANCIENT AND MODERN,

WITH

A BIOGRAPHY OF THE AUTHOR,

BY

GRACE KING.

BIBLIOGRAPHY

BY

WM. BEER,

LIBRARIAN NEW ORLEANS PUBLIC LIBRARY,

TOGETHER WITH AN EXHAUSTIVE INDEX.

FIFTH EDITION.

IN FOUR VOLUMES.

VOL. III.

A FIREBIRD PRESS BOOK

PELICAN PUBLISHING COMPANY
Gretna 1998

Entered according to Act of Congress in the year 1882
By Charles Gayarre

In the clerks office of the District Court of the United States for
the Southern District of New York.

Copyright 1903
by F. F. Hansell & Bro., Ltd

Reprinted 1965
by Pelican Publishing Company

Second printing—1974
ISBN 1-56554-645-7

Manufactured in the United States of America
Published by Pelican Publishing Company, Inc.
1000 Burmaster Street, Gretna, Louisiana 70053

TO

GEORGE BANCROFT,

The Friend

WHO ENCOURAGED HIS LABORS, AND

The Historian

WHOSE FAME IS THE PRIDE OF HIS COUNTRY

THIS WORK

IS GRATEFULLY AND RESPECTFULLY DEDICATED

BY THE AUTHOR.

CONTENTS.

CHAPTER I.
O'REILLY'S ADMINISTRATION.
1769 to 1770.

                                                                                    Page

O'Reilly's Administration—Organization of the Government—Oath of Office—O'Reilly's Proclamation—Duties and Jurisdiction of Public Officers—O'Reilly's Legislation—Its Effects on the Laws previously Existing—O'Reilly's Instructions to Commandants—O'Reilly's Enlightened Views on the Commercial Wants of the Colony—O'Reilly's Liberal Policy—Raising of the Louisiana Regiment—Inauguration of the Cabildo—Concessions of Vacant Lands—Regulations for Grants of Land—New Orleans—Its Annual Revenue—Commercial Regulations—The Capuchins and the Nuns—The French Black Code re-enacted—O'Reilly's Administration approved by the King—O'Reilly's Character, ... 1

CHAPTER II.
UNZAGA'S ADMINISTRATION.
1770 to 1776.

Unzaga's Administration—Commerce of the Colony—Disastrous Hurricane—Religious Quarrels—Father Dagobert—Character of Father Dagobert—Character of Father Génoveaux—Arrival of Spanish Capuchins—Father Cirilo's Despatches on the Clergy and Inhabitants of Louisiana—The Clergy of Louisiana in 1772—The Clergy of Louisiana in 1773—Unzaga's Despatch on the Quarrels of the Clergy—The Colony reconciled to the New Government—Its Interference between Debtors and Creditors—Power of granting Lands where Vested—Defensive Resources of the Colony—Unzaga desires his Recall—Unzaga recommends a Better Organization—End of Unzaga's Administration, ... 42

CHAPTER III.

GALVEZ' ADMINISTRATION.

1777 to 1783.

MIRÒ'S ADMINISTRATION.

1784 to 1785.

Galvez' Administration—Encouragement to Commerce and Agriculture—Joint Despatch of Villars and D'Aunoy—George Morgan's Letter to Galvez—Galvez provides for the Defence of the Colony—Views of Spain as to the American War in 1777—Galvez gives Assistance to the Americans—Captain Willing's Expedition—New Facilities granted to Commerce in 1778—Spanish Colonists from the Canary Islands—The English Trade excluded from the Colony—The Confiscation of Noyan's Estate—Other Colonists from the Canary Islands—Ravages of the Small-Pox and of Hurricanes—Spain declares War against England—Galvez' Military Preparations—Galvez' Address to the Louisianians—Galvez ready to attack the English—Departure of the Expedition—Fort Manchac carried by Storm—Siege of Baton Rouge—Baton Rouge and Natchez taken—Naval Exploit of Vincent Rieux—Good Behavior of the Militia—Good Behavior of the Blacks and Indians—Rewards granted by the Spanish Court—An Epic Poem by Julien Poydras—Galvez attacks Mobile—Surrender of Mobile—Galvez prepares to attack Pensacola—Sounding of the Pensacola Channel—The Spanish Admiral refuses to enter it—Galvez causes the Channel to be sounded—Heroism of Galvez—Siege of Pensacola—Blowing-up of a Redoubt—Capitulation of Pensacola—Insurrection and retaking of Fort Panmure—Retreat of the Insurgents from Natchez—Distress of the Insurgents—Martin Navarro's Circular—Answer of the Colonists—Privileges granted to the Colony—Father Cirilo made a Bishop—Treaty between Spain and other Powers—M'Gillivray the Half-Breed Indian—His Propositions and Disclosures to Spain—A Congress of the Indian Nations—Treaty of Spain with the Indians—Regulations for the Indian Trade—Extraordinary Severity of the Winter of 1784—Galvez Viceroy of Mexico—The Character of Galvez—Death of Galvez, ... 105

CHAPTER IV.

MIRÒ'S ADMINISTRATION.

1785 to 1789.

What is a Juez de Residencia?—Census of 1785—Arrival of Acadian Families—Respite granted to Debtors—Commerce of the Colony—Mirò's View on the same Subject—Navarro's Views on the same Subject—Navarro's Recommendations on the Subject—Royal Order as to the Natchez District in 1786—Mirò's Bando de Buen Gobierno—Arrival of Irish Priests—Navarro's Fears of the Americans—Defenceless State of the Colony—Encouragement to Emigrants—Commercial Distress of the Colony—Navarro's Advice to his Government—Navarro's Fears of American Ambition—Epidemics in the Colony—Mirò conciliates the Indians—Cost of Indian Friendship—Schemes to dismember the United States—Plans of Mirò and Gardoqui—Wilkinson's Visit to New Orleans—Wilkinson's Memorial—George Morgan, Leader of Emigrants—Mirò and Wower D'Argès—Mirò's Views on American Emigration—Mirò advocates Commercial Franchises—Mirò's Instructions to Grandpré—Oath imposed on Emigrants—Great Fire in New Orleans—Public Education in 1788—Spanish Intrigues with Wilkinson—Wilkinson's Letter to Mirò—Major Isaac Dunn—Alexander Leatt Bullit and Harry Innis—Daniel Clark, Wilkinson's Agent—Wilkinson's Flatboats—Spanish Loan to Wilkinson—M'Gillivray's Letter to Mirò—Intrigues in Cumberland District— Census of Louisiana in 1788—Navarro's Memorial—Spanish Intrigues in the West—Colonel Morgan's Memorial—Gardoqui's Letter to Major Dunn—

Page
Oliver Pollock and James Brown—Inundations in Louisiana
—Wilkinson's Intrigues—Col. Marshall and Col. Muter—
Caleb Wallace and Benjamin Sebastian—Intrigues in the
Kentucky Convention—Action of Wilkinson in that Body—
Wilkinson communicates his Views to Spain—Wilkinson's
Advice to Spain—Wilkinson's Apprehensions of Detection—
English Intrigues in the West—Wilkinson dupes Colonel
Connelly—Wilkinson denounces the French—Wilkinson's
Devotion to Spain—Gen. St. Clair's Letter to Major Dunn—
Wilkinson and James Brown—Gardoqui and Major Dunn—
Wilkinson denounces Colonel Morgan—Peter Paulus, Dorsey
and Paulin—Wilkinson's Letter to Gardoqui—Miró's Dealings with Peter Paulus—Miró's Despatch to his Government
—Miró's Instructions to Wilkinson — He recommends to reward Wilkinson, ... 167

CHAPTER V.

MIRÓ'S ADMINISTRATION.

1789 to 1791.

Governor Sevier's Letter to Gardoqui—Dr. James White's Letter to Miró—Miró's Answer—Districts of Miró and Frankland
—Miró and General Daniel Smith—Miró and Gardoqui at
Variance—Miró rebukes Colonel Morgan—Colonel Morgan's
Apology—Surveyor-General Thos. Hutchins—Pierre Foucher
and New Madrid—The Holy Inquisition—Father Antonio de
Sedella—The Cathedral in New Orleans—The South Carolina Company — Moultrie, Huger, Snipes, Washington—
Wilkinson's Advice to the S. C. Company—Sebastian begging Remuneration—Continuation of Wilkinson's Intrigues—
G. Nicholas, S. M'Dowell and Payton Short—Continuation of
Wilkinson's Intrigues — Wilkinson's Wish to become a
Spaniard—Moultrie's Letter to Wilkinson – Miró's Letter to
Wilkinson—Miró's Contemptuous Language—A Lesson to
Traitors—Miró's Distrust of Wilkinson—Sebastian, a Spy on
Wilkinson — Miró praising Wilkinson — James O'Fallon's
Letter to Miró—Plan of the South Carolina Company—
O'Fallon's Credentials—Scheme to set up an Independent
Government —Wilkinson's Opinion of O'Fallon — Miró's

Pag*

Cautious Reserve — Miró and the South Carolina Company—Miró's Suggestions—Spain and the Half-Breed M'Gillivray—The Cabildo's Memorial to the King—Apprehensions of an English War—Negotiations between Spain and the United States—Failure of Miró's Schemes—Revenue of Louisiana in 1790—Miró's Departure—Spanish Domination growing popular, ... 257

CHAPTER VI.

CARONDELET'S ADMINISTRATION.

1792 to 1797.

Carondelet's Administration—Factions in the Colony—Capture of Wm. Augustus Bowles—Life of Wm. Augustus Bowles—M'Gillivray's Death—M'Gillivray's Character—Extension of Commercial Franchises—Jacobinism in Louisiana—Carondelet's Defensive Measures—Fortifications at New Orleans—Spanish Alliance with the Indians—Carondelet's Policy and Views—Interference between Debtors and Creditors—Carondelet favors the Natchez District—Emancipation of Indian Slaves—Great Conflagration in New Orleans—Address of French Jacobins—Intrigues of Genet—Military Resources of the Colony—De la Chaise's Address—De la Chaise's Death—Renewal of Wilkinson's Schemes—Etienne de Boré, the First Sugar Planter—Carondelet's Proclamation—The Carondelet Canal—Encouragement to Emigrants—A Slave Conspiracy—The Madrid Treaty of 1795—Spanish Intrigues in the West—Power, the Agent of Carondelet—Carondelet's Propositions—Carondelet's Appeal to Wilkinson—Failure of Carondelet's Schemes — War declared against England—Gayoso and Ellicott—Gayoso's Subterfuges—Excitement in the Natchez District—The Committee of Public Safety—Gayoso's Concessions—Intendant Rendon's Despatch—Taking of the Balize by the French—Improvements in New Orleans—First Appearance of Yellow Fever—Bishop Penalvert's Despatch—General Victor Collot—The New Orleans Fortifications—The Inhabitants of the Illinois District—General Collot's Arrest—The End of Carondelet's Administration, ... 313

CHAPTER VII.

GAYOSO'S ADMINISTRATION.
1797 to 1799.

CASA CALVO'S ADMINISTRATION
1799 to 1801.

Page

Gayoso's Administration—Gayoso's Bando de Buen Gobierno—Illustrious Strangers in 1798—Duke of Orleans and his Brothers—Captain Guion at Natchez—Formation of the Mississippi Territory—Count Aranda's Prophecy—Reflections on General Wilkinson—Change in Gen. Wilkinson's Views—Daniel Clark appointed Consul—Intendant Morales and his Measures—Morales quarrels with Gayoso—Morales' Despatch—Morales' Complaints—Morales and Wilkinson—Fine imposed on Carondelet—Gayoso's Death—Census of Upper Louisiana—Casa Calvo appointed Governor—Bishop Penalvert's Complaints—Designs of the Americans on Louisiana—Bonaparte and Louisiana—Pontalba's Memoir—Treaty of St. Ildephonso, ... 386

CHAPTER VIII.

SALCEDO'S ADMINISTRATION.
1801 to 1803.

Rufus King's Despatch—Mr. Madison to Mr. Pinckney—Treaty between Spain and France—Livingston's Despatch to Rufus King—Revolutionary Spirit in the Colony—Dread of the Americans—Morales' Proclamation in 1802—Mr. King on the Cession of Louisiana—Livingston to Talleyrand—Livingston to Madison—Treaty of Amiens- Mr. Madison to Mr. Livingston—Mr. King and Lord Hawkesbury—Livingston's Exertions in France—His Views on the Cession of Louisiana—Mr. Livingston's Negotiations—Livingston and Joseph Bonaparte—Daniel Clarke and General Victor—Talleyrand's Assurances—The Right of Deposit at New Orleans—Madison's Despatch on Colonial Officers—The President to Congress—The President to Monroe—Debates in Congress—Mr. Ross in

the Senate—The House of Representatives to the Senate—
Mr. Ross's Resolutions—Mr. White's Speech in the Senate—
Mr. White in the Senate—Mr. Jackson in the Senate—Mr.
Cooke in the Senate—Mr. Morris in the Senate—Mr. Clinton
in the Senate—Mr. Breckenridge's Resolutions in the Senate
—Mr. Griswold's Resolutions in the House—Mr. Randolph's
Motion in the House—Mr. Madison's Despatch to Livingston
—Livingston's Propositions to Talleyrand—Credentials to
Monroe and Livingston—Mr. Livingston's Energetic Address
—Mr. King and Mr. Addington—Livingston's Dealings with
Talleyrand—Talleyrand shrugs his Shoulders—Barbé Mar-
bois's Walk in the Garden—The Struggle of the Diplomatists
—What is Louisiana worth?—The Negotiation fairly opened—
The Way to make a Bargain—Barbé Marbois' Diplomacy
—Bonaparte and his Advisers—M. Marbois in Cabinet Coun-
cil—Decrès in the Council—Bonaparte in the Council—Treaty
of Cession to the United States—Diplomatic Hand-Shaking—
Bonaparte's Prophecy, ... 447

CHAPTER IX.

SALCEDO'S ADMINISTRATION.

1801 to 1803.

Importance of the Cession—Talleyrand's Way of Explaining—
Was West Florida ceded?—French View of the Question—
Spain's Protest—Mr. Madison on the Protest—Casa Irujo to
Mr. Madison—Madison to Pinckney—The French Chargé on
the Protest—The President's Message in 1803—Debates in
Congress—Mr. White in the Senate—Mr. Pickering in the
Senate—Mr. Tracy in the Senate—Mr. Breckenridge in
the Senate—John Quincy Adams in the Senate—Mr. Gris-
wold in the House—Arguments of his Opponents—Thomas
Randolph in the House—Mr. Griswold in the House—Mr.
Dana in the House—Mr. Thomas Randolph in Reply—Mr.
John Randolph in the House—Resolutions adopted—What
Bills finally adopted, ... 527

xii CONTENTS.

CHAPTER X.
SALCEDO'S ADMINISTRATION.
1801 to 1803.

Page

Morales and Casa Irujo in Conflict—Intended Reorganization of the Colony—The Colonial Prefect Laussat—Fears of the Colonists—The French coldly received—Laussat on the State of the Colony—Laussat on the Right of Deposit—Laussat's Proclamation—Address of the Planters—Address of the Inhabitants of New Orleans—Spanish Commissioners' Proclamation—Laussat's Despatch to his Government—Laussat's Discontent—Quarrels between Burthe and Laussat—News of the Cession to the United States—Possession given to the French—Laussat's Proclamation—New Organization of the Colony—Withdrawal of the Spanish Troops—Laussat's Version of what happened—The First Mayor of New Orleans – Laussat's Preparations—Laussat's Embarrassment—Laussat and the Disaffected Militia—Laussat's Distrust of the Spaniards — Laussat's Excitement — Review of Laussat's Course—Splendid Festivities—Claiborne and Wilkinson's Joint Commission—The Americans take Possession—Claiborne's Proclamation—Situation of the Colony in 1803—Louisiana an Incumbrance to Spain—Concluding Remarks, 576

APPENDIX, ...   629

HISTORY OF LOUISIANA.

SPANISH DOMINATION.

CHAPTER I.

O'REILLY'S ADMINISTRATION.

1769 to 1770.

IN a preceding work on the French domination in Louisiana, I have related the cession of that colony to Spain in 1762, the attempt of that power to take possession of its new domain in 1766, the insurrection of the colonists in 1768, who drove away the Spaniards, the arrival of O'Reilly at New Orleans with overwhelming forces, to avenge the insult offered to his Catholic Majesty, the trial and punishment, on the 25th of October, 1769, of the leaders of the insurrection, and the final and complete occupation of the province by the Spaniards. The object of the present work is to record the history of Louisiana, as a Spanish colony, from 1769 to December 1803, when again her destinies were changed, and she was transferred to the United States of America.

O'Reilly, having secured the obedience of the new subjects of Spain, and having, by the terror which the blood he spilt had inspired, guarded against the repetition of any attempt, similar to the one which he had so severely repressed, showed his sense of security by sending away the greater portion of his troops; and, retaining only about 1,200 men, he proceeded to the immediate organization of the province in its military, judicial, and commercial departments. It will be recollected that Louis XV., in his letter to Governor D'Abbadie, after the cession of Louisiana to Spain, had expressed the wish that Louisiana should preserve the laws, institutions, and usages to which it had been so long accustomed, and had declared that he expected from the friendship of his cousin, the king of Spain, that, for the welfare and tranquillity of the colonists, that monarch should give to his officers in that province, such instructions as would permit the inferior judges, as well as those of the Superior Council, to administer justice according to the old laws, forms, and usages of the colony. Such, at first, had been the intention of his Catholic Majesty, but it was changed by the events which occurred in the colony in 1768; and, on the 25th of November, 1769, O'Reilly issued a proclamation,* in which he informed the colonists that, considering the part which the Superior Council had acted in the late disturbances, his Majesty thought proper to abolish that tribunal, and to establish in Louisiana that form of government and that system of administration, which had always succeeded in maintaining tranquillity and subordination in the domains of his Catholic Majesty, and which had secured for them a durable prosperity. Perhaps the king of Spain, who could not decently have disregarded the wishes expressed by the king of France in relation to his royal donation, was not backward to avail himself of the opportunity offered to him by the colonial insurrection, to refuse the continuance of the French organization, and to remodel it in the Spanish

---

* American State Papers, vol. i., p. 363. Miscellaneous.

ORGANIZATION OF THE GOVERNMENT.

style. It was natural for the statesmen of Spain, to think it sound policy to assimilate their new acquisition to their other possessions, and to efface all that might tend to keep up or revive in the colony the recollection and regrets of the past.

Thus O'Reilly, in his proclamation, announced that a Cabildo would be substituted for the Superior Council, and be composed of six perpetual regidores, two ordinary alcaldes, an attorney-general Syndic, and a clerk, over which body the governor would preside in person.*

The offices of perpetual regidor and clerk were acquired by purchase, and, for the first time, at auction. The purchaser was declared to have the faculty of transferring his office to a known and capable person, from whom he was permitted to require in payment one half of its appraised value; but one third only could be received on any subsequent mutation.

Among the Regidores were to be distributed the offices of Alferez Real, or Royal Standard Bearer, of Principal Provincial Alcalde, of Alguazil Mayor, or High Sheriff, of Depositary General, and of Receiver of Fines.

The ordinary Alcalde and the Attorney-General Syndic were to be chosen, on the first day of every year, by the Cabildo, and were always re-eligible, during the two first years, by a unanimous vote, and subsequently by a bare majority. At such elections the votes were openly given and recorded.

The ordinary alcaldes† were, individually, judges within the town of New Orleans, in civil and criminal cases, in which the defendant did not possess and claim the privilege of being tried by a military or ecclesiastical tribunal, in virtue of the *fuero militar*, or *fuero ecclesiastico*.‡

---

* Martin's History of Louisiana. † Ibid.
‡ *Fuero* means privilege—for instance, such as the *fueros*, or privileges granted

These alcaldes, in their chambers, and without any written proceedings, took cognizance of, and summarily decided upon, all judicial matters in which the value of the object in dispute did not exceed twenty dollars. In other cases, they sat in a hall destined for this purpose, and their proceedings were recorded by a notary and a clerk; and when the value of the object in dispute exceeded ninety thousand maravedis ($330 88c.), an appeal lay from their decision to the Cabildo.

This body did not examine itself the judgment appealed from, but chose two Regidores, who, with the Alcalde who had rendered it, revised the proceedings; and, if he and either of the Regidores approved the decision, it was affirmed.

The Cabildo sat every Friday, but the Governor had the power of convening it at any time. In his absence, one of the Alcaldes presided, and, immediately after the adjournment, two Regidores went to his house and informed him of what had been done.

The ordinary Alcaldes had the first seats in the Cabildo, immediately after the Governor; and, below them, the other members sat in the following order: the Alferez Real, or Royal Standard Bearer, the Principal Provincial Alcalde, the Alguazil Mayor, or High Sheriff, the Depositary General, the Receiver of Fines, the Attorney General Syndic, and the Clerk.

The office of Alferez Real was merely honorary, no other function being assigned to the incumbent but the bearing of the royal standard in a few public ceremonies. The Principal Provincial Alcalde had cognizance of offences committed out of the town; the Alguazil Mayor executed personally, or by his deputies, all process from the different tribunals. The Depositary General took

to particular provinces, to corporations, to the military, or to the ecclesiastical body, &c. &c.

charge of all moneys and effects placed in the custody of the law. The functions of the Receiver General of Fines are pointed out by his official denomination. The Attorney General Syndic was not, as may be supposed from his title, the prosecuting officer of the crown. His duty was to propose to the Cabildo such measures as the interest of the people required, and to defend their rights. This was a sort of imitation of the Roman tribune, and shows that, even in those days, and under that form of government which was reputed, not only absolute, but also tyrannic, the people, contrary to the general belief, were admitted to have rights, which were to be advocated and defended. Such at least was the theory, if the practice was different.

The Regidores, or municipal officers, received fifty dollars each, annually, from the treasury. The Principal Provincial Alcalde, the Alguazil Mayor, the Depositary General, the Receiver of Fines, and the Ordinary Alcaldes were entitled, as such, to fees of office.

In certain cases, there was an appeal from the highest tribunal of the province to the Captain General of the island of Cuba; from him, to the Royal Audience in St. Domingo, and thence to the Council of the Indies in Madrid.

The other officers of the province were a Captain General residing in Cuba, and to whom the Governor of the colony seems to have been subordinate; a Governor, clothed with civil and military powers; an Intendant, who had the administration of the revenues, and of all that concerned the naval and commercial department; a Contador, or Royal Comptroller; an Auditor of War and Assessor of Government, who was the legal adviser of the Governor; an Auditor of the Intendancy, who was the legal adviser of the Intendant. There being in those days, in Louisiana, a scarcity of men learned in the law, says Judge Martin in his History, the Auditor of War frequently acted as the counsel, not only of the Governor, but also of the Intendant, of the Cabildo, and of all the other public functionaries. There was a secretary of the governor and a secretary of the intendant, a treasurer of the province, a general storekeeper and a purveyor, a surveyor general, a harbor master, an interpreter of the French and English languages, an Indian interpreter, and three notaries public; besides, a collector, a comptroller, a cashier, an inspector, and a special notary for the custom-house.

Every officer who received a salary of more than three hundred dollars a year, was appointed by the crown; inferior offices to these were in the gift of the governor, or of the intendant, in their respective departments. The governor exercised judicial powers in civil and criminal matters throughout the province, as did the intendant with regard to all that appertained to the revenue and the admiralty; and as did the vicar general in the ecclesiastical department. These officers had, it seems, exclusive jurisdiction in their respective courts. The two former were assisted, as I have already said, by an auditor or assessor, whose opinion they might, on their own responsibility, disregard. It was one of the powers of the governor to make grants of land.

In every parish, says Judge Martin in his History, an officer of the army or militia, of no higher grade than a captain, was stationed as civil and military commandant. His duty was to attend to the police of the parish and preserve its peace. He was instructed to examine the passports of all travelers, and suffer no one to settle within his jurisdiction, without the license of the governor. He had jurisdiction over all civil cases in which the value of the object in dispute did not exceed twenty dollars; in more important cases, he received the petition and answer, took down the testimony, and transmitted the whole to the governor, by whom the record was sent to the proper tribunal. He had the power to punish slaves, and arrest and imprison free persons charged with offences, and was bound to transmit immediate information of the arrest, with a transcript of the evidence, to the governor, by whose order the accused was either discharged, or sent to New Orleans. These parish commandants acted also as notaries public, and made inventories and sales of the estates of the deceased, and attended to the execution of judgments, rendered in New Orleans, against defendants who resided in the country parishes.

The Spanish language was ordered to be employed by all public officers in their minutes; but the use of the French was tolerated in the judicial and notarial acts of the commandants.

The public officers were bound to take the following oath:

" I, * * * * * appointed ... (here followed the designation of the office,) ... swear before God, on the holy cross and on the evangelists, to maintain and defend the mystery of the immaculate conception of Our Lady the Virgin Mary, and the royal jurisdiction to which I appertain in virtue of my office. I swear also to obey the royal ordinances and decrees of his Majesty, to fulfil faithfully the duties of my office, to decide in conformity with law in all the affairs which shall be submitted to my tribunal; and the better to accomplish this end, I promise to consult persons learned in the law, on every occasion which may present itself in this town; and, finally, I swear never to exact other fees than those fixed by the tariff, and never to take any from the poor."

This last clause of the oath is worthy of being recommended to the attention of officers acting under more liberal institutions.

These were the principal features in the organization of the new government.

On the 25th of November, 1769, O'Reilly issued a proclamation making known a set of instructions which he had caused to be prepared by two of his legal advisers, Don Jose Urrustia and Don Felix Del Rey, who acted so conspicuous a part in the prosecution against Lafrénière and his accomplices. These instructions were an abridgment or summary of the rules to be followed in civil and criminal actions, and of the laws of Castile and of the Indies, to which they referred, and to which they might serve as an index. This compendium was intended as a guide to all the functionaries and to the public. It contained also an enumeration of all the offices in the colony, and a definition of all the functions and privileges thereto appertaining. In the preamble to his proclamation, O'Reilly said:—" Whereas the want of jurists in this colony and the little knowledge which the new subjects of his Catholic Majesty possess of the Spanish Laws, may render a strict observance of them difficult (which would be so much at variance with the intentions of his Majesty), we have thought it useful and even necessary to have an abstract made of said laws, in order that it may become an element of instruction or information to the public, and a formulary in the administration of justice, and in the municipal government of this town, until a more general knowledge of the Spanish language be introduced in this province, and until every one be enabled by the perusal of those laws, to know them thoroughly. Wherefore, under reserve of his Majesty's pleasure, we order and command all the judges, the Cabildo, and all other public officers, to conform strictly to what is required by the following articles." This document* is given at length in the Appendix, and is in every way worthy of an attentive perusal. It will be found, with the exception of a few objectionable provisions, to be remarkable for wisdom and humanity, and it would not require much investigation to discover worse legislation in these our days of enlightened morality and progressive knowledge.

The Article 20, of Section I., concerning the Cabildo, runs thus:

"The electors, in the two jurisdictions, being responsible for the injury and detriment which the public may sustain, by the bad conduct and incapacity of the elected in the administration of justice and the management of the public interests, should have for their only objects, in the election of ordinary alcaldes and other officers, the service of God, the king, and the public; and, in order to prevent an abuse of that great trust, their choice should be directed to those persons who shall appear to them most suitable for those offices, by the proofs they may possess of their affection for the king, their disinterestedness, and their zeal for the public welfare."*

With the omission of the word *king*, this article would not be found inapplicable to present circumstances, and might be fitly recommended to that generation of electors who hold now in their hands the destinies of our country.

Article 21 said: "The Cabildo is hereby informed that it must exact from the governors, previous to their taking possession of their office, a good and sufficient

---

* American State Papers, vol. i., p. 368. Miscellaneous.

surety, and a full assurance to this effect—that they shall submit to the necessary inquiries and examinations during the time they may be in employment, and that they shall conform to whatever may be adjudged and determined against them. This article merits the most serious attention of the Cabildo, which is responsible for the consequences that may result from any omission and neglect in exacting the aforesaid securities from the governors."

Considering the age in which it was framed, and the source from which it emanated, this article deserves to be noticed, on account of the check which it intends to impose on the exercise of the executive power.

The section 11, on the ordinary alcaldes, is not without interest. The 4th article of that section says:

"The alcaldes shall appear in public with decency and modesty, bearing the wand of royal justice—a badge provided by law to distinguish the judges. When administering justice, they shall hear mildly those who may present themselves, and shall fix the hour and the place of audience, which shall be at 10 o'clock in the morning, at the Town Hall; and, for the decision of cases in which no writings are required, they shall sit in the evening between 7 and 8 o'clock, at their own dwellings, and in none other."

Art. 13 and 15 read thus: Art. 13—"The ordinary Alcaldes, accompanied by the Alguazil Mayor (High Sheriff), and the escribano (clerk), shall, every Friday, proceed to the visitation of the prisons. They shall examine the prisoners, the causes of their detention, and ascertain how long they have been imprisoned. They shall release the poor who may be detained for their expenses, or for small debts; and the jailor shall not exact from them any release fee. The alcaldes shall not set at liberty any of the prisoners detained by order of the Governor, or of any other judge, without the express consent of said authorities."

"Art. 15. The Governor, with the Alcaldes, the Alguazil Mayor, and the escribano, shall, yearly, on the eve of Christmas, Easter, and Whitsunday, make a general visitation of the prisons, in the manner prescribed by the Laws of the Indies. They shall release those who have been arrested for criminal causes of little importance, or for debts, when such debtors are known to be insolvent, and shall allow them a sufficient term for the payment of their creditors."

These articles are imbued with a spirit of humanity and christianity highly creditable to the legislation of Spain.

The section 3d defines the attributions of the Alcalde Mayor Provincial, and shows that the celebrated institution of the *Santa Hermandad* was established in Louisiana.

The 4th article of this section shows great regard for the comfort and protection of travelers and strangers. It says: "The Alcalde Mayor Provincial shall see that travelers are furnished with provisions at reasonable prices, as well by the proprietors as by the inhabitants of the villages through which they may pass."

The 5th article says: "The principal object of the institution of the tribunal of the Santa Hermandad (holy brotherhood) being to repress disorders, and to prevent the robberies and assassinations committed in unfrequented places by vagabonds and delinquents, who conceal themselves in the woods, from which they sally to attack travelers and the neighboring inhabitants, the Alcalde Mayor Provincial shall assemble a sufficient number of members or brothers of the Santa Hermandad, to clear his jurisdiction of the perpetrators of such evil deeds, by pursuing them with spirit, seizing, or putting them to death."

Section 7th concerns the Procurador General. The article I. is as follows:

"The Procurador General is an officer appointed to assist the people in all their concerns, to defend them, preserve their rights, and obtain justice on their behalf, and to enforce all other claims which relate to the public interest.

"In consequence thereof, the Procurador General, who is appointed solely for the public good, shall see that the municipal ordinances are strictly observed, and shall endeavor to prevent everything by which the said public interest might suffer.

"For these purposes, he shall apply to the tribunals competent thereto, for the recovery of debts and revenues due to the treasury of the town of New Orleans, in the capacity of attorney for said town. He shall pursue these causes with the activity and diligence necessary to discharge him from the responsibility he would incur by the slightest omission.

"He shall see that the other officers of the Council or Cabildo discharge strictly the duties of their offices; that the Depositary General, the Receiver of Fines, and all those who are to give sureties, shall give such as are good and sufficient; and in case said sureties should cease to be good, he shall demand that they be renewed conformably to law.

"He shall be present at, and shall interpose in the division of lands, and in other public matters, to the end that nothing unsuitable or injurious shall occur."

It must be admitted that this whole section is replete with a feeling of liberality and a regard for the interests of the people, which is supposed to appertain only to a republican government.

The section 10, which treats of the jailor and the prisons, breathes not that spirit of ferocity, which is generally believed to be akin to the subject, and characteristic of that age, as well as the attribute of the presumed tyranny of Spanish legislation and officials ; but, on the contrary, it seems to have been framed under the mild influence of modern philanthropy. The provision which prohibits jailors from exacting any fee from the poor, and from receiving any gratuity, either in money or goods, is worthy of commendation. It may not be inappropriate to quote the whole section.

Art. 1. "The jailor shall be appointed by the alguazil mayor, and approved by the governor before entering on the duties of his office. He shall also be presented to the Cabildo to be inducted into office, and to take an oath to discharge faithfully the duties of the said office, to guard the prisoners watchfully, and to observe the laws and ordinances established in this respect, under the penalties therein declared.

Art. 2. "The said jailor must not enter upon the duties of the said office until he shall have given good and sufficient sureties in the sum of two hundred dollars, as a warranty that no prisoner detained for debt shall be released without an order from the judge competent thereto.

Art. 3. "The jailor shall keep a book, in which he shall inscribe the names of all the prisoners, that of the judge by whose order they have been arrested, the cause for which they are detained, and the names of those who may have arrested them. He shall reside in the prison intrusted to his care, and, for each considerable fault committed by him, he shall pay sixty dollars, applicable one half to the royal chamber, and the other to the informer.

Art. 4. "It is the duty of the jailor to keep the prison

clean and healthy, to supply it with water for the use of the prisoners, to visit them in the evening, to prevent them from gaming or disputing, to treat them well, and to avoid insulting or offending them.

Art. 5. "It is likewise the duty of the jailor to take care that the female prisoners are separate from the men; that they be kept in their respective apartments, and that they be not worse treated than their offence deserves, or than is prescribed by the judges.

Art. 6. "With regard to his fees, the said jailor shall confine himself strictly to those which are established; he shall take none from the poor, under a penalty of the value of the same. He shall not, without incurring the same penalty, receive any gratuity, either in money or in goods. He shall avoid entirely either playing, eating, or forming any intimacy with the prisoners under the penalty of sixty dollars, applicable, one third to the royal chamber, one third to the informer, and the remaining third to the poor prisoners."

Persons of noble birth, the military, the municipal and other civil officers, lawyers, physicians, women, and certain other individuals, were exempted from imprisonment for debt.

The section on criminal trials has some remarkable features, among which the art. 14, which says: "The accused, being convicted of the crime, on its being fully established on trial by sufficient proof, or by some other proof in conjunction with his own confession, may be condemned to the penalty provided by law for the same. The said condemnation shall also take place, when two witnesses of lawful age and irreproachable character shall depose that, of their certain knowledge, the accused has committed the crime; but when there shall appear against the accused but one witness, and other indications or conjectures, he shall not be condemned to the penalty provided by law; but some other punishment shall be inflicted as directed by the judge, with due consideration of the circumstances which may appear on the trial. This state of things requires the greatest circumspection, as it must always be remembered, that it is better to let a criminal escape than to punish the innocent."

This provision concerning condemnation on the testimony of one witness, whatever may be said as to the propriety of its policy, is certainly more humane than the law by which we are now governed, and which may send a man to the scaffold on the bare testimony of another. It will also be observed that the well known axiom that "it is better that guilt should go unpunished, than that innocence should suffer unjust punishment," is not confined to the common law of England. It may, moreover, not be amiss here—to remark, in a parenthesis, that the boasted privileges of English liberty existed in some parts of Spain, although destroyed since, long before they were dreamed of in that noble land from which we have borrowed so much of our judicial and political organization.*

The whole chapter concerning appeals is characterized by the desire of bringing lawsuits to a speedy termination—a thing not to be expected, according to public opinion, from Spanish Legislation.

It must be confessed, however, that some of the penalties inflicted, savored of the peculiar temperament of the age and of the exaggerated devotion to the church and the throne which marked the Spanish character at the time; for instance, art. 1 of section v. on punishments, decreed that: "he who shall revile Our Saviour, or his mother the Holy Virgin Mary, shall have his tongue cut out, and his property shall be confiscated, applicable one

---

* See art. Navarre, in the Encyclopædia Britannica, vol. xv., p. 743.

half to the public treasury, and the other half to the informer."

Art. 2d. said: "He, who forgetting the respect and loyalty which every subject owes to his king, shall have the insolence to vilify his royal person, or that of the queen, of the hereditary prince, or of the *infantes* (princes of the blood) or of their sons, shall be punished corporally, according to the circumstances of the crime; and the half of his property shall be confiscated to the profit of the public or the royal treasury, if he have legitimate children; but should he have none, he shall forfeit the whole, applicable two thirds to the public treasury, and the other third to the accuser."

Art. 3. "The authors of any insurrection against the king or the state, or those who, under pretence of defending their liberty and rights, shall be concerned in it, or take up arms therein, shall be punished with death and the confiscation of their property. The same punishments shall also be inflicted on all those who may be convicted of high treason."

The Art. 4. contains a remarkable feature. A plebeian, using opprobrious language to the detriment of any one, was condemned to pay a fine of 1200 maravedis; but should a nobleman have committed the same offence, the penalty for him was 2000 maravedis. This distinction seems to have originated from the impression, that such an offence ought to be more severely punished in one of gentle than of base blood, on account of its being more heinous in one who, on account of his rank, ought to have been more correct in his deportment.

The following articles show at least that the new government was imbued with puritanical severity, and was disposed to check by extreme punishment all infractions against morality.

Art 6. said: "The married woman convicted of adultery, and he who has committed the same with her, shall be delivered up to the husband, to be dealt with as he may please; with the reserve, however, that he shall not put one of them to death, without inflicting the same punishment on the other.

Art. 7. "The man who shall consent that his wife live in concubinage with another, or who shall have induced her to commit adultery, shall, for the first time, be exposed to public shame, and condemned to a confinement of ten years in some fortress; and, for the second time, shall be sentenced to one hundred lashes and confinement for life.

Art. 8. "The same punishment shall also be inflicted on those who carry on the infamous trade of enticing women to prostitution, by procuring them the means of accomplishing the same.

Art. 9. "He who shall be guilty of fornication with a relation in the fourth degree, shall forfeit half of his property to the profit of the public treasury, and shall, moreover, be punished corporally, or banished, or undergo some other penalty, according to the rank of the person and the degree of kindred between the parties. If the said crime be committed between parents and their offspring, or with a professed nun, the same shall be punished with death.

Art. 10. "He who shall commit the detestable crime against nature shall suffer death, and his body shall afterwards be burnt, and his property shall be confiscated to the profit of the public and royal treasuries.

Art. 11. "The woman who shall be publicly the concubine of an ecclesiastic shall be sentenced, for the first time, to a fine of a mark of silver, and to banishment for one year from the town or from the place where the offence may have been committed. The second time, she shall be fined another mark of silver and banished for two years, and, in case of relapse, she shall be punished by one hundred lashes, in addition to the penalties aforesaid.*

Art. 12. "If fornication be committed between unmarried persons, they shall be admonished by the judge to discontinue every kind of intercourse with each other, under the penalty of banishment for the man, and confinement for the woman, during such time as may be necessary to operate a reformation. Should this menace have not the desired effect, the judge shall put the same into execution, unless the rank of the parties requires a different procedure—in which case, the said offence shall be submitted to the consideration of the judges collectively, to apply the remedy which their prudence and zeal for the repression of such disorders may suggest. They shall punish all other offences of debauchery in proportion to their degree, and to the injury occasioned thereby."

Ever after the promulgation of this document, it is to be supposed that all judicial decisions were grounded on the laws of Spain. At a later period, however, it became a question, which was debated in the courts of justice of Louisiana, how far the French laws had been repealed by O'Reilly, and whether he had the authority to abolish them, as the extent of his powers had never been exactly known. But now the question is set at rest, as it is ascertained that O'Reilly was clothed with unlimited authority,† and that all he did in Louisiana was fully confirmed by the king and the council of Indies. In a communication addressed to his government, on the 17th of October 1769, he had said‡, "it seems proper

---

* No penalty was decreed against the ecclesiastic by the civil authorities, because he probably had the privilege of being tried only by the tribunals of his holy order.

† See the Letter of the Marquis of Grimaldi to the Count of Fuentes, at the court of Versailles. Gayarré's Louisiana, 3d series of Lectures, p. 264, vol ii.

‡ En la 3d Fha, en Nueva Orleans, 17 de Oct. de 1769, dice: " Que le parece con-

that this colony be governed by the same laws which prevail in the other dominions of his Majesty in America, and that in its military, judicial, and financial organization, it be, in each of these respective departments, a dependency of the Island of Cuba." The government gave its approbation to these views of O'Reilly.* Fortunately, there was no very great dissimilarity between the fundamental principles of the Spanish and the French jurisprudence, which had the same sisterly origin, and drew their existence from the honored womb of Roman legislation, emphatically called the "Civil Law," and so well known under that name.

O'Reilly had a set of instructions drawn up, which he sent to the parish commandants. From those addressed to de Mézières, who was in command of Natchitoches, I extract the following passage: "The commandant of the Post of Natchitoches shall not omit to employ every means to prevent the trade now going on with the Mexican provinces; and, whereas every officer who commands a post, ought not to be ignorant of anything that occurs within the limits of his jurisdiction, he shall bear the responsibility thereof in every respect. There is nothing which renders a government more respectable and beneficent than the prompt and equitable administration of justice. Therefore do I most particularly recommend the observance of this duty to every commandant, and any want of exactitude in the discharge of official functions I shall consider as a contempt of the authority of the Governor General of this province. Those in command have been clothed with power, only to make their subor-

veniente que dicha colonia se gobierna por las mismas leyes que los demas dominios de S. M. en America, y que en lo militar, judicial y economico dependa de la isla de Cuba."

* See the Records of the deliberations of the Council of the Indies on O'Reilly's acts in Louisiana, which are in manuscript in the office of the Secretary of State at Baton Rouge.

dinates happy, and to endear the government of the king to his subjects by its gentleness and benefits. This end will be accomplished by the impartial administration of justice, by a strict compliance with the orders of the Governor General, and by an enlightened exhibition of firmness and humanity on all occasions. * *
* * * * * * *

"It shall be made known to all the inhabitants that, by the laws of his Majesty, which shall go into operation in this province on the 1st of December, 1769, it is not permitted that Indians be held in slavery; wherefore, from the date of the notification of these presents, no one shall buy, exchange, and barter, or appropriate to himself Indian slaves. They shall neither sell, nor in any way part with, those they now have (unless it be to set them free), until they hear further from his Majesty on this subject. M. de Mézières shall make out an exact list of the Indian slaves who are within his jurisdiction. Said list shall contain the names of the owners, the price which they ask for every one of their Indian slaves, and the exact filiation of said slaves. This will obviate any future abuse on a subject which has so strongly excited the solicitude of our laws. *
* * * * * * *

"I have remarked a considerable number of traders in the census of Natchitoches. These men can have no other object in view than an illicit trade. Therefore I charge M. de Mézières, most particularly, to cause to depart those named Ménars, Poeyfarré, Dartigo, Durand Duvivier and Villars, of whom I know enough to desire that they be dismissed from that post, and be forced to remain in this capital (New Orleans), or be expelled altogether from the province. * * *
* * * * * * *

" M. de Mézières shall cause the inhabitants to make

to their parochial church all the repairs which decency and the security of the edifice require. This is the first duty of every good Christian, and no one has the right nor the power to refuse his contribution thereto. M. de Mézières shall make known to every inhabitant the equity of this contribution, and shall have recourse to compulsory means, only when it shall be absolutely necessary, to enforce the fulfilment of so essential a duty."

It is impossible not to smile at the following passage: " Having been informed by the curate of Natchitoches that, during divine worship, the church is filled with dogs, I request the commandant to prevent the repetition of this breach of decency."

He also gave a set of instructions to the commandants of the *Coast*—that is, all the petty governors at the different posts on the banks of the Mississippi.* In the 16th Article, he said: " The greatest vigilance shall be exercised to oppose the sojourning of men of bad morals in those posts, in order to prevent that any damage or scandal result thereby to the inhabitants; and should there be such men as above described, when the commandants shall fail to change their vicious behavior by admonitions and corrections, then it shall become the duty of said commandants to arrest them, and to send them to the Governor General, with an account of the causes of complaint laid against them."

The 19th Article said : " The aforesaid commandants shall take special care, that the inhabitants carry on no trade with the English vessels which navigate the Mississippi, nor with any of the settlements situated on the territory of his Britannic Majesty, and that the king's subjects do not go out of the limits of this province,

---

* Tenientes particulares de la Costa.

without a written permission from the Governor General. Those acting in violation of the provisions of this article shall be arrested by said commandants and sent to this town (New Orleans), in order that their case be submitted to the further consideration of the government, but the first proceeding shall be to sequestrate their property."

He caused to be framed for the commandant at Arkansas a series of instructions, which it is impossible to read without entertaining a high opinion of his administrative talents, justice and humanity. These instructions descend into the smallest details, and demonstrate that he was well aware, as all truly great minds are, of the importance of apparently unimportant minutiæ.

In the 3d Article, he expressed himself as follows: "It shall be the care of the commandant that every thing offered for sale at that Post (Arkansas), and which may be wanted for the sustenance and support of the soldiers, be sold cheap. There is nothing more indispensably necessary, in order that the soldiers be conscious that nothing is made out of them, and that their chief treats them with the strictest equity. When this is not the case, there never fail to be murmurs of discontent and a deficiency of subordination."

All the regulations which he established, to distribute the customary presents among the Indians, to secure an honest trade between them and the Europeans, and to guard them against deception and oppression, are equally creditable to his head and to his heart.

The 9th Article said: "The commandant shall prevent, as much as may be in his power, that any damage be done to the English who navigate the Mississippi, and shall take care that there be no crossing over of the river, to inflict any injury on the subjects of his Britannic

Majesty; and he shall have recourse to every means, to induce the Spanish Indians to live in peace with the English, and also with the other savage tribes."

Instructions were sent in common to the commandants at the posts of St. Louis and St. Geneviève, as well as to others established on the Missouri and in the Illinois district. The population of St. Louis consisted then of 17 males and 16 females (free), of 12 males and 6 females (slaves); that of St. Geneviève happened to be exactly the same.

The instructions began with this preamble, full of dignity and commendable sentiments: "The great distance between this capital and the Illinois requires proportionate discretion and prudence in the commandant of that remote district. There are three important objects recommended to his special vigilance and attention. Those are: that the domination and government of his Majesty be loved and respected; that justice be administered with promptitude and impartiality and in conformity to law; and that commerce be protected and extended as much as possible. In order to secure ends of such moment, it is necessary that the officer in command should make known, in the most manifest manner, the king's desire to promote and protect the felicity of his subjects, and should also promulgate the express orders which he, the officer in command, has received to discriminate between the good and the wicked, to favor the former in every thing licit, and to prosecute all those who, through bad faith, deceive and ruin their creditors, and who, by their flagitious deportment, disturb public tranquillity."

Articles 3 and 4 show O'Reilly to be a man of high honor and of strict fidelity, in observing the faith of treaties, and in respecting acquired rights.

Article 3 said: "Should any subject of his Catholic

Majesty commit any excess or trespass in the territory of the English, or offer any insult to those of that nation who navigate the Mississippi, the commandant shall do prompt justice, and shall give full and immediate reparation, on the just complaints of the English officer, but without failing to observe the formalities prescribed by law."

Article 4: "The officer in command shall, as much as in his power may be, prevent the Indians who dwell on the king's territory, from inflicting any vexation or extortion on the English who navigate the Mississippi, and from crossing that river to give any offence to the subjects of his Britannic Majesty, and, in every respect, he shall predispose the Indians to be peaceful and humane towards the English and the other nations of savages, and, to that effect, he shall tell them that the principles of our religion and the fidelity of our friendship never permit us to tolerate, that any injury be done to such as are our friends and allies like the English."

It is to be remarked, that O'Reilly proscribed that system of monopolies which the French had adopted in their commercial intercourse with the Indians. Article 7 of the document to which I have referred shows it, and is also a striking proof of the solicitude of the Spanish governor to secure the welfare of the aborigines. "No trader," it said, "shall be permitted to introduce himself in the villages of the Indians who dwell on the territory of his Majesty, unless the commandant is satisfied with his morals and the correctness of his deportment; but said commandant shall not be at liberty to refuse a permit or license to any one who may be known to be an honest man, and, under no pretext, shall he tolerate, authorize, or grant any exclusive privilege or monopoly. He shall uniformly recommend to all the traders, to make known to the Indians the gentleness and equity of our government, and the felicity which it thereby imparts to the subjects of his Majesty."

In Article 9, he went on saying: "The commandant shall acquaint the Indians with the greatness, the magnanimity and the generosity of the king, and shall inform them that they may expect, every year, to receive the usual presents; that his Majesty desires their happiness, and that they must never yield obedience, nor give credence, to any other word than that of the Great Chief, governor general of the province, communicated to them through the officer who shall have been put in command of the post; and he, the said commandant, shall exhort them (with promises of fair rewards), to arrest* and deliver up whatever trader or fugitive who, in furtherance of wicked ends and intentions, may endeavor to inspire them with feelings of distrust towards their true father, and towards that nation which deserves, among all others, the renown of being a magnanimous, pious and justice loving nation, and, in support of the truth of this declaration, he shall communicate to them the order of the king which prohibits that, in his dominions, there be made Indian slaves, even out of the captives of hostile tribes."

Art. 10. "The commandant shall take care, that all the Indians who may come to St. Louis and St. Geneviève be well treated, and be paid an equitable price for the hides they may bring to market, and for whatever other things they may have for sale, and that, in the barters or purchases they may make, they be served with good faith.

---

* Arrestar y traer preso á cualquier tratante ó prófugo que por sus malos fines esparciese entre ellos desconfianzas de su verdadero padre, ni de la nacion que merece, entre todas las del mundo, el renombre de magnanima, piadosa y justiciera, y, en prueba de elló, manifestará la orden del Rey, para que ni aun de las naciones enemigas se sufra en sus estados esclavo Indio.

In this way, they will derive more benefit from their trade with us; they will provide themselves with what their wants require, without its being at the expense of the king; and the English will not reap all the profits of a commerce which ought to be in our hands. The advantages of treating the Indians with equity and benevolence have been made apparent in this town, where, since my arrival, on the occasion of the distribution of the annual presents to them, the chiefs of every nation came to compliment me; and now a number of Indians are daily seen here, with their canoes loaded with provisions, hides, and other things, which they offer at public sale for their just value; and then, they themselves buy in the shops what they want, and return home perfectly contented."

These articles of O'Reilly's instructions show that the Spaniards were not disposed to pursue in Louisiana, towards the Indians, the cruel policy which was attributed to them in their other American domains. The rest of O'Reilly's instructions, on all the subjects which they embrace, are marked with foresight, prudence, liberality, and firmness. They conclude with saying: "The commandants shall have for invariable rules: to keep up the strictest order and economy in all that appertains to the royal treasury, to cultivate the best harmony with the English, to maintain tranquillity and contentment among the inhabitants, to provide for the increase of commerce and its being carried on in good faith, and to take care that the Indians be well treated."

Immediately after his arrival in Louisiana, O'Reilly had taken an enlightened view of the wants of the colony, as appears by a communication of the 17th of October, 1769, which he addressed to the Spanish government, and in which he represents the necessity of favoring commerce, because, without it, the colony could not subsist: "This province," he said, "wants flour, wine, oil, iron instruments, arms, ammunition, and every sort of manufactured goods for clothing and other domestic purposes. These can only be obtained through the exportation of its productions, which consist of timber, indigo, cotton, furs, and a small quantity of corn and rice. In Spain there would be no market for the timber of the colonists, which is one of the most important sources of their revenues. Of all our colonies, the Havana is the only place where this kind of produce could be disposed of. According to my conceptions, the importation of it into that city would be advantageous both to the king and to the island of Cuba. To the king, because he would preserve for the use of his royal navy the cedars which are now employed to make sugar boxes, and because, with the Cuba timber, he could have the lining of his ships and many other works done at a much cheaper rate; to the island, because its inhabitants could cause their sugar boxes and the other works required by them, to be made in Havana at less cost with the Louisiana planks.

"By granting to this province, as formerly to Florida, the benefit of a free trade with Spain and with Havana, its inhabitants would find in that very city of Havana a market for all their produce, and would provide themselves there with all the articles of which they stand in need. The establishing of sugar mills would be increased, by thus affording to the planters of Cuba an outlet for all the rum manufactured by them, and which is lost for want of consumers. The consumption of this article would be considerable here, and every barrel of it would put two dollars into the king's treasury, through the export duty paid in Havana. But, for the better regulation of this trade, and to make it reciprocally advantageous, it seems to me proper and necessary, that the timber, furs, indigo, cotton, corn and rice of this province should pay no entry duty in Havana, and that no other new excise or export tax be imposed on any of the articles which may be exported from Havana to New Orleans.

"It would also be proper, that the vessels belonging to this colony be received in Havana and the ports of Spain on the same condition and footing with Spanish vessels, but with the understanding that no vessels, except they be Spanish, or belong to the colony, shall be admitted in this port, or employed in transporting goods, and that this be recommended to the special care of my successors.

"From Catalonia there would come ships with red wine; here they would take a cargo of timber and other articles for Havana, and they would load with sugar.

"I found the English in complete possession of the commerce of the colony. They had in this town their merchants and traders with open stores and shops, and I can safely assert that they pocketed nine tenths of the money spent here. The commerce of France used to receive the productions of the colony in payment of the articles imported into it from the mother country; but the English, selling their goods much cheaper, had the gathering of all the money. I drove off all the English traders and the other individuals of that nation whom I found in this town, and I shall admit here none of their vessels."

In a despatch of the 1st of March, 1770, O'Reilly took credit to himself for having reduced the annual expenses of the colony, from $250,000 to $130,000, by the economical retrenchments which he had introduced into the administration of the province, and applied to the salaries of its officers; and he informed the government, that the religious wants of the colony would require the permanent employment of eighteen priests. In the same despatch, he said: "I visited and examined in person the most populous parts of this province, by proceeding from this capital to Pointe Coupée, which is one hundred and fifty miles up the river, and I took care, as I progressed along, to convene the inhabitants in every district, at the most convenient place for them, where I listened to their grievances and provided a remedy thereto, by referring them to the arbitration of their best informed neighbors, without having recourse to the judicial tribunals, and, in this way, I gave those people a very favorable opinion of the government of his majesty, and I succeeded in obtaining that the arbitrators named by the respective parties be acceptable to them, on account of their being chosen among the men enjoying the best reputation; and by these means, I have procured that the new government be grateful to the inhabitants.

"I thought it my duty to acquiesce in the prayer of the inhabitants in almost every district, that a surveyor be appointed to measure the lands and determine their limits, but I reduced the salary of that officer to half of what it was formerly, and I decreed that, for the future, it be paid out of the sale of the crops of the inhabitants, at the price fixed for their commodities at New Orleans.

"So far, the concessions of land in this province had been intrusted by his most Christian Majesty to the Governor and to the ordaining commissary, and the concurrence of both was necessary thereto; but I have thought it advisable, that, for the future, the Governor be the only one authorized by the King to make such concessions; and, for the apportionment of the lands belonging to the royal domain, I have appointed a council of twenty-four persons, known for their practical sense and information, and for their sound judgment."

O'Reilly, with striking liberality, and, no doubt, also from motives of sound policy, appointed almost none but Frenchmen to the command of the several posts, even the most distant, and, therefore, all the instructions which he gave them were originally drawn in French. They were afterwards translated into Spanish, and sent to the court of Madrid for its approbation.

In conformity with the orders of the king, a regiment was raised in the colony under the name of "Regiment of Louisiana," and Don J. Estecheria was appointed its Colonel. But this officer having not as yet arrived, Unzaga, who was to succeed O'Reilly as governor of the province, undertook to organize the regiment, and assumed its command provisionally. O'Reilly sent commissions to all those whom Ulloa had, in his despatches, represented as well affected towards Spain, and those commissions were eagerly accepted. There was no want of a keen desire to gird on the sword of command, under a government which granted so many privileges to the wearers of epaulets. The pay of the Spanish troops being greater than that formerly allowed to the French, a certain number of disbanded French soldiers, who had remained in the colony, were tempted to enlist, and the "regiment of Louisiana" was soon complete. It is an admitted fact, that the Creoles of those days were remarkable for their great size, for the stateliness of their bearing, for those peculiarly striking lineaments which constitute the nobility of the face, and for the elegant symmetry of their forms. O'Reilly is said to have been so much struck with this characteristic distinction in the Creole officers of the regiment of Louisiana, that he regretted his inability to take with him some of them to Spain and to Charles III., as a fair specimen of the new subjects acquired by his Catholic Majesty.

The arrival of the Spaniards in New Orleans had produced a considerable increase of population, and the provisions which they expected having been unaccountably delayed, the colony was threatened with famine

The price of flour ran up to twenty dollars a barrel; fortunately, there arrived from Baltimore a brig, with a cargo of flour belonging to one Oliver Pollock, who tendered it to O'Reilly on the terms which that officer might himself determine. O'Reilly refused to avail himself of this liberal offer, insisted on Pollock's specifying his price, and finally agreed to take the whole load of flour at fifteen dollars the barrel. The Spanish governor was so well pleased with Pollock's behavior on this occasion, that he told him he would report it to the king, and assured him that he, Pollock, during his lifetime, should enjoy, for all the merchandise which his brig could carry, a free trade with Louisiana. A very valuable privilege, forsooth, if it had been long enjoyed! But it is not in evidence that such was the case.

The new Cabildo was solemnly inaugurated, and began its sessions on the first day of December, 1769. It was composed of François Marie Reggio, Pierre François Olivier de Vezin, Charles Jean Baptiste Fleuriau, Antoine Bienvenu, Joseph Ducros, and Denis Braud. Jean Baptiste Garic, who had been clerk of the Superior Council, had bought the same office in the Cabildo. Reggio was alferez real, De Vezin principal provincial alcalde, Fleuriau alguazil mayor, or high sheriff, Ducros depositary general, and Bienvenu receiver of fines.

On the 1st of January, 1770, the Cabildo elected as ordinary alcaldes St. Denis and De La Chaise. One was a descendant of the celebrated St. Denis, whose name is so chivalrously connected with the history of Louisiana, and the other was the grandson of the royal commissary De La Chaise, who had come to the colony in 1723, and was a brother-in-law to Villeré, whose tragical death had so recently taken place. These facts seem to prove, that the horror produced by the execution of Lafrénière and his companions was not so great as reported by tradition and that the Spaniards did not think themselves so hated as they have been represented to be, since they intrusted so many important offices and the command of the most distant posts to almost none but Frenchmen. It cannot certainly be denied, that, on their part, it denoted at least confidence and liberality.

Don Luis de Unzaga had been designated to succeed O'Reilly, who had been sent to Louisiana only for temporary purposes. As a preliminary step and a prelude to a transfer of his powers to that officer, O'Reilly, immediately after the organization of the Cabildo, ceded to him the presidency of that body, in which he ceased to appear. About the middle of December, 1769, he had gone up the Mississippi, to visit the establishments at the German Coast, the Acadian Coast, Iberville, and Pointe Coupée. In all the parishes through which he passed, he convened the inhabitants, as he mentions it in one of his despatches, which I have already cited, and invited them to make known their wishes and wants, promising to satisfy them to the utmost of his powers.

On his return to New Orleans, O'Reilly published a set of regulations concerning the concessions of vacant lands:

"Divers complaints and petitions," said he, "which have been addressed to us by the inhabitants of Opeloussas, Attakapas, Natchitoches and other places of this province, joined to the knowledge we have acquired of the local concerns, culture, and means of the inhabitants, by the visit which we have lately paid to the German Coast, to Iberville and Pointe Coupée, with the examination we have made of the reports of the inhabitants assembled by our order in each district, having convinced us that the tranquillity of the said inhabitants and the progress of cultivation required a new regulation, which should fix the extent of the grants of land to be hereafter made, as well as determine the enclosures to be put up, the lands to be cleared, the roads and bridges to be kept in repair by the inhabitants, and specify what is the sort of damage done by cattle for which the proprietors shall be responsible—for these causes, and having nothing in view but the public good and the happiness of every inhabitant—after having advised with persons well informed in these matters, we have regulated all these objects in the following articles."*

After having ordered, that, for the future, grants of land should not exceed a certain extent, and having entered into many minute regulations, he says:

Art. 12—"All grants shall be made in the name of the king, by the Governor General of the province, who will, at the same time, appoint a surveyor to fix the bounds thereof, both in front and in depth, in presence of the ordinary judge of the district and of two adjoining settlers, who shall be present at the survey. The above mentioned four persons shall sign the proces-verbal which shall be made thereof, and the surveyor shall make three copies of the same; one of which shall be deposited in the office of the Escribano of the government and Cabildo, another shall be delivered to the Governor General, and the third to the proprietor, to be annexed to the titles of his grant.

"In pursuance of the powers which the king, our Lord, (whom God preserve!) has been pleased to confide to us by his patent issued at Aranjuez, on the 16th of April, 1769, to establish in the military and in the police departments, in the administration of justice and in the colonial finances, such regulations as should be most conducive to his service and to the happiness of his

* American State Papers, vol. i., p. 876. Miscellaneous.

subjects in Louisiana, under the reserve of his Majesty's approbation, we order and command the governor, judges, cabildo, and all the inhabitants of this province, to conform punctually to all that is required by these regulations.

"Given at New Orleans, the 18th of February, 1770."

It will be observed that O'Reilly, who had come to Louisiana as the delegate of royalty itself, and who was invested, as such, with unbounded powers of legislation, prescribed the manner in which all future concessions of land should be made by the governors of Louisiana, and determined with precision the extent of those concessions, which were not to exceed certain limits. Hence it follows, that it is questionable whether some of those immense grants of land which were made at a later period by the governors of Louisiana had the requisite validity, except it be shown that the limitations assigned by O'Reilly to his successors, in the name of the king, had been subsequently repealed or modified.

By an ordinance of the 22d of February, 1770, O'Reilly provided a revenue for the town of New Orleans. An annual tax of forty dollars was to be levied on every tavern, billiard table, and coffee house, and one of twenty dollars on every boarding house; a duty of one dollar was to be charged on every barrel of brandy brought to the town; and O'Reilly graciously accepted and sanctioned a proposition liberally made by the butchers, to pay an annual contribution of three hundred and seventy dollars into the coffers of the town, to meet municipal expenses. In making this offer, these butchers expressly declared, that they did not mean to justify thereby any alteration on their part, now and thereafter, in the price of meat—which alteration, they said, ought never to take place without extreme necessity. It was estimated that, with all these branches of revenue, the annual income of the town would amount to two thousand dollars.*

As the town was put to considerable expense, to keep up the levee which protected it against inundation, it was authorized to collect an anchorage duty of six dollars from every vessel of two hundred tons and upwards, and half that sum from smaller ones.

On both sides of the public square or *Place d'armes*, from Levee to Chartres and Condé streets, there was a large space of ground facing on St. Peter's and St. Anne's streets, with a front of three hundred and thirty-six feet on both these streets, and eighty-four feet in depth. O'Reilly granted to the town, in the name of the king, the whole of that space of ground, which was soon afterwards sold to Don Andres Almonaster on a perpetual yearly rent.† It is still owned by his daughter, the baroness of Pontalba, who has lately covered it with buildings of an imposing aspect, by which she has considerably embellished the great commercial emporium to which she is indebted for her birth and wealth.

O'Reilly expressly prohibited the purchase of anything from persons navigating the Mississippi, or the lakes, without a passport or license.‡ It was, however, permitted to sell fowls and other articles of provisions to boats and vessels, provided the fowls and provisions were delivered on the bank of the river, and payment received in ready coin.

Persons violating this prohibition were liable to a fine of one hundred dollars, and to the confiscation of the articles so purchased, one third of the whole being the reward of the informer.

---

* Qué con todos los expresados ramos podran ascender los proprios de la ciudad á 2000 pesos fuertes.—See the Records of the deliberations of the Council of the Indies on O'Reilly's acts in Louisiana.

† Martin's History of Louisiana. ‡ Ibid.

No change was effected in the ecclesiastical organization of the province. The old Superior of the capuchins, the reverend father Dagobert, remained in the undisturbed exercise of his pastoral functions, as curate of New Orleans, and in the administration of this southern part of the diocese of Quebec, of which the Canadian bishop had constituted him vicar general. The other capuchins were maintained in the curacies of their respective parishes.

It may be remembered that, in 1726, the Ursuline Nuns, by the agreement which they had made with the India Company, had bound themselves to take charge of the Charity Hospital in New Orleans. Displeased probably with this kind of service, the Nuns had, in the course of time, obtained from the Pope a bull releasing them, it seems, from their obligation, which had become merely nominal, being confined to the daily attendance of two nuns, during the visit of the king's physician.* After having noted down his prescriptions, they withdrew, contenting themselves with the easy task of sending from their dispensary in the convent the medicines he had ordered. The Catholic king, to show his regard for this religious corporation, decided that two of the Nuns should be maintained at his own expense, for each of whom sixteen dollars was to be paid monthly to the convent out of his royal treasury.

Don Joseph de Loyola, who had come to Louisiana with Ulloa, in 1766, as intendant died in 1770, and his functions were discharged ad interim by Don Estevan Gayarre, the royal comptroller, or contador.

Don Cecilio Odoardo arriving with the commission of auditor of war and assessor of government, Jose de Urrustia and Felix del Rey, those two learned men in the law, who had been the advisers of O'Reilly, and who had

---

* Martin's History of Louisiana.

been discharging the duties now imposed on Odoardo, departed for Havana.

Bobé Desclozeaux, who, on the death of Michel de la Rouvillière, in 1759, had acted as commissary general ad interim, remained in New Orleans by order of the king of France, with the consent of the king of Spain, to call in and redeem the paper money which had been emitted by the former colonial administration, and of which a very considerable quantity was still in circulation.

When Louisiana was ceded to Spain, there were pending in France several appeals from the judgments of the Superior Council. On the 6th of April, 1770, the king of France, through his council of state, declared that he could no longer take cognizance of said appeals, because, when parting with Louisiana, he had also parted with the *first and most glorious of his rights, that of rendering justice in that province*, wherefore he ordered that all the cases which might still be on the dockets of any of his courts, be transferred to the tribunals of Spain, by which they were to be decided.

O'Reilly thought it necessary, by a special proclamation, to re-enact the Black Code which Louis XV. had given to the province. This seems to confirm the opinion, that the French laws were considered by the Spanish government as virtually abrogated by the publication of the ordinance subjecting the colony to the laws of the Indies. A short time after, O'Reilly having completed the mission for which he had been clothed with extraordinary powers, and temporarily sent to Louisiana, delivered up the government of the province to Don Louis de Unzaga, and departed, on the 29th of October, 1770.

Judge Martin, in his History of Louisiana, says: " Charles III. disapproved of O'Reilly's conduct, and he received, on his landing at Cadiz, an order prohibiting his appearance at court." This assertion seems to rest only on the very fallible authority of tradition, and is certainly irreconcilable with official documents on record. Thus, on the 28th of January, 1771, the king of Spain sent to his Council of the Indies a communication, in which he informed them, that he submitted to their consideration all the acts of O'Reilly's administration in Louisiana, which he fully approved, but on which, nevertheless, he wished to have the opinion of his faithful council. The answer was: that the council, having carefully examined all the documents to which the king had called their attention, could discover in the acts of O'Reilly nothing which did not deserve the most decided approbation, and which was not a striking proof of the extraordinary genius of that general officer. Would such an encomium have been bestowed on him, if he had been even suspected of having excited the slightest royal displeasure? Not only all his acts, but also all his suggestions were sanctioned, with one solitary exception, which seems to give still more force to the sweeping commendation expressed, as to every thing else, by the king and his council. This exception is relative to the 6th article of section 5 on punishments, in which O'Reilly said: "The married woman convicted of adultery, and he who has committed the same with her, shall be delivered up to the husband, in order that he may do with them what he pleases, with this reserve, however, that he shall not put one of them to death, without inflicting the same punishment on the other." The council declared that this article, "The perusal of which had proved sufficiently disgusting to them, should be considered* as of no effect, and as having never been writ-

* Se considerase como suspenso y no escrito el art. 6, que dice: "La muger casada que adultere y el adultero sean entregados al marido para que haga de ellos lo que quiera, con tal que no pueda matar al uno sin matar al otro." El cual causó bastante repugnancia al tiempo de leerse.

ten." This article, however, had not been devised by O'Reilly, but was borrowed from book 8 of the "Nueva Recopilacion de Castilla" (new digest of the laws of Castile). It is besides well known that O'Reilly remained high in favor at court, until the death of Charles III.

The motto on O'Reilly's coat of arms was: "fortitudine et prudentiâ;" and he seems not to have been deficient in the possession of both these virtues. But there is hardly an instance, when blood shed in a political cause, whatever may have been the just and apparent necessity of it at the time, did not, sooner or later, rise from the earth, to cloud in the eye of the world the fame of the author or adviser of the deed. This has become an historical truth, and is confirmed by what O'Reilly's memory has suffered, in consequence of the execution of Lafrénière and his companions. He was not, however, the blood-thirsty tyrant that he was represented to be, and never, except on this occasion, in the whole course of a long public life, which was exposed to the scrutiny of those who hated him as a foreigner, and envied him as one of the king's favorites, did he ever give the slightest cause to accuse him of not having been always attentive to the dictates of humanity. His talents as a military man, and as an administrator when discharging the functions of a civil officer, cannot be the object of a doubt, and it must even be admitted that they were of a superior order.

When in Louisiana, he was no more than thirty-four or thirty-five years old. There he left a reputation of strict morality and military precision. Fond of pomp, and somewhat ostentatious in all his tastes, naturally gay, and animated with strong sociable dispositions, he, nevertheless, was not addicted to pleasure, and he devoted himself entirely to the business he had on hand. He was exceedingly prompt, exact and active, and he required the same qualifications in his subordinates. By a proper and systematic distribution of his time, to which he inflexibly adhered, he could get on, with astonishing ease and rapidity, through an immense deal of labor, and he left nothing to be done by others which he could do himself. He emphatically was a man of action, a lover of the camp, as his predecessor, Ulloa, was a man of study, a lover of meditation and scientific speculations. It was said that he endeavored, as far as possible, to see every thing with his own eyes, and, when he had to trust others, he never failed to descend into the minutest details of the duties which he expected them to fulfil. Not only was O'Reilly excessively urbane in his social and official intercourse, but distinguished also for the exquisite refinement of those courtly manners which have now almost ceased to be a reality, and the recollection of which will soon fade away into vague and dreamy traditions. But he was of an irritable temper, and liable to fits of haughtiness on the slightest appearance of what he supposed to be premeditated contradiction or opposition. Preserving all the vivacity, excitability, and sprightly wit of the Irish temperament, he was remarkably animated in conversation, and seemed to have a relish and a turn of mind for a good joke. He cultivated with sedulous attention the society of some families with which he seemed to be highly pleased, and which he always treated with deferential courtesy. Escorted by a few dragoons, his carriage was frequently seen driving at a rapid pace up the Coast, where he used, in his moments of leisure, to visit a family residing a few miles from the town, and in which he found himself in an atmosphere reminding him of that of the best European society. One day, when, according to his habit, he had provoked a keen encounter of wits with the lady of the manor being stung by a sharp repartee, his hasty temper betrayed him, and he forgot himself so far as to say, with a tone of command: " Madam, do you forget who I am ?" "No, sir," answered the lady, with a low bow, " but I have associated with those who were higher than you are, and who took care never to forget what was due to others; hence, they never found it necessary to put any one in mind of what they were." Nettled at this proud answer, Count O'Reilly departed instantly, but returned the next day with a good-humored smile, and an apology befitting a gentleman of his rank. Finally, he became a much valued friend, where at first he had merely been a guest, and, to complete the description of his character, it may be sufficient to add, that, whatever may have been some of his errors, he won esteem and affection wherever he was intimately **known.**

CHAPTER II.

UNZAGA'S ADMINISTRATION.

1770 to 1776.

THE departure of O'Reilly for Spain was soon followed by that of the royal comptroller, Don Estevan Gayarre This officer had applied to the court for leave to return to Spain, and to be put on the list of retired pensioners, on account of his many years of service and of his impaired vision. On the 22d of September, 1770, the Marquis of Grimaldi wrote to the royal comptroller a letter in which he informed him that the favor for which he had petitioned (his return to Spain) was granted, and requested him, on his arrival in the Peninsula, to give information of it and of the state of his health to the government, in order that his majesty might determine on calling him to some other employment or allow him to retire, with the pension to which he was entitled. In consequence of this communication, Estevan Gayarre left the colony in the beginning of 1771, carrying away with him more than one document,* showing conclusively the good understanding which had always existed between Aubry and the Spanish authorities, during all the phases of the revolution of 1768, and a certificate in which the French governor testified, in warm terms of acknowledgment and eulogy, to the important services rendered by the comptroller both to the kings of France and Spain. He was succeeded in office by Antonio Joseph de Aguïar;

* See the Appendix.

his son, Don Juan Antonio Gayarre, who had, under him, acted as chief officer in the comptroller's office (1ro official de contadoria), and who on the 23d of September, 1768, notwithstanding he was then only sixteen years of age, had been, on the eve of the insurrection, appointed commissary of war by the intendant Joseph de Loyola, in which office he was subsequently confirmed by O'Reilly on the 5th of January, 1770, remained in the colony to serve under Aguïar. The old contador and companion of Ulloa died in Spain at the close of the century. To complete the sketch which I gave of his life and character, when depicting that of the other actors who appeared on the stage at that eventful period of the history of Louisiana, and also to illustrate the manners and feelings of another age, it may not be inappropriate to give here a short extract from a letter which, in 1796, he wrote from Coruna in Gallicia, to one of his grandsons in Louisiana:

"My son, I may say that I have already one foot in the grave. I have little of earthly goods to bequeathe, or to dispose of, contenting myself with leaving, at my death, what will be necessary to bury me in seven feet of ground, with the little but honorable exhibition of military pomp, within which have shrunk all my vain hopes in this miserable world. Yea, such is this world! Its flitting glories fade away—and there remains nothing but the alternate lassitude and self-torment of thought. Therefore a pure and sound mind ought ever to have its eyes fixed on heaven."*

* Hijo mio, yo estoy yá con el pie en la sepultura y tengo no efectos de considéracion de que testar ni disponer, contentandome yó con que, á mi fallecimiento se halle lo necesario para enterrarme en siete quartas de tierra con la corta y honrada pompa militar con que solo he fundado la esperanza vana de este miserable mundo. Lo que es el mundo! Cesen glorias pasadas—Del pensamiento unas veces fatiga y otras tormento; el spiritu bueno siempre há de estar mirando al cielo.

Don Luis de Unzaga, whom O'Reilly had designated as his successor, was colonel of the regiment of Havana, and was subsequently confirmed as governor of Louisiana, by a royal schedule of the 17th of August, 1772, with a salary of $6000. When he entered upon the duties of his office, he found that the commerce of Louisiana had greatly decreased under the ill-advised policy of Spanish restrictions; for, it will be recollected that, by the royal ordinance which Ulloa had caused Aubry to publish in 1766, the trade of the colony had been confined to Seville, Alicant, Carthagena, Malaga, Barcelona, and Coruna, and that no vessels were to engage in this trade, restricted as it was, but those that were Spanish built and commanded by Spaniards. Even these vessels, when sailing to or from Louisiana, were prohibited from entering any Spanish port in America, except in case of distress, and then they had to be submitted to a strict examination and to heavy charges. It is true that, in 1768, an exemption from duty had been granted by the king to the commerce of Louisiana on foreign and Spanish goods, either when exported from the six ports already mentioned, or when imported into New Orleans; but the exportation of specie or produce from Louisiana was burdened with a duty of four per cent. The colonists had lately obtained a very slight and insufficient mitigation of the evils of which they complained, and it consisted in a permission granted for the admission of two vessels from France annually.

This oppressive system was exceedingly foolish, as it could benefit neither the colony nor the mother country. Which of the goods they most wanted for their consumption could the colonists have procured to advantage, in Seville, Alicant, Carthagena, Malaga, Barcelona and Coruna, the only ports they could trade to? And if procured, how could they have paid for them?

Importations are paid with exportations; and what could they have successfully exported to those ports, that would have defrayed the costs of transportation? Was it their indigo? But it could not have encountered the competition of the indigo of Guatimala, Caraccas and other Spanish possessions, to which it was greatly inferior in quality. Was it their furs and peltries? But these objects were little cared for in the warm climate of Spain. Was it their rice and corn? But this they raised in too small a quantity, and wanted altogether for their own home consumption. Was it their timber and lumber, which was their most important branch of revenue? But what cargo of the kind would have sold sufficiently high in Spain, to cover the bare expenses of transportation across the Atlantic? Moreover, setting all these considerations aside, how could the merchants of New Orleans compete with the English, who had engrossed the contraband trade of the colony, through the facilities afforded them by the privilege of navigating the Mississippi? Their vessels were constantly ploughing the river up and down; and, under the pretence of going to their possessions of Manchac, Baton Rouge and Natchez, the English contrived clandestinely to supply the inhabitants of New Orleans and the planters above and below that town with goods and slaves. They took in exchange whatever their customers had to spare,* and extended to them a most liberal credit, which the good faith of the purchasers amply justified. Besides, they had very large warehouses at Manchac, Baton Rouge and Natchez, and a number of vessels constantly moored a short distance above New Orleans, opposite to the spot now known as the city of Lafayette. To these places the inhabitants of Louisiana used to resort, and to

---

* Martin's History of Louisiana, p. 26, vol. 2.

carry on their contraband dealings, which were hardly if in any way, checked by the Spanish authorities Encouraged by this tacit connivance, the English had gone farther, and had contrived to convert into floating warehouses two vessels, the cabins of which they fitted up as stores, with shelves and counters. These ingeniously devised shops were kept moving up and down the river, stopping, like our present line of coast steamboats, at every man's door, and tempting him and his family with the display of their goods and trinkets. Thus, in this indirect way, the English having monopolized the trade of Louisiana, this colony had, in a commercial point of view, become for its owner an entirely worthless possession.

Without this infraction of the unwise provisions of the commercial and revenue laws of Spain, it is difficult to imagine how the colony could have subsisted, and, therefore, Unzaga acted judiciously for the province and for Spain, when he disregarded the Chinese-like regulations which he was commanded to enforce, and when he winked at their violation. The poor merchants of New Orleans, whose occupation, like Othello's, was gone, were permitted to indulge in impotent clamors, and in slyly whispered insinuations that the Spanish governor had some reason of his own, besides the alleged one of supplying the wants of the colony, for the indulgence which he extended to British traders. But their complaints were as unnoticed as the idle wind, and things went on as usual, without even any show of attempted interruption.

This year (1771) the Marquis of Grimaldi informed Unzaga, that his majesty had consented to what, he, Unzaga, had applied for, that is, that eleven capuchins from the province of Champagne in France be permitted to come to Louisiana, and had granted the prayer of the

Ursuline Nuns—that a church be built as an appendage to their convent.

In the beginning of 1772, Colonel Estecheria arrived, and assumed the command of the regiment of Louisiana. There came also from Spain, at the king's expense, a priest with two assistants, who were sent to instruct the rising generation in the Spanish language, and from Havana, four young women, who took the veil in the convent of the Ursuline Nuns of New Orleans, and who were destined to teach Spanish to young persons of their sex.

The winter of 1772 was made remarkable for its extreme severity, and all the orange trees perished, as in 1748 and 1768.

If the winter had been Siberian-like, the summer which followed showed itself tropical in all its character, and the country was visited by a hurricane, which was much more furious and destructive than all those which had yet been seen, and which, beginning on the 31st of August, lasted to the 3d of September. Strange to say, however, it was hardly perceptible in New Orleans, where the weather retained its serenity, although it was severely felt in the immediate neighborhood of that town. The sea was driven over the islands along the coast of the gulf, and rushed in mountainous waves, not through, but, as it were, over the passes of the Rigolets and Chef-Menteur, to meet Lake Pontchartrain, which rose to a prodigious height. As the wind blew from the sea, all the vessels at the Balize, with the exception of one that foundered, and was lost with all on board, were lifted up like feathers by the joint fury of the warring elements, and blown over into the midst of those swamps of reeds which line the mouths of the Mississippi. Along the sea-coast, from Lake Borgne to Pensacola, the wind ranged from South-South-East; but farther west, it blew with still greater violence from North-North-East and

East. Judge Martin relates, in his History of Louisiana, that a schooner, belonging to the British government, and having a detachment of troops on board, was driven westerly as far as Cat Island, under the western part of which she cast anchor; but the water rose so high, that she parted her cable, and floated over the island. The wind swept with such irresistible power through the woods, that they were almost entirely destroyed within a radius of about thirty miles from the sea-shore. At Mobile, the strong hand of the hurricane seized the vessels, boats, logs and every thing else that were in the bay, and scattered them about the streets of that town, just as a boy, in a mad freak, flings round his playthings. There was such an accumulation of logs in the gullies and hollows about the town and in its lower grounds, that it supplied the inhabitants with fuel during the whole of the ensuing winter.

The foaming sea seemed to have been lashed into nothing but spray, which, rising up to an immense height, was carried inland by the wind to the distance of four or five miles from the shore, where it descended in thick showers. For thirty miles up a branch of the Pascagoula river, called Cedar Creek on account of the number of cedar trees with which its banks were shaded, the tempest prostrated almost every tree, as if myriads of axes had been emulously at work with destructive rage. Some had been torn by the roots and fantastically tossed about, others were broken into splinters, and, among the few that remained standing, some were stripped of every limb, or twisted together, trunks and branches, into a shapeless mass. The awful scene of desolation looked like the work of a million of intoxicated demons. But one of the most astonishing effects of this hurricane remains to be related. Within four weeks after it had been over, such of the mulberry trees as had escaped its fury, produced a second growth of leaves and fruit. They budded anew, blossomed, and, to complete the phenomenon, produced fruit as plentifully as they had done before.

On the 17th of August, 1772, the King granted to the province of Louisiana, some extension of commerce, in conformity with the suggestions made by O'Reilly in his despatch of the 17th of October, 1769, but the favor, after all, was so restricted, that it did not prove of much importance to the welfare of the colony.

The conflict which had sprung up between the Jesuits and Capuchins, in 1755, as to the exercise of spiritual jurisdiction in Louisiana, may not have been forgotten. The Bishop of Quebec had appointed a Jesuit his Vicar-General in New Orleans, but the Capuchins pretended that they had, according to a contract passed with the India company, obtained exclusive jurisdiction in Lower Louisiana, and therefore had opposed therein the exercise of any pastoral functions by the Jesuits. The question remained undecided by the Superior Council, which felt considerable reluctance to settle the controversy by some final action, from fear perhaps of turning against itself the hostility of both parties, although it leaned in favor of the Capuchins. From sheer lassitude there had ensued a sort of tacit truce, when father Hilaire de Géneveaux, the Superior of the Capuchins, who, for one of a religious order proverbially famed for its ignorance, was a man of no mean scholarship and of singular activity, quickened by a haughty and ambitious temper, went to visit Europe, without intimating what he was about, and returned with the title of Apostolic Prothonotary, under which he claimed, it seems, the power to lord it over the Jesuit who was the Vicar-General of the Bishop of Quebec. Hence an increase of wrath on the part of the Jesuits and a renewal of the old quarrel, which ceased only when the Jesuits were expelled from all the French dominions. But the triumph of father Géneveaux was not of long duration; for, in 1766, the Superior Council, finding that he was opposed to their scheme of insurrection, had expelled him as a perturber of the public peace, and father Dagobert had become Superior of the Capuchins. They lived all together in a very fine house of their own, and there never had been a more harmonious community than this one was, under the rule of good father Dagobert.

He had come very young in the colony, where he had christened and married almost everybody, so that he was looked upon as a sort of spiritual father and tutor to all. He was emphatically a man of peace, and if there was anything which father Dagobert hated in this world, if he could hate at all, it was trouble—trouble of any kind —but particularly of that sort which arises from intermeddling and contradiction. How could, indeed, father Dagobert not be popular with old and young, with both sexes, and with every class? Who could have complained of one whose breast harbored no ill feeling towards anybody, and whose lips never uttered a harsh word in reprimand or blame, of one who was satisfied with himself and the rest of mankind, provided he was allowed to look on with his arms folded, leaving angels and devils to follow the bent of their nature in their respective departments? Did not his ghostly subordinates do pretty much as they pleased? And if they erred at times—why—even holy men were known to be frail! And why should not their peccadilloes be overlooked or forgiven for the sake of the good they did? It was much better (we may fairly suppose him so to have thought, from the knowledge we have of his acts and character), for heaven and for the world, to let things run smooth and easy, than to make any noise. Was there not enough of unavoidable turmoil in this valley of tribulations and miseries? Besides, he knew that God was merciful, and that all would turn right in the end. Why should he not have been an indulgent shepherd for his flock, and have smiled on the prodigal son after repentance, and even before, in order not to frighten him away? If the extravagance of the sinning spendthrift could not be checked, why should not he, father Dagobert, be permitted, by sitting at the hospitable board, to give at least some dignity to the feast, and to exorcise away the ever lurking spirit of evil? Did not Jesus sit at meal with publicans and sinners? Why then should not father Dagobert, when he went out to christen, or to marry at some private dwelling, participate in convivialities, taste the juice of the grape, take a hand in some innocent game, regale his nostrils with a luxurious pinch of snuff, and look with approbation at the merry feats of the dancers? Where was the harm? Could not a father sanctify by his presence the rejoicings of his children? Such were perhaps some of the secret reasonings of the reverend capuchin.

By some pedantic minds father Dagobert might have been taxed with being illiterate, and with knowing very little beyond the litanies of the church. But is not ignorance bliss? Was it not to the want of knowledge, that was to be attributed the simplicity of heart, which was so edifying in one of his sacred mission, and that humility to which he was sworn? Is it not written: "Blessed are the poor in spirit; for theirs is the kingdom of heaven." Why should he understand Latin, or so many other musty inexplicable things? Was not the fruit of the tree of knowledge the cause of the perdition of man? Besides, who ever heard of a learned capuchin? Would it not have been a portentous anomaly? If his way of fasting, of keeping the holydays, of saying mass, of celebrating marriages, of christening, of singing prayers for the dead, and of hearing confessions, of inflicting penance, and of performing all his other sacerdotal functions, was contrary to the ritual and to the canons of the church—why—he knew no better. What soul had been thereby endangered? His parishioners were used to his ways? Was he, after fifty years of labor in the vineyard of the Lord, to change his manner of working, to admit that he had blundered all the time, to dig up what he had planted, and to undertake, when almost an octogenarian, the reform of himself and others? Thus, at least, argued many of his friends.

They were sure that none could deny, that all the duties of religion were strictly performed by his parishioners. Were not the women in the daily habit of confessing their sins? And if he was so very mild in his admonitions, and so very sparing in the infliction of harsh penance on them, why not suppose that it was because the Saviour himself had been very lenient towards the guiltiest of their sex? It was the belief of father Dagobert, that the faults of women proceeded from the head and not from the heart, because *that* was always kind. Why then hurl thunderbolts at beings so exquisitely delicate and so beautifully fragile—the porcelain work of the creator—when they could be reclaimed by the mere scratch of a rose's thorn, and brought back into the bosom of righteousness by the mere pulling of a silken string? As to the men, it is true that they never haunted the confessional; but perhaps they had no sins to confess, and if they had, and did not choose to acknowledge them, what could he do? Would it have been sound policy to have annoyed them with fruitless exhortations, and threatened them with excommunication, when they would have laughed at the *brutum fulmen?* Was it not

CHARACTER OF FATHER DAGOBERT.

better to humour them a little, so as to make good grow out of evil? Was not their aversion to confession redeemed by manly virtues, by their charity to the poor and their generosity to the church? Was not his course of action subservient to the interest both of church and state, within the borders of which it was calculated to maintain order and tranquillity, by avoiding to produce discontents, and those disturbances which are their natural results? Had he not a right, in his turn, to expect that his repose should never be interrupted, when he was so sedulously attentive to that of others, and so cheerfully complying with the exigencies of every flitting hour? When the colonists had thought proper to go into an insurrection, he, good easy soul, did not see why he should not make them happy, by chiming in with their mood at the time. Did they not, in all sincerity, think themselves oppressed, and were they not contending for what they believed to be their birthrights? On the other hand, when the Spaniards crushed the revolution, he was nothing loth, as vicar general, to present himself at the portal of the cathedral, to receive O'Reilly with the honors due to the representative of royalty, and to bless the Spanish flag. How could he do otherwise? Was it not said by the Master: "render unto Cæsar the things which are Cæsar's?" Why should the new lords of the land be irritated by a factious and bootless opposition? Why not mollify them, so as to obtain as much from them as possible, in favor of his church and of his dearly beloved flock? Why should he not be partial to the Spaniards? Had they not the reputation of being the strictest catholics in the world.

Such was the character of father Dagobert even in his youth. It had developed itself in more vigorous and co-ordinate proportions, as his experience extended, and it had suggested to him all his rules of action through life. With the same harmonious consistency in all 's parts it had continued to grow, until more than threescore years had passed over father Dagobert's head. It was natural, therefore, notwithstanding what a few detractors might say, that he should be at a loss to discover the reasons why he should be blamed, for having logically come to the conclusions which made him an almost universal favorite, and which permitted him to enjoy "his ease in his own inn," whilst authorizing him to hope for his continuing in this happy state of existence, until he should be summoned to the "bourne whence no traveller returns." Certain it is that, whatever judgment a rigid moralist might, on a close analysis, pass on the character of father Dagobert, it can hardly be denied, that to much favor would be entitled the man, who, were he put to trial, could with confidence, like this poor priest, turn round to his subordinates and fellow-beings, and say unto them: "I have lived among you for better than half a century; which of you have I ever injured?" Therefore, father Dagobert thought himself possessed of an unquestionable right to what he loved so much: his ease, both in his convent and out of it, and his sweet uninterrupted dozing in his comfortable arm chair.

But the Evil One was hovering round the walls of Eden, and desolation was nigh. A short time after the province had become Spanish, and the Superior Council had been abolished, father Génoveaux startled father Dagobert by his sudden reappearance before him. At first, the humble spirit of the old Capuchin quailed, and his heart sank within him, when he saw one, whose resources of mind, love of power, and indomitable pride he but too well knew. But it seemed that misfortune had operated a salutary change in father Génoveaux and the outward man much belied the inward one, if *that* also was not altered, for he looked like one ready to kiss the rod of chastisement. His head was bent as it were with contrition, his eyes were lowly fixed on the ground, his hands were meekly crossed on his breast. In this posture of humiliation, he informed father Dagobert that he had returned to serve where he had formerly ruled, and he begged for admittance, as an humble subordinate, into the holy house from which he had been ignominiously expelled as a superior. With a rather faltering voice, father Dagobert uttered some words of welcome to his unexpected guest, and expressed assent to his prayer. Keen, no doubt, were his misgivings, but they were soon allayed by the conduct of father Génoveaux, who not only gave the example of submission, but who also was the very pattern of apostolic humility. He seemed to have lost sight entirely of the concerns of this world, and, when not engaged in the few ecclesiastical functions which were assigned to him, and which he discharged with the most exact fidelity, he was wrapped up in prayer or in study—particularly the study of the Spanish language—so far, at least, as what father Génoveaux did could be ascertained, for he came out of his cell as little as he could ; and, by keeping so much out of every body's way, he, by degrees, almost ceased to be considered as a thing of life; or if so, certainly there could not be a more harmless sort of creature, or a more insignificant entity in flesh and blood.

These were halcyon days, indeed, the enjoying of which was only marred by the news, that Spanish Capuchins were soon expected. How they would agree with their French brethren, was a question which excited no little anxiety in the breasts of the latter, when, in the beginning of July, 1772, it was positively known that father Cirilo was coming with some few assistants, in the name of the bishop of Cuba, Don Santiago Hechevarria, to investigate into the affairs of the church and the state of religion in the colony; and, on the 19th of the same month, which was consecrated to the celebration of a holyday, father Dagobert, at the head of his Capuchins, and accompanied by a large crowd of people, went in procession to the Levee in front of the public square, where father Cirilo and his companions were received with due honors and with great demonstrations of joy. The next day, the Spanish priests were presented to the Governor, to whom father Cirilo delivered his credentials, and the letters addressed by the bishop to that functionary. Governor Unzaga expressed still warmer satisfaction than the people at the arrival of these ministers of peace and instructors in morals and religion, and declared publicly to father Cirilo, that he was ready to make use of all the powers with which he was clothed, to carry into execution the sacred instructions and mandates of his Grace, the bishop of Cuba.

On the very day of the arrival of the Spanish priests in the colony, father Génoveaux doffed the garb of humility and submission which he had assumed, and proudly raising his head, told father Dagobert, in an insulting tone and very abusive language, that a radical change would soon take place, that ignorance, profaneness, wickedness and dotage would speedily be driven out of the convent and of the country, to yield their usurped power to virtue, learning, religion, active zeal and pious labor. He further added, that the avengers of his wrongs had come at last, and that now was the turn of his enemies to tremble. In order to carry his threats into execution, he immediately ingratiated himself with the Spanish priests, and, being much their superior in intelligence and energy, he became their secret adviser and the prompter of all the manœuvres and attacks from which the French Capuchins had to suffer.

Having landed on the 19th of July at New Orleans, father Cirilo lost no time in prying into the Lord's vineyard, and, on the 6th of August, communicated to his diocesan at Havana the result of his observations, of which I give here a condensed abstract: "The people of this province," said he, "are in general religiously disposed, and seem anxious for the salvation of their souls. They observe a profound silence during divine worship, and, when the Most Holy Ghost is brought out (which is on the principal holydays), both sexes prostrate themselves on the ground. With regard to the women, they are more honest than in Spain, and live more in accordance with the precepts of the church. There are some small things in the morals and in the religious observances of these people, which might be better, but time will remedy these trifling evils. As to the clergy, that is, the French Capuchins, I agree with his Excellency, the Governor, whose despatch to your grace I have seen, in saying that father Dagobert, having had the spiritual government of this province for so long a time, deserves every sort of regard and consideration, and that, on account of his age and services, he is entitled to enjoy the most favorable treatment, and to be permitted to be relieved from his official fatigues. But I cannot allow to pass unnoticed what I have remarked in the deportment of those * * * * * * how shall I designate them? for, certainly, I cannot call Capuchins those whom I consider as unworthy of this holy name. In a true Capuchin, according to the rules and discipline established by St. Francis, there is naught to be seen but austerity and poverty. But such is not the case with these men. In their dress, such, for instance, as their shirts, breeches, stockings and shoes, they resemble the laity much more than members of their religious order. They say that they have a dispensation from the Pope; but of what nature? I have not seen it yet. Whether it is in existence or not, certain it is that the doctrine which we profess, commands us to be satisfied with the strictest necessaries of life and with the extremest poverty. Therefore I do not believe in the grant of any such dispensation by the Popes, beyond what may be absolutely requisite to keep soul and body together. But it never could extend so far as to authorize every one of these fathers, to have a watch in his fob and a clock striking the hour in his room, and another in their refectory which cost two hundred and seventy dollars. Nor do I believe that they have permission from our Sovereign Lords the Popes, to possess so many silver spoons and forks, that it is doubtful whether your Grace owns the like. Not only have they silver spoons of the ordinary size, but they have also small ones, to take coffee with, as if wooden spoons were not good enough for Capuchins! I will not speak of the furniture of their rooms, nor of the luxuries of their table. But be it sufficient to say, that although, since our arrival and on our account, they have somewhat moderated their good living, their table is still reputed to be better than any other in this capital. Hence, what was it before? Very often they do not eat at the common refectory, but invite one another to dine at their private apartments.

"This abuse your grace can remedy, as well as that of their having, to wait upon them at table, so many young mulattresses or negresses who are not married. I cannot put a stop to this scandal, having no authority over them. But I infer from a letter written to me by the Superior of our order in Cataloña, that there is some probability of his being appointed to take charge of this province. With the strength which I might derive from this fact, should it prove to be true, and from your Grace's countenance and support, I would endeavor to make it known that we are capuchins, and to force those who live in violation of our sacred rules and without .caring for God, either to reform their evil ways or to go back whence they came. But, for the present, we can make no innovation, except with regard to the parsonage of this parish, because, in this matter, you can order and dispose as you please, inasmuch as father Dagobert has promised the governor that he would obey all the mandates of your grace, and for this reason, it is agreed between us and the governor, that you commission father Dagobert as the vicar general of this province, until we can learn the French language, because, without its knowledge, it is impossible that we should discharge our functions. But in case your Grace, most excellent sir, should be of opinion that said individual ought not to be appointed vicar general, your Grace might, for the present, postpone all nomination to that office, leaving everything as it is, writing to father Dagobert and to me what you wish to be done in this province, and charging us with the execution of the good intentions of your Grace and of his majesty (whom may God preserve for ever!) And in order that your Grace, the governor and myself may attain our ends with greater facility, and plant here, without noise and opposition, the Lord's vineyard, as it is in Havana, I am of opinion that you should state, when you write, that you are determined to postpone the nomination of the vicar general, until you have the report of him whom you may send to inspect the affairs of the church in this province. Thus, father Dagobert, either through fear, or to please your grace, will execute what your grace will command him to do. It is important to secure his influence, not only because the people of this colony, for thirty years past, have known no other spiritual jurisdiction than that of this father, but also because he has obtained the esteem and affection of all, so that whatever father Dagobert orders is obeyed without reluctance. It seems proper to me that your Grace should write none but joint letters to us both, because father Dagobert does not understand the Spanish language, and God knows to whom he would give your letters to be read. This might produce disturbances, whilst, if I am the person to communicate the contents of your letters to him, I will take care to impress them upon him with prudence and dexterity, and procure that your wishes be complied with. In this way, the governor and myself think that we can obtain all that we desire without trouble and noise.

"If it be discovered that said father does not obey your instructions, I shall give your Grace due information thereof, in order that you may appoint a vicar general; and if you deign to favor my suggestions, you might bestow on him and myself the faculty of granting dispensation, particularly with regard to the publications required before the marriage ceremony can be performed. The first thing you ought to do, is to commission some body who, in the name of your Grace, would take possession, in the manner you may determine, of the church of the Nuns and of the plantation which the capuchins have, in order to show that your Grace is the head of this apostolic see and the administrator of all its possessions. In this way we shall know how matters stand, for it is said that the plantation of the holy fathers is under mortgage. What is certain, is that it yields nothing for want of proper management, and your Grace might, for the future, make such regulations as would prevent the ruin of those fathers from being entirely accomplished.*

"With regard to our parochial and judicial rights and privileges, it is sufficient to refer to the governor's letter to your Grace. As to the administration of the sacraments, I have observed no abuse, but on the contrary, I must say that they are received with great piety—particularly the sacrament of marriage. I must state, however, that there is no preaching every Sunday according to the mandate of the Council; but, at the same time, I must admit that, so far as my information goes, sermons are delivered on the principal holydays of the year. The French capuchins keep three books, one in which they record the baptisms, another the marriages, and in the third, the deaths of the whites and blacks, as they occur; which practice is to be corrected. I must also remark that these books ought to be kept in Spanish, and the governor and myself (for we shall both be always of the same mind) will look to the reforms which it may be proper to introduce in relation to these books.

"As to masses pro populo, it is certain that they are not said; for, these priests take no notice of any of the apostolic bulls and letters which have been issued for these last thirty years. This makes it necessary that your Grace should command them to be complied with, in order that, with your Grace's authority, we may correct these Monks, who have been living to this day, with the same morals which they brought with them on their first arrival in these parts. As to religious conferences, they have no idea of any such thing. But I pass over this point without any further notice, and will only say, that, if our most reverend provincial father of Cataloña be

---

* If capuchins are sworn to poverty and ought not to have silver spoons, why should regulations be made to prevent their *ruin* from being accomplished, and to enable them to retain possession of a plantation and of slaves?

appointed commissioner for this province, I shall take care that this practice, which *we* observe once a week among ourselves, be introduced among the French Capuchins.

"The confessionals, in their shape and construction, are more decent and better than ours in Spain, and, far from changing any thing in them, I would recommend that those which may for the future be made here, be exactly on the same model. What is to be regretted is —that none of these priests confess in these confessionals, but in the vestry, where they sit in an arm chair, by the side of which the penitent kneels. On the first day of this month, when many ladies came to confession, it was done as I have related, with the exception of the Spanish ladies, who were shriven by us—the Spanish ladies confessing in the morning, the French in the evening. On witnessing such an abuse, I could not help asking for its cause, and I was answered that it was owing to the heat. But it is not the less a fact, that I shrove my penitents in the morning, in the confessionals of the church, not in the vestry, and, if I felt the heat, surely I had suffered more from the same cause on other occasions and in other places. With regard to the habits of these priests, I know very little; but I have remarked in them an independent spirit, which is not disposed to obedience and subjection. As to their going to balls, I do not see any probability in it, because the youngest of them is fifty years old; but they frequently attend dinner parties, particularly when they perform marriage ceremonies. This is always done, not in church but in private houses, where they usually remain to enjoy all the pleasures of the feast. This is contrary to our holy habits, and your Grace will order, no doubt, that, henceforth, marriages be celebrated in church, except in case of ill-health in the parties, or for some other important cause; and, above all, that no priest be permitted to accept of any invitation to dinner, or to partake of any convivialities at the houses of those whom he may be called to unite in the bonds of wedlock.

"The report is, that these Capuchins play cards. It is for your Grace to put a stop to a practice, which is so repugnant to the character of a minister of God and especially of a Capuchin. With regard to the Nuns, I cannot give you any information, unless it is that they live as they have always done, without being cloistered, and as if they were not nuns at all. They have for their ordinary confessor, father Prosper, who is seventy-two years old, but very strong and robust, and capable of directing them. As to any violations of rules and discipline, I shall say nothing, and satisfy myself with repeating, that no Pope's bulls and apostolic decretals ever reach this capital. What gives me the greatest concern is, that the slaves live and die in a state of concubinage; and, what is worse, this is to the knowledge and with the consent of their masters, who tolerate their living together like man and wife. This evil must be immediately remedied. When Count O'Reilly was here, he prohibited this kind of scandalous connection, and he succeeded in having forty of these people married coràm facie Ecclesiæ; but, since his departure, it is of this matter as heretofore. The reason which the slaves give for not getting married is, that they are exposed to be sold by their masters and to be thus separated. It seems to me that the most effective way to prevent the commission of such sins, is to impose upon the masters the obligation of watching over the morals of their slaves.

"Our holy fathers have no lack of negroes and mulattresses, since they have eighteen of them in the convent, of both sexes and of different ages, among whom there are but two married couples, when eight women and two men are marriageable, and still are suffered to live in a state of celibacy. Besides, there are two boys and two girls, three of whom are the issue of a mulattress, who has the direction of the convent. This woman has a sister, who is in a delicate situation, and yet who is not known to have a husband. I felt so much solicitude on the subject, that I procured to see, one day, at four o'clock in the morning, a white man sallying out of the chamber of this mulattress, and I am informed by persons of high standing and of great religious zeal, such as the colonel of the regiment and others, that the young negresses and mulattresses, immediately after having attended us at supper, go out of the convent to meet their lovers, and spend with them the greater part of the night. If such of them as live under the immediate inspection of the fathers behave in this way, what must it be with those who live on the plantation? It will be necessary to find a remedy to these scandals. I am of opinion, however, that, to expel all these women from the convent, would be to inflict too painful a blow on father Dagobert. Therefore he might, for the present, be permitted to retain his three black men and three black wenches or mulattresses, provided they are ascertained to be married, or get married—one man and his wife to be for the kitchen, two men to wait on us at table, and their wives, to take care of the house. And, as these women have their dwellings in the yard of the convent, it might be prescribed that, for no motive, and under no pretext whatsoever, they shall be authorized to enter the chambers occupied by the friars. The governor of this province has no black women nor mulattresses to wait upon him! Why should they? Your Grace and other personages of exalted rank require no mulattresses. Why should the French Capuchins need any? I do not hesitate to say, that, in matters of this kind, the glory and service of God is the only thing to be regarded, without caring for worldly considerations. Let these women be expelled from the convent, and be sent to the plantation. There, if they cannot be useful (and I am of opinion that they are not wanted), let them be sold, and let those who may be retained, and who may be of age to wed, take husbands. This would be giving the good example, and let it be understood that, if they work on the plantation, they must be supplied with sufficient food and clothing, as justice requires; and let it not be with them, as it is, if I am correctly informed, with the generality of slaves here, who are furnished by their masters but with one barrel of corn per month, which is less than is given to a horse. This barrel of corn is to be both food and clothing to them; and, as this is impossible, their necessities drive them into prostitution and other shameful vices. But if your Grace should determine that any black woman or mulattress may be retained in the convent, I would suggest the propriety of her being put under lock and key every night, and recommend that the key be delivered to whomsoever you might designate."

The worthy friar Cirilo now goes into details, as to the measures which he thinks most advisable to be adopted for the better administration of the temporalities of the order, and says:

"I think that many other reforms will be necessary in the course of time, but I have mentioned, I believe, all that was most important to be attended to, in order to cure a body which has been diseased from its very creation; for father Dagobert has allowed a free course to the distemper. It is certain that when he came to the colony, all those who saw him then say that he was poorer than we are, and that he had nothing but his breviary and his gown, whilst the king has provided us with all our necessaries. But I know that I am a capuchin; that, as such, I cannot even own any of the things I need, and that only their temporary use is permitted to me. For this reason, as well as to save my soul, and in order that I may not have to answer before God for the souls of others, should it become my lot to organize and reform this mission, I would do the work with the most careful precision, and be the first to give the good example in my person; because, if the said father Dagobert, who has been Superior so long, had been a true capuchin and had behaved as such, there would have been no necessity for reforms in this convent, or mission. In all sincerity I entreat your grace not to think of me as vicar general of this province, not that I anticipate the fate of St. Benoit, who was murdered by the very monks who had elected him their abbot. I do not suspect these to be capable of such a crime, nor do I fear death, because I should be too happy to die for the greater glorification of the Lord; but I think my abilities unequal to the task. I conclude with praying God to enlighten your Grace in this affair, as on those occasions in which you have displayed so much zeal, prudence and gentleness of heart."

The governor's letter, to which father Cirilo refers, had been addressed by that functionary, on the 11th of July, to the bishop of Havana, and contained a detailed and minute statement of the ecclesiastical organization of the province of Louisiana. "Under the king of France, her former master, she enjoyed," said he, "the fullest and most entire liberty. Her inhabitants were subjected to no other authority than that of the laws, and were ruled by no other customs than those of Paris. The principal and almost only act of sovereignty exercised by the king, consisted in appointing the judges. The whole aim of the French government was to people and cause to flourish a country, which gave the promise, through its fertility, of being converted into an immense and profitable realm, when its primitive wildness should have been subdued by the labors of cultivation. In order to accomplish this end, favors and rewards were granted to the colonists, to stimulate their exertions. They met with no impediments, provided they were active, industrious, and laborious, and they were not controled in their religious sentiments, in order that the disturbances which a contrary course would have produced, should not retard the increase of the population. The king used to pay out of his treasury a mission of capuchins, who ministered to the spiritual wants of the colony, under the superintendence of the bishop of Quebec. This bishop appointed for his vicar general a Jesuit, to whom he delegated the authority of granting dispensations with regard to marriage publications, and the impediments to wed arising from the blood relations of the parties. But the friar, Hilaire de Génoveaux, having been made Superior of the mission of capuchins by the provincial of the province of Champagne in France, began to question the Jesuit's powers, which he pretended to be vested in him alone, as the high prelate and curate of this parish. He further asserted that the bishop's jurisdiction was limited to mere acts of supervision. This produced the noise which is the natural consequence of disputes of the kind. In the meanwhile, father Génoveaux went to France, and returned with the title of apostolic prothonotary, on the strength of which he claimed such privileges, that he added new fuel to the Jesuit's rage, and their wranglings were renewed. The Jesuit, in his capacity of vicar general of the bishop of Quebec, asked of the Superior Council the expulsion of his antagonist as a perturber of the public peace and usurper of episcopal jurisdiction, and succeeded in his application. This event and the subsequent exile of the Jesuits were the cause that father Dagobert became the Superior of the mission and the vicar general of the bishop. He is a pacific man, much liked by the people and by those placed under his jurisdiction. Thus stood matters when his Majesty took possession of the province, and his excellency, Count O'Reilly, made no change in its religious organization beyond expelling some Jews and Protestants."

The Governor then went into an enumeration of the priests of the colony, of the places where they were located, and of the functions they discharged. "All those friars," said he, "are excellent men, and give the good example; but among them there are some who are well informed, and others scarcely instructed as to the duties of their sacred calling; all, however, labor zealously to the best of their abilities and knowledge, and they are familiar with the great poverty and destitution of their parishioners. Among them, father Dagobert obtained the esteem of Count O'Reilly and the good will of all the Spaniards by his kindness and the prudence of his deportment. He is beloved by the people, and, on the grounds which I have stated, I consider him entitled to the favor of your Grace."

The Governor goes into many details as to the revenues of the church and the emoluments of the priests, who, to use his expressions, had more than enough to live with as much decency and decorum as their position required. "The Nuns, who are very few," said he, "are supported by the king on the same footing with the capuchins, and his Majesty pays them a pension for a certain number of orphans they educate. They possess a plantation with slaves, and another without any, under the administration of the prioress, who lives cloistered, and under the direction of their chaplain. These plantations are as badly managed, through want of proper knowledge, as that of the capuchins, and they are all a source of expense both to the capuchins and the Nuns, rather than of revenue. The excessive kindness of father Dagobert permits, that there be in the convent of these friars young blackwomen and mulattresses, who are their slaves, and who were born on their plantation. This is contrary to the sacred dispositions of the canons of the church, and the prudence of your Grace will know how to cure this distemper without cauterizing the patient.

"The bishop of Quebec seems to have delegated to his vicar here the faculty of granting dispensations, with regard to marriage prohibitions, and the impediments to wed arising from consanguinity, and also the privilege of permitting the celebration of marriages, according to his judgment, at the residences of the parties either in the country or in the town. But in general that ceremony is performed at church, in conformity with the wishes of the parties themselves. Marriage is a very solemn contract among the French, and a sacrament of felicities (y un sacramento de felicidadas). According to the laws and old customs of the territory, minors cannot marry without the express consent of their parents; such marriages were declared null and clandestine, and reprobated as conducive to seducing away young girls from the legitimate authority under whose keeping they were placed. This is harsh, and your Grace will determine what is suitable in so serious a matter, from which depends public tranquility.

"It is not the practice here to force any one to submit to the Church, and the process of excommunication is held in utter abomination. I assure your Grace, however, that those who live out of the pale of the Church are very few. These people are devout, respectful, and edifying in their deportment when in church. But, to go to confession and receive the sacrament, is a thing unknown with the male part of the population. They look upon it as an act of hypocrisy, and as treating with levity the holiest sacrament, whose mystery they worship with the deepest and humblest veneration. Hence it results that they approach, for the first and last time, the communion table, on reaching the age of puberty.

"The Church here enjoys no immunities and privileges, and its jurisdiction is entirely confined to the spiritual. The affiancing of parties, the nullity or validity of the marriage contract, the granting of a perpetual divorce, or a temporary separation, all this falls under the cognizance of the secular power, to which the clergy itself is subjected for any crime which may be committed by one of its members. Marriage here was considered in the light of a civil contract only, and the clergy, as in France, exercised no judicial prerogative over their fellow-subjects. In order to establish in this province the ecclesiastical jurisdiction without any disturbance or scandal, it would be proper that your vicar-general should be satisfied with making known, verbally, what are the matters, among those of little importance, which he considers to be of his competency, and that he should proceed therein with moderation, without the bustling apparatus of a court of justice, and without costs to the parties. But in cases of a serious nature, such as those which may arise from the act of affiancing, from the alleged validity or nullity of a marriage, or an application for a final divorce, when the parties, or the facts of the case, are of sufficient importance to excite public attention, it would be advisable not to proceed here beyond the taking down of all the testimony required, and to submit it to your Grace, or to your vicar-general in Havana, for adjudication; and, considering that father Dagobert, your vicar-general here, is no jurist, your Grace might advise him to consult, in such matters, my auditor, &c. In this way, should my suggestions meet your approbation, our laws and customs would be introduced insensibly, without clashing too abruptly with those to which the people of this country have been accustomed."

The Governor went on informing the bishop of Havana, that the ecclesiastical registries were in the greatest state of disorder, being kept in the most ridiculous and filthy manner, and recommended the adoption of the plan which was followed in Havana, for the keeping of similar records. He also said that it was customary in the province, to administer to those convicts who were sentenced to death the sacred sacrament of penitence only, but that he saw no inconvenience in following the regulations of the Spanish clergy on the subject.

"It seems proper to me," said he, "that all the Friars who have now some employment, should be retained in the same, and father Dagobert, for one year, in that of vicar-general. In the mean time, the Spanish Friars will have acquired all the knowledge they may want, and then one of them may be selected to succeed the present incumbent, on the ground that a man who has worked so long is entitled to repose. Nevertheless, he will always be glad to officiate, because singing in church is with him a passion. The other Friars will follow his orders, as to the discharge of their sacred functions. It is their duty to take charge of the souls, and, in its accomplishment, they will move to the right or to the left, as the necessity of the case may require, and with that entire submission which is to be expected from the sons of obedience," (hijos de obediencia.)

It is evident, from the tone of these two letters, that father Cirilo was laboring under a delusion, as subsequent events will show, when he said that: "the governor and himself would always be of the same mind." On the

15th of September, he had become much exasperated, and expressed himself as follows to the bishop of Cuba.

"Most illustrious sir, I will proceed to make known to your Grace the circumstances which caused father Dagobert to become the Superior of this province. When Louisiana was ceded to Spain, the chiefs of the insurrection which broke out shortly after, communicated their rebellious intentions to father Hilaire de Génoveaux, who was then the ecclesiastical superior of the colony, and requested him to lend them his assistance in driving the people into the premeditated revolution. He, who fully appreciated the consequences of such an act, would not consent to it, and then they applied to this father Dagobert, to whom they made the same proposition. This friar, who aimed at nothing but power, not only assented to what was asked of him, but did a great many other things. Matters being thus arranged, the chiefs of the sedition seized father Génoveaux, embarked him loaded with chains, and transported him out of the colony Father Dagobert, having thus got rid of his Superior, wrote to the head of the order in Champagne, that this father Génoveaux had run away to the English, and, on this representation, got himself confirmed in the office to which he had been promoted. But, with regard to this father Dagobert, it happens that he has forgotten to notify the faithful of the coming of Ember weeks. His attention being called to this omission, he solved the difficulty by transferring the observance of these sacred days to the week following. We replied to him that we did not feel authorized to pursue such a course, and he then observed: "Very well; you may fast this week, if you please, but the public will on the next." Thus you see that he arrogates to himself more power than is possessed by the Pope, and that he changes, on his own private authority, all the regulations of the church.

After all, these things but confirm the truth of this axiom: *where fails the fear of God, there fails every thing else.* What remains for us to do is to write to the Court, to obtain the dismission of father Dagobert, and, perhaps, of some other persons. I think that it would require very little effort to obtain this dismission, and if, to replace these men, there did not come Capuchins enough from Castile, there would be no lack of them in my province of Cataloña that would come here."

This despatch had hardly been closed, when his indignation, it seems, gathering fresh strength with the passing hour, forced him to resume his pen on the very same day, and to disburthen himself in the following strain: "Illustrious sir, the evils by which we are surrounded compel us to expose the wicked actions which these monsters, rather than Capuchins, perpetrate against our persons,* against God and his holy things.† It is not my intention, most excellent sir, to trouble you with trifles, and therefore, with regard to what concerns ourselves, I shall merely say that the very Spanish name is an object of abomination to these Friars, because they cannot even bear the sight of the things which are of God, and which appertain to our divine religion, and because these Friars or monsters think that we have come to repress the abuses which they love, and to reform their evil ways. Therefore they hate us, and such is the reason why we cannot obtain from them even what is necessary to the so very limited wants of a poor Capuchin—such, for instance, as a table to write on, an humble box wherein to put our wearing apparel, paper, ink, quills and other trifles. When *they* have bags so full of dollars, *we* are obliged to have recourse to our friends to relieve our necessities.

---

* The Spanish Capuchins. † Y sus cosas sagradas.

"What is most deplorable is to see in the convent the concubine of the friars, for such is the reputation she bears. She has three sons, although who her husband is God only knows. They eat at our table and off the plates of father Dagobert, who, without shame, or fear of the world at least, if not of God, permits them to call him papa. She is one of the mulattresses who are kept in the house. She is the absolute mistress of the whole establishment, and the friars have for her so much attachment, that they strive who shall send to the cherished paramour the best dish on the table, before any one of us is allowed to taste it. To witness such things, and to be silent out of the sheerest complaisance, is what gives additional poignancy to our grief. But these sufferings, being supported for the sake of God, to whose service we have consecrated ourselves, will make more meritorious the labors which we have undergone to please our God and our monarch (whom may God have in his holy keeping!). There are, however, greater evils which afflict our hearts, and which are the sins they clearly commit against God and his holy sacraments. Baptism is administered without any of the ceremonies prescribed by the Romish ritual, and the consecrated oil itself is impure and stale. Children are christened when it suits the whim or caprice of their parents, and hence months will elapse previous to the performance of this ceremony. But father Dagobert never fails eating at the house of the parents of the newly christened child. All of which things are unworthy of a man who is the ecclesiastical head of this province. As to the Eucharist, that mystery which makes the angels tremble with awe, we found that the sacramental elements were so full of insects which fed on them, and presented so disgusting an appearance, that it was necessary to fling them into the jakes, as if they had been the veriest filth. So great is the detestable negligence of these men, that I think they are the disciples either of Luther or Calvin! The consecrated oil is never renewed, either because they think that it is incorruptible, or because, like the heretics, they do not believe in the real presence of Christ in the Eucharist after the utterance of the consecrating words; and the proof of it is, that, on our remonstrating with them on this state of things, one of them answered with the greatest serenity that he had kept two years a large consecrated wafer, and had not thought necessary to change it. Nor is less the irreverence with which they behave when they exhibit the Host to the people; for without singing, or burning any incense, they take it out of its small tabernacle, and expose it in the most indecent manner; or, at Vespers, they sing the *Salve Regina*, and also on the first Sundays of every month. The Host being exposed, they sing the *Miserere, de Profundis*, and *requiem*, &c.—which practices are contrary to the rules of the breviary and to the decretals.

"This father Dagobert is a great hand at giving with the sacrament the benediction to the people, whenever it is desired by them. Thus, in a little more than a month, he gave it eight times. He is no less fond of making processions, for which he has no authority, and for which there is no necessity; and, what is still more singular, when thus going out in procession, he abandons the Host without leaving any priest to watch over it. Once I saw him go out with the Viaticum without ordering the bells to be rung, and with as little ceremony as if he was bent only on taking a walk. I say that I have seen him carry the Viaticum but *once*, although many are the deaths that have occurred since I am here. You must also be made to know, most excellent Sir, that the Viaticum is not administered to the blacks, to the mulattoes, nor to the culprits who are sentenced to death and, having asked father Dagobert for the cause of it, I was answered that it was to establish a distinction between the blacks and whites. Did you ever hear a more cruel answer? Moreover, having inquired if he shrove them, he told me that he did, but that they never took the sacrament of the Eucharist. Was there ever such ignorance in any priest? Who will account to God for this neglect and for the sins of these poor people, who are not taught to participate in the blessed sacrament of communion at the hour of their death? Nor is less the indecency with which, in sight of the exposed Host, these priests demean themselves in the choir, where they are seen stuffing their noses with tobacco, crossing one leg on the top of the other, staring round in every direction, scandalizing the people, and moving the very angels to wrath.

"With regard to the sacrament of penitence, as God alone can know how it is administered, we must leave it to Him to express His judgment upon it, when the day shall come. I shall only say that these priests do not know nor ever have known, nor ever will know anything of morals and religion, for since our coming to this colony, we have never known them to remain in their convent beyond the time required to eat and sleep; and with regard to father Dagobert, here is in a few words how he lives: he rises at six in the morning, says or does not say mass (such mass as he says!) preparing himself in this way for the duties of the day. He then goes to church, hardly makes the proper genuflection, claps on his bonnet, says his mass which does not last a quarter of an hour, without any of the prescribed ceremonies, uncovers his head, makes another genuflection as for grace, and taking his three-cornered hat, which is a very superfluous and unworthy appendage for a capuchin, he goes (without thinking of saying any *Ave Maria*, except it be for goodly dollars, and in abundance) to a somewhat suspicious house, where he plays until the dinner hour. When that meal is over, he resumes the occupation in which he was engaged, and continues in it until supper time, so that it is very doubtful whether he complies with divine worship. With regard to extreme unction, I have not been able to ascertain how this sacrament is administered, and I do not know whether it is administered at all, but I believe that they carry it in their purse.*

" With regard to the holy sacrament of marriage, it is in its administration that the greatest abuses are committed. In the first place, we have good grounds to suppose that they observe none of the ceremonies of their ritual, which is the Romish, and I have already remarked that, with the exception of the poor and the blacks, none marry in church, but that our Superior goes about, either in the town or out of it, marrying people in their own houses, where he says mass and remains with them to participate in all the festivities of the occasion. Since my coming here there have been many marriages, but the parties have every time been granted a dispensation for the required publications, for no other purpose than that of getting money, which is his god. I know that all this is to be paid for and well too, because I am informed that thirty dollars have to be given for a mass with a *Libera me Domine*, and one hundred and fifty for a solemn service for the dead. I am not aware of what is paid for the other sacraments. We have never seen these priests celebrate the marriage ceremony for any black couple, except it be for a negro who resided in the house of a Spaniard, and even this was done with a good deal of repugnance on the part

---

* Por que creo que lo traen á la faltriquera.

of father Dagobert, who objected that this was not customary, and that this negro, like all those of his class, was living, to the knowledge of his masters, in a state of concubinage; finally, in order to get the assent of father Dagobert, it was necessary to resort to the authority of the Governor."

Father Cirilo next complains that no care is taken to teach and propagate the Christian doctrine. He enumerates other abuses and ecclesiastical malfeasances, and recommends the introduction of certain reforms and practices. He then winds up saying: " On reading all this, your Grace must be greatly astonished that the Governor has recommended this Father Dagobert to be continued one year in office as vicar-general of this province, and still more—that I should have joined in that recommendation, although I must confess that the Governor had told me that this priest was excessively ignorant, but I could not persuade myself that it was to such an extent. It now appears certain to me that his ignorance is such, that he is incapable of being trusted with the spiritual government of this colony, and therefore I say (and I am supported in my opinion by my companions, by the most respectable people in this province, and by the colonel, whose understanding is of the highest order) that not only ought father Dagobert to be deprived of his charge, but that he ought also to be expelled from the colony, to be punished according to his deserts, and sentenced to a proper penance for his personal faults and the enormous sins which he has caused some of his flock to commit, and for which there are the gravest reasons to believe that those who have died are now in hell.

"Your Grace, knowing so well the good nature and the pacific dispositions of the Governor, will easily conceive how it is that he is desirous of giving satisfaction to these friars, not because he is not fully aware of their misdeeds, not because he does not see that there is no punishment which they have not deserved, and that it would be proper to *drive them out of the land*, as himself has expressed it to me, but because, when these capuchins knew that the Spaniards were coming up the river, they stirred up the town and persuaded the Governor that, if they were sent away, all the people would also depart; whereupon that officer quieted their fears by telling them that the Spaniards were not coming to turn them out of the country. But your Grace must not believe in the general emigration with which we are threatened. It would be confined to a few of father Dagobert's relations, who would starve, if they were not supported by him. This father Dagobert has promised the Governor that he would do all that your Grace would prescribe, and, satisfied with this pledge, the Governor is willing that the friar should remain vicar-general for one year, and that I should then take his place. Perhaps it would be good policy that he who has done so much harm should be the person to repair it. But how can it be expected from one who is not only evil minded, but who is also strongly suspected of some error of faith? With regard to all the promises which he has given to the Governor, I know that he has not kept one; the Governor, however, with his usual good nature, contents himself with saying that the father will in due time redeem his pledges. But should he do so, he would have better reasons to complain of his being deprived of the dignity of vicar-general, and should he remain in office, it would be extremely difficult to reconcile to such a disappointment those who imagine that they will soon see him dismissed, not only all the Spaniards, who would rejoice at such an event, but also a good many of the French, who already perceive the difference which exists between us and those priests. The motive of all the delays to which the Governor resorts is—that he hopes to receive, at every moment, permission to retire from the colony, and he thinks that if he were once out of the way, we and the French capuchins would be forced to come to some understanding. But may it please God that this Governor do not depart before we take possession of the church here, if we are ever destined to do so, because with some other governor (and God only knows what his turn of mind may be!) we should perhaps be obliged to appeal to the court—which we might, without fear of trouble, undertake to do with this governor. The language which I speak is as plain as it is well founded, because, on my mentioning to the Governor what I had written, and on my telling him that I reproached myself with having consented to father Dagobert's being continued in the office of vicar-general for another year, that my conscience upbraided me for having acted with such levity, and that we both should have to account to God for the sins which we had permitted, he approved me in everything, and expressed the opinion (which is mine also) that this father Dagobert being once removed, the evil would be cut by the root; and this said Governor has also confessed to me that he would petition the court for the removal of this friar!

"Under such circumstances, I would advise your Grace either to send here an impartial person to look into the state of the church, or to intrust me with all the necessary powers to go through the work of reform; for, when once in possession of the Lord's vineyard, I shall not lose sight of my obligation to labor therein as I ought, and I shall act accordingly, and in *conformity* with the sentiment of St. Martin and St. Paul who said: "*that they feared no created thing, nor death, nor any et cætera.*" With the information which I have laid before your Grace, it is in your Grace's power to judge of the extent of the work to be done. What is certain is that I cannot believe that father Dagobert is to remain vicar-general.

"I feel much compunction at having been obliged to make your Grace acquainted with the faults of these bad men, which I would have kept from your knowledge, if my motive in disclosing them had not been the glorification of God. I can safely affirm that father Dagobert will not perform any of the things which he has promised to do, nor will remedy any of the existing evils. Thus, on my having inquired why he did not recommend to the public the observance of such holy days as were celebrated in Spain, he answered me, in the presence of many witnesses, that it was because he did not choose to do so, that no one had the right to give him orders, and that nothing should be done in the colony except according to his will. From this you may judge whether we could feel justified in entertaining any hope of operating the slightest salutary reform. I have not failed to throw out a good many insinuations to these priests, but their uniform answer is: *that they are not Spaniards*, and that, besides our mere assertion, they have no other proof that your Grace is the bishop of this diocese. It must be confessed that they have some grounds for this excuse, because the Governor has thought proper to keep in his possession the letter in which your Grace invested me with all the powers which you had given to father Angel. I have since had no further sight of this letter, and it is certain that the Governor has not communicated its contents to these Friars, because things are as they were before, and the perversity of these men is such, that they are not satisfied with being wicked themselves, but that they also wish us to follow their example, and to abstain from fasting and observing the holydays. As an excuse for their doings, they say that they are not Spaniards. I entreat you, whenever you have any orders to give which you wish to be executed, to send them directly to me. I can assure your Grace that they spare no efforts to make me like one of them, and to induce me to wear a shirt and stockings, and to become as lax in my morals and habits as they are. They think that, if they could seduce me, they would have no trouble with my companions. But having voluntarily assumed the heavy burden of a Capuchin's life, and, by leaving my country, having thrown myself into purgatory although still in this world, I will tax myself to the utmost to be true to the position in which I have placed myself, and to discard the world and its allurements, in order not to lose the merits of all my sacrifices by following the example of these priests (which God forbid!). On the contrary, I hope that He may give me the power to reform them, to make them conscious of the wickedness of their life, and to induce them to purify themselves by prayer—prayer!—which is the soul of the priesthood.*

"It is said that these priests have secreted all the silver plate and money which they possess. This is very bad, but of very little importance to us who know that, with the help of the king and of God, we shall never be wanting in any thing, and shall have bread enough to live. I hope that your Grace will soon afford some consolation to the Spaniards, and that you will not oblige us to remain subjected to an unworthy Superior. In thus hoping, I rely on God, who, in every thing, has so far guided your Grace in such a way as to make all your acts redound to His greater glory, &c., &c. I hope that He will fill your breast with His grace, so as to

---

* Que es la alma de los sacerdotes.

enable you to help and direct us in weeding His vineyard here, which requires more labor than if it was to be planted for the first time," &c., &c.

On the 14th of September (1772), father Dagobert wrote to the Bishop to thank his Grace for having appointed him his vicar-general, a dignity which had been already conferred upon him by the Bishop of Quebec, when Louisiana formed a part of that diocese. Father Dagobert gives to the Spanish bishop an account of his ecclesiastical administration, enumerates the reforms which it requires, and, with great humility, expresses his anxious wish to be guided by the superior wisdom of his apostolic chief, whose orders he declares himself ready to execute to the very letter. Father Dagobert's communication to the Bishop is written with great propriety, with dignified subordination and Christian meekness, and is not such a document as could be expected from the individual described by father Cirilo.

On the 26th of the same month, Governor Unzaga wrote to the bishop a despatch in which he denounced the conspiracy which had been formed by *some unquiet spirits against the poor French capuchins, whom they wished to be censured justè vel injustè.* " It has resulted from this persecution," said he, " that father Dagobert, who does not know what it is to complain, spoke of retiring to France with his companions. At first I could not understand what was the cause of this resolution, as I attributed it to his fear of the discipline which your Grace might establish. But, when I was informed of the true state of things, I sent for him and told him to remain quiet, and that your Grace would give him satisfaction. He showed himself contented with this assurance; and promised that, whatever your orders might be, they would be scrupulously and blindly obeyed, and, in the meantime, he begged me to afford him some relief by preventing father Hilaire de Génoveaux from abusing him, as he was in the habit of doing every day. Thus matters stand, and I have left them, on account of their ecclesiastical nature, to the judgment of your Grace, in order that **your** Grace may settle them with that prudence of which so many proofs have already been given. Of this quality father Cirilo does not possess one particle."

The whole letter of the Governor seems to be written in exculpation of father Dagobert, and of the other French capuchins. "I heartily approve," said he to the bishop, "some of the instructions which you have given, and which are such as to secure the rights and interests of the king, and the object of which is to retain his subjects under his rule by conforming as much as possible with their genius, their character, and manners. This is what I call acting in accordance with the spirit of the apostolic mission; this is voluntarily making one's self the servant of *all* in order to gain *many*, and working for the service of God by assuming the garb of the Jew among the Jews, of the pagan among the pagans, and by sharing even in the infirmities of the sick. On the whole, I refer myself to what I have previously communicated to your Grace, and from which your Grace will no doubt infer that many of the synodical regulations cannot be applied to this province without injury to the interests of the king, the number of whose vassals might be diminished considerably, if those regulations were attempted to be carried into execution, and your Grace will easily understand that it is not always that the laws made for one region can be safely adapted to another." This document is certainly a fair specimen of the Spanish governor's prudence and liberality.

On the 14th of November (1772) father Cirilo, whose indignation had, it seems, gathered more intensity from its own broodings, wrote two letters to the Bishop, and brought with additional vehemence fresh accusations against the friars, whom he represented as the most abandoned of all human beings. Those letters, in some of their parts, are very much in the style of certain passages in Juvenal and Suetonius which are hardly compatible with the chastity of modern languages. The oft repeated burden of all of father Cirilo's communications was his professed willingness, in all humility, and for the greater glory of God, with the Bishop's consent, and on his being invested with full powers, to undertake the ungracious and painful task of reforming all the abuses which he described, and reprobated with such indefatigable zeal.

The quarrel of these priests was far from being settled in 1773, and on the 10th of July, Governor Unzaga wrote as follows to the Bishop: "I cannot understand what grounds father Cirilo can have to rest his complaints upon; and, had not your Grace informed me that he complains, I could not have believed it possible; for he and father Dagobert appear now to agree very well and to move in concert in everything they do. With regard to father Dagobert's alleged infraction of your orders, it is true that he has not as yet executed them all, in all their parts, particularly in relation to your command to expel from the convent the black women and no longer to dispense with the required publications for the celebration of marriages. But I never doubted his willingness soon to obey your Grace in these matters, and therefore I felt no hesitation in giving him time for summoning to his aid the necessary fortitude to throw out of doors a set of people whom he has raised and kept about him from the cradle, and I well understand the weakness which causes his delays. If you should take into consideration the difficulty which there is in eradicating practices, usages and customs, and if you knew the individual, you would see clearly that the omission on his part to which your attention has been called, has not been the result of obstinacy but of simplicity. After all, the black women are now kept on the plantation of the fathers during the day, and the dispensations as to marriages are no longer granted.

"In one of your letters, you communicate to me the complaints of the fathers as to the deportment of father Hilaire de Génoveaux. In one of my previous despatches, I made you acquainted with the character of this friar, and with the cause of his expulsion from the colony when under the French domination. I have also mentioned his talents to your Grace with the commendation they deserve, and I have stated that he was entitled to justice at our hands. On his solicitations, the king permitted him to come here in order that he might proceed, in concert with the authorities, to an examination of his case and of the violence which he said was used towards him by the Superior Council of the late French colony, which not only expelled him without cause from the province, but also deprived him of the ecclesiastical dignity with which he was clothed. I therefore took cognizance of this affair, gathered all the documents relating thereto, and referred the case to the king, who is the only competent authority to decide on its merits. I did not neglect at the same time to acquaint your Grace with all its circumstances. The royal decision has not yet been received, and I shall wait for it. For this reason, and because I consider as slanderous the denunciations submitted to your Grace against this friar, I have abstained from interfering with him. It is true that, at first, he joined the Spanish friars against father Dagobert. But, for the present, he keeps aloof from both parties and remains quiet in his chamber, where he devotes himself entirely to study, in the silence of solitude. I repeat that he is a good man, and that his talents make him very useful to the church, although his pride disqualifies him for the position of a chief or superior. Finally, you will think as you please on the subject, but with regard to myself, I know how difficult it is to come to a correct appreciation of the true merits of men of that sacred calling, when they choose to quarrel among themselves.

"In your last communication, you said that you were informed that each of the French capuchins had received one thousand dollars for his share of the perquisites collected during the year for the funeral rites and ceremonies only, and that father Dagobert made light of the bull of the *Santa Cruzada*. Both assertions are false. The first will provoke a smile, and the second, a sorrowful indignation. How is it possible not to laugh at the impudence of the first assertion, when it is known that there is not in New Orleans and its environs a population of two thousand souls of all professions and conditions; and the greater portion of those people are so poor that, when they die, they are buried with no other charges or expenses than four *reales* paid to the man who goes to the graveyard to give them sepulture. The origin of the extraordinary information sent to your Grace proceeds no doubt from the fact that this capital has suffered greatly from the small pox, and that there have been a great many deaths; but many of the dead were black and white children, whose parents were too poor to pay any funeral charges.

"All that I could learn concerning the alleged contempt of father Dagobert for the bull of the *Santa Cruzada** is that, in conversation, he said that it was

---

* The primitive object of the Bull of the Santa Cruzada was to grant indulgences to all Spaniards that would engage personally in waging war against the infidels, or contribute to it by alms. The price of this Bull was fixed at 2ˀ quar-

unknown in France, and that in the Indies it was valuable only on account of the graces and privileges attached to it, &c. &c. I have conveyed to the knowledge of the king that it is obnoxious to his subjects in this province; that all means of persuasion are vain to reconcile them to it; that they consider it as a tribute paid to the clergy; that they look upon it with horror, and that they would prefer to it any other tax or exaction. As the royal intentions of his Majesty are that nothing be done which may be calculated to breed discontent among his subjects, I mention this fact to your Grace that you may govern yourself accordingly."

This letter offended the Bishop, and called for the following explanatory one which Governor Unzaga wrote to him on the 12th of September, 1773: "Most excellent sir, you inform me that the expressions, *I well know how difficult it is to come to a correct appreciation of the true merits of men of that sacred calling, when they choose to quarrel among themselves,* had caused you to look into all the correspondence which lay before you, and that you could find nothing in it that could justify the language which I have used. You conclude with saying that you have submitted the whole of it to the king, and that you are awaiting the decision of his royal wisdom. As I naturally suppose that you have also submitted all my letters to his Majesty, I have nothing to add on this controversy; because 'the exquisitely sagacious judgment with which he is gifted will decide every thing according to the best interests of his royal service. I will merely observe that I do not conceive

---

tos, or 14 to 15 cents No catholic, inhabiting Spain, could abstain from purchasing this Bull, without exposing his orthodoxy to suspicion. When provided with this Bull, he had, among other privileges, that of eating flesh, with the consent of his physician and confessor, and also of using eggs and milk, on days of fast and during Lent.

where you have seen in any part of my correspondence that I have, as you say, characterized as barbarous the language of the Spanish Capuchins, and much less that I have called this colony a French province, in violation of the oath of allegiance which the colonists have sworn to their new prince, who is as celebrated for his equity as for the goodness of his heart. It is to be regretted, most excellent sir, that words do not bear the stamp of the soul of him who uses them. There would not be so many misconceptions in this world. God knows that my heart loves your Grace most tenderly, that my hands press without distrust the generous ones of a prelate, who has long ago honored me with his friendship, and that I would lay down my life to wipe off the expressions which have mortified your Grace. Turn them over and over, on every side, and you will see that they are applicable only to the Friars and to their disputes. I so expressed myself for the discharge of my conscience; and, doubting my ability to act satisfactorily in the premises, I referred all decision thereon to your Grace, as the only competent judge. I entreat your Grace to consider those expressions as having been dictated by an honorable delicacy of feelings, and not to look upon them as the inspirations of a sentiment of irritation which is foreign to my character and incompatible with my official position. It seems to me that the common lot of human nature is for each one to judge for himself and act for the best. If we do not agree in the means to be employed, let us abide by the decision of our sovereign master, who, besides being animated with the tenderest love for his subjects, possesses a mind of such sagacity that he soon discovers what their welfare requires. In all this I do not see any cause of complaint for either of us; at least such is my way of thinking. I attach no importance to the mere fact of prevailing over any body. My interest, in all this affair, is to receive with due veneration the manifestations of the royal intentions, and to comply with them in every point. As soon as they shall be made known to me, I will execute them strictly, according to my habit."

The bishop of Havana, not satisfied with the indifference which he thought that Unzaga had manifested in this religious controversy, had applied to the Marquis de la Torre, governor and captain general of the island of Cuba, and had requested him to stimulate what he called the indolence of the Governor of Louisiana. In reply to a communication from La Torre on this subject, Unzaga wrote a long despatch reciting to the Captain General the causes of all these religious difficulties which, after all, consisted in a mere struggle for power among those priests, in which the interests of the king were not implicated in the slightest degree. He evidently sided with the French Capuchins, in whose favor he showed that his feelings were enlisted, and whom he defended against most of the accusations brought against them. He represented the Spanish Capuchins as being fully as ignorant as the French, and indeed it is impossible to read all he says, without coming to the conclusion that both the French and Spanish clergy in Louisiana, at the time, were not altogether worthy of their sacred mission. "I know the extent of the evil," said he, "but I believe that the application of the remedy is not in my power. To whichever side I might incline, I discover a shoal which prevents me from acting with the activity and firmness which I might otherwise exhibit. If, doing violence to my conscience and honor, I supported father Cirilo, it would be securing the triumph of artifice and malignity, and oppressing innocence. Were I to favor the other side, I should be obliged to remove father Cirilo to the remotest part of the province, and his

Grace, the bishop, might persuade himself that I deprive him of his man, and that I oppose his designs, whilst my most earnest wish is to execute them, provided they do not conflict with the interests of the king, and have not the tendency to cause the province to lose the little which has remained of its former population. It would give much satisfaction, if his Grace would pay a visit to this colony to become acquainted with his flock and with the true state of things. He would soon be undeceived on many points, and perhaps would reform certain abuses. The people here will remain quiet as long as they are gently treated; but the use of the rod would produce confusion and ruin. Their dispositions are the result of the happy state of liberty to which they have been accustomed from the cradle, and in which they ought to be maintained, so far as is consistent with the laws of the kingdom."

Unzaga, after having written this reply marked with so much independence and liberality to the Marquis de la Torre, addressed, on the same day, an elaborate defence of the course he had pursued to the bailiff de Arriaga, one of the king's ministers. In this communication he does not spare the Bishop, whom he accuses of an indiscreet severity which would have depopulated the colony, if he had, as governor, carried his Grace's pastoral instructions into execution. "The first document by which," said he, "the new prelate made himself known to the French Friars was a tissue of phrases, in which he reproached them with having committed crimes. What must have been their feelings towards him when they received such a manifesto against their deportment, and particularly when they saw themselves upbraided for so many acts of a heinous character, which were sheer calumnies! With regard to the people, they found themselves threatened with excommunication if they did not receive the sacrament at Easter, and they had to fear, as consequences of their refusal, to be subjected to temporal punishments, such as imprisonment, confiscation, and even the application of the discipline of the holy office of the Inquisition, under the jurisdiction of which they were not born, and to which they are not accustomed. It was easy for me to foresee, that if the French Capuchins became disgusted with their new position, they would soon take refuge on some English vessel and be followed by a large portion of the population; and, that should any body be excommunicated for not complying with the precept to take annually the sacrament at Easter, the same results would ensue; because the people would run away from the ecclesiastical rod, for which they have no relish.

"One of the chief revenues of the clergy here had been the granting of dispensations, which the Bishop now reserves to himself. But if the heart were to draw within itself all the blood which runs through the different parts of the human body, those parts would wither from want of nutrition. How comes then the Bishop of Cuba, who says that he is not sparing of communicating to his subordinates the powers he possesses, to retain in this case the most valuable? And through what means does he expect the members of his diocese to subsist, except they should be reduced to a state of spirituality and be above the wants of mortality?

"How can he pretend to be serving the king, he who, all the while, is stirring up with a firebrand the patience of his majesty's vassals? He addresses them in a surly tone, and deprives them of their perquisites on the very day that he makes himself known to them! I confess that there are in the province abuses which must be corrected, although I deny the excesses in the existence of which his Grace believes, because he is incorrectly informed. Granting the disease with which the colony is afflicted, it argues only that she wants the attendance of a physician—and the tender nursing of a pastor—a wise physician who will graduate the doses of his treatment in accordance with the temperament of the patient—and a benevolent pastor who will conceal the rod and the shears.

"I had offered my services to his Grace from the beginning; but, far from adopting my views, which were such as to favor the interests of the king, without interfering with the real substance of religion, he agreed with me on trifles and disregarded my opinion on all matters of importance. Hence the discord which is complained of. In order to appease the disorder, I used the authority with which our pious king has invested me, with such measure and propriety as to prevent the public tranquillity from being disturbed. But to those who had been injured by a wrong beginning contentment was not restored.

"Although I am aware of the importance of repressing abuses, and of establishing good habits, because they originate good laws and secure their execution, yet I must affirm that there is here no such moral deformity as has been depicted to his Grace, none which threatens society with the slightest damage, and which could tend to a breach in the observance of those duties that faithful subjects have to discharge towards their prince. Why then all this clamor and outcry? Why this anger? Why this furious persecution which is capable of rousing into resistance submission itself?

"I have acted according to the rules of sound policy, when I have refused to lay a heavy hand on some abuses which, if they are such in the eye of the strict discipline of the church, cannot be held to have that character with regard to society or the body politic, or which deserve at least no other than clerical punishment or repression. What is it to the king, for instance, whether the French Capuchins consider the teal as amphibious and eat it on fast days, and follow other practices quite as insignificant, and which, through immemorial custom, have been thought to be legitimate among these people? There were more important abuses to which I called their attention, and which I have been the first to denounce. I have corrected them through the gentle means of persuasion, and I have obtained most excellent results without noise and scandal, by merely employing the powerful weapon of ridicule, and by clothing with rags what I wished to make contemptible.*

"Nevertheless his Grace, resenting the information I have laid before the Governor of Cuba, puts himself in motion against me, takes up offensive weapons, attacks me on certain expressions to which he has given a meaning for which I am at a loss to account, goes into a critical examination of my correspondence, and, in order to shelter himself, endeavors to prepossess the judgment of your Excellency, and to enlist in favor of his acts the piety of his Majesty."

The Governor proceeds to a review of all the Bishop's acts, which he represents as impolitic and unnecessarily severe, and hints that he might have good grounds to consider himself insulted by the Bishop, who chose to disregard his representations as untrue, and to believe other individuals less entitled than he is to credit and respect. "The people here," said he, "are neither vicious nor addicted to debauchery, nor opposed to our habits, although, in many respects, those habits disagree with their tastes. They have some of their own, as

---

* Ridiculizandolos y vistiendo los de andragos.

other people have, to which they are much attached—and this is very natural. Those habits are not in conflict with the primordial obligations of society; they are not to be eradicated at once, but must be removed gradually and almost imperceptibly.

"His Grace says, that so anxious was he to keep up good harmony between himself and me, that he took care to send all his orders through me, submitting them to my judgment, and that, in this way, I was quite as much the Bishop as the Governor of the province; but the truth is that he wanted to constitute me his executive officer and bailiff (fiscal de vara), rather than his adviser.

"The Prelate exalts the virtues of father Cirilo! I do not know whether the ambition* which lurks beneath the coarse woollen gown of the monk can be held up as a pattern of virtue, but I am sure that, for a monk, to have sown dissension between his brethren and the Prelate who is their Superior, is an act sufficiently mean to make him fall from that pedestal of probity to which his Grace wishes to raise him, on account of his opposition to imaginary licentiousness."

The Governor then takes up one by one all the accusations brought against the French Capuchins, and avers that there is no foundation for them. "What they may do in their cells," said he, "and what their secret sins may be, I cannot tell; but I know that they give no bad examples, and that they inculcate no unsound doctrine. And how many times does it not happen that the preacher's sermons and his acts are at variance! How comes the Prelate to be acquainted with the existence of crimes, which, monstrous as they are represented to be, I have not been able to detect, although I am on the spot. I rely, as a last resort, on the judgment of the

---

* La ambicion oculta bajo el grueso sayal.

king, who will not put faith in the denunciations of certain individuals prompted by personal ambition or baser motives, in preference to the assertions of his governor, whom he knows to be worthy of belief. I trust in the humane intentions of his Majesty, who never loses sight for one moment of the welfare and happiness of his subjects, and who has always striven to introduce the influence of religion and morality in his domains, not by abrupt force, nor by producing affliction and complaints, but through the salutary effects of sweet and mild persuasion, of good example and of wholesome admonition. These are the flowery and pleasant paths through which the Holy Evangelists and their true followers have invariably proceeded in establishing a religion of peace. His Majesty will decide whether the conduct of the Bishop of Havana, who has presented himself sword in hand, is in conformity with the pious intentions of the royal breast, and is worthy of the apostolic ministry.

"An enlightened prudence and a good deal of toleration are necessary here, for although this is a Spanish province, and although Count O'Reilly endeavored to make its inhabitants forget the former domination under which they had lived so long, still I cannot flatter his majesty so much as to say that the people have ceased to be French at heart, and that in them is not to be found that spirit of independence which causes resistance to oppressive laws. But I will affirm that they are susceptible of being submissive and loyal subjects, that they entertain great veneration for their ancient laws, and that the state of felicity which they now enjoy is a guaranty to me that they are not to be suspected of being disposed to fail in their duties towards the crown. Therefore do I endeavor to keep them in the colony, and to secure their love and services to the king, without caring in the least for what I deem to be fooleries.* After the blow which the colonists drew upon themselves by their late revolution, the infliction of another would be tantamount to utter destruction."

Considering that this document was addressed to the Court of Spain, and that it was written against a high dignitary of the church in a country where it is supposed to have possessed for centuries so much power, it is impossible not to be struck with Governor Unzaga's bold language. The Spanish government, which has the reputation of being so considerate and temporizing in all its decisions, acted on this occasion with its usual prudence. It supported the Bishop in all that he had written or done, save a few exceptions, but, at the same time, it abstained from censuring the Governor, and contented itself with signifying to both functionaries that it was confidently expected that they would make some mutual sacrifices of their views for the sake of harmony, and would no longer expose the king's service to suffer in consequence of their dissensions. This hint was taken, it seems; and, whether some compromise or other was effected between the French and Spanish capuchins, peace appears to have spread its broad wings over the convent of this reverend fraternity, and nothing further was heard of their former quarrel.

As the clergy is so important an element in the composition of every social and political organization, I have not deemed it inappropriate to introduce this ecclesiastical episode as an historical illustration of Louisiana in 1772.

In 1773, the colonists were beginning to be reconciled to their new government, which was recommended to them by the mildness of Unzaga's administration. The

* Cuidando poco lo que juzgo por frioleras.

planters, in particular, found considerable resources in the clandestine trade which they carried on with the English, who supplied them with negroes at a cheap price. The heavy sums brought from Vera Cruz to meet the expenses of the government were circulating freely, and, by increasing the amount of specie, had enabled the planters to sell their crops advantageously and to give more extension to their establishments. It is well known that our planters seldom resist the temptation to buy more land or more negroes, when the golden opportunity presents itself. Such had been the case on the present occasion, and, instead of employing the proceeds of their crops to pay their old debts, they had bethought themselves of a different application of their moneys, and even increased their liabilities to their creditors. "Keep thy pen from lender's book, and defy the foul fiend," says Shakspeare, in his poetical wisdom. The planters committed the indiscretion of violating this precept, and could not *defy the foul fiend* that presented himself in the shape of a hurricane, which occasioned such ravages on their plantations, that, when the time came for settlement with their creditors, they could pay neither capital nor interest, but, on the contrary, wanted advances. The creditors stuck to their bond, and wanted, if not their pound of flesh, at least part of it. They became clamorous, and some of them resorted to legal measures to expropriate their creditors. The debtors—including those who could pay and those who could not—entered into a confederacy, and resolved on resistance per fas et nefas. At their head was St. Maxent, a wealthy planter, whose daughter Governor Unzaga had married, and who thought that he could avail himself of this circumstance to set his creditors at defiance. In a Spanish colony, at that time, a governor was almost omnipotent, and, therefore, all the contending parties gathered in earnest supplication round that functionary. In these circumstances, Unzaga acted with the strictest impartiality, and with his customary discretion. He began with forcing his father-in-law to pay every cent of what he owed, and also employed coercion against all those who were able to pay their debts, but who had sought to postpone discharging them by availing themselves of this popular excitement. To the really distress and honest debtors he granted the delays which they required, and even reconciled the creditors to this indulgence, having convinced them that it was favorable to their own interest. The course pursued by the governor in this emergency obtained universal approbation.

By a royal schedule of the 4th of August, 1774, says Judge Martin, in his History of Louisiana, the power of granting lands in the colony was vested in the governor, according to the regulations made by O'Reilly, on the 8th of January, 1770. Hence the question presents itself, whether all grants made by subsequent governors were not null and void, when made in violation of those regulations, if it be not shown that those regulations had been repealed or modified. With regard to the private sale of lands and other immovables, Unzaga had issued, on the 9th of November, 1770, a prohibitory decree, which is of some importance, in relation to the laws governing the transfer of property under the Spanish administration, and which will be found in the Appendix.*

The province continued, in 1775, to be so thinly inhabited, that it was easy for the runaway slaves to conceal themselves for any length of time, even in the vicinity of New Orleans. They had the audacity to form themselves into gangs, which committed great depredations on the plantations. It was found necessary to remedy

---

* See the Appendix.

this pressing evil, and to put a stop to a state of things which served as a fatal example to the rest of the negroes, and Governor Unzaga issued a proclamation, by which he offered an amnesty or free pardon to those slaves who should return voluntarily to their masters, and threatened with severe punishment those who should not avail themselves of the opportunity offered to them to obtain mercy for their past misdemeanors. This measure seems to have had a salutary effect.

In 1776, Don Bernardo de Galvez succeeded Estecheria in the command of the regiment of Louisiana. The year previous, hostilities had broken out between Great Britain and her thirteen colonies of North America, and that great contest had begun which was to give birth to one of the mightiest nations of the present century. There were at that time in New Orleans a number of merchants from Boston, New York, and Philadelphia, whose feelings were strongly enlisted on behalf of their countrymen, who were struggling against oppression. Among them, Oliver Pollock was one of the most conspicuous and most active. They procured a good supply of arms and ammunition for the inhabitants of the western part of Pennsylvania, which they delivered to Colonel Gibson, who had come for it from Pittsburg. This was done with the connivance of the Spanish governor; for Spain, like France, was inimical to Great Britain, and was willing to add fuel to the flames which threatened her old and potent rival.

On the 28th of February, the Court of Madrid had requested Unzaga to specify what were the means of defence which he possessed in the colony, and what would be his plans of operation should he be attacked. On the 19th of June, he answered by sending a detailed statement of the number of troops in the colony, and their equipments—of the munition, provisions, and mate rials of which he could dispose—of the fortifications then existing at New Orleans and in its immediate vicinity, with his reflections relative to the best mode of defence. He commented on the small number of regulars and militia he had under his command, and observed that they were far from being adequate to the protection of a country having more than fifteen hundred miles in extent. He represented the fortifications as insignificant, and their artillery as insufficient. "Besides, as the country was open on all sides," said he, "it was perfectly useless to attempt making a show of resistance in front, when the enemy could attack on the flank and on the rear, without meeting any defence. Two small vessels of war, such as there is one already, being introduced, and taking their station in the rear above New Orleans, would cut off my retreat." He also represented the fortifications at Manchac, Pointe Coupée, Natchitoches, Arkansas, and Illinois, as being equally unavailable, and he informed his government that, in case of war, should he be attacked by superior forces, he would, unless he received contrary orders, retreat to the frontiers of Mexico, leaving it to the treaty of peace that would be concluded in the end, to determine finally on the fate of Louisiana.

He also communicated to his government all the information he had been able to gather, in relation to the designs which he suspected the English to have formed against the colony of Louisiana. "The last news we have," said he, "were brought by the English vessels which navigate this river on their way to the settlements of that nation, and they are of a dubious character; for the insurgents and the royalists make contradictory reports. But, on weighing and comparing them carefully, I have come to the conclusion that it may be correctly estimated that Great Britain now disposes, in the waters of North America, of ninety vessels of war, carrying each from sixteen to fifty guns, and has an army of 25,000 men. It seems that, since the engagement at Boston, the English have not made much progress, and have confined their operations to the blockading of ports, &c., &c., and that the insurgents have taken Montreal, and raised the siege of Quebec, after having lost one thousand men, and the general who commanded them, &c., &c.

" I shall not, however, allow myself to be thrown off my guard, and cease to use those precautions which I ought to resort to in the present circumstances, because I suspect that, at any moment, the royalists and the insurgents may make up their quarrel and unite their forces, in order to take possession by surprise of one of the domains of some European power, and thus to indemnify themselves for their losses and expenses, or in order to carry into execution any other designs, which I shall endeavor to penetrate by using all the means at my disposal ; and, to that effect, I have despatched a trusty man to Philadelphia, who, under the pretext of looking for flour, with a passport, and with permission to transport the flour to Cadiz in a Spanish vessel and with a Spanish crew, will endeavor to discover their designs by stopping at some of their ports."

On the 22nd of the same month, Unzaga, who had been made Brigadier-General, again petitioned the court to be allowed to retire to Malaga, with the pay of Colonel, on account of his advanced age, the bad state of his health and his impaired sight. He represented that he had served the king forty-one years in the army, the eight first years of which in Spain, Italy, and Africa, and the thirty-three remaining years in America, where the royal patronage had bestowed upon him the government of Louisiana, the duties of which he had been performing for more than six years.

On the 13th of August, he again communicated to his government all the information he had been able to collect in relation to the American war, and insisted on having leave of retiring from active service.

"On the 7th of September, he informed his government that he had despatched to Philadelphia a packet commanded by Bartholomew Beauregard, apparently for the purpose of procuring flour for the wants of New Orleans, but really to pry into the designs of the royalists and insurgents.

Unzaga, in a despatch of the 28th of December, called the attention of the government to the prejudice and injuries to which was exposed the safety of the colony from the fact that said colony was dependent, as to its military administration and government, on the Governor and Captain General of the island of Cuba, and, among other reasons, he gave the following:

"In case of war, it is vain to hope for any help from Havana, nor for proper directions or orders from the captain general, who is not acquainted with the country and its localities. For want of such knowledge, the captain general would probably issue no orders, and the governor of Louisiana would then remain inactive, as he would not be willing to incur any responsibility; and thus his hands being tied up, the opportunity of securing the most important successes might be neglected, and the honor of the Spanish arms might be tarnished, the captain general of Cuba excusing himself, on the impossibility in which he would be to act or to give orders, and the governor of Louisiana pleading the want of instructions. I have been, for nearly seven years, the chief officer in command of this province. I have lived in that dependent state to which I allude, and, although I do not say that I have suffered from it, because I have always gloried in serving and obeying with implicit readiness, yet I must assure the king, on my honor, that, under the present colonial organization, the royal interests are liable to be put in jeopardy, and that the governor of this province, whoever he may be, will be exposed to many mortifications, more or less aggravating according to the humor of the captain general of Cuba."

The leave to retire from active service, with permission to reside at Malaga, which Unzaga had prayed for, was refused, and he was appointed Captain General of Caraccas. He had won the esteem and affection of the population, and his departure caused unbounded regrets. His administration had been that of a gentle and indulgent father, and his having dared to connive at the breach by the British of the fiscal and commercial laws of Spain, a strict observance of which would have been fatal, materially increased the prosperity of the colony. His conduct, in this respect, was not absolutely approved by the king's ministers, but it did not deprive him of the confidence of his sovereign, as is fully proved by his promotion.

CHAPTER III.

GALVEZ' ADMINISTRATION.

1777 to 1783.

MIRO'S ADMINISTRATION.

1784 to 1785.

By a royal decree of the 10th of July, 1776, the government and intendancy of Louisiana had been ordered to be provisionally surrendered to Don Bernardo de Galvez, then colonel of the regiment of Louisiana. He entered on the duties of his office, as Unzaga's successor, on the 1st of February, 1777. He was then about twenty-one years old, and his talents, his energy and his activity would have secured him a brilliant career, even had he not possessed other means of success. But to these advantages he joined that of being as powerfully connected as any subject in Spain. His father, Don Mathias de Galvez, was viceroy of Mexico, and his uncle, Don Joseph de Galvez, was almost king of Spain, for he was secretary of state and president of the council of the Indies, and was, as such, next to the crowned heads, the man who wielded the greatest power in Europe.

In 1776, it had been stipulated between the courts of France and Spain that Louisiana should be permitted to trade with the French West India Islands, on condition that the articles which might be wanted from Louisiana for those islands should be purchased (in order to prevent smuggling) by two commissioners appointed by the French government, who should reside in New Orleans. On the 12th of February, 1777, the two French commissioners, Villars and Favre d'Aunoy, arrived in Louisiana. It was through them that all the French vessels which should come to the colony were to get their cargoes. The appointment of Galvez was the signal of a considerable change in the commerce of the province. The English had enjoyed the monopoly of it under Unzaga's administration, but it now passed into the hands of the French. The commissioners of that nation soon obtained from Galvez the grant of more privileges than were conceded in the treaty, and the French vessels were authorized to load not only at New Orleans, but also at any point on the river, provided they brought to the governor a declaration from the planters specifying the articles which they had shipped. Another encouragement was given to the commerce of the province by reducing to one-half the duty of four per cent., which used to be collected on the exportation of its produce. The French paid for the articles they bought, either in specie, bills of exchange, or *Guinea* negroes; the introduction of those that were born in the colonies, or had remained long in them, having been prohibited. Vessels from Louisiana were permitted to bring European produce or goods from the island of Cuba, or from Campeachy. On the 30th of March, 1777, the French commissioners, Villars and Favre d'Aunoy, wrote to their government: " The facilities granted by M. de Galvez to the trade between Louisiana and the French islands, and also the liberal interpretation given by him to the clauses of the treaty, have revived the industry and activity of the merchants and planters, and opened a brilliant prospect to the colony." On the 26th of April, the same commissioners informed their govern ment that Galvez had seized eleven English vessels, richly laden, which were trafficking with the planters on the banks of the Mississippi, and said that, if the governor persisted in the rigor with which he acted against the English, the French commerce in Louisiana would soon acquire a much greater extension.

The Spanish government sought also to give encouragement to agriculture, and informed the colonists that the king would, for the present, purchase tobacco to the amount of eight hundred thousand dollars, if they could raise so much of it, and that, for the future, he would buy their whole crop, however large it might be. A meeting of the planters was convened by the Governor, and they were invited to deliberate on the price at which they could afford to sell their tobacco. It was ultimately agreed to be seven livres a pound for leaf tobacco, and ten livres for tobacco in carots. The Spanish government had two objects in view, in thus fostering the cultivation of tobacco : 1°,—it was to draw from Louisiana, at a low price, all the tobacco necessary to the supply of its Mexican provinces, and thereby to raise its revenue, through the duty which it imposed on this article in those provinces ; 2°,—it aimed at driving the English and the Dutch out of the French market, which they monopolized as to the tobacco trade.

"Enjoying a better climate than Maryland and Virginia," said Villars and d'Aunoy, in one of their despatches, "Louisiana, on account of its extent and fertility, could furnish the universe with tobacco. But its population, if not augmented, will not even permit the accomplishment of the wish entertained by his Catholic Majesty, to supply with its produce the wants of the Mexican market. It is calculated that, in a territory measuring 1500 miles in length, there are hardly 8000 negroes, and that the whites muster from 6000 to 7000 souls only. The lands of Lower Louisiana, where is the great bulk of the population, are favorable to the lumber and timber trade, to the cultivation of rice, corn and indigo, but they are not adapted to tobacco. These considerations have not escaped the attention of the Spanish ministry. They have granted an annual sum of $40,000, to facilitate the establishment of the new colonists who may come to Louisiana, and it is ordered that concessions be made to them, in those parts where it may suit them to settle. But, as Spain herself is wanting in population, and as those of her subjects who come to America show that they have very little disposition to devote themselves to agriculture, her project is to draw here, either from France or from the French colonies, all the population which may be necessary to the execution of her views. The Spanish government acts in conformity with this plan, and requests our coasters to make the inhabitants of St. Domingo and the Windward islands acquainted with the advantages which await them in Louisiana. Considering that the tendency of this scheme, should it succeed, is to deprive France of a useful portion of her subjects engaged in the pursuit of agriculture, we hasten to inform you of it, in order that you may, should you think it advisable, put a stop to an emigration which cannot but be injurious to the interests of France. If it be Frenchmen who are to be relied upon for the cultivation of Louisiana, it seems to us more natural that his most Christian Majesty should resume the possession of this colony. France alone can raise it to that degree of prosperity to which it is entitled." Fully alive to the policy of giving more extension to the agriculture of Louisiana, the Court of Madrid issued a decree permitting the introduction of negroes into that province by French vessels, from whatever ports they might come.

In the mean time, the struggle which was going on between England and her American colonies was watched with intense interest by the Governor of Louisiana, and by the Spanish court, which sent several orders to afford secret assistance to the insurgents. In consequence of the favorable dispositions of Spain, which were conveyed to some of the leaders of the Americans in the West, several large boats had come this year, 1777, from Fort Pitt to New Orleans, where munitions had been collected by Oliver Pollock, with the occult aid of Galvez, for the use of the thirteen United States. "Captain Willing, of Philadelphia, who came in one of those boats," says Judge Martin in his History of Louisiana, "visited the British settlements on the Mississippi, and some of his companions crossed the lakes to Mobile, with the view to induce the inhabitants to raise the striped banner, and join their countrymen in the struggle for freedom. The people of both the Floridas, however, remained steadfast in their attachment to the royal cause. Perhaps those on the Mississippi and in Mobile, who remembered the fate of Lafrénière and his companions at New Orleans, were deterred from rising by the recollection of this late tragedy. The thin and sparse population of both the Floridas, their distance from the provinces engaged in the war, and the consequent difficulty of receiving any assistance from them, had also its influence on the conduct of the inhabitants."

Galvez kept up an active correspondence with Colonel George Morgan, who was in command of Fort Pitt, and who, in a letter of the 22d of April, gave the Spanish Governor a very able and lucid history of all the events which had occurred since the beginning of the Revolution. "Should we be able," said the colonel, "to procure transports in New Orleans, I think that we could easily surprise Mobile and Pensacola, destroy their fortifications, and possess ourselves of all their munitions, unless these ports be better fortified and defended than we imagine. I would pay liberally to have a plan of the fortifications, and correct information as to the garrisons and naval forces which protect these places. If one thousand men were sufficient for the contemplated expedition, and if we could, in New Orleans, purchase or charter vessels, and procure artillery, on as short notice as possible, we could strike the most successful blow in a quarter where it is least expected. But we shall never proceed to any action on the subject, before having previously obtained the permission and co-operation of your excellency, and before having secured all the transports, provisions, &c., of which we may stand in need. If we cannot, however, expect so much at your hands, we flatter ourselves that you will at least permit us to trade freely with New Orleans, and I beg your excellency to inform me by an express messenger of your decision, and this, of course, at my expense."

But Galvez had no idea, for obvious reasons, of permitting the Americans to set their foot, in military array, on the soil of Louisiana, and eluded to give any positive answer to Morgan's proposed plan of attack against the British possessions. He wrote to his government that, considering the turn which the war was taking, he feared the inconveniences which might result from the passage of the belligerents through the neutral territory of Louisiana, and he informed the court of Madrid that, in order to endeavor to protect the Spanish interests on the river, he had caused to be built four boats, carrying, each, one 24 or 18 pounder. "These gunboats," said he, in a despatch of the 2d of June, "will be more useful in the river than two frigates, because, as they will be propelled by wind and oar, they will be more than a match for any vessel of war that may enter the passes of the

Mississippi, considering that those vessels of war, on account of the shallowness of the water, cannot be of a large size, and that their guns must be of a small calibre, such as twelve pounders at most; so that it will always be in our power to choose our position and distance, and to do much injury without receiving any, on account of the wider range of our guns. All agree that one of those gun-boats will be able to sink any vessel of war lying at anchor, or becalmed, which must be the case, almost at every moment, when a vessel comes up the river, on account of the rapidity of the current, and because the wind, which is favorable at one bend of the river, becomes necessarily adverse beyond that point."

On the 10th of July, Galvez sent to his government a minute statement of the fortifications, the garrison, and the other means of defence of Pensacola and Mobile, and of the naval forces attached to these two points. He also informed his government that the Creeks, Choctaws, and Chickasaws, who, he said, formed a population of 25,000 souls, including women and children, had declared that they would remain neutrals in the war between the English and Americans, and would prevent the latter from violating their territory to attack any of the English possessions.

On the 15th of August (1777) the Spanish government informed Galvez: that in case the American colonists should seize the British settlements on the Mississippi, and should be disposed to deliver them up to his Catholic Majesty, he, Galvez, was authorized to receive them in trust or deposit, always taking care that this should not provoke any violent measures on the part of the English, which might be avoided by giving them to understand, that it must be more advantageous for them that those settlements should be, as a deposit, under the domination of the king, than in the possession of the insurgents. But this was anticipating the happening of an event which was not likely to occur, for the Americans would have been very little disposed to avail themselves of the officious proposition of the king of Spain to relieve them from the burden of keeping any of their acquisitions, and they would certainly have been inclined, and would probably have thought themselves able, to retain possession of their conquests, should they have made any.

Some of their incursions in the territory acknowledging the sway of Great Britain, west of the Ohio, and on the banks of the Mississippi, had proved highly successful, and the militia of Virginia had possessed themselves of Kaskaskia, and of some other posts on that river. By an act of the Legislature, the region which Virginia had thus acquired was erected into a county called Illinois, and a regiment of infantry and a troop of horse were raised for its protection, under the command of Colonel Clark. It will be recollected that, by the last treaty of peace between Great Britain and France, the Mississippi had been given to North Carolina as its western limit. But George III. had forbidden any settlement of white people to the west of the mountains of North Carolina. Notwithstanding this prohibition, a considerable number of emigrants from that province had removed to the banks of the Watauga, one of the branches of the Holston. "They had increased to such a degree," says Judge Martin in his History of Louisiana, "that, in 1776, their claim to representation in the convention that framed the constitution was admitted. In 1777, they were formed into a county which had the Mississippi for its western boundary." Thus, at this early period of their history, had the United States extended their dominion and carried their flag and their laws to the banks of that mighty stream over which they were destined to

GALVEZ GIVES ASSISTANCE TO THE AMERICANS.

exercise, in the short space of less than forty years, an exclusive jurisdiction.

In the month of January, 1778, Captain Willing returned to New Orleans for the second time, to enter into communication and concert with Oliver Pollock who, with the permission and support of Galvez, had now openly assumed the character of an agent for the insurgents. The Court of Spain had gradually become less timid in its manifestation of hostility towards Great Britain; and Galvez, encouraged by his government, had gone so far as to give assistance to the Americans in arms, ammunition, provisions, &c., to the amount of seventy thousand dollars. By these means, the posts occupied by the militia of Virginia on the Mississippi had been strengthened, and the frontier inhabitants of Pennsylvania had received material aid and comfort. Under such encouraging circumstances, Willing had not hesitated to increase in New Orleans the crew of his boats; and with most of those same companions who had come down with him, and who were about fifty in number, he engaged in foraging and predatory excursions against the British planters on the Mississippi. This troop captured a small vessel which was at anchor near the mouth of Bayou Manchac, and took possession of the fort, which was evacuated by its garrison of about fifty or sixty men, who crossed the Mississippi and sought refuge on the Spanish side. In the very vessel of which they had possessed themselves, the Americans proceeded up the river to Baton Rouge, stopping at the several plantations on the way, burning all the houses and other buildings, and carrying off the negroes.

A good many of the British planters, on hearing of the approach of these unwelcome visitors, crossed the Mississippi with their most valuable effects and slaves, and sheltered themselves under the Spanish flag, which floated on the right side of the river. The inhabitants on the left bank were scattered about, they were few in number, and therefore could not make any effective resistance. The invaders continued up as far as Natchez their course of devastation, laying waste the plantations, destroying the stock, applying the torch of the incendiary to the edifices, and carrying off such slaves as had not followed their masters in their flight. All the sympathies of the people of Louisiana were in favor of the Americans; "but," says Judge Martin in his history, "this cruel, wanton and unprovoked conduct towards a helpless community was viewed with great indignation and horror, much increased by the circumstance of Willing's having been hospitably received and entertained, the preceding year, in several houses which he now committed to the flames." It must also be added, that most of the sufferers by these acts of vandalism were well known in New Orleans, where they used to resort to supply their wants, or for social intercourse; and that all of them had more or less extensive relations with the Spanish portion of Louisiana, in whose families some of them had married. This contributed to draw from those inhabitants a keener reprobation of the conduct of Captain Willing, who was looked upon as having acted more like an Indian warrior than a civilized enemy.

The Americans, however, did not choose to attempt retaining possession of these posts, or of any portion of the territory they had thus devastated. In connection with these events, Villars and Favre D'Aunoy, the French commissioners at New Orleans, wrote to their government "The Spaniards here see with regret these conquests, because it cuts off their hope of executing them on their own account, and of thereby securing for themselves the exclusive possession of the Gulf of Mexico. Besides, they feel that the mildness and the other advantages of the

NEW FACILITIES GRANTED TO COMMERCE IN 1778.

climate of Louisiana may seduce the Americans, and attract them to a region, from which the communication with the Gulf of Mexico begins to be better and more practically known, presenting but trifling difficulties, &c. Therefore, it is the interest of Spain that France should recover the possession of Louisiana."

Such was not, however, the opinion of the Spanish government, which, to increase the prosperity of the colony, and to bring relief to the distresses from which it was suffering, was disposed to relax the severity of the commercial restrictions under which it was placed. In accordance with this more judicious policy, which was, at last, forcing itself upon the councils of Spain, Galvez, by a proclamation of the 20th of April, 1778, in order to facilitate the sale of the produce of the colony, permitted its exportation to any of the ports of France. This proclamation had been preceded by one issued on the 17th, which granted a similar privilege of trading with any part of the United States.

By a royal order of the 4th of May, 1778, the indemnity to be paid to owners of slaves sentenced to death, perpetual labor and transportation, or of runaway slaves killed in the attempt made to arrest them, was fixed at two hundred dollars a head; but, in this latter case,[*] the indemnity was due only to those who had previously consented to pay a proportion of the price of the slaves thus killed, which proportion was to be deducted from the indemnity.

The province was reviving under the healthful influence of the extension of its commercial franchises, when it received a considerable accession to its population by the arrival of a number of families, transported to Louisiana from the Canary Islands, at the king's expense

---

[*] Martin's History of Louisiana, vol. ii., p. 43.

Some of them, under the command of Marigny de Mandeville, settled at *Terre aux Bœufs*, on a tract of land now included in the parish of St. Bernard; others, under the guidance of St. Maxent, located themselves near Bayou Manchac, at about twenty-four miles from the town of Baton Rouge, where they established a village which they called Galvezton; the rest formed that of Venezuela, on Bayou Lafourche. The government carried its parental solicitude so far as to build a house for each family, and a church for each settlement. These emigrants were very poor, and were supplied with cattle, fowls and farming utensils; rations were furnished them for a period of four years, out of the king's stores, and considerable pecuniary assistance was afforded to them.* Their descendants are now known under the name of *Islingues*, which is derived from the Spanish word, *Isleños*, meaning islanders.

It must not be forgotten that, by an ordinance promulgated when Spain took possession of Louisiana, in 1766, vessels from New Orleans were restricted to sail to six Spanish ports only. Persisting in the new and wiser course of policy into which he had lately entered, the king put Louisiana on the same footing with his more favored colonies, and opened to her vessels any of the ports of the Peninsula to which the commerce of the Indies was permitted. Furthermore, the exportation of furs and peltries from Louisiana was, at the same time, encouraged by an exemption from duty for a period of ten years, and it was only on their re-exportation from Spain that the ordinary duty was to be paid.

This was a step towards liberality, but what seemed to the colonists to be a departure from it was the prohibition of the introduction and reading of a French book,

---

* Martin's History of Louisiana, vol. i., p. 43.

written by Mercier, and entitled: "The year two thousand four hundred and forty." The Governor was instructed to proceed to the destruction of every copy of it which might be found in the province. Another book reprobated by the royal decree was Robertson's History of America. The formidable tribunal of the Inquisition had condemned Mercier's book; and the king, or rather his all-powerful minister, Joseph Galvez, president of the council of the Indies, thought that he had good reasons to prevent his Majesty's subjects from reading certain remarks, or statements of facts, which were contained in Robertson's History, and which he deemed to be false and slanderous. At this time, not only was the king considerate enough to wish that the minds of his subjects should not be contaminated by the perusal of dangerous books, but also was he anxious to secure the allegiance even of the foreigners who resided in his dominions. Thus, a considerable number of individuals from the United States, from West and East Florida, and from other parts, who had settled in New Orleans, were required to depart, or to take an oath of fidelity to his Catholic Majesty. In such a dilemma, the great majority of them chose to swear as they were desired.

For many years, the English had not fared so badly in Louisiana. Now, their trade with the colony was entirely ruined. "The British flag," say Villars and Favre d'Aunoy, in a despatch dated on the 18th of July, 1778, "has not appeared in this river for more than three months, or, at least, it is only to be seen flying at the mast-head of a frigate destined to protect the Manchac settlement. The duties to be paid by our ships, on their coming here, are reduced every day, because the Spaniards are made more tractable by the need in which they stand of our commerce. Finally, the whole trade of the Mississippi is now in our hands."

On the 20th of August, Villars, one of the French commissioners, wrote a despatch in which he informed his government of the steps he had taken, to obtain the reversal of the decree by which the Spanish government had confiscated the property of the brother of Noyan, one of the unfortunate colonists who had been shot by O'Reilly's order. This brother, who was called Bienville after his uncle, the founder of New Orleans, had taken a part in the conspiracy against the Spaniards, and had been sent, as an emissary, to the English commander at Pensacola, to propose, in the name of the insurgents, that the colony be put under the protection of the English as an independent republic. On the death of his elder brother, he assumed the name and title of Chevalier de Noyan. Villars' despatch on the subject is as follows:

"The Chevalier de Noyan, lieutenant of a ship of the line, died in the month of March last, at St. Domingo, where he had gone into copartnership with the Baron de Breteuil. As he was one of the instigators of the revolution of 1768, General O'Reilly, who was clothed with the most extensive powers, ordered the sequestration of his property; but, as it was not sold, and as its revenues were merely deposited in the king's treasury, without being appropriated by him to the royal domain, it was inferred that the object of his Majesty was to deprive the Chevalier de Noyan, for some years, of his income, and thereby to cut him off from the means of living in comfort, but with the reserved intention of putting an end to the punishment by restoring the culprit, on a future day, to the possession of his property. Viewing the case in this light, the Duke de Duras, the Count de

Vergennes, and the Baron de Breteuil, as the kinsmen, the protectors and the friends of the Chevalier de Noyan, repeatedly addressed to the court of Spain, through our ambassador, the Marquis d'Ossun, the most pressing solicitations to obtain a decree raising the sequestration. But these gentlemen pursued, I believe, an impolitic course. They grounded their application on Noyan's innocence, which they could not establish without calling into question the justice of Count O'Reilly, and of the king, who had ratified the conduct of his agent. Therefore did the court of Spain refuse to grant their request. Now that M. de Noyan is dead, is the moment, or never, of making a last effort in the interest of his widow and children. I have prepared for the president of the council of Indies a memorial, which Governor Galvez will forward and will support to the utmost of his power."

This shows that it was then known in the colony, although this knowledge appears to have since faded away, that O'Reilly had come to Louisiana *with the most extensive powers*, and that the king had *approved* the judicial tragedy of which this officer was the author. This despatch, with many other authentic documents, emphatically contradicts the tradition that Count O'Reilly, by putting to death Lafrénière and his companions, had incurred the displeasure of his royal master—which popular belief, like most traditions, is not supported by the unyielding and uncompromising facts which it is the duty of history to record.

In the beginning of the year, 1779, Don Juan Dorotheo del Portege succeeded Don Cecilio Odoardo in the office of auditor of war and assessor of government.

In a despatch of the 15th of January, Galvez informed his government of another accession to the population of Louisiana, by the arrival of 499 individuals from the

Canary Islands, who had come to the colony at the king's expense. They received as favorable a treatment, at least, as their predecessors; nay, greater advantages were granted to them, for it appears that some of the emigrant families, besides the lands, the cattle, rations, pecuniary and other aid given to them, received the splendid donation of between three and four thousand dollars. This certainly was a very handsome beginning at the time, in a new country, offering so many resources. According to the government's direction, these people were transported to the district of the Attakapas, under the command of Bouligny, and formed, on Bayou Teche, a settlement then called New Iberia. They attempted the cultivation of flax and hemp, but without success; and most of them abandoned agricultural pursuits, to confine their industry entirely to the raising of cattle, to which they were naturally invited by the luxuriant and boundless prairies that surrounded them on every side.

Almost at the same time, there came to the province, for its spiritual relief, by the order and at the charge of the king, six capuchin friars, one of whom, named Antonio de Sedella, lived to extreme old age in Louisiana, and died in 1829, leaving behind him a spotless reputation and an honored memory.

One of the most serious afflictions of the colony, in this year, as in the preceding ones, was the small pox, which proved very fatal in New Orleans, and on the plantations above and below. It appears to have been, for many years, in Louisiana, the disease most prevalent and most feared. Hurricanes seem also to have been one of its chief scourges, and their frequency was really astonishing. Galvez, in a despatch of the 15th of January, 1779, speaks of one which had raged from the 7th to the 10th of October, 1778, with such violence, that the sea rose higher than it had ever been known to do before, destroying entirely all the establishments at the Balize, Bayou St. John, and Tigouyou.

But the attention of the inhabitants was diverted from these calamities by stirring events, in which they were called to take a part. Thus, France, having recognised the independence of the United States, had concluded a treaty of alliance and commerce with them and afforded them considerable succor. England, very naturally, considered such proceedings as equivalent to a declaration of war, and hostilities had actually begun, when Spain offered her mediation, and made propositions tending to secure a general peace, which was to be agreed upon in a meeting of the ministers of the belligerent powers at Madrid, including those of the United States. But this was not palatable to the pride of England, and, on the rejection by the cabinet of St. James of the terms offered by Spain, the Catholic King determined to join his cousin of France in the coming struggle against Great Britain. His ambassador left London without taking leave, and the British government, acting with its customary energy and promptitude, immediately issued letters of marque against the ships and subjects of Spain.

On the 8th of May, the King of Spain published a formal declaration of war against Great Britain, and, on the 8th of July, authorized his subjects in America to take their share in the hostilities to be waged against the English and their possessions. No news could have been more welcome to Galvez. He was young, bold, energetic, and he felt that his talents were equal to the career which was opening before him. Availing himself of the occasion with alacrity, he immediately planned an attack against the neighboring English possessions, and submitted it to a council of war. It was composed of men of a less fiery spirit, who rejected his proposition, and recommended that all offensive action be suspended until reinforcements be received from Havana. They also advised that, in the mean time, Galvez should confine all his exertions to the execution of the best measures that might be devised for the defence of the colony.

Galvez' mind was not so constituted as to induce him to submit implicitly to the decision of his advisers, and he acted as men of his temperament usually do in similar circumstances. He had convened a council of war, in the hope that it would agree with him, but as it did not, he resolved to act on his own responsibility. He had discovered by intercepted letters from Natchez, that the English intended to surprise New Orleans,* and he concluded to ward off the blow by being the first to attack, when he was thought to be hardly capable of defence. He labored under the apprehension that, if the English once possessed themselves of both banks of the river down to its mouth, they might then find themselves in a situation to carry the war into New Mexico and the other provinces of New Spain. These were strong considerations, which weighed on his mind, and which stimulated his zeal. Under the pretext of preparing for defence, he proceeded with indefatigable activity to prepare for carrying into execution his secret designs, which he intrusted only to Don Juan Antonio Gayarre, whom he appointed commissary of war for the projected expedition. He had proposed to march against the enemy on the 22nd of August, resolving to call together, previously, on the 20th, all the inhabitants who were at hand, and whom he intended to invite to follow him But, on the 18th, a hurricane, that well-known visiter of

---

* Supplemento á la Gazetta de Madrid de Viernes, 14 de Enero de 1780.

the country, suddenly burst out with such violence, that, in three hours, it destroyed a large number of houses in New Orleans, the greater part of the dwellings and improvements on the banks of the river, for forty miles up and down, swept off like chaff all the crops, killed almost all the cattle, and spread general consternation throughout the province. All the vessels which Galvez had in readiness for the expedition went to the bottom of the Mississippi, with the exception of the frigate, *El Volante*, which was saved by the intrepidity and skill of its commander, Luis Lorenzo de Terrazas.

This was a sad and unexpected reverse, disconcerting all the measures of the Governor. But reflecting that if, in the state of prostration in which the colony was, time was given to the English, whose establishments had not suffered from the hurricane, they could, by calling the Indians to their assistance, take the field with fifteen hundred men, and secure the conquest of the Spanish possessions, he made up his mind to persevere in his original intentions, and ordered the commissary of war, Don Juan Antonio Gayarre, to renew his preparations. But in the exhausted state of the colony, it was not easy to provide all those various elements, the combination of which is necessary to secure the success of the invasion of an enemy's territory, and the commissary of war had to tax his energy and ability to the utmost to satisfy the impatience of his chief. He had to apply himself to his task, day and night, and allow himself no breathing time, until it was completed. Galvez, in order to induce the colonists to join him in the contemplated expedition, in spite of the circumstances of desolation in which the country then was, had recourse to an expedient, "to which," says the supplement to the Madrid Gazette of the 29th of August, 1780, "he was in part indebted for his final success."

With the official communication of the declaration of war, Galvez, who was only governor ad interim, had received intelligence that the king had confirmed him in the government of Louisiana. But he had concealed this fact, in order that it should not be known that he had heard from Madrid. He now convened the inhabitants on the public square at New Orleans, discoursed on the miserable condition of the province, and regretted that, in such untoward circumstances, he had to inform them that war had been declared against Great Britain, and that he had received strict orders to put the colony in a state of defence, because an attack was anticipated. He then showed them his commission as governor of Louisiana under the royal patent. "Gentlemen," said he, addressing them with the energy of language and sentiment which was suited to the occasion, "I cannot avail myself of my commission, without previously swearing before the cabildo, that I shall defend the province; but, although I am disposed to shed the last drop of my blood for Louisiana and for my king, I cannot take an oath which I may be exposed to violate, because I do not know whether you will help me in resisting the ambitious designs of the English. What do you say? Shall I take the oath of governor? Shall I swear to defend Louisiana? Will you stand by me, and conquer or die with your governor and for your king?" So saying, with the left hand he displayed the royal commission, under the broad seal of Spain, and, with the right, he drew his sword with an expression of heroic determination. An immense and enthusiastic acclamation was the answer. "Fear not taking your oath of office," cried the crowd, as if with one voice; "for the defence of Louisiana, and for the service of the king, we tender you our lives, and we would say our fortunes, if we had any remaining." On the spot, Galvez went through the ceremony of his installation, amidst the increasing enthusiasm and shouts of the whole population, and, immediately after, hastened to accelerate his preparations, with the united assistance and efforts of the colonists.

Still concealing his real designs, the governor gave out that he was going to post his troops in those places to which he expected that the first attacks of the English would be directed. He ordered down to New Orleans all the boats which had been spared by the hurricane, at those points on the river where its violence had not been so much felt. One schooner and three gunboats were raised out of the river, into which they had sunk, and the provisions, ammunition and artillery were put in them. The artillery consisted of ten pieces, one twenty-four, five eighteen, and four four-pounders, under the command of Don Julien Alvarez, who, although his health was greatly impaired, took charge with alacrity of the trust reposed in him. This small fleet was to go up the river at the same time with the army, in order to supply its wants. On the 26th of August, Galvez gave the command of New Orleans and of the garrison which was left in it to Lieutenant Colonel Don Pedro Piernas, and delivered up the civil administration of the province, during his absence, to the contador, or comptroller, Don Martin Navarro. He appointed as second in command to himself, in the campaign which he was to undertake, Colonel Don Manuel Gonzales; next in rank came Don Estevan Miró, and Jacinto Panis, with the commissary of war, Don Juan Antonio Gayarré. These were to be under him the principal actors in the expedition.

On the 27th, these arrangements being made, the governor took his departure in the morning, to recruit at the German and Acadian Coasts all the men that he might prevail upon to join him. On the same day, in the afternoon, his small army put itself in motion. It was composed of 170 veteran soldiers, 330 recruits, 20 carabiniers, 60 militiamen, and 80 free blacks and mulattoes, of Oliver Pollock, the agent of the American Congress, with nine of his countrymen, as volunteers—making a total of 670 men, without one single engineer among them, says the Supplement to the Madrid Gazette, which relates all the details of this expedition. They were reinforced on the way by 600 men of every condition and color, besides 160 Indians, who had been gathered up at the German Coast, at the Acadian Coast, at Opeloussas, Attakapas and Pointe Coupée. These troops, when united, formed a body of fourteen hundred and thirty men. Although they were provided with no tents, and with none of those articles which are usually deemed necessary to an army entering upon a campaign, yet they marched on with unabated ardor, and much order, through the thick woods which, at that time, shaded a considerable portion of the banks of the river. With a view to guard against surprises, the colored men and the Indians were ordered to keep ahead of the main body of the troops, at a distance of about three quarters of a mile, and closely to reconnoitre the woods. Next came the veteran troops, whose left was protected by the river and by the artillery of the boats, and whose right rested on the forest. The militia formed the rear guard.

On the 6th of September (1779) the Spaniards came in sight of Fort Manchac, situated at a distance of about one hundred and fifteen miles from New Orleans. But disease and the fatigues of the journey had caused a diminution of more than one third in their number. It was only when he was about a mile and a half from the fort, that Galvez informed his troops of the declaration of war against the English, and of the positive instructions he had received to attack their establishments. This communication was responded to with demonstrations of joy; a general disposition was shown to come to close quarters with the enemy, and there was exhibited a patriotic emulation, as to which should distinguish himself most in the service of the king.

On the 7th, in the morning, the regulars were posted in an advantageous position, with the intention of opposing them to a body of four hundred Englishmen who were said to be coming with artillery and provisions to the relief of Manchac, and the assault was given to the fort by the militia, with complete success. Gilbert Antoine de St. Maxent, brother-in-law to ex-Governor Unzaga, was the first who entered the fort through one of its embrasures. The garrison was composed of a captain, a first lieutenant and a second lieutenant, with twenty privates, of whom one was killed, and five escaped with one of the lieutenants. The rest remained prisoners of war. This certainly was no great exploit.

On the 8th, the inventory of the fort was made; six days of rest were allowed to the troops; and, on the 13th, they resumed their march for Baton Rouge, which is only fifteen miles from Manchac. At a mile and a half from Baton Rouge, the army took its quarters, and the artillery was landed from the boats. Already had Grand Pré, with all the forces which he had been able to bring with him from Pointe Coupée, occupied a position between Baton Rouge and Natchez, in order to interrupt all communication between these two places, as he actually did, after having possessed himself of two English posts, one of which was on Thompson's Creek, and the other on the Amite, forcing their garrisons to surrender themselves prisoners of war.

Governor Galvez, having, with some officers, reconnoitred the fort of Baton Rouge, saw that it would be impossible to carry it by storm, on account of its strength. This fort was surrounded by a ditch, eighteen feet wide and nine in depth; it had, besides, very high walls, with a parapet protected with *chevaux de frise*, and a garrison of four hundred regulars and one hundred militiamen, and was supplied with thirteen pieces of heavy artillery. The governor also considered that the greater portion of his forces consisted of natives of the country, among whom there were many heads of families, and that a victory would be dearly bought by the blood which it would cost, and the desolation it would spread in the colony. Therefore, resisting the repeated and pressing solicitations of his troops to be led to the assault, he resolved to open trenches and establish batteries.

There was near the fort a wood which projected towards it in the shape of a triangle. This, at the first glance, seemed the most favorable spot from which to attack, and this the governor chose, to deceive the enemy, and to divert their attention from the point where he intended to carry on his works. Thither he sent a detachment of militia, supported by the colored companies and the Indians, in order that, under cover of the trees, and during the night, they should make as much noise as possible, and simulate an attack.

The English wasted and spent in vain their ammunition, by firing with ball and grape at that part of the wood from which they thought they would be assailed, whilst, in the meantime, the Spaniards, without being incommoded, were erecting their batteries within musket shot of the fort, behind a garden which concealed their operations. The English discovered the stratagem when it was too late, and when the besiegers had succeeded in sheltering themselves from the shot of their enemies.

On the following day, the 21st of September, at daybreak, the Spanish batteries, under the direction of Don Julien Alvarez, were plied with such accuracy and effect, that, notwithstanding the briskness of the fire of the besieged, the fort was so dismantled by half past three in the afternoon, that the English sent two officers with a flag of truce, to propose articles of capitulation. Galvez would assent to no terms but those he was willing to offer, which were—that the garrison should surrender at discretion, and, at the same time, that Fort Panmure, at Natchez, should be delivered up to him, with its garrison, composed of eighty grenadiers and their officers. The English accepted these conditions, and, after a delay of twenty-four hours which was granted to them (during which they were observed to be engaged in burying a considerable number of dead bodies), they came out with military honors, and marched five hundred paces from the fort, when they delivered up their arms and flags, and remained prisoners of war. The veteran troops, which thus surrendered, consisted of three hundred and seventy-five men. At the same time, Galvez despatched a captain with fifty men, to take possession of Fort Panmure, at Natchez, which is about one hundred and thirty miles distant from Baton Rouge. This fort it would have been very difficult to carry by force, because it was situated on an elevated and steep hill, and was difficult of access. In these two forts of Baton Rouge and Natchez was found a considerable number of militiamen and free negroes, with arms in their hands. They were set free on account of the difficulty of keeping securely so many prisoners.

Whilst the expedition was meeting with so signal a

success, the fortune of war was also declaring itself in favor of the Spaniards in other parts of the province. On Lake Pontchartrain, an American schooner, which had been fitted up at New Orleans by an individual, named Pikle, boarded and captured an English privateer, called the West Florida, and much superior in force to its antagonist. The Spanish gunboats also captured near Galvezton three schooners and a small brig which were returning to Pensacola, one schooner which they met on the Mississippi, and two cutters loaded with provisions, which were coming from Pensacola, through Lakes Pontchartrain and Maurepas, to the relief of the English establishments.

Another English cutter, says the Madrid Gazette from which I quote, was taken in a manner which deserves to be related. One Vincent Rieux, a native of New Orleans, had been put in command of a sloop of war, to cruise in the lakes. On his coming to Bayou Manchac, through which the English used to receive all their supplies from Pensacola, having been informed that one of their barques, well armed, and well laden with provisions and ammunition, was soon expected, he landed his guns, cut down a few trees to form a sort of intrenchment, and kept himself concealed with his crew. When he saw the English close under the muzzles of his guns, he suddenly blazed away at them, and raised with his companions such shouts and yells, that the enemy, persuaded that they had to deal with at least five hundred men, fled below deck. Rieux, availing himself of their panic, rushed on board, closed the hatches, and captured every soul that was in the vessel. The prisoners were: one captain, one first lieutenant, two second lieutenants, fifty-four grenadiers of the Waldeck regiment, and from ten to twelve sailors. It would be difficult to describe their surprise, when they found themselves the captives of fourteen men; these were, every one of them, creoles or natives of Louisiana.

In short, the results of this campaign were highly flattering to the Spanish arms. Eight vessels and three forts had been taken; five hundred and fifty-six regulars, besides a good many sailors, militiamen and free blacks had been made prisoners, among whom were Lieutenant-colonel Dickson aud many other officers. Dickson was the commander general of all the British settlements on the Mississippi, and was in the fort of Baton Rouge, when it surrendered. These remarkable advantages had been obtained, hardly with the loss of any blood on the part of the Spaniards. The Louisiana militia* behaved with extraordinary discipline and fortitude. It was found difficult to restrain their ardor, particularly that of the Acadians, who, at the sight of the British troops, being inflamed with rage at the recollection of their old injuries, were eager to rush on those who had desecrated their hearths, burned their paternal roofs to the ground, and driven them into exile like miserable outlaws and outcasts.

The companies† of free blacks and mulattoes, who had been employed in all the false attacks, and who, as scouts or skirmishers, had proved exceedingly useful, were reported by Galvez to his government as having behaved

---

* Las milicias se emplearon con indecible zelo en todos los trabajos, y en el servicio de la artilleria, dando constantes pruebas de una subordinacion sin limites; pues por ella dexaron muchas veces de arrojarse sobre los enemigos, especialmente las compañias de Acadianos, á quienes enardecia la memoria de las crueldades de los Ingleses en la guerra pasada que les obligaron á abandonar sus domicilios.—Sup. á la Gaz. de Madrid, 14 de Enero de 1780.

† No merecen menos elogio las compañias de negros y mulatos libres que siempre estuvieron ocupados en las abanzadas, falsos ataques y descubiertas, escopeteandose con el enemigo, y portandose en todas ocasiones con tanto valor y generosidad como los blancos.—Sup. á la Gaz. de Madrid, 14 de Enero de 1780.

on all occasions, with as much valor and generosity as the whites.

It seems that even the Indians showed themselves, for the first time, alive to the voice of humanity, and abstained from doing the slightest injury to the fugitives whom they captured, although their immemorial custom was to treat prisoners with the most horrible cruelty*— nay, they had improved so much as to carry in their arms to Galvez, with the most tender care, the children who had taken refuge in the woods with their mothers. This change in their habits was due to the happy influence exercised over them by Santiago Tarascon and Joseph Sorelle, of Opeloussas, who were both well acquainted with their language, and under whose command they had been placed in this expedition.

Having accomplished his purposes, Galvez disbanded the militia and sent them to their homes, with the praises and the rewards which they deserved. Charles de Grand-Pré, brother-in-law of the commissary of war, Don Juan Antonio Gayarre, was left in command of Baton Rouge, with jurisdiction over two officers placed, the one at Fort Bute, on the bank of Bayou Manchac, and the other at Fort Panmure, at Natchez. In order to occupy the posts which he had conquered, Galvez had to draw largely on his regulars, so that he had only fifty of them left in the capital to garrison it, and to watch over the numerous prisoners who had been taken, and over the several tribes of Indians who had come to New

---

* Finalmente los Indios dieron por la primera vez el noble exemplo de humanidad de no haber hecho el mas leve daño á los habitantes Ingleses fugitivos y desarmados, ó que aunque con armas se les rendian, a pesar de la general costumbre que tienen de tratar con la mas horrible crueldad á sus prisioneros ; habiendo llegado hasta el extremo de traer entre sus brazos con agasajo para presentar al gobernador los niños que por temor de su inhumanidad se habian refugiado con sus madres á los montes.—Sup. á la Gaz. de Madrid, 14 de Enero de 1780.

Orleans to compliment the Spaniards on their victory. But although the prisoners had been permitted on parole to be free within the limits of the town, and although it was full of Indians belonging to different tribes, some of which were of the most warlike and haughty temper, there did not occur the slightest disorder in the course of more than twenty days, during which the Spaniards had to trust entirely to the good faith and honor of their Indian allies, and of their English prisoners. The respect which Galvez inspired by his character, talents, energy, and recent achievements was such, that he had no cause to repent of having acted, on this occasion, as he did, and with what might have turned out to be rash imprudence.

Towards the middle of October, there arrived at New Orleans from Natchez the garrison of fort Panmure, and, at the same time, a reinforcement of Spanish troops from Havana. The Spanish court was liberal in granting honors and rewards to all those who had distinguished themselves in this expedition. Galvez was appointed brigadier-general, Colonel Don Manuel Gonzalez was raised to the same grade, and was made Governor of the province of Cumanas; Lieutenant-colonel Mirò, Captain Don Pedro Piernas, and Don Jacinto Panis were promoted. The commissary of war, Don Juan Antonio Gayarré, was appointed Royal Comptroller or Contador for Acapulco, at that time a celebrated port from which the rich Spanish galleons took their departure to spread the wealth of the western over the eastern world.*

The achievements of Galvez fired the poetical vein of a gentleman, named Julien Poydras, who celebrated them in a small poem written in the French language, which was printed and circulated at the king's expense. This gentleman subsequently acquired immense wealth,

* Captain Hall.

was delegated to the congress of the United States by Louisiana, served in its territorial and state legislatures, and, on his death, liberally founded and endowed, by his last testamentary dispositions, several charitable institutions. These acts of benevolence have secured to him more fame than his poetry, and his name has been given to one of the principal streets of New Orleans.

The congress of the Thirteen United Provinces of America saw with much satisfaction the rupture which had occurred between Great Britain and Spain, and availed themselves of this favorable circumstance to send to the court of Madrid a minister, whose instructions were to negotiate a treaty of alliance, and, particularly, to insist on their right to the navigation of the Mississippi to the sea. This right, however, the king of Spain was not willing to admit, and was supported by France in the view which he took of the question. "We are disposed," said in substance the ministers of the Catholic King to the United States, "to acknowledge your independence and to enter into a treaty of alliance and commerce with you; but, if you wish us to consent to your admission into the great family of nations, you must subscribe to the right of Spain to the exclusive navigation of the Mississippi, and consent to our taking possession of both the Floridas and of all the territory extending from the left bank of that river to the back settlements of the former British provinces, according to the proclamation of 1763. No part of this territory ever was included within your limits, and the whole of it, with the Floridas, may be legitimately conquered by his Catholic Majesty, without giving you any ground for remonstrance or complaint. We furthermore expect you to prohibit the inhabitants of your confederacy from making any attempt towards settling in or conquering any portion of the British territory to which we refer

Considering that you have, beyond the mountains, no possessions except the post of Kaskaskia and a few others, which you have momentarily acquired from the British, and which you hold only by a very precarious tenure, what is the navigation of the Mississippi to you in comparison with the importance of your recognition by us as an independent nation, and of the advantages which you will derive from your relations with us, in consequence of a treaty of alliance and commerce?" This pretension was not palatable to the far-sighted policy of the new power which was budding into existence, and these negotiations were still pending at the beginning of the year 1780.

Hardly had Galvez returned to New Orleans after his conquests of Manchac, Baton Rouge and Natchez, when he planned another expedition destined against Mobile, and Don Juan Antonio Gayarré again acted as commissary of war on this occasion. All the preparations for this campaign were made with the greatest activity, and the colonists, who now had implicit faith in the talents and good luck of their governor, whom they thought invincible, assisted him with unremitting ardor, and showed themselves ready to peril their lives and fortunes on his behalf. On the 5th of February, Galvez sailed from the Balize with two thousand men, composed of regulars, of the militia of the colony, and of some companies of free blacks. In the gulf he was overtaken by a storm which crippled, or caused to be stranded on the coast some of his vessels, and greatly damaged his provisions and ammunition. The Governor and the whole expedition were in imminent danger of being wrecked and entirely lost. After some delays, however, and considerable exertions, Galvez succeeded in landing his army, artillery, military stores and provisions, on the eastern point of Mobile river. But this had been done with a great deal of confusion, and with a want of concert which the war of the elements had rendered inevitable. Had General Campbell, who was at Pensacola, at the head of forces superior to the Spanish, marched immediately against them, and made a sudden and vigorous attack, he might have secured an easy victory. So conscious was Galvez of his danger that, notwithstanding his natural daring and his confidence in his own resources, his first impulse was to prepare himself for a retreat by land to New Orleans, leaving his baggage and artillery behind. But those he had sent to reconnoitre the country having brought back the intelligence that there was no appearance of any design on the part of the enemy to sally out of Pensacola, Galvez boldly determined to advance and to attack fort Charlotte, towards which he moved with rapidity, and which he invested without hesitation. Six batteries were immediately erected, and a breach having been made in the walls of the fort, its commander, to avoid an assault which he could not resist, capitulated in conformity with the terms offered by Galvez. This event took place on the 14th of March.

A few days after, General Campbell arrived with a force which would have been sufficient to prevent the capture of the fort, but which was not able to retake it from the Spaniards. He was, therefore, compelled to an inglorious retreat to Pensacola. In the month of May, the commissary of war, Don Juan Antonio Gayarré, returned to New Orleans, through the lakes, on which he was assailed by another storm, which very nearly proved fatal to him. His vessel was struck by lightning, and it was with considerable difficulty that she came into port. A short time after, he departed to take possession of the office of Royal Comptroller, at Acapulco, with which he had been intrusted. The history of this officer now ceases to be connected with Louisiana, but, on his death, which happened in Mexico about the year 1787, his wife and his three sons, who were all natives of Louisiana, returned to the place of their birth. As to Galvez, he was rewarded for his success in the Mobile expedition by the grade of Major-General. He was then twenty-four years old, and therefore had no right to complain, as others frequently do, of the tardiness of promotion.

Encouraged by his past success, Galvez determined to attack Pensacola. But this place was well fortified, and had a very large garrison. His means were not adequate to the execution of his plan, and he had to solicit the Captain-general of Cuba for reinforcements, which were promised, but not sent. Impatient of delay, and mistrusting the intentions of the Captain-general, Galvez sailed for Havana, in order to ask in person for what he desired. The son of the viceroy of Mexico, and the nephew of the president of the Council of the Indies, so well known to be the omnipotent minister of Charles III., was not easily to be refused, and Galvez, having obtained all the troops, ammunition and implements of war which he deemed necessary, sailed on the 16th of October from Havana for Pensacola, but encountered one of those hurricanes which were so frequent in those days. Some of his transports foundered, the rest were dispersed, and he returned to Havana on the 16th of November, having been one month in gathering and collecting the scattered remnants of his fleet, with a perseverance, humanity, and unflinching sense of duty which cannot be too highly commended.

Galvez was not the man to give up any project which he had once formed, and the 28th of February, 1781, found him at the head of a much more formidable expedition than the one which had been disabled by the storm. On that day, he left Havana for Pensacola,*

* Martin's History of Louisiana, vol. ii., p. 54.

with a ship of the line, two frigates, and several transports, on board of which were fourteen hundred soldiers, a competent train of artillery, and abundance of ammunition. The fleet was commanded by Don Jose Cabro de Irazabal.

On the 9th of March,* Galvez landed his troops, ordnance and military stores on the island of St. Rose, and, on the next day, erected a battery to support the fleet when passing over the bar, which attempt was made on the 11th, but soon abandoned, because the admiral's ship got aground. The next day Galvez wrote to Irazabal: "I am uneasy at the risk which the fleet and transports will run, should they remain long exposed to the storms which so frequently prevail on this dangerous coast. Therefore I request you to call the captains of all the ships on board of yours, and to consult them as to the best means of getting the fleet over the bar, as speedily as possible." Irazabal complied with this request, and, in his answer to Galvez, said: "The officers have declared that they are unable to form an opinion on the probable success of a second attempt, as they are without a correct chart of the coast. They complain that the pilots on board of the fleet are incapable of affording any aid, because every account they have given of the soundings has proved erroneous. The officers further add, that, on the first attempt to cross over the bar, their ships nearly lost their rudders; and it is their belief that, if they had persisted in the undertaking, they would soon have come to a position which would have rendered all manœuvres impossible. We had always anticipated that the artillery of the British fort could reach the channel, but now it is demonstrated that it commands, not only the channel over the bar, but

---

* Martin's History of Louisiana, vol. ii., p. 54.

even the island of St. Rose. There are in the fort twenty four pounders, the balls of which would rake, fore and aft, any of our vessels that should attempt to cross the bar, and the direction of the channel is such, that they would be obliged to present successively, as they moved on, their sides, poops and prows to the enemy's guns. Besides, the channel is so narrow, that should the first ship get aground, she would obstruct the passage for the rest, and the rapidity of the current preventing any quick manœuvre, the ships would run foul of each other, before they could turn, even if that were possible. Considering, however, that you deem the crossing of the bar an object of vast importance to the king's service, we have come to the conclusion to send one or two officers, attended by three or four pilots, to sound the channel during the night, as far as Point Siguenza, a fire being ordered to be made on that Point, in order to ascertain the direction. After which a second trial to cross over the bar may be made. But my individual opinion is, that any attempt to attack the British by water would be fruitless, and that the land force ought to be considered by your Excellency as the best and most efficacious means to reduce the fort. Therefore, I beg leave to recommend that it be used without delay."

This answer of the Spanish admiral caused great displeasure to Galvez. He thought that it originated from that feeling of jealousy which but too often springs up between land and naval forces when they are destined to coöperate; and that the officers of the navy, who were his associates in this expedition, being under the impression that he would exclusively reap all the glory in case of success, were disposed rather to thwart than to forward his plans. He replied to Irazabal: " admitting the danger of losing a ship or two, from which, after all, in case of accident, all on board would be easily saved, what would be such a loss in comparison with that of the whole fleet, which is likely to occur, should there be a storm! Therefore I desire that the captains be again called together, and invited to reconsider their former report." In the mean time, in order to rouse and stimulate those officers of the navy whose prudence was so little in accordance with his views, Galvez determined to attempt, with the naval means of which he had the absolute command, what seemed to be denied to him by his more timid associates.*

In compliance with his orders, the brig Galvezton, commanded by Rousseau, which had lately arrived from New Orleans with ordnance, cast anchor near the bar. Rousseau sounded the channel as far as Point Siguenza, during the night of the 15th to the 16th, and reported, the next morning, that there was water enough† in the shallowest part of the channel for the largest ship in the fleet, with her full load. Notwithstanding Rousseau's declaration, the Spanish captains having, as Galvez desired, met on board of the admiral's ship, obstinately persisted in their former decision, and referred the Governor to greatly to that officer's indignation.

So stood matters, when Joseph de Espeleta arrived, on the 16th, from Mobile, with all the regulars which he could draw from that place and its neighborhood, and, on the next day, Don Estevan Miró came from New Orleans with the Louisiana forces. They took their position on the western side of the Perdido.

In the critical situation in which he was placed by the refusal of the Spanish admiral to grant the required assistance, Galvez acted with his usual decision of character Assuming the entire responsibility of his movements,

---

* Martin's History, vol. ii., p. 56.   † Ibid.

and casting aside all reliance on Irazabal, he resolved to act for himself, and independently of him. Without loss of time, he ordered the brig Galvezton, a schooner, and two gunboats, which constituted all the naval forces belonging to his government of Louisiana, and which, as such, were entirely at his disposal, to prepare for crossing the bar. Towards noon,* Captain Rousseau, with his brig, the schooner and gunboats, cast anchor near the bar. At half-past two, the bay of Pensacola presented a stirring spectacle. On land, the Spanish forces were drawn up in battle array, and the beating of their drums, with the notes of other martial instruments, were wafted over the blue waves to the British fort, which echoed back fierce sounds of defiance, whilst that portion of its walls which faced the bay could be distinctly seen to be crowded with the military whom curiosity had gathered together, to watch the manœuvres of the enemy. All being ready for action, Galvez, leaving his army, threw himself into a boat which took him on board of the brig Hardly was he on deck, when, by his orders, the broad flag of Castile was proudly displayed at the main-mast, a salute was fired, all sails set, and the small fleet moved on gallantly. The fort, which seemed to have been patiently waiting for this signal, was immediately in a blaze, and pouring a heavy fire on the daring little vessels which were swiftly sweeping onward, and which, on their side, answered with a brisk cannonade. The aim of the British artillery was principally directed at the brig, on the deck of which stood up Galvez in the midst of a brilliant staff. The brig, the schooner and the gunboats passed by in rapid succession, without receiving much injury, except in their sails and rigging, and Galvez

---

* Martin's History, vol. ii., p. 57.

safely landed at the bottom of the bay under a salute, and amid the enthusiastic acclamations of his troops.

Irazabal and his men had remained the motionless spectators of this bold undertaking. It was evident that he could no longer hesitate to follow this example, under the penalty of being dishonored, and therefore, the next day, he entered the bay, the frigate leading the way, and the convoy forming the rear. The fort kept up a brisk fire* for upwards of an hour, until the hindmost vessel was out of its reach. Very little damage was done to the Spanish fleet, the whole of which thus joined Galvez, with the exception of the Admiral's ship, which that officer sent back to Havana, because she had just been reladen for her return. Whilst the Spanish fleet, under Irazabal, was crossing over the bar, Galvez advanced in an open boat to meet them, passed by the fort amidst a shower of balls which fell thick around him, and repassed it in the same way, at the head of the ships, whose commanders he had thus compelled to action by his heroism. He remained in the midst of the vessels until the last of them had anchored. This feat of Galvez excited the enthusiasm of his countrymen, and was even much admired by the British.

On the same day, at four o'clock in the afternoon, this indefatigable man, so distinguished for his activity and intrepidity, accompanied only by two of his aides, made an effort to cross the bar, to go and confer with Espeleta and Miró, and devise with them a plan of attack. But he long struggled in vain against a strong adverse wind, and he returned to his camp, about midnight, without having been able to accomplish his purpose.

On the next day, the 20th, early in the morning, " he

---

* Martin's History, vol. ii., p. 57.

sent," says Judge Martin in his History of Louisiana, "one of his aides to General Campbell, with a message, in which he informed him that, when the British came to Havana in 1762, their commander intimated to the Captain-General of the Catholic King, that, if any of the King's edifices, ships, or other property were destroyed, the Spaniards would be treated with all the rigor and severity of the laws of war; that the like intimation was now made to the General and all those it might concern, and under the same terms."

Campbell, on the following day, very early in the morning, returned his answer, through one of his officers, whom he sent to Galvez. "Sir," said Campbell to the Spanish general, "an enemy's threats can only be considered as a stratagem. I hope that, in the defence of Pensacola, I shall not forget myself so far as to resort to any measure not justified by the usages of war. I avail myself, however, of this opportunity to make my acknowledgments for the frank intimation I have received, and I give you the assurance that my conduct will be regulated by yours, with regard to the adoption or rejection of certain propositions I have to make in conjunction with the Governor of West Florida."

At noon, the propositions thus alluded to were made known to Galvez. An aide of Campbell's, accompanied by Lieutenant-colonel Dickson, who, it will be remembered, had been taken prisoner the preceding year, at Baton Rouge, and liberated on parole, came in a boat, bearing the flag of truce, and delivered to Galvez letters from Campbell and Governor Chester of West Florida.*
"Humanity," said Campbell, "requires as much as possible that inoffensive individuals be exempted from the disasters which are the necessary incidents of war. Con

---

* Martin's History of Louisiana, vol. ii., p. 59.

sidering, therefore, that the garrison of Pensacola is unable to resist the force brought against it, without the total destruction of the town, and the consequent ruin of its inhabitants, and that its fate depends on that of the redoubt of marine and of Fort George which protect it, I propose that Pensacola shall remain neutral ground; that it shall be used by neither party for protecting itself or annoying its adversary, and that it shall continue to be the safe asylum of women and children, the aged and the infirm, during the siege of the redoubt of marine and Fort George, within which alone I mean to contend for the preservation of the province for the British Crown. This is to the interest of both parties, as it will preserve Pensacola for the victor, whoever he may be. But should this proposition be rejected, and should the Spaniards seek shelter in Pensacola, it will become my duty immediately to destroy that town. I further propose that the Spanish prisoners in my possession be liberated on parole, and on your Excellency's assurance that they shall not be employed in the military or civil service of the Catholic king, during the war, unless they are sooner exchanged."

Galvez, when he had heard of the approach of the British officers sent to him, had commanded his army to be drawn up in arms, in order that the messengers of Campbell and Chester should have a full view of his forces, and might report accordingly to their chiefs. His troops were numerous, fully equipped, well trained, provided with everything necessary to carry on the siege successfully, and he had calculated on the impression which this sight would produce. He received courteously the British officers, and sent them back, after having verbally declared to them that he was too much indisposed to prepare a written answer before the next day.

During the following night, the English set fire to a

few houses near Fort St. George. This circumstance greatly irritated Galvez, who, in the morning, sent his promised answer to Campbell. "Sir," said he, "I consider as a departure from, or a violation of, your proposition conveyed to me yesterday, the burning of the houses which you destroyed last night. This occurrence, with others that have come to my knowledge since the departure of your aide and of Lieutenant-colonel Dickson, has convinced me that those who sent them had no other object than procrastination. I am ashamed of my having been thought a fit object to practise deception upon, and of having confirmed by my credulity the impression which had been received of me. Therefore I make it known to your Excellency that I shall listen to no proposition but that of surrender; and that the conflagration of Pensacola, so long as it is not attributable to any fault of mine, will be contemplated with complete indifference."

Campbell rejoined, says Judge Martin in his history, that the haughty style assumed by the Spanish chief, far from its intended effect, would have that of exciting the utmost opposition to the ambitious views of Spain; that the officer commanding at Fort George had done nothing but his duty, in destroying a few houses near it which afforded protection to the enemy; and that, if the invaders sought to avail themselves of Pensacola, by seeking an asylum there, it would be immediately destroyed.

After a good deal of talking in imitation of Homer's heroes, both the British and Spanish chiefs began to think seriously of coming to blows. Campbell withdrew all his forces into the fort, and Galvez lost no time in tightening the iron belt which encircled it. He approached the British fortifications on one side, while his lieutenants, Miró and Espeleta, did the same operation on the other. The Spaniards set to work in earnest to erect their batteries, which they supplied with a good train of artillery.

In the beginning of April, all being ready on the part of the besiegers, a simultaneous attack was made by the fleet and by the land forces. The fire poured upon the British was really tremendous, and frequently drove them from their guns, to which they returned, however, with that bull-dog tenacity which is the well known characteristic of their nation. They had not been taken by surprise; and, as they had long expected a siege, they had provided themselves with an ample supply of ammunition and provisions. The fortifications were in an excellent state of repair, and defended by a numerous garrison, so that the Spaniards* made but little impression. But, being much annoyed by the guns of the fleet, the English hastily erected a lower battery of heavy cannon, with which they soon drove the ships on the opposite side of the bay. Galvez was thus reduced to his land batteries, with which he did very little execution, and the result of the siege was beginning to be very doubtful, when there happened one of those accidents which so frequently determine the fortune of war. In the first week of May, a powder magazine in one of the advanced redoubts of the English, took fire from a shell and blew up. The redoubt was completely destroyed by the explosion, and a free passage was effected in the very walls of the fort. Galvez availed himself of this golden opportunity, and, by his order, Espeleta, with a strong detachment, immediately took possession of the smouldering ruins, and soon after, opened a brisk fire with four field pieces. At the same time, with Galvez at their head, all the Spanish forces were putting themselves in motion to storm the fort, when a white flag was hoisted

---

* Martin's History, vol ii., p. 61.

up by the English, and an officer came out to propose a capitulation.*

The terms being agreed on, the capitulation was signed on the 9th of May. More than eight hundred men who composed the garrison became prisoners, and the whole province of West Florida was surrendered to Spain. The honors of war, however, were allowed to the garrison. "They were permitted," says Martin, in his history, "to retain their baggage and private property, and were transported to their sovereign's dominions, under a stipulation that they should not serve against Spain or her allies, until duly exchanged. Arthur O'Neal, an Irish officer in the service of Spain, was left in command of Pensacola."

Whilst the Spaniards were meeting with so signal a success in Florida, they lost, at Natchez, fort Panmure, which was taken by some British adherents who had settled in that neighborhood in 1775, under General Lyman. This officer was a native of Connecticut, and had risen to high rank in the service of the British. In 1755, he had been appointed by the king major-general and commander-in-chief of the forces of his native province. In 1762, he was in command of all the colonial American troops which had joined the British expedition against Havana. After a stay of several years in England, whither he had gone to solicit the reward he deserved for his many services, he obtained large grants of land on the Mississippi and Yazoo rivers, where, with a remarkable degree of enterprise and the true spirit of the pioneer, although his grey hairs seemed to unfit him for the undertaking, he had resolved to dare the influence of a climate so different from the one to which he had been accustomed, and to encounter the dangers of a

* Martin's History, vol. ii., p. 61.

struggle with the wilderness, at so many hundred miles from the green valleys of the land of his birth. But, notwithstanding the difficulties which stared him in the face, the intrepid veteran shouldered his household gods, and with his eldest son and a few friends, departed, in 1775, for the banks of the Mississippi, on which he formed a settlement, near fort Panmure, in the district of Natchez. He died a short time after, leaving his adherents in possession of his grants. These men had seen with much regret the British flag succeeded by the Spanish. When they heard that Galvez had dared invade Florida, their patriotism did not doubt of his defeat, and, in the excess of their zeal, they determined to give a proof of their loyalty to their sovereign. They secretly formed the plan of driving away the Spaniards, engaged most of the other inhabitants in the conspiracy, and secured the co-operation of some of the neighboring Indians. On the 22d of April, 1781, they approached fort Panmure in a body, and keeping out of reach of its guns, unfurled the British flag. During the night, they came nearer to the fort,* and brought some artillery to bear upon it, but a heavy fire from the Spanish guns soon forced them to retire. From the 24th to the 28th, hostilities were kept up between the insurgents and the Spaniards, and some gunshots were exchanged, which killed a few men.

"On the 28th," says Martin, in his history, "the commandant of the fort sent one of his officers to the insurgents, to represent to them the danger to which they exposed themselves by a rebellion against their lawful sovereign, recommending to them, at the same time, to deliver up their leaders and disperse, and promising that, if they did so, the royal clemency should be ex-

---

* Martin's History, vol. ii., p. 68.

tended to them. They promised to send an answer the next day. Accordingly, in the morning, a planter came to the fort with a letter from M'Intosh, one of the most respectable inhabitants of the district, informing him that what the messenger would say could be relied on. This man, on being questioned, said the fort was undermined, and would be blown up on the following day. There was a deep valley at a very short distance from the fort, at which the Spaniards had noticed a considerable number of persons during the preceding days, a circumstance which gave some credit to the story. On the 29th, the men, according to the report of the commandant, being exhausted with fatigue and watching, and the provisions and ammunition being nearly consumed, the fort was surrendered, on the garrison being permitted to march to Baton Rouge."

The insurgents had been incited to their enterprise by the report of the appearance of a strong British fleet in the gulf, which, they thought, would cut off Galvez' return to Louisiana. But, soon after the taking of Fort Panmure, they were informed, to their utter dismay, that they had relied on an idle rumor, and their consternation was increased by the news that Pensacola had surrendered to Galvez. The punishment inflicted at New Orleans on Lafrénière and his companions, in 1769, was a recent occurrence with which the insurgents were well acquainted, and they became apprehensive of a similar fate. Resolving not to expose themselves to Spanish resentment, they determined to make the best of their way to Savannah in Georgia, which was the nearest point occupied by the British. It is not easy to conceive an enterprise attended with more difficulties. The fugitives had to cross an immense wilderness inhabited by hostile Indians, and, as they were loyalists, they had to pursue a circuitous route, in order to avoid falling into the hands of the armed bands of the Americans who had shaken off the yoke of the mother country. But they were placed between a choice of evils, and they determined for the perils of the journey.

Numerous and indescribable, indeed, were the hardships encountered by this caravan. They had to carve their way through almost interminable forests, to swim across an infinite number of streams, deep and broad, to scale steep and lofty mountains which seemed to stand up like impassable barriers before them, to risk their lives in the fording of innumerable marshes, to make long and tedious circuits round those through which they dared not go, to sleep in the rugged lap of the wilderness, to suffer from thirst, famine, disease, and the pelting of storms, and to be constantly on the alert against the Indian foe, who, they knew, was hovering around them. The mother's breast dried up under the parched lips of the plaintive infant, who drooped and fell like a withered leaf; the orphan sat weeping on the mother's grave, which he was soon to leave; the wife's wailings were heard for the husband's loss, and the husband's manly cheeks were seen furrowed by tears near the wife's corpse. The aged father gave his last blessing to his family, and sank to rise no more. Sorrowfully indeed journeyed this miserable band, some on horseback, and many, whose horses had died, on foot. The greedy buzzard during the day, and the howling wolf at night, seemed to be instinctively attracted towards them by the hope of anticipated prey. On reaching the limits of the State of Georgia, they separated into two bands. One had the bad luck of falling into the hands of the American insurgents, and the other, having crossed, on a raft, the Alatamaha at its mouth, finally arrived at Savannah in the latter part of October. They had been travelling one hundred and thirty-one days.

Whilst these military operations had been going on, the commerce and agriculture of the province had been completely ruined, so that the inhabitants had been almost driven to despair. On the 24th of August, 1780, as if intended to be the last pound of weight wanting to break the camel's back, a hurricane, much more furious than the one which had prevailed, the year preceding, on the 18th of the same month, swept over the province, destroying all the crops, tearing down the buildings, and sinking every vessel or boat which was afloat on the Mississippi, or the lakes. The disasters were so extensive that, on the 29th, Don Martin Navarro, the Intendant, who, during the absence of the Governor, had been intrusted with the civil administration of Louisiana, addressed to the colonists a circular, which was printed by the king's printer, Antoine Boudousquié, and in which patient fortitude was recommended to those whom the wrath of heaven and of man had afflicted so much. "So far as we are concerned," said he, "we are willing to stretch to the utmost what powers and means we may have, in order to render you effectual services, relieve your distresses, and remedy as much as possible the necessities of the public. In so doing, we are persuaded that we act in conformity with the intentions of his Majesty, to whom we send a faithful and exact description of this last and fatal event. His royal heart will participate in your miseries, and his paternal love will suggest the best means to give the assistance which you require. But,* if in the course of one year and five

---

* Si en el discurso de un año y cinco dias han experimentado ustedes tantos contratiempos y tantas adversidades, aun queda que vencer la mayor, que es la de la conformidad y la paciencia, pues nada diminuye los trabajos como la con-

days you have experienced such a series of misfortunes, there remains yet one difficulty to overcome, it is to conquer those feelings which might be opposed to your resigning yourselves entirely to the will of God, and to your adopting the proper spirit of submission which the circumstances demand; for, nothing contributes more to level down difficulties, and to assuage the pains to which life is subjected, than the determination to conquer the former and bear the latter. All countries have their inconveniences; some suffer from the extreme cold or heat of their climate, and others are convulsed with earthquakes; this one is infested with wild beasts and insects; that one is exposed to inundations; and I know of none which are not occasionally devastated by the fury of storms and hurricanes. Let us put our faith in the divine providence, that will appease our alarms, and remedy the evils with which we are afflicted. Let us give a last proof of our loyalty to our sovereign, by not abandoning a country which we have conquered and preserved, in spite of human foes and of the elements themselves leagued against us. Let us give to God the proof of our perfect resignation, by saying with the holy man Job: 'The Lord gave, and the Lord hath taken away. Blessed be the name of the Lord!'

On the same day, the inhabitants of New Orleans and of its neighborhood returned an answer, in which they thanked Navarro for the consolation which he endeavored to minister to them, and bestowed much praise on

---

stancia con que se sobrablevan. Todas las provincias tienen sus ˙inconvenientes, unas el rigor del clima, otras el de los insectos, otras el de los tremblores de tierra, y todas expuestas á la furia de los uracanes. Esperemos en la divina providencia que calmara nuestras desgracias, demos la ultima prueba de nuestra lealtad al soberano en no abandonar un pays que hemos ayudado á conquistar, á pesar del enemigo comun y contra el torrente de los elementos, y a Dios la de la resignacion, diciendo con Job: Dios nos lo dío, Dios nos lo quitó. Su santissima nombre sea por siempre bendito y alabado.

his administration, and that of Galvez. Then they went on reciting all the sufferings they had experienced in less than two years, from a combination of adverse circumstances, such as war, two hurricanes, inundation, contagion, a summer more rainy and a winter more rigorous than had ever been known, the stagnation of commerce, the ruin of agriculture, the want of capital, the prodigiously high price asked for all the necessaries of life, and they depicted in the most vivid colors the extreme indigence to which they were reduced. "But," said they in conclusion, "we shall endeavor to conform, as much as may be permitted by the frailties of human nature, to your pressing exhortations to patience, and, if we cannot rise to so high a degree, in the possession of this virtue, as the holy man, Job, who was singularly favored by Heaven in this respect, we dare assure you that we shall at least be his match in gratitude, as soon as, through the clouds of the threatening sky which lowers over our heads, we shall see shining forth the sign which will give us the pledge of future security and happiness."

The war with Great Britain, and the capture of the British forts on the Mississippi, had deprived, says Martin in his history, the planters of Louisiana of the great advantages they derived from the illicit trade carried on by British traders. On the representation of Galvez, considerable privileges were granted to the commerce of the province, on the 22d of January, 1782, by a schedule which was published in New Orleans in the spring.

"In the preamble of this document, the king states that his royal solicitude and wishes have been always to secure to his vassals the utmost felicity, and to enable them to enjoy the advantages of a free trade; that he had never lost sight of so important an object in the regulations he had made for the commerce of his vast dominions in the Indies, being firmly persuaded that the protection of trade and industry has a great influence on the wealth and prosperity of a nation. His Majesty then adds, that the province of Louisiana has particularly merited his royal attention, since its annexation to his dominions. His paternal love for its inhabitants had induced him to give them repeated proofs that a change of government had not diminished their happiness. But, notwithstanding the favors and exemptions he had been pleased to grant them, on several occasions, particularly by the regulations of the commerce of the Indies, made on the 28th of October, 1778, experience had shown that the advantages he had contemplated were not realized; and the trade in peltries of that province with the numerous nations of Indians who surround it, and the articles of exportation to Europe which the country produces, demanded new regulations. Accordingly, and with the view of rewarding the zeal and fidelity of the colonists, during the late campaigns for the recovery of the territories lately possessed by Great Britain on the Mississippi and the Gulf of Mexico, the following favors and privileges are granted to the province of Louisiana:

"1° Permission is given, during a period of ten years, to be computed from the day on which peace may be proclaimed, to all vessels of the king's subjects in the province of Louisiana, bound to New Orleans or Pensacola, to sail directly with their cargoes from any of the ports of France in which a Spanish consul resides, and to return thereto with peltries, or the produce of Louisiana or West Florida (except specie, the exportation of which, in this way, is absolutely forbidden), under the express condition that a detailed invoice of all the merchandise on board, signed by the consul, shall be delivered by him, in a sealed cover, to the captain, to be presented by the latter at the custom-house of the place of destination.

"2° In case of urgent necessity in the colony, the existence of which necessity is to be certified by the governor and the intendant, permission is given to the colonists to resort to any port in the French West India islands.

"3° To encourage the commerce of the province to the ports of the Peninsula to which it is allowed, permission is given to export from New Orleans and Pensacola any species of merchandise directly imported there from Spain, to be landed in any port within the king's American dominions to which trade is allowed, paying only the duty with which such merchandise would have been charged on its exportation from the Peninsula, according to the regulations of the 12th of October, 1778; but the exportation of foreign merchandise imported in Louisiana is forbidden.

"4° An exemption from duty is granted, during the same period, on negroes imported into Louisiana or West Florida, and permission is given to procure them in the colonies of neutral or allied powers, in exchange for produce or specie, paying only, for such produce and specie, the duties mentioned in the 7th article.

"5° In order that the colonists may fully enjoy the favors and privileges now granted, they are permitted during the term of two years, to be computed from the proclamation of peace in New Orleans, to purchase foreign vessels free from duty, and such vessels are to be considered as Spanish bottoms.

"6° The exportation of pipe and barrel staves from Louisiana to Spain is permitted free from duty.

"7° It being just that commerce should contribute to the charges of the colony and to the expenses it occasions, a duty of six per cent. is laid on all merchandise exported from, and imported by the king's subjects, in the Peninsula, Louisiana, and West Florida, according to a moderate assessment.

"8° Custom-houses are to be established in New Orleans and Pensacola."

Galvez, whose enlightened mind had not been slow in discovering what would soon have converted Louisiana into a populous and wealthy colony, had recommended that it be granted the privilege of free trade with all the ports of Europe and America.* But neither the Court of Madrid, nor the spirit of the age, was disposed to go so far.

The conquest of Pensacola by the Governor of Louisiana was fully rewarded. He was promoted to the grade of Lieutenant-General, was decorated with the cross of knight pensioner of the royal and distinguished order of Charles III., was made a Count, and received the commission of Captain-general of the provinces of Louisiana and Florida.

Another individual, who had made himself conspicuous in a different field, under Unzaga's administration, was also promoted, about the same time. That was father Cirilo, the former antagonist and reviler of father Dagobert. He was created a bishop *in partibus infidelium*, for the see of the town of Tricali in Greece. But he was appointed co-adjutor to his former patron, Don Jose Estecheveria, who still occupied the see of Cuba, and he was directed to exercise his episcopal functions† in Louisiana.

A simultaneous attack of the French and Spaniards having been planned against the island of Jamaica, Galvez sailed for St. Domingo, where the combined forces were to assemble, and where he was to take the command of those of Spain. On his departure, he intrusted

---

* Villars' despatch of the 20th of May, 1781.
† Martin's History, vol. ii., p. 68.

provisionally, the government of Louisiana to Colonel Mirò.

But the preliminary articles of peace between Great Britain, France, and Spain, were signed at Paris on the 20th of January, 1783, and the definitive treaties between Great Britain, the United States and Spain, were signed at the same city, on the 3d of September of the same year. By this treaty, Spain gained the provinces of West and East Florida, which were ceded to her by Great Britain.

By the same treaty,* Great Britain acknowledged the independence of the United States, and recognized, as their southern boundary, a line to be drawn due east from a point in the river Mississippi, in the latitude of 31 degrees north of the equator, to the middle of the river Apalachicola, or Cataouche; thence, along the middle thereof to its junction with Flint River; thence straight to the head of St. Mary's River; and thence down along the middle of St. Mary's river to the Atlantic ocean. This line became the dividing one between the possessions of Spain and the United States.

By the 8th article of the treaty, the navigation of the Mississippi, from its source to its mouth, was expressly declared to remain for ever free and open to the subjects of Great Britain and to the citizens of the United States. This stipulation was destined to give rise to endless discussions between the two former allies, Spain and the United States—involving the future destinies of Louisiana.

On the 1st of January, 1784, M'Gillivray, a half-breed Indian, who was one of the most influential chiefs of the Talapouches, wrote to Arthur O'Neil, the Spanish governor of Pensacola, to propose a treaty of alliance and

* Martin's History, vol. ii., p. 72.

commerce with the Spaniards. He consequently represented in glowing colors the advantages which Spain would derive from it, and, what is curious, he hints at a scheme which was subsequently adopted by the Court of Madrid, and which was, to separate the Western territories from the rest of the United States.

"Having been informed a few days ago," said he, " by a letter received from St. Augustine, that the definitive treaty of peace between their Catholic and Britannic Majesties was ratified in Paris on the 3rd of September last, I take the liberty to congratulate with you on this fortunate event. As this treaty confirms Spain in the possession of both the Floridas, I solicit, in the name of the Talapouche nation, the beneficent protection of his Catholic Majesty for our persons, and for the land which we claim, and of which we are in actual possession. If the fortune of war has compelled his Britannic Majesty to withdraw from us his protection, nevertheless he had no right to transfer us away, with our property, to any power whatever against our will and inclination.

"Certainly, as a free people, we have the right to choose our protector, and we do not see any one who answers our purposes better than the Sovereign of the two Floridas. I will therefore lay before you a few reasons to demonstrate, that it would be sound policy on the part of Spain to grant us what we desire.

"Since the publication of the general treaty of peace, the American Congress has brought to light a situation of its affairs, showing the debts and revenues of the confederacy. By this statement it appears, that the debts contracted in Europe and America are estimated at more than forty-two millions of dollars, the interest of which is about two millions and a half. The Court of Versailles has urged upon the American Congress the necessity of paying the interest of the money due to

France. In order to raise the necessary funds to meet these claims, the Congress has imposed duties, taxes and contributions, striking alike the Thirteen United States. This expedient has produced so unfavorable an impression, that a good many of their citizens, in order to escape from the burden of taxation, have abandoned their dwellings for the woods,* and have marched towards the Mississippi, in order to unite with a certain number of disbanded soldiers, who are anxious to possess themselves of a considerable portion of the territory watered by this river, and they propose establishing what they call *the Western Independence*, and throwing aside the authority of the American congress. The emigrants are so numerous that, in a short time, it is possible that they may find themselves strong enough to carry into execution their scheme of separation; and, if they once form settlements on the Mississippi, it will require much time, trouble and expense to dislodge them.

"I can assure you that the Americans in the South employ every means in their power to enlist the feelings of the Talapouches on their behalf, and to secure the support of this nation. Should they succeed, the result of their influence will be, that the Indians, instead of remaining the friends of Spain, will become very dangerous neighbors, and will assist the Americans in all the designs which they may form against Pensacola, Mobile, or any part of the adjacent Spanish dominions; and of all these things the Americans speak openly. I will now communicate my views as to the best course to be pursued to frustrate their designs." The course which he advocated was, in substance, to grant to the Tala-

---

* Buscando nueva morada en los bosques, dirigiendo principalmente su viaje al Mississippi para unirse con porcion de vagos soldados que desean poseer gran parte de las tierras de este rio, y piensan establecer lo que ellos llaman, la independencia occidental, fuera de la autoridad del congreso.

pouches as many commercial advantages and other privileges as could be bestowed upon them.

Feeling how important it was to conciliate all the Indian nations, whose hostility or friendship was so intimately connected with the prosperity and safety of Louisiana, the Spaniards invited them to meet in what they called *a congress*, at Pensacola and Mobile, and it was resolved, in order to give more solemnity to the occasion, that this congress should be attended by the governor ad interim, Estevan Miró, by the intendant Navarro, and by Arthur O'Neil, the commander of Pensacola.

On the 30th of May, 1784, the Indian congress was opened with great pomp and the usual ceremonies. The customary presents, with medals and other decorations, were given, and a treaty of alliance and commerce was sealed, much to the satisfaction of the parties. On the 6th of June, a liberal distribution of brandy, powder and every sort of ammunition was made, and after much feasting, McGillivray was dismissed with his Talapouches, who were delighted with their reception by the Spaniards. He had been appointed commissary-general of all the Talapouche tribes, with a monthly salary which was not to be less than fifty dollars.

On the 22d of the same month, Miró presided, at Mobile, over another congress which was composed of the Chickasaws, the Alabamas, the Choctaws and the other smaller nations, who all came with their wives and children. This vast concourse of people was magnificently entertained at the expense of the Spanish government. Rich gifts were showered plentifully, chiefs cajoled—and finally, the same ceremonies which had been gone through at Pensacola, were reënacted at Mobile, only on a larger scale, and the same treaties of alliance and commerce were sworn to and signed.

The 6th article of the treaty with the Talapouches, which was also inserted in all the treaties with the other nations, redounds much to the glory of Spain, on the score of humanity, for which, unjustly no doubt, she is not generally given much credit. This article deserves to be quoted, and reads as follows:

"In conformity* with the humanity and the generous sentiments cherished by the Spanish nation, we (the Indians) renounce for ever the custom of raising scalps, and of making slaves of our white captives; and, in case of our taking any prisoners in consequence of the breaking out of any sudden war against the enemies of his Catholic Majesty, we bind ourselves to treat those prisoners with the kindness to which they are entitled, in imitation of the usages of civilized nations, reserving to ourselves the privilege of exchanging them against an equal number of Indians, or of receiving for them the quantity of goods which may be previously agreed upon, without making the slightest attempt against the lives of those captives."

By the last article of the treaty, it was stipulated in the name of the king, that he confirmed the Indian nations in the possession of the lands which they owned within his dominions, and that, in case they should be deprived of them by any of his enemies, he should then, in consequence of the love which he entertained for his Indian allies, grant them elsewhere, in some of the territories belonging to him, and as an equivalent for their

* En obsequio de la humanidad, y correspondiendo á los generosos sentimientos de la nacion Española, renunciamos pará siempre la practica de levantar cabelleras, ni hacer esclavos á los blancos. Y en caso de que una inopinada guerra contra los enemigos de su Majestad Catolica nos ponga en el caso de hacer algun prisionero, lo trataremos con la hospitalidad que corresponde, á imitacion de las naciones civilizadas, cangeando lo despues con igual numero de Indios, ó recibiendo en su lugar la cantidad de generos, que privatmente se stipulare, sin cometer con ninguno de los expresados prisioneros de guerra el menor atentado á su vida.

loss, the same extent of lands, presenting equal advantages.

In order to avoid all future discussions, and to prevent deceit as much as possible, a minute tariff was agreed upon, in relation to the price and quality of every article which they were to be furnished with, and for which they were to give in return a certain quantity of peltries. The most stringent regulations were also made by the Spanish Governor, to protect the Indians against the malpractices of the traders, who were to be permitted to introduce their merchandise in their villages. These regulations began with this declaration as a preamble: "The trade with the Indian nations is to be conducted on principles of good faith and equity; and those that engage in it shall take care so to demean themselves as to secure, by all the means in their power, the attainment of so important an object, without availing themselves, to avoid these obligations, of the despicable subterfuges of fraud and deceit."

A contract was passed, on the 24th of July, between the Spanish government and James Mather, a resident and merchant of New Orleans, by which this individual bound himself, on certain conditions, to employ two vessels to import all the goods and merchandise wanted for the Indian trade. These two vessels were to navigate under the Spanish flag, and one was to land its cargoes at Pensacola, the other at Mobile. Mather had reserved to himself the privilege of sending his vessels for the supplies he was to procure, either to the Dutch, Danish, or English islands, in America, or to one of the European ports belonging to these three nations. His return cargoes from Pensacola and Mobile were to consist of the productions of the colony.

The fortitude of the inhabitants of Louisiana, to whom the Intendant Navarro, in his circular of the 29th of

August, 1780, had recommended the patience of Job, was put to another trial by the prodigious rigor of the winter of 1784. The months of July and August of the preceding year had been so cool, that the colonists, to their great amazement, had to resort to their winter clothing. White frosts made their appearance in the beginning of September, and continued to be frequent to the 15th of November (1783) when the cold became intense.* There was a constant succession of squalls, and the wind blew with unheard of violence, from the north and north-east, and then from the south, going almost through the whole round of the compass. With rapid transition, the keen northern blast froze the ground, and the warm breath of the southern breeze brought back the genial temperature of the spring. The variations of the weather were such, that, several times, in six hours, Reaumur's thermometer fell from twenty degrees above the freezing point to two and three degrees below it, in a closed room where fire was kept up. On the 13th of February, 1784, the whole bed of the river, in front of New Orleans, was filled up with fragments of ice, the size of most of which was from twelve to thirty feet, with a thickness of two to three. This mass of ice was so compact, that it formed a field of four hundred yards in width, so that all communication was interrupted for five days between the two banks of the Mississippi. On the 19th, these lumps of ice were no longer to be seen. "The rapidity of the current being then at the rate of two thousand and four hundred yards an hour," says Villars, "and the drifting of the ice by New Orleans having taken five days, it follows that it must have occupied in length a space of about one hundred and twenty miles. These floating masses of ice were met by ships in the 28th degree of latitude."

* Villars' despatch, 25th of February, 1784.

Another cause of distress for the poor colonists was the depreciation of the royal paper money, which had been issued at par to meet the expenses of the war, and which had fallen down fifty per cent. of its original value. As if this was not enough, commerce was crippled by a decree of the Court of Spain, which was published in New Orleans, in the beginning of September, and which prohibited foreign vessels from entering the river under any pretext whatever, either stress of weather, or want of provisions, &c. The administration of the colony considered this decree as being a revocation of the schedule of 1776, in relation to the French Islands, and wrote to Spain to obtain further instructions as to the manner of carrying the new decree into execution.

In the beginning of the year, 1785, Galvez was appointed Captain-general of the island of Cuba, of the province of Louisiana, and of the two Floridas. But, on the death of his father, in the summer, he succeeded him in the viceroyalty of Mexico, and was allowed the privilege of retaining the captain-generalship of Louisiana and the Floridas.

Galvez was one of the most popular viceroys that Mexico ever had. He governed that extensive country nine years, with all the powers of absolute and despotic sovereignty; and his administration was so mild, so just and so enlightened, that he became the idol of the people. He had that nobleness of mien, that gracefulness of manner, that dignified, and, at the same time, easy affability for high and low, which, in persons of his rank, never fail to win the heart. He was a man of profuse magnificence in his habits, and the gorgeous displays which he used to make on public occasions, were much to the taste of all classes of the population.

> Then, as I said, the Duke, great Bolingbroke—
> Mounted upon a hot and fiery steed,

THE CHARACTER OF GALVEZ.

> Which his aspiring rider seemed to know—
> With slow, but stately pace, kept on his course,
> While all tongues cried—God save thee, Bolingbroke!
> You would have thought the very windows spake,
> So many greedy looks of young and old
> Through casements darted their desiring eyes
> Upon his visage; and that all the walls,
> With painted imag'ry, had said at once—
> Jesu preserve thee! Welcome, Bolingbroke!
> Whilst he, from one side to the other turning,
> Bare-headed, lower than his proud steed's neck,
> Bespake them thus—I thank you, countrymen:
> And thus still doing, thus he passed along.

His wife, who was a native of Louisiana, was of surpassing loveliness, and as charitable, gracious and intelligent as she was beautiful. She was literally adored by the Mexicans and Spaniards, and she greatly contributed to her husband's popularity.

Galvez had caused to be constructed, at a short distance from his capital, for himself and his successors, as he pretended, on the rock of Chapultepec, which has since become famous in the war of the United States against Mexico, a superb country seat, which had cost him immense sums. Surrounded by large and deep ditches, flanked with strong bastions well supplied with artillery on the side looking towards Mexico, and protected on the northern side by an immense forest, this edifice, whatever might be the name and the disguise given to it, looked more like a fortress than a peaceful seat of rural enjoyment. Immense subterranean vaults, filled with provisions to last many months, and many underground ways, communicated from the castle both with the city and the forest. This pretended country seat was, in fact, an impregnable fortification, and as it could not be intended by Galvez against the people, whose idol he was, and to whom it would have been impolitic, under such circumstances, to show any distrust, it became an object of wondering comments, hints and insinuations. It was even rumored that Galvez, who was the son of a viceroy, and who had succeeded his father in the same capacity, as it were by the regular laws of legitimate succession, was not disposed to relinquish, at the caprice of his sovereign, the power which he considered to be an hereditary heir-loom in his family, and that he was secretly aiming at occupying the throne of Mexico, not as the representative of the king of Spain, but in his own right. It is said that, owing to these vague and probably calumnious whisperings, the Court of Madrid was preparing to recall Galvez, when, in consequence of too much exposure and fatigue in hunting, he died in August, 1794. He was then in the full meridian of life, being only thirty-eight years old. His death was felt to be a great public calamity, and was deplored as such by the whole population of the kingdom of Mexico.

CHAPTER IV.

MIRÒ'S ADMINISTRATION.

1785 to 1789.

GALVEZ was succeeded ad interim by Mirò, and Don Pedro Piernas took the place of Mirò as colonel of the regiment of Louisiana.

One of the first measures of Mirò's administration was one of charity. It is remarkable that leprosy, which is now so rare a disease, was then not an uncommon affliction in Louisiana. Those who were attacked with this loathsome infirmity generally congregated about New Orleans, where they obtained more abundant alms than in any other part of the colony. They naturally were objects of disgust and fear, and the unrestrained intercourse which they were permitted to have with the rest of the population was calculated to propagate the distemper. Ulloa had attempted to stop this evil, by confining some of the lepers at the Balize, but this measure had created great discontent and had been abandoned. Mirò now determined to act with more efficacy in this matter, and, on his recommendation, the cabildo, or council, caused a hospital to be erected for the reception of these unfortunate beings, in the rear of the city, on a ridge of land lying between the river Mississippi and bayou St. John. The ground they occupied was long known and designated under the appellation of *La terre des Lépreux*, or *Lepers' Land*. In the course of a few years, the number of these patients gradually diminished, either by death or transportation, the disease disappeared almost entirely, the hospital went into decay, and *Lepers' Land* remained for a considerable length of time a wild looking spot, covered with brambles, briers, weeds, and a luxurious growth of palmettoes. It is, in our days, a part of suburb Trémé, and is embellished with houses and all the appliances of civilization.

Hardly had Miró entered upon the duties of his office, when he was instructed to inquire into the official acts of one of his predecessors, Governor Unzaga, and to report thereon to his government. When an individual is called upon to discharge these functions, he receives the commission of what is termed in Spanish jurisprudence, *A Juez de Residencia*, or a Judge of Residence. According to the laws of Spain, this inquiry takes place into the official conduct of public functionaries, when they are removed by death or any other cause. It is made at the most important part of the district in which the late officer exercised his jurisdiction; and from the decision of the Judge of Residence there lies an appeal to the Council of the Indies. This law never had the salutary effects which were intended. The object of the legislator was apparent. Power, he thought, is liable to abuse, and great power is vested in all the officers of the Spanish monarchy, within the sphere, high or low, in which each is called to act. Let him know, therefore, that, as soon as he is stript of the power intrusted to his hands, there shall be a thorough investigation of all his acts, private or public; that every one shall have the right and the opportunity to accuse him fearlessly, even from malice, caprice, or envy; let him know that, whilst he is in the discharge of his functions, he is surrounded by the observing vigilance of a whole population, from the ranks of which numerous accusers and witnesses, when he is rendered powerless, may start up to impugn his motives, to blacken his character, to arraign his acts, to bring into broad daylight every circumstance of his life, and to drag him like a culprit before the seat of Justice. This, no doubt, must be an effectual safeguard against his partiality, his cupidity, and his other passions. So schemed theory; but practice told a very different tale. The Judge of Residence could be bribed, intimidated, or otherwise influenced. If not, he found his inquiries generally baffled by the combined efforts of those who ought to have afforded him assistance. There is a sort of free-masonry and sympathetic alliance between all persons in office, which makes them opposed to seeing any one of them subjected to censure. They may quarrel together, but an *esprit de corps* will unite them against any censor that will presume to sit in judgment over any one of them. Thus, when a Spanish functionary went out of office, the Judge of Residence soon discovered that he was opposed by a league of all the other officers of the district in which had officiated the late incumbent, against whom no accuser presented himself, from the fear of having to struggle against the friends he had left behind him, or might have at court, from the unwillingness to incur the displeasure, or excite the suspicions of the other functionaries, and from many other considerations. Besides, not unfrequently, the officer, whose conduct was to be investigated, had been promoted to a more important office, and, although he might have been sent away to some distant part of the Spanish dominions, yet who would run the risk, except under extraordinary circumstances, of incurring the hatred and oppression of a man rising in power? Moreover, the Judge of Residence was himself, generally, a man of ambitious aspirations, and had been, or would be in some responsible office sooner or later, and had been, or would be, on a day to come, subjected, in his turn, to a Judge of Residence. It is natural, therefore, that any one in that position should not have been disposed to give the dangerous example of much scrutiny and severity. Hence the law had become a dead letter, and the appointment of a Judge of Residence was, in most cases, a mere formality. It proved so on this occasion. No complaint was produced against Unzaga, whether there was cause for any or not, and Miró's decision, as a Judge of Residence, on his predecessor's administration, was all that could be desired by that functionary, or by his friends.

In this year, 1785, a census which was taken of the inhabitants of Louisiana gave the following results:

New Orleans,	4,980
Balize to the city,	2,100
At the Terre aux Bœufs,	576
Bayou St. John, and Gentilly,	678
Tchoupitoulas,	7,046
Parish of St. Charles,	1,903
St. John the Baptist,	1,300
St. James,	1,332
Lafourche,	646
do interior,	352
Iberville,	673
Pointe Coupée,	1,521
Opelousas,	1,211
Atakapas,	1,070
New Iberia,	125
Ouachita,	207
Rapides,	88
Avoyelles,	287
Natchitoches,	756
Arkansas,	196
St. Genevieve,	594
St. Louis,	897
Manchac,	77
Galvezton,	242
Baton Rouge,	270
Natchez,	1,550
Mobile,	746
Total,	31,433

This enumeration shows that the population had more than doubled since 1769, when it amounted only to 13,538. The number of free colored persons was about 1,100, and that of the slaves and whites was very near being equally divided. The expenses of the colony were between 400,000 and 500,000 dollars. The Governor had a salary of $10,000; that of the Intendant was $4,000, &c., &c.

The province received, this year, a very considerable accession of population, by the arrival of a number of Acadian families, who, at the expense of the King of France, and in consequence of an arrangement between the courts of Versailles and Madrid, came over to join such of their countrymen as had emigrated to Louisiana. They were granted lands, mostly on both sides of the Mississippi river, near Plaquemines. Some went to the settlement already existing on the Terre aux Bœufs; others established themselves on Bayou Lafourche, and the rest were scattered in the districts of Attakapas and Opeloussas.

It will be recollected that, in 1782, a royal schedule had been issued, which relaxed the restrictions imposed on the trade of the colony. The consequence of it had been, that the commerce of New Orleans had greatly revived, and a number of merchants from France had established themselves in that town. "The planters, however," says Judge Martin in his History, "regretted the time when British vessels plied on the Mississippi, stopping before every house, furnishing the farmer with whatever he wanted, accepting in payment whatever the latter had to spare, and granting a credit almost unlimited in extent and duration. A number of agents had arrived from Jamaica, to collect debts due to merchants of that island, the recovery of which had been impeded during the war. As the trade these creditors had carried on could not now be continued, they pressed for settlement and payment. In some cases, legal coercion was resorted to; but Miró, with as much prudence as Unzaga on a similar occasion, exerted his influence to procure some respite for those who were really unable to comply with their engagements, and allowed a resort to the last extremity against those only whose bad faith appeared to require it. Instances are related, in which, unable to obtain a creditor's indulgence for an honest debtor, he satisfied the former out of his own purse."

Miró exerted himself to obtain as much extension as possible for the commerce of the colony, and applied to the Court of Madrid to recommend its being fostered by more liberal regulations. In a despatch of the 15th of April, 1786, he said: "In Louisiana, there are strong houses which would be able to carry on all its commerce, if they were not restrained by the want of capital, and by the depreciated paper money which the wants of the country require to be put in circulation. This cause prevents them from undertaking the least mercantile speculation which would be attended by much risk. It is, therefore, astonishing that, notwithstanding these adverse circumstances, there should be so much commercial activity on this river, where at least forty vessels are always to be seen at the same time. I say that the operations of the merchants are impeded by the want of capital, because, not having specie at their disposal, they are obliged to purchase the agricultural productions of the country with paper money, and, as the planter sells them his crop at a very high rate, proportioned to the depreciation of the paper offered in payment, they cannot operate any sale of those productions in the European market, without losing thirty or forty per cent., and frequently seventy. This has occasioned losses, which have destroyed the fortunes of many merchants, and hence have originated the numerous creditors by whom some of them are harassed.

* * * * * *

"Commerce is so necessary to the common prosperity of nations, that, without it, and without the relations which it establishes, man would not have arrived at that exalted degree of knowledge and civilization which he possesses; even the Indians, who are ignorant of the laws which regulate civil societies, feel the importance of exchanging the spoils of the chase, either for objects of absolute necessity, or for such articles of luxury as they are acquainted with. * * * *

* * * * * *

"In order that this commerce with the Indians be advantageous, it is necessary, 1st, that it be carried on without interruption; 2d, that it be conducted with as much legality as possible; 3d, that the merchandise be sold at the most equitable price; 4th, that there be always a sufficient number of traders in the Indian villages; 5th, that it be permitted to all to go and trade freely with the Indian nations; 6th, that this commerce be subjected to no favoritism and to no monopoly.

"Should commerce be carried on with them without interruption, they will not think of resorting to any other nation than ours, and from the familiar intercourse which will be established between them and us, there will result friendly relations and ties of good fellowship, which these people are not incapable of forming.

"Besides, should there be established among them open shops, where they could sell their peltries, they would not think of visiting the capital, where they claim presents and rations which are a serious drain upon the Treasury.

"The trade with them must be conducted with the utmost legality, in order to inspire them with sentiments of honesty, which, otherwise, it would be difficult to inculcate in them, because they are always disposed to follow the example of the whites, whose superiority they acknowledge.

"Nothing can be more proper than that the goods they want should be sold them at an equitable price, in order to afford them inducements and facilities for their hunting pursuits, and in order to put it within their means to clothe themselves on fair terms. Otherwise, they would prefer trading with the Americans, with whom they would, in the end, form alliances, which cannot but turn out to be fatal to this province.

"It is important that there should be no want of traders in the Indian villages, not only for obvious commercial purposes, but also to act as spies on the Indians, or to watch the movements of any intruder who might endeavor to pervert them.

"That this trade be open to all, is in accordance with the rights and privileges which are enjoyed by every subject of his Majesty; and to secure its continuation, it is necessary that it be not exclusive, as the Indians would be aware of the disadvantages they would suffer from a monopoly, because there is not a nation so ignorant as not to know, that it can derive no benefits from a commerce not open to competition. Our commerce with the Indians divides itself into two different branches,— the one, embracing all the Mississippi region, extending from New Orleans upwards, and the other radiating from Mobile and Pensacola, through all the country which is dependent on these two places. Those nations who are known under the appellation of Choctaws, Alibamons, Chickasaws, Creeks, Talapouches, and Apalaches, supply themselves at Mobile and Pensacola. Two cargoes, annually, of one hundred and seventy tons each, composed of effects worth sixty thousand dollars, at the European valuation, will be sufficient for Mobile; and two similar cargoes, but worth only forty thousand dollars, will do for Pensacola. The profits derived from this trade may reach twenty-five per cent., provided the price of peltry should keep up in the European market.

"Should it be deemed absolutely necessary to maintain this commerce with the Indians, then the fundamental condition of it must be, that it be not shared, in the slightest degree, if possible, either by the English or French, and that the Indians should know no other traders than the Spaniards. But this must be the work of time."

The celebrated half breed, Alexander McGillivray, the most influential chief among the Talapouches, had been allowed a share in the profits to be derived from the trade carried on at Pensacola, besides the pension of $600 a year, paid him by the Spanish Government. In connection with this circumstance, Navarro observes: "So long as we shall have this chief on our side, we may rely on having established, between the Floridas and Georgia, a barrier which it will not be easy to break through. The Indians are now fully convinced of the ambition of the Americans; the recollection of past injuries still dwells on their minds, and, with it, the fear that these greedy neighbors may one day seize upon their lands, and strip them of a property to which they consider themselves as having a right derived from nature herself.* It ought to be one of the chief points in the policy of this Government to keep this sentiment alive in their breasts.

"With regard to our Indian commerce on the Missis-

* En el dia se mantienen los Indios convencidos de la ambicion de los Americanos; la memoria de las pasadas injurias que les han hecho, subsiste, y con ella el recelo de que, algun dia, se apoderarian de sus tierras, y despojaran de una propri dad que creen pertenecer les por un derecho de naturaleza, en cuyo pensamiento es conveniente y deberá ser el punto principal de nuestro Gobierno hacerles perseverar

sippi, of which New Orleans is the centre, it is now much reduced, although it ought to be the most lucrative of all, because it embraces some of the nations in the province of Texas, and all those of the Arkansas and Illinois districts.

"In relation to Texas, our trade is of very little consequence, on account of the risks with which it is attended. It would much improve, if we could secure peace with the Comanches. Until then, the goods wanted for that trade will not require more than an annual outlay of six thousand dollars.

"The commerce in the district of the Arkansas is subjected to inconveniences of the like nature, and exposes the traders to no little danger on account of the incursions of the Osages.

"The commerce with the Illinois is the easiest, and yet it is of very little importance, because the English, who are in possession of Michilimakinac, three hundred leagues above, introduce themselves with the greatest facility into our possessions, and seize on the richest portion of the trade by forestalling the peltries of the finest quality. We are compelled to be mere lookers-on, when others do what we ought to do ourselves, and we have to undergo the vexation of seeing the trade, which ought to come down the Mississippi, elude our grasp and take the St. Lawrence for its channel. They have also possessed themselves of the trade with all the nations on the river *Aux Moines*, which is eighty leagues above St. Louis, and within the jurisdiction and dependence of the Illinois district. There beavers and otters are to be found in the greatest abundance."

Then Navarro goes on enumerating the remedies he recommends to obviate these evils, and which, if adopted, would, he says: "cause to fall into Spanish hands the manna offered by the trade with the Indians, which is a casket of wealth, of which others have the use, although we hold its key.* The treasures of that mine would then find their way into the coffers of our nation, and our enemies would not wrest from us the bread which should help to our sustenance,† and forty thousand dollars a year would be sufficient to supply all the wants of that trade."

Navarro concludes his despatch with these reflections: "If the province of Louisiana is intended to serve as a barrier against the Americans, it cannot answer this purpose without a considerable increase of its population, and it can acquire the numerous population of which it is susceptible, only through commerce and agriculture. The one requires protection, the other assistance. The former cannot prosper without freedom and unlimited expansion; the latter cannot succeed without laborers. Both are necessary to supply the means of paying the expenses of the colony, to secure the possessions and the rights of the sovereign, and to make his power and arms respectable.‡ These are all my views on this matter."

The whole of this document, of which I have only given a few extracts and the condensed spirit, is replete with good sense and liberality, and is a strong proof of Navarro's distinguished qualifications.

On the 5th of April, 1786, the king issued a royal order, by which he approved the conduct of Mirò, who, in the preceding year, had granted, in the districts of Baton Rouge and Natchez, which had been conquered by the Spaniards, some indulgence and extension of time to the British subjects, in relation to their selling their

---

* De que tenemos la llave, y otras la utilidad.

† Entonces sigue que la mina de este comercio fluirá en los cofres de la nacion, y no veremos que nos arrancan de las manos, nosotros enemigos, el pan que ha de servir á sustentarnos.

‡ Es cuanto puedo informar en este asunto.

property, collecting their debts, and removing away their persons and effects. The king declared his will that permission to remain be granted to such of them as might desire it, provided they took an oath of allegiance and fidelity to him, and promised not to move out of their respective districts without the permission of the governor. "Those who neglected to take the oath," says Judge Martin in his History of Louisiana, "were to depart by sea for some of the colonies of North America; and if they were unable to defray the expenses of the voyage, it was to be paid by the king, who was to be reimbursed, as far as possible, by the sale of their property.

"The king further ordered that, at Natchez and other places where it might be done conveniently, parishes be formed, and put under the direction of Irish clergymen, in order to bring over the inhabitants and their families to the Catholic faith, by the mildness and persuasion it recommends. For this purpose, the king wrote to the Bishop of Salamanca to choose four priests, natives of Ireland, of approved zeal, virtue and learning, from among those of his university, to be sent to Louisiana at the king's expense.

"Mirò, on whom the provisional government had devolved on the departure of Galvez, now received a commission of governor, civil and military, of Louisiana and West Florida, and issued his *Bando de buen gobierno*, on the 2d of June.

"A *Bando de buen gobierno* is a proclamation, which the governor of a Spanish colony generally issues on assuming its government, to make known the principles by which he intends to direct his conduct, and to introduce necessary alterations in the ordinances of police.

"In this document, Mirò begins by stating that religion being the object of the wise laws of Spain, that a reverent demeanor in church being a consequence of it, and that the bishop having lately published an edict with regard to the respect and devotion with which the faithful are to attend the celebration of the holy mysteries, the proceedings of the vicar-general against delinquents will receive every necessary aid from the government. Working on the Sabbath and other holy festivals is prohibited, except in cases of necessity, without the license of the vicar. He forbids also the doors of shops or stores being kept open during the hours of divine service, and the dances of slaves on the public squares on those days, before the close of the evening service.

"He declares his intention to proceed with severity against all persons living in concubinage. He observes, that the idleness of free negro, mulatto, and quarteroon women, resulting from their dependence for a livelihood on incontinence and libertinism, will not be tolerated. He recommends them to renounce their mode of living, and to betake themselves to honest labor; and declares his determination to have those who neglect his recommendation sent out of the province, warning them that he will consider their excessive attention to dress, as an evidence of their misconduct.

" He complains that the distinction which had been established in the head-dress of females of color is disregarded, and urges that it is useful to enforce it; he forbids them to wear thereon any plumes or jewelry, and directs them to have their hair bound in a kerchief.

" He announces that the laws against gambling and duelling, and against those who carry about their persons dirks, pistols, and other weapons, shall be rigorously enforced.

" The nightly assemblages of people of color are prohibited.

" The inhabitants of the city are forbidden to leave

it, either by land or by water, without a passport, and those who leave the province are to give security for the payment of their debts.

"Persons coming in, by land or water, are to present themselves to the Government House.

"Those who harbor convicts, or deserters from the land or naval service, are to be punished.

"Any large concourse of people without the government's consent is inhibited.

"None are to walk out at night without urgent necessity, and not then without a light.

"No house or apartment is to be rented to a slave.

"Tavern-keepers are to shut their houses at regular hours, and not to sell spirituous liquors to Indians, soldiers, or slaves.

"Purchases from soldiers, Indians, convicts, or slaves are prohibited.

"Regulations are made to prevent forestalling, to hinder hogs from running at large in the streets, to restrain the keeping of too great a number of dogs, and to secure the removal of dead animals.

"Measures are taken to guard against conflagrations, to drain the streets, and to keep the landing on the Levee unobstructed.

"Verbal sales of slaves are forbidden."

According to one of Mirò's despatches, the revenue resulting from the import and export duties at New Orleans amounted, this year, to 585,063 *reales de plata*, that is about $72,000.

In the beginning of 1787, the districts of Opeloussas and Atakapas, which, on account of the thinness of their population, had, so far, been intrusted to the care of one officer, had become so considerable, that it was deemed expedient to divide them into two separate commands Nicholas Forstall was appointed commander of the

Opeloussas district, and the Chevalier de Clouet, who had before presided over both, was left in charge of Atakapas.

It may not have been forgotten, that the king had requested the Bishop of Salamanca to choose from the Seminary of that town four Irish priests, who were to be sent to Louisiana, and who were to settle among the Protestant and Anglo-Saxon subjects of his Majesty, in the hope, no doubt, of converting them to the Catholic faith. These priests arrived in 1787, and were established at Baton Rouge, Natchez, and other posts in the territory conquered over Great Britain by Galvez.

At that time, Spain began to look with earnest solicitude at the growing power which, under the appellation of the United States of America, had taken its rank among the nations of the earth, and the western settlements of which had come into collision with those of the Spaniards in Florida and Louisiana. Thus the State of Georgia claimed an immense territory on the east side of the Mississippi, from Loftus heights northward, for several hundred miles, which region was in the possession of Spain, with a population estimated at about ten thousand souls. Georgia had sent commissioners to New Orleans in the autumn of 1785, demanding the surrender of that territory and the recognition of the line stipulated in the treaty of 1783. The Spanish authorities of Louisiana had denied having any power to act on the subject, which was properly referred by the respective parties to the governments of Spain and of the United States.

Besides, the Mississippi was the natural outlet for the commerce of the American people in the western settlements, and that commerce was pouring down upon New Orleans, as it were with the waves of that mighty river The duties which were collected by the Spanish authorities were considered as oppressive and unjust. The sturdy flat-boatmen of Ohio and Kentucky, on their return home, had always a long list of seizures, confiscations, fines, imprisonments, extortions, or vexatious delays to publish, and those tales, which probably in many cases were exaggerated, kept in constant agitation a population, who considered that they derived from nature itself a right to the free navigation of the Mississippi. It was the highway to the sea given to them by God, and they were determined to have it. Hence the excitement went up to such a degree, that an open invasion of Louisiana was talked of, and a forcible seizure of New Orleans contemplated. But before resorting to these extreme measures, the patriotic yeomanry of the West had applied to Congress, and urged upon that body the necessity of obtaining from Spain by negotiation, at least such commercial privileges as were indispensable to the very existence of the western settlements. These were circumstances of sufficient importance to secure the most vigilant attention, on the part of the Spanish functionaries at New Orleans.

Thus, on the 12th of February, 1787, Navarro, the Intendant, wrote to his government: "The powerful enemies we have to fear in this province are not the English, but the Americans, whom we must oppose by active and sufficient measures. It is not enough to have granted Louisiana a restricted commerce for ten years; it is indispensable to use other resources. It is of little importance that her productions should go to France or anywhere else, if we are incapable of turning them to our profit. When we cannot supply her with articles manufactured by ourselves, it is of no consequence if her wants in that respect are satisfied by other nations, provided this toleration contributes, as it does, to the daily increase of the white and black population of this colony, extends commerce, quickens industry, spreads the domain of agriculture, and gives rise to a state of things, which, in a few years, will be productive of considerable sums to the king. Without this toleration, and without the commercial franchises granted by the royal schedule of the 22d of January, 1782, this country would have been a desert, when it is calculated to become one of the most important portions of America.

"There is no time to be lost. Mexico is on the other side of the Mississippi, in the vicinity of the already formidable establishments of the Americans. The only way to check them is with a proportionate population, and it is not by imposing commercial restrictions that this population is to be acquired, but by granting a prudent extension and freedom of trade.*

"I address your Excellency from the fulness of the patriotic spirit with which I am animated. I have no other object in view than the interest of my sovereign. I consider the province of Louisiana as a portion of his royal domain, and I wish that I could, with every power of reasoning which I may possess, succeed in demonstrating the necessity of developing the strength and vitality of this province, because, from every one of those innumerable settlements which command us from their natural position, I see clouds rising and threatening us with a storm that will soon burst upon this province, and the damage would be still greater, if unfortunately the inundation extended itself to the territories of New Spain."†

---

* No hay que perder tiempo. Mejico está de la otra orilla del Mississippi, en las immediaciones de estos hoy formidables establecimientos de Americanos. El modo de contrarestarlos es una poblacion proporcionada, y esta no se forma con restricciones, sino con alguna prudente libertad en el comercio.

† Hablo a vuestra Excellencia lleno del espiritu patriotico de que estoy revestido; mis intenciones son los intereses de mi soberano. Miro la provincia de la Luisiana como una porcion de su propriedad, y quisiera persuadir con toda mi razon a que se fomente, pues en cada pueblo de los inumerables que nos dominan por natural situacion, se prepara contra esta provincia un nublado que descar-

In the month of March, Governor Mirò, in a despatch to the Marquis of La Sonora,* secretary of state, and president of the council of the Indies, commented with much earnestness on the defenceless state of the colony, and represented the Plaquemine Turn as the best spot to be fortified. He sent the estimate of the expenses which would be required for the erection of some batteries and a small fort at that locality, and which the engineers had put down at $37,000.

In consequence of the treaties of alliance and commerce concluded with the Indians at Mobile and Pensacola, in 1784, and in order to carry them into execution, and supply them with the objects of trade which were necessary to their wants, commercial privileges had been conceded to William Panton at Pensacola, and to James Mather at Mobile, who, in consideration of these privileges, had stipulated with the Spanish government to satisfy the Indians. But the goods which were to the taste of these people, and which could be procured with more ease than any other, were to be obtained in England only, and therefore the ships of these two merchants had been permitted, as an exception, to resort to the port of London. The Spanish government, however, soon took umbrage at the liberties which it had granted, and in August, 1786, they had been considerably curtailed or impeded by a royal decree. Panton and Mather remonstrated with vivacity, and represented that, if those restrictions were not repealed, they would remove themselves, their families and their effects to some other more favored spot than were Pensacola and Mobile under the pernicious influence of the unwise regulations of Spanish policy. On the 24th of March, Governor

gará algun dia, y seria mucho mas el perjuicio, si por desgracia inundase las tierras de Nueva España.

* A title recently conferred upon the celebrated minister, Don José Galvez.

Miró, and the Intendant Navarro, in a joint despatch, backed the reclamations of Panton and Mather, and commented at length on the importance of conciliating the Indians, and of keeping up with them as extensive a trade as possible, at a time when they were in arms to defend their territories against the encroachments of American ambition.

Alive to the policy of increasing the population of Louisiana, Governor Miró somewhat relaxed the restrictions upon the river trade, reduced the transit duties, and encouraged emigration from the west to the Spanish possessions on the Mississippi, particularly to the parishes of West Florida. He therefore granted permission to a number of American families to settle in Louisiana, and to introduce the utensils, effects and provisions of which they might stand in need, except brandy and sugar, on their paying a duty of six per cent. Desirous of ascertaining the number of Acadians who had settled in Louisiana, he ordered a census of them to be made, and in was found that, in 1787, that population amounted to 1,587 souls.

The province of Louisiana would soon have become a desert, if it had been limited to trading with Spain only, and if the Spanish restrictions on its commerce had been strictly enforced; but the colonial government had winked at its infractions, and, for some time, a lucrative trade had been carried on, not only on the Mississippi, but also, and principally, with the city of Philadelphia. Gardoqui, the Spanish minister sent to the United States, had himself connived at it; suddenly, however, either from the corrupt motives attributed to him, or from whatever other cause, he reprimanded Navarro with extreme severity on the infractions of the laws of Spain, added that he had informed his court of these facts, and forced the Intendant to proceed to the harshest measures against such delinquencies. This produced a crisis by which the colony was greatly distressed, and a great portion of the population was reduced to such extremities, that the Intendant informed his government, on the 10th of October, 1787, that he had assumed the responsibility of continuing to the Acadians, for two months more, their rations, which were to have been suspended. The annual donations in money, provisions and other articles to the Acadians, the *Isleños*, or emigrants from the Canary Islands, and to the Indians, were a heavy drain on the Spanish treasury, for they amounted to 1,733,381 *reales de plata*, or about $173,338. To this is to be added a debt of $760,779, which the Spanish government had contracted in Louisiana during the war against the English, and which remained to be paid. It is not astonishing therefore that Navarro, in a despatch of the 19th of December, 1787, addressed to Valdès, the successor of the Marquis de la Sonora, should have made an energetic description of the misery which prevailed in the colony. He represented that there was a complete stagnation of affairs; that there were no sales of any kind; that foreigners and particularly the European French had ceased to make any investments, as formerly, on real estates, which now could not be disposed of, even for a mere nominal price, and that commerce, agriculture, and every branch of industry was completely withered and destroyed.

"It is certain," said he, "that this province requires different regulations from those which his gracious Majesty has established for his other possessions in America, and that to submit Louisiana to the same regimen is to operate her ruin. Every one of the Spanish colonies has its peculiar productions and a commerce incidental thereto. Is it not probable that, to subject them to the same uniform system, is to clip the wings of progress?* The peculiar position of Louisiana ought to exclude her from the application of that system of uniformity. I have been serving his Majesty in this colony for about twenty-two years, not without prejudice to my health. During all this time, I have not ceased to observe the various changes and vicissitudes which have been fatal to its prosperity, and I have never omitted to mention them to the government, not however without the constant apprehension of their not being attended to, on account of the little importance of the individual who framed these representations.

"The commercial franchises which his Majesty had granted in his schedule of the 22d of January, 1782, and the latitudinarian extension which was given to them, were sufficiently powerful to impart to this colony the development which it needs. But there soon intervened certain restrictions, which are diametrically opposed to the concessions made, and which a subaltern officer cannot disregard without exposing himself to disapprobation and disgrace.

"Thus the permission which had been given to purchase negroes from the colonies of our allies and of neutrals, and to introduce them here, after having paid for them, either with our productions, or with money, on which was to be levied an export duty of 6 per cent only, was a proof of his Majesty's solicitude and predilection for Louisiana. But there presents itself a difficulty, which destroys all the graciousness of the grant: for instance, the law 30, tit. 27, lib. 9, de la Recopilacion de Indias decrees, that no foreigner shall be permitted to sell on credit in the Indies any object of commerce. If this law is to be extended to Louisiana, it follows as a

---

* Cortar las alas del progreso.

natural consequence, that the importation of negroes must cease, and, from that moment, we must expect that this colony, which promises to become one of the most considerable in America, is soon to be the poorest and the most miserable.

"Nobody doubts but that the wealthiest nations consider *credit* as the tutelar deity of commerce, and that all, without a solitary exception, skilfully avail themselves of it, to execute their designs and secure the progressive development of their resources, and that the most prosperous is the one which has the most of it. It is notorious that there are no commercial enterprises which do not rest mainly on credit, and that, if it were required that they should be carried on with specie and cash payments only, mercantile speculations would be extremely rare. In such matters reputation is wealth, honesty is security, and this is the current coin which facilitates the most important operations of commerce. Without these powerful auxiliaries, a country which should be in want of capital, would have no means of progressing, and would eternally remain in its beggarly condition, should it be prohibited by legislation from having recourse to credit.

"Louisiana is, in appearance, greatly protected, but she is not so in reality, and she is far from being ranked among the provinces that are rich, and if even those cannot trade without credit, how can it be done by this one, which is in its cradle and swaddling clothes?

"Relying on the good faith of the colony, the merchant uses credit to buy negroes in the islands of friendly powers, sells them here on a credit of one year or more; and this course benefits him, and enriches the planter by giving him hands with which he can increase his crops and procure his means of payment; and agriculture being thus fostered, secures to the king an augmentation of revenue in proportion to that of the province. These are the effects of credit."

Navarro then goes on analysing the causes of the decline of the colony, and pointing out every commercial restriction to which he attributes it, and, among those causes, he mentions the apprehensions which are produced by the threats of the Americans. He concludes with enumerating the means which are calculated to people the country and make it satisfied with its government.

"It is necessary," said he, "to keep in mind that, between this province and the territories of New Spain, there is nothing but the feeble barrier of the Mississippi, which it is as easy to pass as it is impossible to protect, and that, if it be good policy to fortify this province by drawing a large population within its limits, there are no other means than that of granting certain franchises to commerce, leaving aside, as much as possible, all restrictions and shackles, or at least postponing them to a future time, if they must exist. In addition, the government must distinguish itself by the equity of its administration, the suavity of its relations with the people, and the disinterestedness of its officers in their dealings with the foreigners who may resort to the colony. This is the only way to form, in a short time, a solid rampart for the protection of the kingdom of Mexico.

"It is an incontestable axiom, that every remedy ought to be proportioned to the evil to which it is to be applied; and the danger which threatens us from the proximity of the Americans is of such a nature, that it will soon be too late to ward it off, if we do not now guard against it by the most efficacious measures. Even if the territory of New Spain should never be the object of the ambition of the Americans, they ought to be for us a cause of constant distrust and apprehension, because they are not unaware that the river de Arcas is not distant from New Mexico, and that there are mines in the Ouachita district. These are powerful motives for a nation restless, poor, ambitious, and capable of the most daring enterprises."* It is evident that the Intendant Navarro was not deficient in perspicacity, and that the distinguishing traits of the American character had soon made themselves known to the rulers of Louisiana.

The province had, in this year 1787, produced a sufficient quantity of corn, rice, and other grains for its home consumption, but it had made only half a crop of indigo, which was the chief staple of the colony. To increase the distress of the colonists, the summer was marked by fevers, which frequently and easily assumed a malignant type. There was also an epidemic catarrh, from which few were exempt, and by which many were seriously incommoded. The small pox infested the whole province, and those whom fear prevented from being inoculated became the victims of their prejudices. All those who were attacked by the contagion, either died, or were dangerously sick. The inoculation was fatal only to very few, but this was enough to confirm in their systematic opposition those who declaimed against this wise and humane practice. This disease had struck such terror into the Acadian families, that, when one of their members was attacked by the disease, they used to abandon him to solitude and to his fate, leaving him to his own resources, but supplying him with all the provisions and other articles they supposed he would need, although breaking off all communication with him, and thereby depriving him of their assistance. Some of

---

* Poderosos motivos para una nacion inquieta, pobre, ambiciosa y arriscada.

them, however, who were established in Feliciana, and who numbered eighty persons of both sexes and of all ages, had the fortitude to have themselves inoculated, and not one of them had cause to repent having taken that determination.*

Always haunted by the fear of their restless neighbors, the Spaniards spared no means to conciliate the Indians, in order to interpose them between themselves and the objects of their apprehension, and succeeded in drawing to New Orleans thirty-six of the most influential chiefs of the Choctaws and Chickasaws, whom they cajoled and feasted, and whose friendship and alliance they secured. Governor Mirò received them with great pomp, gave them rich presents, harangued them, smoked the pipe with them, and made a liberal distribution of medals and collars. But the regent of the Chickasaws (the king being a minor) would not permit himself to be decorated with a medal, saying that such insignia might be honor-conferring distinctions for his warriors and the inferior classes of his people, but that, with regard to himself, he was sufficiently distinguished by his blood and birth, and that to act as the friend and ally of the Spaniards, and to acknowledge himself the son of the Great Father, who was on the other side of the water, meaning the king of Spain, it was sufficient that he should have received his banner and his presents; "which is a manifest proof," wrote Navarro, "of the existence of the pride and point of honor, observable even among the barbarous and uncivilized nations." The Governor took them to a public ball, with which they seemed to be delighted, expressing the belief that all the beautiful ladies present were sisters, and had

* Navarro's despatch of the 19th of December, 1787.

fallen from heaven.* The Governor also entertained them with a military parade and field manœuvres, which they surveyed with much attention and with demonstrations of pleasure. Finally they were fully won over by such arts, and they returned to their villages with Spanish hearts. Impressed with this flattering conviction, Navarro wrote to his government: "All these nations are entirely devoted to us, and I can also safely affirm, that the Americans will not gain much ground with them."† This boasted friendship of the Indians was not without being felt by the Spanish treasury, and it appears, from an account rendered on the 5th of January, 1788, that the amount of the sums spent in presents to the Indians, from 1779 to 1787 inclusive, rose up to about $300,000.

It is in 1787, that the History of Louisiana becomes connected in a remarkable manner with that of the United States, by the formation of a great scheme, the object of which was the dismemberment of the confederacy so lately established. The first Federal Union, which was conceived under the pressure of circumstances admitting of no delay, was weak in the very bones and marrow of its organization, and, although it had carried the United States triumphantly through the war of independence, it was inadequate to the ultimate purposes which it had in view, and was threatened with dissolution on account of its inherent imperfections. The western people, particularly, were exceedingly dissatisfied. They were then separated from the Atlantic states by an immense distance, by the intervening barrier of a wilderness

---

* Creyendo las Señoras bajadas del Cielo y suponiendolas todas hermanas.—Navarro's despatch.

† Y podemos ya con seguridad afirmar que todas estas naciones estan á nuestra devocion, y tambien decir que los Americanos no haran por este lado mucho progreso.

and high mountains, by a difference of pursuits, of habits, and interests, and they felt less than any other portion of the United States the force of the ties which bound them together, and the necessity of that union. They had repeatedly laid their grievances and wrongs before the general government, and obtained no redress. They had in vain petitioned Congress to secure for them the free use of the Mississippi, without which it was useless for them to till the ground, since they had no market for their produce. The growing population of that newly settled region became intensely excited, and the bold and sturdy yeomen of the West determined to take their case into their own hands. But if they were unanimous as to that, they were divided as to the means of accomplishing their object, and they had even split into five different parties.

"The first (Judge Martin's History, vol. ii., p. 101) was for being independent of the United States, and for the formation of a new republic, unconnected with the old one, and resting on a basis of its own, and a close alliance with Spain.

"Another party was willing that the country should become a part of the province of Louisiana, and submit to the admission of the laws of Spain.

"A third desired a war with Spain and the seizure of New Orleans.

"A fourth plan was to prevail on Congress, by a show of preparation for war, to extort from the Cabinet of Madrid what it persisted in refusing.

"The last, as unnatural as the second, was to solicit France to procure a retrocession of Louisiana, and to extend her protection to Kentucky."

Well informed of the condition of things then existing, Governor Miró, in Louisiana, and the Spanish Minister, Gardoqui, at Philadelphia, were both pursuing the same object, which was—to draw to Louisiana as much of the western population as could be induced to emigrate, and even to operate, if possible, a dismemberment of the confederacy, by the secession of Kentucky and of the other discontented districts from the rest of the United States. Both these Spanish functionaries were partners in the same game, and yet they were unwilling to communicate to each other the cards they had in hand. Each one was bent upon his own plan, and taking care to conceal it from the other; each one had his own secret agents unknown to the colleague whom he ought to have called to his assistance. There was a want of concert, arising perhaps from jealousy, from the lack of confidence, from ambition, from the desire of engrossing all the praise and reward in case of success, or from some other cause. Be it what it may, the consequence was, that the schemes of these two men frequently counteracted each other, and resulted in a series of measures which were at variance and contradictory, and which seemed inexplicable to him who had not the key to what was going on behind the curtain.

Among the most influential and popular men in the west, through whose co-operation Mirò hoped to accomplish his object, was General James Wilkinson, who had already acquired considerable reputation in the military service of the United States, and who had lately emigrated to that section of the country. This individual had some friends among the merchants of New Orleans, with whom he corresponded, and on whose influence with the Spanish Colonial government, backed by his own talents, address and management, he confidently relied in his hope to be able to open a lucrative trade between that town and the western country, which trade would be exclusively conducted by or through himself, and would thus secure to him a rapid and large fortune.

General Wilkinson had therefore descended to New Orleans, in the garb of a merchant and speculator, with a cargo of tobacco, flour, butter and bacon. Orders had been issued to seize and confiscate the boat and its load, when Wilkinson, having had an interview with Governor Miró, was permitted to sell his cargo without paying any duty. Several other interviews followed, and Wilkinson was hospitably feasted by the Spanish Governor, who became every day more friendly and condescending, and who granted to his guest permission to introduce into Louisiana, free of duty, many western articles of trade which were adapted to its market. Wilkinson remained in New Orleans during the months of June, July, and August, and sailed in September for Philadelphia. Many wondered at the intimacy which had grown up, during this time, between Miró and Wilkinson, and sly hints and insinuations were thrown out. as to its nature and tendency.

"While Colonel Wilkinson was in New Orleans, in June, 1787," says Butler in his History of Kentucky, "Governor Miró requested him to give his sentiments freely in writing, respecting the political interests of Spain and the inhabitants of the United States dwelling in the regions upon the western waters. This he did at length in a document of fifteen or twenty pages, which the Governor transmitted to Madrid, to be laid before the King of Spain. In this document he urges the natural right of the western people to follow the current of the rivers flowing through their country to the sea. He states the extent of the country, the richness of the soil, abounding in choice productions, proper for foreign markets, to which they have no means of conveying them should the Mississippi be shut against them. He sets forth the advantages which Spain might derive from allowing them the free use of the river. He proceeds to show the rapid increase of population in the western country, and the eagerness with which every individual looked forward to the navigation of that river. He describes the general abhorrence with which they received the intelligence that Congress was about to sacrifice their dearest interest by ceding to Spain, for twenty years, the navigation of the Mississippi; and represents it as a fact that they are on the point of separating themselves entirely from the Union, on that account. He addresses himself to the Governor's fears by an ominous display of their strength, and argues the impolicy of Spain in being so blind to her own interest as to refuse them an amicable participation in the navigation of the river, thereby forcing them into violent measures. He assures the Spanish Governor that, in case of such alternative, "Great Britain stands ready, with expanded arms, to receive them," and to assist their efforts to accomplish that object, and quotes a conversation with a member of the British parliament to that effect. He states the facility with which the province of Louisiana might be invaded by the united forces of the English and the Americans, the former advancing from Canada by the way of the Illinois river, and the latter by way of the Ohio river; also, the practicability of proceeding from Louisiana to Mexico, in a march of twenty days; that in case of such invasion, Great Britain will aim at the possession of Louisiana and New Orleans, and leave the navigation of the river free to the Americans. He urges forcibly the danger of the Spanish interests in North America, with Great Britain in possession of the Mississippi, as she was already in possession of the St. Lawrence and the great lakes. He concludes with an apology for the freedom with which he had expressed his views by the Governor's particular request; that such as they are, they are from a man *whose head may err, but whose heart cannot deceive.*"

So much for Wilkinson's ostensible doings. But it leaked out at the time and passed current among those who pretended to be well informed, that Wilkinson had delivered to the Spanish Governor a memorial containing other representations which were kept from the public eye.

In the mean time, Gardoqui, the Spanish minister at Philadelphia, was acting in conformity with his cherished plan of fomenting emigration from the American settlements into Louisiana, and one of his chief agents was an individual named Pierre Wower d'Argès. For this purpose, he, with the authorization of his court, invited the people of Kentucky and those who dwelt on the Cumberland river to establish themselves in West Florida and the Florida district of Lower Louisiana, under the protection of Spain, and he made them liberal grants of land, conceding them also considerable privileges and favors. The Americans who should settle in Louisiana were to be permitted to introduce slaves, stock, provisions for two years, farming utensils and implements, without paying any duty whatever, and, as to any other kind of property, it might be imported and offered for sale, on paying a duty of 25 per cent. They were also promised the free use of their religion. These conditions proved sufficient allurements for many Americans, who, with their families, removed to Louisiana and became Spanish subjects. Colonel George Morgan, who had proposed to lead a large number of emigrants, had obtained from Gardoqui the concession of a vast tract of land about seventy miles below the mouth of the Ohio, on which he subsequently laid the foundation of a city, which he called New Madrid, in compliment to the Spaniards.

Pierre Wower d'Argès had arrived at New Orleans, and applied to Mirò for the support of Gardoqui's views and plans. Mirò, who found them not agreeing with his own, was greatly mortified, and, in a despatch which he addressed, on the 8th of January, 1788, to Valdès, the minister and secretary of state for the department of the Indies, said: "I fear that they may clash with Wilkinson's principal object, as I shall attempt to demonstrate by the following observations. In the first place, D'Argès having presented himself here with very little prudence and concealment, it may turn out that Wilkinson, in Kentucky, being made aware of the mission of this agent, may think that we are not sincere, and that, endeavoring to realize his project without him, we use him merely as a tool to facilitate the operations of D'Argès. Under this impression, and under the belief that D'Argès may reap the whole credit of the undertaking in case of success, it may happen that he will counteract them; for this reason, I have been reflecting for many days, whether it would not be proper to communicate to D'Argès Wilkinson's plans, and to Wilkinson the mission of D'Argès, in order to unite them and to dispose them to work in concert. But I dare not do so,* because D'Argès may consider that the great projects of Wilkinson may destroy the merit of his own, and he may communicate them to some one, who might cause Wilkinson to be arrested as a criminal, and also because

---

* Pero no me atrevo á abrasar el primer partido, por que puede D'Argès considerar que los grandes projectos de Wilkinson destruirian el merito del suyo, y precipitarse (lo que cabe en lo posible), á confiarlos á alguno capaz de influir á que se arestase Wilkinson como criminal, y tambien por que este se disgustariá mucho de que otro tuviese parte en una confianza de que depende su vida y honor, como el mismo expresa en su memoria.

Wilkinson may take offence at another being admitted to participate in confidential proceedings, upon which depend his life and honor, as he expresses himself in his memorial.* Being precluded by these reasons from opening myself on the subject with D'Argès, I thought that I was bound to be equally discreet with Wilkinson, until I knew what are the intentions of his Majesty with regard to the latter.   *   *   *
    *   *   *   *   *   *

"The delivering up of Kentucky unto his Majesty's hands, which is the main object to which Wilkinson has promised to devote himself entirely, would for ever constitute this province a rampart for the protection of New Spain. Hence I consider as a misfortune the project of D'Argès, because I look upon the commercial franchises which he has obtained for the western colonists, and the permission given to the people to introduce any kind of articles into Louisiana, on their paying a duty of twenty-five per cent., as destructive of the great design which has been conceived.

"The western people would no longer have any inducement to emigrate, if they were put in possession of a free trade with us. This is the reason why this privilege should be granted only to a few individuals having influence among them, as is suggested in Wilkinson's memorial, because on their seeing the advantages bestowed on these few, they might be easily persuaded to acquire the like by becoming Spanish subjects."

Miró also objected to the imposition of the duty of twenty-five per cent. on certain articles to be introduced by the American settlers in Louisiana, because he said that, if Wilkinson was to be believed, Great Britain

---

* This cannot be the memorial openly given to Miró by Wilkinson, and to which Butler refers in his History of Kentucky, but must be the other secret document of which the existence was rumored at the time.

made them much more liberal propositions, with which those of Spain would not compare advantageously. With regard to the religious toleration granted by Gardoqui, Miró observed that it was too extensive. "It will be sufficient," said he, "to promise the emigrants that they shall not be forced to become Catholics, because, if they are told that their religion is to be tolerated, they will infer that they are permitted to practise it freely, which would authorize them to take along with them their ministers, whose absence would, on the contrary, favor the frequent conversions which the Irish priests would make, and which, otherwise, would be much more difficult. I can conceive of but one case which would justify granting to those people the free exercise of their religion—that is, if Kentucky could not be prevailed upon to give herself up to His Majesty without this condition.

"Your Excellency informs me that the agent D'Argès will give it to be understood in Kentucky, with dexterity and prudence, without committing himself at all, that, until the question of boundaries be definitively settled, the Spanish government will permit those inhabitants and colonists to send down their produce to New Orleans, &c., and Your Excellency goes on saying, that there are good grounds for expecting that many merchants in Spain and even in Havana will come to this port to enjoy this lucrative commerce, particularly if the franchises hitherto granted to foreigners were curtailed. This part of Your Excellency's communication obliges me to represent, on the strength of the knowledge which I have of this province, that its prosperity would be immediately checked, if the slightest restrictive alteration were added to the royal schedule of the 22d of January, 1782, which allows the colonists to supply their wants from France and its colonies, and that the greater the number of emigrants we shall obtain from

Kentucky and the rest of the United States, the greater necessity there will be for those franchises, in order that there should be no lack of the goods necessary to supply the wants of the new comers; for, to these franchises we are indebted for the aggrandizement into which this province has been expanding itself since they were granted. It would be inopportune to repeat at length the reasons which determined His Majesty to bestow those favors, and I shall confine myself to the principal one, which is, that deer skins and indigo, which are the two most important returns of trade from this country to France, have not, to this day, been adapted to the commerce of Spain, because the importation of those skins into the Peninsula gives no profit, and that the indigo of Louisiana is inferior to that of Guatimala, which is chiefly used in the kingdom. The only articles the Americans could furnish for the commerce of Spain and Havana, would be flour, hemp, materials for cordage, and wrought iron. With regard to flour, it would be necessary for Your Excellency to consider, whether its exportation to Havana would not be prejudicial to the provinces of New Spain, which now supply that market," &c. &c.

On the 20th of February, Mirò sent to his government a copy of the instructions which he had given to Lieutenant-colonel Charles de Grandpré, Governor of Natchez, in relation to the 1582 Kentuckian families, which Pierre Wower d'Argès was expected to lead to that district. In that document Governor Mirò said to Grandpre: "You will make concessions of land to every family on its arrival; to each family not owning negroes at all— six arpens fronting a Bayou or water-course, with forty in depth, making a total of two hundred and forty arpens; to such as may have two, three, or four slaves, or be composed of four or six adult and unmarried sons, capable of working—ten arpens in front by forty in depth; to such as have from ten to twenty negroes—fifteen arpens by forty, and to those owning more than twenty negroes, twenty arpens by forty.

"As to religion, you are already aware that the will of his Majesty is, that they be not disturbed on that account, but I think it proper that they be made to understand, that this toleration means only that they shall not be compelled to become Catholics; and it is expedient that this information be conveyed to them in such a manner, as to convince them that they are not to have the free exercise of their religion—that is—that they are not to build churches, or have salaried ministers of their creed—which is the footing on which have been placed the settlers who have preceded them.

"I herewith forward to you a copy of the oath which you will require of them. You will take notice of its last clause, by which they bind themselves to take up arms against those who may come as enemies from the settlements above; you will then, after having assured them that they shall not be troubled in matters of religion, inform them that the object of peopling Louisiana is to protect it against any invasion whatever which may be directed against it from the aforesaid settlements; that this is to their own interest, since, under the Spanish domination, they cannot fail to be happy, on account of its mild and impartial administration of justice, and because they will have no taxes to pay; and besides, that the royal treasury will purchase all the tobacco which they may raise. Whilst presenting to them these considerations, you will carefully observe the manner in which they shall receive them, and the expression of their faces. Of this you will give me precise information, every time that you send me the original oaths taken."

The form of the oath was as follows: "We, the under

signed, do swear on the Holy Evangelists, entire fealty, vassalage and lealty to his Catholic Majesty, wishing voluntarily to live under his laws, promising not to act, either directly or indirectly, against his real interest, and to give immediate information to our commandants of all that may come to our knowledge, of whatever nature it may be, if prejudicial to the welfare of Spain in general, and to that of this province in particular, in the defence of which we hold ourselves ready to take up arms on the first summons of our chiefs, and particularly in the defence of this district, against whatever forces may come from the upper part of the river Mississippi, or from the interior of the continent." Grandpré, however, had not to attend to these particulars, having been shortly after superseded by Lieutenant-colonel Gayoso de Lemos.

Such had been the efforts made to increase the population of Louisiana, when its prosperity was suddenly checked by a terrible visitation. On the 21st of March, 1788, being Good Friday,* at half past one in the afternoon, a fire broke out in New Orleans, in the house of the military treasurer, Vicente Jose Nuñez, and reduced to ashes eight hundred and fifty-six edifices, among which were the stores of all the merchants, and the dwellings of the principal inhabitants, the Cathedral, the Convent of the Capuchins, with the greater portion of their books, the Townhall, the watch-house, and the arsenal with all its contents. Only seven hundred and fifty muskets were saved. The public prison was also burnt down, and time was hardly left to save the lives of the unfortunate inmates. Most of the buildings that escaped the conflagration were those which fronted the river. The wind was at the time blowing from the south with extreme violence, and rendered nugatory all attempts to stop the

---

* Miro's despatch of the 1st of April, 1788.

progress of the devouring element. The imagination can easily conceive the scene of desolation; almost the whole of the population of the smouldering town was ruined, and deprived even of shelter during the whole of the following night. But, the next morning, Governor Miró furnished those who desired it with tents, and distributed rations of rice, at the expense of his Majesty, to all those who applied for it. They were found to amount to about seven hundred persons. Many took refuge with those whose dwellings had not been consumed, every sort of assistance was tendered to the sufferers, and on this melancholy occasion, were displayed to advantage those feelings of compassion and generosity which lie latent in the human heart.

One of Miró's first cares was to send to Philadelphia three vessels consigned to Gardoqui, to procure, in as short a time as possible, provisions, nails, medicaments, and other objects of indispensable necessity, which were to be resold at equitable prices. The Spanish minister was invited to grant permission to such other vessels as would come to New Orleans with these articles, and $24,000 were remitted to him for the purchase of three thousand barrels of flour. Miró sent to the Court of Spain a detailed account of the losses occasioned by this conflagration, and put them down at $2,595,561.

On the 1st of April, 1788, Governor Miró wrote to his government a despatch containing a curious account of the state of public education in Louisiana. "It seems," said he, " that in 1772, there came from Spain Don Andreas Lopez de Armesto as director of the school which was ordered to be established at New Orleans, Don Pedro Aragon as teacher of grammar (maestro de syntaxis), Don Manuel Diaz de Lara as professor of the rudiments of the Latin language, and Don Francisco de la Celena as teacher of reading and writing (maestro de primeras lettras). But the Governor, Don Luis de Unzaga, found himself greatly embarrassed as to the establishment of those schools, because he knew that the parents would not send their children to them, unless they were driven to it by the fear of some penalty Considering, however, that it was not proper to resort to violence, he confined himself to making the public acquainted with the benefits they would derive from the education which the magnanimous heart of his Majesty thus put within their reach. Nevertheless, no pupil ever presented himself for the Latin class; a few came to be taught reading and writing only; these never exceeded thirty, and frequently dwindled down to six. For this reason, the three teachers taught nothing beyond the rudiments."

Miró goes on saying, that the late conflagration having destroyed the school-house, Don Andres Almonaster had offered, as a substitute, free of charge, and as long as it should be wanted, a small edifice containing a room thirteen feet in length by twelve in width, which would suffice for the present, because, since the occurrence of the fire, many families had retired into the country, so that the number of pupils had, by that event, been reduced from twenty-three to twelve. He also proposes the construction of a more respectable school-house, the cost of which he estimates at $6,000.

"The introduction of the Spanish language in this colony," he observes, "is an object of difficult attainment, which it will require much time to accomplish, as the like, with regard to any language, has always happened in every country passing under the domination of another nation. All that has been obtained so far is, that all the proceedings of the courts of justice in the town be conducted in Spanish. But we have not succeeded so well in the other posts and dependencies, where French only continues to be spoken. Even in this town, the books of the merchants, except of those Spanish born, are kept in that language. For this reason, as those who have no fortune to leave to their sons aspire to give them no other career than a mercantile one, for which they think that reading and writing is sufficient, they prefer that this be taught them in French, and thus there were, before the fire, eight schools of that description, which were frequented by four hundred children of both sexes."

On the 11th of April, Mirò and Navarro informed the cabinet of Madrid, in a joint despatch, that they had received a communication in cypher from Wilkinson, in which he conveyed to them the agreeable intelligence that, after a painful and long journey, he had safely returned from the North to the West, across the mountains; that all his predictions were on the eve of being accomplished; that, as he had foretold, Kentucky had separated itself from Virginia, and that the rest would follow of course as Spain desired. Wilkinson's letter had been brought by one of his boats, which was soon to be followed by the remainder of them. The following is a part of Wilkinson's letter, alluded to in Mirò and Navarro's despatch:

"I have collected much European and American news, and have made various interesting observations for our political designs. It would take a volume to contain all that I have to communicate to you. But I despatch this letter with such haste, and its fate is so uncertain, that I hope you will excuse me for not saying more until the arrival of my boats; and, in the mean time, I pray you to content yourselves with this assurance: *all my predictions are verifying themselves, and not a measure is taken on both sides of the mountains which does not conspire to favor ours.* I encountered great difficulties in crossing the mountains," &c., &c.

"I must, however, let you know that I met in Richmond an old companion in arms, a friend of mine, and at present a member of Congress, who had just arrived from New York, and who communicated to me that, a few days before his departure, he had been informed by Gardoqui of my gracious reception at New Orleans by the Governor, &c. &c.

"In consequence of this, and considering that Gardoqui has spies all over the United States, I thought that, in order to prevent his suspicions, and divert his investigations from the quarter to which they might be directed, it was prudent on my part to write him a complimentary letter, in which I broached some ideas which may give rise to a correspondence between us, and the result of which I shall communicate to you.

"I beg you to be easy, and to be satisfied that nothing shall deter me from attending exclusively to the object we have on hand, and I am convinced that the success of our plan will depend on the disposition of the court.

"I take leave of you with the most ardent prayers to the Almighty for your spiritual and temporal welfare, and I beg to subscribe myself your unalterably devoted friend, and your most faithful, humble and obliged servant."

On the 15th of May, Miró wrote to urge upon the government the necessity of buying for the account of the king a larger quantity of tobacco. "If it be not possible," said he, "that Spain should consume tobacco to the amount of a few more millions of pounds, I fear that the new colonists with whom this province is peopling itself will consider as without foundation the hopes which rested on the cultivation of this plant, and which made them believe that they would find among us a prosperity, the expected enjoyment of which had induced them to prefer the domination of His Majesty to any other. This alone, I conceive, can make happy all the population which extends from Natchez inclusively to the regions above. I am so convinced of it, that I feel compelled to say, that there is no means more powerful to accomplish the principal object we have in view in the memorial which has been laid before His Majesty, than the promise that the government will take as much as six millions of pounds of their tobacco, instead of the two millions which are now bought from them."

On the 15th of May, Wilkinson wrote from Kentucky the following letter to Miró and Navarro: "My dear and venerated Sirs, I have for the second time the pleasure of addressing you, and I flatter myself that some time ago you received my first communication, which I sent by express in a pirogue with two oarsmen, and the answer to which I am continually expecting.

"Major Isaac Dunn, the bearer of this despatch, and an old military companion of mine, came to settle in these parts during my absence. The reliance which I put in his honor, his discretion and his talents, has induced me, after having sounded his dispositions with proper caution, to choose him as a fit auxiliary in the execution of our political designs, which he has embraced with cordiality. He will therefore present himself in order to confer with you on those points which require more examination, and to concert with you those measures which you may deem necessary to expedite our plan; and, through him, I shall be able to receive the new instructions which you may deem expedient to send me. I have also chosen him to bring me back the product of the present cargo of my boats. For these reasons, permit me to recommend him as one worthy of your entire confidence, and as a safe and sagacious man, who is profoundly acquainted with the political state of the American Union, and with the circumstances of this section of the country. I desire that he be detained in Louisiana as little as possible.

"On the first day of January of the next year, 1789, by mutual consent, this district will cease to be subjected to the jurisdiction of Virginia. It has been stipulated, it is true, as a necessary condition of our independence, that this territory be acknowledged an independent State by Congress, and be admitted as such into the Federal Union. But a Convention has already been called to form the constitution of this section of the country, and I am persuaded that no action on the part of Congress will ever induce this people to abandon the plan which they have adopted, although I have recent intelligence that Congress will, beyond a doubt, recognize us as a Sovereign State.

"The Convention of which I have spoken will meet in July. I will, in the mean time, inquire into the prevailing opinions, and shall be able to ascertain the extent of the influence of the members elected. When this is done, after having previously come to an understanding with two or three individuals capable of assisting me, I shall disclose so much of our great scheme as may appear opportune, according to circumstances, and I have no doubt but that it will meet with a favorable reception; because, although I have been communicative with no more than two individuals, I have sounded many, and wherever it has seemed expedient to me to make known your answer to my memorial, it has caused the keenest satisfaction. Colonel Alexander Leatt Bullit and Harry Innis, our attorney-general, are the only individuals to whom I have intrusted our views, and, in case of any mishap befalling me before their accomplishment, you may, in perfect security, address yourselves to these gentlemen, whose political designs agree entirely with yours. Thus, as soon as the new government shall be organized and adopted by the people, they will proceed to elect a governor, the members of the legislative body and other officers, and I doubt not but that they will name a political agent with power to treat of the affair in which we are engaged, and I think that all this will be done by the month of March next. In the meantime, I hope to receive your orders, which I will do my utmost to execute.

"1 do not anticipate any obstacle from Congress, because, under the present federal compact, that body can neither dispose of men nor money, and the new government, should it establish itself, will have to encounter difficulties which will keep it weak for three or four years, before the expiration of which I have good grounds to hope that we shall have completed our negotiations, and shall have become too strong to be subjected by any force which may be sent against us. The only fears I have, proceed from the policy which may prevail in your Court. I am afraid of a change in the present ministry, and in the administration of Louisiana, of the possibility of which event you are better judges than I can be, and I beg you to be explicit with me on the subject.

"In my last, I mentioned a letter which I had addressed to Gardoqui. I took the precaution to put it open into the hands of the Baron De Zillier,* in Philadelphia, my relation and trusty friend, who has since written to me that, after mature reflection, he had thought it best not to deliver it.

* Quere, Villiers?

"I have applied* to Mr. Clark, my agent in New Orleans, with regard to sending me merchandise by the way of the Mississippi. This is of the utmost importance for the accomplishment of our wishes, because the only tie which can preserve the connection of this section of the country with the Atlantic States is the necessity under which we are, to rely on them altogether for the supply of such articles as are not manufactured among us; and when this people shall find out that they can procure them more conveniently through this river, the dependent state in which they are will cease, and with it all motives of connection with the other side of the Apalachian mountains. Our hopes will then be turned towards you, and all obstacles in the way of our negotiations will have been removed; for which reasons, I flatter myself that you will find it expedient to favor this measure, and will have the kindness to grant to Mr. Clark the necessary protection to carry it into execution.

"Referring you to the preceding observations, and to the information which Major Dunn will give as to what I may have omitted, I beg you to accept my wishes for your happiness, and to believe me to be, with the highest and warmest personal respect and esteem, your obedient, humble and ready servant."

On the 15th of June, Miró sent to Spain a copy of Wilkinson's letter with the following observations:

"The flatboats of Brigadier-General Wilkinson have just arrived with a cargo which cost seven thousand

---

* Most of these despatches, if not all, were originally in cypher; they are to be found at length and in Spanish in the archives of Spain. Copies made in compliance with a resolution of the Legislature of the State of Louisiana, under the supervision of M. de Gayangos, a gentleman distinguished for his learning and literary works, and also under the direction of his Excellency Romulus Saunders, who was then the U. S. Minister Plenipotentiary at Madrid, are deposited in the office of the Secretary of State at Baton Rouge.

dollars in Kentucky, under the care of Major Dunn, who has delivered me the letter of which I forward a translation. It will make you acquainted with the state in which is the principal affair mentioned in my confidential despatch No. 13. This Major confirms all of Wilkinson's assertions, and gives it out as certain, that, next year, after the meeting of the first assemblies in which Kentucky will act as an independent State, she will separate entirely from the Federal Union; he further declares that he has come to this conclusion from having heard it expressed in various conversations among the most distinguished citizens of that State : *that the direction of the current of the rivers which run in front of their dwellings points clearly to the power to which they ought to ally themselves,* but he declares that he is ignorant of the terms on which this alliance will be proposed. The said Brigadier-general, in a private letter addressed to me, adds that he flatters himself with the prospect of his being the delegate of his State to present to me the propositions offered by his countrymen, and that he hopes to embrace me in April next.

"From the beginning, he had informed me that he was not possessed of any pecuniary means. Here an individual, on the recommendation of the Intendant Navarro, had loaned him three thousand dollars. He now begs me not to seize his cargo, as he has pledged the product of its sale to refund that sum, and to pay his crew and the amount due on the tobacco which he had bought on credit, and as the balance is to enable him to support himself without embarrassment, which will contribute to preserve and increase his influence in his State.

"Although his candor, and the information which I have sought from many who have known him well, seem to assure us that he is working in good earnest, yet I am

aware that it may be possible that his intention is to enrich himself at our expense, by inflating us with hopes and promises which he knows to be vain. Nevertheless, I have determined to humor him on this occasion, &c. &c. * * * * * *
* * * * * * *

"As you may have seen, Wilkinson had promised a volume of information when his flatboats should come down. He has kept his word, and transmitted to me various newspapers containing articles on the Mississippi, the letters of the American, Sullivan, which Don Diego Gardoqui must have communicated to you, and a paper of his own, full of reflections on the new federal government, the establishments on the Ohio, and the navigation of the Mississippi, of which the only passage worthy of occupying your Excellency's attention is the last one, in which he says to me, that 'If Sullivan presents himself on this side of the Apalachian mountains, I may rest assured that his journey will soon be at an end, and that there will be obstacles in his way, to prevent him from becoming troublesome to this province, as he boasts of.'"

On the same day, Mirò forwarded to his government the copy of a letter addressed, on the 25th of April, by McGillivray, the chief of the Talapouches and the pensioned ally of the Spaniards, to the Governor of Pensacola: "I must inform you," said the Indian chief, "that since the departure of Garion with my last letters, two delegates from the district of Cumberland have arrived with proposals of peace to this nation. They represented to me that they were reduced to extremities by the incursions of our warriors, and that, to obtain peace and our friendship, they were disposed to submit to whatever conditions we might choose to impose; and, presuming that it would have a powerful influence with me and would secure them my favor, they added that they would throw themselves into the arms of his Majesty as subjects, and that Cumberland and Kentucky are determined to free themselves from their dependence on Congress, because that body cannot protect either their persons or their property, or favor their commerce, and they therefore believe that they owe no obedience to a power which is incapable of benefiting them.

"These deputies desired to know my sentiments on the subject of their propositions; but as it embraces important political questions, I thought proper not to divulge my views. My answer was, that, in the first great council held by this nation, these matters would be considered, and that, in the mean time, all hostilities would cease, and that peace would be finally established, when its conditions should be agreed upon." McGillivray's correspondence, if proceeding from his own pen, denotes in that half-breed a man of considerable education and of singular abilities, not supposed generally to exist in those of his race and position.

Commenting on this letter in a despatch of the 15th of June, Miró said: "I consider as extremely interesting the intelligence conveyed to McGillivray by the deputies, on the fermentation existing in Kentucky with regard to a separation from the Union, &c.   *   *
*   *   *   *   *   *

"Concerning the propositions made to McGillivray by the inhabitants of Cumberland to become the vassals of his Majesty, I have abstained from returning any precise answer," &c., &c.   *   *   *   *
*   *   *   *   *   *

"As it may happen, however, that deputies may soon come here from that part of the country, I beg your Excellency to prescribe to me the course which I am to pursue as the most agreeable to his Majesty."

Whilst all these intrigues were on foot, the population

of Louisiana was steadily increasing, and Colonel Peter Brian Browin,* among others, with a number of families. provided with passports from Gardoqui, had arrived to settle in the district of Natchez. A census was taken this year, 1788, and presented the following results:

City of New Orleans,	5,338
From the Balize to the city,	2,378
At the Terre aux Bœufs,	661
On the Bayous St. John and Gentilly,	772
Barataria,	40
Tchoupitoulas,	7,589
Parish of St. Charles,	2,381
St. John the Baptist,	1,368
St. James,	1,559
Lafourche,	1,164
do interior,	1,500
Iberville,	944
Pointe Coupée,	2,004
Opeloussas,	1,985
Atakapas,	2,541
New Iberia,	190
Ouachita,	232
Rapides,	147
Avoyelles,	209
Natchitoches,	1,021
Arkansas,	119
St. Genevieve,	896
St. Louis,	1,197
Manchac,	284
Galvezton,	268
Baton Rouge,	682
Feliciana,	730
Natchez,	2,679
Mobile,	1,468
Total,	42,346

There were about as many whites as there were slaves, and the free colored persons numbered about 1,700. In 1785, the census had given a total of 31,433 souls; thus the increase had been considerable, and would appear still more so, if it be true, as it was then asserted, that

---

* The name is thus spelt in the Spanish manuscript.

this last census was short of the real number, and that the population at the time ought to have been computed at least at 45,000 souls.

This year, Miró, who, it will be recollected, had been appointed, in 1785, Judge of Residence to inquire into the official acts of Unzaga, received a commission to the same effect with regard to Galvez, under whom he had served, who had led him to victory, whom he loved as his chief and companion in arms,—Galvez, who now was the powerful Viceroy of the kingdom of Mexico, and whose uncle* had been so recently the omnipotent minister of the King of Spain! It seems that the minister who signed this commission and sent it to Miró, can hardly be supposed to have refrained from a smile at the mockery he was perpetrating.

In the spring of 1788, Martin Navarro, the gifted Intendant of Louisiana, who had won the esteem, respect, and attachment of all classes, during his long residence in the colony, left it for Spain, and the two offices of Intendant and Governor were united in the person of Miró. Considering the importance of the great scheme of which Miró was one of the main springs, it was thought necessary to facilitate his operations by exposing him to no interference with his authority on the part of a colleague in power. Besides, to appoint a new Intendant would have been to initiate another person, who might lack prudence and discretion, into secrets which it was good policy to keep within the breasts of as few individuals as possible, and this might have been objected to by Wilkinson and his associates, as endangering their safety. Navarro's last official despatch was a memorial which was to be submitted to the king, and in which, at the request of the Minister of the Department of the

---

* Jose de Galvez, Marquis de la Sonora, died in 1786.

Indies, he expressed his views in relation to Louisiana. In this document, the Intendant depicted in vivid colors the dangers which Spain had to apprehend for her American colonies, from the thirteen provinces that had lately become independent and had assumed their rank among the nations of the earth, under the appellation of the United States of America. He dwelt with peculiar emphasis on the ambition and the thirst of conquest which his keen eye could already detect in the breast of the new-born giant, who, as he predicted with remarkable accuracy, would not rest satisfied until he extended his domains across the continent, and bathed his vigorous young limbs in the placid waves of the Pacific. When was there a truer prophet? And how was this dread event, so clearly foreseen, to be prevented?—By severing the Union—by dividing from the Atlantic States the boundless West, where so much power was already slumbering in the lap of the wilderness. To effect this, was not, in his opinion, very difficult, if the propitious circumstances, then existing, were turned to advantage without loss of time, and by the use of proper means. "Grant," said he, "every sort of commercial privileges to the masses in the western region, and shower pensions and honors on their leaders." This memorial produced a deep impression at Madrid, and confirmed the government of Spain in the policy which it had begun to pursue.

D'Argès had, in consequence, received instructions from Gardoqui and from the Count of Florida Blanca, one of the members of the Cabinet of Madrid, to do all that was in his power to procure the dismemberment of the American Union. He had come to solicit assistance and co-operation from Miró; but, to his great astonishment, he was detained in New Orleans by the Governor, under various pretexts, and not permitted to ascend the Mississippi, on his way to the West. In a despatch of the 7th of August, addressed to the Count of Florida Blanca, Mirò explained his reasons for so doing. "Being obliged," said he, "to conceal from D'Argès the true cause of Wilkinson's visit to New Orleans, I told him only, that the General had presented to the Court a memorial approved by me, in favor of the district of Kentucky, with a view to opening a trade between this colony and that province. He cannot conceive why I am losing, as he thinks, so much time, and why I do not hasten to avail myself of the permission given by your Excellency to carry on an enterprise, to which he would join his contribution of labor, at the propitious moment when the inhabitants of Kentucky are framing the Constitution of that State. His intentions are praiseworthy, if sincere, as I believe them to be. But my mind, although not very acute, has not been without detecting that the jealous ambition of a man easily produces feelings of enmity in his breast, and that, when two individuals work together in the same undertaking, the first who discovers that his companion is to reap all the merit of the success, if obtained, is apt, instead of contributing to it, to use for its defeat the very knowledge and experience which he has acquired in the matter.

"My not permitting D'Argès to ascend the river will not be productive of any injury to the royal service, and his being allowed to be in competition with Wilkinson, when they cannot be made acquainted with their reciprocal mission, would produce results of a serious nature, and, thus, I hope to obtain the approbation of your Excellency for detaining him here, until I receive the instructions of his Majesty on the main question."

On the 28th of August, Mirò wrote to his Government "In compliance with the orders given by the American

Brigadier-General, James Wilkinson, to his agent here, this individual has invested the product of the sale of tobacco, with an additional sum of money, in merchandise, with which he has loaded a boat. This cargo, which has required an outlay of $18,246 and six reals, is composed of eatables and dry goods destined for the Kentucky market.

"The establishment of this trade is of the utmost consequence for the success of our great project, which I disclosed and explained in the confidential despatch No. 13, to which is annexed the memorial of the said Brigadier, because it is exceedingly important that the Western people should see, before declaring themselves for a change of domination, that the true channel through which they have to be supplied with the objects of their wants, in exchange for their own productions, is the Mississippi."

Mirò explains at length the facilities of that commerce, and demonstrates how much more advantageous it would be for the Western people than that which they have been forced to carry on, across the mountains, with the Atlantic States.

"The great obstacle," continues he, "which Wilkinson's agent, who is also interested in this commercial adventure, has to encounter, is the difficulty to ascend as far up as the falls of the Ohio without being attacked by the Indians, but I have encouraged him to attempt it at all hazards, and I have proposed to him to send two expresses to Wilkinson, one through the Talapouche territory, and the other through the Chickasaw nation, to notify the General of the coming up of his boat, in order that he may send an armed one to the mouth of the Ohio, which, with the twenty rowers who man this boat, will, I hope, be sufficient protection to secure its safety. I have written to Wilkinson not to sell the goods at a higher price than what they cost here, because it is highly important that this first essay should inspire the inhabitants of Kentucky with the most flattering hopes.

"I have good reasons to expect that the arrival of this boat will produce the most agreeable sensation among these people, and will make them feel more keenly that their felicity depends on the concession of such commercial facilities by his Majesty, and for the acquisition of which I conceive that there are few sacrifices which they would not make; and therefore I hope with the utmost confidence, that his Majesty will approve all that I have done, on this and other occasions—which course has secured to me the most profound tranquillity in this province, whilst I am waiting for instructions in so great and important an affair."

On the 7th of September, Colonel Morgan addressed from New Jersey to Gardoqui, a very curious memorial, in which he proposes to establish on certain conditions an immense colony near the mouth of the Ohio. Those conditions he stipulates at length, and declares that, if they are strictly adhered to, the population which he will draw to that settlement will, in ten years, amount to at least one hundred thousand souls. He expatiates on the advantages which would result therefrom to Spain, and, in return for what he promises to do, he desires that the rank of colonel enjoyed by him in the army of the United States, against whose government he expresses himself with some bitterness of feeling, and which he accuses of having acted with bad faith towards him, be secured to him; that he be granted a concession of twenty miles square, with a pension for the rest of his life, and that other boons and advantages be guarantied to himself and to his family.

On the 4th of October, Gardoqui answered Colonel

George Morgan from New York, expressing the warmest opprobation of that gentleman's plan of colonization, and informing him that he had forwarded it to be submitted to the king, and that he doubted not but that all that was applied for would be granted. "As you seem anxious," said he, "not to lose any time, I forthwith transmit a passport, and letters for the Spanish authorities, so that you may go at once, and examine the territory in which you contemplate making your settlement. On your arrival at New Orleans, you will act in concert with the Governor, who will give you all the facilities you desire, and, in your progress through the West, on your way to the capital of Louisiana, you will assure the inhabitants of his Majesty's desires to grant them all the favors and privileges which may secure their prosperity."

Gardoqui, on the 7th of the same month, wrote also to Major Dunn, to entreat him to make his fellow-citizens acquainted with the sincere wish which he, Gardoqui, entertained, *to procure*, as he expressed it, *the happiness of that Western world, provided they should understand their own interests, and second his operations without loss of time.**

On the 3d of November, Mirò thus expressed himself in a despatch to the Minister Don Antonio Valdès, in relation to the grand scheme of dismembering the Union: "This affair proceeds more rapidly than I had presumed, and some considerable impetus is given to it by the answer of Congress to the application of Kentucky to be admitted into the Union as an independent State. That answer is, that the new federal government which is soon to go into operation will take their wishes into

---

* Procurar la dicha de los habitantes de ese mundo occidental, siempre que conozcan sus propios intereses, y segunden mis movimientos, sin perdida de tiempo.

consideration, and will act thereon. This information Don Diego Gardoqui must have communicated, but he did not what follows.

"Oliver Pollock, a citizen of Philadelphia, who arrived here three days ago, in a vessel from Martinique, has declared to me that Brown, a member of Congress, who is a man of property in Kentucky, told him in confidence that, in the debates of that body on the question of the independence of that Territory, he saw clearly that the intention of his colleagues was, that Kentucky should remain under the jurisdiction of Congress, like the county of Illinois, and that a Governor should be appointed by them for that province as for the other; but that, as this was opposed to the welfare of the inhabitants of Kentucky, he was determined to return home (which he did before Pollock's departure from Philadelphia), and, on his arrival, to call for a general assembly of his fellow citizens, in order to proceed immediately to declare themselves independent, and to propose to Spain the opening of a commercial intercourse with reciprocal advantages; and that, to accomplish this object, he would send to Pollock the necessary documents, to be laid before me and to be forwarded to your Excellency. He requested Pollock to prepare me for it in anticipation.

"Your Excellency will therefore rest assured that Brown, on his arrival in Kentucky, finding Wilkinson and his associates disposed to surrender themselves up to Spain, or at least to put themselves under her protection, will easily join them, and it is probable, as Wilkinson has already foretold it, that, next spring, I shall have to receive here a deputation appointed in due form.

"I acted towards Pollock with a great deal of caution, and answered him as one to whom had been communicated some new and unlooked for information, giving him to understand, that I could not pledge to him my support before seeing the documents which he expected," &c., &c.

These intrigues, of which Louisiana was the focus, were the most interesting events which marked her history in the year 1788. In the course of the same year, the fortitude of the colonists, whose number Spain was so anxious to increase, had been sorely tried by inundations which had devastated the post of St. Genevieve, at Illinois, and the districts of Manchac, Baton Rouge, and other settlements. The principal sufferers were the Acadians, to whose relief the Colonial government found itself obliged to come, to the amount of $12,000.* The Bonnet Carré Levee, which is now a cause of so much expense and danger, possessed the same characteristics in 1788. The inhabitants of the German coast petitioned Miró to come to their assistance, and one Antoine Peytavin proposed to borrow from the royal Treasury, on giving good security, the sum of $16,000 payable in six years, and on binding himself to stop the crevasse at that spot, and to reconstruct a strong embankment, provided the full property of the lands, the front of which he would have to protect, be made over to him.

On the 12th of February, 1789, Wilkinson wrote from Lexington, Kentucky, to Governor Miró : "Immediately after having sent you my despatch by Major Dunn, I devoted all my faculties to our political designs, and I have never since turned aside from the pursuit of the important object we have in view. If subsequent events have not come up to our expectations, still I conceive that they are such as to inspire us with flattering hopes

* Miró's despatch, August 28th, 1788.

of success in due time, and, although in the conjectural opinions which I presented to you and Navarro, I may, in some particulars, have been deceived, you will yet see that, in the main, I expressed myself with a prophetic spirit, and that important events have occurred, to confirm the accuracy of my sentiments.

"When Major Dunn left Kentucky, I had opened myself only to the Attorney General Innis, and to Colonel Bullitt, who favor our designs, and indirectly I had sounded others, whom I also found well disposed to adopt my ideas. But, having made a more strict examination, I discovered that the proposed new government of the United States had inspired some with apprehensions, and others with hopes—so much so that I saw that this circumstance would be a cause of some opposition and delay. I also perceived that all idea that Kentucky would subject itself to Spain must be abandoned for the present, and that the only feasible plan to the execution of which I had to direct my attention was that of a separation from the United States, and an alliance with Spain, on conditions which could not yet be defined with precision. I considered that, whatever be the time when the separation should be brought about, this district being then no longer under the protection of the United States, Spain might dictate her own terms; for which reason, I embraced without delay this last alternative.

"The question of separation from the United States, although discussed with vehemence among the most distinguished inhabitants of this section of the country, had never been mentioned, in a formal manner, to the people at large, but now was the time for making this important and interesting experiment, and it became my indispensable mission to do so. I had to work on a ground not yet prepared for the seed to be deposited in it, and I felt that, to produce a favorable impression, I had to proceed with reserve, and avoid with the utmost care any demonstration which might be calculated to cause surprise or alarm. For these motives, I gave an equivocal shape to the expression of my design, speaking of it in general terms, as being recommended by eminent politicians of the Atlantic coast, with whom I had conversed on this affair, and thus, by indirect suggestions and arguments, I inspired the people with my own views, without presenting them as such, because it would have been imprudent in me to divulge them under the existing circumstances, and I can give you the solemn assurance that I found all the men belonging to the first class of society in the district, with the exception of Colonel Marshall, our surveyor, and Colonel Muter, one of our judges, decidedly in favor of separation from the United States and of an alliance with Spain. At first, these two men had expressed this same opinion with warmth, but now their feelings have taken a different direction from private motives of interest and personal pique; for which reasons I have very little to dread from their influence; but, at the same time, I foresaw that they would avail themselves of the opposition made by some literary demagogues, who were under the influence of fear and prejudice. Nevertheless, I determined to lay the question before our Convention, and I took the necessary measures accordingly.

"I was thus occupied until the 28th of July, on which day our Convention met at Danville, in conformity with the ordinance you saw in the Gazette which I sent you by Major Dunn. The Honorable Samuel McDowell, President of the Convention, had, the day before, received a packet from the Secretary of Congress, containing an account of the proceedings of that body on the subject which excited our solicitude,—that is, our intended separation from the State of Virginia.

"You will remember that, in my memorial, I was of opinion that the Atlantic States would not consent to the admission of this district into the Union, as an independent State, but, on my return from New-Orleans, I was induced to alter my opinion from the information which I received through persons of the highest authority, and, under that new impression, I wrote you by Major Dunn. Thus we were not prepared for an unexpected event, of which we could have received no premonition. You will at first sight discover, on perusing the aforesaid paper No. 1, that this Act of Congress was passed with the intention to gain time, amuse and deceive the people of this district, and make them believe that they could rely on the good dispositions of the Atlantic States, until the formation of the new government, when our opponents flatter themselves that it will be able to check our designs. Unfortunately, this artifice produced but too much effect on the members of this Convention, and confirmed the apprehensions of others.

"From this proceeding of Congress it resulted, that the Convention was of opinion, that our proposed independence and separation from Virginia not being ratified, its mission and powers were at an end, and we found ourselves in the alternative, either of proceeding to declare our independence, or of waiting according to the recommendation of Congress. This was the state of affairs, when the Honorable Caleb Wallace, one of our Supreme Judges, the Attorney-General Innis, and Benjamin Sebastian proposed a prompt separation from the American Union, and advocated with intrepidity the necessity of the measure. The artifice of Congress was exposed, its proceedings reprobated, the consequences of depending on a body whose interests were opposed to ours were depicted in the most vivid colors, and the strongest motives were set forth to justify the separation.

The arguments used were unanswerable, and no opposition was manifested in the course of the debates. It was unanimously conceded that the present connection was injurious to our interests, and that it could not last any length of time. Nevertheless, sir, when the question was finally taken, fear and folly prevailed against reason and judgment. It was thought safer and more convenient to adhere to the recommendation of Congress, and, in consequence, it was decided that the people be advised to elect a new Convention, which should meet in the month of November, in conformity with the ordinance which you will find in the Gazette, No. 2.

"I am afraid of fatiguing you with these details, but I felt that it is my duty, in an affair of so much importance, to relate facts as they have occurred. You may also blame me for having raised this question so soon, and at a time when I had grounds to doubt of its being decided favorably, but I flatter myself that my intentions justify my course of action.

"To consolidate the interests and confirm the confidence of our friends,* to try our strength, to familiarize the people with what we aim at, to dissipate the apprehension which important innovations generally produce, and to provoke the resentment of Congress with a view to stimulate that body into some invidious political act, which might excite the passions of the people; these are the motives which influenced me, and on which I rely for my justification.

"The last Convention was legally elected, and met at Danville in the month of November, in conformity with

---

* El consolidar los intereses, y establecer la confianza de nuestros amigos; el probar nuestras fuerzas; familiarizar el pueblo con el asunto; desvanecer el terror que las novedades interesantes generalmente inspiran; y el excitar el resentimiento del Congreso con la esperanza de inducir a este cuerpo á algun acto de politica invidiosa que pudiese irritar los animos del pueblo, estos son los motivos que me influyeron y à los que dejo mi justificacion.

the decree above-mentioned. Marshall and **Muter had** in the mean time, been scattering distrusts and apprehensions calculated to do injury to our cause. It is evident, however, that it has acquired considerable force ; but, in order to elicit an unequivocal proof of the dispositions of that assembly, I submitted to its examination my original memorial and the joint answer of yourself and Navarro. I received, in the terms which you will find in the Gazette, No. 3, the unanimous thanks of that body, in token of its approbation of my conduct on that occasion. Some of our friends urged me to avail myself of this opportunity to revive the great question, but I thought that it was more judicious to indulge those who, for the moment, wish only that a new application be made in relation to the independence and separation of Kentucky from Virginia, and that a memorial be addressed to Congress on the necessity of obtaining the free use of the navigation of the Mississippi. I assented to these last propositions the more readily, that it was unanimously resolved that, should any of them be rejected, then the people would be invited to adopt all the measures necessary to secure for themselves a separate government from that of the United States, because it would have become evident that Congress had neither the will nor the power to satisfy their hopes. I determined therefore to wait for the effects which will result from the disappointment of those hopes, and on which I rely to unite the country into one opinion. This is the basis on which the great question now rests, and the Convention has adjourned to the next month.

"'Thus, Sir, if we review the policy favored by the inhabitants of Kentucky, we see that the most intelligent and the wealthiest relish our designs, which are opposed by only two men of rank, who, controlled by their fears of silly demagogues, and filling their followers with hopes from the expected action of the new Congress, have caused the suspension of the measures we had in view to unite the people, and thus to secure the success of our plans without involving the country in violent civil commotions.

"There are three conditions which are requisite to perpetuate the connection of this section of the country with the Atlantic States. The first, and the most important, is the navigation of the Mississippi; the second, which is of equal consequence, is the admission of this district into the Union as an independent State, and on the same footing with the others; the third, and the last, which is of less moment, is the exemption from taxes until the befalling of the two events previously mentioned. Now, Sir, as two of these conditions are inadmissible, either by the Atlantic States or by Spain, can any one hesitate to declare what will be the consequences? With due deference, I say, No; because, as it is not rational to suppose the voluntary casting away of property, that another may profit by it, so it is not to be presumed that the Eastern States, which at present have the balance of power in their favor in the American government, will consent to strip themselves of this advantage, and increase the weight of the Southern States, by acknowledging the independence of this district and admitting it to be a member of the Federal Union. That the people of Kentucky, as soon as they are certain of their being refused what they claim, will separate from the United States, is proclaimed even by Marshall, Muter, and their more timid followers.

"The same effect will be produced by the suspension of the navigation of the Mississippi, which lies entirely in the power of Spain, and which must reduce this section of the country to misery and ruin; and as it has been stipulated that the operations of the Federal Government shall be uniform, the new Congress will have to lay taxes, without exception whatever, over the whole country submitted to its jurisdiction. The people here, not having the means of paying those taxes, will resist them, and the authority of the new government will be set at naught, which will produce a civil war, and result in the separation of the West from the East.

"This event is written in the book of destiny. But if, to produce it, we trust solely to the natural effect of political measures, we shall experience some delay. It is in the power of Spain, however, to precipitate its accomplishment by a judicious coöperation; and permit me here to illustrate the observations which I presented some time ago to yourself and Navarro, in my answer to your inquiries as to the nature of that coöperation.

"As long as the connection between the Americans of the East and of the West on this side of the Apalachian mountains shall produce reciprocal benefits, and an equal security to their common interests and happiness, the Union will maintain itself on a solid foundation, and will resist any effort to dissolve it; but, as soon as it shall be ascertained that one section of the confederacy derives from the Union more advantages than the other, and that the blessings of a good government—such as peace and protection—cannot be equally distributed, then harmony will cease, and jealousies will arise, producing discord and disunion. In order to aid the favorable dispositions of Providence, to foment the suspicions and feelings of distrust already existing here, and inflame the animosity between the Eastern and Western States, Spain must resort to every artifice and other means which may be in her power.

"I have stated that the navigation of the Mississippi, and its admission as an independent State and a member of the Union, are rights claimed by the people of this part of the country, and constituting one of the principal conditions under which its connection with the Atlantic States is to continue. Hence it follows, that every manifestation of the power of Spain and of the debility of the United States, every evidence of the resolution of the former to retain exclusively for herself the right of navigation on the Mississippi, and every proof of the incapacity of the latter, will facilitate our views. Every circumstance also that will tend to impede our admission as an independent State will loosen the attachment of many individuals, increase the discontent of the people, and favor the execution of our plan.

"Until I devoted myself entirely to the affair in which we are engaged, I confess that I could not discover the aim of the first treaty proposed by Gardoqui to Congress, but it seems to me now that I can penetrate its policy. I consider it as profoundly judicious, and I am of opinion that it ought to be renewed and vigorously carried on, until its objects be attained, cost what it may, because, besides that the proposed relinquishment of the right of navigating the Mississippi would immediately disrupt the Union, and separate for ever the West from the East, the sanction of the treaty by Congress would make our situation so truly desperate, that Great Britain would not venture to intervene in our favor, and all our hopes would rest on the liberality of Spain.

"Whilst this affair is pending, Spain ought to consider the navigation of the Mississippi as one of the most precious jewels of her crown. For, whatever power shall command that navigation, will control all the country which is watered by that river and by those streams which fall into it. This control will be as effective and complete as that of the key upon the lock, or that of the citadel over the exterior works which it commands. The grant of this boon ought to be looked upon as the price of our attachment and gratitude, and I beg leave to be permitted to repeat, that there must be known no instance of its being extended to any other than those who understand and promote the interests of Spain in this part of the country. I entreat you, Sir, to believe, that this question of navigation is the main one on which depends the union of the West and East, and that, if Congress can obtain the free use of the Mississippi, and if Spain should cede it without condition, it would strengthen the Union, and would deprive Spain of all its influence on this district.

"The sanguine spirit of an American impels him to construe in his favor everything that is left doubtful, and therefore Spain cannot act with too absolute precision on this important question. You must not forget, Sir, that such was my first impression, in which I have been daily confirmed by subsequent observations and experience. The concessions of the Americans will be in proportion to the energy and power exhibited by Spain; but were she to yield, she would lose much in dignity and consideration, and she would breed in the Americans a spirit of pride and self-importance quite incompatible with our designs. Thus, the privileges conceded to emigrants are an obstacle in the way of our great undertaking, because, as they were bestowed before they were asked for, and as they were entirely unexpected, they have been considered here by many as the effects of fear, and as a prelude to the removal of all restrictions whatever on our commerce.

"The generality of our population are constantly discussing and fostering these ideas, and as long as the hopes they have conceived on this subject are kept up, it is a circumstance which will militate in favor of the Union, and will delay the effect of my operations.

"With due deference I may be permitted to say, that,

to people the banks of the Mississippi with Americans ought to be an object of secondary importance to the interests of his Catholic Majesty, because there is no necessity to transplant a population which can be controlled and governed on the soil where it grows naturally. The engrafted branch retains the primitive qualities of the parent trunk. Moreover, if Spain can establish colonies of Americans on the Mississippi, there is no reason why she should not have them also on the Ohio. It is an incontestable fact, worthy of your attention, that the emigrants who have come down the Ohio, in order to settle in Louisiana, are insolvent debtors and fugitives from justice, and are poor and without principles. Such people are not only unworthy vassals, but also ought to be looked upon as dangerous characters, against whom it is prudent to be on one's guard.

"But, sir, should unforeseen events produce results contrary to my wishes, to my logical deductions and to my hopes, should an obstinate resistance to forming a connection with Spain, or should an unexpectedly hostile disposition manifest itself in these settlements, then the true policy would be to make of emigration the principal object to be obtained, and Spain would always have the power, through some agents of an eminent rank here, to draw to her the most respectable portion of the population of this district. Hundreds have applied to me on this subject, who are determined to follow my example, and I do not deceive myself, nor do I deceive you, sir, when I affirm that it is in my power to lead a large body of the most opulent and most respectable of my fellow-citizens whither I shall go myself at their head, and I flatter myself that, after the dangers I have run and the sacrifices which I have made, after having put my honor and my life in your hands, you can have no doubts of my favorable dispositions towards the interests of his Catholic Majesty, as long as my poor services shall be necessary.

"After having read these remarks, you will be surprised at being informed, that lately I have, jointly with several gentlemen of this country, applied to Don Diego Gardoqui for a concession of land, in order to form a settlement on the river Yazoo. The motive of this application is to procure a place of refuge for myself and my adherents, in case it should become necessary for us to retire from this country, in order to avoid the resentment of Congress. It is true that there is not, so far, the slightest appearance of it, but it is judicious to provide for all possible contingencies.

"These observations are sincere and well meant, and although I still continue to be without any answer from the Spanish Ministry, I consider myself bound in honor to proceed in my undertaking until I obtain favorable results. Ardent are my wishes and strong are my hopes, but may not both be illusive? Is it not possible that Great Britain may have accomplished her desires, by exchanging Gibraltar for the two Floridas and the Island of New-Orleans? It is a rumor which is afloat in America, and I must confess that it fills me with anxiety; for I have a very recent proof that that power turns its attention to this country with the utmost earnestness, and sets in motion every sort of machinery to secure its aim, because, whilst William Eden is negotiating in Madrid with his Excellency the Count of Florida Blanca, Lord Dorchester, the Governor of Canada, scatters his emissaries in this district, to win over the people to the interests of Great Britain. The document No. 4 contains an authentic copy of the letter of General St. Clair, Governor of the Northern portion of the territory of Ohio, to Major Dunn. That letter, sir, is the proof that the part which I play in our great enterprise, and the dangers to which I am exposed for the service of his Catholic Majesty, are known; and it will serve at the same time to evidence the correctness of the information which I gave in my memorial in relation to the designs of Great Britain. Whence and how General St. Clair has acquired any knowledge of the views of Spain, I cannot guess, unless he should have inferred them from the indiscreet zeal of Don Diego Gardoqui, which may have hurried that gentleman into confidential communications to persons unworthy of that trust, and even to strangers, as must have been demonstrated to you by the extract of his letter to Colonel Morgan, which you will find in the paper marked No. 5, and which is now circulating over the whole of this district. So far as I am concerned, having shared in this important affair, I will endeavor to discharge with fidelity the part assigned to me, without being deterred by the fear of consequences, always relying on the generosity of his majesty, who will indemnify me or my family for whatever loss of fortune I may incur

"The British Colonel Connelly, who is mentioned in General St. Clair's letter, arrived at Louisville in the beginning of October, having travelled from Detroit through the woods, to the mouth of the river Big Miami, from which he came down the Ohio in a boat. My agent in that town (Louisville) gave me immediate information of that fact, and of the intention which Connelly had to visit me. Suspecting the nature of the negotiation he had on hand, I determined, in order to discover his secret views, to be beforehand with him, and to invite him here. Consequently he came to my house on the 8th of November. I received him courteously, and, as I manifested favorable dispositions towards the interests of his Britannic Majesty, I soon gained his confidence—so much so—that he informed me that Great Britain, desiring to assist the American settlers in the West, in their efforts to open the navigation of the Mississippi, would join them with ready zeal, to dispossess Spain of Louisiana. He remarked that the forces in Canada were not sufficient to send detachments of them to us, but that Lord Dorchester would supply us with all the implements of war, and with money, clothing, &c. . . . to equip ten thousand men, if we wished to engage in that enterprise. He added that, as soon as our plan of operation should be agreed upon, these articles would be sent from Detroit, through Lake Erie, to the river Miami, and thence to the Wabash, to be transported to any designated point on the Ohio, and that a fleet of light vessels would be ready at Jamaica to take possession of the Balize, at the same time that we should make an attack from above. He assured me that he was authorized by Lord Dorchester to confer honors and other rewards on the men of influence who should enter on that enterprise, and that all those who were officers in the late continental army, should be provided with the same grade in the service of Great Britain. He urged me much to favor his designs, offering me what rank and emoluments I might wish for, and telling me at the same time that he was empowered to grant commissions for the raising of two regiments which he hoped to form in Kentucky. After having pumped out of him all that I wished to know, I began to weaken his hopes by observing that the feelings of animosity engendered by the late revolution were so recent in the hearts of the Americans, that I considered it impossible to entice them into an alliance with Great Britain; that, in this district, particularly in that part of it where the inhabitants had suffered so much from the barbarous hostilities of the Indians, which were attributed to British influence, the resentment of every individual was much more intense and implacable.

In order to justify this opinion of mine and induce him to go back, I employed a hunter, who feigned attempting his life. The pretext assumed by the hunter was the avenging of the death of his son, murdered by the Indians at the supposed instigation of the English. As I hold the commission of a Civil Judge, it was, of course, to be my duty to protect him against the pretended murderer, whom I caused to be arrested and held in custody. I availed myself of this circumstance to communicate to Connelly my fear of not being able to answer for the security of his person, and I expressed my doubts whether he could escape with life. It alarmed him so much, that he begged me to give him an escort to conduct him out of our territory, which I readily assented to, and on the 20th of November, he recrossed the Ohio on his way back to Detroit. I did not dismiss him without having previously impressed upon him the propriety of informing me, in as short a time as possible, of the ultimate designs of Lord Dorchester. As this man was under the protection of the laws of nations, and as he carefully avoided to commit any offence against our government, I considered the measure I had resorted to as the most appropriate to destroy his hopes with regard to this country, and I think that the relation he will make on his return to Canada will produce the desired effect. But should the British be disposed to renew the same attempt, as it may very well turn out to be the case, I shall be ready to oppose and crush it in the bud.

"Thus, sir, you see realized the opinions I expressed in my memorial relatively to the views which Great Britain had on this part of the country. But whilst I reveal to you the designs of that power, permit me a few reflections on the conduct of France with regard to these settlements. I know that the family compact will compel her to assist Spain against any hostility whatever. May not Spain, however, be exposed to suffer from the subtle policy and machinations of the most intriguing and the craftiest of all nations? It is to my knowledge that the Court of Versailles has, for years past, been collecting every sort of information on this district, and that it would give a great deal to recover its possessions on the Mississippi. In the year 1785, a Knight of St. Louis, named D'Argès,* arrived at the falls of the Ohio, gave himself out for a naturalist, and pretended that his object was to inquire into the curious productions of this country, but his manner of living contradicted his assertion. He made few acquaintances, lived very retired, and during one year that he remained here, he never went out of Louisville, where he resided, farther than six miles. On his perusing the first memorial which the people of this district presented to the Legislature of Virginia on the question of separation, he expressed his admiration that there should be in so new a country a writer capable of framing such a composition, and, after having made some reflexions on the progressive importance of our settlements, he exclaimed with enthusiasm: '*Good God! my country has been blind, but its eyes shall soon be open!*' The confidential friend of this gentleman was a Mr. Tardiveau, who had resided many years in Kentucky. D'Argès used to draw drafts on M. de Marbois, then Consul of France at New York, and, finally, he lived as one who belonged to the family of Count de Moustier, the French minister, and I am informed from a good source, that he presented to this same Count de Moustier a very elaborate memorial on these settlements, which was forwarded to the Court of France.

"Perhaps, sir, you will think this information frivo-

* The same of whom Miró speaks, and who was one of the secret agents of the Spanish Government.

lous, but I am sure you will believe that it proceeds from my devoted zeal for the interests of Spain. Please remember that trifles as light as air frequently are, for the faithful and the zealous, proofs as strong as those of Holy Writ.

"Before closing this letter, I shall take the liberty to observe that, in order to secure the success of our schemes, the most entire confidence must be reposed in your agent here, because, without it, his representations will be received with suspicion, and his recommendations disregarded, or executed with tardy precaution,—which is capable of defeating the most ably devised plan. Whether I possess that confidence or not is what I am ignorant of, but the Almighty, who reads the hearts of all men, knows that I deserve it, because nobody ever undertook a cause with more honest zeal and devotion than I have this one. You may therefore conceive the anxiety which I feel on account of the silence of your government on my memorial, and I infinitely regret that some communication, in relation to this part of the country, should not be transmitted through Louisiana, because I know that the negotiation may be conducted through that channel with more secrecy and with better results.

"I deem it useless to mention to a gentleman well versed in political history, that the great spring and prime mover in all negotiations is *money*. Although not being authorized by you to do so, yet I found it necessary to use this lever, in order to confirm some of our most eminent citizens in their attachment to our cause, and to supply others with the means of operating with vigor. For these objects I have advanced five thousand dollars out of my own funds, and half of this sum, applied opportunely, would attract Marshall and

Muter on our side, but it is now impossible for me to disburse it.

"I shall not write you again before the month of May unless some unexpected event should require it. At that time, I will inform you of the decision of Virginia and of Congress on our last application, and I do not doubt but that our affairs will soon assume a smiling aspect."

General St. Clair's letter to Major Dunn, to which Wilkinson alluded in his preceding communication, was dated December 5, 1788. "Dear Dunn," said he, "I am much grieved to hear that there are strong dispositions on the part of the people of Kentucky to break off their connection with the United States, and that our friend Wilkinson is at the head of this affair. Such a consummation would involve the United States in the greatest difficulties, and would completely ruin this country. Should there be any foundation for these reports, for God's sake, make use of your influence to detach Wilkinson from that party."

On the 14th of February, 1789, two days after he had written the despatch to Miró, in which he said that he would remain silent until the month of May next, unless some unforeseen circumstance should require him to resume his pen, Wilkinson thus addressed the Spanish Governor:

"My much esteemed and honored friend: having written to you on the 12th instant, with all the formality and respect due to the Governor of Louisiana as the representative of his Sovereign, I will now address the man I love and the friend I can trust, without ceremony or reserve.

"If you have felt some surprise, perplexity and disquietude produced by the silence of the ministry on my memorial, and if you have not yet received satisfactory news from our dear friend, Don Martin Navarro,* I believe that I may say to you that you ought to be satisfied, because it seems that our plan has been eagerly accepted. Don Diego Gardoqui, about the month of March last, received from his court ample powers to make with the people of this district the arrangements he might think proper, in order to estrange them from the United States and induce them to form an alliance with Spain. I received this information, in the first place, from Mr. Brown, the member of Congress for this district, who, since the taking into consideration of our application to be admitted into the Union has been suspended, entered into some free communications on this matter with Don Diego Gardoqui. He returned here in September last, and, finding that there had been some opposition to our project, he almost abandoned the cause in despair, and positively refused to advocate in public the propositions of Don Diego Gardoqui, as he deemed them fatal to our cause. Brown is one of our deputies or agents; he is a young man of respectable talents, but timid, without political experience, and with very little knowledge of the world. Nevertheless, as he firmly perseveres in his adherence to our interests, we have sent him to the new Congress, apparently as our representative, but in reality as a spy on the actions of that body. I would myself have undertaken that charge, but I did not, for two reasons: first, my presence was necessary here, and next, I should have found myself under the obligation of swearing to support the new government, which I am in duty bound to oppose.

"The intrusting of that negotiation to Don Diego Gardoqui in preference to you has been a most unfor-

---

* It will be remembered that Navarro had returned to Spain the preceding year.

tunate circumstance, because this gentleman does not use his powers with prudence. He gives passports to everybody, and, instead of forming connections with men of influence in this district, who should be interested in favoring his designs, he negotiates with individuals who live in the Atlantic States, who therefore have no knowledge of this section of the country, and have no interest in it.

"When Major Dunn arrived at Philadelphia, he found that his wife and children had gone to Rhode Island. In his journey thither, he passed through New York, and Don Diego Gardoqui sent for him and put him several questions on the circumstances relative to this district and the object of his last voyage to New Orleans. Gardoqui plied Dunn with the most friendly offers; he said that he would not confine his good intentions to the granting of passports, but would render what services might be necessary; that he would also act with equal liberality towards Dunn and Dunn's friends; and would bestow upon them much more important favors than could the Governor of Louisiana, because he had more extensive powers. The Major, with much prudence, warded off his inquiries, and promised writing him from this district. But Gardoqui's eagerness rose to such a pitch, that he pursued the Major to Philadelphia with a letter, the original of which I inclose to you (No. 1). The Major, in his visit to Gardoqui, discovered that there were various individuals and companies who courted the favor of the Minister, in order to obtain the faculty of making settlements on the Mississippi and participate in the advantages of our commerce. When Dunn reached Kentucky and gave me this information, it struck me it was necessary that he should return immediately to New York, and see Don Diego Gardoqui, in order to change this Minister's ideas, which, if persisted in, would be contrary to our great designs, and in order to suggest to him the true policy which he ought to pursue. With a view to removing every cause of distrust or unfavorable impressions from Gardoqui's mind, I wrote to him the letter of which I send you a copy (Doc. No. 2), and I flatter myself, my esteemed friend, that it will meet your approbation. The Major carries with him a petition, to obtain, on the Yazoo and the Mississippi, the concession of land to which I alluded in my last letter. It is the most advantageous site to form a settlement above Natchez. That petition is signed by Innis, Sebastian, Dunn, Brown and myself. Our intention is to make an establishment on the ground mentioned in my communication of the 12th, and with a view to destroy the plan of a certain Colonel Morgan.

This Colonel Morgan resides for the present with his family, in the vicinity of Princeton in New Jersey, but twenty or twenty-five years ago he used to trade with the Indians at Kaskaskia, in copartnership with Baynton and Whaiton. He is a man of education and possesses an intelligent mind, but he is a deep and thorough speculator. He has already become twice a bankrupt, and according to the information which I have lately received, he is now in extremely necessitous circumstances, &c. &c. He was sent by a New Jersey Company to New York, in order to negotiate with Congress the purchase of a vast tract of land comprising Cahokia and Kaskaskia. But whilst this affair was pending, he found it to his interest to deal with Don Diego Gardoqui, and he discovered that it was more advantageous for him to shift his negotiation from the United States to Spain. The result was, that he obtained, forsooth, the most extraordinary concession, which extends along the Mississippi, from the mouth of the St. Francis river to point *Cinq*

Hommes, in the West, containing from twelve to fifteen millions of acres. I have not seen Morgan, nor am I acquainted with the particulars of his contract, but I have set a spy after him since his coming to these parts and his going down the river to take possession of his *new province*, and through that spy, I have collected the following information: "that the intention of Morgan is to build a city on the west bank of the Mississippi, as near the mouth of the Ohio as the nature of the ground may permit; that he intends selling his lands by small or large lots for a shilling an acre; that Don Diego Gardoqui pays all the costs of that establishment, and has undertaken to make that new town a free port, to intercept all the productions of this country, on the most advantageous terms he may be able to secure from our people. Morgan departed from here, in the beginning of this month, to take possession of his territory, to survey it, and fix the site of the town, which will be called New Madrid. He took with him two surveyors, and from forty to fifty persons besides; but not one of them was from Kentucky. This is all that he could do. In a political point of view Morgan's establishment can produce no good result, but, on the contrary, will have the most pernicious consequences; because the Americans who may settle there, will, on account of their proximity to, and their constant intercourse with their countrymen, of this side of the river, retain their old prejudices and feelings, and will continue to be Americans as if they were on the banks of the Ohio. On the other side, the intention of detaining the productions of this vast country at a point so distant from their real market, whilst the Americans shall remain the carriers of that trade, cannot fail to cause discontents and to embroil the two countries in difficulties. Probably it will destroy the noble fabric of which we have laid out the foundations, and which we are endeavoring to complete. If it be deemed necessary to keep the Americans at a distance from Louisiana, let the Spaniards at least be the carriers of the produce they receive in their ports, and of the merchandise which is acceptable to the Americans. In this way will be formed an impenetrable barrier, without any costs to the king, because, in less than thirty years, his Catholic Majesty will have on the river thirty thousand boatmen at least, whom it will be easy to equip and to convert into armed bodies, to assist in the defence of the province, from whatever quarter it may be threatened.

"I am informed that Morgan intends visiting you, as soon as he shall have finished the survey of the lands conceded to him. Permit me to supplicate you, my most esteemed of friends, not to give him any knowledge of my plans, sentiments or designs. It is long since he has become jealous of me, and you may rest assured that, in reality, he is not well affected towards our cause, but that he allows himself to be entirely ruled by motives of the vilest self interest, and therefore that he will not scruple, on his return to New York, to destroy me. One of the objects of Major Dunn, in seeing Gardoqui, is to sound him on this affair, and I doubt not but that he will do so successfully. I expect him back in the beginning of April, he having departed from here on the 17th of January, and I having heard of his safe arrival on the other side of the mountains. Immediately after his return, I shall either go in person and visit you, or I shall send you an all-trusty friend.

"As Don Diego Gardoqui has given passports to all those who applied for any, you must expect that various individuals will come down the river in the course of the season, but you must take care, my honored friend, to repose confidence in none but such as will deliver you a 'etter from me, because I will furnish with one every man of merit, veracity and influence. I presume that there must now be in New Orleans a certain Peter Paulus, who is sent from Philadelphia, where he kept soul and body together by being an obscure tavern keeper. There are now here a Mr. Dorsey and a Mr. Paulin, with passports from Gardoqui and letters for you from Dr. Franklin and Thomas Miflin, Governor of Pennsylvania. These two individuals are citizens of Philadelphia, where they kept a dry goods store. Having both become bankrupts, they brought some effects to Kentucky, and have exchanged them for productions of the country, which they will carry down to New Orleans, in order to make a few dollars out of his Catholic Majesty and take them back to their families at Philadelphia. Such are, my esteemed friend, the new comers who produce Gardoqui's credentials. Your own judgment must tell you that they can have no weight in the important question we have on hand. Why then should they have rewards and privileges? And such men have the audacity to suppose that they will obtain leave from you to do whatever they please!

"Herein inclosed (Doc. No. 3), you will find two Gazettes which contain all the proceedings of our last Convention. You will observe that the memorial to Congress was presented by me, and perhaps your first impression will be that of surprise at such a document having issued from the pen of a good Spaniard. But, on further reflection, you will discover that my policy is to justify in the eye of the world our meditated separation from the rest of the Union, and quiet the apprehensions of some friends in the Atlantic States, the better to divide them, because, knowing how impossible it is that the United States should obtain what we aspire to, not only did I gratify my sentiments and inclinations, but I also framed my memorial in such a style as was best calculated to excite the passions of our people; and convince them that Congress has neither the power nor the will to enforce their claims and pretensions. Thus having energetically and publicly represented our rights and lucidly established our pretensions, if Congress does not support them with efficacy (which you know it cannot do, even if it had the inclination), not only will all the people of Kentucky, but also the whole world, approve of our seeking protection from another quarter.

"Your favoring the fitting out of the boat destined for this part of the country will, no doubt, meet the approbation of his majesty, because truly, my friend, this is an important point gained to convince the people of Kentucky that, instead of sending their money across the mountains in order to purchase their various necessities, they can with advantage procure them in New Orleans, in exchange for their produce and on better terms. Adieu, my dearest friend! To-morrow I go to the falls of Ohio, in order to despatch my boats."

The letter to Gardoqui, to which Wilkinson alluded, and of which he sent a copy to Miró, had been written on the 1st of January, 1789, and was couched in these terms: "Sir, I venture to address you this letter, under the supposition that my correspondence will not be undervalued in your estimation, when you are informed that, although not personally known to you, I have been one of the first and most active agents to promote the political designs which you seem to entertain in relation to this country; that, in support of those projects which aim at securing the reciprocal happiness of the Spaniard of Louisiana and of the American of Kentucky, I have* voluntarily sacrificed my domestic felicities, my time,

---

* He sacrificado voluntariamente mis domesticas felicitades, tiempo, bienes, comodidades, y lo que es mas importante, abandoné al hacer my fama personal y caracter político.

my fortune, my comforts, and, what is more, have given up promoting my personal fame and political character. In the pursuit of the object which I have in view, I trespass upon your attention under the firm persuasion that you will excuse the liberty I take, and which originates from my zeal for the prosperity of Louisiana and Kentucky, and that, whatever be the result of this affair, what I am going to communicate to you will remain for ever locked up in your breast.

"You may not have forgotten that, during the winter of 1787, the Baron de Steuben applied to you, in order to obtain a passport for a gentleman who wished to visit Louisiana, by descending the river Mississippi. You, at first, gave your assent, but withdrew it afterwards. I do not know whether my name was mentioned to you at the time, but the evidence resulting from my having possession of the very letter in which you excused yourself to the Baron, and which he sent to me, in order to show why his application on my behalf had no effect, will convince you that he who now addresses you is the same individual for whom the Baron acted. Your refusal, however, did not put an end to my design, and I determined to venture on visiting New Orleans, ostensibly for commercial purposes, but in reality for the following reasons:

"An intimate knowledge and a comparative analysis of the relative local circumstances of the Atlantic and Western States did not leave in my mind the slightest doubt, even on the very threshold of my investigation, that their interests were of an opposite character and their policy irreconcilable. Having established my family in Kentucky, where I had acquired a large tract of land, I foresaw that I had nothing to hope from the Union. Under this impression, I considered that it was my duty to look anywhere else, for the patronage and protection which the prosperity and happiness of our extensive establishments required imperatively. With this view,* I entered the jurisdiction of the government of Louisiana, and also with the determination to run the risk of encountering judicial difficulties,† in case my propositions were rejected, and then to open a negotiation with Great Britain, which had already been active in the matter. But, truly, the manner in which the Governor and the Intendant received me removed all my apprehensions, and led to a free and reciprocal communication of confidential thoughts and sentiments. Really, their urbanity and caressing attentions to me‡ inspired my heart with the warmest attachment for their persons, whilst my observations in relation to the clemency, the justice and energy of their government forced me to make comparisons, which were far from being favorable to the turbulent licence in which we live. With the permission of these gentlemen, I reduced to writing my views on the situation, circumstances, aspirations and interests of the country in which I live, on the policy of the Atlantic States in reference thereto, and on the designs of Great Britain, with copious reflections on the true interest of his Catholic Majesty and the system he ought to pursue in order to secure and extend his colony of Louisiana. This essay or memorial, according to my express desire, was forwarded direct from New Orleans to Madrid, in September, 1787. As this affair was to me of the utmost importance, and as I was not acquainted with your poli-

---

* Con este intento me dirijé al gobierno de la Luisiana, determinado al mismo tiempo en la alternativa de que, si se desechasen mis proposiciones, correría el riesgo de una contestacion civil, y abriría una negociacion con la Gran Bretaña, por la que se habian dado ya pasos sobre el asunto.

† He alludes, no doubt, to the expected seizure of the cargo of tobacco with which he had gone down to New Orleans, without passport or permission.

‡ Sus urbanas y cariñosas atenciones.

tical views, I refused my consent to its being communicated to you, and I trusted to the honor and discretion of the Spanish ministry for my security, in case my propositions should be disapproved.

"The negotiation having commenced in this way, I expressed the desire to know its result through no other channel. This disposition of my mind proceeded from my reliance on Mirò and Navarro, and from the opinion which I have not yet relinquished, that this affair may be managed through them in such a way as entirely to avoid exciting the suspicions of Congress. But it seems that the Cabinet of Madrid has deemed proper to pursue the ordinary and regular course, and that you have received powers in the premises. This makes it absolutely necessary for the success of our plans, that I should open a correspondence with you, and I flatter myself that these circumstances will justify the step which I take, in the eyes of my dear and honorable friends Don Estevan Mirò and Don Martin Navarro, because you may rest assured that, for no human consideration, I would run the risk of losing their friendship or good opinion.

"On my return from Louisiana, I went through Virginia last winter, and wrote to you a complimentary letter, the object of which was to open a correspondence with you. But it was intercepted; hence the necessity of my going into these details, in order to make fully known to you the individual who now aspires to your confidence.

"In conclusion, I beg leave to refer myself in general terms to my friend, Major Dunn, who will present to you various authentic documents in relation to your plan, and which it would be imprudent to mention in writing. I hope that you will not blame this precaution on my part, if you reflect on the fluctuation and mutability of human affairs; because, if the Court of Spain, as the rumor runs, has unfortunately ceded the Floridas and the island of New Orleans to Great Britain, a new theatre will be open for new actors, and other measures must be taken. It is not necessary* to suggest to a gentleman of your experience and knowledge, that man, throughout the world, is governed by private interest, however variously modified it may be. Some men are avaricious, some are vain, others are ambitions. To detect the predominant passion, to lay hold and to make the most of it, is the most profound secret of political science.

"The Major will communicate to you what we have agreed upon in relation to the application which he is to lay before you. He will tell you in detail the measures which I have taken in this district, the effects they have produced, and the present temper of the people, and if you can have faith* in the system which he will develop to you, and if you help it on with vigor, I pledge, from to-day, my life, fame, and fortune, to answer for the success which I promise."

Peter Paulus, of whom Wilkinson speaks in his letter of the 14th of February, had arrived in New Orleans. He had with him thirty-four persons, and, for having procured them to emigrate, he obtained as a reward $350 from Governor Miró. He offered to bring to Louisiana three thousand families on certain conditions, among which one of the principal was, that the king of Spain should pay all the expenses incidental to their removal,

---

* No es necesario sugerir á un caballero de los conocimientos y experiencia de V. S. que el genero humano, en cualquiera parte, se gobierna por su propio interés, aunque variamente modificado. Unos son sordidos, algunos vanos, otros ambiciosos; escoger, tomar y sacar ventajas de la pasion predominante es lo mas profundo de la ciencia politica.

† Y si V. S. puede fiarse al sistema que le esplicara y apoyarle vigorosamente, desde luego empeño mi vida, fama y fortuna para responder del suceso.

and that the trial by jury be allowed to the new colonists. "This," said Miró, "I have positively refused, because it would cost millions to his Majesty. But I had a long conversation with Paulus,† in which I explained to him the advantages which the Ohio people would find in establishing themselves in the province, wherefore those who had the most means among them ought immediately to take that step, because they would infallibly, in a few years, reach a state of opulence. I endeavored also to convince him, that no monarchy in the world could go to the immense expense of maintaining and supporting the ever increasing number of families that would indubitably present themselves, if they were granted the assistance which was solicited for them, and which they were given to understand that they would obtain. I remarked to him that, if, without any aid, the stream of emigration continued to flow so abundantly from the Atlantic states to this side of the Apalachian mountains, the emigrants had stronger motives to rely on their own resources when coming to this province, where lands were given to them gratis, and where the industrious were sure to become prosperous under a mild government, which would afford them support and protection, and where they would enjoy the advantage of an easy outlet for their produce.

"This Peter Paulus is a Dutchman by birth; he appears to be fifty years old; his face seems to indicate that he is an honest man, and his language, although dull and unpolished, is stamped with much apparent sincerity. The families he proposes to bring along with him are Germans, who reside a considerable distance above Kentucky.*

But Paulus replied, that he had been induced by

---

* Miró's despatch of the 15th of March, 1789.   † Probably in Pennsylvania.

Gardoqui and his agents to hold out very different hopes to the emigrants, and that if, on his return to them, he altered his language, they would consider him as an impostor.

Regretting the imprudence of Gardoqui, who had allowed his zeal to incite him to a course which might be fatal to his Majesty's interest, and on which he commented at length in one of his despatches to his government, Governor Mirò said to Paulus : " I have no power to send any emissary to promote emigration from the United States, and therefore I cannot encourage your pretensions, nor those of the people you represent. I can only receive the foreigners who may come spontaneously and of their own free will, to swear themselves the vassals of his Catholic Majesty. To them surveyed lands shall be granted gratis, in proportion to the laborers of whom each family may consist. The smallest concession shall not be less than 200 arpens—400 to families of four to ten laborers, and 800 to those numbering from ten to fifteen hands or more."

Although not willing to pay for the expenses of emigration on so large a scale, Governor Mirò consented to certain disbursements, in order to increase the population of Louisiana. For instance, the vessel, the Conception, having arrived from Philadelphia, with 173 emigrants, he established 133 of them in the Feliciana district at the cost of the royal treasury.*

On the 11th of April, he forwarded to Madrid, with his comments, Wilkinson's two letters, which I have quoted, and the documents annexed to them. In that communication he represents, that he shares Wilkinson's opinion that the independence of the Western people, under the protection of, and in close alliance with, Spain,

* Mirò's despatch of the 15th of March, 1789.

would be more to the interest of his Majesty than their annexation to his domains, on account of the expenses and responsibilities which such an acquisition would entail on Spain, and also on account of the jealousies and opposition which it would elicit from foreign powers. He urgently presses the cabinet of Madrid to send him instructions as to the course to be pursued by him, in case the Western people should declare their independence and send delegates to him. He further remarks that he is totally unprepared to supply them with the ammunition, arms, and other implements of which they may stand in need to resist any action of the Federal Government, should it attempt to coerce them into submission.

"In the paragraph B.," said he to the Minister, " you will find an account of the bold act which General Wilkinson has ventured upon, in presenting his first memorial in a public convention. In so doing, he has so completely bound himself, that, should he not be able to obtain the separation of Kentucky from the United States, it has become impossible for him to live in it, *unless he has suppressed, which is possible, certain passages which might injure him.* Nevertheless, on account of the opposition made by Marshall and Muter to Wilkinson's plan, the Convention determined that new memorials be presented to Virginia and to Congress, to obtain the independence of Kentucky, its admission into the Union, and the free navigation of the Mississippi. On these two first questions, I disagree with Wilkinson as to their solution, and I am of opinion that the independence of these people from Virginia and their reception into the Union will be conceded to them, and that the answer of Congress on this subject is not deceitful, because the right of Kentucky to what she claims is incontestable, and is derived from the articles of confederacy on which the United States established their first government."

Miró declared that, with Wilkinson, he thought it was a stroke of bad policy on the part of the Spanish government, to have granted to the inhabitants of Kentucky the use of the navigation of the Mississippi, although under the restriction of a duty of fifteen per cent., because, rather than being deprived altogether of that channel for the exit of their produce, they would not have hésitated to renounce all allegiance to Congress. He informed his government that he had lately written in cypher to Wilkinson, through one Jennings, a confidential agent, that emigration to Louisiana was to be encouraged by all means, whilst, at the same time, the other plan of the independence, or annexation of Kentucky, was to be steadily kept in mind. "You will render a great service to the king," he wrote to Wilkinson, "if you induce to come down here a large number of families, having some property and not needing pecuniary assistance, but only lands. It is proper, however, that you should remain in that district, in order to insist on the plan of an alliance with Spain, until it be effected or be given up; because, according to the answer received from the Court, you are now our agent, and I am instructed to give you to hope that the king will reward your services as I have already intimated to you."*

He continues saying, that Wilkinson seems averse to this mode of peopling the colony, but that he, Miró, cannot share Wilkinson's views in that respect, and that the emigrants have more means, and are of a better character, than Wilkinson gives them credit for. He

* Pero conviene se mantenga V. S. en ese distrito, para instar sobre el projecto de la conexion, hasta que se verifique, ó desvanesca; pues que ya segun la repuesta de la Corte, es V. S. nuestro agente, y se me ordena le de á V. S. esperanzas de que el Rey lo recompensará como ya le tengo insinuado.

confirms what Wilkinson relates of the intrigues of the English in Kentucky, and dwells on the service rendered by Wilkinson, in driving away Colonel Connelly with so much diplomatic skill and by a well-devised subterfuge. He recommends that the five thousand dollars which Wilkinson declared having spent for the benefit of Spain be refunded to him, and that he be further intrusted with the two thousand five hundred dollars which he asked for, to corrupt Marshall and Muter.

In the mean time, Wilkinson's launches had arrived in New Orleans, and, in that same despatch of the 11th of April, Miró informed the Spanish government that he had bought from the General, for the account of the royal treasury, 235,000 pounds of tobacco, for which transaction he begged the approbation of his Majesty, " on the ground that it was important to keep the General contented." *

* Mediante á lo mucho que importa el tener contento al dicho Brigadier.

CHAPTER V.

MIRÒ'S ADMINISTRATION.

1789 to 1791.

WE have seen the part which Wilkinson and others were acting in Kentucky, in favor of Spain. But in the western settlements of North Carolina a strong party had also sprung up, which was operating with equal force, in the same direction and under the same influence.

In 1786, the western portion of North Carolina, which was called the Washington district, had declared itself independent, and had constituted itself into the State of Frankland, which organized its government, and elected Colonel John Sevier as its first Governor. But Congress interfered in favor of North Carolina, the authority of which was maintained, and the new State of Frankland terminated its brief career in 1787. This first attempt in the West to throw off openly the allegiance due to the parent State had roused intense excitement for and against it, and the secessionists, still persevering in their former designs, were watching for the opportunity to renew them. Thus, on the 12th of September, 1788, ex-governor John Sevier had written to Gardoqui,* to inform him that the inhabitants of Frankland *were unanimous in their vehement desire to form an alliance and treaty of commerce with Spain, and put themselves under her protection.* Wherefore, he begged for ammunition, money, and whatever other assistance Mirò could

---

* A copy of which letter was immediately forwarded by Gardoqui to Mirò.

grant, to aid the execution of the contemplated separation from North Carolina, pledging the faith of the State of Frankland for the payment of whatever sums Spain might advance, and whatever expenses she might incur, in an enterprise which would secure to her such durable and important results. "Before concluding this communication," said Sevier, "it is necessary that I should mention that there cannot be a moment more opportune than the present, to carry our plan into execution. North Carolina has refused to accept the new constitution proposed for the confederacy, and therefore a considerable time will elapse before she becomes a member of the Union, if that event ever happen."

The settlers on the Cumberland river, who were also under the jurisdiction of North Carolina, were deeply interested in the navigation of the Mississippi, and therefore were equally influenced by the motives which were operating so powerfully on the people of Kentucky and other portions of the West. The name of Mirò given to a district which they had lately formed, shows which way their partiality was leaning at that time.

Doctor James White was one of the most active agents employed by Gardoqui to operate on the Western people, and this individual had come to Louisiana to enter into an understanding with Mirò on the execution of the mission with which he had been intrusted. In a communication which he addressed to Mirò, on the 18th of April, 1789, he said, "With regard to Frankland, Don Diego Gardoqui gave me letters for the chief men of that district, with instructions to assure them that, if they wished to put themselves under the protection of Spain and favor her interests, they should be protected in their civil and political government, in the form and manner most agreeable to them, on the following conditions:

"1º—It should be absolutely necessary, not only in order to hold any office, but also any land in Frankland, that an oath of allegiance be taken to his Majesty, the object and purport of which should be to defend his government and faithful vassals on all occasions, and against all his enemies, whoever they might be. 2º—That the inhabitants of that district should renounce all submission or allegiance whatever to any other Sovereign or power. They have eagerly accepted these conditions, and the Spanish minister has referred me to your favor, patronage and assistance to facilitate my operations. With regard to Cumberland, what I have said of Frankland applies to it with equal force and truth."

On the 22d of the same month, White again wrote to Mirò, saying: "M. Gardoqui has informed me that,[*] considering I was in the service of Spain, my expenses would be paid out of the royal treasury." He concludes with asking about four hundred dollars,[†] to facilitate his dealing decently and commodiously with those he was to influence. This sum was immediately granted.

Mirò, in answer[‡] to White's application, delivered to him a paper beginning with this preamble: "Considering the representation of James White in favor of the districts of Frankland and Mirò, formerly Cumberland, in whose welfare he has manifested much interest, I authorize him to make known what his Catholic Majesty, moved by no other motive than that of generosity, is disposed to do for the inhabitants of the said districts." This document contained an enumeration of the favors and advantages to be granted to such as would emigrate to

---

[*] M. Gardoqui me aseguró que siendo mi servicio conexo con el de S. M. su tesoro me satisfaria los gastos.

[†] Requirirá como quatro cientos pesos para facilitarme el tratar con aquellos gentes comoda y decentemente.

[‡] Mirò's communication to White, on the 20th of April, 1789.

Louisiana, and of the conditions annexed to them. It further conceded to the people of Frankland and Cumberland the privilege to carry their produce down the Mississippi to the market of New Orleans, provided they should pay a per centage of 15 per cent., which Miró reserved himself the right of reducing as he might please, on behalf of such men of influence among them as might solicit that favor and be made known to him by White.

"But," said he, "with regard to the proposition of that gentleman (James White) in relation to the wish expressed by the inhabitants of Cumberland and Frankland to connect themselves with Spain after their separation from the United States, I can neither assist, nor foment such a scheme, on account of the good harmony which exists between his Catholic Majesty and the United States. Nevertheless, it is for the inhabitants of the aforesaid districts to seek after what suits them best, and, should they succeed in securing for themselves a complete independence from the United States, then his Majesty would grant them, out of his royal beneficence, all the favor, help, and advantages which might be adapted to their condition, and compatible with the interests of the Spanish monarchy." This passage is another proof of the aversion which Miró felt, either from jealousy, or from prudence, and perhaps from both, to permit Gardoqui and his agents to take any share in the intrigues which, with Wilkinson, he was carrying on, to detach the Great West from the rest of the Union.

On the 23d, he wrote to the General: "My esteemed friend—I thought of writing to you at full length through Major Dunn, but his return having taken place sooner than I expected, I could not write as I wished, for want of time; because, although working from seven in the morning until dinner time, and from five o'clock in the afternoon until eleven o'clock at night, I cannot discharge all the official duties which have accumulated on my hands, &c."* In this letter, he earnestly recommends Wilkinson to favor emigration, particularly of families having good morals and some property. "Notwithstanding the press of time," says he, "I must communicate to you a new circumstance in our affairs, but it is necessary that your lips be for ever sealed as to the names of the individuals I shall make known to you, in order that the confidence I thus repose in you shall never turn out to be prejudicial to them, and at the same time I assure you, most positively, that I have not unfolded to anybody our relations, nor have I ever mentioned you, although I was compelled to speak of the state of things in Kentucky.

"Don Diego Gardoqui drew to the interests of Spain James White, a member of Congress, who has possessions in the district of Mirò, formerly Cumberland, and sent him to the State of Frankland, in order to incite its inhabitants to separate themselves from the United States and to form an alliance with us. Having returned to New York, he informed Gardoqui that the affair was progressing favorably, that the principal inhabitants were ripe for a separation, and that, after having effected it, they would swear allegiance to Spain, obligating themselves to form no alliance or connection whatever with any other power, and to take up arms for the defence of the province of Louisiana from whatever quarter be the attack, and only reserving the privilege of governing themselves."

Mirò then informed Wilkinson that he had authorized White to proceed immediately to the districts of Mirò and Frankland, in order to communicate to the inhabitants the document which I have already quoted.

---

* He had then to fulfil the functions both of Governor and Intendant united in one person.

"I have just received," continued he, "two letters, one from Brigadier General Daniel Smith, dated on the 4th of March, and the other from Colonel James Robertson, with date of the 11th of January, both written from the district of Miró. The first letter was carried by a militia officer, named Fagot, a confidential agent of General Smith, and informed me that the inhabitants of Cumberland, or Miró, would, in September, send delegates to North Carolina, in order to solicit from the legislature of that State an act of separation, and that, as soon as this should be obtained, other delegates would be sent from Cumberland to New Orleans with the object of placing that territory under the domination of his Majesty.*

"I have replied to both in general terms, referring them to my answer to White, who carries my letters to these gentlemen.

"You see, by the tone of this confidential communication, that I still continue to hold you as the principal actor in our favor, and therefore I hope that, gathering all the information which you may deem necessary, you will give me your opinion on this affair, and all the explanations which may throw light on it, in order that I may shape my course accordingly. I wish also to hear what you have to say as to the importance of those districts, which I do not think of much consequence, although I could not help acting as I have, the said White having been sent to me by Don Diego Gardoqui. It is proper that you be made acquainted with all this affair in case it should be deemed useful to induce those aforementioned districts to act in concert with Kentucky when that province shall have achieved her separation from the United States.

---

* Se nombrarán otros dirigidos á esta capital con el objeto de entregarse bajo el dominio de S. M.

"I am waiting with the greatest anxiety for your letters, in order to know what has occurred since your last, and God grant that I may, in a short time, embrace you as the delegate from that State. Command your most affectionate friend, &c."

The next day, Miró wrote to General Daniel Smith in vague terms, referring him for particulars to White. "The giving of my name to your district," said he, "has caused me much satisfaction, and I feel myself highly honored by that compliment. It increases my desire to contribute to the development of the resources of that province and the prosperity of its inhabitants, &c., &c.

"I am extremely flattered at your proposition to enter into a correspondence with me, and I hope that it will afford me the opportunity of being agreeable to you."

On the 30th of April, Governor Miró sent to Antonio Valdès, one of the Spanish ministers, a detailed account of all that I have related, and spoke rather slightingly of the pretended services rendered by White under the direction of Gardoqui. "The inhabitants of Frankland," said he, "had already thrown off the mask before White's arrival among them, and would most certainly, as is proved by John Sevier's letters, have had recourse to me, without the interference of the doctor. In that same State of Frankland, opinions are divided in such a way, that part of the inhabitants (I do not know whether it is the majority) wish to remain subjected to Congress and to North Carolina. Therefore I consider that, to meddle with them, cannot be of much advantage to us. Nevertheless, we must not reject their advances.

"The answer which I have given to White, and which he is to show to the principal men of Miró and Frankland, is so framed, that, should it miscarry, it will afford no cause of complaint to the United States; but verbally, I have energetically recommended to him to use the most strenuous efforts to procure the desired separation. Mirò concludes with asking for the approbation of his Majesty in relation to all he had done, and urgently solicits instructions as to his course of action, on the emergency of the arrival of delegates from the discontented districts.

On the 20th of May, Mirò addressed to his government a long despatch, in which he commented on the impolicy of the conditions and extent of the concession of land made by Gardoqui to Colonel Morgan, a little below the mouth of the Ohio. One of the conditions was, that the emigrants to that region should have the right of self-government. Mirò called the attention of the cabinet of Madrid to the danger of thus having an *imperium in imperio*, a government within a government, and pointed out the results which would inevitably flow from such a state of things. "Experience has demonstrated," said he, "that, in this province, large concessions of land to an individual have never produced the desired effect of procuring population," &c. &c. He then goes on complaining of the ambiguity with which Gardoqui had written to him on the circumstances attending the plan of colonization entertained by Colonel Morgan, who had come to New Orleans to carry it into execution, with the expected approbation and concurrence of the Governor of Louisiana.

Three days after (on the 23d of May), Mirò wrote to Morgan, that great had been his surprise, on reading the papers submitted to him; that the extent of territory conceded was much larger, and that the favors and privileges attached to the grant were much more exorbitant, than he had been informed. He declared them completely inadmissible, and enumerated the conditions on which he, Mirò, would allow Morgan to establish his contemplated colony. "You see," said he, "how different they are from those you have proposed, and, truly it is to me a matter of deep regret, because, having been made acquainted with the fine qualities for which you are distinguished, I was awaiting your arrival with impatience, and with the hope of being able to approve your plan. I am therefore much disappointed at being obliged to resist its execution, because it would be extremely prejudicial to the welfare and interest of the kingdom to permit the establishment of a republic within its domains; for as such I consider the government which you have conceived, although retaining some shadow of submission to his Majesty.

"I also infinitely regret, that you have gone so far as to cause to be circulated through the whole population of the Ohio and Kentucky districts the report that so extensive a territory had been granted to you, and that, under the impression that such a grant was final and valid, you have drawn the plan of a city, and given it a name (which is the exercise of a power appertaining to the sovereign alone), and, what is worse, that you have called it *our city*, in your letter to certain gentlemen at Fort Pitt, whilst Don Diego Gardoqui authorized you to do no more than survey the lands. How wide a difference is there between what you did and what you had a right to do!" Assuming, however, a gentler tone, Miró told Morgan that he attributed the imprudence of his acts to an excess of zeal to serve the King; that he authorized him, should he be disposed to continue his services to his Majesty, to induce as many families as possible to come and settle in Louisiana, and particularly in the Natchez district, but only under the conditions that he had made known to him; and that, should he, Morgan, be successful in that operation, the king would reward him in a befitting manner. Miró further promised him a concession of one thousand acres of land for himself, and the same quantity for every one of his sons Morgan was also informed that a fort would be constructed by the Spaniards at the place which he had chosen for the town of New Madrid, that a detachment of soldiers would soon be sent there, and that its commander would be instructed to receive favorably all the emigrants that should present themselves.

The next day, Morgan sent to Miró a reply, in which he apologized for the course he had pursued. He said that, if he had erred, it was with the best intentions and from sheer ignorance, and he thanked the Governor for attributing what he had done to its true motive—an excessive zeal to serve his Majesty. "As I have always kept up the character of a man of honor," said he, "I am sure you will remain convinced that I shall never act, knowingly, in violation of the laws and will of his Majesty.

"Among the inducements which I have to leave my native country, must be ranked the desire of increasing my fortune, and establishing my family in peace, under a safe and secure government. If you have occasionally read the acts of Congress, you may have seen that my father-in-law Baynton, myself and my partners were unjustly dispossessed by the State of Virginia of the largest territorial estate within its limits, and that it was not in the power of Congress to protect us, although that honorable body manifested the best disposition to do so. These circumstances, and the wish to recommend myself to the kind notice of the King, prompted me to my last undertaking, and I am now disposed to accept the conditions which you do me the honor of proposing, under the hope of acquiring one day the favor of his Majesty."

On the 12th of June, Miró informed his government of all his transactions, and observed that, had he acqui-

ceed in Morgan's plan of colonization, an independent republic would soon have been formed in Louisiana by the new settlers, and the provinces of New Spain endangered. "On such conditions," said he, "I would myself undertake to depopulate the greater part of the United States, and draw all their citizens to Louisiana, including the whole Congress itself. Already has Thomas Hutchins, their surveyor-general and principal geographer, written to Daniel Clark, a merchant and resident of this town, begging to be informed whether Morgan's propositions were accepted by me, because, disregarding the office and the salary he now enjoys, he would become the subject of his Catholic Majesty, being under the impression, as he declares, that New Jersey, with the districts of Fort Pitt and of Kentucky, would be deprived by emigration of their best inhabitants.

"The circumstance of their governing themselves, whilst the King should pay their magistrates, would attract here a prodigious multitude of people, but they would never imbibe any affection for our government, or for Spanish customs, and, on the slightest dispute in relation to the jurisdiction exercised over them by the Governor of Louisiana, they would declare themselves independent, and, what is worse, having the free use of their respective religions, they never would become catholics. * * * * *
* * * * * *

"As it is probable that, towards the end of the year, there shall arrive a considerable number of emigrants at the projected establishment of New Madrid, and, as it might be prejudicial to allow them to settle there by themselves, without any control, and in order to do away with the idea which they may have of governing themselves, I have resolved to construct a fort at that place, so that a multitude of new-comers be not abandoned to their own caprice and their own resources without protection and without the administration of justice."

In conformity with the intention manifested in this letter, Governor Miró, in the month of July, sent Pierre Foucher, a lieutenant of the regiment of Louisiana, with two sergeants, two corporals and thirty soldiers, to build a fort at New Madrid, and to take the civil and military command of that district. His instructions were *to govern those new colonists in such a way as to make them feel that they had found among the Spaniards the state of ease and comfort of which they were in quest.*

Miró's diplomacy and administration of Louisiana had been thought worthy of a reward, and in the month of May, he had been informed that he had been promoted to the grade of brigadier-general. He had immediately returned his thanks for that favor, and, in that despatch, commenting on the military resources of the colony, he had observed that the regiment of Louisiana, which ought to have been two thousand strong according to the royal ordinance, did not muster more than 1,258 men.

In the month of July, he communicated to his government certain propositions made by Colonel Morgan for the cultivation of flax and hemp, and he recommended that the whole quantity which Morgan should be able to raise be purchased on account of the royal treasury. He also sent at the same time a memorial from William Butler, in which this gentleman proposed to conduct to Louisiana forty-six families of emigrants, well provided for, on condition that he be permitted to import one hundred thousand dollars' worth of merchandise.

In the beginning of this year, 1789, Louisiana had learned that she had passed under the sceptre of another monarch. The benevolent and wise Charles III. had died on the 14th of December, 1788, and had been succeeded by his son Charles IV. On the 7th of May, the usual funeral rites were performed in New Orleans in honor of departed royalty, with as much pomp and solemnity as the finances of the colony could afford On the 8th, the conventional grief of the preceding day was forgotten, and the whole city wore an aspect of joy equally as sincere. The new Sovereign was proclaimed in due form, amidst repeated discharges of artillery and musketry; the ships in the harbor paraded their gayest colors; a great review of the troops took place, with the ordinary enlivening music of military instruments; the authorities dined in state, and toasted the new King's health; the people, to whom theatrical exhibitions were given at the cost of the government, shouted to the top of their lungs, and the whole city was illuminated at night. Never was rejoicing more ill-timed, since the man who had ascended the throne, and to whose care were to be committed the destinies of one of the most extensive and glorious kingdoms of the world, was perhaps one of the weakest in intellect among his fellow beings.

It appears that, soon after the death of Charles III., who was far from being a bigoted king, an attempt was made to introduce the much dreaded tribunal of the Inquisition into the colony. The reverend Capuchin, Antonio de Sedella, who had lately arrived in the province, wrote to the Governor to inform him that he, the holy father, had been appointed Commissary of the Inquisition; that in a letter of the 5th of December last, from the proper authority, this intelligence had been communicated to him, and that he had been requested to discharge his functions with the most exact fidelity and zeal, and in conformity with the royal will. Wherefore, after having made his investigations with the utmost secrecy and precaution,* he notified Miró that, in order to carry, as he was commanded, his instructions into perfect execution in all their parts, he might soon, at some late hour of the night, deem it necessary to require some guards to assist him in his operations.

Not many hours had elapsed since the reception of this communication by the Governor, when night came, and the representative of the Holy Inquisition was quietly reposing in bed, when he was roused from his sleep by a heavy knocking. He started up, and, opening his door, saw standing before him an officer and a file of grenadiers. Thinking that they had come to obey his commands, in consequence of his letter to the Governor, he said: "My friends, I thank you and his Excellency for the readiness of this compliance with my request. But I have now no use for your services, and you shall be warned in time when you are wanted. Retire then, with the blessing of God." Great was the stupefaction of the Friar when he was told that he was under arrest. "What!" exclaimed he, "will you dare lay your hands on a Commissary of the Holy Inquisition?"—"I dare obey orders," replied the undaunted officer, and the Reverend Father Antonio de Sedella was instantly carried on board of a vessel, which sailed the next day for Cadiz.

Rendering an account of this incident to one of the members of the Cabinet of Madrid, Governor Miró said in a despatch of the 3d of June :† "When I read the communication of that Capuchin, I shuddered. His Majesty has ordered me to foster the increase of population in this province, and to admit in it all those that would emigrate from the banks of those rivers which empty themselves into the Ohio. This course was

---

* Sigilo y cautela.

† Al leer el oficio del dicho capuchino me estremecí.—Miró's Despatch.

recommended by me, for the powerful reasons which I have given in confidential despatches to the most excellent Don Antonio Valdès, and which your Excellency must have seen among the papers laid before the Supreme Council of State. This emigration was to be encouraged under the pledge, that the new colonists should not be molested in matters of religion, provided there should be no other public mode of worship than the Catholic. The mere name of the Inquisition uttered in New Orleans would be sufficient, not only to check immigration, which is successfully progressing, but would also be capable of driving away those who have recently come, and I even fear that, in spite of my having sent out of the country Father Sedella, the most fatal consequences may ensue from the mere suspicion of the cause of his dismissal." Considering the dread in which the holy tribunal of the Inquisition had always been held in Spain, the energy with which Miró acted on this occasion cannot be too much admired.

In the same despatch, Miró informed his government of the laying of the first brick for the foundation of the cathedral which the munificence of Don Andres Almonaster intended to erect for the town, at the estimated cost of $50,000. This building, when completed, became the tomb of its founder on his death, which happened not long after. Although this monumental and venerable relic of the past was pulled down, in 1850, in the mere wantonness of vandalism, to make room for the upstart production of bad taste, yet the stone which covered the mortal remains of the pious founder of the destroyed temple has at least been respected, and still retains his coat of arms and proud motto:

<pre>
         A pesar de todos
         Venceremos á los Godos.
</pre>

* * * * *

> In spite of all
> We will conquer the Goths.

In this year, 1789, a powerful company, composed of Alex. Moultrie, Isaac Huger, Major William Snipes, Colonel Washington and other distinguished gentlemen, had formed itself at Charleston, South Carolina, and had purchased from the State of Georgia an immense territory, including, it is said, at least 52,900 square miles, and extending from the Yazoo to the neighborhood of Natchez on the banks of the Mississippi. This territory was partly claimed by the Choctaws, the Chickasaws, and Spain. On the 1st of October, the gentlemen whom I have named wrote to Captain Cape, one of their agents and associates, not to lose one minute, and, in concert with Colonel Holder, to take possession of the land, in virtue of their contract with Georgia. "The main thing which remains to be done," said they, "to complete the transaction, is to form a settlement." On the same day, they also wrote to Colonel Holder in Kentucky: "We can inform you with much satisfaction, that there is not the slightest obstacle in the way of the affair in which you are a partner, and that everything is already settled with our sister State of Georgia and with all parties concerned here.* But we are all convinced that there remains yet a very essential thing to be done without delay, and which would have the most important results in the future, if executed promptly—that is, *to take possession of, and settle the land at once.* Therefore we most earnestly entreat you, our good friend, not to postpone this operation for an instant, and to come down as soon as possible with your complement of emigrants, and form the establishment as agreed upon. Our title and right are already secured, but should you promptly effect

---

* All these documents are retranslated from a Spanish translation.

a settlement, we could show the world that our plan has been put in execution, by which means we could carry on several operations which would marvellously increase your profits in this speculation, as well as greatly benefit all our associates, who must remain in a state of inaction as long as we do not form a settlement. * *
* * * * * * *

"I do not doubt but that you will lose no time in writing to our friends of the Choctaw nation, in order to inform them of your having to be their neighbor and ally, as well as the friend of all the Indians, whose attachment to us shall, we dare say, be cultivated and fostered by all possible means, as being essential to our interests and pacific views.

"With regard to our friends the Spaniards, we hope that you will, without delay, communicate to them your departure, and our firm intention to cultivate and even to court their friendship as much as possible, giving them with sincerity all the information they may desire on any subject, because it is neither our interest nor our wish to deceive them, as we consider their interests and ours as intimately connected and inseparable. We desire being useful to them, and we hope that, in return, they will be to us what we shall be to them. When nations are mutually and reciprocally bound together by the same interests, their alliance is maintained by the strongest ties, and their motives and views can never disagree. We confidently flatter ourselves that we shall form a highly advantageous rampart for Spain, and that we shall ourselves feel that it is our interest that such should be the case. * * * * *
* * * * * * *

"At all events, take possession, exhibit this letter and even our contract to the Spaniards, and conceal nothing from them."

18

On the 4th of January, 1790, Wilkinson, to whom all this affair had been communicated, with a view, no doubt, to secure his assistance, wrote to Messrs. Moultrie, Huger, Snipes, and Washington, with his usual characteristic keenness, and begged leave, after a long preamble on his disinterestedness and the honesty of his intentions, to make, as he observed, a few trifling observations on the measures they had adopted, and to suggest the preliminary dispositions which would be indispensably necessary to secure the complete accomplishment of their plans. Alluding to the letters which I have quoted, and which were exhibited to him by Captain Cape, he said that they appeared to be of so extraordinary a nature, that he remarked to that gentleman that he would not hesitate to pronounce them forgeries, if the proofs of their authenticity were not so strong.* He further informed Messrs. Huger, Washington, Snipes, and Moultrie, that, on his last trip to New Orleans, he had had a frank and free intercourse with Governor Miró; that he had discussed with that Spanish functionary the whole affair, and had finally ascertained what was the sole basis on which a settlement might be formed in that latitude, &c."†

* * * * * *

"It is a stupendous enterprise," wrote Wilkinson, "well worthy of the attention it has attracted, and if it be successfully executed, it will procure immense wealth for the interested parties. But there are difficulties to conquer, which are proportioned to the importance and magnitude of the object. The foundations on which this enterprise must necessarily rest, are *active funds*, and the agencies of several gentlemen of the best education and

---

* Despues de leer las expresadas cartas fué, que si estas no tenian fuertes pruebas de autenticidad, desde luego las pronunciaba por falsas.

† Y en fin quedé instruido del solo plan sobre que podia formarse un **estable** cimiento en estos **parajes**.

manners, as well as gifted with political sagacity and with those talents which secure popularity. It is impossible that, under present circumstances, you should effect your establishment before next autumn. In the meantime, a gentleman of distinction, and clothed with full powers, ought to be sent to New Orleans to negotiate for the company, and to secure to them the good will and services of Governor Mirò, without which you may abandon your project as being totally impracticable. Should you gain the friendship of that officer, his influence would facilitate your negotiations with the Choctaws, to occupy and possess peaceably the desired ground, &c.

* * * * * *

"Whatever be the reception you may give to this letter, I know that my duty is to undeceive you with regard to the presumed concession which Mr. Woods pretends to have from the Choctaws. Believe me, gentlemen, when I tell you that his title is not worth a pinch of snuff. I hate all deceit, and hence the information which I impart to you. Nevertheless, permit me to observe, that you must take care to give no cause of jealous complaints to those individuals who have possessed themselves of your confidence in this affair. An offended friend becomes the worst of enemies, and an active enemy, however obscure he may be, can obstruct the best conceived designs.

"After these observations, gentlemen, it only remains for me to say that I desire to co-operate with you as your agent," &c., &c.

Whilst Wilkinson was thus eager to embark in this new scheme, his agents in Kentucky for his other designs were pressing him for money. On the 5th of January, Sebastian was addressing him in the following strain: "As my attention to this affair takes up the greater portion of my time, and prevents me from following any other pursuit, I certainly hope to obtain from the Spanish government at least some indemnification, if not a generous reward for my services. On principle, I am as much attached to the interests of Louisiana as any one of the subjects of his Catholic Majesty. But you know that my circumstances do not permit me to engage in his service and to abandon every other occupation, without the prospect of remuneration." This letter was immediately communicated by Wilkinson to Miró, to whom he submitted also all the documents he had procured concerning the enterprise of Moultrie and his associates. In connexion with this subject, he wrote from Lexington to the Spanish Governor, on the 20th of January: "The documents No. 1, 2, 3, will inform you of the purchase which a company, composed of distinguished men, has made from the State of Georgia, of a vast territory contiguous to the Mississippi. Mr. Cape, to whom I have loaned three thousand dollars, is consequently in my dependence. Holder, on account of his being under my protection, cannot do any harm, and both are insignificant creatures. Turning this affair over in my mind, I became apprehensive lest it should become prejudicial to our other plans, and, after mature reflection, I determined to address Messrs. Moultrie, Huger, and Snipes, who are gentlemen of rank and fortune (as you will see per Doc. No. 4), with a view to obtain the agency of that affair, and to induce the Company to sue for your protection. If I succeed, I am persuaded that I shall experience no difficulty in adding their establishment to the domains of his Majesty, and this they will soon discover to be their interest. I hope that the step I have taken will meet your approbation. It would have been necessary to do a little more, but I had no time to consult you and ascertain your opinion. This is the reason for which I have undertaken to place in your hands the whole control of this affair. You will have the opportunity to modify the plan of the Company as your judgment and prudence will suggest, and the interest of the King may require. I will keep you well informed of every movement which I shall observe, and it will be completely in your power to break up the projected settlement, by inciting the Choctaws to incommode the colonists, who will thus be forced to move off and to establish themselves under your government."

Six days after, Wilkinson wrote to Miró in a less flattering tone. It seems that clouds had arisen and obscured the sun of their hopes. "The general permission," said he, in a despatch of the 26th, "to export the products of this country through the Mississippi river, on paying a duty of 15 per cent., has worked the consequences which I feared, because, every motive of discontent having thus been removed, the political agitation has subsided, and to-day there is not one word said about separation. Nor are the effects produced by this pernicious system less fatal in relation to our plan of fostering emigration to Louisiana. Every year, the inhabitants and landholders of these parts had ever present to their minds the terrible prospect of seeing their produce perish in their hands for want of a market, but now they no longer have any such apprehensions on account of the ready outlet they find at New Orleans for the fruits of their labor—which circumstance has diffused universal satisfaction in this district, &c. * *

* * * * * *

"The pruriency of emigration has been soothed and allayed by the spirit of trade which engrosses general attention, and there are many, at this very moment, who are preparing cargoes for New Orleans, and who, under the pretext of settling in Louisiana, will procure to elude the payment of the aforesaid duty. I will not dismiss this subject without assuring you, that I make incessant efforts to accomplish the views of his Majesty, and, although I have to conquer immense difficulties, yet I flatter myself that, if you confine the privilege of the present free commerce to those who will readily and really emigrate, I shall be able to effect a strong settlement at the Walnut Hills, &c., &c. * *

* * * * * * *

"On my arrival here, I discovered a great change in those who had been so far our warmest friends. Many, who loudly repudiated all connection with the Union, now remain silent. I attribute this, either to the hope of promotion, or to the fear of punishment. According to my prognostic, Washington has begun to operate on the chief heads of this district. Innis has been appointed a federal judge with an annual salary of one thousand dollars; George Nicholas, district attorney; Samuel McDowell, son of the president of the Convention, and Marshall, have been appointed to offices somewhat resembling that of Alguazil Mayor; and Payton Short, the brother of our chargé d'affaires at Versailles, is made a custom-house officer. But he has resigned, and probably will visit you in the spring. I do not place much reliance on George Nicholas and Samuel McDowell. But I know that Harry Innis is friendly to Spain and hostile to Congress, and I am authorized to say that he would much prefer receiving a pension from New Orleans than from New York. Should the King approve our design on this point, it will have to be broached with much delicacy, caution and judgment, &c. * *

* * * * * * *

"And I fear that we can rely on a few only of my countrymen, if we cannot make use of liberal donations, &c

* * * * * * *

"I know that Colonel Morgan happens now to be in New Jersey, where I believe that he is awaiting the results of the promises of Don Diego Gardoqui. Doing justice to the Colonel,* I must inform you that he is for ever the friend of Spain, and the advocate of our plans But I fear that, owing to peculiar embarrassments of his own, he will not be able to effect his settlement at *L'Anse à la Graisse* (New Madrid) as promptly as he hopes. He is as badly treated as I am by the dependents of General Washington and by the friends of Congress. I see that all those who are put in office are the enemies of Spain, and that all the friends of Congress are hostile to me, because I openly praise the former, and publicly blame the latter. All those who go down the Mississippi as traders are my enemies, because they envy my position, and the favor and protection which you grant me. But you may rest assured that the constant persecution of Congress cannot produce the slightest impression on my attachment and zeal for the interests of Spain, which I shall always be ready to defend with my tongue, my pen, and my sword."†

Relatively to the Convention which, he said, was to meet in Kentucky in June next, and the members of which were to be elected in May, he expressed himself as follows: "I will pay strict attention to its proceedings, and I will present myself to that assembly, with the intention of doing all that may be in my power, to promote the interest of our cause, in which I shall be warmly assisted by our good friend Sebastian, who is now my principal aid, because, although Harry Innis is also our

---

* Wilkinson is here in direct contradiction with himself, see p. 245. But he may have had reasons to change his sentiments and language.

† Pero puede Vs. vivir convencido que el universal maltrato del congreso no puede hacer la menor impression en el amor y zelo que tengo por los intereses de la España que estaré siempre pronto á defender con mi lengua, pluma y espada.

friend, yet the office which he holds renders it improper for him to work openly. At present, all our politicians seem to have fallen asleep. Buoyed up by the privilege of trade which has been granted to them on the Mississippi, the people think of nothing else than cultivating their lands and increasing their plantations. In such circumstances it is impossible that I should, with any chance of success, press upon them the important question which I had proposed to myself on my arrival here.

"I am justified in saying that Congress strongly suspects my connection with you, and that it spies my movements in this section of the country. Consequently, an avowed intention on my part to induce these people here to separate from the Union, before the majority of them show a disposition to support me, would endanger my personal security, and would deprive me of the opportunity of serving you in these parts. My situation is mortally painful, because, whilst I abhor all duplicity, I am obliged to dissemble. This makes me extremely desirous of resorting to some contrivance that will put me in a position, in which I flatter myself to be able to profess myself publicly the vassal of his Catholic Majesty, and therefore to claim his protection, in whatever public or private measures I may devise to promote the interest of the Crown."

The change to which Wilkinson alludes in this communication is to be attributed to the confidence inspired to all by the wise and firm administration of Washington, who had been installed into office on the 4th of March, 1789, as first President of the United States, under that new Constitution which had just been framed by the people thereof, "to form a more perfect union, establish justice, insure domestic tranquillity, provide for the common defence, promote the general welfare, and secure the blessings of liberty to themselves and their posterity," and which was beginning to accomplish these objects.

It appears that the emigrants whom Colonel Morgan had attracted to L'Anse à la Graisse, or New Madrid, had not long remained satisfied with their leader, for they had sent John Ward to New Orleans as their delegate, to present to Miró* a memorial signed by them, and in which they complained of the state of complete anarchy in which they lived, and of the exactions of Colonel Morgan. "We also beg you," they said, "to permit us to remark, that the method adopted for settling this district is very prejudicial to the interests of the King, and also to those of the inhabitants of New Madrid, his subjects. Therefore, we conclude with assuring you, that if we cannot obtain satisfaction with regard to what we represent to you through Mr. Ward, our agent, we shall be obliged, relying on our right and the just support of our friends, to abandon a country and a climate with which we are highly pleased."

On the 27th of February, Alex. Moultrie replied to Wilkinson's letter of the 4th of January, accepting with many compliments the offer of his services, and entreating him to use his best efforts in order to accelerate and perfect the great enterprise of the South Carolina Company, but informing him that the agency of the company could no longer be disposed of, as it had been some time ago granted to Dr. O'Fallon, who was the bearer of Moultrie's letter to Wilkinson. But it is evident from a communication addressed by Miró to Wilkinson, on the 30th of April, that this gentleman could not do much for the South Carolina speculators who had applied to him. " I return to you many thanks," said Miró, " for the letter you have written to Messrs. Moultrie, Snipes, Huger, and

* Miró's despatch of the 27th of January, 1790.

Washington, although you have rendered them a greater service than to me, by the wholesome advice which you have administered to them. It would be exceedingly painful to me to march with arms in my hands against citizens of the United States, with which my court frequently recommends me to keep on the best terms of harmony and friendship. But, in order to avoid, once for all, every cause of trouble and misunderstanding on this subject, I beg you to communicate to these gentlemen my following declarations:

"1º—Spain is in possession of all that she conquered from Great Britain in the last war, and consequently, of the territory which these gentlemen have obtained from the State of Georgia, and therefore, so long as the question of limits shall not be settled, every attempt to seize on any portion of the land to which we have a previous right of possession, will be an act of hostility which we must resist.

"2º—The concession of land from the Choctaws and Chickasaws founded on the treaty of Hopewell and Seneca, in 1786, is a chimera." Miró then goes on saying, that the chiefs themselves who had signed that treaty had signified to the American Commissioners that they had no such powers, and had furthermore declared, that it was only after having been made drunk, that they had put their seals to it. He also informs Wilkinson that the Choctaws had proclaimed, that they would not permit the Americans even *to walk over their lands*, because they were afraid of their being gradually usurped by the well-known rapacity of those intruders. The tone of this letter is very different from the affectionate style in which Miró usually addressed Wilkinson, and indicates that he resented Wilkinson's letter of the 26th of January, in which he was informed of the change which had occurred in the feelings of the people of Kentucky, and of the almost undoubted destruction of all his hopes and plans.

In a second despatch to Wilkinson, dated on the same day (30th of April), Miró comments on the reasons given by that gentleman, to account for the revulsion of sentiments which was described to have taken place among the Western people. "Your countrymen," said he, "will soon find out that the advantages they expect from the navigation of the Mississippi, on their paying an import duty of 15 per cent. when entering Louisiana, and an export duty of 6 per cent. when leaving it, amount to nothing. So far, tobacco has been the only produce of any importance which they have brought to New Orleans, and which the king has reserved to himself the privilege of buying. Should he not choose to do so, on the ground that the article wanted is not furnished in sufficient quantity, or is not of the quality required, it would remain a dead weight in the hands of the owner. Several individuals, who are now here, have discovered this to be the case. With regard to your supposition that they will elude paying the duty of 15 per cent. under the pretext of coming to settle in Louisiana, it is without any sort of foundation whatever, and you may rest assured that I shall take care that the law be executed on that point." He then enumerated in detail the preventive measures which he had imagined, more effectually to defeat the anticipated fraud.

"I therefore confidently hope," continued he, "that, with your characteristic perseverance, making use of the information which I give you, and which will be confirmed by your countrymen on their return, you will be able to revive our political designs, by sowing broad-cast, and causing to germinate among your people, such ideas as will seem to you best calculated to establish the conviction, that the welfare of the inhabitants of Kentucky depends, either on their forming a close and strong connection with Spain, or on their seeking to better their fortune by becoming denizens of Louisiana."

With regard to that passage in Wilkinson's letter in which he said that he had become an object of suspicion to his government, and that his situation was mortally painful, because, whilst abhorring duplicity, he was obliged to dissemble, wherefore he was seeking for the occasion of professing himself publicly the vassal of his Catholic Majesty, in order to claim his protection in whatever public or private measures he might devise to promote the interests of the crown, Miró replied :* "I much regret that General Washington and Congress suspect your connection with me, but it does not appear to me opportune that you declare yourself a Spaniard, for the reasons which you state. I am of opinion that this idea of yours is not convenient, and that, on the contrary, it might have prejudicial results. Therefore, continue to dissemble and to work as you promise, and as I have above indicated." In this letter, all the caressing epithets and other expressions so plentifully used, on other occasions, are dropped, and the words, *my dearest friend,* or any other approaching their meaning, are studiously excluded, and Miró's despatch terminates merely with the commonplace salutation so familiar in Spanish phraseology : "Dios guarde a Vs. muchos años." "God preserve you many years."

In travelling over these historical grounds, here have we come to a point from which a rich scene of practical morality is displayed before us. "You may rest assured," had written Wilkinson, "that the constant persecution

---

* Siento mucho se desconfie el general Washington y el Congreso, de la conexion di Vs. conmigo; pero no me parece oportuno que Vs. se declare Español a fin de que nuestra corte pueda sostenerle. Soy de parecer que esta idea no puede ser conveniente, y que al contrario podria acarrear prejudiciales resultas. Disimule Vs. pues, y trabaje como promete y arriba le indico.

of Congress cannot produce the slightest impression on my attachment and zeal for the interests of Spain, which I shall always be ready to defend with my tongue, my pen, and my sword." So far, so good, and "Thank you, dearest friend," had replied Spanish interest. "But I am anxious to become a Spaniard on the first opportunity that shall present itself," said Wilkinson, proceeding a step further.—"You! a Spaniard, Sir! Oh, no! that cannot be. Continue to dissemble, and to work under ground, as you are bound to do. Retain your American tongue, your American pen, and your American sword. You can serve us better in that guise." Thus spoke Spanish pride and Spanish honor. Is there on record a more striking specimen of withering contempt?

On the 22d of May, Mirò wrote to the minister, Don Antonio Valdès, to render him an account of his last transactions and correspondence with Wilkinson. "Although," said he, "I thought with Wilkinson that the commercial concessions made to the Western people might deter them from effecting their separation from the United States, because I supposed they would prefer losing the defalcation produced in the value of their crop by the payment of the duty of fifteen per cent., to running all the risks of a revolution, yet I never imagined that the effects would be so sudden, and that the large number of influential men, whom Wilkinson, in his previous letters, had mentioned as having been gained over to our party, would have entirely vanished, as he now announces it, since he affirms having no other aid at present than Sebastian.

"I consider that I am exposed to err in expressing an opinion on the acts of a man, who works at six hundred leagues from this place, and who has undoubtedly rendered, and is still rendering services to his Majesty, as I have explained it in my other despatches. But the

great falling off which I observe in his last letter induces me to believe that, full of good will and zeal, and persuaded, from the experience of past years, that he could bring round to his own opinions the chief men of Kentucky, he declared in anticipation that he had won over many of them, when he had never approached them on the main question, and that, encountering, at this time, instead of facilities, invincible obstacles, and, above all, personal risks should he declare himself, he has availed himself of the motive which he puts forth, to cover his precipitation, &c. &c.   *   *   *   *
   *   *   *   *   *   *   *

"Nevertheless, I am of opinion that said brigadier-general ought to be retained in the service of his Majesty, with an annual pension of two thousand dollars, which I have already proposed in my confidential despatch No. 46, because the inhabitants of Kentucky, and of the other establishments on the Ohio, will not be able to undertake anything against this province, without his communicating it to us, and without his making at the same time all possible efforts to dissuade them from any bad designs against us, as he has already done repeatedly."

Miró concludes his letter with recommending that a pension be granted to Sebastian, "because I think it proper," said he, "to treat with this individual, who will be able to enlighten me on the conduct of Wilkinson, and on what we have to expect from the plans of the said brigadier-general."*

Thus every thing was done according to the most approved rules laid down in the code of corruption: "set a thief to catch a thief, and a spy after another

---

* Por que creo muy conveniente el tratar con este individual que podrá aclararme mucho la conducta del expresado brigadier y lo que se puede esperar de sus proyectos.

spy." Thus Wilkinson was employed to watch the Kentuckians, and Sebastian to betray his confederate Wilkinson. Not a link wanting in the chain of infamy.

In a second despatch of the 22d of May, Mirò communicates to the same minister all the information he had received on the plan of colonization formed by the South Carolina Company, and all he had done in relation to that matter. "You will observe," said he, "that Messrs. Alex. Moultrie, William Clay, Snipes, and Huger, members of that Company, recommend to Colonel Holder to cultivate the alliance of the Indian nations, and to communicate to us all the operations of said Company, together with their intention to court our friendship, because they consider their interests and ours as inseparably connected, and conclude with charging their agent to *take possession at all events.*

"From the whole texture of their letter to Holder it is to be inferred, that they believe themselves authorized to form an Independent State, because there is not in it one word which indicates the least subordination to the United States. On the contrary, they flatter themselves *that they will serve as a barrier or rampart for the protection of Louisiana,* which circumstance could not happen, unless they formed a sovereign State."

Mirò praised Wilkinson for the part he had acted on that occasion, and for having so much discouraged the South Carolina Company, that their operations were suspended for the moment. "I mention this fact the more readily on his behalf," said he, "that I spoke less favorably of him in my preceding communication." Mirò closed his despatch with asking for instructions on the subject, and said that, in the mean time, should the South Carolina Company attempt to take possession of the territory which they pretended to have purchased from Georgia, he would oppose that usurpation with such forces as he could command, and with the assistance of the Indians, and that his first step would be to occupy a strong military position at "Walnut Hills," at the mouth of the Yazoo.

On the 24th of May, James O'Fallon, who styled himself the "General Agent in the Western settlement for the company of South Carolina relatively to the Yazoo territory," wrote from Lexington to Governor Miró a letter, which, notwithstanding its length, I shall quote almost in full, on account of the curious developments which it contains.

"The detention," said he, "which I shall probably experience in Kentucky, where I have just arrived on my way to New Orleans; the importance of the mission for which I am sent to you, not only with regard to the Spanish Empire in general, but also particularly with regard to Louisiana and West Florida, as well as in relation to the interests in the Yazoo territory of the South Carolina Company, whose general agent I have the honor to be, in virtue of a unanimous nomination, under the seal and formal diploma of the chief director and of the other proprietors of an extensive territorial concession in the vicinity of your government, finally granted to them by the State of Georgia; the weighty political bearing of my negotiation with you, and the propriety of your being made acquainted with the general design of our plan, before my arrival and my presenting to you my full credentials, with other authentic documents, which clothe me with the most extensive and confidential powers, and which I shall communicate to you with my characteristic frankness; the obligations resulting from the public situation in which I am, as well as my natural disposition to contribute to the glory and prosperity of the Crown which you serve (which disposition is quite notorious at the Spanish Court, through the information afforded by its minister at New York and the Governor of St. Augustine, who, from abundant experience, can testify to it):—All these motives now prompt me to address you, in order to give in advance the following intelligence. which you will examine in your moments of leisure.

"The affair which I have the honor to lay before you is pregnant with events of the greatest importance, which must promptly and inevitably be brought forth, if opportunely favored by the court of Spain and yourself, and which are such, that, even in the eye of the most indifferent, they must assume proportions of the most considerable magnitude. This great project was conceived by myself, a long time ago. Through my persuasion and influence the members of the General Company, who, in particular, are all dissatisfied with the present Federal Government, have, immediately and spontaneously, fallen in with my plan, for the execution of which, considering that it was my conception, they have appointed me their delegate as one of the twenty proprietors of the concession, with plenary powers to complete it, as you will see after my arrival. At the same time that this important affair was in agitation, and progressing among the most influential members of the Legislature of Georgia, the Company was honoring me with their entire confidence; and, without their having suspected in the beginning what I was aiming at, I insensibly prevailed upon them to acquiesce in my political views (after the obtaining of the concession), and led them to consent to be the slaves of Spain,* under the appearance of a free and independent State. forming a rampart for the adjoining Spanish territories, and establishing with them an eternal, reciprocal alli

* Esclavos de la España

ance, offensive and defensive. This, for a beginning, when once secured with the greatest secrecy, will serve, I am fully persuaded, as an example to be followed by the settlements on the western side of the mountains, which will separate from the Atlantic portion of the confederacy, because, on account of the advantages which they will expect from the privilege of trading with our colony, under the protection of Spain, they will unite with it in the same manner and as closely as are the Atlantic States with France, receiving from it every assistance in war, and relying on its power in the moment of danger. In order to induce the Company to pursue this course, I refused to take any share in the enterprise under any other conditions; and, in order to confirm their hostility to Congress, which then was acting despotically, as well as to the President and his ministers, who were opposing their pretensions, I used indirect means, which decided them to form the resolution of separating themselves from the Union, and of removing with their families, dependents, and effects, to their conceded territory, with the determination, if Spain favored them, not to subject themselves, nor the numerous colony which they will soon form, to the administration of Congress or of Washington. The individuals interested in that concession are gentlemen of the greatest influence, power, and talent, among the most gifted in the confederacy; and they are sure of having, within eighteen months after the date of their first settlement, ten thousand men established on their territory and capable of bearing arms. All that they desire from the Spanish Crown for their projected establishment, is a secret co operation, which, in reality, will soon ripen into a sincere friendship. I assure you that Spain will obtain everything from them in return, except the sacrifice of their liberty of conscience and of their civil government. I affirm all this, because I am authorized to do so by the plenary powers which they have given me, both in writing and verbally, as will appear by my secret instructions, which I shall communicate to you with the utmost sincerity on my arrival. For I intend, in my proceedings, to keep aloof from all dissimulation whatever.

"Whilst the Company was making the most strenuous efforts to obtain their concession, in which two years were secretly employed, I was corresponding with Don Diego Gardoqui in New York, and with the Governor of East Florida, through my intimate friend, Captain Charles Howard, the Secretary of that province. At the same time, at the request of the same minister, I was confidentially engaged in obtaining for the court of Spain information of the highest importance, in relation to Great Britain and the United States, and was also working to procure the emigration of ten thousand Irish, American, and German families to the deserts of East Florida. In order to bring these affairs to an end, I was preparing to follow that minister to Madrid, when, in spite of Congress and the President, the Legislature of Georgia, as it were unanimously, conceded to the South Carolina Company, the Virginia Company, and the Tennessee Company, the territories which they had respectively sued for in the vicinity of your government: in consequence of which, these Companies found themselves incorporated and organized by an act of that Legislature, and, by virtue of said incorporation and organization, were empowered, under the sanction of the new federal constitution and authorities, and against the will and wishes of the President and of some of his ministers, to treat and negotiate in relation to the contemplated colonization.

"In this conjuncture, I fully informed the minister Gardoqui, and the Governor of St. Augustine, of the circumstances that had occurred, and of the intention of a few members of the Company to have recourse to Great Britain for their own private views and benefit. It was in my power to cause that disposition to evaporate, and, the better to obtain this result, I abandoned the project of introducing families into West Florida. I then succeeded in persuading them as I wished, and, with the view of conciliating the interests of the company with those of Spain, I consented to be appointed their general agent to negotiate with you, as I have already expressed it above, and thereby be enabled to treat for the establishment of the new colony, combining their interests with those of Louisiana, on principles of reciprocal advantage and defence.

"These premises being taken for granted, it remains for me to inform you that, some time in June next, I intend to depart for New Orleans in order to have frank, sincere and unreserved conferences with you on these matters. I will do nothing without your approbation and consent, because I aim at nothing else than serving the interests of Spain, to which I am hereditarily attached, abandoning all other pursuit, more lucrative for my family, in order merely to follow the bent of my inclination. I need not say to you how much the Company and myself rely on your honor, secrecy, and good will, on which depends our security, as you may infer from what I have so ingenuously related. The Company waits only for your determination, in order to carry its plan into execution in a short time, &c., &c.

* * * * * *

"The plan of the Company, with your co-operation, will contribute not a little to procure the utmost credit for your administration, immortalizing your name as that of one of the most useful vassals of the crown of Spain, and the political father of Louisiana. Events will soon happen, in which I must inevitably act with you in conformity to all your desires."

On the 20th of June, Wilkinson wrote from Frankfort, Kentucky, to Governor Miró: "Sir, since my last letter of the 20th of May, I have had several favorable occasions to converse with Dr. O'Fallon, general agent of the South Carolina Company in Yazoo, and I have the satisfaction to be able to assure you that his plan, his principles and his designs agree perfectly with ours. At the beginning, he operated with much precaution, concealing his true intentions, until having sounded me, and I not fearing to unbosom myself to him, he opened to me his breast, and I found his sentiments to be so uniformly like mine, that he won much on my confidence. I believe, however, that it is my duty to inform you, that he appears to be a man of a light character, although he is not lacking in education and intelligence, because, at his time of life, being forty-five years old, and with many gray hairs, he allows his flightiness and puerile vanity to peep out. But, if the sentiments which he invariably expresses are to be believed (and I am inclined to put faith in them), he is a great friend to Spain.

"He writes to you, by this occasion, in terms which, I flatter myself, will be agreeable to you. I have induced him to do so, because I thought it proper that you should have a pledge for his not retracting the sentiments which he has manifested to me and by which he has gained my confidence."

On the 10th of August, Miró sent to his government copies of all the preceding correspondence, and a detailed account of what he had done in relation to the important matters which had been submitted to his consideration. "O'Fallon's propositions," said Miró, "which he alleges to be founded on credentials which he will exhibit on his arrival, require the most serious reflections, because it is necessary to weigh the advantages resulting from their being accepted, with the danger of permitting such a settlement in such close contiguity with the possessions of his Majesty, or to speak more to the point, of taking, as it were, a *foreign State to board with us.* I will therefore presume to offer to you a few observations, which my very limited intelligence suggests to me, in order that they may serve as materials which may be of some use to you in proposing to his Majesty what you may deem best. With regard to myself, I consider as too hazardous my venturing to express a precise and positive opinion on so delicate a subject."

After this exceedingly modest exordium, Miró proceeds to handle with some assurance what he had apparently approached with such timidity. He said that, according to a plan transmitted to him by General Wilkinson, the inferior limit of the territory conceded to the South Carolina Company was at a water-course called Cole's Creek, eighteen miles above Natchez; extending to the 33d degree of latitude, thirty miles above the mouth of the Yazoo. "The whole of which territory," said Miró, "belongs to his Majesty, from the bank of the Mississippi to landward, for 120 miles, east and west, more or less, where begin the possessions of the Indians. These lands are very rich, particularly those belonging to his Majesty. The United States have not consented so far to have their limits determined in that region, and maintain the right which, in their opinion, they derive from their treaty of peace with Great Britain, unduly granting them a portion of the banks of the river Mississippi, down to the 31st degree, which is to be found at thirty-six miles below the fort of Natchez. They labor with incessant ardor to gain the Indian nations, because, no doubt, they look upon them as a barrier which now prevents them from taking possession of the territory which they claim; whilst these tribes would help them to it, if friendly. Should the plan of colonization of the South Carolina Company be permitted to be carried into execution, all the hopes of the United States would vanish, or at least they would find it no trifling enterprise to send an army in order to gain their point, and the territory still retained by his Majesty would extend to eighteen miles above Natchez, which is the most populous portion of the whole district.

" But should the proposition made by the South Carolina Company be rejected, Louisiana would be in continual danger of being attacked, without the co-operation of Congress, by the sole forces of the Company, which will easily find in the settlements on the Ohio such individuals as it is easy to incite unto war by tendering them the hope of plunder. In that case, the expenses which his Majesty would have to incur in the defence of his possessions would be a matter of serious consideration.

" Among the other advantages likely to result from the formation of that new and independent State, which would soon have a large population, may be ranked the extension of commerce it would procure for New Orleans, if declared a free port, to which all nations would then resort. A slight duty on exports and imports would, in a few years, secure to his Majesty a large revenue.

" With regard to the territory granted to the Virginia Company in the Yazoo district, it extends from the 33d degree, which is the upper limit of the other Company, to 34° 40´ north, comprehending, on account of the sinuosities of the Mississippi, 120 miles along its banks by 120 in depth. I do not think that we have a positive right to those lands, which are the hunting grounds of the Chickasaws, who could, with justice, oppose the settlement contemplated by the Virginia Company. As the leaders in this Company act from the same motives which influence the first, to wit, the South Carolina Company, what I have said as applicable to the former, is equally so to the latter, inasmuch as they would both pursue the same course. This would also prove true in relation to the Tennessee Company, whose concession runs from the mouth of the Tennessee river to about 120 miles back, and belongs to the territory bought from the Chickasaws and Cherokees. The course pursued by these three Companies would reopen a favorable field in Kentucky and the other Ohio settlements for the operations of Wilkinson, who, so far, has been working without much success. These are the advantages to be expected.

" But I think that it would be preferable for Spain to people that territory on her own account, rather than yield it to the South Carolina Company. Its soil is richer than that of any other portion of this province, and I know that there are many in America who have their eyes fixed on it, particularly on the part called Walnut Hills. Hence it results, that it would be of the utmost importance to people that district with subjects of his Majesty, because, if once thickly inhabited, its population would contribute to the defence of Louisiana against any of the machinations of the settlements on the Ohio, or of the Virginia Company on the Yazoo, whose colony would be contiguous, should their plan be carried into execution. It is true that emigration to this province is slower than we ought to have expected, from the numerous offers to bring families here. Colonel Morgan has contented himself with making a publication to excite emigration, but he has remained inactive in his residence of New Jersey, without in the least prosecuting his plan of an establishment below the mouth of the Ohio, whither he had promised to move immediately, nor has he written one word. General Wilkinson says that Morgan has been checked in his enterprise by the commercial privilege granted to Kentucky.

"Should the proposition of the South Carolina Company be refused, the government ought to look for means to foster emigration. This leads me to renew the propositions which I have made, to declare New Orleans a free port for all the European nations, and even for the United States of America, and to clothe me with the power, either to restrain, or stop altogether, as I may deem it opportune, the commerce of Kentucky and the other settlements on the Ohio. You will then see Louisiana densely peopled in a few years, his Majesty defraying all the expenses of the colony out of the duties which will be collected in his name, and out of the profits made on his tobacco purchases, which he will be able to effect at still lower prices, although tobacco now sells here for less than in any other of his dominions.

"I believe that I am not in error when I affirm, that to confine Louisiana to trade with our nation, would be to ruin her. At this very moment, France has the real monopoly of the commerce of this colony, although theoretically and legally it ought to be exclusively in the hands of the subjects of his Majesty. The colonists, to whom goods and merchandise are consigned, have no interest in them, and merely lend their names to the true importers. Therefore, if the Spaniards have no share in this trade, the whole profits of which are enjoyed by the French, would it not be more advantageous to have it divided between the English, the Dutch, &c., through whose competition the inhabitants of Louisiana would have their wants supplied at a much cheaper rate, and would sell their produce higher These commercial franchises would, as I have said before, greatly increase the population, and thereby secure to his Majesty the possession of Louisiana, which is the key of the kingdom of New Spain.*

"This policy I recommend, in case the proposition of the South Carolina Company be rejected, but should it be accepted, I think the same policy equally advantageous; because, should a colony be established by that Company in the territory it has obtained from Georgia, it is to be feared that the conformity of language, manners, and religion, the free and public exercise of which would be permitted, would draw thither a considerable number of the families now established in the Natchez district, thereby increasing the forces and power of the new State. So great an evil would require an extraordinary remedy, and the only efficacious and applicable one would be the grant of a free trade to Louisiana. The magnitude of the peril to be obviated would have to conquer the reluctance felt to make this concession."

Another danger had also struck Miró, and impressed him with serious misgivings. Where was the proof that the Company was sincere in its intentions, and would adhere to its propositions? Would it not devise some means of eluding them? Had it not perhaps, in anticipation, prepared to do so, and would it not be ready for the excuse in due time? Were it to take possession of the extensive domain which it claimed as its own, and were it to establish there a large population, how could it be dispossessed if the occasion required it? But should these apprehensions not be well founded, and not be confirmed by the subsequent actions of the South Carolina

* Llave del Reyno de Nueva España.

colonists, would there not be a serious cause for fearing that, from the impulse of a natural affection, they would be disposed to support the United States in their still pending territorial pretensions to the 31st degree of latitude, and to the navigation of the Mississippi?

"Besides," continued Miró, "it is self-evident that it would be extremely perilous to have, so close to us, so powerful a neighbor, who might, without our being able to prevent him, prepare for the conquest of this province, by insensibly providing himself with artillery, and all the other implements he might require to execute his design. The Crown could not resist an enterprise of the kind, without going to an expense which it is not able to incur. Therefore, should it be determined not to adopt the remedy which I have proposed (the grant of free trade), it is now less difficult to prevent the establishment contemplated by the South Carolina Company, than it would be to meet successfully the fatal results which it may have, and we had better prepare ourselves to act accordingly."

Miró then suggested, that it might be proper to pursue a middle course between rejecting and admitting the propositions of the Company. It consisted in permitting them to colonize the aforesaid territory, on condition that they should declare themselves the subjects of his Catholic Majesty, and submit to the same regulations imposed on all emigrants. In Miró's mind, however, sprang up another dark misgiving. "These people," he said, "are imbued with the conviction that those lands belong to them by purchase, and, in order to obtain them, they may momentarily accept of all sorts of conditions. But would they not violate them, as soon as they should find themselves powerful enough to do it with impunity?

"I will now." continued Miró, "communicate to you

the measures which I have resorted to, in order to prevent any one of the three Companies from carrying its scheme into execution." He then goes on explaining, how he had excited the hostility and secured the opposition of all the Indian tribes to the Americans. "I have recommended them," says he, "to remain quiet, and told them, if these people presented themselves with a view to settle on their lands, then to make no concessions and to warn them off; but to attack them in case they refused to withdraw; and I have promised that I would supply them with powder and ball, to defend their legitimate rights."

With regard to O'Fallon, Miró informed his government that he would so demean himself, as to permit that individual to retain some hopes of success in his mission, and added that he would endeavor to induce O'Fallon to accompany him to Havana, whither he intended to go in October, to confer with the Captain-General on the interesting matters which he had to manage.

In those important conjunctures, McGillivray, the famous chief of the Talapouches, found himself much courted by the Spaniards and the Americans. He had been invited by Washington to cease his hostilities, and to repair to New York, to confer on the articles of a definitive treaty of peace. The wily chief availed himself of this circumstance with considerable skill, to raise himself in the estimation of Miró, and to put his services at a higher price. He wrote to that Governor that, although he should conclude a treaty of peace with the Federal Government, yet he would ever remain faithful to his old friends the Spaniards, and he asked from the Court of Madrid many favors, with an annual stipend of fifteen thousand dollars to carry on hostilities against the projected establishment of the South Carolina Company, if not against the United States. But he obtained only a pension of two thousand dollars, with a regular salary for his interpreters, and the promise of ammunition, arms, and other military supplies in case of need.* The whole correspondence of this half-breed Indian warrior and diplomatist evinces a remarkable degree of shrewdness, information, and talent.

Thus it is seen that Louisiana had been, for several years, the focus of very important intrigues, the object of which was no less than to destroy the great American confederacy which had just been formed, and which was soon destined to operate so powerfully on the rest of the civilized world. But the mass of the population of the colony had been ignorant of, and was indifferent to, the plots, schemes, and diplomacy of their rulers. A cause of agitation and an object of more immediate consequence to them, was a royal schedule, issued on the 31st of May, 1789, in relation to the education and occupation to be given to slaves, and the manner they were to be treated, in all the dominions of his Catholic Majesty. Some of the regulations it contained proved exceedingly unpalatable in Louisiana, and the Cabildo or Council remonstrated on them, on the 23d of July, 1790, in a document which they addressed to the King. His Majesty, it seems, had ordered that chaplains should, on every plantation, attend to the religious education of the negroes. The colonists observed, that this could not be complied with for several reasons; and they might have rested satisfied with the first, which was—that there were not priests enough, even to fill the curacy of every parish; the next was—that there were few planters that were not considerably in debt on account of recent inundations and conflagrations, and of the scarcity and exorbitant price of every necessary of life, wherefore the

* Miró's despatch of the 10th of August, 1790. McGillivray's letter to Miró, May 8th, 1790.

great majority had not the means of paying the salary which it would be requisite to give to so respectable a class of men; and besides, that a good many of the plantations were distant from each other—which circumstance would prevent the same chaplain from officiating on them; that the greater number of the planters were very poor, and their houses too uncomfortable to afford proper accommodation for the ministers of the Gospel.

With regard to the article of the schedule which required the sexes to be kept separate, they said that it was impossible to conform to it without the greatest inconveniences, because the works to be executed on a plantation frequently required that all the hands be kept together, in order to use them to the best advantage according to circumstances; that to divide the hands would increase the costs and trouble of supervision; that most of the planters had only a few negroes, with whom they and their sons worked in the field, and that they could not afford to separate the males from the females, because they would have no distinct occupation to give to them respectively; that the slaves labor under the inspection of their masters, and of the sons, or overseers of their masters; that the work is proportioned to the sex, the strength, the age, and the health of each of them, and that no abuses have resulted from both sexes working together; that even admitting that the vigilance of their superiors should be at fault, the slaves would be prevented from indulging in certain excesses by the fatigues of the body, which are their best corrective, although their labors are moderate, and ample time is allowed them for their own benefit and purposes, according to the intentions of his Majesty.

In relation to the amusements which the slaves were permitted to enjoy on every holiday, after having discharged their religious duties, without their being permitted to go from one plantation to another, the Cabildo remarked that this could be applicable to the large estates only. "But," said they, "where there are only three or four slaves, how could they divert themselves, if the sexes were separated? Would they not grow desperate when hearing the distant sounds of dancing and music, without being able to join in the festival?" &c. &c.

As to the prohibition in relation to the working of negroes on holidays, the Cabildo observed that it was, occasionally, impossible to do otherwise, because it became necessary, at times, not to keep the Sabbath, in order not to lose the fruits of the labors of the whole year; but that the negroes were either compensated for it in money, or were allowed other days of rest in the place of those which had been taken away from them.

As to the article in the royal schedule which enjoined the marriage of the slaves, the Cabildo declared that it was the most critical and difficult of all the obligations imposed by the King upon the planters, because the master would frequently not have the means of buying the female that his slave might choose, or the master of the female might also not be in a situation to purchase the male; and, besides, because such forced sales and purchases would give rise to frauds, heart-burnings, and many other inconveniences which are self-evident and need no description. "On the other hand," they said, "negroes have an almost insuperable aversion to marriage, and the efforts which have been made to establish and encourage that institution among them have always proved fruitless. The habits, contrary to it, among those living machines, are so powerful, that all attempts to persuade them to receive from the church that sacrament have been foiled so far. To force it upon them would produce general discontent, and perhaps the worst consequences.* The masters would infallibly lose some of their slaves, who would run away, if any compulsion was used to make them contract real marriages, on account of their conviction that it would be subjecting them to the evils of a double servitude, and that marriage is a source of disgusts and miseries produced by the continual discords which it breeds among those of their class, and from which celibacy is free, in which opinion they are confirmed by a long experience.

"Although the article 10," continued the Cabildo, "relative to the prevention of excessive punishments by the masters and overseers, is dictated by the spirit of prudence and those feelings of humanity which are natural to the soul of your Majesty, still it offers, sire, to the indocile and unquiet character of the negroes a vast field for machinations against their masters, by inducing them to institute against said masters continual lawsuits founded on complaints suggested to them by their dissatisfied and rebellious humor, and on pretexts which they will invent according to their own fancy and to suit their own purposes. Notwithstanding that the enlightened uprightness of the tribunals is a guaranty in favor of the masters, that they shall not be punished without well authenticated causes, still when the complaints against them shall have been proved to be malicious, no chastisement inflicted on the negroes can be a sufficient indemnification for the loss of time and other damages which they shall suffer, whilst their slaves,

---

* Siendo mas poderosa la costumbre contraria en esta gente maquinal que todas las persuasiones con que se intente reducirlos a desposarse por la Iglesia; de modo que el obligarlos a ello seria indubitablemente un motivo, no solo de general descontento sino acaso de pesimas consequencias. Estos amos perderian infaliblemente algunos de sus esclavos que se irian profugos, si se les quisiese sugetar a contraer verdaderos matrimonios, por la preocupacion que reina entre ellos de ser esa una doble esclavitud, y un manantial de disgustos por las discordias continuas que tienen los casados de esta clase, y de que viven exentos los que no lo son, acreditado uno y otro por larga experiencia entre los negros.

under the pretext of suing for justice, will abandon their labors, and will compel their masters to suspend the cultivation of their estates, in order to account for their conduct, or that of their overseers. To this must be added the disgrace of their being confronted with their own slaves. It would be enough to discourage a large number of the planters, and cause them to renounce the pursuits of agriculture in order to avoid seeing themselves so frequently and so causelessly exposed to vexations and contumelies."

This is a mere condensed abstract from the long publication addressed by the Cabildo or Ayuntamiento of Louisiana to the King, and which is an interesting document, well worthy of an entire perusal, as embodying the views and feelings of the community on the peculiar organism of an institution, which has so entwined itself round the very vitals of the Southern States, that, be it continued, modified, or extinguished, it must, in its ultimate results, exercise for centuries, if not for ever, socially and politically, for good or for evil, the most direct, powerful, and incessant influence on their condition, their prosperity, and their very existence.

It seems that Miró, during his long residence in Louisiana, had not become sufficiently enamored with it to forget good old Spain, and that he had applied several times to be permitted to return to the land of his ancestors and of his birth. On the 12th of October, he wrote again to the Count de Campo Alanga, the minister of the department of the Indies, to be employed at home in that department, and he founded his pretensions on his knowledge of the French and English languages, and his long and familiar acquaintance with the affairs of America, on which he had obtained, as he alleged, the most minute and varied information during his protracted residence on that continent. "I have now had the honor," said he, " of serving the King, always with distinguished zeal, for thirty years and three months, of which, twenty-one years and eight months in America, until the state of my health requires my return to Europe."

This year, the people of Louisiana again suffered extensively from the inundations of the Mississippi. They were also greatly disquieted by the apprehensions of a war with Great Britain, on account of the high grounds taken by that power towards Spain in regard to the settlement at Nootka Sound. An invasion of Louisiana by the British from Canada was a cause of serious fears in the colony, and became a subject of consideration even for the General Government of the United States. Washington had to turn his attention to the course he would pursue, should a passage be asked by Great Britain for her troops through the territory of the United States, or should that passage be effected without permission. These circumstances were considered by the United States as the most favorable they could have, to press their claim to the navigation of the Mississippi; and Carmichael, their chargé-d'affaires at Madrid, was instructed, not only to urge this demand with the most tenacious earnestness, but also to aim at putting the use of that river beyond the reach of molestation or dispute for the future, by obtaining for the United States the island of New Orleans and the Floridas. The United States were not then ready to give millions for such an acquisition, " but," said they to Spain, " the friendship of the United States gained by this liberal transaction, and the security which that friendship would procure for the dominions of Spain on the West of the Mississippi, would be a fair and sufficient equivalent for the desired cession. Not only would the United States have no object in crossing that stream, but their real interest would also require that Spain should retain the immense possessions she claimed to the West of it.* Besides, the navigation of the Mississippi is of such absolute necessity to the United States, that they must, sooner or later, acquire it, either through separate action and by the exertion of their own individual power, or in conjunction with Great Britain. This is the decree of Providence, written on the very map of the Continent of America, and therefore it cannot be resisted by human agency, however obstinate and powerful it may be in its opposition. Was it not the part of wisdom to anticipate an irresistible event, and make the most of it, by gently and peacefully facilitating its accomplishment, which otherwise would inevitably be brought about by violence?"—Such was the language of the United States, but it failed to obtain from Spain the boon which they craved. She, probably, had some misgivings as to the duration of their promised friendship, if they once extended their empire to the left bank of the Mississippi, from the mouth of the Ohio to the Gulf of Mexico. Some sudden and unexpected cause of quarrel might easily occur from the very proximity of the two flags, which the width only of the river would separate; and should thus the two nations bend their necks to drink from the same stream, one of them might complain that the already turbid waters of the Mississippi were made still more so by the other, and might turn into reality the fable of the wolf and the lamb. As to the assertion that the United States would never have any interest nor feel any temptation to cross the river, it is probable that Old Spain shook her experienced head at the boldness of the declaration and at the credulity which it implied on her part. She well knew, on the contrary

* Martin's History of Louisiana, vol. ii., p. 105.

that, if the young giant of the wilderness once planted his foot on the left bank of the mighty river, he would ere long leap across it, as if it were a puny rivulet, and that, in the exulting consciousness of his growing and unconquerable strength, and, with the rough club borrowed from his native forests, beating down the flag and crushing the polished panoply of chivalrous and time-honored Spain, he would soon stride across Texas towards the fat provinces of Mexico and the halls of the Aztec emperors. She could well read the book of destiny, but she thought that she had no immediate interest in hastening the events which were registered in that immortal record of the decrees of Providence.

The year 1791 found Mirò still the unwilling governor of Louisiana. But his intrigues in the West and South, to operate a dismemberment of the territory of the Union, seem to have been slackening, either from the expectation that he was soon to be recalled, or from distrust in his agents and doubts of the final success of his efforts.

Having been blamed for the quantity of tobacco which he had bought, the preceding year, for the account of the government, he wrote to the Cabinet of Madrid, on the 17th of January, to explain the motives by which he had been influenced, and to show that the King had obtained a considerable pecuniary gain by that operation; and, on the 20th of April, he returned to the same subject, recommending large purchases of tobacco, and expressing the opinion, that the carrying on of an extensive trade with the West would be the only means of protecting Louisiana against the resentment of the American settlements on the Ohio.

It appears by another of Mirò's despatches, that the whole revenue derived by the Government from the commerce of Louisiana, including the net produce of the seizure and sale of contraband goods, amounted, in 1790, to 529,304 silver reales, or $66,163.

On the 18th of May, the King, alarmed at the revolutionary ideas which seemed to spread with fearful rapidity, had recourse to an expedient, which provokes a smile, and which does not redound much to the credit of the inventive faculties of the royal brains, or of those of his advisers. It consisted in the prohibition of the introduction into Louisiana of boxes, clocks, and coin, stamped with the figure of a woman dressed in white and holding a banner in her hand, with this inscription: *American Liberty*. It was feared that there might be a tongue and a voice in these inanimate objects. So much for the year 1791. But, in 1852, where is in the world the humble cottage and the royal palace in which the influence of American Liberty is not felt, despite the proscription of this hateful inscription?

The French revolution, which had commenced in 1789, had produced one in St. Domingo in 1791, in that part of the island which belonged to France. The negroes, who, by a decree of the National Convention sitting in Paris, had been assimilated to the whites, being stimulated to go beyond the granted equality, and to claim, not only superiority over their brethren who could not boast of a black skin, but also the exclusive enjoyment of life and property to their detriment, rose upon those who had been their former masters, and butchered them without distinction of age or sex. Those who escaped from the tender mercies of the new-fledged, dark-faced freemen and citizens of France, fled to Cuba, Jamaica, the United States, and Louisiana. Among the refugees who sought an asylum in New Orleans, was a company of comedians from Cape Français, who opened a theatre a short time after their arrival. From that circumstance dates the origin of regular dramatic exhibitions in New Orleans. The new comers sought to make a living in the best way they could, and more than one wealthy sugar planter, more than one pampered son of fortune, in days which had vanished like a dream, were seen opening humble schools, and became teachers of the alphabet, and of dancing, fencing, or fiddling. They were not few, those who were reduced even to lower occupations. But they generally bore their misfortunes with becoming fortitude and dignity, and some rose again to rank and wealth.

The administration of Miró terminated with the year 1791. This officer sailed for Spain, where he continued his military career, and, from the rank of Brigadier General, rose to that of *Mariscal de Campo*, or Lieutenant General. "He carried with him," says Judge Martin in his History of Louisiana, "the good wishes and the regrets of the colonists." Miró was not a brilliant man, like his predecessor Galvez, but had a sound judgment, a high sense of honor, and an excellent heart. He possessed two qualities which are not always found together—suavity of temper and energy; he had received a fair college education, possessed several languages, was remarkable for his strict morality and his indefatigable industry, and joined to his other qualifications the long experience of one who had not lived in vain. He was a native of Catalonia, and had some of the distinguishing traits of character of the population of that province. He left Louisiana entirely reconciled to the Spanish domination, which had been gradually endeared to the inhabitants by the enlightened and wise deportment of almost every officer who had ruled over them. Another circumstance had contributed to operate a sort of fusion, and establish bonds of friendship and consanguinity between the two races. Thus, the most eminent among the Spaniards had, either from the shrewd inspirations of policy, or from the spontaneous impulse of the heart, allied themselves to the families of the natives. Governor Unzaga had married a Maxent, Governor Galvez, her sister; the commissary of war, Don Juan Antonio Gayarré, the son of the royal comptroller, had married Constance de Grandpré; the intendant Odoardo, her sister; Bouligny, who since became Colonel of the regiment of Louisiana, a D'Auberville; Colonel Piernas, a de Porneuf; Governor Miró, a Macarty; Colonel, and afterwards, Governor Gayoso de Lemos, a Miss Watts; and so on with many others whom it is unnecessary to mention. These were remarkable examples, which had never been given by the French Governors, and but seldom by the other high dignitaries of Louisiana, before it became a Spanish colony.

CHAPTER VI.

CARONDELET'S ADMINISTRATION.

1792 to 1797.

FRANÇOIS LOUIS HECTOR, Baron de Carondelet, a colonel of the royal armies of Spain, succeeded Miró, on the 30th of December, 1791, as governor and intendant of the provinces of Louisiana and West Florida. When he received this appointment, he was governor of San Salvador in the province of Guatimala. He was a native of Flanders, and had, by his acknowledged ability and unremitting exertions and zeal, risen to rank and importance in the service of Spain.

According to Spanish usage, the Baron, shortly after entering upon the duties of his office, published his "Bando de Buen Gobierno," on the 22d of January, 1792. "Among the new regulations which it introduced," says Judge Martin in his History of Louisiana, "it provided for the division of the city of New Orleans into four wards, in each of which an Alcalde de Barrio, or commissary of police, was to be appointed. In order to procure to government a knowledge of all the inhabitants, and every stranger among them or in the city, it was made the duty of all persons renting houses or apartments, to give the names of their new tenants to the Alcalde of the district, on the first day of their occupation, or, at farthest, on the succeeding one. The Alcaldes de Barrio were directed to take charge of fire engines and their implements, and to command the fire and axemen companies, in case of conflagration. They were also empowered to preserve the peace, and to take cognizance of small debts.

"In one of his first communications to the Cabildo, the Baron recommended to them to make provision for lighting the city and employing watchmen. The revenue of the corporation did not amount, at this period, to seven thousand dollars. To meet the charges for the purchase of lamps and oil, and the wages of watchmen, a tax of one dollar and twelve and a half cents was to be laid on every chimney.

"In a letter to the minister, the Baron, this year, mentioned that the population of New Orleans was under six thousand.

"Having received instructions from the King to attend to the humane treatment of slaves in the province, he issued his proclamation, establishing the following regulations:

"1°—That each slave should receive, monthly, for his food, one barrel of corn, at least.

"2°—That every Sunday should be exclusively his own, without his being compelled to work for his master, except in urgent cases, when he must be paid for or indemnified.

"3°—That, on other days, they should not begin to work before daybreak, nor continue their labors after dark; one half hour to be allowed for breakfast, and two hours for dinner.

"4°—Two brown shirts, a woollen coat and pantaloons, and a pair of linen pantaloons and two handkerchiefs, to be allowed, yearly, to each male slave, and suitable dresses to every female.

"5°—None to be punished with more than thirty lashes, within twenty-four hours.

"6'—Delinquents to be fined in the sum of one hun

dred dollars, and, in grave cases, the slave to be sold away to another."

On the 27th of April, Carondelet wrote to his government: "When I arrived at New Orleans, I found it divided into two factions—the one headed by Governor Mirò and backed by the Bishop, the assessor of the Intendancy, Don Manuel Serrano, &c.; and the other, composed of the Contador, or royal comptroller Don Jose Orue, the vicar Felix Portillo, who is a capuchin, Don Jose Ortega, &c. The most influential among the French had sided with one or the other party, according to the promptings of their own private interest, so that this capital was full of discord and animosities. Having shown myself indifferent to both parties, and quite resolved to punish those who should prove intractable, I succeeded in effecting a reconciliation, at least ostensibly, with the exception of the comptroller and the assessor, who could not be brought to be on friendly terms with each other." He therefore recommended that both be sent out of the colony with their advisers. A summary manner of reëstablishing harmony! He further said that the comptroller accused Mirò of having embezzled the funds of the King, but that this accusation had so far remained without proof.

On the 23d of July, he also informed his government of the reasons which had induced him to prohibit the introduction of negroes from Jamaica and the French Islands, leaving to the traders in that kind of commodity the faculty of providing themselves with it on the coasts of Africa. The Governor had adopted this measure at the solicitation of the members of the Cabildo, who were afraid of the importation of slaves infected with a spirit of insurrection.

Louisiana had always carried on a brisk trade with that portion of the island of St. Domingo which belonged to the French, and she therefore suffered considerably in consequence of the revolution operated by the blacks in that hitherto prosperous colony. In the month of August, she found herself threatened almost with famine, and she was relieved only by the arrival of one thousand barrels of flour, for which the Baron de Carondelet had sent in haste to Philadelphia.

On the 15th of September, he communicated to the court of Madrid the details of an important capture which he had made some months previous, in the person of William Augustus Bowles. This individual was a native of Maryland, and the manner in which he began life shadowed forth what he would be in riper years. Thus, instead of assisting his countrymen, who were struggling for their independence, he, at the age of fourteen, entered the British army as a foot soldier. His first steps in the military career seem to have been marked with signal success; for, a year after, in 1777, notwithstanding his extreme youth, we find him in Jamaica with the grade of ensign, and, as such, having the honor of bearing the proud banner of England. This was luck indeed for an American boy of fifteen! Shortly after, he went with his regiment to Pensacola, and there the scene changes. William Bowles became guilty of such an act of insubordination, that he was deprived of his rank. In a fit of disgust, it is said that the young man stript himself of his English uniform, contemptuously flung it into the sea, and fled to the Indians, among whom he lived several years, and whose language he acquired to perfection. He married the daughter of a chief of the Creek nation, was naturalized among them, and became himself a chief, a great warrior, and therefore an influential man. In 1781, when Galvez besieged Pensacola, Bowles* the deserter secured his pardon, and

* Pickett's History of Alabama, vol. ii., p. 115.

regained the good graces and favor of the English, by leading a party of Creeks to the assistance of General Campbell. But Bowles got tired at last of his Indian wife, of his Indian popularity, and of his Indian life, which, probably, did not afford him sufficiently ample scope for the versatility of his genius. Now he bids a long and glad farewell to the hospitable wilderness which had sheltered him, and he is next seen in New York. What is he doing there? Why—forsooth, he has joined a company of actors, and is amusing himself with eliciting the applause of enraptured audiences, or perhaps is swearing oaths of deadly hatred at those spectators, whose evidences of disapprobation remind him of the hisses of those snakes which he left far away in the shady woods of Alabama. He followed that company of players to New Providence, where he continued to exercise the same profession, and, occasionally, tried his hand at painting portraits. Whether as a comedian, a painter, an American Tory, an ex-British officer, an Indian chief, or something else, it is certain that he won the confidence of Lord Dunmore, Governor of the Bahamas, who appointed him an English agent, to establish on the Chattahouchie a commercial house, with the view of entering into competition with the celebrated one of Panton in Pensacola, which was under the patronage of the Spanish authorities. True to his mission, Bowles soon began to deal and intrigue among the Indians with his characteristic daring and address. He counteracted the influence of Panton, he undermined the power of McGillivray, and gave great annoyance to the Georgians, who resorted, however, with their customary decision, to a summary mode of redress, and sent him word, on a certain day when they had lost patience, that, if he did not depart within twenty-four hours, they would cut off his ears. Not wishing to incur this penalty, he hastily returned to New Providence, from which he was deputed to England by Lord Dunmore with a delegation of Creeks, Seminoles, and Cherokees, to enlist in their favor the protection of the British government, and secure its assistance in repelling American aggression. He and his Indian companions were well received at court, and their friendship was gained by valuable presents. Bowles did not disappoint his English allies, and on his return to America, says Pickett in his History of Alabama, " began a piratical war upon the coasting vessels of Panton, having taught his warriors to navigate the gulf. He captured some of the vessels, laden with arms and ammunition, ran them up in bayous, where he and an abandoned set of white men from the prisons of London, together with hosts of savages, engaged in protracted debaucheries, and, day and night, made the woods echo with horrid oaths and panther screams." And yet this man is represented as having possessed the most winning address, and a gentleness of mien which did not exclude, when the occasion required it, the imposing and stern aspect of command. His was the sweetest of smiles, femininely beautiful, and apparently indicative of the bubbling well of human kindness within, " with the dark eye-brow that shaded at times the glance of fire." He was one of those impassioned beings, of those " demons in act, but gods at least in face," whom the Rembrandt of poetry—Byron—delighted to paint.

With Panton's merchandise, which he lavishly distributed among the Indians, Bowles regained his former popularity and influence among the Creeks, and became so bold as to accuse McGillivray of treachery to his own tribe, and attempt to overthrow that chieftain and usurp his place. But McGillivray was fully his match, and went to New Orleans to arrange with Carondelet the capture of his restless enemy. The Court of Madrid had instructed the Governors of Louisiana and of Pensacola, either to bribe Bowles into an alliance with Spain, or to seize him and his accomplices or supporters. "Considering," said Carondelet, in a despatch of the 15th of September, "how important it was to the interests of his Majesty, to the security of these provinces, and the prosperity of the kingdom, to stifle, even in the very womb of conception, the dangerous intentions of this adventurer, to keep up the friendship of the Talapouches or Creeks, and to remove from their minds the erroneous impressions which he might have made on them, I took the most efficacious means to have him arrested in compliance with the orders of the King, and on the 12th of March, he was brought to me in this city, from which I sent him to Havana, where he embarked, on the 22d, in the frigate the Mississippi; which took to Spain my predecessor, the Brigadier-general, Don Estevan Miró. I also caused to be transported to Havana Wm. Cunningham and Henry Smith, who were his accomplices in robbing the stores of William Panton at the Apalaches.

* * * * * * *

"I have pursued my plan with perseverance, and I have succeeded in quieting almost all the Indians. I have, to all appearances, taken the most adequate measures to capture all the companions and accomplices of Bowles, and I will not desist from the prosecution of this object, until it be accomplished, since on its success depends, not only the tranquillity of these provinces, but also the security of the Mexican empire, for which they are a natural rampart, and barrier of protection.* I cannot close this letter, without observing to your excellency that, by all means, the presence of Bowles in this latitude must be guarded against, and that he must be carefully detained

---

* Sino tambien la seguridad del imperio Mejicano de que son el antemural y natural barrera.

in Europe." This sufficiently shows, without comments, the fears which the daring and talents of this adventurer had excited in the Spanish Government, and the importance to which he had risen as a prisoner of state.

Bowles was carried to Madrid, where he was imprisoned, and treated with alternate kindness and severity, but he was neither seduced nor intimidated. The government repeatedly offered him his liberty, with pecuniary and military rewards, if he chose to abandon the English service and enlist in that of Spain, by using his influence with the Creeks, to assist the Spaniards in Louisiana and the Floridas. Bowles was proof against all temptation, and has the merit of having remained true to his plighted faith. Seeing that nothing could be gained from his stubborn resistance, the ministry caused him to be transported to the island of Manilla in the Pacific Ocean, where he remained until February, 1797. In this year, for reasons unknown, perhaps with a view that he should be more securely guarded, as war had then broken out between Spain and England, he was ordered back to the Peninsula. "But," says Pickett in his History of Alabama," he contrived on his way to escape, at Ascension Island, and reached Sierra Leone, where the English Governor gave him a passage to London. Mr. Pitt and the Duke of Portland provided for his necessities in a munificent manner." Then, if we follow this personage in his romantic career, we see him leading a corsair's life, and privateering in the Gulf of Mexico, in a light English schooner, against the commerce of Spain, and particularly against the fat boxes of merchandise of Panton, the wealthy Pensacola merchant. Much to the relief of his victims, he was wrecked on the coast of Florida; but nothing daunted, if he had to discontinue his operations on the blue waves of the sea, it was to renew them in the wilderness of the continent. He soon joined again the Creeks, by whom he was heartily welcomed back, as if he had been a chief of their own tribe and race, and with them, he began hostilities against the Americans and the Spaniards, towards whom he entertained an equal animosity. He marched upon the town of St. Marks, captured the fort, and again plundered stores which belonged to Panton, of whom he seemed destined to be the scourge. He conducted his foraging expeditions with such skill, activity and energy, that he became far and wide an object of terror, and the name of Bowles remained a household word, but too familiar to the frightened imagination of almost every woman and child in the settlements of the hardy pioneers of Alabama and Florida. He had at last made himself so troublesome, that the Americans and the Spaniards, who distrusted each other, and whose interests were opposed in so many things, easily agreed on one point—which was—the necessity of their combining to get rid of their implacable foe, and they secretly offered a large reward for his capture. This temptation was so powerful, that it could not be resisted; and Bowles' own warriors seized and pinioned him, at a grand festival to which he had unsuspiciously resorted. During the night which followed this act of treachery, gnawing apart the ropes with which he was bound, he escaped in the most miraculous manner, to the great astonishment of the Indians. But, being retaken by his pursuers, he was conveyed to Mobile, and thence to Havana, where he subsequently died in one of the dungeons of the Moro Castle. Such was the romantic and eventful life of this remarkable adventurer, who, for several years, had maintained himself in a position to exercise some considerable influence on the destinies of Louisiana.

McGillivray did not survive long the first capture of his rival, Bowles, which, as already stated, was effected in the beginning of the year 1792, and of which he had been one of the main instruments. On his return from New Orleans, late in the summer of that very year, he was taken ill, at Mobile, of a fever, which revived old constitutional diseases, and brought on a crisis, of which he died a short time after. William Panton, the far-famed Pensacola merchant, of whom he was the friend, and to some extent the partner, and whose commercial dealings with the Indians he had so long and so faithfully promoted, wrote to Lachland McGillivray, the father of the chieftain, who was still living at Dunmaglas in Scotland, an interesting letter on the death of his son.* "Your son, Sir," said Panton, "was a man that I esteemed greatly. I was perfectly convinced that our regard for each other was mutual. It so happened, that we had an interest in serving each other, which first brought us together, and the longer we were acquainted, the stronger was our friendship.

"I found him deserted by the British, without pay, without money, without friends, and without property, saving a few negroes, and he and his nation threatened with destruction by the Georgians, unless they agreed to cede them the better part of their country. I had the good fortune to point out a mode by which he could save them all, and it succeeded beyond expectation, &c.

* * * * * *

"He died on the 17th of February, 1793, of complicated disorders—of inflamed lungs and the gout on the stomach. He was taken ill on the path coming from his cow-pen, on Little river, where one of his wives, Joseph Curnell's daughter, resided, and died eight days after his arrival here (Pensacola). No pains, no attention, no cost was spared to save the life of my friend,

---

* Pickett's History of Alabama, vol. ii., p. 141.

but fate would have it otherwise, and he breathed his last in my arms, &c.   *   *   *   *
*   *   *   *   *   *   *

"He died possessed of sixty negroes, three hundred head of cattle, with a large stock of horses, &c.   *
*   *   *   *   *   *   *

"I advised, I supported, I pushed him on, to be the great man. Spaniards and Americans felt his weight, and this enabled him to haul me after him, so as to establish this house with more solid privileges than, without him, I should have obtained. This being the case, if he had lived, I meant, besides what he was owing me, to have added considerably to his stock of negroes. What I intended to do for the father, I will do for his children. This ought not to operate against your making that ample provision for your grandson and his two sisters, which you have it in your power to make. They have lately lost their mother, so that they have no friends, poor things, but you and me. My heart bleeds for them, and what I can, I will do. The boy, Alleck, is old enough to be sent to Scotland, to school, which I intend to do, next year, and then you will see him."

Such was the end of the man, whom the Spaniards had considered as one of their most valuable allies, to protect Louisiana against the approach of the Americans. McGillivray was one of those interesting characters who have now become so scarce, and who, in the early days of the history of America, presented in their persons the curious spectacle of the combined qualities and defects of the wild Indian and the educated white man of the Caucasian race—what is called a half-breed—a compound of night and day—a moral, intellectual and physical twilight—the blending of colors and races—the offspring of the embraces of civilization and barbarism—the embodiment of the spirit of the wilderness still retaining its nature and propensities, although somewhat tamed and refined by the tuition of morality, the revelations of religion, and the soothing influence of the arts and sciences. He, himself, seemed to delight in showing, by his usual dress, the opposite elements which composed his organization; for that dress was a striking mixture of the Indian and European garb. When he travelled among the whites, it was always with befitting dignity, and with two servants, one of whom was a half-breed, and the other a negro. When moving on the territory of his nation, he was followed, like a chief, by an Indian escort. In imitation of more powerful rulers, he had several places of residence, if not palaces, where he entertained his visitors with the most liberal hospitality. His two favorite seats were at Hickory Ground, and at little Tallase. The historian Pickett, who, being a native of Alabama, has had a better opportunity than any one else, to procure the fullest information concerning this distinguished chieftain of the land where he dwells, thus describes his person:

"General McGillivray was six feet high, spare made, and remarkably erect in person and carriage. His eyes were large, dark and piercing. His forehead was so peculiarly shaped, that the old Indian countrymen often spoke of it. It commenced expanding at his eyes, and widened considerably at the top of his head. It was a bold and lofty forehead. His fingers were long and tapering, and he wielded a pen with the greatest rapidity. His face was handsome, and indicative of quick thought and much sagacity. Unless interested in conversation, he was disposed to be taciturn, but even then was polite and respectful." Pickett calls him the Talleyrand of Alabama. If, as a barbarian, he delighted in the plurality of wives, and thereby was pointedly opposed in taste to his exquisitely civilized prototype, who never could bear to live with the only one he had taken to his bosom, he certainly had, if small and great things can be assimilated, some diplomatic resemblance with the celebrated statesman of France. For he succeeded in persuading the Americans, the British and the Spaniards, that he was serving them all, whilst he was serving himself only, and, which is better, perhaps his own people. The individual who, Proteus-like, could in turn—nay more, who could at the same time, be a British Colonel, a Spanish and American General, a polished gentleman, a Greek and Latin scholar, and a wild Indian Chief with the frightful tomahawk at his belt and the war paint on his body, a shrewd politician, a keen-sighted merchant, a skilful speculator, the emperor of the Creeks and Seminoles, the able negotiator of treaties with Washington in person and other great men, the writer of papers which would challenge the admiration of the most fastidious—he, who could be a mason among the Christians, and a pagan prophet in the woods; he, who could have presents, titles, decorations showered at the same time upon him from England, Spain and the United States, and who could so long arrest their encroachments against himself and his nation, by playing them, like puppets, against each other, must be allowed to tower far above the common herd of men. He was interred with masonic honors in the splendid garden of William Panton, in the town of Pensacola.* He was much regretted by the Spaniards, but his death literally spread desolation among his people, and one of them, on pronouncing a funeral oration to his memory, might, with truth, had he known anything of Hebrew history and of Latin language, have applied to him what was said of one of the Machabei: Fleverunt eum omnis populus

---

* Pickett's History of Alabama, vol. ii., p. 142.

Israel planctu magno, et lugebant dies multos, et dixerunt: quo modo cecidit vir potens, qui salvum faciebat populum Israel!

If the intelligence of the capture of Bowles had been grateful to the ministers of Madrid, they were not as well pleased with the information which they received from Carondelet, in a despatch of the 20th of December, in which they were made to understand that the materials for the military defence of Louisiana were in the most wretched state, and that it was impossible to do what was absolutely necessary to put them in a proper condition, without an expenditure of at least $250,000. The revenue received through the custom-house at New Orleans, amounted, this year (1792), to $89,499.

On the 1st of January, 1793, the King issued an ordinance approving the prohibitory measure which Carondelet, on the recommendation of the Cabildo, had adopted concerning the importation of slaves into Louisiana from Jamaica and the French West India Islands; and, at the same time, wishing to encourage the slave trade from Africa, his Catholic Majesty granted great privileges to such of his subjects as would engage in it with Spanish vessels.

On the 9th of June, the King issued another ordinance, continuing, increasing and extending the commercial franchises which had been conceded by the royal schedule of 1782.* This wise policy was extremely favorable to the commerce of New Orleans, which, besides, had hitherto been fostered by the enlightened liberality of the Spanish Governors, who had always connived at the violation of those stringent and ill-devised commercial regulations of Spain, which, in her colonies, absolutely confined all trade to her natural born

---

* Martin's History of Louisiana, vol. ii., p. 118.

subjects, or to such as were naturalized and residing in her dominions. Particularly since the conflagration which had destroyed New Orleans in 1788, Miró had openly disregarded the positive instructions of the minister of finances, had thrown open the port of New Orleans to a brisk trade with Philadelphia, and had extended the same patronage to foreign merchants residing in the province, although not naturalized, and the same policy was still very properly pursued by the Baron de Carondelet. It must be said that the King, on being informed of the necessities of Louisiana, approved of the disregard of his own laws by his own representatives. "After this," says Judge Martin in his History of Louisiana, "the officers of the custom-house contented themselves with the simple declaration of an individual, generally the consignee, that he was owner of the vessel. No oath was administered; the production of no document was required; the declaration was even accepted from an individual who did not reside in the province, on his asserting that he meant to do so, or on his producing a licence to import goods. No one was thereby deceived, but the custom-house officers were furnished with a pretext for registering as a Spanish bottom, and thus preserve an appearance of compliance with the law. So little attention was paid to this, that, at times, the Governor and Intendant certified that a vessel was American property, while she appeared on the custom-house books as a Spanish vessel." A strange anomaly, indeed, coupled with a still more curious one—that of the King of Spain's preference to approve the violation of his superannuated, moth-eaten and obnoxious laws, than consent to their repeal or modification.

The hope of quiet and prosperous times was thus smiling on the inhabitants of Louisiana, when they were violently agitated by the news that Louis XVI. had perished on the scaffold on the 21st of January, 1793, and that the King of Spain had declared war against the new French Republic. Although the fate of the august victim was deplored, yet the feelings of the majority of the population of Louisiana were in favor of the new order of things which was expected to be established in France, in the hope that a free government, resting on a solid basis, would succeed the bloody anarchy which they considered as having only a temporary and transitory existence. They were not also without secret hopes of being re-annexed to France, by a more vigorous and enlightened government than the one which had given them away to Spain; and even one hundred and fifty of them were bold enough to sign a petition openly addressed to the French Government, and praying for their being replaced under the protection of France. The sympathies of the colonists were not concealed; at the theatre, the celebrated French hymn, "La Marseillaise," was frantically asked from the orchestra, and in some of the tippling-shops of New Orleans, which were resorted to by such spirits as rejoice in the atmosphere of these places, the jacobinical song of "*Ça ira—ça ira, les Aristocrates à la lanterne,*" was vociferated with a degree of boldness which showed they thought that help was at hand, and that punishment would hesitate to visit them. The Baron's critical situation may easily be imagined. "He prepared and promoted," says Judge Martin in his History of Louisiana," the subscription of a paper, in which the colonists gave assurance of their loyalty to, and affection for, the Catholic King, and bound themselves to support his government in Louisiana. He put a stop to the practice which had of late been introduced, of entertaining the audience at the theatre with the exhibition of certain martial dances to revolutionary airs. He caused six individuals who had manifested their approbation of the new French principles, and evinced a desire of seeing them acted upon in Louisiana, to be arrested and confined in the fort. At the intercession of several respectable inhabitants of New Orleans, he promised to liberate them; but, believing afterwards that he had discovered new causes of alarm, which rendered a decisive step necessary, he shipped them for Havana, where they were detained during a twelvemonth."

These circumstances required that Louisiana be put on such a footing as to meet all emergencies, and, on the 30th of September, Carondelet informed his government that the fortifications and all the other necessary materials for the protection of the colony had been allowed to go to ruin; that the amount of the annual expenditure fixed for Louisiana by O'Reilly, in 1769, at the rate of $115,000, had not been sufficient to answer all the exigencies; and that, although, since 1784, the budget of the province had been carried up to $537,869, and had been so kept up to the present day, still, for some cause or other, unknown to him, the fortifications and artillery had been so neglected, that they were unfit for any practical use; and that, to comply with the royal order of October, 1791, requiring Louisiana to be put in an ordinary state of defence, would demand an annual appropriation of $100,279, over and above the regular budget, in order to cover the expenses to be occasioned by an increase of troops, as four additional battalions would be absolutely necessary.

In these difficult conjunctures, it was of the utmost importance to secure the friendship of the Indians, and therefore all the efforts of Carondelet were bent towards strengthening old alliances with them, and making new ones. These efforts were crowned with success, and, on the 28th of October, he had the satisfaction, through his agent and representative, Colonel Gayoso de Lemos, Governor of Natchez, to make a reciprocally defensive and offensive treaty, between Spain on one side, and the Chickasaws, the Creeks, the Talapouches, the Cherokees, and the Alibamons on the other. The treaty of 1784 was ratified in all its points, and these different Indian nations, forming a confederacy for their mutual assistance, bound themselves never to act in any thing which might have a bearing on the interest, security or welfare of the parties to the treaty, without first obtaining the consent of them all, and the approbation of the Governor of Louisiana. In return for the protection which Spain promised to extend over all these nations, they obligated themselves to contribute, to the utmost of their power, to maintain his Catholic Majesty in possession of the provinces of Louisiana and of the two Floridas. Spain, being the patron of all these nations, was to negotiate with the United States, in order to have the limits of the territories of every one of said nations, respectively fixed between them and the United States, so as to avoid any further cause for quarrel and dissension. The other articles of the treaty were concerning the distribution of presents to the several tribes, and other objects of minor importance.

On the 18th of January, 1794, Carondelet wrote to the ministry a despatch, in which he informed them that he was erecting, without the assistance of one solitary engineer, considerable fortifications, or repairing old ones, at several points of the colony, and particularly around New Orleans. He observed that they would not only protect the city against the attack of an enemy, but also keep in check its inhabitants themselves, who had lately shown a disposition to embrace the new-fangled doctrines of France, and had manifested the desire of returning under her domination. "I am every day on horseback before dawn," said he, "in order to visit the works, to urge the laborers, and to attend to all my other innumerable duties." He added that, if New Orleans had not been awed by the forts which he had caused to be constructed, its population would have rebelled, and a revolution have taken place. "By the exertion of the utmost vigilance, and at the cost of sleepless nights," said he, "by frightening some, by punishing others, by driving several out of the colony, and particularly those Frenchmen who had lately come among us, and who had already contaminated the greater part of the province with their notions and maxims of equality, by intercepting the letters and papers of a suspicious character, and by dissembling with all, I have obtained more than I had hoped, considering that the whole colony is now in a state of internal tranquillity." He further remarks that, with regard to his secret and confidential despatches, he has nobody about him that he could venture to trust with the copying of them; that the obligation imposed upon him by the order of the King, to transcribe for, and to submit to, the Captain-general of the island of Cuba, of which Louisiana is a dependency, all the documents he has to forward to the Secretary of State at Madrid, multiplies his labors to an enormous extent, and that the most robust man could not resist the wear and tear of such a life; that the secretary of the government of the colony, Don Armesto, is an indefatigable man, but that it is physically impossible that he should do all that is to be done, and that the King's service would be materially benefited, if the Captain-general resided in Louisiana.

The Baron de Carondelet further expressed some feelings of proud satisfaction at the late treaty which he had concluded with the Talapouches, the Chickasaws and other nations, and in virtue of which he could, at any time, as he declared, oppose, if necessary, twenty thou sand Indians to the Americans, for the trifling annual expenditure of ten thousand dollars. But, by another of his despatches, dated on the 24th of February, it appears that the pensions and presents given to the Indians amounted to the yearly and pretty round sum of $55,000.

In this long and very able despatch, the Baron reviews the situation of the colony, and proposes to abandon the fort of Natchez, which is commanded by neighboring heights and can really be of no avail in a case of emergency, for the one at the Walnut Hills, which is situated one hundred and twenty miles higher on the river, and which he describes as being in an infinitely stronger position, and as being the key of the province. He says that, on any sudden invasion by the French, should they come down the river, he could oppose to them fifteen hundred men from the Natchez district and from the upper parts of the colony; he represents, that his salary, which is nominally $6,000, but which in reality is reduced to $4,757, on account of certain deductions to be made from it, is not adequate to the exigencies of his rank and to his official expenses; he calls the attention of the government to various improvements to be made and abuses to be reformed, to the propriety of increasing the salary of some officers and diminishing that of others, of creating some offices and of suppressing several; he proposes the digging of a canal from the ditches that run along the ramparts with which the town is encircled to Bayou St. John, about a mile back towards the swamps; he represents that this work would not cost more than $30,000, and would be of immense utility, as it would give through Bayou St. John and the lakes, an opening to the commerce of New Orleans with Mobile and Pensacola, and would drain the putrid waters stag nating around it and producing those epidemics which are so fatal to its prosperity. "Should this drainage not be executed," said he, "it will be necessary to abandon the town in less than three or four years; for the inundations of the Mississippi, which, on the breaking of any one of its levees or dykes in this neighborhood, cover almost all the streets of New Orleans, gradually raise by their deposits the adjacent lands, and thus make of the town a sort of sink, which will have no outlet for its waters." It appears from very curious documents accompanying this despatch, and giving the most detailed accounts of the annual expenses of the colony, including the Mobile and Pensacola districts, that they had, by degrees, ascended to $776,304 in 1793, on which the Baron proposed a reduction of $239,023. The receipts of the custom-house, which constituted the most important part of the revenue, had not produced, this year, more than $76,815. The military expenses alone amounted to $438,436; as to the pay of the clergy, it was only $12,866. Besides the regular expenses of the government, the supplying of Pensacola and Mobile with goods for the trade with the Indians required an annual disbursement of $80,000—that is, $40,000 for each one of these towns.

On the 17th of May, 1794, the Baron de Carondelet wrote to his government to beg the King to step in between the inhabitants of Natchez and their creditors, so as to allow to the former some delays to pay their debts, and thus prevent them from being ruined by litigation.

"Since my taking possession of this government," said he, " my continual and all engrossing occupations in maintaining public tranquillity, and in putting in a regular state of defence this province, which is open on all sides, and which, from the date of the administration of my immediate predecessor to the present day, has not ceased to be threatened by the ambitious designs of the Americans, have consumed and absorbed all my time for almost two years; and the war lately declared against France has, finally, much increased my anxieties and trouble in a colony, which is mostly occupied by French people, and which has been repeatedly exposed to invasions, both by sea and from the upper part of the Mississippi. These causes have prevented my submitting sooner to your consideration a subject, which is of so very delicate a nature." Carondelet then informs the minister, that the Natchez district was originally peopled by English and American emigrants, who settled it since the treaty of peace concluded in 1783; that they engaged in the cultivation of tobacco, under the flattering prospect of selling annually to the royal treasury two hundred thousand pounds of this their only produce; that they had contracted large debts for the acquisition of negroes and of other things required by their agricultural pursuits; that, in 1789, on account of unfavorable circumstances, they had not been able to meet their obligations, and had obtained delays from their creditors on certain conditions; but that most of them had not been able to comply with those conditions, on account of the insufficiency of the crops, of the difficulty of selling them, and of several other untoward events, among which was the promulgation of the royal schedule of 1790, declaring that the government had reduced to forty thousand pounds the quantity of tobacco which it would purchase for the future. Carondelet further stated that, if the law was permitted to have its course, these people, rather than allow themselves to be utterly ruined, would take refuge with their negroes on the territory of the Indians and the Americans; that they had recently undertaken, with many difficulties to be overcome, the cultivation of cotton and indigo; that it was necessary to consider that they formed a protection against the expected French and American invasions; that they had lately acted like zealous and faithful subjects, when three hundred of them, at the close of the last year, came down to New Orleans to offer their services, on this province being threatened with an invasion through the Balize; that this example had repressed the machinations of the numerous lovers of changes and innovations who are to be found in the colony, had invigorated the timid and wavering, and confirmed the loyal, the honest, and the courageous, in their good sentiments; wherefore he recommended that the king be advised to interpose his authority between the debtors and their creditors, and to grant to the former a delay for payment, until the gathering in of the crop of 1800, provided partial and annual payments be made in the mean time.

Taking into consideration the complaints of Carondelet as to the multiplicity of his duties, the government, separating the two offices of intendant and governor, which it had united under the administration of Miró and since the departure of Navarro, appointed as intendant Don Francisco de Rendon, who had been employed as Secretary of legation for Spain in the United States. He was installed into office on the 26th of August, 1794.

In consequence of Louisiana having been detached from the bishopric of Havana and erected into a distinct see, this year was also marked by the arrival of another high dignitary, the new bishop, Don Luis de Peñalvert y Cardenas, who established his residence in New Orleans, and two canons were added to the clergy of the province.

It may not have been forgotten, that O'Reilly had declared it to be contrary to the mild and beneficent laws of Spain, that the Indians be held in a state of bondage, and that the inhabitants of Louisiana would have to prepare for the emancipation of those of that race whom they had so far considered as their lawful property, but that the execution of this measure should be suspended, until the King should finally decide upon it in his royal wisdom. No steps had ever since been taken in the matter; the King had been silent; and the Indian slaves had remained contented with their situation, when suddenly, in 1793 and 1794, they, almost in a body, startled Governor Carondelet by applying for their freedom. In a despatch of the 17th of May, he commented at length on the danger of acquiescing in their demands, represented the ruinous effects it would have for their owners, and recommended, if not a direct refusal, at least measures of compromise, which would postpone the evils of emancipation, if not retard them so as to render them nugatory. "There are many reasons to suspect," said he, "that the movement observable among the Indian slaves who have lately made a rush to claim their freedom according to the tenor of our laws, is attributable to the suggestions of certain secret agents, who do not lose any opportunity of exciting in these provinces the dissensions which have produced the ruin of the French colonies."

On the 10th of December, Carondelet informed the Court of Madrid that, on the 8th of that month, a conflagration, but too well favored by a strong north wind, and originating in Royal street, through the imprudence of some children playing in the court-yard of one François Mayronne, which was adjacent to a hay store, had consumed in three hours two hundred and twelve of the most valuable dwellings and magazines, the property of private individuals, as well as edifices of the greatest value belonging to the government. The losses of the merchants were immense; for only two stores were spared by the devouring element. The materials owned by the Crown, and destroyed by this conflagration, were also considerable. "It seems," said Carondelet, "that the sufferings inflicted on the colony by three hurricanes in fourteen months were not enough." He further stated that, although the conflagration of 1788 had consumed a larger number of buildings, still the pecuniary losses on this occasion were much heavier. To form any idea of what they were, it must be remembered that Governor Miró estimated those incurred in 1788, at $2,595,561. The province was again threatened with famine, for almost all the provisions had been destroyed, and not more than one thousand barrels of flour remained for the consumption of the inhabitants and of the troops. Fortunately, the fire did not reach the cathedral, which was the gift of Don Andres Almonaster to the city, and which had just been completed. In order the better to avoid for the future the recurrence of such calamities, Carondelet recommended that premiums be granted by his Catholic Majesty to such of his subjects in New Orleans as should rebuild with terraced roofs, or with roofs made of tiles instead of shingles as formerly.

It may not be uninteresting to remark here, before closing the recital of those events which happened in 1794, and which are connected with the history of Louisiana, that the first regular newspaper published in the colony made its appearance this year, under the name of "Le Moniteur de la Louisiane," or "The Monitor of Louisiana."

The internal condition of Louisiana was certainly sufficient to give occupation to the Baron de Carondelet, but the dangers which threatened her from abroad were of such magnitude, as to fill him with the keenest anxieties, and deeply to impress him with the heavy responsibility which circumstances had prepared for him

In the beginning of the year 1794, a society of French Jacobins, established in Philadelphia,* had caused to be printed, and circulated in Louisiana the following address:

"LIBERTY, EQUALITY.

"The Freemen of France to their brothers in Louisiana: 2d year of the French Republic.

"The moment has arrived when despotism must disappear from the earth. France, having obtained her freedom, and constituted herself into a republic, after having made known to mankind their rights, after having achieved the most glorious victories over her enemies, is not satisfied with successes by which she alone would profit, but declares to all nations that she is ready to give her powerful assistance to those that may be disposed to follow her virtuous example.

"Frenchmen of Louisiana, you still love your mother country; such a feeling is innate in your hearts. The French nation, knowing your sentiments, and indignant at seeing you the victims of the tyrants by whom you have been so long oppressed, can and will avenge your wrongs. A perjured king, prevaricating ministers, vile and insolent courtiers, who fattened on the labors of the people whose blood they sucked, have suffered the punishment due to their crimes. The French nation, irritated by the outrages and injustices of which it had been the object, rose against those oppressors, and they disappeared before its wrath, as rapidly as dust obeys the breath of an impetuous wind.

"The hour has struck, Frenchmen of Louisiana; hasten to profit by the great lesson which you have received.

"Now is the time to cease being the slaves of a govern

* Carondelet's despatch of the 28th of February, 1794.

ment, to which you were shamefully sold; and no longer to be led on like a herd of cattle, by men who with one word can strip you of what you hold most dear—liberty and property.

"The Spanish despotism has surpassed in atrocity and stupidity all the other despotisms that have ever been known. Has not barbarism always been the companion of that government, which has rendered the Spanish name execrable and horrible in the whole continent of America? Is it not that nation who, under the hypocritical mask of religion, ordered or permitted the sacrifice of more than twenty millions of men? Is it not the same race that depopulated, impoverished and degraded whole countries, for the gratification of an insatiable avarice? Is it not the nation that has oppressed and still oppresses you under a heavy yoke?

"What have been the fruits of so many crimes? The annihilation, the disgrace, the impoverishment, and the besotting of the Spanish nation in Europe, and a fatal lethargy, servitude, or death for an infinite number of the inhabitants of America.

"The Indians cut down the tree whose fruits they wish to reach and gather. A fit illustration of despotism! The fate of nations is of no importance in the eye of tyranny. Everything is to be sacrificed to satisfy capricious tastes and transient wants, and all those it rules over must groan under the chains of slavery.

"Frenchmen of Louisiana, the unjust treatment you have undergone must have sufficiently convinced you of these sad truths, and your misfortunes must undoubtedly have deeply impressed your souls with the desire of seizing an honorable opportunity of avenging your wrongs.

"Compare with your situation that of your friends— the free Americans. Look at the province of Kentucky, deprived of outlets for its products, and yet, notwith standing these obstacles, and merely through the genial influence of a free government, rapidly increasing its population and wealth, and already presaging a prosperity which causes the Spanish government to tremble.

"Treasure up in your minds the following observations; They divulge the secret springs of all despotic governments, because they tear off the veil which covers their abominable designs. Men are created and born to love one another, to be united and happy, and they would be so effectually, if those who call themselves the images of God on earth—if kings—had not found out the means of sowing discord among them and destroying their felicity.

"The peopling of Kentucky has been the work of a few years; your colony, although better situated, is daily losing its population, because it lacks liberty.

"The Americans, who are free, after consecrating all their time to cultivating their lands and to expanding their industry, are sure to enjoy quietly the fruits of their labors, but, with regard to yourselves, all that you possess depends on the caprice of a viceroy, who is always unjust, avaricious, and vindictive.

"These are evils which a firm determination, once taken, can shake off. Only have resolution and energy, and one instant will suffice to change your unhappy condition. Wretched indeed would you become, if you failed in such an undertaking! Because, the very name of Frenchmen being hateful to all kings and their accomplices, they would, in return for your attachment to us, render your chains more insupportable, and would persecute you with unheard of vexations.

"You quiver, no doubt, with indignation; you feel in your hearts the desire of deserving the honorable appellation of freemen, but the fear of not being assisted and of failing in your attempt deadens your zeal. Dismiss such apprehensions: know ye, that your brethren the French, who have attacked with success the Spanish Government in Europe, will in a short time present themselves on your coasts with naval forces; that the republicans of the western portion of the United States are ready to come down the Ohio and Mississippi in company with a considerable number of French republicans, and to rush to your assistance under the banners of France and liberty; and that you have every assurance of success. Therefore, inhabitants of Louisiana, show who you are; prove that you have not been stupified by despotism, and that you have retained in your breasts French valor and intrepidity; demonstrate that you are worthy of being free and independent, because we do not solicit you to unite yourselves with us, but to seek your own freedom. When you shall have the sole control of your actions, you will be able to adopt a republican constitution, and being assisted by France so long as your weakness will not permit you to protect or defend yourselves, it will be in your power to unite voluntarily with her and your neighbors—the United States—forming with these two republics an alliance which will be the liberal basis on which, henceforth, shall stand our mutual political and commercial interests. Your country will derive the greatest advantages from so auspicious a revolution; and the glory with which you will cover yourselves will equal the prosperity which you will secure for yourselves and descendants. Screw up your courage, Frenchmen of Louisiana. Away with pusillanimity—ça ira—ça ira—audaces fortuna juvat."

The distribution of this inflammatory address in Louisiana, through secret agents, caused great alarms to the Baron de Carondelet. These alarms were increased by his knowledge of the efforts made by Genet, the French

Minister near the government of the United States, to set up against Louisiana an expedition composed of Frenchmen and Americans, of which he himself was to be the commander-in-chief. Genet had speculated on the prejudices of the Western people, and had sent, particularly to Kentucky and Tennessee, active, enthusiastic, and intelligent agents, who, circulating among the hardy population and the remotest pioneers of the West, discoursed glibly on the innumerable advantages which would accrue to these people, if they separated from the rest of the United States, if they helped to enfranchise Louisiana by an invasion, and if they formed with her an alliance under the protection of France. For enterprises of this kind, fiery and adventurous spirits are always at hand, in all countries and in all ages ; and the French emissaries in the West and South seduced a considerable number of men, who immediately prepared for the execution of the undertaking in which they had enlisted. Armed bands had been gathered on the southern frontier of Georgia, and even a large body of Creek warriors was in readiness to join the invaders. It was feared at the same time, that an attack would be made from the Ohio settlements, and that the spring flood of the Mississippi would bring down the enemy, borne swiftly onward by the rising waters of that river. An individual, of the name of Clark, was the main actor in all these military preparations in the South, and Auguste de la Chaise, a native of Louisiana, and a grandson of the King's former ordaining commissary (commissaire ordonnateur) who had come to the colony in 1723, had been sent by Genet to Kentucky to recruit forces, and was to be the leader of those invaders who were to descend the Ohio and Mississippi.

The Baron, when such dangers threatened him, did not sleep at his post. He completed the fortifications of

New Orleans, strengthened others already existing throughout the province, and mustering all his forces, organized them to meet the expected conflict. According to a report made by him to his government, he could rely, as fit for military service in the colony, on about six thousand militia-men, and he affirmed that, within three weeks, three thousand of them could be concentrated at any one point in the province. Not trusting entirely to these means of defence, he had recourse to the politic arts of the diplomatist, and in order to appease the hostility of the Western people, he removed some of the restrictions which cramped their trade, granted again important privileges to some enterprising and influential men among them, and prepared himself to renew Miró's former scheme of winning over that restless and energetic population to the dominion of Spain. The firm and loyal interference of Washington prevented the attack which was threatened from the Ohio districts, checked the intrigues of Genet, and relieved the apprehensions of the Spanish authorities in Louisiana. The Governor of Georgia also issued his proclamation against the unlawful enterprise meditated under Clark, with the assistance of the Creeks, against East Florida. De la Chaise, who, of all the agents employed by Genet, was the one most feared by Carondelet, on account of his rash intrepidity, his indefatigable activity, his zeal for France, and his exquisite address, and because, being a native of Louisiana and belonging to one of its most powerful families, he exercised considerable influence in the colony, seeing that he had to abandon all the hopes he had conceived to wrest Louisiana from the domination of Spain, retired from Kentucky, and took service in the French army, after having laid before the democratic society of Lexington the following communication:[*]

[*] American State Papers, vol. i., p. 931.

"Citizens,

"Unforeseen events, the effects of causes which it is unnecessary here to develop, have stopped the march of two thousand brave Kentuckians, who, strong in their courage, in the justice of their rights, in the purity of their cause, and in the general assent of their fellow-citizens, and convinced of the brotherly dispositions of the Louisianians, waited only for their orders to go and take away, by the irresistible power of their arms, from those despotic usurpers the Spaniards, the possession of the Mississippi, secure for their country the navigation of it, break the chains of the Americans and of their French brethren in the province of Louisiana, hoist up the flag of liberty in the name of the French republic, and lay the foundation of the prosperity and happiness of two nations destined by nature to be but one, and so situated as to be the most happy in the universe.

"Citizens: The greater the attempts you have made towards the success of that expedition, the more sensible you must be of the impediments which delay its execution, and the more energetic should your efforts be towards procuring new means of success. There is one from which I expect the greatest advantages and which may be decisive—that is, an address to the national Convention, or to the Executive Council of France. In the name of my countrymen of Louisiana, in the name of your own interest, I dare once more ask you this new proof of patriotism.

"Being deprived of my dearest hopes, and of the pleasure, after an absence of fourteen years and a proscription of three, of returning to the bosom of my family, my friends, and my countrymen, I have only one course to follow—that of going to France and expressing to the representatives of the French people the cry, the general wish of the Louisianians to become part of the

French republic—informing them, at the same time, of the most ardent desire which the Kentuckians have had, and will continue to have for ever, to take the most active part in any undertaking tending to open to them the free navigation of the Mississippi.

"The French republicans, in their sublime constitutional act, have proffered their protection to all those nations who may have the courage to shake off the yoke of tyranny. The Louisianians have the most sacred right to it. They are French, but have been sacrificed to despotism by arbitrary power. The honor, the glory, the duty of the National Convention is to grant them their powerful support.

"Every petition or plan relative to that important object would meet with the highest consideration. An address from the Democratic Society of Lexington would give it a greater weight.

"Accept, Citizens, the farewell, not the last, of a brother who is determined to sacrifice everything in his power for the liberty of his country, and the prosperity of the generous inhabitants of Kentucky. Salut en la patrie.

"AUGUSTE LA CHAISE."

This gentleman perished in an ambuscade in St. Domingo, in the year 1803, a short time after he had been raised to the grade of General. Had not death stopped him in his career, when he was still in the meridian of life, it is to be presumed from what he had already accomplished, that he would have risen to higher honors, and might have left behind him a memory of which his native country, Louisiana, would have been proud.

As soon as the danger of an invasion had passed away, the Baron de Carondelet began to throw impediments in the way of the western trade, which he had temporarily favored, and again imposed restrictions calculated to facilitate the operations of those agents whom he had sent to Kentucky to tempt the people into a separation from the United States and an alliance with Spain, by which the much desired outlet of the Mississippi would be secured to them. The times were highly auspicious for the intrigues of Spain. Not only were the inhabitants of Kentucky and Tennessee weary of struggling against such obstacles to their commerce, and irritated against the Federal Government that could not remove them, but Western Pennsylvania also had been thrown into a ferment by the "excise on distilled spirits," giving rise to what is commonly called, in American history, "the Whisky Insurrection," which had taken such proportions as to require the presence of an army of twelve thousand troops from the Eastern States to quell it. Almost all the tribes of the North-western Indians, at the instigation of the English, were waging open war against the United States; and the General Government was embarrassed by tedious and vexatious negotiations with Great Britain, Spain, and even their old ally France—which negotiations assumed at times an angry tone, leading to the belief that hostilities might perhaps ensue. England in the North-west, and Spain in the South, seemed to unite in pressing with all their weight on both flanks of the West, to break it loose from the Federal Government, and force it into a permanent separation. Lord Dorchester had sent from Canada, and the Baron de Carondelet, from Louisiana, numerous emissaries who were emulously at work to heat and exasperate the different parties then existing in Kentucky, and to produce a state of feeling which might be favorable to their views.

Carondelet's chief emissary was Thomas Power, an Englishman by birth, but naturalized a Spanish subject.

and very zealous in the service of his adopted country. This man was intelligent, cautious, and had a natural disposition to intrigue. He was thought by the Baron de Carondelet to be a fit subject to be employed on the hazardous mission of sowing the seeds of sedition in the West, and was sent thither under the pretence of collecting materials for a natural history of that section of the country, but really to revive with Wilkinson, Innis, Sebastian, and others, the plots which had been carried on under Miró's administration.

Whilst these fruitless intrigues were afoot and were engrossing the attention of the Baron de Carondelet, the year 1794 was marked by an event which was to convert the fields of Louisiana into as fertile mines of wealth as ever lay hid in the bowels of the earth. So far, the results of the agricultural labors of the colonists had been insignificant. To the cultivation of indigo they had, hitherto, mostly addicted themselves, and for several consecutive years it had been sadly unsuccessful. Hurricanes had repeatedly swept over the land, and other strange vicissitudes in the seasons had destroyed the crops. As it were to complete the ruin of the unfortunate planters, an insect had lately made its appearance, and invariably attacked the indigo plant. Every year it devoured the leaves with incredible rapidity, and left nothing but the naked stems standing, to mock the eye of the farmer and to remind him of the extent of his losses. Particularly in the years 1793 and 1794, these ravages had been so general, that the whole province had been thrown into a state of consternation and despair. What was to be done? Rice and corn were produced for the wants of the country only, and were not exported with much advantage. As to cotton, it hardly repaid the labor of cultivation, on account of the inexperience of the planters and of the difficulty which was then felt in separating the seed from the wool. The manufacture of sugar had been abandoned since 1766, as being unsuited to the climate, and only a few individuals continued to plant canes in the neighborhood of New Orleans, to be sold in the market of that town. It is true that two Spaniards, Mendez and Solis, had lately given more extension to the planting of that reed, but they had never succeeded in manufacturing sugar. One of them boiled its juice into syrup, and the other distilled it into a spirituous liquor, of a very indifferent quality, called taffia.

When the whole agricultural interest of Louisiana was thus prostrated, and looking round for the discovery of some means to escape from annihilation, when the eager and anxious inquiry of every planter was: "What shall I do to pay my debts and support my family?"—the energy of one of the most spirited and respected citizens of Louisiana suddenly saved her from utter ruin, and raised her to that state of prosperity which has increased with every successive year.

That individual was Etienne de Boré, who was born in the Illinois district of Louisiana in 1740, and who had gone back to France with his parents when he was only four years old. He was of a distinguished Norman family, being lineally descended of Robert de Boré, who was, in 1652, one of the king's counsellors, director general of the post-office department, and one of the stewards of the king's household,* &c. Etienne de Boré, when his age permitted it, entered into that privileged body of the king's household troops, called the "mousquetaires," or guardsmen. None could be a "mousquetaire" unless he was noble by birth; every "mousquetaire" had the grade of captain, and the Captain of a company of

---

* Conseiller de roi, controleur general des postes, et maitre des courriers de **Paris** à Orléans, maitre d'hotel de la maison du roi, &c.

"mousquetaires" had the rank of Lieutenant General Etienne de Boré had left the mousquetaires in 1772, to assume the command of a company of cavalry. But the circumstance of his having, the year before, married in Paris the daughter of Destréhan, the ex-treasurer of Louisiana when it was a French colony, operated a change in his career, by inducing him to return to Louisiana, where his wife had some property. Etienne de Boré had settled on a plantation which was situated on the left bank of the Mississippi, six miles above New Orleans. There he had, like the majority of the planters, given his attention to the cultivation of indigo, and he had also seen his hopes blasted, and himself and family threatened with entire ruin.

In these critical conjunctures, he determined to renew the attempts which had been repeatedly made to manufacture sugar. He immediately prepared to go into all the expenses and incur all the obligations consequent on so costly an undertaking. His wife warned him that her father had, in former years, vainly made a similar attempt; she represented that he was hazarding on the cast of a die all that remained of their means of existence; that, if he failed, as was so probable, he would reduce his family to hopeless poverty; that he was of an age, being over fifty years old, when fate was not to be tempted by doubtful experiments, as he could not reasonably entertain the hope of a sufficiently long life to rebuild his fortune, if once completely shattered; and that he would not only expose himself to ruin, but also to a risk much more to be dreaded—that of falling within the grasp of creditors. Friends and relations joined their remonstrances to hers, but could not shake the strong resolve of his energetic mind. He had fully matured his plan, and was determined to sink or swim with it. There are circumstances in a man's life when he must know

THE FIRST SUGAR PLANTER. 349

how to play, coolly and sagaciously, a desperate game. Boré felt it, and braced up his strength to fling himself on "the tide which, if taken at the flood, was to lead him to fortune, or if not, was to wreck him among the shoals of life."

Purchasing a quantity of canes from Mendez and Solis, he began to plant in 1794, and to make all the other necessary preparations, and, in 1795, he made a crop of sugar which sold for twelve thousand dollars—a large sum at that time. Boré's attempt had not been without exciting the keenest interest; many had frequently visited him during the year, to witness his preparations; gloomy predictions had been set afloat, and, on the day when the grinding of the cane was to begin, a large number of the most respectable inhabitants had gathered in and about the sugar-house, to be present at the failure or success of the experiment. Would the syrup granulate? Would it be converted into sugar? The crowd waited with eager impatience for the moment when the man who watches the coction of the juice of the cane, determines whether it is ready to granulate. When that moment arrived, the stillness of death came among them, each one holding his breath, and feeling that it was a matter of ruin or prosperity for them all. Suddenly the sugar-maker cried out with exultation: "It granulates!" and the crowd repeated: "It granulates!" Inside and outside of the building one could have heard the wonderful tidings, flying from mouth to mouth, and dying in the distance, as if a hundred glad echoes were telling it to one another. Each one of the bystanders pressed on, to ascertain the fact on the evidence of his own senses, and, when it could no longer be doubted, there came a shout of joy, and all flocked around Etienne Boré, overwhelming him with congratulations, and almost hugging the man whom they called their saviour—the saviour of

Louisiana. Fifty-seven years have elapsed, and an event, which produced so much excitement at the time, is very nearly obliterated from the memory of the present generation; but it may be permitted to the filial piety of a grandson to record in these pages, with an honest pride, the indebtedness of his native country to a cherished ancestor.

The population of Louisiana had been steadily increasing, notwithstanding the obstacles and even calamities which had retarded its progress, and, in the beginning of 1795, the Cabildo made a representation to the King on their inadequacy to fulfil their duties, and prayed for the creation of six additional offices of "regidor," which petition was subsequently granted.

If the fears of an immediate attack had disappeared, the excitement produced in Louisiana by the French revolution, the intrigues of Genet, and the rumors of an invasion by De la Chaise, who was thought to be coming, as he had promised, "to give freedom to the land of his birth," had not entirely subsided. In such circumstances, says Judge Martin in his History of Louisiana, the Baron thought that the strictest vigilance was required in New Orleans, and availed himself of some nocturnal depredations, to issue a proclamation enforcing a severe police and directing the shutting of the gates at an early hour.

In this proclamation he complained of "the success with which evil-minded, turbulent and enthusiastic individuals, who certainly had nothing to lose, had spread false rumors, calculated to give rise to the most complete distrust between the Government and the people, whereby the province was threatened with all the disasters to which the French colonies had fallen a prey."

After this, the proclamation announces that* "to

* Martin's History of Louisiana, vol. ii., p. 127.

restore order and public tranquillity, Syndics, chosen among the most notable planters, are to be appointed, residing within about nine miles of each other, to be subordinate to the commandant, to whom they are to give weekly accounts of every important occurrence.

"It is made the duty of every one having the knowledge, even by hearsay, of any offence, or seditious expressions tending to excite alarm or disturb public tranquillity, to give immediate notice to the Syndic, commandant or governor.

"Every assemblage of more than eight persons, to consult on public matters, is absolutely forbidden.

"Every individual is bound to denounce to the commandant any Syndic guilty of the offence of making use of any seditious expressions.

"Every traveller, found without a passport, is immediately to be arrested, and carried before the Syndic, who is to examine and send him to the commandant.

"Every traveller, possessed of the knowledge of an important event, is first to give notice of it to the Syndic, who is to take a note of it, register the name of said traveller, and afterwards, according to the circumstances, permit or forbid the communication of the event, giving information of it to the commandant.

"Syndics* are to order patrols from time to time.

"At the same time," says Monette in his History of the Valley of the Mississippi, "Baron de Carondelet was laudably exerting himself to enlarge, beautify and fortify the city. Early in May, 1794, he had given public notice of his intention to open a canal in the rear of the city, for the double purpose of draining the marshes and ponds in that vicinity, and establishing a navigable communication with the sea. This canal, communicating

---

* American State Papers, vol. i., p. 877.

with the Bayou St. John, would effectually accomplish the latter object, to the great commercial advantages of New Orleans, while it would also remove one great source of annoyance and disease proceeding from the generation of innumerable swarms of mosquitoes and march miasma from the stagnant pools.

"To accomplish this important undertaking for the advantages of the city, he proposed to accept the voluntary contribution of such slave labor as the planters and others in the vicinity might be willing to give. The month of June had been announced as the time for beginning the work, at which time sixty negro slaves were sent by the patriotic inhabitants, and the canal was commenced. The work progressed rapidly; but the depth of the canal was only six feet. The convicts and a few slaves continued to labor upon the work during the remainder of the year, until the canal was opened to the intersection of the Bayou St. John, through which a navigable route lay to Lake Pontchartrain. The following year, the plan of making the canal navigable up to the city was concurred in, and the Governor made a second call upon the patriotism and public spirit of the people for additional labor. To this call a generous response was given, and one hundred and fifty negroes were sent to expedite the work. The excavation was now made to the width of fifteen feet, with a depth sufficient to admit small vessels to the vicinity of the ramparts on the rear of the city. In November, the Governor made one more call for aid from the planters within fifteen miles of the city, assuring them that, with eight days' work from the same number of hands, he would be able to render the canal navigable for small vessels up to the 'basin,' which had been excavated near the ramparts of the city. The labor was cheerfully contributed, and the canal was in successful operation during the following winter, 1796. Early in the spring, a number of schooners came up and moored in the basin. Thus, in the autumn of 1795, was there a navigable canal route from the city, by way of the Lakes, to the sea. In honor of the projector and patron, the Cabildo, by a decree, designated it as 'Canal Carondelet,' a name which it retains to this day." It will be recollected that this same work had been projected and begun, in 1727, by Governor Perier, but soon relinquished.

The revolution in France had been favorable to the increase of the population of Louisiana, which had been recruited by the arrival of some French royalists, who had fled from the anger of their former vassals. Such emigrants were acceptable to the crown of Spain, and among the most conspicuous were the Marquis de Maison Rouge, the Baron de Bastrop, and Jacques Céran de Lassus de St. Vrain, an officer of the late royal navy of France, who had emigrated like so many others of the nobility. They proposed* plans for the removal of a number of their countrymen to Louisiana from the United States, where they had sought an asylum. Their propositions were accepted—twelve square leagues were granted to Bastrop, on the banks of the Ouachita, thirty thousand superficial acres were appropriated to Maison Rouge's establishment, and De Lassus de St. Vrain obtained a concession of ten thousand square *arpens*. These grants were made on certain conditions, which were never complied with, and a full title never vested in the grantees, who, by their birth, habits and tastes, were not qualified to carry such plans into execution and to become pioneers in the wilderness.

"The encouragement thus given by the colonial go

---

* Martin's History of Louisiana, vol. ii., p. 128.

vernment," says Judge Martin, "was not confined to a grant of land. It covenanted to pay two hundred dollars to every family, composed of at least two white persons, fit for the labors of agriculture, or the mechanical arts necessary in a settlement of the kind, such as carpenters, blacksmiths, &c. Four hundred dollars were allowed to families having four laborers, and proportionately to those having only an artisan or laborer. They were to be assisted with guides and provisions from New Madrid to the Ouachita district. Their baggage and implements of agriculture were to be transported from New Madrid at the King's expense. Each family, consisting of at least two white persons fit for the pursuits of agriculture, was entitled to four hundred acres of land, with a proportionate increase to more numerous families. Settlers were permitted to bring European servants, to be bound to them for six or more years, and who, at the expiration of their time of service, were to receive grants of land in the same proportion."

A few months after, the King gave his approbation to this agreement between the Spanish authorities and the French royalists. These were laudable efforts on the part of the Spanish government, but they proved completely abortive.

Thus was that government pursuing, with all the means in its power, the wise policy of increasing the white population, when the colony was discovered to be threatened with a very serious danger. The news of the success of the St. Domingo revolution, and of the rebellion of those who might be called the white slaves of France against their masters, had not been without penetrating into the very cabins of the blacks of Louisiana, who thought that they were authorized to do the same thing for themselves; and, accordingly, a conspiracy was formed on the plantation of Julien Poydras, one of the wealthiest planters, who was travelling in the United States. The estate of Poydras was situated in Pointe Coupée, an isolated parish, distant one hundred and fifty miles from New Orleans, and where the number of the negroes was considerable—from which circumstances they had derived much encouragement. The conspiracy had extended itself throughout the whole parish, and the 15th of April had been the day selected for the massacre. All the whites were to be indiscriminately butchered, with the exception of the adult females, who were to be spared to gratify the lust of the conspirators. A disagreement as to the hour at which the rising should take place gave rise to a quarrel among the leaders, and one of them, through his wife, sent information to the commandant of the parish of all the details of the plot. The ringleaders, among whom were three whites, were immediately arrested and put in prison. The blacks rose and flew to the rescue of their chiefs; a conflict ensued, in which twenty-five of them were killed. The trial of the rebellious slaves was rapidly got through; twenty-three were hung all along the banks of the river down to New Orleans, and their corpses remained for some days dangling from their gibbets, as a warning to the rest of their population; thirty-one were severely flogged; and the three whites, who certainly were the guiltiest, and who ought to have been punished with more rigor than the miserable and ignorant beings* they had deluded, were only sentenced to leave the colony. This event produced great alarm among the inhabitants, who did not know how far the ramifications of the conspiracy had extended, and the apprehensions continued to be such, that, on the 29th of February of the following year, the Cabildo petitioned

---

* The Intendant Rendon's despatch of the 15th of June, 1795

the King, to obtain from him that the importation of slaves into Louisiana be completely prohibited, and in the mean time, the Baron, in compliance with their wishes, issued a provisional proclamation to that effect.

Such was the state of affairs in Louisiana, when the negotiations which had been so long pending between the United States and Spain were brought to a close, by a treaty signed at Madrid, on the 20th of October, 1795.

The principal stipulations of the treaty, which related to Louisiana, were, says Monette in his History of the Valley of the Mississippi, as follows:

"The *second* article stipulates that the future boundary between the United States and the Floridas shall be the thirty-first parallel of north latitude, from the Mississippi eastward to the Chattahoochy River; thence along a line running due east, from the mouth of Flint River to the head of St. Mary's River, and thence down the middle of that river to the Atlantic Ocean, and that, within six months after the ratification of the treaty, the troops and garrisons of each power shall be withdrawn to its own side of this boundary, and the people shall be at liberty to retire with all their effects, if they desire so to do.

"The *third* article stipulates that each party, respectively, shall appoint one commissioner and one surveyor, with a suitable military guard of equal numbers, well provided with instruments and assistants, who shall meet at Natchez, within six months after the mutual ratification of the treaty, and proceed thence *to run and mark* the said Southern boundary of the United States.

"The *fourth* article stipulates that the middle of the Mississippi River shall be the Western boundary of the United States from its source to the intersection of the said line of demarcation. The King of Spain also stipu lates that the whole width of said river, from its source to the sea, shall be free to the people of the United States.

"The *fifth* article stipulates, that each party shall require and enforce peace and neutrality among the Indian tribes inhabiting their respective territories.

"The King of Spain stipulates and agrees to permit the people of the United States, for the term of three years, to use the port of New Orleans as a place of deposit for their produce and merchandise, and to export the same free from all duty or charge, except a reasonable consideration to be paid for storage and other incidental expenses; that the term of three years may, by subsequent negotiation, be extended; or, instead of that town, some other point in the island of New Orleans shall be designated as a place of deposit for the American trade. Other commercial advantages were likewise held out as within the reach of negotiation. The treaty was duly ratified by the Senate in March following, and the Federal Executive proceeded to make the necessary arrangements for the fulfilment of all its stipulations on the part of the United States."

By this treaty the Southern boundary of the United States, as settled by their treaty of peace with Great Britain, was recognised, and also the principle so tenaciously advocated—that free ships make free goods.

"But," continues Monette, "although Spain suspended her restrictions upon the river trade after this treaty had been ratified, it was quite apparent that the King never intended to surrender the territory east of the Mississippi, and north of latitude 31, provided any contingency should enable him to hold possession. He had been compelled, by the pressure of political embarrassment, both in Europe and in America, to yield a reluctant assent to the treaty, as the only means by which he could preserve the province of Louisiana from invasion, and conciliate the hostile feelings of the Western people of the United States. The provincial authorities in Louisiana seemed to view the late treaty on the part of Spain as a mere measure of policy and court finesse, to propitiate the neutrality of the Federal Government and satisfy the American people, until her European embarrassments should have been surmounted. Spain, incited by France, had been upon the verge of a war with Great Britain; and already the British authorities in Canada had planned an invasion of Upper Louisiana, by way of the Lakes and the Illinois River, whenever hostilities should be formally proclaimed. To prevent this invasion was one object to be gained by the treaty of Madrid, which would put the neutral territory of a friendly power in the way of invasion."

Whilst the negotiations had been carried on between Spain and the United States, the Baron de Carondelet had not been inactive, and had been striving to secure success to his favorite plan of separating the West from the rest of the Union. His chief agent, Power, had informed him that the same influential individuals in Kentucky, who had been in secret correspondence with Governor Miró, such as Wilkinson, Innis, Murray, Nicholas, &c., were disposed to renew their former relations with the Spanish Government, and that some of them would be ready to meet at the mouth of the Ohio any officer of rank that should be sent to them. In consequence of this communication, Carondelet chose for this delicate mission the Governor of Natchez, Gayoso de Lemos, who proceeded to New Madrid, whence he despatched Power to make the preliminary arrangements for the interview with Sebastian, Innis, and their other associates. Power met Sebastian at Red Banks. This individual told the Spanish emissary, that Innis had been prevented by some family concerns from leaving home, that, as the courts of Kentucky were then in session, the absence of Nicholas—a lawyer in great practice—would excite suspicion, and that Murray,* having lately become an habitual drunkard, was unfit for any kind of business and could not be trusted. This was a great disappointment for Power; but Sebastian went down with him to meet Gayoso, who, in the mean time, had employed the men of his escort in erecting a small stockade fort, on the right bank of the river, opposite the mouth of the Ohio, in order to cause it to be believed that the construction of this fortification had been the object of his journey. Sebastian declared to Gayoso that he was authorized to treat in the name of Innis and Nicholas, but seems to have said nothing about Wilkinson. Gayoso proposed to him that they should together visit the Baron de Carondelet; this was assented to, and Power, Sebastian, and Gayoso departed for New Orleans, where they arrived early in January, 1796, and, in the beginning of the spring, Sebastian and Power sailed together for Philadelphia, no doubt on a mission from the Spanish Governor.

Power soon returned to Kentucky, and submitted to those whom he expected to seduce the following document:

"His Excellency, the Baron de Carondelet, &c., Commander-in-chief and Governor of his Catholic Majesty's provinces of West Florida and Louisiana, having communications of importance, embracing the interests of said provinces, and at the same time deeply affecting those of Kentucky and of the Western country in general, to make to its inhabitants, through the medium of the influential characters in this country, and judging it, in

---

* Martin's History, vol. ii., p. 126.

the present uncertain and critical attitude of politics, highly imprudent and dangerous to lay them on paper, has expressly commissioned and authorized me to submit the following proposals to the consideration of Messrs. Sebastian, Nicholas, Innis and Murray, and also of such other gentlemen as may be pointed out by them, and to receive from them their sentiments and determination on the subject.

"1º—The above mentioned gentlemen are to exert all their influence in impressing on the minds of the inhabitants of the Western country, a conviction of the necessity of their withdrawing and separating themselves from the Federal Union, and forming an independent government wholly unconnected with that of the Atlantic States. To prepare and dispose the people for such an event, it will be necessary that the most popular and eloquent writers in this State should, in well-timed publications, expose, in the most striking point of view, the inconveniences and disadvantages that a longer connection with and dependence on, the Atlantic States, must inevitably draw upon them, and the great and innumerable difficulties in which they will probably be entangled, if they do not speedily recede from the Union ; the benefits they will certainly reap from a secession ought to be pointed out in the most forcible and powerful manner ; and the danger of permitting the federal troops to take possession of the posts on the Mississippi, and thus forming a cordon of fortified places round them, must be particularly expatiated upon. In consideration of gentlemen devoting their time and talents to this object, his Excellency, the Baron de Carondelet, will appropriate the sum of one hundred thousand dollars to their use, which shall be paid in drafts on the royal treasury at New Orleans, or, if more convenient, shall be conveyed at the expense of his Catholic Majesty into this country, and held at their disposal. Moreover, should such persons as shall be instrumental in promoting the views of his Catholic Majesty hold any public employment, and in consequence of taking an active part in endeavoring to effect a secession shall lose their employments, a compensation, equal at least to the emoluments of their respective offices, shall be made to them by his Catholic Majesty, let their efforts be crowned with success, or terminate in disappointment.

"2°—Immediately after the declaration of independence, Fort Massac shall be taken possession of by the troops of the new government, which shall be furnished by his Catholic Majesty, without loss of time, with twenty field pieces, with their carriages and every necessary appendage, including powder, balls, &c., together with a number of small-arms and ammunition, sufficient to equip the troops that it shall be necessary to raise. The whole to be transported at his expense to the already mentioned Fort Massac. His Catholic Majesty will further supply the sum of one hundred thousand dollars for the raising and maintaining of said troops, which sum shall also be conveyed to, and delivered at, Fort Massac.

"3°—The northern boundary of his Catholic Majesty's provinces of East and West Florida shall be designated by a line commencing on the Mississippi, at the mouth of the river Yazoo, extending due east to the river Confederation or Tombigbee; *provided, however*, that all his Catholic Majesty's forts, posts or settlements on the Confederation or Tombigbee, are included on the south of such a line; but should any of his Majesty's forts, posts or settlements fall to the north of said line, then the northern boundary of his Majesty's provinces of East and West Florida shall be designated by a line beginning at the same point on the Mississippi, and drawn in such a direction as to meet the river Confederation or

Tombigbee, six miles to the north of the m st northern Spanish fort, post or settlement on the said river. All the lands to the north of that line shall be considered as constituting a part of the territory of the new government, saving that small tract of land at the Chickasaw Bluffs, on the eastern bank of the Mississippi, ceded to his Majesty by the Chickasaw nation in a formal treaty concluded on the spot in the year 1795, between his Excellency Don Manuel Gayoso de Lemos, Governor of Natchez, and Augliakabee, and some other Chickasaw chiefs; which tract of land his Majesty reserves for himself. The eastern boundary of the Floridas shall be hereafter regulated.

"4°—His Catholic Majesty will, in case the Indian nations south of the Ohio should declare war or commence hostilities against the new government, not only join and assist it in repelling its enemies, but also if said government shall, at any future period, deem it necessary to reduce said Indian nations, extend its dominion over them, and compel them to submit themselves to its constitution and laws, his Majesty will heartily concur and coöperate with the new Government in the most effectual manner in attaining this desirable end.

"5°—His Catholic Majesty will not, either directly or indirectly, interfere in the framing of the constitution or laws which the new government shall think fit to adopt, nor will he, at any time, by any means whatever, attempt to lessen the independence of the said government, or endeavor to acquire an undue influence in it, but will, in the manner that shall hereafter be stipulated by treaty, defend and support it in preserving its independence.

"6°—The preceding proposals are the outlines of a provisional treaty, which his Excellency the Baron de Carondelet is desirous of entering into with the inhabitants of the Western country, the moment they shall be in a situation to treat for themselves. Should they not meet entirely with your approbation, and should you wish to make any alterations in, or additions, to them, I shall, on my return, if you think proper to communicate them to me, lay them before his Excellency, who is animated with a sincere and ardent desire to foster this promising and rising infant country, and at the same time promote and fortify the interests of his beneficent royal master, in securing, by a generous and disinterested conduct, the gratitude and affections of a just, sensible and enlightened people.

"The important and unexpected events that have taken place in Europe since the ratification of the treaty concluded on the 27th of October, 1795, between his Catholic Majesty and the United States of America, having convulsed the general system of politics in that quarter of the globe, and, wherever its influence is extended, causing a collision of interests between nations formerly living in the most perfect union and harmony, and directing the political views of some states towards objects the most remote from their former pursuits, but none being so completely unhinged and disjointed as the cabinet of Spain, it may be confidently asserted, without incurring the reproach of presumption, that his Catholic Majesty *will not carry the above mentioned treaty into execution;* nevertheless, the thorough knowledge I have of the disposition of the Spanish government justifies me in saying that, so far from its being his Majesty's wish to exclude the inhabitants of this Western country from the free navigation of the Mississippi, or withhold from them any of the benefits stipulated for them by the treaty, it is positively his intention, as soon as they shall put it in his power to treat with them, by declaring themselves independent of the Federal Government and establishing one of their own, to grant them privileges far more extensive, give them a decided preference over the Atlantic States in his commercial connections with them, *and place them in a situation infinitely more advantageous, in every point of view, than that in which they would find themselves, were the treaty to be carried into effect.*"

To back these tempting offers and to smoothe difficulties, money had been sent up the Mississippi and the Ohio, and Power, who had several interviews with Wilkinson, delivered to him ten thousand dollars, which had been carried up, concealed in barrels of sugar and bags of coffee. Wilkinson had just been appointed Major-general of the United States in the place of Wayne, who had died recently, and Power was directed to avail himself of his intercourse with Wilkinson, to ascertain the force, discipline, and temper of the army under that general, and to report thereon to Carondelet. The Spanish Governor, through his agent, made also a strong appeal to Wilkinson's ambition. "The Western people," said he, "are dissatisfied with the excise on whiskey;* Spain and France are irritated at the late treaty, which has bound so closely together the United States and England; the army is devoted to their talented and brilliant commander; it requires but firmness and resolution on your part to render the Western people free and happy. Can a man of your superior genius prefer a subordinate and contracted position as the commander of the small and insignificant army of the United States, to the glory of being the founder of an empire—the liberator of so many millions of his countrymen—the Washington of the West? Is not this splendid achievement to be easily accomplished? Have you not the con

---

* Martin's History of Louisiana, vol. ii., p. 145.

fidence of your fellow citizens, and principally of the Kentucky volunteers? Would not the people, at the slightest movement on your part, hail you as the chief of the new republic? Would not your reputation alone raise you an army which France and Spain would enable you to pay? The eyes of the world are fixed upon you; be bold and prompt; do not hesitate to grasp the golden opportunity of acquiring wealth, honors, and immortal fame. But should Spain be forced to execute the treaty of 1795, and surrender all the posts claimed by the United States, then the bright vision of independence for the Western people, and of the most exalted position and imperishable renown for yourself, must for ever vanish."

But all these allurements failed to produce their expected effects. Time, Washington's administration, and a concourse of favorable circumstances, had consolidated the Union; and Wilkinson and his associates, whatever might have been their secret aspirations, were too sagacious not to see what almost insuperable obstacles existed between the conception and execution of such dangerous schemes. Therefore, on his return to New Orleans, Power made to his Spanish employer an unfavorable report on what he had observed. He remarked, in the words used by Judge Martin in his History of Louisiana, that whatever might have been, at any previous time, the disposition of the people of Kentucky, they were now perfectly satisfied with the General Government, and that their leading men, with a few exceptions, manifested an utter aversion to the hazardous experiments heretofore thought of—especially as their own Government had now obtained for them, by the late treaty, the principal object which they expected to attain by a separation from the Union.

In the meantime, Spain had concluded a treaty of

peace with France, and, on the 7th of October, 1796, had declared war against Great Britain, mentioning as one of her grievances, the late treaty which that power had made with the United States, and which was alleged to be a great infringement on the rights of the Spanish Crown. The attention of the Governor of Louisiana was called to the gathering of a considerable number of troops on the southern frontier of Canada—which circumstance had given rise to the report that an invasion of Louisiana was contemplated. The Minister of the Catholic King near the United States communicated to the President his fears on the subject, and requested that in conformity with the late treaty and the law of nations, the United States, as neutrals, should take the necessary measures to oppose effectually the intended violation of their territory.

The Baron had determined not to deliver up to the United States the posts ceded by the treaty of 1795, until the failure of his last attempt to detach the Western country from the Union should be fully ascertained, for in case of success, of course the treaty would have been annulled by the disruption of the American confederacy. Therefore, when the Spanish authorities heard of the approach of Andrew Ellicott, who had been appointed, under the treaty, commissioner for the United States, they had recourse to every artifice to postpone the execution of its stipulations. Ellicott arrived at Natchez on the 24th of February, 1797, and proposed to Gayoso, who was the other commissioner on the part of Spain, that they should proceed immediately to the discharge of their respective duties. But Gayoso replied that the fort was not ready to be surrendered; that certain preliminaries could be settled at New Orleans only, where the American commissioner refused to go; that the stipulations of the treaty were not sufficiently explicit, and that doubts had risen in the Baron de Carondelet's mind as to their interpretation; that it was questionable whether all the forts and edifices were to be delivered up in their integrity to the United States, or razed and abandoned, in conformity with formal treaties which Spain had made with the Chickasaws, who had ceded to her the lands at the Chickasaw Bluffs, Walnut Hills, and Tombigbee, on certain conditions that would be violated, if the treaty of 1795 were interpreted in the manner favored by the American government; and that the ultimate orders of his Catholic Majesty, or of his minister plenipotentiary near the United States, should be waited for in a matter of so much importance. Not satisfied with putting forth these pretexts for procrastination, Gayoso proceeded to strengthen the fortifications at Natchez, Walnut Hills, and the other posts above, under the apparent apprehension of Indian hostilities and of an invasion from Canada; and the meeting of the commissioners for establishing the line of demarcation, as provided for by the treaty, was indefinitely postponed. It was alleged that,* as the treaty of 1795 contained no guaranty of property to those who desired to retire beyond the American jurisdiction, it would be necessary to settle that point by a new treaty. At another time it was seriously urged, that a scrupulous observance of the treaty of Madrid could not be demanded, because the United States had not acted in good faith towards Spain in conceding to Great Britain, by the treaty of London, November 19, 1794, the free navigation of the Mississippi, although this concession had been made nearly a year previous. These objections were not presented in a body, but were sprung up one after the other, and evidently to gain time. The course

---

* Monette's Valley of the Mississippi, vol. ii., p. 523.

pursued by the Spanish authorities gave rise to an excited correspondence between them and the American officers; and the people of the district, who, being of Anglo-Saxon descent, and emigrants from the United States, had all their sympathies enlisted in favor of their countrymen, became highly incensed. On their showing some signs of resistance, two of them were arrested on the 9th of June, 1797, and confined within the Spanish fort. As this evinced on the part of Gayoso a determination to enforce vigorously the authority of Spain, in a country which he ought already to have abandoned, the people flew to arms and drove the Governor to seek an asylum in the fort. Public meetings were held, violent speeches delivered, extreme measures contemplated, and Lieutenant Pope, who commanded the military escort of the commissioner, Andrew Ellicott, declared that he would for the future *repel by force any attempt made to imprison those who claimed the privilege of citizens of the United States. He also notified the people of his intentions, and assured them of his protection and support against any arbitrary military force which might be brought to operate against them, or in any way to infringe their rights as American citizens.*

"At this time," says Monette, who relates these events with great accuracy, and whose narration I can do no better than partly to borrow, " it was supposed that Gayoso might order reinforcements from other posts on the river, to aid in maintaining his authority. Lieutenant Pope had resolved to permit no such reinforcement, and called on the people to sustain him in repelling an attempt to reinforce the garrison in Fort Panmure.

"On the 14th of June, Governor Gayoso issued his proclamation, exhorting the people to a quiet and peaceable submission to the authority of his Catholic Majesty until the difficulties between the two governments could be properly arranged. At the same time, he promised the utmost lenity, and a pardon to all who repented of their misdeeds, and, as an evidence of repentance, abstained from all acts calculated to disturb the public peace.

"The people, already highly irritated by delays and disappointed hopes, took great exceptions to the word 'repentance,' as highly offensive to free citizens of the United States. Things now assumed a serious aspect, and the opposition to Spanish authority had taken a regular form of rebellion. A number of respectable militia-companies were organized, and ready to take the field at the first notice, and open hostilities seemed inevitable. Both parties were in a continual state of preparation to repel force by force. Gayoso made great efforts to reinforce his garrison, but without success, while the militia were drilling throughout the settlements. Confined to the walls of his fortress, and too weak for offensive operations, he interceded with the American commissioner to use his influence in calming the popular excitement. But Colonel Ellicott felt little sympathy for the unpleasant position which he had brought upon himself.

"In the meantime a public meeting had been announced to be held at Benjamin Bealk's, on the Nashville road, eight miles from Natchez. This meeting was assembled on the 20th of June, and was attended by many of the inhabitants. The subject of the existing difficulties was discussed, and the meeting dispersed after appointing a "Committee of Public Safety" consisting of seven prominent men, to represent the people thereafter in any negotiation with the Spanish authorities. No measures adopted by the Spanish Governor should have the force of law until the concurrence of this Committee should render it obligatory.

"Up to this time, the Spanish commandant, as well as the American, kept an active patrol continually on duty; and during the greater portion of the time since the month of May, a heavy piece of ordnance in the Spanish fort had been brought to bear upon the American commissioner's tent, which was in full view.

"On the 18th of June, while all was excitement and apprehension, the Governor, confined within the narrow limits of the fort, desired an interview with the American Commissioner at the house of Captain Minor. To meet this appointment, Gayoso, in great trepidation, having left the fort by a circuitous route, made his way through thickets and cane brakes to the rear or north side of Minor's plantation, and thence through a corn field to the back of the house, and entered the parlor undiscovered. Such were the visible marks of anxiety in his person, that Colonel Ellicott says his feelings never were more excited than when he beheld the Governor. The humiliating state to which he was reduced by a people whose affections he had courted, and whose gratitude he expected, had made a strong and visible impression upon his mind and countenance. His having been educated with high ideas of command and prerogative served only to render his present situation more poignant and distressing.

"The Committee of Public Safety, agreeably to their instructions, presented themselves before Gayoso in their official capacity, for his recognition and approbation. He did not hesitate to recognize them as representatives of the people, and cheerfully acceded to their demand, that none of the people should be injured or prosecuted for the part they had taken in the late movements against the Spanish authority; also, that they should be exempt from serving in the Spanish militia; unless in case of riots or Indian hostilities. The proceedings of the public meeting, the recognition of the Committee by the Governor, and his acquiescence in their demands, had all tended greatly to quiet public apprehensions and to allay the popular excitement.

"Yet there were persons in the Committee whose fidelity to the United States was suspected by Colonel Ellicott; and one of them was particularly objectionable to him and Lieutenant Pope. In order to insure harmony, he prevailed upon the Governor to dissolve the Committee, and to authorize the election of another, by proclamation—which should be *permanent*. A new Committee, consisting of nine members, was accordingly elected about the first of July, "permanent in its character," and created by virtue of the Spanish authority. The organization of this Committee was highly gratifying to Colonel Ellicott, who declared that *this Committee was the finishing stroke to the Spanish authority and jurisdiction.*" And so it was; the concessions made by Gayoso were ratified by Carondelet, and a sort of truce ensued between the two adverse parties.

Leaving, for the present, matters as they stand under this compromise, I shall proceed to notice some facts which had occurred in the meanwhile, and which are to be briefly chronicled.

It appears by a despatch of the Intendant Rendon, dated on the 28th of April, 1795, that the expenses of the province had amounted in 1794 to $864,126, and that the custom-house revenue had not given more than $57,506.

On the 15th of June, he describes* the sad condition

---

* Manifiesta el triste estado á que está reducida la provincia por falto de recursos. El estado, (dice) á que los hurricanes y incendio han traido esta provincia y lo exhaustas de caudales que se hallan las Reales Cajas para subvenir á los indispensables gastos que me ocasionen las repetidas expediciones de fondos á que nos obligan las tentativas que la sedienta ambicion de nuestros enemigos forman para apoderarse de estas posesiones y abrirse paso á Nueva-España: Los

to which the colony had been reduced by the want of capital, by the disasters produced by conflagration and the repeated occurrence of hurricanes, by the exhaustion of the royal treasury in Louisiana, drained by the incessant demands of funds which the Spanish authorities had to meet in order to counteract the schemes of the insatiable ambition of their enemies to possess themselves of the territories of Spain, with a view of opening to themselves a passage to the Mexican provinces; by the fortifications which they had been obliged to erect, increase, or strengthen throughout the colony to repel such designs; by the creation of a small fleet of galleys which protected the navigation of the river; by the immense disbursements to which they were subjected by the avidity of their Indian allies, and other innumerable and extraordinary contingencies which daily occurred, which had reduced them to the most deplorable indigence, deprived them of the means of attending to numerous objects urgently requiring their immediate consideration, and prevented them from maintaining, in all their integrity, the authority of the Government and the honor of the arms of the King. "All that remains for me to do," said he, "is to repeat my most earnest entreaties that the necessary funds be sent to me as promptly as possible."

On the 30th of November, he informed his Government that a French privateer, called "La Parisienne," with six guns and a crew of forty-five men, commanded

diferentes puestos y fortificaciones que ha sido forzoso aumentar en oposicion á sus designios, una escuadra de galeras que defiende la navegacion del Rio, immensos dispendios que se hacen en las tribus Indias nuestras aliadas, y otras inumerables extraordinarias evocaciones que casi diaramente ocurren, habiendonos reducido á la mas deplorable indigencia por faltarnos ya todo medio para atender á tantos y tan urgentisimos objetos, y mantener con el honor debido la autoridad del Gobierno y de las armas del Rey. Solo me queda el recurso de reiterar á V. E. mis mas eficaces ruegos, á fin de que se sirva franquearme con la mayor brevedad los fondos necesarios, &c.

by Captain Alexander Bolchoz, had taken possession of the post of the Balize, at the mouth of the Mississippi, on the 13th of October preceding. The French occupied that post until the 21st, when, on hearing of the approach of Spanish forces from New Orleans, they retired after having destroyed everything they could. The French vessel had presented herself under the Spanish flag, and the chief pilot, named Juan Ronquillo, with sixteen men out of the twenty who were stationed at the Balize, having gone out to meet her, were made prisoners, and twenty of the French, well armed, availed themselves of the Spanish boat to go ashore, and easily overpowered the four men who had remained to guard the post.

In the same despatch, Rendon said that the cultivation of tobacco had been abandoned in all the districts of the province with the exception of Natchitoches, ever since his Majesty had reduced to one hundred and twenty thousand pounds the quantity which he would buy annually.

In another communication of the 30th of January, 1796, he stated the revenue of the custom-house in 1795 to have been $114,932—a little more than double of what it had been the year previous—which is, no doubt, to be attributed to the removal of the apprehensions of a revolution and the cessation of the state of uncertainty existing in 1793 and 1794.

In April, 1796, Don Francisco Rendon departed from New Orleans for the province of Zacatecas, of which he had been appointed Intendant, and his successor in Louisiana was Don Juan Ventura Morales, who, on the 17th of July of the same year, informed his government of some changes which had been effected in the comptroller's department (contaduria), and by which, on the resignation of Don Francisco Arroyo, Don Carlos Anastasio Gayarré, the grandson of the Contador Don Estevan Gayarré, who had come with Ulloa in 1766, had taken Arroyo's place, and Don Manuel Hoa had succeeded Gayarré. For these changes he begged the royal approbation.

Until the year 1796, the city of New Orleans had never been lighted at night except by the moon, and had been guarded by occasional patrols only, when circumstances required it. But, on the 30th of March of that year, the Baron wrote to his government that, considering the frequent and almost inevitable robberies which were perpetrated in a city of six thousand souls, by a multitude of vagabonds of every nation, he had, as proposed before, imposed a tax of nine reales a year on every chimney, to provide for the expenses of the police; that he had formed a body of thirteen serenos,* or watchmen, and established eighty lamps; that the keeping up of these thirteen watchmen and eighty lamps would cost $3,898 annually; and that to meet these expenses, he had to call for a proportionate contribution, which he had apportioned among all the inhabitants of New Orleans. To make this tax lighter, he proposed that eighteen hundred feet in depth of that part of the commons fronting the rear of the city and nearest to the fortifications, which were unproductive of any revenue to said city, because they were inundated six months in the year, be divided into lots of sixty feet front by one hundred and fifty in depth, and conceded to such of the inhabitants as should offer to cultivate them into gardens, on condition of their paying annually a certain sum to defray the expense of lighting up the streets— which sum would be so much to be deducted from what the city had now to pay.

---

* A sereno is a night watch, so called from his announcing in a loud voice from time to time the state of the weather, and from his frequently crying out· 'Sereno," fair weather.

These were decided improvements calculated to meliorate the condition of New Orleans, which, unfortunately, was visited, it is said for the first time, with the yellow fever in the fall of the year 1796. That autumn proved, besides, very sickly in every other way.

The Intendant Ventura Morales, in a despatch of the 31st of October, speaks of it in the following terms: "An epidemic which broke out in the latter part of August, and which is prevalent to this day, has terrified and still keeps in a state of consternation the whole population of this town. Some of the medical faculty call it a malignant fever; some say that it is the disease so well known in America under the name of 'black vomit,' and, finally, others affirm that it is the yellow fever which proved so fatal in Philadelphia, in the autumn of 1794. Although the number of deaths has not been excessive, considering that, according to the parish registry, it has not yet reached two hundred among the whites since the breaking out of the epidemic, and considering that many died from other diseases, still it must be admitted that the loss of lives is very great, because, although those who died out of the precincts of the town, and the protestants who perished (and they were numerous), have not been registered, nevertheless the number of deaths exceeds, by two thirds, those which occurred in the same lapse of time, in ordinary years.

"A peculiarity to be remarked in the disease is, that it attacks foreigners in preference to the natives, and what is singular, it seems to select the Flemish, the English, and the Americans, who rarely recover, and who generally die the second or third day after the invasion of the disease. Such is not the case with the Spaniards and the colored people, with whom the recipe of Dr. Masderall has produced marvellous effects."

As to the sanitary condition of the morals and religion

of the inhabitants Bishop Peñalvert had said in a despatch of the 1st of November, 1795:

"Since my arrival in this town, on the 17th of July, I have been studying with the keenest attention the character of its inhabitants, in order to regulate my ecclesiastical government in accordance with the information which I may obtain on this important subject.

"On the 2d of August, I began the discharge of my pastoral functions. I took possession without any difficulty of all the buildings appertaining to the church, and examined all the books, accounts, and other matters thereto relating. But as to re-establishing the purity of religion, and reforming the manners of the people, which are the chief objects El Tridentino* has in view, I have encountered many obstacles.

"The inhabitants do not listen to, or if they do, they disregard, all exhortations to maintain in its orthodoxy the Catholic faith, and to preserve the innocence of life. But, without ceasing to pray the Father of all mercies to send his light into the darkness which surrounds these people, I am putting into operation human means to remedy these evils, and I will submit to your Excellency those which I deem conducive to the interests of religion and of the state.

"Because his Majesty tolerates here the Protestants, for sound reasons of state, the bad Christians, who are in large numbers in this colony, think that they are authorized to live without any religion at all. Many adults die without having received the sacrament of communion. Out of the eleven thousand souls composing this parish, hardly three to four hundred comply with the precept of partaking at least once a year of the Lord's supper. Of the regiment of Louisiana, there are not above thirty,

---

* The Bishop alludes to the disciplinary rules established by the Council of Trent.

including officers and soldiers, who have discharged this sacred duty for the last three years. No more than about the fourth part of the population of the town ever attends mass, and on Sundays only, and on those great holydays which require it imperiously. To do so on the other holydays they consider as a superfluous act of devotion to which they are not bound. Most of the married and unmarried men live in a state of concubinage, and there are fathers who procure courtezans for the use of their sons, whom they thus intentionally prevent from getting lawful wives.* The marriage contract is one which, from a universal custom, admitting only of a few accidental exceptions, is never entered into among the slaves. Fasting on Fridays, in Lent, and during *vigilias y temporas*, is a thing unknown; and there are other mal-practices which denote the little of religion existing here among the inhabitants, and which demonstrate that there remains in their bosoms but a slight spark of the faith instilled into them at the baptismal font.

"I presume that a large portion of these people are vassals of the king, because they live on his domain, and accept his favors. But I must speak the truth. His Majesty possesses their bodies and not their souls. Rebellion is in their hearts, and their minds are imbued with the maxims of democracy; and had they not for their chief so active and energetic a man as the present governor, there would long since have been an eruption of the pent-up volcano; and should another less sagacious chief ever forget the fermenting elements which are at work under ground, there can be no doubt but that there would be an explosion.

"Their houses are full of books written against religion and the state. They are permitted to read them

* Hay padres que proporcionan las mancebas á sus hijos para distraerles los matrimonios.

with impunity, and, at the dinner table, they make use of the most shameful, lascivious, and sacrilegious songs.

"This melancholy sketch of the religious and moral customs and condition of the flock which has fallen to my lot, will make you understand the cause of whatever act of scandal may suddenly break out, which, however, I shall strive to prevent; and the better so to do, I have used and am still using some means, which I intend as remedies, and which I am going to communicate to your Excellency.

"The Spanish school, which has been established here at the expense of the crown, is kept as it ought to be; but as there are others which are French, and of which one alone is opened by authority and with the regular license, and as I was ignorant of the faith professed by the teachers and of their morality, I have prescribed for them such regulations as are in conformity with the provisions of our legislation.

"Excellent results are obtained from the Convent of the Ursulines, in which a good many girls are educated; but their inclinations are so decidedly French, that they have even refused to admit among them Spanish women who wished to become Nuns, so long as these applicants should remain ignorant of the French idiom, and they have shed many tears on account of their being obliged to read in Spanish books their spiritual exercises, and to comply with the other duties of their community in the manner prescribed to them.

"This is the nursery of those future matrons who will inculcate on their children the principles which they here imbibe. The education which they receive in this institution is the cause of their being less vicious than the other sex. As to what the boys are taught in the Spanish school, it is soon forgotten. Should their education be continued in a college, they would be confirmed in their religious principles, in the good habits given to them, and in their loyalty as faithful vassals to the crown. But they leave the school when still very young, and retire to the houses of their parents mostly situated in the country, where they hear neither the name of God nor of King, but daily witness the corrupt morals of their parents."

The Bishop goes on enumerating the means and expedients through which he hopes to remedy all the evils which he thus energetically describes. So much for the representation made of Louisiana by the Bishop Don Luis de Peñalvert y Cardenas, in the year of our Lord 1795.

There is another delineation of Louisiana from the pen of the French general Victor Collot, who visited that province in 1796, and who gives a most minute description of its military resources and of its fortifications at the time. The character of the work which he published may be said to be almost entirely strategic. It is evident that this superior officer had received from his government a mission which he had fully the ability to execute. He points out the two rivers of the Arkansas and of the Grands Osages as being the keys of Mexico; "for," says he, "although these two rivers are separated from each other at their mouths by a distance of more than six hundred miles; although the first empties itself into the Mississippi, and the second into the Missouri, yet, as the river des Grands Osages runs south-east, and the river of the Arkansas north-east, they come so near one another at their sources, that they are separated only by a narrow valley, at the extremity of which is Santa Fé.

"From the point where ceases the navigation of the river of the Arkansas to Santa Fé, there are sixty miles, and from the point where ceases the navigation of the river des Grands Osages, there are from one hundred and fifteen to one hundred and twenty miles.

"Thus, supposing two bodies of troops, one of which would muster in the State of Indiana, at the mouth of the river of the Illinois, and opposite that of the Missouri, and the other in the State of Tennessee, at the "Ecores à Margot," a little above the river of the Arkansas, the first ascending the Missouri and the river of the Grands Osages, the second that of the Arkansas, they might both arrive within an interval of very few days, at the same given point (Santa Fé), as they would have about the same facilities of navigation and the same distance to run over. The difficulties to be overcome by the column on the right, in ascending the Missouri for ninety miles, and in moving on land sixty miles more than the column on the left, would be more than compensated by the facility which it would find in going up the river of the Grands Osages, which is much less rapid than that of the Arkansas ; and, considering that from the head of these two rivers, the ground, from its nature, presents neither mountains nor rivers which might be serious obstacles, one may easily appreciate how important it is for Spain that these two passages be closed."

General Collot also gives a description of the fortifications of New Orleans. "At the superior extremity of the city, when facing the river," said he, "is a draining canal which runs from the Mississippi in the direction of Lake Pontchartrain. Its width is twenty-four feet by eight in depth.* This canal, by the means of a sluice, supplies with water the ditches of the city.

"Its defensive works consist in five small forts and a great battery, which are distributed in the following manner:

---

* This is a singular error: there never was such a canal; it was merely in contemplation.

THE NEW ORLEANS FORTIFICATIONS. 381

" On the side which fronts the river, and at both extremities, are two forts which command the road and the river. Their shape is that of a regular pentagon, with a parapet eighteen feet thick, coated with brick, with a ditch and covered way. In each of these forts are barracks for the accommodation of one hundred and fifty men, and a powder magazine. Their artillery is composed of a dozen twelve and eighteen-pounders.

" Between these two forts, and in front of the principal street of the city, is a great battery, commanding the river with its guns, and crossing its fires with the two forts.

" The first of these forts—that is, that on the right, which is most considerable—is called St. Charles, the other St. Louis.

" In the rear, and to cover the city on the land side, are three other forts. They are less considerable than the two first. There is one at each of the two salient angles of the long square forming the city, and a third between the two, a little beyond the line, so as to form an obtuse angle.* These three forts have no covered way and are not revetted,† but are merely strengthened with friezes and palisades. They are armed with eight guns and have accommodations for one hundred men. The one on the right is called *Fort Burgundy*, that on the left *St. Ferdinand*, and that of the middle *St. Joseph*.

" The five forts and the battery cross their fire with one another, and are connected by a ditch of forty feet in width by seven in depth. With the earth taken out of the ditch, there has been formed on the inside a parapet three feet high, on which have been placed, closely serried, a line of twelve feet pickets. Back of these pickets is a small causeway. The earth has been cast

---

* Un angle obtus.   † Ne sont pas revêtus.

so as to render the slope exceedingly easy and accessible Three feet water are always kept up in the moats, even during the driest season of the year, by means of ditches communicating with the draining canal.

"It cannot be denied that these miniature forts are well kept and trimmed up. But, particularly on account of their ridiculous distribution, and also on account of their want of capaciousness, they look more like playthings intended for babies than military defences. For there is not one which cannot be stormed, and which five hundred determined men would not carry sword in hand. Once master of one of the principal forts, either St. Louis or St. Charles, the enemy would have no need of minding the others, because, by bringing the guns to bear upon the city, it would be forced to capitulate immediately, or be burnt up in less than an hour, and have its inhabitants destroyed, as none of the forts can admit of more than one hundred and fifty men. We believe that M. de Carondelet, when he adopted this bad system of defence, thought more of securing the obedience of the subjects of his Catholic Majesty, than of providing a defence against the attack of a foreign enemy, and, in this point of view, he may be said to have completely succeeded."

General Collot describes also the fort at the Plaquemine Turn; he says that it is provided with twenty pieces of artillery of various calibre, and that it can accommodate three hundred men.

He further gives the following description of the inhabitants of the Illinois District: "On the American side, there are still to be found some Frenchmen, to wit: at Kaskaskias, at Rock's Prairie (prairie du rocher), at Piorias on Red River, at Dog's prairie (prairie du chien), near Wisconsin, at Chicago on Lake Michigan, and at the Post of Vincennes on the Wabash.

"Most of these people are a compound of traders, adventurers, wood runners, rowers and warriors—ignorant, superstitious and obstinate—whom no fatigues, no privations, no dangers can stop in their enterprises, which they always carry through. Of the qualities which distinguish the French, they have retained nothing except courage.

"When at home, and in the privacies of their ordinary life, their character is very much like that of the Aborigines, with whom they live. They are therefore indolent, lazy and addicted to drunkenness, cultivating the earth but little or not at all; the French which they speak has become so corrupt, that it has degenerated into a sort of jargon, and they have even forgotten the regular division of the months, and of time itself, according to the calculations of civilization. If you ask them when a particular event happened, they will answer, that it was when the waters were high, when the strawberries were ripe, or in the corn and potato season. Should it be suggested to them to change anything for the better, even in matters which are acknowledged by them as being defective, or should any improvement be recommended to them in agriculture, or in some of the branches of commerce, their only answer is: *it is the custom; so it was with our fathers. I get along with it —so, of course, will my children.* They love France and speak of it with pride."

General Collot, on his way to New Orleans from the upper country, had stopped to visit Etienne Boré at his sugar plantation, six miles above New Orleans, where he was arrested by order of the Baron de Carondelet, who had sent up fifty dragoons by land and an armed boat by the river. The General was put in the boat, and taken down to New Orleans, where he was imprisoned in Fort St. Charles; on the next day, he was called upon by the Governor, who proposed to him a house in town, which he might occupy on parole, and with a Spanish soldier at his door. The General, having accepted the proposition, left the fort for his new lodgings in the Governor's carriage, which had been politely tendered to him. On the 1st of November, the General, from whom some of his maps, drawings and writings had been taken away, was conveyed on board of one of the King's galleys, and, being accompanied by a captain of the regiment of Louisiana, who was not to lose sight of his person, was transported to the Balize, where he was deposited in the house of the chief pilot, Juan Ronquillo, "situated," says he, "in the midst of a vast swamp, and from which there was no issuing except in a boat." He remained at this dismal spot, until the 22d of December, when he embarked on board of the brig Iphigenia for Philadelphia. It is evident from the General's own relation of his visit to New Orleans that he was not permitted to examine the fortifications of that place, and that he must have described them from hearsay.

The Baron de Carondelet wrote to citizen Adet, who was the representative of the French republic near the government of the United States, in order to justify the course which he had pursued towards General Collot. His reasons were :*

1°—The silence of the minister, who had neglected to notify him, the Governor, of the approach of the General.

* In a despatch of the 10th of December, 1796, the Intendant Morales says: No habiendo tenido por conveniente este Gobernador que el general de la Republica Francesa Jorge Victor Collot que se introdujo en esta provincia por el Ohio, acompañado de su ayudante de campo, tenga comunicacion con estos moradores ni que se instruya del Estado de defensa de la ciudad, tomé el partido de enviarle al puesto de la Baliza, a esperar ocasion para embarcarle para cualquiera puesto de los Estados Unidos.

2°—A confidential communication which he, the Baron de Carondelet, had received from Philadelphia, warning him that General Collot was intrusted with a secret mission, against which the Spanish authorities were to be on their guard.

3°—The information given by one of his subaltern officers, that General Collot was reconnoitring the province.

4°—The alarm and excitement which the presence of that superior officer had caused in the colony, and which originated from the rumor mentioned in the American newspapers—that Louisiana was soon to become a French possession.

Etienne Boré was known for his extreme attachment to the French interest, which he was at no pains to conceal, and it is said that the Baron seriously thought of having him arrested and transported to Havana, but that he was deterred by the fear of producing a commotion by inflicting so harsh a treatment on so distinguished a citizen, who, by his personal character, his rank, his family connections, and the benefit he had lately conferred on his country by the introduction of a new branch of industry, commanded universal sympathies and exercised the widest influence.

In the fall of 1797, the Baron de Carondelet departed for Quito, on his having been appointed President of the Royal Audience of the province of that name. The Baron was a short-sized, plump gentleman, somewhat choleric in his disposition, but not destitute of good nature. He was firm and prudent, with a good deal of activity and capacity for business, and he has left in Louisiana a respected and popular memory.

CHAPTER VII.

GAYOSO'S ADMINISTRATION

1797 to 1799.

CASACALVO'S ADMINISTRATION.

1799 to 1801.

BRIGADIER-GENERAL GAYOSO DE LEMOS had been installed into office on the 1st of August, 1797, but it was only in the month of January, 1798, that, in conformity to established usage, he published his Bando de Buen Gobierno—a sort of charter, or programme, making known the principles and regulations on which the Governor thought that a *good government* ought to be established, and by which he was to be guided in his future administration. It contained nothing worthy of any special notice.

Shortly after, he addressed to the Commandants at the different posts throughout the colony the following set of instructions, in relation to grants of lands:

" 1°—Commandants are forbidden* to grant land to a new settler, coming from another spot where he has already obtained a grant. Such a one must either *buy* land, or obtain a grant from the *Governor himself.*

" 2°—If a settler be a foreigner, unmarried, and without either slaves, money, or other property, no grant is

---

* Martin's History of Louisiana, vol. ii., p. 153.

to be made to him, until he shall have remained four years in the post, demeaning himself well in some honest and useful occupation.

"3°—Mechanics are to be protected, but no land is to be granted to them, until they shall have acquired some property, and a residence of three years, in the exercise of their trade.

"4°—No grant of land is to be made to any unmarried emigrant, who has neither trade nor property, until after a residence of four years, during which time he must have been employed in the culture of the ground.

"5°—But if, after a residence of two years, such a person should marry the daughter of an honest farmer, with his consent, and be by him recommended, a grant of land may be made to him.

"6°—Liberty of conscience is not to be extended beyond the first generation; the children of the emigrant must become Catholics; and emigrants, not agreeing to this, must not be admitted, but expelled, even when they bring property with them. This is to be explained to settlers who do not profess the Catholic faith.

"7°—In Upper Louisiana, no settler is to be admitted, who is not a farmer or a mechanic.

"8°—It is expressly recommended to Commandants, to watch that no preacher of any religion but the Catholic comes into the province.

"9°—To every married emigrant of the above description two hundred arpens may be granted, with the addition of fifty for every child he brings.

"10°—If he brings negroes, twenty additional arpens are to be granted him for each: but, in no case, are more than eight hundred arpens to be granted to an emigrant.

"11°—No land is to be granted to a trader.

"12°—Immediately on the arrival of a settler, the

oath of allegiance is to be administered to him. **If he** has a wife, proof is to be demanded of their marriage; and, if they bring any property, they are to be required to declare what part belongs to either of them; and they are to be informed that the discovery of any wilful falsehood in this declaration will produce the forfeiture of the land granted them, and of the improvements made thereon.

" 13°—Without proof of a lawful marriage, or of the absolute ownership of negroes, no grant is to be made for any wife, or negro.

" 14°—The grant is to be forfeited, if a settlement be not made within the year, or one tenth part of the land put in cultivation within two.

" 15°—No grantee is to be allowed to sell his land, until he has produced three crops on a tenth part of it; but, in case of death, it may pass to an heir in the province, but not to one without, unless he come and settle on it.

" 16°—If the grantee owes debts in the province, the proceeds of the first four crops are to be applied to their discharge, in preference to that of debts due abroad. If, before the third crop be made, it becomes necessary to evict the grantee, on account of his bad conduct, the land shall be given to the young man and young woman, residing within one mile of it, whose good conduct may show them to be the best deserving of it; and the decision is to be made by an assembly of notable planters, presided over by the Commandant.

" 17°—Emigrants are to settle contiguous to old establishments, without leaving any vacant lands between— in order that the people may more easily protect each other, in case of any invasion by the Indians, and that the administration of justice, and a compliance with police regulations, may be facilitated."

In the beginning of this year, 1798, New Orleans was visited by three illustrious strangers, the Duke of Orleans, with his two brothers, the Duke of Montpensier and the Count of Beaujolais, who were striking examples of those remarkable vicissitudes of fortune with which the annals of history are so replete. The royal fugitives who had thus come to claim the hospitality of the humble town which, under the patronage of their ancestors, had been founded in the wilderness, on the distant bank of the Mississippi, were the descendants of the celebrated regent, Duke of Orleans, and, through him, of Louis XIII., king of France. They were of a race which, without interruption, had given monarchs to that kingdom for centuries; and if there ever was a house that could boast of pretensions to durability, it was theirs, so profoundly and ineradicably laid had seemed to be its foundations in the very depths, not only of the broad kingdom of France, but also of the whole continent of Europe. There was a day, however, when "the rain descended, and the floods came, and the winds blew, and beat upon that house, and it fell, and great was the fall of it!" Men, who had suddenly been precipitated so low from the heights of a prosperity which seemed destined to be the everlasting and lawful possession of their family by the prescriptive right derived from so many centuries, were certainly fit objects of sympathy in their misfortune, and they met with a generous and warm-hearted reception, both from the Spanish authorities and from the inhabitants of Louisiana. Costly entertainments were given to them, and they spent several weeks in New Orleans and its neighborhood. They appeared to take much interest in the destinies of a colony which was the creation of France, and they examined minutely the sugar plantation which had been lately established by Etienne Boré, near the city. When a "mousquetaire," or guardsman in the household troops of Louis XV., and watching over the safety of the majesty of France, little did he dream that the day would come when three princes of the blood would be his guests in the wilderness of America! What strange events will not time bring on, and how shifting are the scenes in which it delights! The Count of Beaujolais and the Duke of Montpensier soon slept in the tomb; but the other fugitive exile—the Duke of Orleans—whose father's head had fallen on the scaffold, ascended the throne of France, and the planter's grandson became, in his turn, in the gorgeous halls of royalty, the guest of him who had been the planter's guest. But again "the rain descended, and the floods came, and the winds blew, and beat upon the king's house, and it fell, and great was the fall of it," for it was not strong, and not "built upon a rock." Now are the king's children exiles and wanderers on the face of the earth. Will it be the decree of capricious fortune that one of them shall taste the hospitality which his royal father enjoyed in Louisiana in 1798?

But, to return to events having a more direct bearing on the destinies of the colony, it must here be recorded that Colonel Charles Grandpré had been appointed by the Spanish authority to take the command at Natchez, in the place of Brigadier-General Gayoso de Lemos, who had now become Governor of Louisiana. But Grandpré's energy, and the little favor with which he looked upon the Americans, being well known, the "Permanent Committee of Public Safety" declared unanimously that his presence would not be acceptable, and might be the cause of a dangerous outbreak. Under such circumstances, it was thought prudent to leave the command of that post to Captain Minor, who was then acting as civil and military commandant ad interim. Captain Minor, as Gayoso had done before, recognized the powers of the

'Permanent Committee," and this concession **restored** so much harmony between the two parties, that Lieutenant Pope, with the men under his orders, retired a few miles from Fort Panmure into the interior.

In the meantime, General Wilkinson, who was the commander-in-chief of the American army, thought that it was opportune to make some demonstration that would satisfy the Federal Government of the sincerity of his zeal, gratify the impatience of the Western people, and so far operate upon the Spanish authorities as to induce them to evacuate the forts of which they were still in possession. In consequence of this determination, he sent Captain Guion at the head of a detachment, with orders to assume the command of Natchez. He also intrusted Captain Guion with a despatch for Gayoso, in which he said of the bearer: "This officer's experience and good sense, and the powers with which he is clothed by the President of the United States, conspire to promise a happy result to his command, in which I flatter myself I shall not be disappointed." In obedience, no doubt, to the instructions which had been given to him by Mr. Wilkinson, and perhaps from his own sense of propriety, Guion, on his arrival at Natchez, behaved towards the Spaniards in the most conciliatory manner. He checked any public manifestation of disrespect to them, and exerted himself to the utmost to allay the excitement which prevailed in the district. He almost annihilated the authority of the "Permanent Committee of Public Safety," which had adopted, he thought, imprudent and improper measures, and he went even so far as to threaten* to break it up by force. But Guion's liberality and the amiableness of his deportment towards the Spaniards did not seem to accelerate their movements, and to procure their desired removal from the

---

* Monette's History of the Valley of the Mississippi, vol. i., p. 530.

forts Panmure and Nogales (or Walnut Hills), which were the only remaining ones to be evacuated—so that Guion himself, becoming impatient, declared that he would not wait further than the 1st of April, 1799, and would then attack the forts.

But, at last, the Spaniards having lost, as it has been seen by Power's report to Carondelet, all hopes of operating a dismemberment of the Union, an order was sent by the court of Madrid to comply with the stipulations of the treaty, to have the line of demarcation surveyed, and to surrender the ceded territory. Thus, on the 23d of March, Fort Nogales, at Walnut Hills, was evacuated, and its garrison came down to Natchez, where they remained until the 29th, when, during the night, the Spaniards, without having given any previous notice to the Americans, abandoned the fort, after having sent all their artillery, ammunition, baggage, &c., on board of the boats and galleys they had on the river. By daybreak, the Americans entered the fort, which they discovered to be vacant, and the gates of which had been left open.

In virtue of an act of Congress approved on the 10th of May, 1798, the territory thus surrendered by the Spaniards was organized into a territorial government, and designated as the "Mississippi territory." On the 26th of the same month, General Wilkinson arrived with the federal forces at Natchez, where he established his head-quarters, and, shortly after, removed to the well known spot on the river, called "La Roche à Davion" by the French, "Loftus's Heights" by the English, and, subsequently, Fort Adams by the Americans, from the fortifications which were then begun by Wilkinson.

Thus were defeated all the schemes and efforts of Spain to protect her American colonies against the encroachments which she foresaw; and from the day when her feeble hand thus relinquished the grasp of so important a portion of her dominions in Louisiana, may be said to date the rapid decay of her power on the continent which she claims to have discovered, and where she had accomplished so much. The danger that threatened Spain in America had long been foreseen by one of her ablest statesmen, the Count of Aranda, who, in the cabinet council which was convened in Madrid by the King to determine whether Spain, after the revolution of 1768 which had resulted in the expulsion of Governor Ulloa from Louisiana, should persist in accepting the donation of that province by the French King and make the necessary efforts to recover its possession, had so strenuously spoken in the affirmative, on the ground of the urgent necessity of establishing a permanent barrier between the growing power and ambition of the northern British colonies and the wealthy but weak provinces of Mexico. After signing the treaty of Paris, in 1783, the same minister had submitted to his Catholic Majesty a secret memoir,* in which he declared that the independence of the British colonies filled his mind with grief and fear, and expressed his belief that both France and Spain acted in opposition to their interests when they espoused the cause of those colonies, because he regarded the existence of the United States of America as highly dangerous to the Spanish American possessions, and, on this subject, used the following very remarkable language:

"This federal republic is born a pigmy, if I may be allowed so to express myself. It has required the support of two such powerful States as France and Spain to obtain its independence. The day will come when she will be a giant, a colossus formidable even to these

* De Bow's Review May number, 1847, p. 411

countries. She will forget the services she has received from the two powers, and will think only of her own aggrandizement. The liberty of conscience, the facility of establishing a new population upon immense territories, together with the advantages of a new government (meaning free, no doubt), will attract the agriculturists and mechanics of all nations, for men ever run after fortune; and, in a few years, we shall see the tyrannical existence of this very colossus of which I speak.

"The first step of this nation, after it has become powerful, will be to take possession of the Floridas in order to have the command of the Gulf of Mexico, and, after having rendered difficult our commerce with New Spain, she will aspire to the conquest of that vast empire, which it will be impossible for us to defend against a formidable power established on the same continent, and in its immediate neighborhood. These fears are well founded; they must be realized in a few years, if some greater revolution, even more fatal, does not sooner take place in our Americas."

In conclusion, he proposed, as the best means of averting this imminent danger, that Spain should relinquish the Americas and establish therein three of the Infantes, one to be king of Mexico, one of Peru, and the other of Costa Firme, retaining under the dominion of the mother country only Porto Rico and Cuba; and he recommended that a treaty of commerce be entered into between France and Spain in relation to these countries, from the advantages of which Great Britain should be excluded.

These views explain the tenaciousness with which, to the last moment, Spain held fast to every inch of the ground which she considered as constituting a rampart against the anticipated aggressions of her great northwestern neighbor. In relation to her late intrigues with

Wilkinson, in which she had engaged in the vain hope of crippling, when still in the cradle, the new-born giant pointed out to her by Count Aranda, Monette says, in his History of the Valley of the Mississippi: "The temerity of this last intrigue, put in operation by the Governor of Louisiana, astonishes every reflecting mind. But General Wilkinson was a talented and ambitious man; he had received many favors from the Spanish governors nearly ten years before; he had received exclusive privileges in the commerce with Louisiana, a long and confidential intercourse had existed between him and Governor Miró; he was known to have indulged a predilection for Spanish authority, and was ambitious of power and distinction; he was now at the head of the western armies, and, with the power and influence of his station, he might effectually bring about a separation of the West, the formation of a new republic, of which he himself might be the supreme ruler, and conduct the alliance with Spain. Such may have been the reasonings of Baron de Carondelet, at this late period.

"But General Wilkinson had already proceeded too far in his treasonable intrigues and correspondence with the Spanish Governor, and the suspicions of his own government rested upon him. The brilliant prospects and the bright hopes of becoming the head of a new confederation, had vanished from his imagination, and he was anxious to retain his command, and with it his standing as a patriotic citizen of the United States. Hence, in the summer of 1797, he had given to Power a cold reception; he had informed him that the time for a separation had passed by; that now the project of the Baron de Carondelet would be chimerical in the extreme; that the Western people, by the late treaty, had obtained all they desired, and that now they entertained no wish for an alliance with either Spain or France; that the political ferment which existed four years previously had entirely subsided; and that, far from desiring an alliance with Louisiana under the Spanish Crown, the people of Kentucky, prior to the treaty of Madrid, had proposed to invade Louisiana with an army of ten thousand men, to be put in motion upon the first open rupture between the two governments; and that now they were highly exasperated at the spoliations committed upon the American commerce by French privateers, who brought their prizes into the port of New Orleans for condemnation and confiscation. He gave it as his opinion that the Governor-general would therefore consult his own interest, and the interest of his Catholic Majesty, by an immediate compliance with the terms of the treaty.

"General Wilkinson also complained that his connection and his correspondence with the Spanish Governor had been divulged; that all his plans had been defeated, and the labor of ten years had been lost; that he had now burned all his correspondence and destroyed his cyphers, and that duty and honor forbade a continuance of the intercourse. Yet he still indulged the hope of being able to manifest his confidence in the Baron; for it was probable that he would receive from the Federal Government the appointment of Governor over the Natchez district, after its surrender agreeably to treaty, when he should not want an opportunity of promoting his political projects."

Although Spain had been drawn into the wars which desolated the European continent, still Louisiana had felt none of their direful consequences, and had continued to enjoy an uninterrupted tranquillity, which was only marred by the fears resulting from the rapid extension of the American settlements. She could already see the shadows of the coming giant shooting across her bosom and darkening her sky.

The commerce of New Orleans, however, had been steadily increasing, particularly with the United States, and this circumstance was deemed sufficient to require the appointment of an official agent by the Federal Government, to protect their commercial interests. "Besides," says Colonel Ellicott, in his journal, "the French privateers had now become very troublesome to the trade of the United States in the West Indies, and about the Gulf of Mexico. A number of our captured vessels were taken into the port of New Orleans, condemned, and confiscated with their cargoes at a trifling price, our seamen treated in the most shameful manner, and our trade otherwise brought into great jeopardy." This induced the American commissioner, Colonel Ellicott, to prevail upon the Governor of Louisiana to recognize Daniel Clark, Jr., as consul for the United States until the President should make a regular appointment, which was shortly after conferred on Evan Jones, with Huling as vice-consul.*

In consequence of the close proximity of the American and Spanish posts, a convention was entered into between Governor Gayoso and General Wilkinson for the mutual surrender of deserters, and also an agreement, somewhat of the like nature, was made between the Governor of the Mississippi territory, at Natchez, and Don Jose Vidal, Commandant of the Spanish post, on the opposite side of the river, for the reciprocal surrender of fugitive slaves. The animosity which had existed between the American and Spanish authorities seemed to have disappeared entirely, and to have given way to an amicable intercourse and to good feelings.

* Monette's Valley of the Mississippi, vol. i, p. 540.

In commemoration of this happy change, the Spanish Commandant, Don Jose Vidal, gave the name of "Concord" to the fort which was erected on the west side of the river, in front of Fort Panmure on the east side, and the present parish of Concordia derives its appellation from this circumstance. The village of Vidalia now existing opposite Natchez, is so called from the old Spanish Commandant, Don Jose Maria Vidal.

Under the royal decree, of the 24th of August, 1770, the civil and military governors of Louisiana had alone been empowered to make concessions of the lands belonging to the Crown; but, on the 21st of October, in the year 1798, the King of Spain thought proper to vest that power exclusively in the Intendant of the provinces of Louisiana and West Florida.

In consequence of this royal schedule, the Intendant Morales issued, on the 17th of July, 1799, a set of regulations, to which the concessions of land should hereafter be subjected.* These regulations were considered at the time inimical to the Americans, and calculated to prevent their emigration into Louisiana. Another measure adopted by Morales was looked upon as still more hostile and as the harbinger of future oppressive acts, aimed at crippling the commerce of the United States.

It will be recollected that, by the treaty of Madrid concluded in October, 1795, between Spain and the United States, the citizens of the latter power had secured to themselves the right of deposit in New Orleans for their western produce, for the space of three years, to be counted from the date of the ratification of the treaty, and that his Catholic Majesty had bound himself, at the expiration of the three years, to extend the time, or to designate *some other suitable point* within

---

* See the Appendix.

the island of New Orleans, to serve as a place of deposit.* The Intendant Morales, considering that *three years* had elapsed since the ratification of the treaty between his Sovereign and the United States, issued an order,† prohibiting the use of New Orleans as a place of deposit by the western people, but without designating *any other suitable point.* When this measure became known in the West, it excited the most intense indignation, and an expedition against New Orleans was openly contemplated. President Adams himself had been obliged to make some demonstrations in the way pointed out by the current of popular opinion, and had ordered three regiments of the regular army to concentrate on the Ohio, and to wait for further orders. Twelve additional regiments were ordered to be raised by Congress, and other preparations were made, which seemed to indicate that an immediate campaign was projected against Louisiana.

When, to meet such dangers, all the resources of the colony should have been carefully husbanded, and when the greatest harmony should have prevailed among the Spanish officers, a misunderstanding of a serious nature had sprung up between the Intendant Morales and Governor Gayoso—between the purse and the sword. On the 31st of January, 1799, Morales, in a despatch to his government, complained bitterly of the temper of the Governor, of his mode of thinking, of his disposition to indulge in useless expenses, and said that, in such circumstances, he, Morales, could not have it in his power to serve the King as effectually as he wished.‡ On the 31st of March, he again complained that the

---

* Monette's Valley of the Miss., vol. i., p. 543.
† Martin's History of Louisiana, vol. ii., p. 158.
‡ Dice que es tal el caracter del gobernador, tal su modo de pensar, y tan propenso á hacer gastos inutiles que no podrá servir á su Majestad, como e deseará.

Governor illegally assumed powers which belonged to the Intendant; that he, Morales, was obliged to yield to many of the Governor's unjust exigencies, in order to avoid scandalous disputes, and that he had in vain made to that officer confidential observations on the subject; he further went on animadverting with severity on several acts of Gayoso's administration . "The* Governor's natural disposition," said Morales, "to waste what he owns as well as what he borrows, and to cause those about him to do the same, and his desire to increase his prerogatives and power, and to show himself generous at the expense of the King, are much more the causes of all the defensive preparations which he requires, than his fear of the invasion from the Americans, which serves as a pretext for his demands." He then recites in detail the reasons why he thinks that the Americans have given up all ideas of attacking Louisiana, ever since they have been put in possession of the ceded territory, and he comments on the smallness of Wilkinson's forces, which do not exceed four hundred men. He complains also of the orders issued and of the measures taken by Gayoso, in relation to the galleys and boats which constituted the naval resources of the colony. "Without knowing more than I do† in this matter," writes Morales,

---

* Su propension natural á gastar lo suyo, y lo que pide prestado, y a hacer gastar á quantos le circundan, y el deseo de tener objetos en que extender sus facultades, y manifestarle generoso á costa del Rey, eran mas bien los agentes de los preparativos de defensa que exigía, que los recelos de invasion de parte de los Americanos a cuya sombra se solicitaban.

† Sin entender mas que yo, se cree este gobernador sobresaliente á los mejores generales de marina. Aquellas cosas han producido entre nosotros contestaciones bastante agrias y desagradables, hasta el punto de pretender que la Intendencia, sin hablar palabra, se someta á todos sus caprichos, depreciando cuantas razones se alegan para evitar á S. M. gastos inútiles. Creo de absoluta y indispensable necesitad que el Rey se digne tomar una de dos determinaciones que son: ó cohartar las facultades de este gobernador en los terminos que sean de su real agrado: ó con el conocimiento que doy de la situacion de estas Reales Cajas proporcionar á la Intendencia medios para que pueda llenar los deseos de este gefe.

'the Governor thinks himself superior in nautical knowledge to the best marine officers. These things have produced between us sufficiently bitter and disagreeable discussions, and the Governor goes so far as to pretend, that the Intendant must submit to all his caprices, without having one **w**ord to say, when he, the Governor, treats with contempt all the reasons which are laid before him to avoid drawing his Majesty into fruitless expenses. For these reasons, I think it indispensably necessary that the King should do one of these two things: either confine the powers of this Governor within the limits which his Majesty may deem proper to prescribe, or, taking into consideration the information I have given as to the condition of the royal treasury in this colony, supply me with the means of satisfying the exigencies of this officer."

Morales, among the sources of unnecessary expenses which he enumerates, mentions the establishment* of couriers between Pensacola and Savannah, the costs of which he has not as yet been able to ascertain. "But, so far," says he, "they have been of no further use than procuring gazettes from that section of the country; and we all know what faith is to be put in the news to be found in the northern gazettes, in which any one may insert what he pleases for four reals."

On the 30th of April, 1799, Morales wrote to his government to acknowledge having received from the Viceroy of New Spain $434,238, to pay the expenses of the preceding year, 1798, and also $50,000, which were due for the budget of 1797.

The misunderstanding between Gayoso and Morales

---

* Los correos que van y vienen de Pansacola á Savannah, que aun no sé á quanto asciende el gasto. Solo produjó hasta ahora gacetas de aquel parage, y es sabido al credito que puede darse á las noticias de las gacetas del norte, donde por qua : reales cada uno puede poner lo que mas acomoda á sus ideas.

went on daily increasing, and, in a despatch of the 31st of May, the Intendant observed,* that, considering it was no longer possible for him to continue to be in a state of open warfare against the Governor, he found himself under the necessity of supplicating his Majesty to relieve him from discharging the functions of Intendant, and to transfer him to some other point of his Majesty's dominions in America. He then goes on giving "minute and positive proofs," as he says, "of the violence and tyranny exercised towards him by the Governor, who transgresses that moderation and urbanity† with which those in authority ought to be treated, who insults and threatens the intendancy, and commits all the excesses which are recited."

The Federal Government had ordered Wilkinson to Washington, to confer with him upon all the important matters relating to the West and to Louisiana, on which he was supposed to possess the most extensive information. He accordingly descended the Mississippi from Natchez, and departed from New Orleans for New York. In a despatch of the 10th of July, Morales speaks of Wilkinson's late visit to that town, and communicates to his government all the intelligence he has been able to obtain in relation to the political views of the United States concerning Louisiana, by pumping the American general. "Concealing," says Morales, "what we know‡ of his reprehensible deportment towards us, we have given him as kind and as favorable a welcome as his

---

* Dice que no siendole posible por mas tiempo el continuar en pugna abierta con aquel gobernador, se ve en la precision de suplicar á S. M. se sirva relevarle del cargo de intendente y trasladarle á otro punto de los dominios de America.

† Contraviniendo á lo que prescriben la moderacion y urbanidad con que deber ser tratadas las personas constituidas en mando, insultando y amenazando á la intendencia, y cometiendo los demas excesos que refiere.

‡ —— Disimulandolo que sabemos su reprensible manejo con respeto á nosotros lo hemos obsequiado en los mejores terminos que permite el pais, y exigia su caracter, &c., &c.

rank required and our means permitted in this country. On the eve of his departure, I prevailed upon him to furnish me with a copy of the instructions which he had left with Major Cushing, his successor, as to the manner in which this officer was to demean himself towards the Spaniards. They simply amount to this,—that the American officers are, by all possible means, to cultivate our friendship and to preserve the good understanding which so fortunately exists between the two powers.

" It would not be justifiable to draw favorable or unfavorable conclusions from the mere outward show of such demonstrations.* But, as there are certain moments when the individuals of that nation are in the habit of opening their hearts, I will not conceal from your Excellency, that, in those moments of effusion, when the General was with persons who possessed all his confidence, he manifested the same sentiments which I communicated in my confidential despatch of the 31st of May last, No. 23. In a few words, the policy of the United States may be said to be reduced to these two points : 1°—to prevent France and England taking possession of this province by cession, or by the force of arms ; 2°—to repress any scheme of separation which may be entertained by the States of Kentucky and Tennessee. The General gave it even to be understood, that he thought it proper, and therefore would propose to the President—that he should return with full authority to help us with all the forces under his command in case the English should invade the colony, provided we do not, in the mean time, declare war against them, the

---

* No puede formarse juicio, ni deducir consequencias adversas ni favorables de semejantes exterioredades; pero con todo, como los individuos de esta nacion suelen tener momentos en que su corazon se difunde, no ocultaré á V. E, que en los que ha tenido dicho general con personas que juzgaba de su confianza, ha manifestado lo mismo que expuse á V. E., en mi representacion reservada del 31 Mayo ultimo No. 23.

Americans, because it is more to the interest of the United States that this province remain under the domination of Spain. But, to accomplish the two objects they have in view, the forces which they possess at the posts they have occupied are very limited."

According to the provisions of the Spanish Jurisprudence, and to time-honored custom, Gayoso had received the commission of Judge of Residence to inquire into the acts of his predecessor. It seems that, on this occasion, it did not turn out to be an idle and unmeaning formality, and Judge Martin, in his History of Louisiana, records as follows the result of the investigation: "One act of the Baron's administration was deemed reprehensible. He had been deluded by an excess of zeal for what he conceived to be the public good, into taking upon himself the responsibility of condemning to death a slave, who had killed his owner. The fact was proved, but Vidal, the assessor of government, conceived that the circumstances which attended it, did not bring the case under any law authorizing a sentence of death, and had recommended a milder one. At the solicitation of a number of respectable planters, and of the owner of the slave, Marigny de Mandeville, a knight of St. Louis and a Colonel of the Militia, who represented to the Baron that an example was absolutely necessary, especially so soon after the late insurrection, he disregarded the opinion of his legal adviser, and ordered the execution of the slave. It was thought the life of a human being, although a slave, ought not to depend on the opinion of a man, in any case where its sacrifice was not expressly ordered by law. A fine of five hundred dollars was imposed on and paid by the Baron."

In a despatch of the 25th of July, Morales informed his government of the death of Gayoso, in the following terms: "On the 18th inst., it pleased God* to put an end to the life and government of Brigadier-General Don Manuel Gayoso de Lemos. He died of a malignant fever, of the nature of those which prevail in this country during the summer, and the dangerous character of which was known only a few hours before it terminated fatally. He had no time to lose in fulfilling the last duties of the Christian, and in making his testamentary dispositions. A short time before expiring, he reconciled himself with me, and we exchanged a reciprocal pardon for the causes of complaint we had given to each other in the accomplishment of what we had thought our respective duties."

Governor Gayoso died extremely poor, leaving nothing to his heirs but a large amount of debts. He was a spendthrift, in the full sense of the word. Having been educated in England, he had adopted some of the habits peculiar to that country, particularly that of indulging too much in the pleasures of the table. It is said that Wilkinson's last visit to New Orleans proved fatal to Gayoso. They had long been on a footing of intimacy strengthened by a similarity of tastes; and, on their recently coming together, they had carried to an excess their convivialities, which had predisposed Gayoso to the disease that carried him off in his forty-eighth year. On his sudden death, Don Francisco Bouligny, who was the Colonel of the regiment of Louisiana, assumed the military administration of the colony, and the auditor, Don Jose Maria Vidal, the civil and political government.†

---

* El 18 del corriente fué Dios servido poner fin al gobierno del Brigadier Don Manuel Gayoso de Lemos. Una calentura maligna de las que ofrece este pais en la estacion de verano, no conocida por los facultativos hasta algunas horas antes de su fallicimiento le quitó la vida, habiendo sido forzoso andar de priesa para que cumpliese con las obligaciones de christiano y que hiciera testamento. Poco antes de expirar se reconcilió conmigo, y quedaron reciprocamente remitidas las quejas personales á que dió lugar el cumplimiento de la que cada uno entendia ser su obligacion.

† Morales' despatch of the 25th of July, 1799.

CENSUS OF UPPER LOUISIANA.

The post of New Madrid was, this year, annexed to Upper Louisiana, of which a census was made by order of its commandant-general, Charles Dehault De Lassus, which presented the following results:

St. Louis,	925
Carondelet,	184
St. Charles.	875
St. Fernando,	276
Marais des Liards,	376
Maramec,	115
St. Andrew,	393
St. Genevieve,	949
New Bourbon,	560
Cape Girardeau,	521
New Madrid,	782
Little Meadows,	72
Total,	6,028

The white population* numbered 4,948 souls; the free colored 197; the slaves 883.

The commerce of that part of the country had also increased in proportion to the augmentation of the population. Its crops amounted to 265,047 bushels of wheat, about the same of Indian corn, and 28,627 pounds of tobacco. Thirteen hundred and forty quintals of lead were produced from the mines, and about one thousand barrels of salt from the salt wells. The fur trade, which was carried on entirely through New Orleans, gave annually about $75,000.

On being informed of Gayoso's death, the Marquis de Someruelos, Captain-General of the island of Cuba and of Louisiana, sent over the Marquis de Casa Calvo to be the governor ad interim of the colony. This gentleman entered on his functions in the fall of the year.

On the 15th of October, Morales wrote to his government that, having heard of the appointment of Don

---

* Martin's History of Louisiana, vol. ii., p. 172.

Ramon de Lopez y Angullo to the office of Intendant in Louisiana, which he, Morales, had filled ad interim for three years and a half, and considering himself no longer capable of discharging the duties of his own office of contador, he begged his Majesty to allow him to retire with such a grade and pension as his Majesty might think proper to favor him with.

Casa Calvo, a short time after his arrival, transmitted to the Captain-General of Cuba, who, in his turn, forwarded it to Madrid, a petition from several proprietors of landed estates, soliciting that the unlimited introduction of negroes be again permitted, which Casa Calvo recommended as being required by the agricultural interest. On the 23d of November, the cabinet of Madrid answered: "that, permission having lately been given to the French citizens Cassagne, Huguet, Raimond & Co., to introduce into the colony five thousand negroes free of duty, it had been resolved in council not to go farther."

I shall close what relates to this year (1799) with a despatch of the Bishop of Louisiana, Don Luis de Peñalvert y Cardenas, on the state of religion and morals in the colony. "The emigration from the western part of the United States and the toleration of our government," said he, "have introduced into this colony a gang of adventurers who have no religion and acknowledge no God, and they have made much worse the morals of our people by their coming in contact with them in their trading pursuits. A lodge of freemasons has been formed in one of the suburbs of the city, and counts among its members officers of the garrison and of the civil administration, merchants, natives and foreigners. Their secret meetings on fixed days, on which they perform their functions, as well as other circumstances, give to this association a suspicious and criminal appearance.

"The adventurers I speak of have scattered themselves over the districts of Attakapas, Opeloussas, Ouachita and Natchitoches in the vicinity of the province of Texas in New Spain; they employ the Indians* on their farms, have frequent intercourse and conversations with them, and impress their minds with pernicious maxims in harmony with their own restless and ambitious temper, and with the customs of their own western countrymen, who are in the habit of saying to such of their boys as are distinguished for a robust frame, whilst patting them on the shoulder: *you will be the man to go to Mexico.*

"Such is the case with the upper part of the Mississippi, with the district of Illinois and the adjacent territories, in which there has been a remarkable introduction of those adventurers, who penetrate even into New Mexico. This evil, in my opinion, can only be remedied by not permitting the slightest American settlement to be made at the points already designated, nor on any part of the Rio Colorado.

"The parishes which were religiously disposed are losing their faith and their old customs; the number of those Christians who receive the sacrament at Easter decreases; and the people turn a deaf ear to the admonitions of their clergy.

"It is true that the same resistance to religion has always manifested itself here, but never with such scandal as now prevails. The military officers and a good many of the inhabitants live almost publicly with colored concubines, and they do not blush at carrying the illegitimate issue they have by them to be recorded in the parochial registries as their *natural children.*"

* Arman sus caserias con los Indios, tienen confabulaciones, les imprimen maximas prejudiciales conforme á su caracter inquieto, ambicioso, y á los vinculos que observan con sus paisanos del Oeste, quienes tienen la costumbre de palmear el hombro de sus niños quando son muy robustos, diciendoles *you will go to Mexico.*

The Bishop goes on saying that the magistrates, whose duty it ought to be to give a good example to the people, are the first to violate all the precepts of religion and morality.

On the 1st of January, 1800, the new Intendant, Don Ramon Lopez y Angullo, entered on the duties of his office. He was a knight pensioner of the royal and distinguished order of Charles III.

This year had, it seems, been intended by Providence to be the beginning of a new era for Louisiana, since it gave rise to a series of events and negotiations which ultimately terminated her existence as an European colony, and raised her to the dignity of a Sovereign State by her incorporation with the great American confederacy. This new power had determined on the acquisition, by force if necessary, of New Orleans at least, if not of the whole of Louisiana. But it was felt that, to conduct this enterprise successfully, it was indispensable to refrain from awakening the suspicions of Spain; and therefore, under cover of preparing for the difficulties which might arise from its differences with France at the time, the American government had added twelve regiments to the army, and had ordered three of them, as I have already stated, to the mouth of the Ohio, with instructions to have in constant readiness a sufficient number of boats, to carry down the contemplated expedition to New Orleans. But this plan was abandoned, or postponed, on account of the evident determination of the people not to reelect as president the individual who had been at the head of the government for nearly four years. It was thought more prudent to leave to his successor, who would come fresh from the people, and to the unimpaired vigor of a new administration, the management of so important an undertaking

In the meantime, the extraordinary man who ruled the destinies of France had fixed his eyes on Louisiana, which he resolved to acquire, as one of the elements of the great system he had devised to carry to the highest degree of splendor the commerce, navigation and manufactures of the country he had made so illustrious by war. In furtherance of the views which he had conceived, he had ordered his ministers to collect from all valuable sources the most minute information on the resources of Louisiana. There is extant on this subject a very remarkable *memoir*, submitted to the First Consul of the French republic by M. de Pontalba, who had long resided in the colony and occupied in it a distinguished official position. He gives a very accurate topographic description of the Western country, and then says of its inhabitants: " All this proves that the only commercial outlet for their produce is the Mississippi; that Louisiana can never cease to be the object of their ambition, as they depend upon her in the most absolute manner; that their position, the number of their population, and their other means, will enable them to invade this province whenever they may choose to do so, and that, to preserve her, it is necessary to conciliate and control them by keeping up intelligences with the most influential men among them, and to grant them privileges, until this province be sufficiently strong to defend herself with her own resources, against the torrent which threatens her. Should its waters be let loose, there is no doubt but that they would sweep every thing on their passage; for the Kentuckians, single handed, or allied with the inhabitants of the neighboring districts, may, when they choose, reach New Orleans with twenty or thirty thousand men, transported on large flatboats which they are in the daily habit of constructing to carry their produce to market, and protected by a few gun-boats loaded with more provisions than they would need. The rapidity of the current of the Ohio and of the other rivers which discharge themselves into it, makes it an easy undertaking, and the paucity of their wants would accelerate its execution. A powder horn, a bag of balls, a rifle, and a sufficient provision of flour—this would be the extent of their military equipment; a great deal of skill in shooting, the habit of being in the woods and of enduring fatigue—this is what makes up for every deficiency.

"More or less extraordinary means, in accordance with the degree of importance attached to Louisiana, must be resorted to, in order to save her from the irruption by which she is threatened. Should she be appreciated in proportion only to the revenue she now yields to the metropolis, it will be found out that the 6 per cent. duty on exports and imports, which is the sole one existing in the colony, does not produce one hundred thousand dollars a year, and that the annual expenses of the King of Spain for that province rise up to five hundred and thirty-seven thousand dollars.

"What entitles Louisiana to peculiar attention is the fact of her being a port in the Gulf of Mexico, where no other power than Spain has any; but what gives her still more value, is her position in relation to the kingdom of Mexico, whose natural barrier is the Mississippi.

"It is necessary to make this barrier an impenetrable one. It is the surest means of destroying for ever the bold schemes with which several individuals in the United States never cease filling the newspapers, by designating Louisiana as the high road to the conquest of Mexico, particularly ever since the occurring of differences with regard to its limits.

"The long discussion relating to those limits between

the United States and Louisiana, which was terminated in 1797, proceeded from an equivocation in the treaty of peace of 1783, which equivocation was, no doubt, purposely introduced by England, in order to breed a subject of discord between Spain and the United States. Otherwise it would have been necessary to express, that his Catholic Majesty should order the surrender to the United States of the district and fort of Natchez, which he then occupied by right of conquest.

"When England possessed her thirteen colonies and part of the province of Louisiana, the limits of Georgia being marked in the maps as running east and west from the sea to the Mississippi, the district of Natchez was included within them; but the inhabitants of that post having represented that, on the appeal cases from their courts, they were obliged to resort to Georgia, his Britannic Majesty declared that the district of Natchez would henceforth be placed under the jurisdiction of the Governor of Pensacola, and be incorporated with Western Florida, which was under the government of that officer. In this way, that province became extended to the Chaterpé line, which had been drawn by the English, the Chickasaws and Choctaws, from the territory of Mobile, at 135 miles from the fort of that name on the western bank of the Tombecbee, to the Yazoo River, at fifteen miles from its junction with the Mississippi. So that, Western Florida, having been ceded to his Catholic Majesty by Great Britain in the peace treaty of 1783, was thus transferred away in all its integrity, and with all its dependencies at the time of the cession, of which Spain, however, was already in possession by the right of conquest, and which she had never agreed to surrender.

"The English, in the same peace treaty which they concluded at the same time with the United States, abandoned to them all that was marked in the old maps as a part of the United Provinces, as far as the Mississippi, without *excepting that part of it which his Britannic Majesty had already detached and annexed to Western Florida;* and the line which was determined in that treaty, by running in the middle of the Mississippi to the 31st degree of latitude, surrendered to the United States all the east side of that river as far as the spot lying opposite the mouth of the Red River, 36 miles below Natchez, and by running west and east from that point to the river St. Mary, left to them all the district of Natchez, which was the most populous portion of Louisiana, thus restricting the possession of Spain towards Mobile to a sandy territory which did not extend beyond six miles, and reducing the country back of Pensacola to thirty miles of barren soil.

"Ever since the year 1785, the United States had aimed at taking possession of Natchez and all the territory which was assigned to them by the said treaty. Spain had constantly opposed such pretensions, and had succeeded, through her intelligences with the western provinces of the United States and through her negotiations, in suspending the hostilities with which she had often been threatened, and in eluding the unfounded claims of the United States down to the year 1797, when she was obliged to accede to them in order not to expose herself to the loss of the whole province.

"As the Americans therefore are in possession of these new frontiers, it becomes more urgent than ever to secure a barrier for the protection of Mexico. There are two ways to accomplish this object. The first is, to establish in Louisiana a population sufficiently large to defend her against all attacks; the second is, to form a union with Kentucky and the other districts of the Western Country, with the obligation on their part to serve as a rampart against the United States; and, until it be possible to execute one or the other of these propositions, my opinion is, that, by all possible means, peace must be preserved with the United States.

"This is what the Spanish Government has never ceased doing from 1787 to the present time. It was assisted in this policy by a powerful inhabitant of Kentucky, who possesses much influence with his countrymen, and enjoys great consideration for the services he has rendered to the cause of liberty, when occupying high grades in the army of the United States; who, from that time, has never ceased to serve Spain in all her views; and who will put the same zeal at the command of France, because he thinks with reason that an intimate union between her and Louisiana is more advantageous to his country (Kentucky), than its present relations with the United States.

"This individual,* whose name I shall not mention in order not to expose him, but which I shall make known when his services shall be wanted, came to New Orleans in 1787. He informed the Spanish Government of the state of things then existing in Kentucky and the adjoining districts, and of the efforts which the inhabitants of those provinces were making to obtain their independence and the free navigation of the Mississippi. He also declared that there was a general disposition among those people to place themselves under the protection of Spain, should Congress refuse to do justice to their claims.

"It is on that refusal that this inhabitant of Kentucky had founded all his hopes, and, in that case, he had offered to declare himself the vassal of his Catholic Majesty He promised, as such, to give information of all that the inhabitants of that region would undertake for

---

* General Wilkinson.

or against Louisiana, and he proposed, as another means, to promote emigration from the Western Districts adjoining Louisiana, in order to increase our strength. It is with these dispositions that he went back.

"He returned to New Orleans, in 1789, to renew to the government his propositions to employ all the means in his power to procure for his district of Kentucky its independence from the United States, by forming with Spain an alliance exclusive of all other nations, and actively to foment, at the same time, emigration to Louisiana.*

"He notified the Spanish Government, in 1791, that his hopes of success for his schemes had vanished. He attributed the cause of it to the granting by Spain to the inhabitants of Kentucky of permission to take down their produce to New Orleans, and to sell it there on paying a duty of 15 per cent. He pretended that the fertility of their soil amply indemnified them for the payment of that duty, and, the next year, he wrote that all ideas of emigration from his district had been entirely given up, ever since the inhabitants of Kentucky knew that his Catholic Majesty had declared that, for the future, instead of purchasing annually two millions of pounds of tobacco from the emigrants, he would take only forty thousand pounds.

"It results from all this, that Spain could not succeed in gaining over to her side the people of Kentucky. The same motives have stopped the emigration which might with reason have been expected, considering that Louisiana, which contained twenty thousand souls in

---

* This note is to be found at the bottom of the page in the original manuscript; "Four times, from 1786 to 1792, preparations were made in Kentucky and Cumberland to attack Louisiana, and, every time, this same individual caused them to fail through his influence over his countrymen. I make these facts known to show that France must not neglect to enlist this individual in her service."

1782, and forty-five thousand in 1792, numbers now more than seventy thousand, including, however, the district of Natchez, which was surrendered to the Americans in 1797.

"The individual above mentioned gave the unwise advice to place the people of those districts under the absolute dependence of Spain, by preventing them from having any trade whatever with Louisiana, and by depriving them of the navigation of the Mississippi. He hoped that the majority of the Thirteen States would accede to it. He thought that, by this means, it would be possible to check the excessive and alarming emigration from the Atlantic States towards their western territory, and presumed that the inhabitants of that terri tory not being supported by the Federal Government in their pretensions, it would then become easy to induce them to seek their welfare by throwing themselves into the arms of Spain.

"All these designs have miscarried (and indeed it could hardly have been otherwise) because, instead of opposing the pretensions of said districts, the United States, on the contrary, energetically favored them, and addressed, in 1792, to the Court of Madrid a memorial in which they represented that, unless they chose to expose themselves to losing one half of their territory, they could not turn a deaf ear to the continual clamors of the inhabitants of the West, who solicited, o er and above the free navigation of the Mississippi, the possession of a spot on the lower part of the river, where their boats might discharge their produce and take in the goods which they wanted—adding that should this place of depot be fixed at New Orleans, it might give rise to difficulties and discussions.

"The Congress, by such means, secured the affection of those people to such an extent, that it became no longer possible to think of forming the union above mentioned, although, for a certainty, that western population would have been the happier in consequence of it. Spain also lost all hope of peopling Louisiana, before coming to arrangements with the United States.

"In order to prolong that negotiation (and this infinitely suited the Court of Spain) several propositions were made to Congress. First, it was represented that, on account of the delicate situation of the Western country, his Majesty, through humanity, had granted to the inhabitants thereof the privilege of selling their produce at New Orleans, and that, although it was on their paying in kind a duty of 15 per cent., yet this was more advantageous than if they resorted to direct exportation by sea, since they sold for eight dollars at New Orleans a barrel of flour which cost no more than three dollars at Monongahela, and since the ships that might come through the Atlantic to the Mississippi, in order to take that produce, would pay for it a much less price; but that, in order to do away with all pretexts for any contraband trade and with the discussions to which it might give rise, his Majesty permitted the free navigation of the Mississippi to the inhabitants of the Western country, who might easily cause to be constructed on their rivers schooners or any other craft, in which they might transport their produce to the ports of the United States or to such harbors of the foreign colonies as may admit it. This proposition was rejected, and the United States persisted in demanding the opening of the Mississippi to the American ships, and the possession of a post at a convenient spot on the bank of that river.

"This negotiation was again prolonged by new propositions—such as the one opening the river up to the Plaquemine Turn, which is thirty miles from the Balize, provided the ships should not load from the banks of the river, but from those flatboats in which the Western people carry their produce, and which might conveniently come up to the sides of the ships.

"As Congress refused to abate one jot of their pretensions, Spain, in order not to lose more, found herself compelled to grant them the free navigation of the river; and, instead of conceding to them the post which they demanded, consented to their being put in possession of the above mentioned territory, which they claimed under their treaty with Great Britain. This was done in 1797, after the prolonged negotiation I have described

"Now that the Americans, in consequence of these transactions, possess more than eighteen hundred miles of the eastern bank of the Mississippi, from the 31st degree, in front of the mouth of Red River, to the 42d degree, it becomes more important than ever to people the Western side, which is better susceptible of numerous and flourishing establishments such as New Madrid, the banks of the St. Francis, the Arkansas, the Ouachita, and Red River, together with the posts of Natchitoches, Attakapas, Opeloussas, &c.

"All these districts, on becoming populous, might defend the province, by easily concentrating their forces at the point where it might be required according to circumstances. The lands watered by these rivers are the most fertile in America, and afford us room for the finest establishment, which would be of an immense extent, and which would be contiguous to the kingdom of Mexico.

"These were the points which the court of Spain was afraid of stocking with population on account of the neighborhood I have mentioned, and there are extant in the archives of Louisiana the most precise orders not to permit the establishment of any family on the Ouachita river, through which there is the most direct communication with Mexico.

"The Spanish possessions in Louisiana, being thus reduced by these new limits, do not extend on the east bank of the Mississippi, beyond the 31st degree, at a point which is thirty-six miles below Natchez, as I have already said above. But, notwithstanding this, the United States cannot look upon the Chickasaw, Choctaw, Alibamon, and Creek nations as belonging to them, because these nations, who are entirely devoted to us, besides that they have always received presents from Great Britain, as the proprietor of Florida, have renewed the sort of dependence to which they have subjected themselves in exchange for the protection of Spain. At a Congress which the government of Louisiana held in May, 1784, at Pensacola, with the Creeks, and in June, at Mobile, with the other nations, there was a treaty made to that effect in thirteen articles—which treaty was afterwards approved by the court.

"The United States will answer to this—that they also have made treaties with the Chickasaws and Choctaws at Hopewell and Seneca, in 1786. But those pretended treaties are imaginary and null.

"On the side of the Chickasaws, a chief, with a small number of warriors, came to Hopewell; and only some Choctaw chiefs—the only ones who had not delivered up their English medals to the Spanish government, came to Seneca—all of them without any powers from their respective nations. This is what these same chiefs declared when they since came to give up the aforesaid medals to the government, and to take those of the king of Spain. The king of the Chickasaws and his principal chiefs disapproved also the act of the above mentioned chief.

"It is very important that the aforesaid nations remain under the protection of France, in the same way they were under that of Spain, because they serve as a barrier against the United States, on a space of nine hundred miles which it would be necessary to go over through those nations, in order to come in that direction from the provinces of Georgia and South Carolina.

"I do not doubt but that the Americans would oppose with all their power the extending of the protection of France over those nations, as they have always opposed Spain, by sending commissioners, every year, to endeavor to detach those Indians from her. They never could succeed in these attempts. They could only gain over to their side the Indian chief of whom I have spoken, with the men of his village. None others allowed themselves to be persuaded by the letters which were written to them by the minister of war, Knox, by Dr. Franklin, and even by General Washington. They delivered those letters to the Governor of Louisiana in proof of their fidelity; but, as it may be possible that the United States shall think proper to use force against them, and as it is against the law of nations to prevent these people from choosing their protector, justice and the interest of France require that she should offer them her assistance according to the exigencies of the case.

"Should even the United States undertake to form establishments on the territory of the aforesaid nations, as they have already attempted it, it is not doubtful but that those nations would oppose it with all their might, and that they would call in the aid of the government of Louisiana, which ought then to assist them with all its forces, in order not to risk the loss of so essential a barrier.

"Those nations have always been disposed to repel by force all attempts to invade their territory. This is what has occurred between the Cherokees, the Creeks, the Talapouches and the United States: the Indians claimed for their limit the Cumberland river, the Americans, the Okony. It is for this cause that they have been constantly at war until 1791, at which time the half-breed Alexander McGillivray was called to New York by President Washington, with divers Creek chiefs. They then framed a treaty of peace, which the nation refused to ratify, because McGillivray had ceded more territory than his instructions authorized him to do. It was even contrary to the thirteen articles of the treaty we* had concluded at the congress held at Pensacola in 1784, with the Creek nation.

"The cession made by McGillivray gave up to the Americans a considerable portion of the best lands of the Creeks, who opposed it, and have, ever since, constantly opposed the taking possession of those lands by the Americans. France ought to assist them in their resistance, and, to do so successfully, it would be proper that, on taking possession of Louisiana, the French government should call together a congress of that nation at Pensacola. Although such an operation would be expensive, on account of the presents which it is the custom to give the Indians on such occasions, and because they are to be supplied with provisions whilst they stay at the place where they have been convened, and on their way back, still such a measure is indispensable. In this congress, the French Governor will know what influence has been retained by McGillivray† over those people since the treaty which they disapproved. He will make them feel how much more advantageous to them is the protection of France, which they have not

---

* Pontalba had been in the employ of Spain.
† It seems that McGillivray's death, which occurred in 1793, had not reached Pontalba, who had retired to France before the happening of that event.

forgotten, than that of the United States, who aim at nothing else than invading their lands.

"The Choctaws and Alibamons, seeing the Creeks convened in congress, will ask for one in their turn. It will be indispensable to grant it, in order to check the constant efforts made by the United States to detach them from the government of Louisiana, towards which they feel considerable affection, and under the protection of which they have always been placed.

"During the French domination, the Governor of Louisiana used to convene a Congress of those nations, every year at Mobile. The consequence is, that their old men speak of that time with grateful remembrance, and those people will see the return of their former protectors with a satisfaction equal to the umbrage which the United States will take at it.

"Notwithstanding the advantages which the Americans have obtained by the establishment of the limits above designated, there is a circumstance which will always keep the inhabitants of the West in the dependence of Louisiana, and which will render their emigration to it advantageous to them, although the lands they now possess are of extreme fertility—and that is, the difficulty which they experience, on account of the distance at which they are, in exchanging their produce for the commodities they want, although they have the free use of the navigation of the river, because the most valuable produce they have for sale is their tobacco and flour, which do not fetch a high price on the Atlantic coast, so that the inhabitants of the West would be obliged to give them away almost for nothing to those ships which would come to the Mississippi and buy them; otherwise, the profits would fall short of the expenses of fitting up those ships. Besides, the sellers would not be able to take any merchandise in exchange for their produce, on account of the considerable cost to which they would be put in order to take them up the Mississippi and the Ohio; for there are eighteen hundred and ninety-nine miles from the post of Plaquemine, which is situated thirty miles from the mouth of the Mississippi, to Louisville, which is the first establishment in Kentucky. Communication by land is still less practicable, although shorter by half. So that the only course to be pursued by the inhabitant of Kentucky, is to sell his produce to the American ships, payable in specie; next, to go himself to Philadelphia, there to buy the commodities he may want; then transport them three hundred miles by land to fort Pitt; and thence convey them home by a navigation of seven hundred and five miles on the Ohio.

"Evidently it is not to be presumed that any farmer could undertake such an operation, and that any merchant of the Atlantic coast could speculate on the produce of the West, when the trade is subject to such difficulties. Therefore, how much more advantageous is it to the inhabitants of the West, to settle lower down on the Mississippi, or at least, to form a union with Louisiana, in order to have the privilege of selling their produce to the best advantage in New Orleans?

"These circumstances are very powerful motives to induce the inhabitants of Kentucky, whose example would shortly be followed by those of the other Western districts, to separate themselves from the United States in order to form an alliance with France, under the obligation of their defending Louisiana in case of an attack from the United States.

"As Spain has granted them all that they have asked for, and as it is to be presumed that they will engage in no hostility, France will have time to mature this scheme, and the inhabitants of Kentucky will also have time to convince themselves that they cannot be happy and prosperous either without this alliance, or without the conquest of Louisiana. Either one or the other of these events is commanded by the nature of the country. It is for France to provide for the one, in order to avoid the other. To succeed in this, it is necessary to employ a man who should appreciate the importance of success, as well as the situation of those Western provinces in relation to Louisiana and the United States, and who should renew the intelligences which the Government of Louisiana had with the individual of whom I have spoken.

"Whilst attending to the execution of this project, it would be of the greatest importance to employ, at the same time, extraordinary means to people Louisiana, so that she might ultimately defend herself with her own resources. Should this be accomplished, the desired alliance would become less necessary, perhaps even useless for France, and, on the contrary, would be solicited by the above mentioned districts.

"At first sight, it seems dangerous to people Louisiana with aliens, but its singular position in relation to the inhabitants of the banks of the Ohio is such, that it may be considered as their home; for it may be set down as an axiom, that it would be easier for these inhabitants to invade Louisiana from those districts, than to rebel, if they were settled within its limits—with this difference in the first case, that invasion would be to them a source of glory, and that, when embarking on the Ohio, being favored by the rapidity of the current, they would operate a junction of their forces in Louisiana before it be known there that they had formed any such design; whilst having once emigrated and being received among us, with a promise of fidelity on their part to the republic, those who should meditate a rising could not carry their scheme into execution without its being known beforehand, and, instead of acquiring the laurels which may be won in legitimate warfare, would expose themselves to the ignominious death of traitors. Besides, it is not to be presumed that those people, who have lived under a precarious government which did not protect them, who have been incessantly apprehensive of dangers from Indian hostilities and deprived of every sort of commerce, may become unfaithful, when they shall be, by the operation of their own free will, established under another government that will protect them, secure an outlet for their produce, abstain from exacting any tax from them, and settle their differences without intermeddling with their domestic affairs, or with their religion.

"As soon as by such means the affection of the first generation shall have been secured, the succeeding ones will of course know no other country than the one in which they shall have been born, and it will then be left to the wisdom of government to imprint on the tender and impressive hearts of youth the true sentiments of patriotism and justice.

"Such motives determined the king of Spain, in 1790, to cause to be sent to the Governor of Louisiana a sufficient quantity of provisions to enable him to receive all the emigrants that should come from the aforesaid districts. He authorized that officer to make concessions of land to them, and divide those settlements into eighteen mile districts, in the centre of which there should be a church, a house for the commandant and an Irish curate, but with instructions not to disturb them in the exercise of their religion.

"My chief aim is to indicate the means of peopling Louisiana, the principal of which are the purchase of all the tobacco to be raised by the emigrants and the most unlimited extension of commerce. If my propositions seem to be exaggerated, let that exaggeration be attributed to the conviction in which I am—that *Louisiana is the key of America,* and therefore of the highest importance. In this respect, she has, for a long time past, been the object of the ambition of the United States; so that they would be deeply disgusted if they saw her pass into the hands of so preponderating a power as France; and they would have invaded her long ago if they had foreseen such an event.

"The purchase of the tobacco raised by the emigrants could not be burdensome to France. Spain used, before the war, to buy annually two millions of pounds of tobacco at New Orleans, although she consumed but little of it.

"I know in the most positive manner, from information given to me by the officer who is personally intrusted with this administration in Spain, that, after reserving the sixty thousand pounds which are sufficient for the consumption of Spain, because she uses none but the rappee, she exported the rest, every year, to Holland and France, and that, according to the returns of the bills of sales, the royal treasury was greatly benefited by that operation. This circumstance induces me to propose this means as the one which promises to be the most successful, without being onerous to the republic.

"The crops of tobacco made by said inhabitants were bought, in 1790 and 1791, at the rate of 8c. per pound, by the Spanish government, which derived considerable profit from it; and those inhabitants were themselves so well satisfied with that price, that I know they would deem themselves exceedingly happy if the government would now buy the same quantity of tobacco at six cents instead of eight. Should it be extended to four millions of pounds a year, it would be sufficient to attract a good many emigrants to Louisiana; for, from Red River to New Madrid, the raising of tobacco is the only culture which can reward the labor of the farmer—which circumstance convinces me that the purchase of this article by the government would powerfully contribute to increase the population of that part of Louisiana.

"France will easily find an outlet for those four millions of pounds of tobacco, considering* that, if Spain made money by the operation when she paid eight cents per pound, France, paying only six cents for the same article, would sell it cheaper, and would therefore easily find, not only a home market, but also one in Holland and in Spain.

"It would not be necessary for France to make any advances to accomplish this object, because she might enter into an arrangement with Spain, by which that power would, annually, send $240,000 from Vera Cruz to Louisiana, to be reimbursed to her in Europe after the sale of the tobacco by France. This arrangement would be equally advantageous to Spain, because she would receive that sum without risk, with a little delay, to be sure—but that delay would be compensated by the saving of the costs of transportation.

"Should this measure be adopted, it would become necessary to establish regulations determining the quantity of tobacco to be bought from every new settler, in the way in which it was done by the Spanish government. Such was the plan which it followed, and which was interrupted by the war.

"The commercial intercourse granted by the King to the inhabitants of Louisiana, although limited to the ports of France and of her colonies in time of peace, and extended to the ports of the United States in time of war, is fully sufficient to provide that province with the

---

* Probably, the agents employed by Spain made money, but it is to be doubted whether any considerable part of it found its way to the coffers of the government.

merchandise of which she may stand in need, and to procure an outlet for her commodities, with the exception of her tobacco, which the royal treasury used to purchase, but it is not sufficient to promote a rapid increase of population."

M. de Pontalba then goes on with an enumeration of all the means best calculated to attract, in a short time, a large number of emigrants—among which means is the grant of free trade, if possible, with all the nations of the world—and says, that the duty of six per cent., which is the only one hitherto levied by the government, would, in that case, on account of the development which the resources of Louisiana would require, be soon amply sufficient to cover, and more than cover, the five hundred and thirty-seven thousand dollars which are the expenses of the present colonial administration.

"The means," says he, "which have, so far, been used to people Louisiana, instead of being onerous to the public treasury, have turned to its advantage; but what would be a still more powerful lever, would be the appropriation of three millions of francs to be loaned in the Western country in this way: to every emigrant one hundred francs to facilitate his voyage, and to provide for the first expenses of his establishment, on condition that this sum shall be reimbursed in three years, the head of every family and the last surviving member of it being responsible in solido; and should this sum be advanced to unmarried men (provided they be laborers and not vagabonds), four of them would be required to become parties to this obligation under the same conditions. This would provoke emigration, and I doubt not that, in less than two years, that sum of three millions of francs would thus have been employed, and would have procured thirty thousand individuals. The government may rest assured, that there would be no loss, or hardly any, in this operation. I do not mention the immense profit which would subsequently accrue from the increase of duty on imports and exports.

"The emigrants from Kentucky and the adjacent districts, being active and industrious farmers, would, when leaving their country, where they have no outlet for their produce, sell their lands to come and clear better ones which they would get for nothing, in a province where the government secures to them a lucrative sale of the fruits of their industry. Not only would they be promptly in a situation to liberate themselves, but they would cause the government, by which they would have been enticed away and protected, to feel the effects of the easy circumstances which it would have secured to them.

"This is not all. After having granted to Louisiana all that might be in her power, France would still have done nothing for her, if she did not give her, as governor, an honest, frank, just and good man, who, by his conciliating temper, would gain the affection of the inhabitants. They are of a mild, sensitive and remarkably grateful temper. The statement of one fact alone will be sufficient to show how much I ought to insist upon this point.

"After having done, in order to remain French, more than it was then permitted to subjects to do, after having seen the solicitations of their delegates rejected by the court of France, the inhabitants of Louisiana, after having deliberated among themselves, came to the resolution of relying on nothing else than their courage —which was the sole resource remaining to them. The result was the expulsion of the Spanish Governor, Ulloa.

"O'Reilly arrived with an army. He had caused himself to be preceded by words of peace, of indulgence, and forgetfulness of the past. The colonists, abandoned by the mother country, thought that they were no longer bound to nurse and preserve for her the love which she rejected. They gave themselves up to the hope of an endurable condition under a new master, and received him without resistance. O'Reilly's conduct is but too well known. It exasperated every heart, and caused the new domination to be abhorred.

"The Count of Galvez made his appearance, and inspired the public with confidence; for he was distinguished for the affability of his manners, the sweetness of his temper, the frankness of his character, the kindness of his heart and his love of justice. Receiving, in 1779, the news of the declaration of war against the English, he convened the colonists around him. "Let them who love me follow where I lead," said he; and the next day, fifteen hundred creoles, among whom were many heads of families, gathered round him, and were ready to march to the enemy.

"The English were attacked before they knew that an expedition had been formed against them, and all their establishments on the Mississippi were carried sword in hand,* before the artillery which was following us was half way on the road to its destination. These are the men of Louisiana, who are, undoubtedly, well worthy of returning to the bosom of France. What is it that can not be expected from them, when they shall be under the influence of the great man who is going to acquire and govern Louisiana!" &c., &c.   *   *   *
*   *   *   *   *   *   *

After going into the exposition of the defensive measures which are to be adopted for the protection of Louisiana, M. de Pontalba thus resumes his observations:

---

* This is not correct, the fort at Baton Rouge having been bombarded and carried only by the artillery. See page 129 of this volume.

"Louisiana in the hands of France, may be called to the most brilliant destinies. What a series of prosperities does not promise to her the preponderance of the republic! And what a source of wealth would she not be for the metropolis! To secure this, all that is necessary is, to adopt a proper combination of all the means which ought to make her prosperous.

"No situation in the universe offers so many advantages as hers, and what remains to do is to know how to use them. The fertility of her immense territory, the abundance of her rich agricultural products which now secure to the planter an interest of 25 per cent. on the capital invested—these are her least advantages.

"New Orleans, the capital of Louisiana, is the only outlet for the most fertile of all countries, the extent of which in length exceeds six thousand miles, and the population of which marches onward with gigantic strides. That town must, of course, serve as a place of *dépôt* for the products of that immense country.

"France holds in her hands the key of Mexico when she possesses Louisiana, since her frontiers on the west side of the Mississippi extend beyond Natchitoches to the gates of St. Antonio, which is a dependency of Mexico.

"The effeminate people that occupy the more than fifteen hundred miles of territory which lie between that point and Mexico would easily become the prey of the first invader who should present himself even with moderate forces. But Spain, when ceding Louisiana to France, rightly sees in her naught but a protector, who is more capable than she is of guarding Mexico against the invasion with which that country is threatened; and a suitable return and equivalent for this protection must necessarily be, one day, the granting by Spain to Louisiana of permission to trade freely with all her ports in the Gulf of Mexico.

"Spain, by this means, would remove any temptation that France might have of invading Mexico; for it becomes more advantageous for France to trade with that country through Louisiana than to acquire its possession. Now, should Louisiana enjoy the privilege of free trade both with France and the Mexican provinces, what portion of the earth would be more highly favored? Where is the province that would offer so many advantages? From every part of the world there would be thereto a rush of men led by ambition and the desire of bettering their condition; and less than ten years would be sufficient to people that province, so as to make her formidable to her neighbors.

"The western districts of the United States, which are now tenanted by individuals of all nations, would soon be deserted, and would retain only such of their inhabitants as should not be able to find lands in Louisiana. It is then that these people will hasten to detach themselves from the United States, from which Nature has separated them by a chain of mountains, and will solicit, if not their annexation to the Republic, at least their independence under the protection of France. All that is necessary for this is, so to favor the inhabitant of Louisiana as to make him love the government that protects him, and to render precious to him the domination that makes him happy; then, both his interest and inclination will urge him to defend that government and domination.

"Almost all the Louisianians are born French, or are of French origin. It is with rage in their hearts that they lost their nationality. and although the truly paternal domination of the King of Spain has, ever since an honorable catastrophe on the taking possession of the province by O'Reilly, secured their happiness, although it has preserved them from similar disasters to those which have devastated St. Domingo, still it is with enthusiasm that they would again become French, if they had no apprehensions as to the organization to be established among them in relation to the blacks, whose emancipation would destroy the fortune of all, annihilate all the means of existence, and be the presage of the greatest misfortune.

"Louisiana cannot dispense with the slave trade. The excessive heat prevailing during the five months in which the hardest works are to be executed on the plantations, does not allow the use of free and white labor and renders the blacks indispensable.

"The enterprise of the inhabitants has been checked for several years; otherwise, the number of the blacks would have considerably increased. On hearing the news of the St. Domingo insurrection, the negroes made an attempt to follow that example. They were repressed, and their ringleaders punished. The authorities then thought prudent to prohibit the introduction of that kind of population into the province, in order not to augment the number of slaves until the restoration of peace. This measure has saved the colony, because the activity of the colonists, the great advantages they have derived from the cultivation of the sugar-cane for the last five years, would have induced them to increase the number of the blacks to such an extent, that they would not have been able to keep them in subjection and would have become their victims.

"Since that time, the number of whites who have been attracted by the prosperity of the province has increased so much, that the government has, for a year past, revoked the preceding measure, but only in relation to the negroes coming directly from Africa.

"It is apparent that any innovation operating against the slave trade system would undermine the very foundations of the prosperity of the colony.

"The inhabitant of Louisiana, if made easy on this point and in relation to the imports and the duties to be paid thereon, would give half of his blood to be replaced under French domination, and would shed the last drop of the remaining half to defend that domination.

"The facility with which man can supply his wants in that colony is such, that two hours of daily labor are sufficient to procure him all the means of existence. The necessities of life are satisfied with hardly any trouble or expense. Several districts, such as those of Attakapas, Opeloussas and Natchitoches, furnish the colonists with thousands of heads of cattle—so that an ox, weighing from seven hundred to eight hundred pounds, costs no more than four dollars. Flour comes from the western provinces of the United States in such abundance, that bread is not higher than in France.

"The crops of rice and corn are so abundant, that the average price of a barrel of rice of one hundred and eighty pounds is from four to five dollars, and that of corn from forty to fifty cents, and this is what constitutes the main food of the planter and of his negroes. Every sort of game and fish is so plentiful, that they scarcely fetch any price at all. An exception must be made as to wages, which are very high. It is the case with every newly settled country in which population has not yet become dense.

"The products of this province consist of sugar, indigo, tobacco, cotton, rice, corn, millet, essences, common furs, timber, boards, planks, shingles, and boxes for the Havana sugar.

"The want of success in the cultivation of indigo,

which, for the last few years, has been almost everywhere the prey of insects, the small results obtained from any other agricultural labor, have determined the planters to try again the experiment which had previously failed—that of establishing sugar cane plantations. Formerly, there was considerable difficulty to be surmounted. It had always been thought that winter was a great obstacle to that culture. Experience has proved the contrary.

"The sugar cane, which requires in the West India islands eighteen months to reach its perfect maturity, is fit for use in Louisiana in seven months. It begins to spring up in March, towards the end of the winter, and is cut at the end of October.

"The impression was, that the planters would have, for the manufacture of sugar, no more time than the month of November and part of December, when the winter should happen to be mild, because the canes would be spoiled, if frosted when standing in the field. To obviate this danger, it would have been necessary for the inhabitant who occupies fifty negroes in ploughing his land, in planting and weeding his canes, to have four mills and more than two hundred negroes, to cut and grind them before the setting in of winter.

"Notwithstanding this, the planters did not give way to discouragement, and experience has demonstrated that the sugar cane which, at St. Domingo, becomes sour two days after its being cut, continues sound in Louisiana, when cut down and covered with its stubble on the ground, until it be manufactured into sugar. It is an invaluable advantage, which secures the success of sugar estates in Louisiana, and is the cause that its cultivation in this province has become as rich a branch of industry and gives as much hope as in any of the most important colonies.

"It is in 1795, that, with a small gang of thirty negroes, the first sugar plantation was established, and with such success, that the individual* who had made the undertaking, sold his crop of brown sugar to the Americans, in 1796, for twelve thousand dollars. The quality of that sugar was found at least equal to that of Martinique. This was enough to excite the emulation of all the planters who had some means, so much so, that, notwithstanding the difficulty of procuring, in time of war, sets of kettles—notwithstanding the prohibition of the introduction of negroes, which checked the increase of cultivation, there are, to-day, more than sixty sugar estates in Louisiana, which produce, annually, four millions of pounds of sugar, which yield from twenty to twenty-five per cent. on the capital invested.

"This sketch is sufficient to give an idea of the progress which this branch of industry is destined to make, as soon as the colony shall enjoy the blessings of peace.

"The districts of Attakapas and Opeloussas, situated at one hundred and seventy-four miles from New Orleans, on the banks of the Teche and Vermillion, which lie on the right side of the Mississippi, are of an immense extent, and the sugar cane succeeds there as well as on the river, and also in the Lafourche district and others.

"The indigo would be one of the most advantageous products of Louisiana, if it could be cultivated successfully; but it is exposed to so many casualties, that it has been abandoned by most of the inhabitants. Thus, this crop which rose, some years ago, to three hundred thousand pounds, has been reduced to one-third, and the cultivation of that plant diminishes every day, since the establishment of sugar plantations. But the impression is, that the sugar cane destroys the insects which are noxious to the indigo, and a piece of land, which has for

* Jean Etienne Boré.

a long time been used for the cultivation of the sugar cane, may with success, it is thought, be turned over to the cultivation of the indigo. This article goes directly, in times of peace, to the ports of France, and can go nowhere else. It is there that it is always sold to the best advantage. It is worth from seven to nine francs the pound.

"The district of Natchitoches is the only one which is addicted to the cultivation of tobacco ever since the district of Natchez belongs to the Americans, when the new demarcation of limits took place in 1797. The quantity of tobacco thus produced rises to two hundred thousand pounds. In time of peace, the greater portion of it is exported to France, and the rest to Vera Cruz and Campeachy.

"The exportation of cotton from Louisiana does not exceed two hundred thousand pounds. This branch of agricultural industry is profitable enough (since the invention of certain mills to separate the seed from the silk) to justify small planters in consoling themselves for not having sufficient forces to go into the planting of the sugar cane.

"That cotton is very fine, but the silk is short. In time of peace, the whole of it is sent to France, where it is no doubt used to better advantage than anywhere else, since it sells there better than in any other country.

"There goes out of Louisiana, annually, more than one hundred thousand dollars' worth of furs, consisting principally of deerskin. Bear and beaver skins, together with the hides of wild beeves, and particularly furs of a fine quality are comparatively scarce. They meet with a ready sale in the ports of France.

"Louisiana supplies St. Domingo with a great deal of timber, planks, shingles, boards, essences, &c. She cannot sell them at so low a price as the Americans, because wages are twice as high there as in the United States, because also the quality of the wood being harder requires more labor, and because the voyages from Louisiana are longer.

"Nevertheless, it is evident that it is more advantageous for St. Domingo to be supplied with timber from Louisiana than from the United States. In the first place, the quality is infinitely better; in the next, the Americans, when introducing cargoes of timber into the French colonies, carry also thither a great quantity of dry goods, manufactured either by themselves, or by the English, and take molasses in return to the amount of only one-half of their exports, as the other half of the return cargo is always in specie, whilst the vessels coming from Louisiana, far from draining St. Domingo of specie, bring a good deal of it, in order to purchase their return cargoes, which consist of goods of French manufacture, and also of wines and eatables. The shipowners are satisfied with a slight profit on the timber, which covers the expenses of freight. The cargoes of timber are a mere pretext, because every vessel sailing with a cargo of this nature, valued for instance at fifteen thousand livres, comes back from St. Domingo with a cargo of merchandise worth three or four times as much, and everybody knows that, with every cargo of timber, there goes in[*] contraband a sufficient quantity of dollars to pay for a return cargo, and, if those ships had not this object in view, their timber cargo would be an insufficient consideration to induce them to undertake such voyages. This trade, which has been interrupted since the war, will take more extension under the domination of France, when the exportation of specie shall no longer be prohibited.

---

[*] The exportation of specie from Louisiana was prohibited.

"The trade which occupies most ships in Louisiana is that of boxes, with which this province supplies the island of Cuba. Havana alone consumes two hundred thousand sugar boxes, which constitute about fifty cargoes. Those boxes, at fifty cents a-piece, give to the planters a revenue of one hundred thousand dollars; to the carriers, as much for the freight; and to the merchants engaged in that trade, a profit of twenty-five thousand dollars. This is not all. It must also be taken into consideration, that there is not one of the vessels employed in carrying those boxes which does not smuggle into Havana a certain quantity of articles of French manufacture, and which does not return to New Orleans with twice the value of its cargo in specie, doubled as it is by the profits of the sale and freight.

"These sugar boxes were formerly made at Havana with the cedar-wood, which is very common there. But Spain, since she possesses Louisiana, has, in order to favor her, permitted her to supply the island of Cuba and the other harbors in the Gulf of Mexico with the boxes required for the sugar crops; and since that permission, such boxes are no longer made in the Spanish establishments, where the quality of the wood being much harder, they cannot be furnished so cheap as by Louisiana.

"If the moment has not yet come to insist upon obtaining for Louisiana from Spain the grant of a free trade with the harbors in the Gulf of Mexico, France ought not at least to give up the sugar box trade with Havana, which Louisiana now enjoys. Since her cession to Spain, more than thirty saw mills have been constructed near New Orleans, on the banks of the Mississippi, to supply that trade, and these saw mills, should they be deprived of that outlet, would become valueless. Besides, these boxes, as I have said, constitute the freight of all the vessels which trade with Havana, and it would therefore deprive this colony of a precious commercial resource.

"It was to reward the inhabitants of Louisiana for the zeal they displayed in 1779 and 1780, when they conquered under General Galvez the English settlements on the Mississippi, and the towns of Mobile and Pensacola, that his Catholic Majesty granted them the privilege of free trade with France. His Majesty, should he be reminded of this fact, would not come to the harsh conclusion of depriving them of so interesting a branch of commerce as the supply of those sugar boxes, of which they have been in possession for the last thirty-four years—that is—ever since they have been under Spanish domination. The benefit which accrues from it to the island of Cuba deserves also some consideration.

"About ten thousand barrels of rice are annually exported from Louisiana to St. Domingo and Havana.

"The chief resource of the province of Louisiana is the money which is spent there by the government for the pay of its agents and officers. Five hundred and thirty-seven thousand dollars are annually sent to New Orleans from Mexico in three ships, which arrive at a regular interval of four months. This sum is divided among so many persons employed by the government, that each one consumes what he receives, so that it soon goes into the pockets of the farmer who feeds him, and of the merchant who supplies his other wants. The whole ends in finding its way into the coffers of the merchant, who supplies the farmer, whose crop, besides, is generally insufficient to pay his debts to said merchant.

"This sketch demonstrates pretty clearly that Louisiana still remains a burden to the metropolis, since the annual disbursements of Spain to keep up that colony amount to four hundred and thirty-seven thousand dollars, over and above the revenue derived through its custom-house. From that sum there may be deducted one hundred thousand dollars, which are uselessly spent at Pensacola. There remains a deficit of three hundred and thirty-seven thousand dollars, which the success alone of sugar-making in the colony justifies the government in the hope of being able to cover in a few years, as soon as a general peace shall permit the slave trade to be resumed, and as soon as the government shall take it in hand to people Louisiana.

"These are about all the articles of exportation which are supplied by Louisiana, in return for the objects of importation which she receives from France in time of peace. There may be added to the above statement about one hundred thousand dollars, in return for the commodities which are smuggled from Louisiana into the harbors of the Gulf of Mexico; and, in time of peace, it is the commerce of France and St. Domingo which gets hold of all this specie, in exchange for wines, oils, soaps, eatables and other articles of French manufacture.

"The planter does not hoard up, however considerable may be the result of his agricultural labors. After having consumed so much of it as is necessary to supply his wants, he employs the rest in improving his estate. Ambition and activity are his characteristics; all that he requires is encouragement.

"The only taxes known in Louisiana are a duty of six per cent. on the exports, valued according to a very moderate estimation. The same duty is paid on all foreign imports.

"Spain has, so far, retained possession of this colony for political reasons. It is onerous to her, as it was onerous to France during all the time that the latter power possessed it, since the custom-house duty, which is here the only source of revenue, does not produce annually one hundred thousand dollars, and since the ordinary expenditure required by the colony rises up every year to five hundred and thirty-seven thousand dollars, without including the extraordinary expenses.

"The inhabitants of Louisiana, as subjects of the King of Spain, have the right to carry to all the ports of the Gulf of Mexico the products of their soil, and when they resort to Havana, Cuba, Vera Cruz and Campeachy, only for the apparent purpose of selling their boxes, timber and tobacco, they smuggle in a considerable quantity of merchandise of French manufacture, such as silk stuffs, ribbons, muslins, lawns, lace and jewels, and the vessels engaged in that trade always bring back to Louisiana four times more dollars than the apparent value of their outward cargoes. Those harbors in the Gulf of Mexico furnish nothing for return cargoes beyond dollars and Campeachy wood. This last article will only serve as ballast for the ships returning to France.

"If, in consequence of the cession of Louisiana to France, Spain closed to that province all her harbors in the Gulf of Mexico, this measure would deprive the colony of the principal resources which constitute its present prosperity, and the exports not being commensurate with the imports which it requires, its commerce would decay, and the colony itself would receive a blow which would keep it palsied, until it should become sufficiently peopled to enable it to produce more than she imports.

"Louisiana wants working hands. Give her population, and she will become an inexhaustible source of wealth for France. Give her population, whatever be the means employed, but give her population.

"Here is an estimate of what that province gives

annually in return for the commodities she receives from France and St. Domingo in time of peace, but which, in time of war, she has permission to procure, wherever she can, in the ports of neutral or allied powers.

4,000,000 lbs. sugar at $8 per 100 lb.	$320,000
4,000 barrels of molasses, at $15 each	60,000
100,000 lbs. indigo	100,000
200,000 lbs. tobacco	16,000
Furs of divers kinds	100,000
Timber, &c., furnished to St. Domingo in time of peace	50,000
200,000 boxes, annually sent to Havana, and sold for	225,000
2,000 barrels of rice, annually exported to St. Domingo, Cuba, and Campeachy, at the average price of	50,000
Dollars, imported by the Government to meet the annual expenses of the colony	537,000
(The extraordinary expenses of the Government absorb the amount of the Custom-house duties, amounting to one hundred thousand dollars.)	
The returns for the contraband commodities introduced by the vessels of Louisiana into the Spanish ports of Cuba and of the Gulf amount to	500,000
Total in dollars	$1,958,000

"In time of peace, it is the commerce of Bordeaux, Marseilles and Nantes which absorbs all this capital, and the whole trade is even engrossed by vessels from these ports. As soon as they have deposited their cargoes at New Orleans, they avail themselves of the time required for the sale of those cargoes and the collecting of the debts due to them, to make a voyage to Havana, or Vera Cruz. They carry thither a cargo of sugar-boxes, and never fail to dispose at the same time of the objects of luxury which they bring from France for that purpose, and, on their return to New Orleans, they find their cargoes for Europe ready prepared.

"It is only since the war with Great Britain does not prevent any intercourse with France, that the King of Spain has allowed the province of Louisiana to trade with neutral nations, because the Court of Madrid could not but be aware that the colony could not do without that foreign trade. Whereupon, it has so turned out that the United States now monopolize the commerce of Louisiana, which, by this means, has hardly suffered at all during the long period of the European wars.

"It would be much to the interest of France and Louisiana to prohibit the introduction of timber from the United States into the French colonies. Then the price of the Louisiana timber, which is better, would be kept up, and the merchants of the province, instead of exporting thither twenty cargoes of timber annually, would send two hundred, and, instead of taking for their return cargoes melons and dollars, as do the Americans, would bring back French dry goods and French liquids, which they would pay for in specie, because the sale of their timber cargoes would not be of sufficient amount to supply them with return cargoes. Besides, wages will diminish in Louisiana in proportion to the increase of population, and consequently its timber will become cheaper.

"By this sketch it appears, that the objects of exportation from Louisiana amount at present to $1,958,000; but, from the moment that France shall be in possession of it, if that province is not permitted to continue its commerce of sugar-boxes in the Gulf of Mexico, the importation will be limited to the agricultural products of its soil, the value of which amounts now to about $696,000; but then the deficit will be $1,260,000, which it now receives from its trade in boxes and its appendages, and also from the disbursements of Spain to meet the necessary expenses of the colonial administration.

"I must not omit to say, that every sort of paper money, by causing the ruin of this province, would in the end become onerous to the government, and profitable only to some stockholders, who are always interested in proposing its issue. The government will easily procure funds in Louisiana, by resorting to bills of exchange on the national treasury at home. It is useless to say, that this resource would fail from the very moment they should not meet with ready payment on their becoming due.

"The good intelligence which exists between France and Spain would also afford to the former the resource of drawing to advantage, for the expenses of the colony, dollars from Vera Cruz, on making reimbursements for them in Europe. Spain would find it to her interest to receive her capital without other costs and risks than those of transportation from Vera Cruz to New Orleans.

"This is all the information which I have been able to gather during a residence of eighteen years in Louisiana, where I was employed by the government in a superior office," &c., &c.

This able document gives so very faithful a delineation of Louisiana, at the time, by one whose authority is inferior to none, that I felt justified in transcribing it at length. It holds up also to France golden visions of maritime power which would have given her a wonderful preponderance in America, but which she was not destined to realize.

Pontalba's memoir was presented on the 15th of September, 1800, and, on the 1st of October, a treaty was concluded at St. Ildephonso, the third article of which is in these terms: "His Catholic Majesty promises and engages to retrocede to the French Republic, six months after the full and entire execution of the above conditions and stipulations relative to his Royal Highness, the Duke of Parma, the colony or province of Louisiana, with the same extent that it now has in the hands of Spain, and that it had when France possessed it, and such as it ought to be after the treaties subsequently entered into between Spain and other states." The stipulation relative to the Duke of Parma was, that as a compensation for that Duchy and its dependencies, which were ceded to France by that prince, who belonged to the Spanish branch of the house of Bourbon, and as a compensation also for the cession which the King of Spain made of Louisiana to the same power, the Duke of Parma should be put in possession of Tuscany, which was to be erected into a kingdom, under the name of Etruria, by the great king maker and king destroyer, Napoleon Bonaparte. As France was then at war with England, the treaty was carefully concealed from the knowledge of the public, because Louisiana might have been easily attacked and conquered by the English, who were masters of the sea.

CHAPTER VIII.

SALCEDO'S ADMINISTRATION.

1801 to 1803.

DON JUAN MANUEL DE SALCEDO, a Brigadier-General in the armies of Spain, arrived in Louisiana about the 15th of June, 1801, to act as governor of the provinces of Louisiana and West Florida; and his predecessor, the Marquis de Casa Calvo, who, it will be remembered, had entered on the duties of his office in the fall of 1799, sailed immediately for Havana.

The Americans, as neighbors, had always been considered as very unsafe for Louisiana, and one of Salcedo's first measures was directed to check what he thought to be the dangerous designs of some men belonging to that nation. Thus, in a despatch of the 13th of July, he informed his government that he had sent up to Natchitoches all that was necessary to arm and equip the militia of that district,* " with the view of counteracting the projects of the American bandit, Philip Nolan, who had introduced himself into the interior of the provinces of New Spain, with thirty-six armed men."

Although it had been the policy of the head of the French government to conceal from the public his transactions with the court of Madrid in relation to Louisiana,

---

* Con el fin de contrarestar los designios del bandido Americano, Felipe Nolan, el cual se habia introducido en las provincias internas de Nueva España con treinte y seis hombres armados.

still some knowledge of it had at last transpired, and Mr. Rufus King, the United States Minister at London (for they had none at the time at Paris), wrote the following despatch to the Secretary of State at Washington, on the 29th of March, 1801: "In confirmation of the rumors of the day, Carnot's answer to Bailleul, published during the exile of the former, states the project which had been discussed in the Directory, to obtain from Spain a cession of Louisiana and the Floridas. A reference to that performance, copies of which I, at the time, sent to the department of State, will show the manner in which it was expected to obtain the consent of Spain, as well as afford a clue to the views of France in seeking this establishment. What was then meditated has, in all probability, since been executed. The cession of Tuscany to the Infant, Duke of Parma, by the treaty between France and Austria, forms a more compact and valuable compensation to this branch of the house of Spain than was formerly thought of; and adds very great credit to the opinion which, at this time, prevails both at Paris and London, that Spain has, in return, actually ceded Louisiana and the Floridas to France. There is reason to know that it is the opinion of certain influential persons in France, that nature has marked a line of separation between the people of the United States living upon the two sides of the range of mountains which divides their territory. Without discussing the considerations which are suggested in support of this opinion, or the false consequences, as I wish to believe them, deduced from it, I am apprehensive that this cession is intended to have, and may actually produce, effects injurious to the Union and consequent happiness of the people of the United States. Louisiana and the Floridas may be given to the French emigrants, as England once thought of giving them to the American Tories · or they may constitute the reward of some of the armies which can be spared at the end of the war.

"I learn that General Collot, who was a few years ago in America, and a traveller in the Western country, and who, for some time, has been in disgrace and confinement in France, has been lately set at liberty; and that he, with a considerable number of disaffected and exiled Englishmen, Scotchmen, and Irishmen, is soon to proceed from France to the United States. Whether their voyage has any relation to the cession of Louisiana is a matter of mere conjecture; but, having heard of it in connexion with that project, I think proper to mention it to you.

"What effect a plain and judicious representation upon this subject, made to the French government by a minister of talents and entitled to confidence, would be likely to have, is quite beyond any means of judging which I possess; but on this account, as well as on others of importance, it is a subject of regret that we have not such a character at this time at Paris."

On the 1st of June, Mr. King, resuming the same subject, said: "On this occasion, among other topics of conversation, his Lordship (Hawkesbury) introduced the subject of Louisiana. He had, from different quarters, received information of its cession to France, and very unreservedly expressed the reluctance with which they should be led to acquiesce in a measure that might be followed by the most important consequences. The acquisition might enable France to extend her influence and perhaps her dominion up the Mississippi, and through the lakes, even to Canada. This would be realizing the plan, to prevent the accomplishment of which, the Seven Years' War took place; besides, the vicinity of the Floridas to the West Indies, and the facility with which the trade of the latter might be interrupted, and the islands even invaded, should the transfer be made, were strong reasons why England must be unwilling that the territory should pass under the dominion of France. As I could not mistake his Lordship's object in speaking to me on this subject, I had no difficulty or reserve in expressing my private sentiments respecting it; taking for my text the observation of Montesquieu, 'that it is happy for trading powers, that God has permitted Turks and Spaniards to be in the world, since of all nations they are the most proper to possess a great empire with insignificance.' The purport of what I said was, that we are contented that the Floridas remain in the hands of Spain, but should not be willing to see them transferred, except to ourselves."

On the 9th of June, Mr. Madison, the Secretary of State, addressed Mr. Pinckney, the American Minister at Madrid, in these terms: "On different occasions since the commencement of the French revolution, opinions and reports have prevailed, that some part of the Spanish possessions, including New Orleans and the mouth of the Mississippi, had been or was to be transferred to France. Of late, information has been received through several channels, making it probable that some arrangement for that purpose has been concerted. Neither the extent of the cession, however, nor the consideration on which it is made, is yet reduced to certainty and precision. The whole subject will deserve and engage your early and vigilant inquiries, and may require a very delicate and circumspect management."

Alarmed at the consequences of a cession of Louisiana by Spain to France, the government of the United States lost no time in sending a minister to France, and gave that important mission to Robert R. Livingston. On the 28th of September, 1801, the Secretary of State wrote to him: "From different sources information has been received that, by some transaction concluded, or contemplated, between France and Spain, the mouth of the Mississippi, with certain portions of adjacent territory, is to pass from the hands of the latter to the former nation. Such a change of our neighbors in that quarter is of too momentous concern not to have engaged the most serious attention of the Executive. It was accordingly made one of the subjects of instruction to Mr. Pinckney, our minister plenipotentiary at the Court of Madrid. You will find an extract of the passage hereto annexed, No. 1. A paragraph connected with the same subject, in a letter to Mr. King, is also extracted and annexed, No. 2. In these extracts you will see the ideas entertained by the Executive, and the general considerations which it is presumed will have most tendency to dissuade the parties from adhering to their object. As soon as you shall have prepared the way by the necessary inquiries at Paris, it will be proper for you to break the subject to the French Government, and to make the use of those considerations most likely to give them full weight."

When the anxieties of the United States Government were thus excited, preliminaries of peace were signed between France and England, on the 1st of October, 1801; and the former power was secretly preparing to avail itself of its treaty with Spain in relation to Louisiana, of the 1st of October, 1800, which had been renewed in all its dispositions on the 21st of March, 1801. Mr. King, the American Minister at London, succeeded in procuring a copy of that secret treaty, and forwarded it to Washington city, with the following note to the Secretary of State, dated on the 20th of November: 'If the annexed copy of the treaty* between France and

---

* Annals of Congress, Session of 1803, p. 1017. Appendix.

Spain, respecting the establishment of the Prince of Parma in Tuscany, be genuine, of which I have no reason to doubt, you will perceive the value which these powers seem to have placed upon Louisiana, the cession whereof to France is confirmed by the 7th article of this treaty.

"I am in hopes that I shall be able to obtain and send you a copy of the treaty ceding Louisiana to France. This would enable us to determine whether it includes New Orleans and the Floridas. * * *
* * * * * * *

"It is not a little extraordinary that, during the whole negotiation between France and England, not a word was mentioned on either side respecting Louisiana, though this government was not ignorant of the views of France in this quarter."

In the meantime, Mr. Livingston had arrived in Paris, where his presence was so much wanted, and on the 12th of December, said in a despatch to Mr. Madison: "In addition to what I wrote yesterday, I have only to mention, that I am more and more confirmed, notwithstanding what I there say of the minister's assurance, that Louisiana is a favorite object, and that they will be unwilling to part with it on the condition I mentioned Speaking of the means of paying their debts to one of their ministers, yesterday, I hinted at this. His answer was: 'None but spendthrifts satisfy their debts by selling their lands;' adding, however, after a short pause, 'but it is not ours to give.'"

On the 30th of the same month, Mr. Livingston communicated his views to Mr. Rufus King at London, on the important subject which so keenly excited the attention of the government of the United States: "I took occasion," said he, "on my first private audience of the Minister of Exterior Relations, to press him directly upon the subject, taking the common reports as a foundation to my inquiry. He explicitly denied that anything had been concluded, but admitted that it had been a subject of conversation. I know, however, from a variety of channels, that it is not a mere matter of conversation, but that the exchange has actually been agreed upon; that the armament destined, in the first instance, for Hispaniola, is to proceed to Louisiana, provided Toussaint makes no opposition. General Collot, whom you may have seen in America, was originally intended for governor of the province, but he is, at present, out of favor. I think it probable the minister will justify his concealment to me, by its not having been definitively closed with Spain, as this, though determined between the two governments, may form an article in the general treaty. His absence (being at Lyons) prevents my coming to something more explicit with him. That Spain had made this cession (which contravenes all her former maxims of policy), cannot be doubted · but she is no longer a free agent.

"I wish to know from you in what light this is seen by England. It will certainly, in its consequences, be extremely dangerous to her, as it will give an almost unbounded power to her rival.

"It puts Spain in a perpetual state of pupilage, since she must always tremble for the safety of her colonies, in case of rupture. To avoid this evil, she must grant every commercial and political advantage to France. Her manufactures will find their way, through this channel, into every part of the Spanish territory, to the exclusion of those of Britain. Our Western territory may be rendered so dependent upon them as to promote their political views, while the interest they have always nurtured with the Indians, and the natural character of the peasantry of Canada, may render the possessions of Britain very precarious, to say nothing of the danger which must threaten her islands, in case a respectable establishment should be made by France in Louisiana, which will not fail to be the case, as the territory is uncommonly fine, and produces sugar, and every article now cultivated in the islands.

"I suggest these hints, that they, with many others which may occur to you, may be made use of with the British ministry, to induce them to throw all the obstacles in their power in the way of a final settlement of this business, if it is not already too late. You know, however, the importance of not appearing yourself, or permitting me to appear much opposed to it, if you find the thing concluded, since it might be made use of to embroil us with France, and Britain will have sufficient address to endeavor to keep up a mutual jealousy, if possible, between us."

"On the following day (31st of December), he wrote to Mr. Madison: "The business of Louisiana is very disagreeable to Spain, as far as I can learn. If it should be equally so to Britain, perhaps it may meet with some obstacles. It is a favorite measure here. Marbois told me yesterday it was considered important to have an outlet for their turbulent spirits; yet would not explicitly acknowledge that the business had been concluded."

"In the fall of this year, the Intendant of Louisiana, Don Ramon de Lopez y Angullo, surrendered his office into the hands of Don Juan Ventura Morales, the comptroller, who was to fulfil his functions ad interim, and prepared to depart for Spain. But, in settling his accounts, it seems that he got into serious difficulties with his successor, who brought some accusation against him before the Spanish ministry. In answer to it, Lopez complained bitterly of Morales, who, he said, threw* in

---

* Formando un dilatado proceso por la cosa mas clara, insignifican'e, infundada é injusta, y como la astucia y perversa malignidad de su corazon, y del asesor

his way interminable delays and litigation on the clearest and most insignificant points, and on grounds which were unfounded and unjust. " Wherefore," continued he, " considering that the crafty and intense malignity of Morales and of his satellite, the assessor (Serano) who is also my mortal enemy, know no bounds, I again beg your excellency (the minister in Spain) to suspend your decision until," &c., &c.

Governor Salcedo seems not to have been very well pleased with the spirit which prevailed in the colony; for, in a despatch of the 2d of March, 1802, he violently complained of the choice made by the Cabíldo, or city council of New Orleans, of one Jose Martinez de la Pedrera, as their assessor, and he even begged leave to drive him out of the colony. He represented that this individual, ever since his arrival from Bayamo, had busied himself in raising up parties, in fomenting dissensions and in breathing the fire of discord into the breasts of the principal members of the community, and had treated with proud contempt the only two men learned in the law who were to be found in the province. He added : "It is important to repress* the pen and tongue of the said Pedrera, who is a bold man, and a dangerous character among a population, the larger portion of which is composed of foreigners, disagreeing in their religious opinions and customs, whose natural dispositions are opposed to a prudent and gentle submission to the laws, and who are anxious to introduce innovations harmonizing with the maxims of liberty which favor, as they

---

satelite suyo, y tambien enemigo mortal mio, no tienen limites, reitero á V. E. la suplica que le tengo hecha de que suspende su juicio, &c., &c.

* Que es importante contener la pluma y la lengua del dicho Pedrera, hombre audaz, en un pais compuesto por la mayor parte de estrangeros de penetracion, de religion y costumbres diversas, contrarios por naturaleza á la prudente y moderada sujecion á las leyes, y ansiosos de introducir novedades analogas á las maximas de libertad que se figuran favorecer su antojo y su capricho.

imagine, their tastes and caprices." The Governor probably alluded in this despatch to the Americans, whose number was daily increasing in New Orleans.

The fact is, that rumors of the cession of Louisiana to France had reached that province, and had produced a deep sensation and a variety of feelings among its motley population. The Americans were not the least excited, and showed themselves very hostile to the contemplated measure. That class of the population had always been looked upon with a suspicious eye by the Spanish Government, which now became more averse than ever to permitting their number to increase, particularly on account of the critical situation in which Louisiana was placed; for this reason, the Baron de Bastrop having ceded to Moorhouse,* a citizen of the United States, a part of the large grant he had obtained from the Baron de Carondelet, in 1796, on the Ouachita, the king disapproved of this arrangement, and, by a royal decree of the 18th of July, 1802, forbade the grant of any land in Louisiana to a citizen of the United States.

Acting under the influence of the same policy, and in order to prevent the afflux of Americans to New Orleans at a time which involved peculiar difficulties, the intendant Morales issued an order suspending the right of deposit at that town, by a proclamation of the 16th of October, 1802. This measure was extremely prejudicial to New Orleans, where it almost produced a famine by stopping the supplies of flour and other Western produce necessary for the daily sustenance of its population.

When this news reached the Western people, they were fired with indignation at an act which suspended their commerce with New Orleans, and deprived them of an outlet without which they could hardly exist.

* Martin's History of Louisiana, vol. ii., p. 180.

Numerous appeals, petitions, and even violent threats were addressed to the general government on the subject, and the protracted embarrassments of the West were exposed to the whole people of the United States in so impressive a manner, as to command their deep attention and to force the government into immediate and energetic action. Here is a specimen of the language used on the occasion: "The Mississippi," said the Western people, "is ours* by the law of nature; it belongs to us by our numbers, and by the labor which we have bestowed on those spots which, before our arrival, were desert and barren. Our innumerable rivers swell it, and flow with it into the Gulf of Mexico. Its mouth is the only issue which nature has given to our waters, and we wish to use it for our vessels. No power in the world shall deprive us of this right. We do not prevent the Spaniards and French from ascending the river to our towns and villages. We wish in our turn to descend it without any interruption to its mouth, to ascend it again, and exercise our privilege of trading on it and navigating it at our pleasure. If our most entire liberty in this matter is disputed, nothing shall prevent our taking possession of the capital, and, when we are once masters of it, we shall know how to maintain ourselves there. If Congress refuses us effectual protection, if it forsakes us, we will adopt the measures which our safety requires, even if they endanger the peace of the Union and our connection with the other States. No protection, no allegiance."

Serano, the assessor of the intendancy, having died on the 1st of December, 1802, Morales, in consequence of this event, says Judge Martin in his History of Louisiana, closed the tribunal of affairs and causes relating to

---

* Barbé Marbois' History. Translation from the French. Philadelphia edition. 1830. P 215.

the grants of royal lands and the compositions thereto appertaining, because the ordinance for the intendants of New Spain provided that, for conducting the affairs of that tribunal and substantiating its acts, there should be the concurrence of such a character. This measure also produced no small inconvenience to the public.

But let us return to Europe and see what was passing there in relation to Louisiana. The American ministers had not been sleeping at their posts, and Mr. Livingston had, on the 13th of January, 1803, thus addressed the Secretary of State at Washington: "My former letters left you little doubt on the subject of the cession of Louisiana. By the inclosed copy of the late treaty between France and Spain, you will find that it is a transaction of pretty long standing.

"The absence of the minister prevents my applying to him for the former treaty, which he will hardly know how to give me after absolutely denying that any had been formed on the subject. By the secrecy and duplicity practised relative to this object, it is clear to me that they apprehend some opposition on the part of America to their plans."

Two days after, Mr. King communicated also his views on the subject to Mr. Madison: "I have before mentioned to you that the cession of Louisiana (of which it seems to me we can have no doubt, notwithstanding what may be said to amuse us) was not once a topic of inquiry or discussion in the negotiation of the preliminaries;* and, for the same reason that it was not heard of on that occasion, Lord Hawkesbury has recently informed me that it had not been, and would not be mentioned at Amiens.† It is impossible for me to sup-

---

* The preliminaries of peace agreed to between France and England on the 1st of October, 180.

† The place where the representatives of England and France had met to discuss the terms of a definitive peace between the two nations.

pose collusion in this affair, and my persuasion, after the most careful attention, is, that England abstains from mixing herself in it, precisely from those considerations which have led her to acquiesce in others of great importance to the balance of Europe, as well as her own repose, and upon which she has been altogether silent."

The studied reserve of the Spanish and French governments, and the mystery with which they had shrouded this late transaction, were but too well calculated to excite the anxieties of the American Ministers at Paris, Madrid, and London, and they were exceedingly desirous of ascertaining whether the treaty of cession between France and Spain included not only Louisiana but also the two Floridas. On the 20th of February, Mr. Livingston addressed to the Minister of Exterior Relations the following note : "The undersigned, &c., * * * has seen, with some concern, the reserve of the French government, with respect to the cession they have received from Spain of Louisiana.

" He had hoped that they would have found a propriety in making such frank and open communications to him, as would have enabled him to satisfy the government of the United States, that neither their boundary, nor the navigation of the Mississippi, secured by their treaties with Spain, would be, in any way, affected by the measure. It would also have been very satisfactory to him to have taken such arrangements with the Minister of Exterior Relations as would have had a tendency to dissipate the alarms the people of the Western territory of the United States will not fail to feel, on the arrival of a large body of French troops in their vicinity; alarms which will be increased by the exertions of those powers that are interested in keeping the two Republics from cementing their connexion. The policy of the former government of France led it to avoid all ground of controversy with the United States, not only by declining to possess any territory in their neighborhood, but also by stipulating never to hold any. The undersigned does not, by this reference to the 6th article of the treaty of 1778, mean to claim any rights under it, since by the convention of Paris, September 30th, 1800, it is understood to be revoked; but merely to lead the French government to reflect, how far a regard to the same policy might render it conducive to the mutual interest of both nations to cover, by a natural barrier, their possessions in America, as France has invariably sought to do in Europe.

" The undersigned prays the Minister of Exterior Relations (if the request is not inconsistent with the views of the government), to inform him whether East and West Florida, or either of them, are included in the treaty made between France and Spain; and to afford him such assurances, with respect to the limits of their territory and the navigation of the Mississippi, heretofore agreed on between Spain and the United States, as may prove satisfactory to the latter.

" If the territories of East and West Florida be included within the limits of the cession obtained by France, the undersigned desires to be informed how far it would be practicable to make such arrangements between their respective governments as would, at the same time, aid the financial operations of France, and remove, by a strong natural boundary, all future causes of discontent between her and the United States."

On the 26th of the same month, Mr. Livingston informed Mr. Madison that he had received no reply to the above note; that he had discovered, however, that the projected establishment in Louisiana was disapproved by every statesman in France, as one that would occasion a great waste of men and money, excite enmities with the United States, and produce no possible advantage to the French nation. But he added that it was a scheme to which the French Consul was extremely attached; and therefore, that those about him felt themselves compelled to support it; and that General Bernadotte was understood to be designed for the command of the new colony, and to have asked ten thousand troops.

Notwithstanding all his exertions, the American minister continued to remain in the dark in relation to the designs of France on Louisiana and the Floridas, as appears by a communication which he addressed on the 24th of March, to the Secretary of State at Washington: "On the business of Louisiana," said he, "they have, as yet, not thought it proper to give me any explanations, though I have omitted no opportunity to press the subject in conversation, and ultimately by the note sent you on the 26th of February, with the copy of another note enforcing the above, to which I have as yet received no answer.

"The fact is, they believe us to be certainly hostile to the measure, and they mean to take possession of Louisiana as early as possible, and with as little notice to us as they can.

"They are made to believe this is one of the most fertile and important countries in the world; that they have a much greater interest with the Indians than any other people; that New Orleans must command the trade of our whole Western country; and, of course, that they will have a leading interest in its politics. It is a darling object with the first consul, who sees in it a means to gratify his friends; and to dispose of his armies. There is a man here, who calls himself a Frenchman, by the name of Francis Tatergem, who pretends to have great interest with the Creek nations. He has been advanced to the rank of a general of division. He persuades them that the Indians are extremely attached to

France, and hate the Americans; that they can raise twenty thousand warriors; that the country is a paradise, &c. I believe him to be a mere adventurer; but he is listened to, and was first taken up by the old directors."

On the 24th of April, although another month had elapsed, Mr. Livingston had gained no ground, and again repeated to Mr. Madison: "The business most interesting to us, that of Louisiana, still remains in the state it was. The minister will give no answer to any inquiries I make on that subject. He will not say what their boundaries are, what are their intentions, and when they are to take possession."

In the meantime, however, a definitive treaty of peace between Spain, France, and Great Britain, had been signed at Amiens on the 25th of March, and this circumstance, which opened the ocean to Bonaparte's contemplated expedition in relation to Louisiana, keenly increased the anxieties of the United States, and they began to assume a tone which shows the deep feeling of the country on the subject. On the 1st of May, Mr. Madison wrote the following despatch to Mr. Livingston: "The conduct of the French Government in paying so little attention to its obligations under the treaty, in neglecting its debts to our citizens, in giving no answers to your complaints and expostulations, which you say is the case with those of other foreign ministers also, and particularly in its reserve as to Louisiana, which tacitly contradicts the language first held to you by the Minister of Foreign Relations—gives tokens as little auspicious to the true interests of France herself, as to the rights and just objects of the United States.

"The cession of Louisiana to France becomes daily more and more a source of painful apprehensions. Notwithstanding the treaty of March, 1801, and notwithstanding the general belief in France on the subject, and the accounts from St. Domingo that part of the armament sent to that island was eventually destined for Louisiana, a hope was still drawn from your early conversations with Mr. Talleyrand, that the French Government did not mean to pursue the object. Since the receipt of your last communications, no hope remains but from the accumulating difficulties of going through with the undertaking, and from the conviction you may be able to impress, that it must have an instant and powerful effect in changing the relations between France and the United States. The change is obvious; and the more it can be developed in candid and friendly appeals to the reflections of the French Government, the more it will urge it to revise and abandon the project. A mere *neighborhood* could not be friendly to the harmony which both countries have so much an interest in cherishing; but if a *possession of the mouth of the Mississippi* is to be added to the other causes of discord, the worst events are to be apprehended. You will consequently spare no efforts, that will consist with prudence and dignity, to lead the councils of France to proper views of this subject, and to an abandonment of her present purpose. You will also pursue, by prudent means, the inquiry into the extent of the cession—particularly whether it includes the Floridas as well as New Orleans—and endeavor to ascertain the price at which these, if included in the cession, would be yielded to the United States. I cannot, in the present state of things, be more particular on this head than to observe that, in every view, it would be a most precious acquisition, and that, as far as the terms could be satisfied by charging on the acquisition itself the restitutions and other debts to American citizens, great liberality would doubtless be indulged by this government."

In England, Mr. King had not been inactive and had

written a note to Lord Hawkesbury, inquiring whether the British government had received from the governments of France and Spain any communication relating to the cession of Louisiana, and whether his Britannic Majesty had, in any manner, acquiesced in, or sanctioned the same, so as to impair or affect the stipulations concerning the free navigation of the Mississippi. "In a word," said Mr. King, "I entreat your Lordship to open yourself on this occasion, with that freedom which, in matters of weighty concern, is due from one friendly nation to another, and which, in the present instance, will have the effect to do away all those misconceptions that may otherwise prevail in respect to the privity of Great Britain to the cession in question."

To this communication Lord Hawkesbury gave the following answer, on the 7th of May: "It is impossible that so important an event as the cession of Louisiana by Spain to France should be regarded by the King in any other light than as highly interesting to his Majesty and to the United States, and should not render it more necessary than ever that there should subsist between the two governments that spirit of confidence which is become so essential to the security of their respective territories and possessions.

"With regard to the free navigation of the Mississippi, I conceive that it is perfectly clear, according to the law of nations, that, in the event of the district of Louisiana being ceded to France, that country would come into possession of it, subject to all the engagements which appertained to it at the time of cession; and that the French government could consequently allege no colorable pretext for excluding his Majesty's subjects, or the citizens of the United States, from the navigation of the river Mississippi.

"With regard to the second question in your letter, I

can have no difficulty in informing you that no communication whatever has been received by his Majesty from the government of France or Spain, relative to any convention or treaty for the cession of Louisiana, or the Floridas; I can, at the same time, most truly assure you that his Majesty has not in any manner, directly or indirectly, acquiesced in or sanctioned the cession.

"In making this communication to you, for the government of the United States, I think it right to acquaint you that his Majesty will be anxious to learn their sentiments on every part of this subject, and the line of policy which they will be inclined to adopt, in the event of this arrangement being carried into effect."

It seems by a despatch of Mr. Livingston, of the 20th of May, that the French government was still continuing to hold the same conduct with respect to his inquiries in relation to its designs on Louisiana, and would not acknowledge that it had formed any specific plan with regard to that province, or that any troops were going out; but assurances were given to him, in general terms, that nothing should be done that could afford any just ground of complaint to the United States, and that, on the contrary, the vicinity of the French would promote mutual friendship between them and the Americans.

At last, on the 28th of May, Mr. Livingston felt authorized to write to Mr. Madison that he had acquired information on which he could depend, in relation to the intention of the French government with respect to Louisiana. "Bernadotte," said he, "is to command, Collot, second in command; Adet is to be prefect; but the expedition is delayed until about September, on account (as Talleyrand expressed himself to Bernadotte) of some difficulty which he did not explain: but which,

I have no doubt, has arisen from the different apprehensions of France and Spain relative to the meaning of the term Louisiana, which has been understood by France to include the Floridas, but probably by Spain to have been confined to the strict meaning of the term. This is why I could never get an answer to my questions relative to the extent of the cession; and upon which the French government had probably no doubt, till we started it. Believing, if this conjecture as to the cause of the delay of the expedition was right, that no time should be lost in throwing obstructions in the way of its conclusion, I wrote a note of which the inclosed is a copy, with the double purpose of alarming Spain, and furnishing her statesmen with arguments, arising from the good faith owed us, against giving their cession the construction France would wish." The note to which Mr. King alludes here was addressed by him to Chevalier D'Azara, ambassador of His Catholic Majesty at Paris.

"On the 30th of July, Mr. Livingston informed the Secretary of State at Washington, that he was earnestly engaged in preparing a lengthy memorial on the subject of the mutual interest of France and the United States relative to Louisiana, by which he hoped to convince France that, both in a commercial and political view, the possession of it would be disadvantageous to her. "In my last," said he, "I hinted to you my suspicions that France and Spain did not understand each other on the subject of Louisiana, and communicated to you my letters to the Spanish ambassador, calculated to sound this business and interpose some difficulties to its execution. His answer confirmed my opinion. I have since received, verbally, his explicit assurance that the Floridas are not included in the cession; and I have been applied to, by one of the ministers here, to know what we understand,

in America, by Louisiana. You can easily conceive my answer. * * * * * *
* * * * * * *

"The French, you know, have always extended it to South Carolina and all the country on the Ohio. Since the possession of the Floridas by Britain, and the treaty of 1763, I think there can be no doubt as to the precise meaning of the terms. * * * *
* * * * * * *

"In the present state of things, until the point is settled, I think it probable the expedition to Louisiana will be postponed. In the meantime, all that can be done here will be to endeavor to obtain a cession of New Orleans, either by purchase, or by offering to make it a port of entry to France, on such terms as shall promise advantages to her commerce, and give her hopes of introducing her manufactures and wines into our Western country. An arrangement of this sort, if they listen to it, would certainly be beneficial to both countries, and only hurtful to Britain."

On the 10th of August, he said: "Our own affairs have advanced but little, since the whole attention of those in power is turned to objects nearer home. I have had several conferences on the subject of Louisiana, but can get nothing more from them than I have already communicated. I have thought it best, by conversation and by writing, to pave the way, prior to my application, till I know better to what object to point. For this purpose, I have written the inclosed essay, which I have translated, and of which I have struck off twenty copies; I have placed some of them in such hands as I think will best serve our purposes. Talleyrand has promised me to give it an attentive perusal; after which, when I find how it works, I will come forward with some proposition. I am very much at a loss, however, as to what terms you would consider it as allowable to offer, if they can be brought to sale of the Floridas, either with or without New Orleans; which last place will be of little consequence, if we possess the Floridas, because a much better passage may be formed on the east side of the river. I may, perhaps, carry my estimate of them too high; but, when I consider, first, the expense it will save us in guards and garrisons, the risk of war, the value of duties, and next what may be raised by the sale of lands, I should think them a cheap purchase. I trust, however, that you will give me some directions on this head, and not leave the responsibility of offering too much or too little, entirely at my door. I speak, in all this business, as if the affair of the Floridas was arranged with Spain; which, I believe, is not yet the case."

It seems that Spain was desirous that the Duchy of Parma should be annexed to Tuscany, which had been erected into the kingdom of Etruria in favor of one of her princes; that she might, for such a consideration, have been willing to let the Floridas go with Louisiana; and that some negotiation to that effect was on foot at that time.

On the 1st of September, Mr. Livingston resumed the interesting topic, in a despatch to Mr. Madison, in which he said: "I yesterday made several propositions to the minister on the subject of Louisiana. He told me frankly that every offer was premature; that the French government had determined to take possession first; so that you must consider the business as absolutely determined on. The armament is what I have already mentioned, and will be ready in about six weeks. I have every reason to believe the Floridas are not included. They will, for the present at least, remain in the hands of Spain. There never was a government in which less could be done by negotiation than here. There is no people, no legislature, no counsellors. One man is everything. He seldom asks advice, and never hears it unasked. His ministers are mere clerks; and his legislature and counsellors parade officers. Though the sense of every reflecting man about him is against this wild expedition, no one dares to tell him so. Were it not for the uneasiness it excites at home, it would give me none; for I am persuaded that the whole will end in a relinquishment of the country, and transfer of the capital to the United States." Subsequent events showed, shortly after, that Mr. Livingston had proved a true prophet on this occasion.

On the 28th of October, he wrote to the President of the United States: "I had, two days ago, a very interesting conversation with Joseph Bonaparte, having put into his hands a copy of the memoir on Louisiana, which I sent the Secretary of State. I took occasion to tell him that the interest he had taken in settling the differences between our respective countries had entitled him to our confidence, and that I should take the liberty to ask him his advice in matters that were likely to disturb the harmony that subsisted between our respective republics. He seemed pleased at the compliment, and told me he would receive with pleasure any communication I could make, but, as he would not wish to appear to interfere with the minister, he begged my communications might be informal and unsigned—exactly what I wished, because I should act with less danger of committing myself, and of course, with more freedom. He added, "you must not, however, suppose my power to serve you greater than it actually is; my brother is his own counsellor; but we are good brothers; he hears me with pleasure, and as I have access to him at all times, I have an opportunity of turning his attention to a particular subject that might otherwise be passed over." I then asked him whether he had read my notes on Louisiana. He told me that he had, and that he had conversed upon the subject with the First Consul, who, he found, had read them with attention, and that his brother had told him that he had nothing more at heart than to be upon the best terms with the United States. I expressed to him my apprehensions of the jealousies that would naturally be excited from their vicinity, and the impossibility of preventing abuses in a military government established at so great a distance from home.

"Wishing to know whether the Floridas were included (which, however, I had pretty well ascertained before), I told him that the only cause of difference that might arise between us, being the debt and Louisiana, I conceived that both might be happily and easily removed by making an exchange with Spain, returning them Louisiana, retaining New Orleans, and giving the latter and the Floridas for our debt.

"He asked me whether we should prefer the Floridas to Louisiana? I told him that there was no comparison in their value, but that we had no wish to extend our boundary across the Mississippi, or give color to the doubts that had been entertained of the moderation of our views; that all we sought was security, and not extension of territory. He replied, that he believed any new cession on the part of Spain would be extremely difficult; that Spain had parted with Trinidad and Louisiana with great reluctance."

On the 11th of November, Mr. Livingston hastened to write to Mr. Madison; "France has cut the knot. The difficulty relative to Parma and Placentia, that stopped the expedition to Louisiana, has ended by their taking possession of the first, as you see by the enclosed paper. Orders are given for the immediate embarkation of troops (two demi-brigades) for Louisiana; they will sail in about twenty days from Holland. The government here will give no answer to my notes on the subject. They will say nothing on that of our limits, or of our right under the Spanish treaty. Clarke has been presented to General Victor as a merchant from Louisiana. The General did not probably conceal his views, which are nothing short of taking exactly what they find convenient. When asked what they meant to do as to our right of *entrepôt*, he spoke of the treaty as waste paper; and the Prefect did not know that we had any such right, though it had been the subject of many conversations with the Minister, and of three different notes. The sum voted for this service is two millions and a half of francs ($500,000); as to the rest, they expect to compel the people to support the expenses of the government, which will be very heavy, as the number of the officers, civil and military, with their suite, is great; and they are empowered to draw; so that the first act of the new government will be the oppression of this people and our commerce. I believe you may add to this an early attempt to corrupt our people, and, if I may judge by the temper which the General will carry with him, an early attempt upon the Natchez, which they consider as the rival of New Orleans. If you look back to some of my letters on this subject, you will see my opinion of the necessity of strengthening ourselves by friendships at home, and by alliance abroad. No prudence will, I fear, prevent hostilities ere long; and, perhaps, the sooner their plans develop themselves the better."

On the very same day he went on saying: "After writing mine of this date, I called on the Minister and insisted on some positive answer to my notes. He told me that he was expressly instructed by the First Consul to give me the most positive assurances that the treaties we had entered into with Spain or them, relative to Louisiana, should be strictly observed. When I expressed my surprise that their officers should not be informed on that head, though on the eve of departing, he assured me that they would be furnished with copies of the treaties, and directed to conform strictly to them. I asked why these assurances were not given to me in the usual form, by replying to my notes? He said that he hoped that there would be no difficulty on that head, when the consul should arrive (he is now absent). I have stated this that you might, by comparing this conversation with the contents of the letter, and the information derived from Clarke's conversation with the general, draw your own inferences. I shall endeavor to-day to see Joseph Bonaparte, though he has all along assured me that it was the Consul's intention to cultivate our friendship, and by no means to do anything that might endanger it. It will, however, be well to be on our guard, and, above all, to reinforce the Natchez, and to give it every possible commercial advantage. If we can put ourselves in a situation to prevent the danger of hostility, I think we may hope that the dissatisfaction of the inhabitants, the disappointment of the officers, and the drain of money which the establishment will occasion, will facilitate our views after a short time."

On the 27th of November, Mr. Madison addressed the American minister at Madrid in relation to the proclamation of Morales which prohibited the deposit at New Orleans of American effects, as stipulated by the treaty of 1795, and closed the Mississippi to the external commerce of the United States from that port. He observed that this proceeding was so direct and palpable a violation of that treaty, that, in candor, he could not but impute it rather to the Intendant solely than to the instructions of his government. He added, that the

Spanish Minister at Washington took pains to impress this belief, and that it was favored by private accounts from New Orleans, mentioning that the Governor did not concur with the Intendant; "but," said Mr. Madison, "from whatever source the measure may have proceeded, the President expects that the Spanish government will neither lose a moment in countermanding it, nor hesitate to repair every damage which may result from it. You are aware of the sensibility of our Western citizens to such an occurrence. This sensibility is justified by the interest they have at stake. *The Mississippi to them is every thing. It is the Hudson, the Delaware, the Potomac, and all the navigable rivers of the Atlantic states, formed into one stream.* The produce exported through that channel, last year, amounted to one million six hundred and twenty-two thousand six hundred and seventy-two dollars from the districts of Kentucky and Mississippi only, and will probably be fifty per cent. more this year, from the whole Western country. Kentucky alone has exported, for the first half of this year, five hundred and ninety-one thousand four hundred and thirty-two dollars in value, a great part of which is now, or will shortly be, afloat for New Orleans, and consequently exposed to the effects of this extraordinary exercise of power. Whilst you presume, therefore, in your representations to the Spanish government, that the conduct of its officer is no less contrary to its intentions than it is to its good faith, you will take care to express the strongest confidence that the breach of the treaty will be repaired in every way which justice and a regard for a friendly neighborhood may require.   *   *

*   *   *   *   *   *

"In the meantime," continued Mr. Madison, "it is to be hoped that the Intendant will be led to see the error which he has committed, and to correct it before a very great share of its mischief will have happened. Should he prove as obstinate as he has been ignorant or wicked, nothing can temper the irritation and indignation of the Western country but a persuasion that the energy of their government will obtain from the justice of that of Spain the most ample redress.

"It has long been manifest that, whilst the injuries to the United States, so frequently occurring from the colonial officers scattered over our hemisphere, and in our neighborhood, can only be repaired by a resort to their respective sovereigns in Europe, it will be impossible to guard against most serious inconveniences. The instance before us strikes with peculiar force, and presents an occasion on which you may advantageously suggest to the Spanish government the expediency of placing in their minister on the spot, an authority to control or correct the mischievous proceedings of their colonial officers towards our citizens; without which any one of fifteen or twenty individuals, not always among either the wisest or best of men, may, at any time, threaten the good understanding of the two countries. The distance between the United States and the old continent, and the mortifying delay of explanations and negotiations across the Atlantic on emergencies in our neighborhood, render such a provision indispensable, and it cannot be long before all the governments of Europe, having American colonies, must see the policy of making it."

It is evident that there was a march of events which, if not checked, would soon have brought on a crisis of the most serious nature. Mr. Livingston had now been twelve months in Paris, and had not been so fortunate as to receive a conclusive answer in any one of the affairs that he had had to transact with the Minister of Exterior Relations. This state of things was becoming intolerable, and was certainly offensive to the dignity of a nation which, though comparatively weak at the time, still had the consciousness of its growing strength and of its proud destinies. In relation to the unjustifiable delays and mysterious reserves on the part of France, Mr. Livingston, on the 24th of December, thus wrote to a French statesman: "Congress are now in session; they will infer from every paper submitted to them by the President, that the French government are disposed to show them but little attention. The obscurity that covers the designs of France on Louisiana (for not the least light can I, officially, obtain on the subject) will double their apprehensions; this, added to the clamors of ruined creditors, and the extreme severity with which some of their citizens have been treated in St. Domingo, and the extraordinary decisions of the Council of Prizes, &c., will leave a fair field for the intrigues of the enemies of France, and even enlist the best patriots of America on their side."

A few days before (15th December) the President of the United States, in a message to Congress, had thus expressed his sentiments to that body on this interesting subject: "The cession of the Spanish province of Louisiana to France, which took place in the course of the late war, will, if carried into effect, make a change in the aspect of our foreign relations, which will doubtless have just weight in any deliberations of the Legislature connected with that subject." Such language was sufficiently significant, and was abundantly justified by existing circumstances.

Let us now avert our eyes from the diplomatic circles of Europe, and turn them to the legislative halls of Congress in Washington. On the 23d of December, 1802, the President sent to the House of Representatives a message, in which he said in relation to the subject which engrossed public attention: "That he was aware of the obligations to maintain in all cases the rights of the nation, and to employ for that purpose those just and honorable means which belong to the character of the United States;"—to which that body, shortly after, replied: "That relying, with perfect confidence, on the wisdom and vigilance of the Executive, they would wait the issue of such measures as that department of the government should have pursued for asserting the rights of the United States—holding it to be their duty, at the same time, to express their unalterable determination to maintain the boundaries and the rights of navigation and commerce through the river Mississippi, as established by existing treaties."

Before the gathering of the storm, which already darkened the horizon, it became the pilot who held the helm of the State to look round for all the resources he had at hand, and, on the 10th of January, 1803, the President wrote to Mr. Monroe: "I have but a moment to inform you, that the fever into which the Western mind is thrown by the affair at New Orleans, stimulated by the mercantile and generally the federal interest, threatens to overbear our peace. In this situation, we are obliged to call on you for a temporary sacrifice of yourself, to prevent this greatest of evils in the present prosperous tide of affairs. I shall to-morrow nominate you to the Senate, for an extraordinary mission to France, and the circumstances are such as to render it impossible to decline; because the whole public hope will be rested on you."

The Senate having sanctioned the nomination, Mr. Jefferson again wrote, on the 13th, to the distinguished man in whom he reposed such implicit confidence "All eyes are now fixed on you; and were you to decline, the chagrin would be great, and would shake your feet the high ground on which you stand with the public. Indeed I know nothing which would produce such a shock; for on the event of this mission depend the future destinies of this Republic. If we cannot, by a purchase of the country, ensure to ourselves a course of perpetual peace and friendship with all nations, then, as war cannot be far distant, it behoves us immediately to be preparing for that course, without, however, hastening it; and it may be necessary (on your failure on the continent) to cross the channel. We shall get entangled in European politics, and, figuring more, be much less happy and prosperous. This can only be prevented by a successful issue to your present mission. I am sensible, after the measures you have taken for getting into a different line of business, that it will be a great sacrifice on your part, and that it presents, from the season and other circumstances, serious difficulties. But some men are born for the public. Nature, by fitting them for the service of the human race on a broad scale, has stamped them with the evidences of their destination and their duty."*

On the 14th of February (1803) Mr. Ross, from Pennsylvania, said in the Senate: "He was fully aware that the Executive of the United States had acted; that he had sent an Envoy Extraordinary to Europe. This was the peculiar province, and, perhaps, the duty of the President. He would not say that it was unwise in this state of our affairs to prepare for remonstrance and negotiation, much less was he then about to propose any measure that would thwart negotiation or embarrass the President. On the other hand, he was convinced that more than negotiation was absolutely necessary, that more power and more means ought to be given to the President, in order to render his negotiations efficacious

---

* Barbé Marbois's History of Louisiana.

Could the President proceed further even if he thought more vigorous measures proper and expedient? Was it in his power to repeal and punish the indignity put upon the nation? Could he use the public force to redress our wrongs? Certainly not. This must be the act of Congress. They are now to judge of ulterior measures; they must give the power, and vote the means to vindicate, in a becoming manner, the wounded honor and the best interests of the country.

"To the free navigation of the Mississippi, we had an undoubted right from nature, and from the position of our western country. This right and the right of deposit in the island of New Orleans, had been solemnly acknowledged and fixed by treaty in 1795. That treaty had been in actual operation and execution for many years; and now, without any pretence of abuse or violation on our part, the officers of the Spanish Government deny that right, refuse the place of deposit, and add the most offensive of all insults, by forbidding us from landing on any part of their territory, and shutting us out as a common nuisance.

"By whom has this outrage been offered? By those who have constantly acknowledged our right, and now tell us that they are no longer owners of the country! They have given it away, and, because they have no longer a right themselves, therefore, they turn us out, who have an undoubted right. Fortunately for this country, there could be no doubt in the present case; our national right had been acknowledged, and solemnly secured by treaty. It was violated and denied without provocation or apology. The treaty then was no security. This evident right was one, the security of which ought not to be precarious; it was indispensable that the enjoyment of it should be placed beyond doubt. He declared it, therefore, to be his firm and mature opinion, that so important a right would never be secure, while the mouth of the Mississippi was exclusively in the hands of Spaniards. Caprice and enmity occasion constant interruption. From the very position of our country, from its geographical shape, from motives of complete independence, the command of the navigation of the river ought to be in our hands.

"We are now wantonly provoked to take it. Hostility in its most offensive shape has been offered by those who disclaim all right to the soil and the sovereignty of that country—an hostility fatal to the happiness of the Western World. Why not seize then what is so essential to us as a nation? Why not expel the wrongdoers? Wrongdoers by their own confession, to whom by seizure we are doing no injury. Paper contracts, or treaties, have proved too feeble. Plant yourselves on the river, fortify the banks, invite those who have an interest at stake to defend it; do justice to yourselves when your adversaries deny it; and leave the event to Him who controls the fate of nations.

"Why submit to a tardy, uncertain negotiation, as the only means of regaining what you have lost—a negotiation with those who have wronged you; with those who declare they have no right, at the moment they deprive you of yours? When in possession, you will negotiate with more advantage. You will then be in the condition to keep others out. You will be in the actual exercise of jurisdiction over all your claims; your people will have the benefits of a lawful commerce. When your determination is known, you will make an easy and an honorable accommodation with any other claimant. The present possessors have no pretence to complain, for they have no right to the country by their own confession. The Western people will discover that you are making every effort they could desire for their protection. They will ardently support you in the contest, if a contest becomes necessary. Their all will be at stake, and neither their zeal nor their courage need be doubted.

"But after negotiation shall have failed, after a powerful, ambitious nation shall have taken possession of the key of your Western country, and fortified it; after the garrisons are filled by the veterans who have conquered the East, will you have it in your power to awake the generous spirit of that country and dispossess them? No; their confidence in such rulers will be gone; they will be disheartened, divided, and will place no further dependence upon you. They must abandon those who lost the precious moment of seizing, and for ever securing their sole hope of subsistence and prosperity; they must then, from necessity, make the best bargain they can with the conqueror."

On the 15th, a confidential message was brought from the House of Representatives to the Senate, transmitting to that body a bill which had passed the House, "to enable the President of the United States to commence with more effect a negotiation with the French and Spanish governments, relative to the purchase of the island of New Orleans, and the provinces of East and West Florida." This bill placed two millions of dollars at the disposal of the President, and the impression got abroad that this sum was to be used to secure the assistance of some powerful personages in Paris and Madrid in the negotiation which was to be opened with France and Spain.

On the 16th, Mr. Ross again took the floor, and continued to urge that the American people should take redress into their own hands, without loss of time. "I know," said he, "that some gentlemen think there is a mode of accomplishing our object, of which, by a most

* The obligation of secrecy which had been imposed.

extraordinary proceeding,* I am forbidden to speak on this occasion; I will not, therefore, touch it. But I will ask honorable gentlemen, especially those from the Western country, what they will say, on their return home, to a people pressed by the heavy hand of this calamity, when they inquire: What has been done? What are our hopes? How long will this obstruction continue? You answer: We have provided a remedy, but it is a secret! We are not allowed to speak of it there, much less here; it was only communicated to confidential men in whispers, with closed doors; but, by and by, you will see it operate like enchantment; it is a sovereign balsam which will heal your wounded honor; it is a potent spell, or a kind of patent medicine, which will extinguish and for ever put at rest the devouring spirit which has desolated so many nations of Europe. You never can know exactly what it is: nor can we tell you precisely the time it will begin to operate; but operate it certainly will, and effectually too! You will see strange things by and by; wait patiently, and place full faith in us, for we cannot be mistaken!—This idle tale may amuse children. But the men of that country will not be satisfied. They will tell you that they expected better things of you, that their confidence has been misplaced, and that they will not wait the operation of your newly invented drugs; they will go and redress themselves."

Then Mr. Ross read the following series of Resolutions:

"*Resolved*, That the United States have an indisputable right to the free navigation of the river Mississippi, and to a convenient place of deposit for their produce and merchandise in the island of New Orleans.

"That the late infraction of such their unquestionable right is an aggression hostile to their honor and interest.

"That it does not consist with the dignity or safety of this Union to hold a right so important by a tenure so uncertain.

"That it materially concerns such of the American citizens as dwell on the Western waters, and is essential to the union, strength and prosperity of these States, that they obtain complete security for the full and peaceable enjoyment of such their absolute right.

"That the President be authorized to take immediate possession of such place or places, in the same island, or the adjacent territories, as he may deem fit and convenient for the purposes aforesaid; and to adopt such other measures for obtaining that complete security as to him in his wisdom shall seem meet.

"That he be authorized to call into actual service any number of the militia of the States of South Carolina, Georgia, Ohio, Kentucky, Tennessee, or the Mississippi territory, which he may think proper, not exceeding fifty thousand, and to employ them, together with the military and naval forces of the Union, for effecting the objects above mentioned.

"That the sum of five millions of dollars be appropriated to the carrying into effect of the foregoing resolutions, and that the whole or any part of that sum be paid or applied, or warrants drawn in pursuance of such directions as the President may, from time to time, think proper to give to the Secretary of the Treasury."

These resolutions were seconded by Mr. Wells, from the State of Delaware. They were taken up on the 23d of February, and Mr. White, from the same State, supported them to their fullest extent. "As to the closing of the port of New Orleans against our citizens," said he, "the man who can now doubt, after viewing all the accompanying circumstances, that it was the deliberate act of the Spanish or French government, must have locked up his mind against truth and conviction, and be determined to discredit even the evidence of his own senses. But, Sir, it is not only the depriving us of our right of deposit by which we have been aggrieved; it is by a system of measures pursued antecedent and subsequent to that event, equally hostile and even more insulting. I have in my hand a paper, signed by a Spanish officer, which, with the indulgence of the chair, I will read to the Senate.

"'*Advertisement.* Under date of the 16th inst. (December, 1802) the Intendant-general of these provinces tells me that the citizens of the United States of America can have no commerce with his Majesty's subjects—they only having the free navigation of the river for the exportation of the fruits and produce of their establishments to foreign countries, and the importation of what they may want from them. As such I charge you, so far as respects you, to be zealous and vigilant, with particular care that the inhabitants neither purchase nor sell anything to the shipping, flat-bottomed boats, barges, or any other smaller vessels that may go along the river, destined for the American possessions, or proceeding from them, &c.

"'CARLOS DE GRANDPRÉ.'

"These are the measures that have been adopted by the Spaniards—excluding us from their shores for the distance of two hundred and seventy miles—treating us like a nation of pirates, or banditti, whom they feared to trust in their country. Spain has dared us to the trial, and now bids us defiance; she is yet in possession of that country; it is at this moment within your reach and within your power; it offers a sure and easy conquest; we should have to encounter there only a weak, inactive and unenterprising people; but how may a few months vary this scene, and darken our prospects! Though not officially informed, we know that the Spanish provinces on the Mississippi have been ceded to the French, and that they will as soon as possible take possession of them. What may we then expect? When, in the last extremity, we shall be drawn to arms in defence of our indisputable rights, where now slumbers on his post with folded arms the sluggish Spaniard, we shall be hailed by the vigilant and alert French grenadier, and in the defenceless garrison that would now surrender at our approach, we shall see unfurled the standards that have waved triumphant in Italy, surrounded by impregnable ramparts, and defended by the disciplined veterans of Egypt.

"I am willing to attribute to honorable gentlemen the best of motives; I am sure they do not wish to involve this country in a war, and, God knows, I deprecate its horrors as much as any man; but this business can never be adjusted abroad; it will ultimately have to be settled upon the banks of the Mississippi; and the longer you delay, the more time you waste in tedious negotiations, the greater sacrifices you make to protract a temporary and hollow peace, the greater will be your embarrassments when the war comes on; and it is inevitable, unless honorable gentlemen, opposed to us, are prepared to yield up the best interest and honor of the nation. I believe the only question now in our power to decide, is whether it shall be the bloodless war of a few months, or the carnage of years.

"These observations are urged upon the supposition that it is in the power of the government to restrain the impetuosity of the Western people, and to prevent their doing justice to themselves, which, by the by, I beg to be understood as not believing, but expressly the contrary. They know their own strength ; they know the feebleness of the enemy ; they know the infinite importance of the stake, and they feel, permit me to say, sir, with more than mere sensibility, the insults and injuries they have received, and I believe will not submit, even for the approaching season, to their present ruinous and humiliating situation. You had as well pretend to dam up the mouth of the Mississippi, and say to its restless waves, ye shall cease here, and never mingle with the ocean, as to expect they will be prevented from descending it. Without the free use of the river, and the necessary advantages of deposit below our line, their fertile country is not worth possession, their produce must be wasted in the fields or rot in their granaries. These are rights not only guaranteed to them by treaty, but also given to them by the God of nature, and they will enforce them, with or without the authority of government; and let me ask, whether it is more dignified for the government to lead or follow in the path of honor? One it must do, or give up that Western country."

Those who were opposed to these Resolutions urged that it was necessary to exhaust every means of negotiation before adopting measures which would lead to hostilities, and that it was indispensable, before doing any thing, to ascertain whether the King of Spain would sanction the act of his Intendant at New Orleans. Among those who took a prominent part against these "Resolutions," was Mr. Jackson of Georgia. "What is the course," said he, "which we have to pursue? Is it to go immediately to war, without asking for redress? By the law of nations, and the doctrines of all writers on them, you are not justified, until you have tried every possible method of obtaining redress in a peaceable manner : it is only in the last extremity, when you have no other expedient left, that a recourse to arms is lawful and just; and I hope the United States will never forfeit their character for justice by any hasty or rash steps, which they may, too late, have to repent of, —when they can have recourse to another method which may procure a redress of the wrong complained of.

"I am, myself, of opinion that New Orleans must belong to the United States; it must come to us in the course of human events, although not at the present day; for I do not wish to use force to obtain it, if we can get a redress of the injury done to us; yet it will naturally fall into our hands by gradual but inevitable causes, as sure and certain as manufactures arise from increased population and the plentiful products of agriculture and commerce. But let it be noticed that, if New Orleans, by a refusal of justice, falls into our hands by force, the Floridas, as sure as fate, fall with it. Good faith forbids encroachment on a pacific ally; but if hostility shows itself against us, interest demands it; Georgia in such case would not do without it. God and nature have destined New Orleans and the Floridas to belong to this great and rising empire. As natural bounds to the South, are the Atlantic, the Gulf of Mexico, and the Mississippi, and the world at some future day cannot hold them from us.

"Sir, we have been told much by the gentleman from Delaware of Bonaparte; that he is the hero of France, the conqueror of Italy, and the tyrant of Germany, and that his legions are invincible. We have been told that we must hasten to take possession of New Orleans whilst in the hands of the sluggish Spaniards, and not wait until it is in the iron grasp of the Cæsar of modern times. But much as I respect the fame and exploits of that extraordinary man, I believe we should have little more to fear from him, should it be necessary in the end to contend with him for the possession of New Orleans, than from the sluggish Spaniards. Bonaparte, Sir, in our Southern country, would be lost, with all his martial talents; his hollow squares and horse artillery would be of little service to him in the midst of our morasses and woods, where he would meet, not with the champaign country of Italy—with the little rivulets commanded by his cannon, which he could pass at leisure—not with fortified cities which command surrounding districts—but with rivers miles wide, and swamps, mortal or impenetrable to Europeans. With a body of only ten thousand of our expert riflemen around him, his laurels would be torn from his brow, and he would heartily wish himself once more safe on the plains of Italy.

"What, Sir, would be forty or fifty thousand French, in those impenetrable forests, to the hosts which would be poured down the Mississippi? But should Bonaparte send an army of forty thousand men here, and should they not be destroyed by our troops, they would, within twenty years, become Americans, and join our arms; they would form connexions with our females, intermarry with them, and insensibly change their habits, their manners, and their language. No other people can long exist in the vicinity of those of the United States, without intermixing and ultimately joining with them.

"The sacred name of Washington has been unnecessarily appealed to, on this as on many other occasions, and we have been boastingly told that, in his time, no nation dared to insult us. Much, Sir, as I revere his memory, acknowledging him among the fathers of his country—was this the fact? Was he not insulted—was not the nation insulted under his administration? How came the posts to be detained after the definitive treaty with Great Britain? What dictated that inhuman deed to stir up horror and destruction among us—Lord Dor chester's insolent and savage speech to the hordes of Indians on our frontiers, to massacre our inhabitants without distinction? Were those not insults? Or have we tamely forgotten them? Yet, Sir, did Washington go to war? He did not; he preferred negotiation and sent an envoy to Britain; peace was obtained by a treaty with that nation—I shall not inquire at what price—but these were the steps taken by him. Shall we then not negotiate? Shall we not follow the leading feature of our national policy? I hope we shall, and by doing so, we shall become unanimous. We are all actuated, I hope, by one view, but we differ on the means; let us do justice by requiring our neighbor to do justice to us, by a restoration of our rights; let us show the nations of the earth we are not anxious for war, that scourge of mankind; that we bear patiently our injuries, in hopes of redress, and that nothing but absolute denial of justice, which will be additional insult, shall induce us to it. But, Sir, if forced to war, contrary to our policy and wishes, let us unsheathe the sword and fling away the scabbard, until our enemies be brought to a sense of justice, and our wrongs are redressed."

Mr. Cocke, from Tennessee, rose also to advocate peaceful measures: "When the gentleman from Pennsylvania" (Mr. Ross), said he, "opened his war project, his resentment appeared to be wholly confined to Spain; his sole object, the securing of the navigation of the Mississippi and of our right to a convenient place of deposit on that river. We were told by that gentleman that we are bound to go to war for this right which God and nature had given the Western people. What are we to understand by this right given by God and nature? Surely not the right of deposit, for that was given by treaty; and, as to the right of navigation, that has been neither suspended nor brought into question.

But we are told by the same gentleman, that the possession of New Orleans is necessary to our complete security. Leaving to the gentleman's own conscience to settle the question as to the morality of taking that place, because it would be convenient, I beg to inform him that the possession of it would not give us complete security. The island of Cuba, from its position and the excellence of its harbors, commands the Gulf of Mexico as completely as New Orleans does the river Mississippi, and, to give that complete security he requires of the President, the island of Cuba must likewise be taken possession of."

Mr. Morris, of New York, maintained the doctrine that Spain had justified the United States in seizing upon New Orleans, by her having made the cession of it without their consent. "Had Spain," said he, "the right to make this cession without our consent? Gentlemen have taken it for granted that she had. But I deny the position. No nation has a right to give to another a dangerous neighbor without her consent. This is not like the case of private citizens; for there, when a man is injured, he can resort to the tribunals for redress; and yet, even there, to dispose of property to one who is a bad neighbor is always considered as an act of unkindness. But as between nations, who can redress themselves only by war, such transfer is in itself an aggression. He who renders me insecure; he who hazards my peace, and exposes me to imminent danger, commits an act of hostility against me, and gives me the rights consequent on that act. Suppose Great Britain should give to Algiers one of the Bahamas, and contribute thereby to establish a nest of pirates near your coasts, would you not consider it as an aggression? Suppose, during the late war, you had conveyed to France a tract of land along the Hudson's river and the northern route by the lakes into Canada, would not Britain have considered and treated it as an act of direct hostility? It is among the first limitations to the exercise of the rights of property, that we must so use our own as not to injure another; and it is under the immediate sense of this restriction that nations are bound to act towards each other."

He further said that the possession of Louisiana by the ambitious ruler of France would give him in the new world the preponderance he had already obtained in the old; that it became the United States to show that they did not fear him who was the terror of all; and that it specially behoved this young and growing republic to interpose, in order to revive the energy and resistance of the half conquered nations of Europe, and to save the expiring liberties of mankind. To this his colleague, Mr. Clinton, replied in the following strain: "Sublime as these speculations may appear to the eyes of some, and high sounding as they may strike the ears of many, they do not affect me with any force. In the first place, I do not perceive how they bear upon the question before me; it merely refers to the seizure of New Orleans, not to the maintenance of the balance of power. Again: of all characters, I think that of a conquering nation least becomes the American people. What, Sir! shall America go forth, like another Don Quixote, to relieve distressed nations, and to rescue from the fangs of tyranny the powerful States of Britain, Spain, Austria, Italy, the Netherlands? Shall she, like another Phaeton, madly ascend the chariot of Empire, and spread desolation and horror over the world? Shall she attempt to restrain the career of a nation which my honorable colleague represents to have been irresistible, and which he declares has appalled the British lion and the imperial eagle of the house of Austria? Shall she wantonly court destruction, and violate all the maxims of policy which ought to govern an infant and free Republic? Let us, Sir, never carry our arms into the territories of other nations, unless we are compelled to take them up in self-defence. A pacific character is of all others most important for us to establish and maintain. With a sea coast of two thousand miles, indented with harbors and lined with cities, with an extended commerce, and with a population of six millions only, how are we to set up for the avengers of nations? Can gravity itself refrain from laughter at the figure which my honorable colleague would wish us to make on the theatre of the world? He would put a fool's cap on our head and dress us up in the particolored robes of a harlequin, for the nations of the world to laugh at; and, after all the puissant knights of the times have been worsted in the tournament by the *Orlando Furioso* of France, we must then, forsooth, come forward and console them for their defeat by an exhibition of our follies! I look, Sir, upon all the dangers we have heard about the French possessions of Louisiana, as visionary and idle. Twenty years must roll over our heads before France can establish in that country a population of two hundred thousand souls. What in the meantime will become of your Southern and Western States? Are they not advancing to greatness with a giant's stride? The Western waters will then contain on their borders millions of free and hardy republicans, able to crush every daring invader of their rights. A formidable navy will spring from the bosom of the Atlantic States, ready to meet the maritime force of any nation. With such means, what will we have to fear from the acts or from the arms of any power, however formidable?"

On the 25th of February, Mr. Ross's resolutions were rejected by a vote of fifteen to eleven, and the following resolutions, of a milder character, which had been proposed as amendments by Mr. Breckenridge, of Kentucky, were unanimously adopted:

"*Resolved*, That the President of the United States be, and he is, hereby authorized, whenever he shall judge it expedient, to require of the Executives of the several States to take effectual measures to arm and equip, according to law, and hold in readiness to march, at a moment's warning, eighty thousand effective militia, officers included.

"That the President may, if he judges it expedient, authorize the Executives of the several States to accept, as part of the detachment aforesaid, any corps of volunteers, who shall continue in service for such time not exceeding — months, and perform such services as shall be prescribed by law.

"That —— dollars be appropriated for paying and subsisting such part of the troops aforesaid, whose actual service may be wanted, and for defraying such other expenses as, during the recess of Congress, the President may deem necessary for the security of the territory of the United States.

"That —— dollars be appropriated for erecting, at such place or places on the Western waters as the President may judge most proper, one or more arsenals."

These resolutions were referred to Messrs. Breckenridge, Jackson and Sumter, to bring in a bill accordingly. On the 26th, Mr. Breckenridge reported by a bill entitled "An Act directing a detachment from the militia of the United States, and for erecting certain arsenals;" and, on the 28th, it was adopted.

Let us now enter the hall of the House of Representatives and ascertain what had there occurred in relation to the same subject.

On the 17th of December, 1802, John Randolph of Virginia moved the following resolution:

"That the President of the United States be requested to cause to be laid before this house such papers as are in the possession of the department of state, as relate to the violation, on the part of Spain, of the treaty of friendship, limits and navigation, between the United States of America and the King of Spain;" and this resolution was agreed to unanimously. On the 22d, in compliance with this resolution, the President laid before the house the required information. On the 31st, the President made another communication in relation to the same subject, which, together with his preceding message of the 22d, was referred to a committee of the whole house on the state of the Union. On the 4th of January, 1803, Mr. Griswold made the following motion:

"*Resolved*, That the President of the United States be requested to direct the proper officer to lay before this house copies of such official documents as have been received by this government, announcing the cession of Louisiana to France, together with a report explaining the stipulations, circumstances and conditions under which that province is to be delivered up; unless such documents and report will, in the opinion of the President, divulge to the house particular transactions not proper at this time to be communicated."

On the 5th, Mr. Griswold called up his resolution respecting Louisiana, and the question to take into consideration was carried by 35 to 32.

Mr. Randolph moved that it be referred to the Committee of the Whole on the state of the Union, to whom had been committed the message of the President respecting the shutting up of the port of New Orleans to the Americans, and the violation of the treaty existing between Spain and the United States, on the ground that the discussion on both questions might embrace points nearly connected. Mr. Randolph's motion was carried, and the House expressed " their unalterable determination to maintain the boundaries and the rights of navigation and commerce through the river Mississippi, as established by existing treaties." But the Committee of the Whole reported on the 11th of January against Mr. Griswold's resolution, and it was consequently lost by a vote of 51 to 35, as it was thought that, if carried, it might interfere with the negotiations already begun by the President. The other proceedings and discussions in the House on this subject were of comparatively little importance, and the excitement there seems to have been less than in the Senate. After having thus exhibited the interest it took in the cession of Louisiana by Spain to France, Congress adjourned on the 4th of March.

In the meanwhile, the Executive had not been inactive, and Mr. Madison had written, on the 10th of January (1803), to the United States' minister at Madrid: " You will find by the printed documents herewith transmitted, that the subject (what had taken place at New Orleans), engaged the early and earnest attention of the House of Representatives; and that all the information relating to it, possessed by the Executive prior to the receipt of that letter,* was reported in consequence of a call for it. You will find, also, that the House has passed a resolution explicitly declaring that the stipulated rights of the United States on the Mississippi will be inviolably maintained. The disposition of many members was to

---

* A letter from the Governor of Louisiana to Governor Claiborne, in which it is stated that the measure of the Intendant closing the port of New Orleans to the Americans was without instructions from his government, and admitted that his own judgment did not concur with that of the Intendant

give the resolution a tone and complexion still stronger. To these proofs of the sensation which has been produced, it is to be added, that representations, expressing the peculiar sensibility of the Western country, are on the way from every quarter of it to the government. There is, in fact, but one sentiment throughout the Union with respect to the duty of maintaining our rights of navigation and boundary. The only existing difference relates to the degree of patience which ought to be exercised during the appeal to friendly modes of redress. In this state of things it is to be presumed that the Spanish government will accelerate, by every possible means, its intervention for that purpose; and the President charges you to urge the necessity of so doing with as much amicable decision as you can employ."

On the 18th of the same month, Mr. Madison thus addressed Mr. Livingston in Paris: "In these debates (of Congress), as well as in indications from the press, you will perceive, as you would readily suppose, that the cession of Louisiana to France has been associated with the violation, at New Orleans, of our treaty with Spain, as a ground of much solicitude. Such, indeed, has been the impulse given to the public mind by these events, that every branch of the government has felt the obligation of taking the measure most likely, not only to reestablish our present rights, but also to promote arrangements by which they may be enlarged, and more effectually secured. In deliberating on this subject, it has appeared to the President that the importance of the crisis called for the experiment of an extraordinary mission, carrying with it the weight attached to such a measure, as well as the advantage of a more thorough knowledge of the views of the government, and the sensibility of the people, than would be otherwise conveyed.

"Mr. Monroe will be the bearer of the instructions under which you are jointly to negotiate. The object of them will be to procure a cession of New Orleans and the Floridas to the United States; and consequently the establishment of the Mississippi as the boundary between the United States and Louisiana."

Previous to these instructions, Mr. Livingston had, on the 10th of January, sent a note to the Minister of Exterior Relations, in which he proposed that France should cede to the United States West Florida, New Orleans, and a certain portion of the territory of Louisiana: "These propositions, with certain accompaniments," said Mr. Livingston, in a despatch to Mr. Madison of the 18th of February, "were well received, and were some days under the First Consul's consideration; I am now lying on my oars in hopes of something explicit from you. From the best accounts I can receive from Holland, the armament (destined for Louisiana) will be detained there till about the last of March, so that you will not have them in New Orleans till June; a precious interval, of which you may think it prudent to avail yourselves."

On the 27th of February, Mr. Livingston submitted to the First Consul a memoir detailing the reasons for which he urged the cession of a portion, at least, of Louisiana by France to the United States. "That France," said he, "will never derive any advantage from the colonization of New Orleans and the Floridas, is fairly to be presumed, from their having been possessed, for more than a century past, by three different nations.* While the other colonies of these nations were increasing rapidly, these have always remained weak and languid, and an expensive burden to the possessors. Even at this mo-

---

* The French, the English, and the Spaniards.

ment, with all the advantages that New Orleans has derived from foreign capital, and an accession of inhabitants from the United States, which has brought its free population to about seven thousand souls, the whole of the inhabitants east of the Mississippi does not more than double that number; and those, too, are for the most part poor and miserable; and there are physical reasons that must for ever render them inadequate to their own support, in the hands of any European nation. These provinces are, however, important to the United States because they contain the mouths of some of their rivers, which must make them the source of continual disputes. The interest that the United States attach, Citizen First Consul, to your friendship, and the alliance of France, is the principal cause of their anxiety to procure your consent to their accession of that country, and to the sacrifices that they are willing to make to attain it. They consider it as the only possible ground of collision between nations whom so many other interests unite. I cannot, then, Citizen First Consul, but express my doubt of any advantage to be derived to France from the retaining of that country in its whole extent; and I think I could show that her true interest would lead her to make such cessions out of them to the United States as would at once afford supplies to her islands, without draining the money of France, and rivet the friendship of the United States, by removing all ground of jealousy relative to a country of little value in itself, and which will be perpetually exposed to the attacks of her natural enemy, as well from Canada as by sea."

On the 2d of March, Mr. Madison forwarded to Messrs. Livingston and Monroe their credentials to treat with the government of the French Republic on the subject of the Mississippi and the territories eastward thereof and without the limits of the United States. "The object in view," said he, "is to procure, by just and satisfactory arrangements, a cession to the United States of New Orleans and of West and East Florida, or as much thereof as the actual proprietor can be prevailed on to part with." The principles and outlines of the plan on which the ministers were authorized to treat were annexed to their credentials.

In the meantime, Mr. Livingston was very pressing in his endeavors to obtain from Bonaparte the recognition of the right of the Americans to use New Orleans as a place of deposit, and, on the 16th of March, he addressed an energetic note on that subject to the Minister of Exterior Relations:

"The First Consul," said he, "has done me the honor, through you, to inform me that he proposes to send a minister to the United States to acquire such information as he may deem necessary, previous to his taking any measure relative to the situation in which the acquisition of Louisiana will place France with respect to the United States. If, Sir, the question related to the formation of a new treaty, I should find no objection to this measure. On the contrary, I should readily acquiesce in it, as that which would be best calculated to render the treaty mutually advantageous. But, Sir, it is not a new treaty for which we now press (though one mutually advantageous might be made), but the recognition of an old one, by which the United States have acquired rights, that no change in the circumstances of the country obliges them to relinquish, and which they never will relinquish but with their political existence. By their treaty with Spain, their right to the navigation of the Mississippi is recognized, and a right of depôt granted, with a provision, on the part of the King of Spain, to revoke this right, if, within three years, he found it prejudicial to his interests, in which case he is to assign another equivalent establishment. The King of Spain has never revoked that right; but, after having made the experiment of its effects upon his interests for three years, he has continued it. The United States have, by this continuance, acquired a permanent and irrevocable right to a depôt at New Orleans, nor can that right now be called in question, either by Spain or by any other nation to whom she may transfer her title. Even the assignment of another equivalent establishment cannot, at this day, be forced upon the United States, without their consent. The time allowed by Spain has passed, and she has preferred to have the depôt at New Orleans to placing it elsewhere; and I will venture to say, that, in so doing, she has acted wisely; for New Orleans derives its whole value from its being the market for American produce, and their principal port of entry; and, if this consideration was important to Spain, it is infinitely more so to France, the produce of whose agriculture and manufactures will then find a ready exchange for the raw materials of the United States. Under these circumstances, at the very moment that Spain is about to relinquish the possession of that country to France, she violates her treaty without any apparent interest, and leaves the country with a stain upon her character.

"In what situation, Sir, are we now placed? An armament is about sailing for New Orleans; that port has been shut by the order of Spain; the French commandant will find it shut. Will he think himself authorized to open it? If not, it must remain shut till the Envoy of France shall have arrived in America, and made the necessary inquiries, and transmitted the result of those inquiries to the First Consul. In the meanwhile, all the produce of five States is left to rot upon their hands. There is only one season in which the navigation of the

Mississippi is practicable. This season must necessarily pass before the Envoy of France can arrive and make his report. Is it supposable, Sir, that the people of the United States will tranquilly wait the progress of negotiations, when the ruin of themselves and their families will be attendant on the delay? Be assured, Sir, that, even were it possible that the government of the United States could be insensible to their sufferings, they would find it as easy to prevent the Mississippi from rolling its waters into the ocean as to control the impulse of the people to do themselves justice. Sir, I will venture to say, that, were a fleet to shut up the mouths of the Chesapeake, Delaware and Hudson, it would create less sensation in the United States than the denial of the right of depôt at New Orleans has done, &c. I can never bring myself to believe, that the First Consul will, by deferring for a moment the recognition of a right that admits of no discussion, break all those ties which bind the United States to France, obliterate the sense of past obligations, change every political relation that it has been, and still is, the earnest wish of the United States to preserve, and force them to connect their interests with those of a rival power; and this, too, for an object of no real moment in itself. Louisiana is, and ever must be, from physical causes, a miserable country in the hands of an European power."

Whilst these negotiations were going on, war was on the eve of breaking out again between Great Britain and France, notwithstanding the hollow peace of Amiens, and, on the 2d of April, Mr. King wrote from London to the Secretary of State at Washington: "In a late conversation with Mr. Addington, he observed to me, if the war happen, it would, perhaps, be one of their first steps to occupy New Orleans. I interrupted him by saying, I hoped the measure would be well weighed before it should be attempted; that, true it was, we could not see with indifference that country in the hands of France; but, it was equally true, that it would be contrary to our views, and with much concern, that we should see it in the possession of England; we had no objection to Spain continuing to possess it; they were quiet neighbors, and we looked forward without impatience to events which, in the ordinary course of things, must, at no distant day, annex this country to the United States. Mr. Addington desired me to be assured that *England would not accept the country, were all agreed to give it to her;* that, were she to occupy it, it would not be to keep it, but to prevent another power from obtaining it; and, in his opinion, this end would be best effected by its belonging to the United States. I expressed my acquiescence in the last part of his remark, but observed, that, if the country should be occupied by England, it would be suspected to be in concert with the United States, and might involve us in misunderstandings with another power, with which we desired to live in peace. He said: *If you can obtain it, well, but if not, we ought to prevent its going into the hands of France, though you may rest assured,* continued Mr. Addington, *that nothing shall be done injurious to the interests of the United States.* Here the conversation ended."

On the 11th of the same month, Mr. Livingston, whose exertions were incessant, wrote from Paris to the Secretary of State at Washington. "My notes will tell you how far I have officially pressed the government on the subject of Louisiana. I have omitted no means, in conversation, of eradicating their prejudices in its favor; and I informed you that I had reason to think that I had been successful with all, unless it was the First Consul, to whom I addressed myself in the letter and essays that you have seen, and which were attentively read by him, as well as several informal notes to his brother (Joseph). I had reason to think that he began to waver; but we had nothing to offer but money and commercial advantages: of the latter, I did not think myself entitled to be liberal; and of the first, I found in them a certain degree of reluctance to treat, as derogatory to the dignity of the government. The affair of New Orleans gave me two important strings to touch: I endeavored to convince the government that the United States would avail themselves of the breach of the treaty to possess themselves of New Orleans and the Floridas; that Britain would never suffer Spain to grant the Floridas to France, even were she disposed, but would immediately seize upon them as soon as the transfer was made; that, without the Floridas, Louisiana would be indefensible, as it possesses not one port even for frigates; and I showed the effect of suffering that important country to fall into the hands of the British, both as it affected our country and the naval force of all Europe.

"These reasons, with the possibility of war, have had, I trust, the desired effect. M. Talleyrand asked me this day, when pressing the subject, whether we wished to have the whole of Louisiana. I told him, no; that our wishes extended only to New Orleans and the Floridas; that the policy of France should dictate (as I had shown in an official note) to give us the country above the river Arkansas, in order to place a barrier between them and Canada. He said that, if they gave New Orleans, the rest would be of little value; and that he would wish to know 'what we would give for the whole.' I told him it was a subject I had not thought of, but that I supposed we should not object to twenty millions, provided our citizens were paid. He told me that this was too low an offer, and that he would be glad if I would reflect upon it, and tell him to-morrow. I told him that, as Mr. Monroe would be in town in two days, I would delay my further offer until I had the pleasure of introducing him. He added, that he did not speak from authority, but that the idea had struck him. I have reason, however, to think that this resolution was taken in council on Saturday. On Friday, I received Mr. Ross's motion. I immediately sent it to Mr. Talleyrand, with an informal note, expressive of my fears that it would be carried into effect; and requesting that General Bernadotte* might not go till something effectual was done. I also translated it and gave it to General Bernadotte, and pressed upon him the necessity of asking express instructions, in case he should find the island in possession of the Americans. He went immediately to Joseph Bonaparte. These, I believe, were exciting causes to the train we are now in, and which I flatter myself we shall be able, on the arrival of Mr. Monroe, to pursue to effect. I think, from every appearance, that war is very near at hand; and, under these circumstances, I have endeavored to impress the government that not a moment should be lost, lest Britain should anticipate us."—Mr. Livingston added in a postscript: "Orders are gone this day to stop the sailing of vessels from the French ports; war is inevitable; my conjecture as to their determination to sell is well founded. Mr. Monroe is just arrived here."

On the 13th, Mr. Livingston, returning to the same subject, said in a despatch to the Secretary of State: "By my letter of yesterday (he means his letter of the 11th), you learned that the Minister (Talleyrand) had asked me whether I would agree to purchase Louisiana,

---

* General Bernadotte had received the appointment of Envoy Extraordinary and Minister Pleripotentiary to represent France at Washington.

&c., &c. On the 12th, I called upon him to press this matter further. He then thought proper to declare that his proposition was only personal, but still requested me to make an offer; and, upon my declining to do so, as I expected Mr. Monroe the next day, he shrugged up his shoulders and changed the conversation. Not willing, however, to lose sight of it, I told him that I had long been endeavoring to bring him to some point, but, unfortunately, without effect; that I wished merely to have the negotiation opened by any proposition on his part; and, with that view, had written him a note which contained that request, grounded upon my apprehension of the consequence of sending General Bernadotte without enabling him to say a treaty was begun. He told me he would answer my note, but that he must do it evasively, because Louisiana was not theirs. I smiled at this assertion, and told him that I had seen the treaty recognizing it; that I knew the Consul had appointed officers to govern the country; and that he had himself told me that General Victor was to take possession; that, in a note written by the express order of the First Consul, he had told me that General Bernadotte was to treat relative to it in the United States, &c. He still persisted in saying that they had it in contemplation to obtain, but had it not. I told him that I was very well pleased to understand this from him, because, if so, we should not commit ourselves with them in taking it from Spain, to whom, by his account, it still belonged; and that, as we had just cause of complaint against her, if Mr. Monroe concurred in opinion with me, we should negotiate no further on the subject, but advise our government to take possession. He seemed alarmed at the boldness of the measure, and told me he would answer my note, but that it would be evasively. I told him I should receive any communication from him with pleasure, but that we were not disposed to trifle; that the times were critical, and, though I did not know what instructions Mr. Monroe might bring, I was perfectly satisfied they would require a precise and prompt notice; that I was very fearful, from the little progress I had made, that my government would consider me as a very indolent negotiator. He laughed, and told me he would give a certificate that I was the most importunate he had met with.

"There was something so extraordinary in all this, that I did not detail it to you till I found some clue to the labyrinth, which I have done, as you will find, before I finish this letter; and the rather, as I was almost certain that I could rely upon the intelligence I had received of the resolution to dispose of the country

"This day Mr. Monroe passed with me in examining my papers; and while he and several other gentlemen were at dinner with me, I observed the Secretary of the Treasury (Barbé Marbois) walking in my garden. I sent out Colonel Livingston to him; he told him he would return when we had dined. While we were taking coffee, he came in; and, after being some time in the room, we strolled into the next, when he told me he heard that I had been at his house two days before, when he was at St. Cloud; that he thought I might have something particular to say to him, and had taken the first opportunity to call on me. I saw this was meant as an opening to one of those free conversations which I had frequently had with him. I accordingly began on the subject of the debt, and related to him the extraordinary conduct of the Minister (Talleyrand), &c., &c. He told me that this led to something important that had been cursorily mentioned to him at St. Cloud (where the First Consul was then residing); but, as my house was full of company, he thought I had better call on him any time before eleven that night. He went away, and I followed him a little after, when Mr. Monroe took leave. He told me that he wished me to repeat what I had said in relation to Mr. Talleyrand's requesting a proposition from me as to the purchase of Louisiana. I did so; and concluded with the extreme absurdity of his evasions of that day, and stated the consequence of any delay on this subject, as it would enable Britain to take possession, who would readily relinquish it to us. He said that this proceeded upon the supposition of her making so successful a war as to be enabled to retain her conquests. I told him that it was probable that the same idea might suggest itself to the United States; in which case it would be their interest to contribute to render her successful; and I asked him whether it was prudent to throw us into the scale. This led to long discussions of no moment to repeat. We returned to the point: he said, that what I had told him led him to think that what the Consul had said to him on Sunday, at St. Cloud (the day on which, as I told you, the determination had been taken to sell) had more of earnest than he thought at the time; that the Consul had asked him what news from England? As he knew he read the papers attentively, he told him that he had seen in the London papers the proposition for raising fifty thousand men to take New Orleans (Mr. Ross's proposition in the Senate). The Consul said he had seen it too, and had also seen that something was said about two millions of dollars being disposed among the people about him, to bribe them, &c., and then left him; that afterwards, when walking in the garden, the Consul came again to him, and spoke to him about the troubles that were excited in America, and inquired how far I was satisfied with his last note.

"He (Marbois) then took occasion to mention his sorrow that any cause of difference should exist between our countries. The Consul told him in reply: *Well! you have the charge of the treasury; let them give you one hundred millions of francs, and pay their own claims, and take the whole country.* Seeing by my looks that I was surprised at so extraordinary a demand, he added that he considered the demand as exorbitant, and had told the First Consul that the thing was impossible; that we had not the means of raising that. The Consul told him we might borrow it. I now plainly saw the whole business: first, the Consul was disposed to sell; next, he distrusted Talleyrand, on account of the business of the supposed intention to bribe, and meant to put the negotiation into the hands of Marbois, whose character for integrity is established. I told him that the United States were anxious to preserve peace with France; that, for that reason, they wished to remove the French possessions to the west side of the Mississippi; that we would be perfectly satisfied with New Orleans and the Floridas, and had no disposition to extend across the river; that, of course, we would not give any great sum for the purchase; that he was right in his idea of the extreme exorbitancy of the demand, which would not fall short of one hundred and twenty-five millions of francs;* that, however, we would be ready to purchase, provided the sum was reduced to reasonable limits. He then pressed me to name the sum. I told him that this was not worth while, because, as he only treated the inquiry as a matter of curiosity, any declarations of mine would have no effect. If a negotiation was to be opened, we should (Mr. Monroe and myself) make the offer after mature reflection. This compelled him to declare, that, though he was not authorized expressly to make the inquiry from me, yet if I could mention any sum

---

* On the supposition that the claims of American citizens against the government of France amounted to twenty-five millions of francs.

that came near the mark and that could be accepted, he would communicate it to the First Consul. I told him that we had no sort of authority to go to a sum that bore any proportion to what he mentioned; but that, as he considered the demand as too high, he would oblige me by telling me what he thought would be reasonable. He replied that, if we would name sixty millions, and take upon us the American claims, to the amount of twenty more, he would try how far this would be accepted. I told him that it was vain to ask anything that was so greatly beyond our means, &c. &c.

"He frankly confessed that he was of my sentiments; but that he feared the Consul would not relax. I asked him to press this argument upon him, together with the danger of seeing the country pass into the hands of Britain. I told him that he had seen the ardor of the Americans to take it by force, and the difficulty with which they were restrained by the prudence of the President; that he must easily see how much the hands of the war party would be strengthened, when they learned that France was on the eve of a rupture with England. He admitted the weight of all this. But, says he, you know the temper of a youthful conqueror; everything he does is rapid as lightning; we have only to speak to him as an opportunity presents itself, perhaps in a crowd, when he bears no contradiction. When I am alone with him, I can speak more freely, and he attends; but this opportunity seldom happens, and is always accidental. Try, then, if you cannot come up to my mark. Consider the extent of the country, the exclusive navigation of the river, and the importance of having no neighbors to dispute you—no war to dread. I told him that I deemed all these to be important considerations, but there was a point beyond which we could not go, and that fell far short of the sum he mentioned.

* * * * * * *

"Thus, Sir, you see a negotiation is fairly opened, and upon grounds which, I confess, I prefer to all other commercial privileges; and always to some a simple money transaction is infinitely preferable. As to the quantum, I have yet made up no opinion. The field opened to us is infinitely larger than our instructions contemplated; the revenue is increasing, and the land more than adequate to sink the capital, should we even go to the sum proposed by Marbois; nay, I persuade myself, that the whole sum may be raised by the sale of the territory west of the Mississippi, with the right of sovereignty, to some power in Europe, whose vicinity we should not fear. I speak now without reflection, and without having seen Mr. Monroe, as it was midnight when I left the treasury office, and is now near three o'clock. It is so very important that you should be apprised that a negotiation is actually opened, even before Mr. Monroe has been presented, in order to calm the tumult which the news of war will renew, that I have lost no time in communicating it. We shall do all we can to cheapen the purchase; but my present sentiment is that we shall buy. Mr. Monroe will be presented to the minister to-morrow, when we shall press for as early an audience as possible from the First Consul. I think it will be necessary to put in some proposition to-morrow. The Consul goes in a few days to Brussels, and every moment is precious."

On the 17th, Mr. Livingston thus resumed the subject in a despatch to his government: "On waiting," said he, "upon the Minister (Talleyrand), we found M. Marbois there, who told me he had come to communicate to the Minister what had passed between us, and that he greatly regretted the not being able to bring us to such an offer as he might mention to the First Consul. I told him that it was unnecessary to repeat what would compel us to limit our offers to a much more moderate sum, as I had already detailed them at large; and he knew they exceeded our means, &c. * * *

* * * * * *

"The next day, Mr. Monroe and myself, after spending some time in consultation, determined to offer fifty millions, including our debts. We presumed it would be best only to mention forty in the first instance. This I accordingly did, in a conference I had on the 15th with M. Marbois. He expressed great sorrow that we could not go beyond that sum, because he was sure that it would not be accepted, and that perhaps the whole business might be defeated, which he the more feared, as he had just received a note from the Minister (Talleyrand), indicative of the Consul's not being quite pleased that he had so greatly lowered his original proposition. He said that he saw our situation, and he knew that there was a point beyond which we could not go safely to ourselves or the President; but he wished us to advance to that point. He said that he would, if I wished, go that very day to St. Cloud, and let me know the result, &c., &c.

"The next morning, which was yesterday, I again called to see him. He told me that he had been to St. Cloud; that the Consul received his proposition very coolly; and that I might consider the business as no longer in his hands, since he had given him no further powers, &c., &c. * * * * *

* * * * * * *

"I dined with the Second Consul yesterday; and, in the evening, M. Marbois came in. I took him aside, and asked him if anything further had passed. He said no; but that, as he was to go to St. Cloud the next day it was possible that the Consul might touch upon the subject again; and that, if he did not, I might consider the plan as relinquished; and that, if I had any further proposition to make, it would be well to state it. I then told him that, on further consideration with Monroe, we had resolved to go to the greatest possible length, and that we would give fifty millions. He said that he had very little hopes that anything short of his propositions would succeed; but that he would make the best use of the arguments I had furnished him with, if an opportunity was offered; and, if nothing was done the next day, I might conclude that the Consul had changed his sentiments; that having given the kingdom of Etruria, whose revenues were twenty-five millions, in exchange for this country, it was natural that the first Consul should estimate it beyond its real value."

Now, that we have seen the American side of the question, let us penetrate into the councils of France, and listen to the recital of these transactions, as told by M. Marbois, in his History of Louisiana. "That province," said he, "was at the mercy of the English, who had a naval armament in the neighboring seas, and good garrisons in Jamaica and the Windward Islands. It might be supposed that they would open the campaign by this easy conquest. The First Consul had no other plan to pursue, when he abandoned his views respecting Louisiana, than to prevent the loss which France was already sustaining, being turned to the advantage of England. He, however, conceived that he ought, before parting with it, to inform himself respecting the value of an acquisition, which was the fruit of his own negotiations, and the only one that had not been obtained by the sword.

"He wished to have the opinion of two ministers, who had been acquainted with those countries, and to one of whom the administration of the colonies was familiar

He was in the habit of explaining himself without preparation or reserve, to those in whom he had confidence.

"On Easter Sunday, the 10th of April (1803), after having attended to the solemnities and ceremonies of the day, he called those two counsellors to him, and, addressing them with that vehemence and passion which he particularly manifested in political affairs, said: 'I know the full value of Louisiana, and I have been desirous of repairing the fault of the French negotiator who abandoned it in 1763. A few lines of a treaty have restored it to me, and I have scarcely recovered it, when I must expect to lose it. But if it escapes from me, it shall one day cost dearer to those who oblige me to strip myself of it, than to those to whom I wish to deliver it. The English have successively taken from France: Canada, Cape Breton, Newfoundland, Nova Scotia, and the richest portions of Asia. They are engaged in exciting troubles in St. Domingo. They shall not have the Mississippi, which they covet. Louisiana is nothing in comparison with their conquests in all parts of the globe, and yet the jealousy they feel at the restoration of this colony to the sovereignty of France, acquaints me with their wish to take possession of it, and it is thus they will begin the war. They have twenty ships of war in the Gulf of Mexico; they sail over those seas as sovereigns, whilst our affairs in St. Domingo have been growing worse every day, since the death of Leclerc. The conquest of Louisiana would be easy, if they only took the trouble to make a descent there. I have not a moment to lose in putting it out of their reach. I know not whether they are not already there. It is their usual course, and, if I had been in their place, I would not have waited. I wish, if there is still time, to take away from them any idea that they may have of ever possessing that colony. I think of ceding it to the United States. I can scarcely say that I cede it to them, for it is not yet in our possession. If, however, I leave the least time to our enemies, I shall only transmit an empty title to those republicans whose friendship I seek. They only ask of me one town in Louisiana; but I already consider the colony as entirely lost, and it appears to me, that in the hands of this growing power, it will be more useful to the policy and even to the commerce of France, than if I should attempt to keep it.'

"One of these ministers had served in the auxiliary army sent by France to the United States during their revolution. The other had, for ten years, been in the public employ, either as secretary of the French Legation to the Continental Congress, or as the head of the administration of St. Domingo.

"'We should not hesitate,' said the last Minister (Barbé Marbois) 'to make a sacrifice of that which is about slipping away from us. War with England is inevitable. Shall we be able with inferior naval forces to defend Louisiana against that power? The United States, justly discontented with our proceedings, do not hold out to us a solitary haven, not even an asylum, in case of reverses. They have just become reconciled with us, it is true, but they have a dispute with the Spanish government, and threaten New Orleans, of which we shall only have a momentary possession. At the time of the discovery of Louisiana, the neighboring provinces were as feeble as herself. They are now powerful, and Louisiana is still in her infancy. The country is scarcely at all inhabited; you have not fifty soldiers there. Where are your means of sending garrisons thither? Can we restore fortifications that are in ruins, and construct a long chain of forts upon a frontier of four hundred leagues? If England lets you undertake these things, it is because they will drain your resources, and she will feel a secret joy in seeing you exhaust yourself in efforts of which she alone will derive the profit. You will send out a squadron; but, while it is crossing the ocean, the colony will fall, and the squadron will, in its turn, be in danger. Louisiana is open to the English from the north by the great lakes, and if, to the south, they show themselves at the mouth of the Mississippi, New Orleans will immediately fall into their hands. Of what consequence is it to the inhabitants whom they are subject to, if their country is not to cease to be a colony? This conquest would be still easier to the Americans; they can reach the Mississippi by several navigable rivers, and to be masters of the country it will be sufficient for them to enter it. The population and resources of one of these two neighbors every day increase, and the other has maritime means sufficient to take possession of every thing that can advance her commerce. The colony has existed for a century, and, in spite of efforts and sacrifices of every kind, the last account of its population and resources attests its weakness. If it becomes a French colony and acquires increased importance, there will be in its very prosperity a germ of independence, which will not be long in developing itself. The more it flourishes, the less chance shall we have of preserving it. Nothing is more uncertain than the future fate of the European colonies in America. The exclusive right which the parent States exercise over these remote settlements becomes every day more and more precarious. The people feel humbled at being dependent on a small country in Europe, and will liberate themselves, as soon as they have a consciousness of their own strength.

"The French have attempted to form colonies in several parts of the continent of America. Their efforts have everywhere proved abortive. The English are patient and laborious; they do not fear the sol.tude and silence of newly settled countries. The Frenchman, lively and active, requires society; he is fond of conversing with neighbors. He willingly enters on the experiment of cultivating the soil, but, at the first disappointment, quits the spade or axe for the chase.

"The First Consul, interrupting these observations, asked how it happened that the French, who were incapable of succeeding in a continental colony, had always made great progress in the West Indies. Because, replied the minister, the slaves perform all the labor. The whites, who would be soon exhausted by the heat of the climate, have, however, the vigor of body and mind necessary to direct their operations.—'I am again,' said the First Consul, 'undecided as to maintaining or abolishing slavery. By whom is the land cultivated in Louisiana?'—'Slavery,' answered the minister, 'has given to Louisiana half her population. An inexcusable imprudence was committed in suddenly granting to the slaves of St. Domingo a liberty for which they had not been prepared. The blacks and whites have both been the victims of this great fault. But, without inquiring at this day how it would be proper to repair it, let us acknowledge that the colonies where slavery is preserved are rather burdensome than useful to France. At the same time, let us beware how we abandon them. They have not the means of governing themselves. The Creoles are French; they have been encouraged in that mode of culture, and in that system which now causes their misfortunes. Let us preserve them from new calamities. It is our duty to provide for their defence, for the administration of justice and for the cares of government. But, for what good purpose would you subject yourself to still greater embarrassments in Louisiana? You would there constantly have the colonial laws in collision with those at home. Of all the scourges that have afflicted the human race, slavery is the most detestable; but even humanity requires great precautions in the application of the remedy, and you cannot apply it, if Louisiana should again become French. Governments still half resist emancipation: they tolerate in secret what they ostensibly condemn, and they are themselves embarrassed by their false position. The general sentiment of the world is favorable to emancipation; it is in vain that the colonists and planters wish to arrest a movement which public opinion approves. The occupation of Louisiana—a colony with slaves—will occasion us more expense than it will afford us profit.

"'But there is another kind of slavery of which this colony has lost the habit: it is that of the exclusive system. Do you expect to reëstablish it in a country contiguous to one whose commerce enjoys the greatest liberty? The reign of prohibitory laws is over, when a numerous population has decided to throw off the yoke. Besides, the productions which were so long possessed exclusively by a few commercial people, are ceasing to be privileged articles. The sugar cane and the coffee tree are everywhere cultivated, and at a very small expense. Every people expects to raise on its own account all the provisions adapted to its territory and climate. There are on the globe, between the tropics, lands a thousand times more extensive than our islands, and susceptible of the same kind of culture. Monopoly is rendered impossible when the productions are so multiplied, and the Louisianians will not permit it to enslave their commerce. Would you subdue resistance by force of arms? The malcontents will find support in the neighborhood, and you will make the United States, with whom reciprocal interests ought to connect us for centuries, enemies of France. Do not expect from the

Louisianians any attachment for your person. They render homage to your fame and to your exploits; but the love of nations is reserved for those princes whom they regard as the authors of their happiness; and, whatever may be your solicitude with respect to theirs, it will be for a long time, and perhaps for ever, without effect. These colonists have lost the recollection of France; they are of three or four different nations, and hardly regard Louisiana as their country. Laws which are incessantly varying, chiefs who cannot know those whom they are sent to govern and are not known by them, changes effected according to the unsettled interests of the ruling state or the inexperience of Ministers, the continual danger of becoming belligerents in quarrels to which they are really strangers; such are the causes which have for a hundred years extinguished in their hearts every sentiment of affection for masters who are two thousand leagues distant from them, and who would exchange or convey them away like an article of merchandise. In order that a country should exist and possess citizens, the certainty of stability must be united with the feeling of prosperity. The Louisianians, on hearing that they had again become French, must have said to one another: *This change will not last longer than the others.* If, Citizen Consul, you, who have, by one of the first acts of your government, made sufficiently apparent your intention of giving this country to France, now abandon the idea of keeping it, there is no person that will not admit that you only yield to necessity; and even our merchants will soon acknowledge that Louisiana free, offers to them more chances of profit than Louisiana subjected to a monopoly. Commercial establishments are at this day preferable to colonies, and even without commercial establishments it is but to let trade take care of itself.'

"The other Minister (Decrès) was of a totally opposite opinion: 'We are still at peace with England,' said he; 'the colony has just been ceded to us, it depends on the First Consul to preserve it. It would not be wise in him to abandon, for fear of a doubtful danger, the most important establishment that we can form out of France, and despoil ourselves of it for no other reason than the possibility of a war: it would be as well, if not better, that it should be taken from us by force of arms. If peace is maintained, the cession cannot be justified, and this premature act of ill-founded apprehension would occasion the most lively regrets. To retain it would, on the other hand, be for our commerce and navigation an inestimable resource, and to our maritime provinces the subject of universal joy. The advantages which we have derived from the colonies are still present to every mind. Ten flourishing cities have been created by this trade; and the navigation, opulence, and luxury which embellished Paris are the results of colonial industry. There can be no marine without colonies; no colonies without a powerful marine. The political system of Europe is only preserved by a skilfully combined resistance of many against one. This is as necessary with respect to the sea as to the land, if it is not intended to submit to the tyranny of a universal sovereignty over commerce and the loss of the immense advantages of a free navigation. To this you will not submit; you will not acknowledge by your resignation that England is the sovereign mistress of the seas, that she is there invulnerable, and that no one can possess colonies except at her good pleasure. It does not become you to fear the Kings of England. If they should seize on Louisiana, as some would have you fear, Hanover would be immediately in your hands as a certain pledge of its restoration. France, deprived of her navy and her colonies, is stripped of half her splendor, and of a great part of her strength. Louisiana can indemnify us for all our losses. There does not exist on the globe a single port, a single city susceptible of becoming as important as New Orleans, and the neighborhood of the American States already makes it one of the most commercial in the world. The Mississippi does not reach there till it has received twenty other rivers, most of which surpass in size the finest rivers of Europe. The country is at last known, the principal explorations have been made, and expenses have not been spared, especially by Spain. Forts exist: some fertile lands suitable to the richest kinds of culture are already fully in use, and others only await the necessary labor. This colony, open to the activity of the French, will soon compensate them for the loss of India.

" 'The climate is the same as that of Hindostan, and the distance is only a quarter as great. The navigation to the Indies, by doubling the Cape of Good Hope, has changed the course of European trade, and ruined Venice and Genoa. What will be its direction, if, at the Isthmus of Panama, a simple canal should be opened to connect the one ocean with the other? The revolution which navigation will then experience will be still more considerable, and the circumnavigation of the globe will become easier than the long voyages that are now made in going to and returning from India. Louisiana will be on this new route, and it will then be acknowledged that this possession is of inestimable value.

" 'A boundless country belongs to us, to which the savages possess only an imaginary right. They overrun vast deserts, with the bow in their hand, in pursuit of wild beasts. But the social state requires that the land should be occupied, and these wandering hunters are not proprietors. The Indian has only a right to his subsistence, and this we will provide for him at a small expense.

"'All the productions of the West Indies suit Louisiana. This variety of products has already introduced large capitals into countries that were so long an uninhabited wilderness. If we must abandon St. Domingo, Louisiana will take its place. Consider likewise the injury which it may do us, if it becomes our rival in those productions of which we have so long had the monopoly. Attempts have been made to introduce there the vine, the olive, and the mulberry tree; and these experiments, which Spain has not been able to prevent, have but too well succeeded. If the colony should become free, Provence and our vineyards must prepare for a fearful competition with a country new and of boundless extent. If, on the other hand, it is subjected to our laws, every kind of culture injurious to our productions will be prohibited.

"'It is even for the advantage of Europe that France should be rich. So long as she shared with England the commerce of America and Asia, the princes and cabinets that consented to be subsidied, profited by their competition in their offers. What a difference it will make to them all, if there is to be no more competition, and if England alone is to regulate this traffic of amity among princes! Alone rich, she alone would give the law.

"'Finally, France, after her long troubles, requires such a colony for her internal pacification; it will be for our country what, a century ago, were for England the settlements which the emigrants from the three kingdoms have raised to so high a degree of prosperity; it will be the asylum of our religious and political dissenters; it will cure a part of the maladies which the revolution has caused, and be the supreme conciliator of all the parties into which we are divided. You wil. there find the remedies for which you search with so much solicitude.'

"The First Consul terminated the conference without making his intentions known; the discussions had been prolonged into the night. The Ministers remained at St. Cloud; and, at day-break, he summoned the one who had advised the cession of Louisiana, and made him read the despatches that had just arrived from London. His ambassador informed him that naval and military preparations of every kind were making with extraordinary rapidity.

"'The English,' said Napoleon, 'ask of me Lampedousa, which does not belong to me, and at the same time wish to keep Malta for ten years. This island, where military genius has exhausted all the means of defensive fortification to an extent of which no one without seeing it can form an idea, would be to them another Gibraltar. To leave it to the English would be to give up to them the commerce of the Levant, and to rob my southern provinces of it. They wish to keep this possession, and have me immediately to evacuate Holland.

"'Irresolution and deliberation are no longer in season. I renounce Louisiana. It is not only New Orleans that I will cede, it is the whole colony without any reservation. I know the price of what I abandon, and have sufficiently proved the importance that I attach to this province, since my first diplomatic act with Spain had for its object its recovery. I renounce it with the greatest regret. To attempt obstinately to retain it, would be folly. I direct you to negotiate this affair with the envoys of the United States. Do not even await the arrival of Mr. Monroe; have an interview this very day with Mr. Livingston. But I require a great deal of money for this war, and I would not like to commence it with new contributions. For a hundred years France and Spain have been incurring expenses for improvements in Louisiana, for which its trade has never indemnified them. Large sums, which will never be returned to the treasury, have been lent to companies and to agriculturists. The price of all these things is justly due to us. If I should regulate my terms according to the value of these vast regions to the United States, the indemnity would have no limits. I will be moderate, in consideration of the necessity in which I am, of making a sale. But keep this to yourself. I want fifty millions, and for less than that sum I will not treat; I would rather make a desperate attempt to keep these fine countries. To-morrow, you shall have full powers.' The new plenipotentiary then made some general observations on the cession of the rights of sovereignty, and upon the abandonment of what the Germans call the *souls*, as to whether they could be the subject of a contract of sale or exchange. Bonaparte replied: 'You are giving me in all its perfection, the ideology of the law of nature and nations. But I require money to make war on the richest nation of the world. Send your maxims to the London market; I am sure that they will be greatly admired there, and yet no great attention is paid to them when the question is the occupation of the finest regions of Asia.

"'Perhaps it will also be objected to me that the Americans may be found too powerful for Europe in two or three centuries; but my foresight does not embrace such remote fears. Besides, we may hereafter expect rivalries among the members of the Union. The confederations that are called perpetual, only last till one of the contracting parties finds it to his interest to break them, and it is to prevent the danger to which the colonial power of England exposes us, that I would provide a **remedy**.

The Minister made no reply. The First Consul continued: "Mr. Monroe is on the point of arriving. To this minister, going a thousand leagues from his constituents, the President must have given, after defining the object of his mission, secret instructions, more extensive than the ostensible authorization of Congress, for the stipulation of the payments to be made. Neither this minister, nor his colleague, is prepared for a decision which goes infinitely beyond anything that they are about to ask of us. Begin by making them the overture, without any subterfuge. You will acquaint me, day by day, hour by hour, of your progress. The cabinet of London is informed of the measures adopted at Washington, but it can have no suspicion of those I am now taking. Observe the greatest secrecy, and recommend it to the American Ministers; they have not a less interest than yourself in conforming to the counsel. You will correspond with M. de Talleyrand, who alone knows my intentions. If I attended to his advice, France would confine her ambition to the left bank of the Rhine, and would only make war to protect the weak states and to prevent any dismemberment of her possessions. But he also admits that the cession of Louisiana is not a dismemberment of France. Keep him informed of the progress of this affair."

Thus it is seen that, according to Marbois's own account, Bonaparte had determined, on the 10th of April, to part with Louisiana, and that he was as anxious to *sell* as the American Ministers to *purchase*. Both parties, being in such dispositions, could not fail to come promptly to some definite conclusion, despite the little coquetting and by-play acted on the part of Messrs. Marbois and Talleyrand, as described by Mr. Livingston, and which no doubt were intended to enhance the value of the commodity they had to dispose of.

The treaty of cession* was signed on the 30th of April. Louisiana was transferred to the United States, with all its rights and appurtenances, as fully and in the same manner as they had been acquired by the French Republic from Spain, on condition of the Americans consenting to pay to France eighty millions of francs, twenty millions of which should be assigned to the payment of what was due by France to the citizens of the United States. Some commercial advantages were besides stipulated in favor of France.

Article 3 of the treaty, which reads as follows: "The inhabitants of the ceded territory shall be incorporated in the Union of the United States, and admitted as soon as possible, according to the principles of the Federal Constitution, to the enjoyment of all the rights, advantages and immunities of citizens of the United States; and in the meantime they shall be maintained and protected in the free enjoyment of their liberty, property, and the religion which they profess"—was, wrote Marbois, prepared by the First Consul himself, who said on that occasion: "Let the Louisianians know that we separate ourselves from them with regret; that we stipulate in their favor every thing that they can desire, and let them, hereafter, happy in their independence, recollect that they have been Frenchmen, and that France, in ceding them, has secured for them advantages which they could not have obtained from an European power, however paternal it might have been. Let them retain for us sentiments of affection; and may their common origin, descent, language, and customs, perpetuate the friendship."

As soon as the Ministers had signed the treaty, writes the same author, who had acted so conspicuous a part in that important event, they rose and shook hands, when

* See the Appendix.

Mr. Livingston, expressing the satisfaction which they felt, said: "We have lived long, but this is the noblest work of our whole lives. The treaty which we have just signed has not been obtained by art or dictated by force; equally advantageous to the two contracting parties, it will change vast solitudes into flourishing districts. From this day the United States take their place among the powers of the first rank; the English lose all exclusive influence in the affairs of America. Thus one of the principal causes of European rivalries and animosities is about to cease. However, if wars are inevitable, France will hereafter have in the New World a natural friend, that must increase in strength from year to year, and one which cannot fail to become powerful and respected in every sea. The United States will re-establish the maritime rights of all the world, which are now usurped by a single nation. These treaties will thus be a guarantee of peace and concord among commercial states. The instruments which we have just signed will cause no tears to be shed: they prepare ages of happiness for innumerable generations of human creatures. The Mississippi and Missouri will see them succeed one another, and multiply, truly worthy of the regard and care of Providence, in the bosom of equality, under just laws, freed from the errors of superstition and the scourges of bad government."

As to the First Consul, when he was informed of the conclusion of the treaty, he sententiously and prophetically said: "This accession of territory strengthens for ever the power of the United States; and I have just given to England a maritime rival, that will sooner or later humble her pride."

Thus closed these negotiations, which I have thought of sufficient interest to be related in detail, and which eventuated in the most important treaty perhaps ever signed in the nineteenth century, if it be judged by its consequences to the United States and to the rest of the world. Among those consequences were the extension of the area of freedom, an immense accretion to the physical and moral power of the great American Republic, and the subsequent acquisition of the Floridas, Texas, California, and other portions of the Mexican territory. Other results, at least of equal magnitude, may be clearly foreseen, and it may be permitted to the pride of patriotism to hope for the realization of Bonaparte's prevision: "that the day may come when the cession of Louisiana to the United States shall render the Americans too powerful for the continent **of Europe.**"

CHAPTER IX.

SALCEDO'S ADMINISTRATION.

1801 to 1803.

As it has been seen, the treaty of cession was signed on the 30th of April. On the 7th of May, Mr. King wrote from London to Mr. Livingston and Monroe: " In case of war, it is the purpose of this government (the British government), to send an expedition to occupy New Orleans. If it be ceded to us, would it not be expedient openly or confidentially to communicate the fact here ? I have reason to be satisfied that it would prevent the projected expedition. I shall remain here till the 14th, in hopes that I may receive your answer, which may be expedited by a courier, should the communication be deemed prudent." The answer was: " We have the honor to inform you that a treaty has been signed (the 30th April) between the Minister Plenipotentiary of the French government and ourselves, by which the United States have obtained the full right to and sovereignty in and over New Orleans and the whole of Louisiana, as Spain possessed the same. If you should find it necessary to make any communication to the British government on this subject, you may likewise inform them, that care has been taken so to frame the treaty as not to infringe upon any of the rights that Great Britain might claim in the navigation of the Mississippi." Mr

King immediately communicated this information to the British government, and, in reply, Lord Hawkesbury said: "I have received his Majesty's commands to express to you the pleasure with which his Majesty has received this intelligence."

In laying before the Secretary of State all the details of this negotiation, Mr. Livingston observed: "As I believe that, next to the negotiation that secured our independence, this is the most important the United States have ever entered into, I thought that every thing that led to it might interest you and the President." And, in a joint despatch of the 13th of May, Messrs. Livingston and Monroe remarked: "An acquisition of so great an extent was, we well know, not contemplated by our appointment; but we are persuaded that the circumstances and considerations which induced us to make it, will justify us in the measure to our government and country. * * * * *
* * * * * * *

"We found, as we advanced in the negotiation, that M. Marbois was absolutely restricted to the disposition of the whole, that he would treat for no less portion, and, of course, that it was useless to urge it. On mature consideration, therefore, we finally concluded a treaty on the best terms we could obtain for the whole. *
* * * * * * *

"We adjust by it the only remaining known cause of variance with this powerful nation; we anticipate the discontent of the great rival of France, who would probably have been wounded at any stipulation of a permanent nature which favored the latter, and which it would have been difficult to avoid, had she retained the right bank. We cease to have a motive of urgency at least, for inclining to one power, to avert the unjust pressure of another. We separate ourselves in a great measure from the European world and its concerns, especially its wars and intrigues. We make, in fine, a great stride to real and substantial independence, the great effect whereof will, we trust, be felt essentially and extensively in all our foreign and domestic relations. Without exciting the apprehension of any power, we take a more imposing attitude with respect to all. The bond of our union will be strengthened, and its movements become more harmonious by the increased parity of interests which it will communicate to the several parts which compose it."

It will be recollected that when the cession of Louisiana by Spain to France was heard of, the Ministers of the United States in Paris, London, and Madrid, had made inquiries to ascertain whether the Floridas were included in the cession as part of Louisiana, and had expressed the opinion that they were not. But that opinion underwent a change, at least with regard to a portion of the Floridas, soon after the signing of the treaty of cession transferring the same province to the United States, such as it had been acquired from Spain, and Mr. Livingston, on the 20th of May, wrote as follows to Mr. Madison on this subject: "I informed you long since, that, on inquiring whether the Floridas were within the cession of Spain, I was told by M. Marbois he was sure that Mobile was, but could not answer farther. I believed his information incorrect, because I understood that Louisiana, as it then was, made the object of the cession; and that since the possession of the Floridas by Britain, they had changed their names. But the moment I saw the words of the treaty of Madrid, I had no doubt but it included all the country that France possessed by the name of Louisiana, previous to their cession to Spain, except what had been conveyed by subsequent treaties. I accordingly insisted with M.

Marbois, at the time we negotiated, that this would be considered as within our purchase. He neither assented nor denied, but said that all they received from Spain, was intended to be conveyed to us. That my construction was right, is fairly to be inferred from the words of the treaties, and from a comment upon them contained in the Spanish Minister's letter to Mr. Pinckney, in which he expressly says, that France had recovered Louisiana as it formerly belonged to her, saving the rights of other powers. This leaves no doubt upon the subject of the intention of the contracting parties. Now, it is well known that Louisiana, as possessed by France, was bounded by the river Perdido, and that Mobile was the metropolis. For the facts relative to this, I refer you to Raynal and to his maps. I have also seen maps here which put the matter out of dispute.

"I called this morning upon M. Marbois for a further explanation on this subject, and to remind him of his having told me that Mobile made a part of the cession. He told me that he had no precise idea on the subject, but that he knew it to be an historical fact, and that on that only he had formed his opinion. I asked him what orders had been given to the Prefect who was to take possession, or what orders had been given by Spain, as to the boundary, in ceding it? He assured me that he did not know; but that he would make the inquiry, and let me know. At four o'clock I called for Mr. Monroe to take him to the Minister of Foreign Affairs (Talleyrand); but he was prevented from accompanying me. I asked the minister (Talleyrand) what were the east bounds of the territory ceded to us? He said he did not know; we must take it as they had received it. I asked him how Spain meant to give them possession? He said, according to the words of the treaty.—But what did you mean to take?—I do not know.—Then you mean that we shall construe it our own way?—I can give you no direction; you have made a noble bargain for yourselves, and I suppose you will make the most of it.

"Now, Sir, the sum of this business is, to recommend to you, in the strongest terms, after having obtained the possession that the French commissary will give you, to insist upon this as a part of your right, and to take possession, at all events, to the river Perdido. I pledge myself that your right is good; and, after the explanations that have been given here, you need apprehend nothing from a decisive measure. Your ministers here, and at Madrid, can support your claim; and the time is peculiarly favorable to enable you to do it without the smallest risk at home. It may also be important to anticipate any designs that Britain may have upon that country. Should she possess herself of it, and the war terminate favorably for her, she will not readily relinquish it. With this in your hand, East Florida will be of little moment, and may be yours whenever you please. At all events, proclaim your right and take possession."

On the 7th of June, Messrs. Livingston and Monroe again said in a joint despatch to Mr. Madison: "We are happy to have it in our power to assure you, that, on a thorough examination of the subject, we consider it incontrovertible that West Florida is comprised in the cession of Louisiana."

Let us now see the view taken of this question by the French negotiator. It cannot be done better than by quoting his own language. "The American negotiators," said he, "easily agreed on the declaration contained in the first article: *The colony or province of Louisiana is ceded by France to the United States, with all its rights and appurtenances, as fully and in the same manner as*

they have been acquired by the French Republic, by virtue of the third article of the treaty concluded with his Catholic Majesty at St. Ildephonso, on the 1st of October, 1800. Terms so general, seemed, however, to render necessary some explanations, relative to the true extent of Louisiana, &c. * * * * * *
* * * * * * *

"There were some historical and diplomatic researches on the first occupation and earliest acts of sovereignty. But they were only attended with the results usual in such cases. Travellers and historians had not left on this subject any but vague and general notions; they had only narrated some accidents of navigation, some acts of occupation, to which contradictory ones might be opposed. According to old documents, the bishopric of Louisiana extended to the Pacific ocean, and the limits of the diocess thus defined were secure from all dispute. But this was at the most a matter in expectancy, and the Indians of those regions never had any suspicion of the spiritual jurisdiction which it was designed to exercise over them. Besides, it had no connection with the rights of sovereignty and property. One important point was, however, beyond all discussion; according to the then existing treaties, the course of the Mississippi, in descending this river to the 31st degree of north latitude, formed the boundary line, leaving to the United States the country on its left bank; to the right, on the other hand, there were vast regions without well defined boundaries, although France had formerly included a great part of them in what was called Upper Louisiana. This was particularly the case with the territories to the south of the Missouri.

"The limits of Louisiana and Florida, to the south of the 31st degree, were not free from some disputes, which possessed importance on account of the neighborhood of the sea, and the embouchure of the rivers. However this country (Florida), disregarded by the European powers that successively possessed it, was scarcely mentioned in the conferences. France had only the smallest portion of it. The name of Florida could not have been inserted without preparing great difficulties for the future.

"The boundary to the north and north-west was still less easy to describe. Even the course of the Mississippi might give rise to some border disputes; for that great river receives, beyond the 43rd degree, several branches, then regarded as its sources. A geographical chart was before the plenipotentiaries. They negotiated with entire good faith; they frankly agreed that these matters were full of uncertainty, but they had no means of quieting the doubts. The French negotiator said: 'Even this map informs us that many of these countries are not better known at this day, than when Columbus landed at the Bahamas; no one is acquainted with them. The English themselves have never explored them. The circumstances are too pressing to permit us to concert matters on this subject with the court of Madrid. It would be too long before this discussion could be terminated, and perhaps that government would wish to consult the Viceroy of Mexico. Is it not better for the United States to abide by a general stipulation, and since these territories are still at this day, for the most part, in possession of the Indians, await future arrangements, or leave the matter open for the treaty stipulations that the United States may make with them and Spain? In granting Canada to the English at the peace of 1763, we only extended the cession to the country that we possessed. It is, however, as a consequence of that treaty, that England has occupied territory to the West, as far as the great Northern Ocean.' Whether the American plenipotentiaries had themselves desired what was proposed to them, or that these words afforded them a ray of light, they declared that they kept to the terms of the 3rd article of the treaty of St. Ildephonso, which was inserted entire in the first article of the treaty of cession.

"M. Marbois, who offered the draft, said several times: '*The first article may in time give rise to difficulties, that are at this day insurmountable. But if they do not stop you, I, at least, desire that your government should know that you have been warned of them.*'

"The French negotiator, in rendering an account of the conference to the First Consul, pointed out to him the obscurity of this article and the inconveniences of so uncertain a stipulation. He replied: '*that if an obscurity did not already exist, it would perhaps be good policy to put one there.*'

Whatever was the true territorial extent of Louisiana, whether it included part of the Floridas or not, Spain immediately protested against the treaty of cession, and her Minister at Washington, the Marquis de Casa Irujo, addressed the following note to the Secretary of State on the 4th of September: "Through the medium of the ambassador of the King my master, in Paris, it has come to his royal knowledge, that that government has sold to that of the United States the province of Louisiana, which his Majesty had retroceded to the French Republic. This information has occasioned to the King, my master, no small surprise, seeing that the French Government had contracted with his Majesty the most solemn engagements never to alienate the said province. In order to convince the Government of the United States of the nature of these engagements, I take the liberty here to insert a paragraph of a note presented on the 22d of July, 1802, by M. de St. Cyr, ambassador of the French Republic, at Madrid, to the Secretary of State of his Majesty, as follows:

"*His Catholic Majesty has appeared to wish that France should engage not to sell nor alienate in any manner, the property and the enjoyment of Louisiana. Its wish in this respect is perfectly conformable with the intentions of the Spanish Government; and its sole motive for entering therein was because it respected a possession which had constituted a part of the French territory. I am authorized to declare to you in the name of the First Consul that France will never alienate it.*"

"The mere reading of the paragraph which precedes will convince you as well as the President of the United States, that the sale of Louisiana which France has lately made is a manifest violation of the obligations contracted by her with his Catholic Majesty, and that France wants the powers to alienate the said province without the approbation of Spain, as is seen incontestably in the above recited note of the ambassador St. Cyr, authorized by his government.

"The King, my master, charges me to inform this government, as soon as possible, of this important circumstance; and, in compliance with his royal will, I hasten to acquaint you therewith, in order that it may, as soon as possible, come to the knowledge of the President of the United States."

On the 27th of the same month (September), the Marquis de Casa Irujo returned to the subject, and said in a communication to Mr. Madison: "On the 4th current, I had the honor to intimate to you the extraordinary surprise with which the King, my master, had heard of the sale of Louisiana, made to the United States, in contravention of the most solemn assurances given in writing to his Majesty, by the ambassador of the French Republic near his person, and with the consent and approbation of the First Consul. The King, my master, charges me again to remind the American

Government, that the said French ambassador entered, in the name of his Republic, into the positive engagement that France never would alienate Louisiana, and to observe to it that the sale of this province to the United States is founded in the violation of a promise so absolute that it ought to be respected; a promise without which the King my master would, in no manner, have dispossessed himself of Louisiana. His Catholic Majesty entertains too good an opinion of the character of probity and good faith which the Government of the United States has known how to obtain so justly for itself, not to hope that it will suspend the ratification and effect of a treaty which rests on such a basis. There are other reasons no less powerful, which come to the support of the decorum and respect which nations mutually owe each other. France acquired from the King, my master, the retrocession of Louisiana under obligations whose entire fulfilment was absolutely necessary to give her the complete right over the said province; such was that of causing the King of Tuscany to be acknowledged by the Powers of Europe; but, until now, the French Government has not procured this acknowledgment, promised and stipulated, either from the Court of London, or from that of St. Petersburgh Under such circumstances, it is evident that the treaty of sale entered into between France and the United States does not give to the latter any right to acquire and claim Louisiana, and that the principles of justice as well as sound policy ought to recommend it to their government not to meddle with engagements, as contrary in reality to their true interests, as they would be to good faith and to their good correspondence with Spain."

Mr. Madison communicated these notes to Mr. Livingston at Paris, to whom he said in a despatch of the 6th of October: "The objections to the cession, advanced by Spain, are in fact too futile to weigh either with others or with herself. The promise made by the French ambassador, that no alienation should be made, formed no part of the treaty of retrocession to France; and, if it had, would have no effect on the purchase by the United States, which was made in good faith, without notice from Spain of any such condition, and even with sufficient evidence that no such condition existed. The objection drawn from the failure of the French government to procure from other powers an acknowledgment of the King of Etruria, is equally groundless. This stipulation was never communicated either to the public or to the United States, and could, therefore, be no bar to the contract made by them. It might be added, that, as the acknowledgment stipulated was, according to the words of the article, to precede possession by the King of Etruria, the overt possession by him was notice to the world that the conditions on which it depended had either been fulfilled, or had been waived. Finally, no particular Powers, whose acknowledgment was to be procured, are named in the article; and the existence of war between Great Britain and France, at the time of the stipulation, is a proof that the British acknowledgment, the want of which is now alleged as a breach of the treaty, could never have been in its contemplation.

"But the conduct of the Spanish government, both towards the United States and France, is a complete answer to every possible objection to the treaty between them. That government well knew the wish of the United States to acquire certain territories which it had ceded to France, and that they were in negotiation with France on the subject; yet the slightest hint was never given that France had no right to alienate, or even that an alienation to the United States would be disagreeable to Spain. On the contrary, the minister of his Catholic

Majesty, in an official note, bearing date May 4th last gave information to the minister of the United States at Madrid, *that the entire province of Louisiana, with the limits it had when held by France, was retroceded to that power, and that the United States might address themselves to the French government in order to negotiate the acquisition of the territories which would suit their interest.* Here is at once a formal and irrevocable recognition of the right as well of France to convey, as of the United States to receive, the territory which is the subject of the treaty between them. More than this cannot be required to silence, for ever, the cavils of Spain at the titles of France, now vested in the United States; yet, for more than this, she may be referred to her own measures at New Orleans, preparatory to the delivery of possession to France; to the promulgation, under Spanish authority at that place, that Louisiana was retroceded, and to be delivered to France; and to the orders signed by his Catholic Majesty's own hand, now ready to be presented to the government of Louisiana, for the delivery of the province to the person duly authorized by France to receive it.

"In a word, the Spanish government has interposed two objections only to the title conveyed to the United States by France. It is said, first, that the title in the United States is not good, because France was bound not to alienate. To this it is answered, that the Spanish government itself referred the United States to France, as the Power capable, and the only Power capable, of conveying the territory in question. It is said, next, that the title in France herself is not good. To this, if the same answer were less decisive, the orders of the King of Spain for putting France into possession are an answer that admits of no reply." * * *

* * * * * * *

Mr. Madison added: "The rightful limits of Louisiana are under investigation. It seems undeniable from the present state of the evidence, that it extends eastwardly as far, at least, as the river Perdido; and there is little doubt that we shall make good both a western and northern extent highly satisfactory to us."

On the 12th of October, the Marquis de Casa Irujo addressed to Mr. Madison another communication, in which he resumed the argument to prove that Spain was right in protesting against the execution of the treaty of cession: "I have received," said he, "your letter of the 4th current in reply to those which I had the honor to write to you on the 4th and 27th of the last month; and as, without entering into the examination of the powerful reasons which, in the name of the King my master, I unfolded therein, against the sale of Louisiana, you refer generally to the explanations which, as you inform me, the minister of the United States near his Majesty is to make at Madrid, I shall at present confine my observations to that which you are pleased to make to me, founded upon certain expressions which you cite to me from an official letter of the Secretary of State of the King my master, to the above mentioned American minister in Spain. The expressions are the following:

"*By the retrocession made to France of Louisiana, this power has recovered the said province with the limits which it had, and saving the rights acquired by other powers. The United States can address themselves to the French government to negotiate the acquisition of territory which may suit their interests.**

"These expressions, which you consider as an explicit

---

* Por la retrocesion hecha á la Francia de la Luisiana, recobró esta potentia dicha provincia con los limites con que la tubo, y salvos los derechos acquiridos por otras potencias. La de los Estados Unidos podrá dirigirse al gobierno Fran cès para negociar la adquisicion de territorios que convengan à su interes.

and positive acknowledgment of the right of the United States and France to enter into the engagements which they afterwards did, do not, in my opinion, weaken, in any manner, the foundation and the force of the representations which I have had the honor to make to you against the sale of Louisiana.

"There is an expression among those you cite, which will suffice to refute the inference you draw from them, and it is that *of saving the rights acquired by other powers*. Although the general form of this expression gives, in other respects, much latitude to its true meaning, it is indubitable that Spain having made the retrocession of Louisiana to France, under certain conditions and modifications, Spain has the undoubted right to claim their execution. Of this nature was the stipulation that France should not sell nor alienate Louisiana in any manner whatever, and likewise the solemn and positive accession and declaration of the French government adhering to the wishes of Spain; consequently this expression destroys the possibility that, according to existing circumstances, the French government should possess the right of selling the said province, or the government of the United States that of buying it.

"There is another consideration still stronger, and which is not at all subject to the interpretation of equivocal expressions. It is evident that the engagement entered into by France with Spain not to alienate Louisiana in any manner, is much older in date than the official letter of M. Cevallos, whose expressions you are pleased to cite to me. In that letter, those which you have scored: *that the United States can address themselves to the French government to negotiate the acquisition of the territory which may suit their interests*, neither signify nor can signify any thing but a deference towards France, whose government alone is now concerned to give a decisive answer to the requests of the United States,—an answer analogous and conformable to the nature of the previous engagements which had been entered into with Spain. The repugnance of the Spanish government may likewise be recognised to give to that of the United States a necessary negative, at a time when it found itself united with them by bonds of the most sincere friendship.

"Other interpretations of equal force may be derived from the obvious meaning of the expressions of the official letter of the Secretary of State of his Majesty mentioned by you; but as those which I have just made are, in my opinion, conclusive, I abstain from entering upon others in detail, and I take the liberty to call to them the attention, as well of yourself as of the President of the United States, in order that you may be more and more convinced of the reason and justice with which the King, my master, objects to the ratification of a treaty founded upon a manifest violation of the most sacred engagements entered into by France."

Mr. Madison communicated to Mr. Pinckney, the American Minister at Madrid, all the arguments which he had used to refute the pretensions of Spain, and said: "The President thinks it proper, that they should, without delay, be conveyed to the Spanish government, either by a note from you or in conversation, as you may deem most expedient, and in a form and style best uniting the advantages of making that government sensible of the absolute determination of the United States to maintain their right, with the propriety of avoiding undignified menace and unnecessary irritation.

"The conduct of Spain, on this occasion, is such as was, in several views, little to be expected, and as is not readily explained. If her object be to extort Louisiana from France, as well as to prevent its transfer to the

United States, it would seem that she must be emboldened by an understanding with some other very powerful quarter of Europe. If she hopes to prevail on France to break her engagement to the United States, and voluntarily restore Louisiana to herself, why has she so absurdly blended with the project the offensive communication of the perfidy which she charges on the First Consul? If it be her aim to prevent the execution of the treaty between the United States and France, in order to have for her neighbor the latter instead of the United States, it is not difficult to show that she mistakes the lesser for the greater damage against which she wishes to provide. Admitting, as she may possibly suppose, that Louisiana, as a French colony, would be less able, as well as less disposed, than the United States, to encroach on her southern possessions, and that it would be too much occupied with its own safety against the United States to turn its force on the other side against her possessions, still it is obvious, in the first place, that, in proportion to the want of power in the French, the colony would be safe for Spain; that compared with the power of the United States, the colony would be insufficient as a barrier against the United States; and, in the next place, that the very security which she provides, would itself be a source of the greatest of all the dangers she has to apprehend. The collisions between the United States and the French would lead to a contest, in which Great Britain would naturally join the former, and in which Spain would, of course, be on the side of the latter; and what becomes of Louisiana and the Spanish possessions beyond it, in a contest between the powers so marshalled?—An easy and certain victim to the fleets of Great Britain and the land armies of this country. A combination of these forces was always, and justly, dreaded by both Spain and France. It was this danger which led both into our revolutionary war, and much inconsistency and weakness is chargeable on the projects of either which tend to re-unite for the purposes of war, the power which has been divided. France, by returning to her original policy, has wisely, by her late treaty with the United States, obviated a danger which would not have been very remote. Spain will be equally wise in following the example; and, by acquiescing in an arrangement which guards against an early danger of controversy between the United States, first with France, and then with herself, and which removes to a distant day the approximation of the American and Spanish settlements, provides in the best possible manner for the security of the latter, and for a lasting harmony with the United States. What is it that Spain dreads? She dreads, it is presumed, the growing power of this country, and the direction of it against her possessions within its reach. Can she annihilate this power? No. Can she sensibly retard its growth? No. Does not common prudence then advise her to conciliate, by every proof of confidence and friendship, the good-will of a nation whose power is formidable to her; instead of yielding to the impulses of jealousy, and adopting obnoxious precautions which can have no other effect than to bring on, prematurely, the whole weight of the calamity which she fears? Reflections, such as these, may, perhaps, enter with some advantage into your communications with the Spanish government; and, as far as they may be invited by favorable occasions, you will make that use of them."

It had been thought proper to communicate to M. Pichon, the French Chargé-d'Affaires at Washington, the tenor of the notes from the Marquis de Casa Irujo, and, in reply, M. Pichon addressed to the Secretary of State, on the 14th of October, the following note:

"The undersigned, to whom the Secretary of State has been pleased to communicate the proceedings of the Minister of his Catholic Majesty to the United States, in relation to the treaty by which the French Republic has ceded Louisiana to the United States, thinks that he owes it to his own government as well as to the American government, to present to Mr. Madison the observations of which those proceedings, as far as they attack the rights and even the dignity of the French government, have appeared to him susceptible.

"The Court of Madrid, according to the notes of its Minister, considers the cession made by France to the United States as irregular and invalid: 1°—because France has renounced the right of alienating the territories in question: 2°—because the treaty of St. Ildephonso, by which Spain retroceded those territories to France, has not been fully executed with respect to the acknowledgment of the King of Etruria—an acknowledgment which was one of the conditions of the retrocession to be fulfilled by France.

"On the first point, the undersigned will observe that the treaty of St. Ildephonso retrocedes Louisiana in full sovereignty, and without any limitation as to the future domain of France. To operate a limitation so essential as is that to which the Court of Madrid appeals, nothing less would have been necessary, according to the nature of contracts in general and of treaties in particular, than a stipulation to this effect inserted in the treaty itself. A promise made fifteen months after the signature of this pact, and which might, on one side, have been yielded to the solicitations of one of the contracting parties, and, on the other, dictated by the dispositions which might then exist in the other party, but which ulterior circumstances might have changed—such a promise cannot create in favor of Spain a right sufficient to enable her to charge with invalidity the transactions which have contravened it. The contrary pretensions would certainly confound all the principles relative to the nature of obligations, and would destroy the solemnity of treaties. These general reasonings would receive a new force from the circumstances which are peculiar to different nations in relation to the subject of pacts; but the undersigned will not enter into the examination of these circumstances, under the persuasion that general principles sufficiently repel the pretensions of the Court of Madrid.

"On the second point, the objections of that Court do not appear to the undersigned to be better founded. It is known that the King of Etruria was placed on the throne since the treaty of St. Ildephonso. We have a right to suppose, that his Catholic Majesty was satisfied from that period with the measures and efforts employed by France to cause the title of this Prince to be acknowledged by the other nations. It is at least what might be concluded from facts within the knowledge of the whole world. In the treaty of Amiens, concluded on the 27th of March, 1802, Great Britain did not acknowledge the King of Etruria. Notwithstanding the silence of the Court of London, on so solemn an occasion, that of Madrid ordered, in the month of October following, the delivery of the colony to France, as is proved by the royal cedula, which the undersigned has received and exhibited to Mr. Madison; a cedula, which, as all the world knows, was long ago forwarded to the Captain General of Cuba, who sent the Marquis de Casa Calvo to New Orleans to superintend its execution.

"To these conclusive observations the undersigned

will add, that the Court of Madrid might have been informed in the course of the month of February last, by its Minister to the United States, that the American government was sending to Paris a Minister Extraordinary, in order to negotiate with the French Government the acquisition of New Orleans If the Court of Madrid had seen, in the object of this mission, an injury offered to its rights, what prevented it, after being thus early apprised, from informing thereof the Minister of the United States at Paris, and the French government, and from interposing, before the conclusion of the treaty, its intervention in a form adapted to suspend it? It does not appear that that court has taken, at Paris, any steps of this nature. To suppose it, would be inconsistent with the instructions which the undersigned has received from his government, to accelerate as much as is in his power the execution of the treaty concluded on the 30th of April last, between the French Republic and the United States.

"The undersigned therefore hopes, that the American government will not see in the proceedings of the court of Madrid, in order to obstruct the execution of this treaty, any thing but specious reasonings, and will proceed to its execution with the same earnestness which the French government has employed on its part. The undersigned has received the necessary orders to exchange the ratifications and effect the taking of possession of Louisiana by France, and its transfer to the United States. He does not presume that the court of Madrid would wish to oppose the execution of the first orders. This supposition would be as contrary to its loyalty as to the dignity of the French government. In any event, as soon as the ratifications are exchanged, the undersigned will proceed without delay, in concert with **the** commissary appointed for that purpose by the First

Consul, to the delivery of the colony to the persons whom the President of the United States shall appoint to take possession of it."

On the 17th of October, Congress assembled at Washington agreeably to the proclamation of the President of the United States, who, in his message, thus referred to the purchase of Louisiana:

"Congress witnessed, at their late session, the extraordinary agitation produced in the public mind by the suspension of our right of deposit at the port of New Orleans, no assignment of another place having been made according to treaty. They were sensible that the continuation of that privation would be more injurious to our nation than any consequences which could flow from any mode of redress; but, reposing just confidence in the good faith of the government whose officer had committed the wrong, friendly and reasonable representations were resorted to, and the right of deposit was restored.

"Previous, however, to this period, we had not been unaware of the danger to which our peace would be perpetually exposed, whilst so important a key to the commerce of the Western country remained under a foreign power. Difficulties too were presenting themselves as to the navigation of other streams, which, arising within our territories, pass through those adjacent. Propositions had therefore been authorized for obtaining, on fair conditions, the sovereignty of New Orleans, and of other possessions in that quarter, interesting to our quiet, to such extent as was deemed practicable; and the provisional appropriation of two millions of dollars, to be applied and accounted for by the President of the United States, intended as part of the price, was considered as conveying the sanction of Congress to the acquisition proposed. The enlightened government of France saw, with just discernment, the importance to both nations of such liberal arrangements as might best and permanently promote the peace, interests, and friendship of both; and the property and sovereignty of all Louisiana, which had been restored to them, has, on certain conditions, been transferred to the United States, by instruments bearing date the 30th of April last. When these shall have received the constitutional sanction of the Senate, they will, without delay, be communicated to the Representatives for the exercise of their functions, as to those conditions which are within the powers vested by the Constitution in Congress. Whilst the property and sovereignty of the Mississippi and its waters secure an independent outlet for the produce of the Western States, and an uncontrolled navigation through their whole course, free from collision with other powers and the dangers to our peace from that source, the fertility of the country, its climate and extent promise, in due season, important aids to our treasury, an ample provision for our posterity, and a wide spread for the blessings of freedom and equal laws.

"With the wisdom of Congress it will rest to take those ulterior measures which may be necessary for the immediate occupation and temporary government of the country; for its incorporation into our Union; for rendering the change of government a blessing to our newly adopted brethren; for securing to them the rights of conscience and of property; for confirming to the Indian inhabitants their occupancy and self-government, establishing friendly and commercial relations with them; and for ascertaining the geography of the country acquired."

On the 26th of October, a bill to enable the President to take possession of the territories ceded by France to the United States, by the treaty concluded at Paris on the 30th of April, was adopted in the Senate by a vote in the affirmative of 26 to 6 in the negative. Those who voted against the bill were John Quincy Adams and Timothy Pickering from Massachusetts, James Hillhouse and Uriah Tracy from Connecticut, Simeon Olcott and William Plumer from New Hampshire.

On the 2d of November, the Senate resumed the second reading of a bill entitled: "An act authorizing the erection of a stock to the amount of eleven millions two hundred and fifty thousand dollars, for the purpose of carrying into effect the convention of the 30th of April, 1803, between the United States and the French Republic." The bill had come up from the House of Representatives, where it had passed on the 29th of October. On the question: Shall the bill pass?—Mr. James White, from Delaware, moved that the further consideration of the bill be postponed until the second Monday in December next, stating as the ground of the motion he had the honor to make, that the question was then involved in much difficulty and doubt. He could not accede to the immediate passage of the bill, "because," said he, "by the day I have named, the Senate would be able to act more understandingly on the subject, as it would then probably be ascertained whether we are likely to obtain the quiet possession of New Orleans and Louisiana under the treaty or not, and there would still remain a great sufficiency of time to make the necessary provisions on our part for carrying the treaty into execution, if it should be deemed necessary.

"Admitting then," continued he, "that his Catholic Majesty is hostile to the cession of this territory to the United States, and no honorable gentleman will deny it, what reasons have we to suppose that the French Prefect, provided the Spaniards should interfere, can give to us peaceable possession of the country? He is acknowledged there in no public character, is clothed with no authority, nor has he a single soldier to enforce his orders. I speak now from mere probabilities. I wish not to be understood as predicting that the French will not cede to us the actual and quiet possession of the territory. I hope to God they may, for possession of it we must have,—I mean of New Orleans, and of such other positions on the Mississippi as may be necessary to secure to us for ever, the complete and uninterrupted navigation of that river. This I have ever been in favor of; I think it essential to the peace of the United States and to the prosperity of our Western country. But as to Louisiana, this new, immense, unbounded world, if it should ever be incorporated into this Union, which I have no idea can be done but by altering the Constitution, I believe it will be the greatest curse that could at present befall us; it may be productive of innumerable evils, and especially of one that I fear even to look upon. Gentlemen on all sides, with very few exceptions, agree that the settlement of the country will be highly injurious and dangerous to the United States; but, as to what has been suggested of removing the Creeks and other nations of Indians from the Eastern to the Western banks of the Mississippi, and making the fertile regions of Louisiana a howling wilderness, never to be trodden by the foot of civilized man, it is impracticable. The gentleman from Tennessee (Mr. Cocke) has shown his usual candor on this occasion, and I believe with him, to use his strong language, that you had as well pretend to prohibit the fish from swimming in the sea, as to prevent the populating of that country after its sovereignty shall become ours. To every man acquainted with the adventurous, roving, and enterprising temper of our people, and with the manner in which our Western country has been settled, such an idea must be chimerical. The inducements will be so strong, that it will be impossible to restrain our citizens from crossing the river. Louisiana must and will become settled, if we hold it, and with the very population that would otherwise occupy part of our present territory. Thus our citizens will be removed to the immense distance of two or three thousand miles from the capital of the Union, where they will scarcely ever feel the rays of the General Government; their affections will become alienated; they will gradually begin to view us as strangers; they will form other commercial connections, and our interests will become distinct.

"These, with other causes that human wisdom may not now foresee, will in time effect a separation, and I fear our bounds will be fixed nearer to our houses than the water of the Mississippi. We have already territory enough, and when I contemplate the evils that may arise to these States from this intended incorporation of Louisiana into the Union, I would rather see it given to France, to Spain, or to any other nation of the earth, upon the mere condition that no citizen of the United States should ever settle within its limits, than to see the territory sold for a hundred millions of dollars, and we retain the sovereignty. * * * * *
And I do say that, under existing circumstances, even supposing that this extent of territory was a desirable acquisition, fifteen millions of dollars was a most enormous sum to give." Mr. Wells, of the same State, took the same view of the question with his colleague, Mr. White.

Mr. Pickering, from Massachusetts, spoke also against the bill, as he thought that Congress was not bound to carry the treaty into execution: "The Constitution, and the laws of the United States," said he, "made in pursuance thereof, and all treaties made, or which shall be made under the authority of the United States, shall be the supreme law of the land. But a treaty, to be thus obligatory, must not contravene the Constitution, nor contain any stipulations which transcend the powers therein given to the President and Senate. The treaty between the United States and the French Republic, professing to cede Louisiana to the United States, appears to me to contain such an exceptionable stipulation—a stipulation which cannot be executed by any authority now existing. It is declared in the 3d article, *that the inhabitants of the ceded territory shall be incorporated in the Union of the United States.* But neither the President and Senate, nor the President and Congress, are competent to such an act of incorporation. I believe that our administration admitted that this incorporation could not be effected without an amendment of the Constitution; and I conceive that this necessary amendment cannot be made in the ordinary mode by the concurrence of two thirds of both houses of Congress, and the ratification of the legislatures of three fourths of the several States. I believe the assent of each individual State to be necessary for the admission of a foreign country as an associate in the Union: in like manner as in a commercial house, the consent of each member would be necessary to admit a new partner into the company; and whether the assent of every State to such an indispensable amendment would be attainable, is uncertain. But the articles of a treaty are necessarily related to each other, the stipulation in one article being frequently the consideration for another. If, therefore, in respect to the Louisiana treaty, the United States fail to execute, and within a reasonable time, the engagement in the 3d article, *to incorporate that territory into the Union*, the French government will have the right to declare the whole treaty void. We must then abandon the country, or go to war to maintain our possession.

* * * * * * *

"But," added Mr. Pickering, "I have never doubted the right of the United States to acquire new territory, either by purchase or by conquest, and to govern the territory so acquired as a dependent province; and in this way might Louisiana have become a territory of the United States, and have received a form of government infinitely preferable to that to which its inhabitants are now subject."

Mr. Tracy, from Connecticut, followed in the same line of argument, objecting also to what he called giving a commercial preference to the ports of the ceded territory over the other ports of the Union, in conformity with the 7th article of the treaty, which stipulated, that the ships of France and Spain should be admitted for twelve years into the ports of Louisiana, free of foreign duty. He concluded with the following sentiments: "We can hold territory; but to admit the inhabitants into the Union, to make citizens of them and States, by treaty, we cannot constitutionally do; and no subsequent act of legislation, or even ordinary amendment to our Constitution, can legalize such measures. If done at all, they must be done by universal consent of all the States or partners of our political association; and this universal consent I am positive can never be obtained to such a pernicious measure as the admission of Louisiana, of a world—and such a world—into our Union. This would be absorbing the northern States, and rendering them as insignificant in the Union as they ought to be, if, by their own consent, the new measure should be adopted."

Mr. Breckenridge, from Kentucky, made in support of the bill, one of the most eloquent speeches of the session. Alluding to the treaty he said: "If my opinion were of any consequence, I am free to declare that this transaction, from its commencement to its close, not only as to the mode in which it was pursued, but as to the object achieved, is one of the most splendid which the annals of any nation can produce. To acquire an empire of perhaps half the extent of the one now possessed, from the most powerful and warlike nation on earth, without bloodshed, without the oppression of a single individual, without in the least embarrassing the ordinary operations of your finances, and all this through the peaceful forms of negotiation, and in despite too of the opposition of a considerable portion of the community, is an achievement of which the archives of the predecessors, at least, of those now in office, cannot furnish a parallel.

"The gentleman from Massachusetts has told us, that this acquisition will, from its extent, soon prove destructive to the Confederacy.

"This is an old, hackneyed doctrine—that a republic ought not to be too extensive. But the gentleman has assumed two facts, and then reasoned from them: first, that the extent is too great; and secondly, that the country will soon be populated. I would ask, Sir, what is his standard extent for a republic? How does he come at that standard? Our boundary is already extensive. Would his standard extent be violated by including the island of Orleans and the Floridas? I presume not, as all parties seem to think their acquisition, in part or in whole, essential. Why not then acquire territory on the west, as well as on the east side of the Mississippi? Is the goddess of liberty restrained by water courses? Is she governed by geographical limits? Is her dominion on this continent confined to the east side of the Mississippi? So far from believing in the doctrine that a republic ought to be confined within narrow limits, I believe, on the contrary, that the more extensive its dominion, the more safe and more durable it will be. In proportion to the number of hands you intrust the precious blessings of a free government to, in the same

proportion do you multiply the chances for their preservation. I entertain, therefore, no fears for the Confederacy, on account of its extent.   *   *   *
*   *   *   *   *   *   *

"But nothing so remote is more clear to me, than that this acquisition will tend to strengthen the Confederacy. It is evident, as this country has passed out of the hands of Spain, that whether it remained with Spain, or should be acquired by England, its population would have been attempted. Such is the policy of all nations but Spain. Whence would that population come? Certainly not from Europe. It would come almost exclusively from the United States. The question, then, would simply be: *Is the confederacy more in danger from Louisiana, when colonized by American people under American jurisdiction, than when populated by Americans under the control of some foreign, powerful, and rival nation?* Or, in other words, whether it would be safer for the United States to populate this country when and how they pleased, or permit some foreign nation to do it at their expense?"

The adoption of this bill was advocated by Mr. John Quincy Adams, who yet had voted, on the 26th of October, against the passage of the bill to enable the President to take possession of the territories ceded by France to the United States.

"It has been argued," said Mr. Adams, "that the bill ought not to pass, because the treaty itself is an unconstitutional act, or, to use the words of the gentleman from Connecticut, an extra-constitutional act; because it contains engagements which the powers of the Senate were not competent to ratify, the powers of Congress not competent to confirm, and, as two of the gentlemen have contended, not even the legislatures of the number of States requisite to effect an amendment of the Constitution, are adequate to sanction. It is therefore, say they, a nullity; we cannot fulfil our part of its conditions, and on our failure in the performance of any one stipulation, France may consider herself absolved from the obligations of the whole treaty on her. I do not conceive it necessary to enter into the merits of the treaty at this time. The proper occasion for that discussion is past. But, allowing even that this is a case for which the Constitution has not provided, it does not in my mind follow, that the treaty is a nullity, or that its obligations, either on us or on France, must necessarily be cancelled. For my own part, I am free to confess, that the 3d article and more especially the 7th, contain engagements placing us in a dilemma, from which I see no possible mode of extricating ourselves but by an amendment, or rather an addition to the Constitution. The gentleman from Connecticut (Mr. Tracy), both on a former occasion, and in this day's debate, appears to have shown this to demonstration. But what is this more than saying, that the President and Senate have bound the nation to engagements which require the coöperation of more extensive powers than theirs, to carry them into execution? Nothing is more common in the negotiations between nation and nation, than for a minister to agree to and sign articles beyond the extent of his powers. This is what your ministers, in the very case before us, have confessedly done. It is well known that their powers did not authorize them to conclude this treaty; but they acted for the benefit of their country, and this house, by a large majority, has advised to the ratification of their proceedings. Suppose then, not only that the ministers who signed, but the President and Senate who ratified this compact, have exceeded their powers. Nay, suppose even that the majority of States competent to amend the Constitution in other cases, could not amend it in this, without exceeding their powers—and this is the extremest point to which any gentleman on this floor has extended his scruples—suppose all this, and there still remains in the country a power competent to adopt and sanction every part of our engagements, and to carry them entirely into execution. For, notwithstanding the objections and apprehensions of many individuals, of many wise, able and excellent men in various parts of the Union, yet such is the public favor attending the transaction which commenced by the negotiation of this treaty, and which, I hope, will terminate in our full, undisturbed and undisputed possession of the ceded territory, that I firmly believe if an amendment to the Constitution, amply sufficient for the accomplishment of everything for which we have contracted, shall be proposed, as I think it ought, it will be adopted by the legislature of every State in the Union. We can therefore fulfil our part of the convention, and this is all that France has a right to require of us. France never can have the right to come and say: *I am discharged from the obligations of this treaty, because your President and Senate, in ratifying it, exceeded their powers;* for this would be interfering in the internal arrangement of our government. It would be intermeddling in questions with which she has no concern, and which must be settled altogether by ourselves. The only question for France is, whether she has contracted with the department of our government authorized to make treaties; and this being clear, her only right is to require that the conditions stipulated in our name be punctually and faithfully performed. I trust they will be so performed, and will cheerfully lend my hand to every act necessary for the purpose. For I consider the object as of the highest advantage to us; and the gentleman from Kentucky himself (Mr. Breckenridge), who has displayed with so much eloquence the immense importance to the Union of the possession of the ceded territory, cannot carry his ideas further on that subject than I do."

Finally, the bill passed on the 3d of November, by a vote of 26 to 5. Those voting in the negative were: James Hillhouse and Uriah Tracy from Connecticut, Pickering from Massachusetts, Wells and White from Delaware.

Descending from the Senate into the Lower House let us now see what had been done there.

On the 24th of October, Mr. Griswold, from Connecticut, moved the following resolution:

Resolved,—*That the President of the United States be requested to cause to be laid before this house a copy of the treaty between the French Republic and Spain, of the 1st of October, 1800, together with a copy of the deed of cession from Spain, executed in pursuance of the same treaty, conveying Louisiana to France (if any such deed exists); also copies of such correspondence between the government of the United States and the government or minister of Spain (if any such correspondence has taken place), as will show the assent or dissent of Spain to the purchase of Louisiana by the United States; together with copies of such other documents as may be in the department of state, or any other department of this government, tending to ascertain whether the United States have, in fact, acquired any title to the province of Louisiana by the treaties with France, of the 30th of April, 1803.*

He believed it would be admitted that, by the express terms of the treaty, the United States had neither acquired new territory nor new subjects.[*] "It appears," said he, "by that treaty, that Spain stipulated to cede to France, upon certain conditions, the province of Lou-

---

[*] Annals of Congress by Gales and Seaton.

isiana. The treaty between the United States and the French government does not ascertain whether these terms have been complied with by France, or whether the cession has been actually made by Spain to France. All that appears is a *promise* made by Spain to cede. If the terms stipulated by France have not been complied with, and Spain has not delivered the province to France, then it results that France had no title, and of consequence that the United States have acquired no title from France. If this be correct, the consequence will be that we have acquired no new territory or new subjects, and that it is perfectly idle to spend time in passing laws for possessing the territory, and governing the people. This point not being ascertained by the language of the treaty, it may be important to obtain documents that may satisfy the House whether the United States have acquired new territory or new subjects. In the treaty lately concluded with France, the treaty between France and Spain is referred to; only a part of it is copied. The treaty referred to must be a public treaty. In the nature of things it must be the title-deed for the province of Louisiana. The Government must have a copy of it. As there is but a part recited, it is evidently imperfect. It becomes therefore necessary to be furnished with the whole, in order to ascertain the conditions relative to the Duke of Parma; it also becomes necessary to get the deed of cession; for the promise to cede is no cession. This deed of cession, I also presume, is in the possession of Government. It is also important to know under what circumstances Louisiana is to be taken possession of, and whether with the consent of Spain, as she is still possessed of it. If it is to be taken possession of with her consent, the possession will be peaceable, and one kind of provision will be necessary; but if it is to be taken possession of in opposition to Spain, a different provision may be necessary. From these considerations I think it proper in the House to call upon the Executive for information on this point."

This Resolution was violently opposed by the friends of the administration on the ground that, in the present stage of the proceedings respecting the treaty and convention with France concerning Louisiana, it was improper to embarrass the business by an unseasonable* call upon the Executive for papers; that the President had already communicated various information on this subject, in his message on the first day of the session; that additional information was given in his message of the 21st, wherein he told the House that the ratification and exchanges had been made; that this message was accompanied with the instrument of cession and covenant concluded at Paris between the American ministers and the agents of the French Republic; that this information was already on the tables of the House; that the President had put the House in possession of it from his own sense of duty; that he had communicated such intelligence as he had received; and that if he was possessed of anything else needful for the examination of the House, it was to be presumed that the chief magistrate of the Union would have spontaneously imparted it; that although the right of the House to request the President to give copies of the papers mentioned in the Resolution under debate was acknowledged, yet that this opposition to it arose merely from their persuasion that those papers were unnecessary, and that some of them were impossible to be had; that, although it might be agreeable to examine these papers as matters of rational curiosity, or as documents of authentic history, yet that this was not

---

* Annals of Congress by Gales and Seaton.

the time for these secondary researches, however amusing they might be; that graver objects demanded the immediate attention of the House, and that there might be danger in delay; that the operation of the Resolution, if adopted, would certainly be to procrastinate and embarrass; and that it was impossible to discern what good would be wrought at the present time by agreeing to it; that there was an additional reason, and that a very weighty one, for refusing the motion at this stage of the proceedings; that the treaty, by its express terms, "must be ratified in good and due form, and the ratifications exchanged within six months after execution;" that the date of this deed of cession was the 30th of April last; consequently, that the limited time would expire on the 30th of the current month; and that this procrastinating Resolution had been sprung up so late as the 24th; that the treaty of cession had been officially made and officially ratified by the constitutional authorities; that it was now laid before the whole world; and that it would be more honorable for those who did not relish it to come boldly forward, and deny the propriety of carrying the treaty into effect, than to assail it in secret ambushes, than to fight it behind entrenchments and under covered ways, in order to conceal their hostility to that great national measure from the public view.

Mr. Thomas Randolph, from Virginia, opposed the Resolution, "because," said he, " I do not conceive that the nation or the House entertain a doubt of our having acquired new territory and people to govern. Could I for a moment believe that even a minority, respectable as to numbers, required any other evidence of this fact than the extract from the treaty which has just been read, I would readily concur with the gentleman from Connecticut (Mr. Griswold), in asking of the Executive, whether indeed we had a new accession of territory and

of citizens, or, as that gentleman has been pleased to express himself, *subjects to govern.* * * *
* * * * * * *

"The treaty which we are now called upon to sanction, has been hailed by the acclamations of the nation. It is not difficult to foresee, from the opinions manifested in every quarter, that it will receive the cordial approbation of a triumphant majority of this House. If such be the general opinion—if we are not barely satisfied with the terms of this treaty, but lost in astonishment at the all-important benefits which we have so cheaply acquired, to what purpose do we ask information respecting the detail of the negotiation? Has any one ventured to hint disapprobation of the conduct of the ministers who have effected this negotiation? Has any one insinuated that our interests have been betrayed? If, then, we are satisfied as to the terms of the treaty, and with the conduct of our ministers abroad, let us pass the laws necessary for carrying it into effect. To refuse—to delay, upon the plea now offered, is to jeopardize the best interests of the Union. Shall we take exception to our own title? Shall we refuse the offered possession? Shall this refusal proceed from those who so lately affirmed, that we ought to pursue this very object at every national hazard? I should rather suppose the eagerness of gentlemen would be ready to outstrip the forms of law in making themselves masters of this country, than that, now, when it is offered to our grasp, they should display an unwillingness, or at least an indifference, for that which so lately was all important to them. After the message which the President has sent us, to inquire of him if indeed we have acquired any new subjects, as the gentleman expresses it, who render the exercise of our Legislative functions necessary, would be nothing less than a mockery of them, of this solemn business, and of ourselves."

In the course of the lengthy debate to which this "Resolution" gave rise, various amendments were proposed, and, at last, the final question was taken on the adoption of the original motion amended as follows:

Resolved—*That the President of the United States be requested to cause to be laid before the House, a copy of the treaty between the French Republic and Spain, of the 1st of October,* 1800, *together with a copy of any instrument in possession of the Executive, showing that the Spanish government has ordered the province of Louisiana to be delivered to the Commissary or other agent of the French government.*

The question was lost by a vote of 57 yeas to 59 nays.

On the 25th (October), the House resolved itself into a Committee of the Whole to take into consideration the motion to adopt the necessary measures to carry the treaty of cession into effect.

In opposition to this motion, Mr. Griswold from Connecticut observed: " By the 3d article of the treaty it is declared—*That the inhabitants of the ceded territory shall be incorporated in the Union of the United States, and admitted as soon as possible, according to the principles of the Constitution, to the enjoyment of all the rights, advantages, and immunities of citizens.* It is, perhaps, somewhat difficult to ascertain the precise effect which it was intended to give the words which have been used in this stipulation. It is, however, clear, that it was intended to incorporate the inhabitants of the ceded territory into the Union, by the treaty itself, or to pledge the faith of the nation that such an incorporation should take place within a reasonable time. It is pro per, therefore, to consider the question with a reference to both constructions.

"It is, in my opinion, scarcely possible for any gentleman on this floor to advance the assertion that the President and Senate may add to the numbers of the Union by a treaty whenever they please, or, in the words of the treaty, may *incorporate in the Union of the United States* a foreign nation who, from interest or ambition, may wish to become a member of our government. Such a power would be directly repugnant to the original compact between the States, and a violation of the principles on which that compact was formed. It has been already well observed that the Union of the States was formed on the principle of a copartnership, and it would be absurd to suppose that the agents of the parties, who have been appointed to execute the business of the compact, in behalf of the principals, could admit a new partner, without the consent of the parties themselves. And yet, if the first construction is assumed, such must be the case under this Constitution, and the President and Senate may admit at will any foreign nation into this copartnership without the consent of the States.

"The government of this country is formed by a Union of States, and the people have declared that the Constitution was established: *to form a more perfect union of the United States.* The United States here mentioned cannot be mistaken. They were the States then in existence, and such other States as should be formed within the then limits of the Union, conformably to the provisions of the Constitution. Every measure, therefore, which tends to infringe the perfect union of the States herein described, is a violation of the first sentiment expressed in the Constitution. The incorporation of a foreign nation into the Union, so far from tending to preserve the Union, is a direct inroad upon it; it destroys the perfect union contemplated between the original parties, by interposing an alien and a stranger to share the powers of government with them

"The Government of the United States was not formed for the purpose of distributing its principles and advantages to foreign nations. It was formed with the sole view of securing those blessings *to ourselves and our posterity*. It follows from these principles that no power can reside in any public functionary to contract any engagement, or to pursue any measure, which shall change the Union of the States. Nor was it necessary that any restrictive clause should have been inserted in the Constitution to restrain the public agents from exercising these extraordinary powers, because the restriction grows out of the nature of the government. The President, with the advice of the Senate, has undoubtedly the right to form treaties, but in exercising these powers, he cannot barter away the Constitution, or the rights of particular States. It is easy to conceive that it must have been considered very important by the original parties to the Constitution, that the limits of the United States should not be extended. The Government having been formed by a union of States, it is supposable that the fear of an undue or preponderating influence, in certain parts of this Union, must have had great weight in the minds of those who might apprehend that such an influence might ultimately injure the interests of the States to which they belonged; and, although they might concert to become parties of the Union as it was then formed, it is highly probable they would never have consented to such a connexion, if a new world was to be thrown into the scale, to weigh down the influence which they might otherwise possess in the national councils.

"From this view of the subject, I have been persuaded that the framers of the Constitution never intended that a power should reside in the President and Senate to form a treaty by which a foreign nation and people shall be incorporated into the Union, and that this treaty, so far as it stipulates for such an incorporation, is void.

"But it has been said that the treaty does not in fact incorporate the people of the ceded territory into the Union, but stipulates that they shall be incorporated and admitted according to the principles of the Federal Constitution. Or, in other words, the treaty only pledges the faith of the nation that such an incorporation shall take place. On this point I will observe, that there is no difference in principle between a direct incorporation by the words of a treaty, and a stipulation that an incorporation shall take place; because, if the faith of the nation is pledged in the latter case, the incorporation must take place, and it is of no consequence whether the treaty gives the incorporation, or produces the law which gives it; in both cases, the treaty produces the effect; and the question still returns: Does there exist, under the Constitution, a power to incorporate into the Union by a treaty or by a law, a foreign nation or people? If it shall be admitted that no such power exists without an amendment to the Constitution, and if it shall be said that the treaty-making power may stipulate for such an amendment, it will be a sufficient answer to say: That no power can reside in any of the national authorities to stipulate with a foreign nation for an amendment to the Constitution. The constituted authorities of our Union have been created to execute the Constitution, not to change or stipulate for changing it, and they can in no case lay the States under the smallest obligation to make the smallest change. Stipulations, therefore, of this nature, which create no obligation, are void. * *

* * * * * * *

"Although I am unwilling to detain the Committee at this late hour, and desire not to delay the wishes of the majority, yet I must be permitted again to refer the Committee to the 7th article of the treaty. This article declares, that the ships of France and Spain, together with their cargoes, being the produce or manufacture of those countries, shall be admitted into the ports of the ceded territory on the same terms, in regard to duties, with American ships. It is certainly worth the consideration of the Committee, whether this article is consistent with the provisions of the Constitution. As our laws now stand, the ships of France and Spain are liable to an extra tonnage duty, and their cargoes to a duty of ten per cent. advance, when arriving in the Atlantic ports. The treaty declares that, in the ports of the ceded territory, this extra duty of import and tonnage shall cease. The treaty does not, and probably cannot, repeal the law which lays this extra duty in the Atlantic States, but those duties must still be collected. The constitution, however, declares in the 8th section of the First Article that: '*all duties, imposts, and excises, shall be uniform throughout the United States,*' and in the 9th section of the same Article, it is said that: '*no preference shall be given, by any regulation of commerce, or revenue, to the ports of one State over those of another.*' By the treaty, however, the uniformity of duties is destroyed, and, by this regulation of commerce contained in the treaty, a preference is certainly given to the ports of the ceded territory over those of the other States. Gentlemen who advocate the constitutionality of the treaty will scarcely say that the ceded territory is no part of the United States, and not embraced by the provisions of the Constitution, because such an assertion, while it avoided one difficulty, would plunge them into another equally fatal, and prove that the third Article is void and, of course, that the cession itself is a nullity."

Another gentleman from Connecticut (Mr. Dana), declared that if the inhabitants of the ceded territory were now, or should hereafter be, admitted into the Union, it would be a violation of that clause of the Constitution which relates to the establishment of an uniform rule of naturalization, since those people would be converted from foreigners to citizens, not in the mode prescribed by the naturalization laws.

Mr. Gaylord Griswold, from New York, denied that there existed in the United States, as such, a capacity to acquire territory, and contended that, by the constitution, they were restricted to the limits which existed at the time of its adoption. He said: "In the 3d section of the 4th article of the Constitution we read: '*New States may be admitted by the Congress into this Union.*' Congress therefore may admit new States, but, according to my construction of this article, this power is confined to the territory belonging to the United States at the formation of the Constitution—to the territory then within the United States. Existing territory, not within the limits of any particular States, may be incorporated in the Union. I maintain, therefore, that the power to *incorporate new territory* does not exist; and that, if it did exist, it belonged to the Legislature, and not the Executive, to incorporate it in the Union. If this were the case, it was the duty of the House to resist the usurped power by the Executive."

The other speakers on this side of the question travelled over the same ground, and paraphrased the same arguments, asserting that if the United States could acquire territory, it was not to make it a part of the Confederacy as a State, but to hold it as a colony for ever, or as a sort of subordinate dependency.

In reply, Mr. Thomas Randolph, from Virginia, said: "That not only did the Constitution not describe any particular boundary, beyond which the United States could not extend, but that their boundary was unsettled on their north-eastern, southern and north-western frontiers at the time of its adoption—nay, that they were without limits beyond the sources of the Mississippi; that the United States had the undeniable power of setting limits, and therefore of extending them; that, in proof of that power, the recent acquisitions on the side of Canada and at the Natchez could be cited; that Congress had expressed, in their own acts, a solemn recognition of the principle, that the United States in their federative capacity might acquire, and that they had acquired, territory; that there had been no usurpation of power by the Executive on this occasion; that if the Government of the United States possessed the constitutional power to acquire territory from foreign States, the Executive, as the organ by which the Union communicates with such States, must be the prime agent in negotiating such an acquisition, and then initiate the business to Congress by message; that he had so done in the present instance, and therefore had not been guilty of any invasion of the privileges of that body; that if the United States could acquire territory by conquest, which could not be denied, they could by purchase, as that power was a necessary appendage to all independent governments; that the alleged preference given to New Orleans over the other parts of the Union did not present a constitutional difficulty, because it must be considered as the price paid for the ceded territory; that by the treaty no preference was given to one State over another, because Louisiana was a Territory and not a State; that a complete discretion was left to the United States as to the time and manner of incorporating that territory into the Union, and that it was not necessary to do so within the twelve years during which France and Spain were to enjoy the privileges granted by the treaty; that the preference of American ships over foreign ships was a legal regulation; and that those who were so tender with regard to the Constitution might have it in their power entirely to get rid of the constitutional difficulty, by taking off from the ships of Spain and France such duties as were higher than the duties paid by American vessels, so as to put all the American ports on the same level with New Orleans.

"When I say this," continued Mr. Thomas Randolph, "I speak for them, and not for myself; nor shall I move to take off these heavy duties, as I do not feel the force of the constitutional objections urged by gentlemen. The article of the treaty, so often quoted, shows that no preference is given to one port over another. Yet, by turning to our statute books, it will be perceived that, at present, there are some ports entitled to benefits which other ports do not enjoy; that they are set apart for particular objects; and particularly for the entry of articles brought from beyond the Cape of Good Hope. According, therefore, to the doctrine of this day, this is a violation of the Constitution."

Mr. Smilie, from Pennsylvania, thought that the right of annexing territory was incidental to all governments; that such a power must be vested in some of the departments of the government of the United States; that clearly it was not vested in the States individually, as they were expressly divested of that right by being deprived of the power of forming treaties and making war; but that it could reside in the General Government only.

Mr. Rodney, from Delaware, said: "That, by the Constitution, Congress had power to lay and collect taxes, duties, imposts and excises, to pay the debts and provide for the common defence and general welfare of the United States; and that within the fair meaning of this general provision was included the power of increasing our territory, *if necessary for the general welfare or common defence.*"

Mr. John Randolph, from Virginia, said that a sense of duty alone could have induced him to rise at that late hour. But he wished to call the attention of the Committee to a stipulation in the treaty of London. Here Mr. Randolph read an extract from the 3rd article of that treaty, whereby the United States were pledged not to impose on imports in British vessels from the British territories in America, adjacent to the United States, any higher duties than would be paid upon such imports, if brought into the American Atlantic ports in American bottoms. "In this case," he said, "gentlemen could not avail themselves of the distinction taken by his friend from Maryland (Mr. Nicholson), between a territory and a state, even if they were so disposed—since the ports in question were ports of a state. The ports of New York on the Lakes were as much parts of that State as the city of New York itself; they had their customhouse officers, were governed by the same regulations as other ports, and duties were exacted at them; yet, under the article of the British treaty which had just been read, British bottoms would and did enter *them* subject to no higher duties than were paid by American bottoms in the Atlantic ports. Mr. Randolph said that he did not mean to affirm that this exemption made by the treaty of London was constitutional, so long as a distinction prevailed between American and British bottoms in other ports. He had never given a vote to carry that treaty into effect—but he hoped the gentlemen from Connecticut (Mr. Griswold and Mr. Dana), both of whom he believed had done so—one of whom at least he knew had been a conspicuous advocate of that treaty—he hoped that gentleman (Mr. Griswold) would inform the Committee how he got over the constitutional objection to this article of the treaty of London, which he had endeavored to urge against that under discussion. How could the gentleman, with the opinion he now holds, agree to admit British bottoms into *certain ports*, on the same terms on which American bottoms were admitted into American ports generally? Thereby making that *very difference*—giving that very *preference* to those particular ports of certain states, which he tells us cannot constitutionally be given to the port of New Orleans,—although that port is not within any state, and, if his (Mr. Griswold's) doctrine be correct, not even within the United States!

"Another gentleman from Connecticut," continued Mr. John Randolph, "had declared that if the inhabitants of the ceded territory were now, or should hereafter be admitted into the Union, it would be a violation of that clause of the Constitution which relates to the establishment of an uniform rule of naturalization, since those people will be converted from foreigners to citizens, not in the mode prescribed by our naturalization law. I wish to know in what manner the subjects of Great Britain settled around our Western posts were admitted to the privilege of citizenship. Whether it was not done by treaty, and not in the mode prescribed by law? How did the people at Natchez become entitled to the rights of citizens? Although born out of our allegiance, the moment our government was established over them, did they not possess of right a security for their lives and property? Could they not demand trial by jury in case of criminal prosecution? When I speak of their acquiring the rights of citizens, I do not mean in the full extent in which they are enjoyed by citizens of any one of the particular States, since they possessed not the right of self-government, but those rights of personal liberty, of personal security and of property, which are among the dearest privileges of our citizens. A stipulation to incorporate the ceded territory does not imply that we are bound ever to admit them to the non-qualified enjoyment of the privileges of citizenship. It is a covenant to incorporate them into the Union—not on the footing of the original States, or of States created under the Constitution—but to extend to them, according to the principles of the Constitution, the rights and immunities of citizens, being those rights and immunities of jury trial, liberty of conscience, &c., &c., which every citizen may challenge, whether he be a citizen of an individual state, or of a territory subordinate to and dependent on those States in their corporate capacity. In the mean time, they are to be protected in the enjoyment of their existing rights. There is no stipulation, however, that they shall ever be formed into one or more States."

The Committee now rose, the Speaker resumed the chair, and the following resolutions were reported:

1°—Resolved, *That provision ought to be made for carrying into effect the treaty and conventions concluded at Paris on the 30th of April, 1803, between the United States of America and the French Republic.*

2°—Resolved, *That so much of the message of the President, of the 21st, as relates to the establishment of a provisional government over the territory acquired by the United States, in virtue of the treaty and conventions lately negotiated with the French Republic, be referred to a Select Committee; and that they report by bill or otherwise.*

3°—Resolved, *That so much of the aforesaid conventions as relates to the payment by the United States of sixty millions of francs to the French Republic, and to the payment by the United States of debts due by France to citizens of the United States, be referred to the Committee of Ways and Means.*

These resolutions were carried by a vote of 90 yeas to 25 nays. The nays were: 1 from Vermont, 9 from Massachusetts, 5 from Connecticut, 3 from New York, 2 from New Hampshire, 1 from Maryland, and 4 from Virginia.

On the 28th, the bill from the Senate entitled: "An Act to enable the President of the United States to take possession of the territories ceded by France to the United States, &c., with the amendments proposed by the House, was passed by a vote of 89 yeas to 23 nays. It read as follows:—

Sect. 1.—*Be it enacted, that the President of the United States be, and he is hereby, authorized to take possession of and occupy the territory ceded by France to the United States, by the treaty concluded at Paris, on the 30th of April last, between the two nations; and that he may, for that purpose, and in order to maintain in the said territory the authority of the United States, employ any part of the army and navy of the United States, and of the force authorized by an act passed the 3d day of March last, entitled: "An Act directing a detachment from the Militia of the United States, and for erecting certain arsenals," which he may deem necessary; and so much of the sum appropriated by the said act as may be necessary is hereby appropriated for the purpose of carrying this act into effect; to be applied under the direction of the President of the United States.*

Sect. 2.—*And be it further enacted, that, until the expiration of the present session of Congress, or unless provision be sooner made for the temporary government of the said territories, all the military, civil and judicial*

WHAT BILLS FINALLY ADOPTED.

powers exercised by the officers of the existing government of the same, shall be vested in such person and persons, and shall be exercised in such manner, as the President of the United States shall direct, for maintaining and protecting the inhabitants of Louisiana in the full enjoyment of their liberty, property and religion.

On the 29th, the House adopted by a vote of 85 yeas to 7 nays, " an Act authorizing the creation of a stock to the amount of eleven millions two hundred and fifty thousand dollars, for the purpose of carrying the treaty of cession into effect," &c., &c.

Such were the congressional proceedings on this **memorable occasion.**

CHAPTER X.

SALCEDO'S ADMINISTRATION.

1801 to 1803.

I HAVE endeavored, in the two preceding chapters, to relate with fidelity, and with as much condensation as the nature of the subject would admit, all the transactions relative to Louisiana, which, in 1802 and 1803, had occurred in the United States, France and Spain. I shall now call the attention of the reader to the events which, in the meantime, had happened in the colony itself, and those which were the result of the transactions I have recorded. Thus, on the 26th of November, 1802, the Marquis de Casa Irujo, the Minister of Spain at Washington, had written to the Intendant, Morales, and represented to him the fatal consequences of his having closed the port of New Orleans to the Americans as a place of deposit, and of his having refused them the free navigation of the Mississippi, "giving," said the Minister, "to the citizens* of the United States good cause for claiming indemnities in return for the serious damages which their commerce will inevitably suffer." On the 15th of January, 1803, Morales answered with some tartness: "That the orders alluded to by the

---

* Dando á los ciudadanos de los Estados Unidos lugar á reclamaciones de indemnizacion por los graves perjuicios que indispensablemente han de recibir en su comercio.

Minister emanated solely from the Intendancy, and had been issued notwithstanding the opposition of the Governor, with whom he, the Intendant, had, in consequence thereof, had some difficulties; and that he assumed the whole responsibility of the measure, the object of which had been to strike at the root of the infinite irregularities and abuses, which were the result of *the right of deposit* granted to the Americans at New Orleans."*

It appears from a despatch of the same officer, that the revenue accruing to the King's treasury, from every source in the colony, amounted, in 1802, to $121,041. "The revenue," observed the Intendant, "would have been much more considerable, if it had not been for the contraband trade carried on by the flatboats which come down the river."

On the first day of March, says Judge Martin in his History of Louisiana, the King disapproved of the order of Morales, prohibiting the introduction and deposit of goods, wares and merchandise from the United States in the port of New Orleans, and ordered that the United States should continue to enjoy their right of deposit in New Orleans, without prejudice of his right to substitute some other spot on the banks of the Mississippi.

On the 23rd of the same month, the Cabildo had completed all the preparations necessary to receive and supply with provisions the large body of troops expected with General Victor. On the next day, by the arrival of a vessel from Havre, the colonists were put in possession of the documents which gave them information of the new form of government intended for Louisiana. Its principal officers were: a Captain-General, with a salary of 70,000 francs; a Lieutenant-Captain-General,

---

* Que el (El intendente) habia tomado aquella medida y aceptaba para si solo la responsabilidad, deseando cortar de raiz los **infinitos obstaculos y abusos que** resultaban del dicho deposito.

who was to command in Upper Louisiana, with a salary of 20,000 francs; two Brigadier-Generals, each with 15,000 francs a year, and two Adjutant-Commandants, with 9,000 francs each. The Colonial Prefect had a salary of 50,000 francs. Next to the Colonial Prefect in the civil department, came the Commissary of Justice.

"The Captain-General* was commander-in-chief of the land and naval forces, and had the care of the exterior and interior defence of the colony. He provisorily filled vacancies in military offices, according to the order of advancement, as far as the grade of chief of division or squadron (chef de division ou d'escadre), and proposed to the Minister proper persons to fill higher grades. He delivered passports, regulated the bearing of arms, and corresponded with the governors of other colonies, whether belonging to allies, neutrals or enemies. With the Colonial Prefect he regulated the works to be done on the fortifications, and the new roads to be opened; and, finally, exercised all the powers formerly granted to governors-general. He was forbidden to interfere with the attributions of the Colonial Prefect, or of the Commissary of Justice; but was authorized to require from either of them information on any matter relative to the service. Power was given him to suspend provisorily the execution of laws, in whole or in part, on his responsibility, after having consulted the Colonial Prefect, or the Commissary of Justice, according to the nature of the case.

"Copies of every deliberation were to be sent yearly to the Minister.

"Vacant lands were to be granted by the Captain-General and Colonial Prefect; but, in case of disagreement, the opinion of the former was to prevail.

---

* Martin's History of Louisiana, vol. ii., p. 182.

"Vacancies in the departments of the Colonial Prefect and Commissary of Justice were to be filled by the Captain-General on their nomination; but no appointment was final until confirmed by the First Consul.

"In case of the absence of the Captain-General, he was to be represented by the Colonial Prefect, or by the highest military officer.

"The Colonial Prefect's powers extended to the administration of the finances, the general accountability and destination of all officers of administration. He was exclusively charged with the police of the colony, including all that related to taxes, receipts and expenditures, the Custom House, the pay of the troops, the public stores, agriculture, navigation, commerce, the census, the suppression of contraband trade, the police of slaves, highways, levees, public instruction and worship, the press, and generally all the powers formerly exercised by Intendants and ordaining Commissaries (Commissaires ordonnateurs). In the assessment of taxes he was to consult three merchants and three planters. In case of absence, he was to be represented by the officer of administration next in rank.

"The Commissary of Justice had the superintendence of all the courts of justice and their ministerial officers: he was to have an eye to the regular administration of justice, the safety and salubrity of jails as well as the conduct of officers and clerks, and was intrusted with the police of vagrants. He might preside and vote in any court of justice, he was to require monthly statements of every case tried from the President and clerks of each court, and he communicated them to the Captain-General. He was authorized to make rules for the administration of justice, and, with the consent of the Captain-General, to order them to be observed. Agents of government were not suable for any matter relating to their offices.

nor could any citizen in the public service be arrested without the Commissary's *fiat*, and said Commissary was to give an account of his proceedings in this respect to the Minister. He was to prepare a civil and criminal code, and submit it to the Captain-General and Colonial Prefect for their examination, and transmit it, with the procès-verbal of their deliberations thereon, to the Minister." Such were the principal outlines of a government which was destined to be never carried into execution.

On the 26th of March, the Colonial Prefect Laussat arrived at New Orleans, and was received with the customary honors on such occasions, by the Spanish Governor and Intendant, round whom had assembled, for the reception of the French Dignitary, all the Clergy of New Orleans, and the principal officers of the regular troops, of the militia, and of the civil administration. The circumstance called for an address from the new ruler of the land, and he expressed those conciliating sentiments which were expected to flow of course from his lips. The French Government,* he said, would have but one object in view, which was the prosperity of the colony; this had been the sole aim of the French Consul in making this important acquisition; order was to be rigidly maintained; laws and customs were to be respected; treaties with the Indian nations were to be observed; and no change was intended in the public worship and in the organization of the clergy, over which the most liberal protection was to be extended. Notwithstanding the suavity of these promises, a good deal of excitement prevailed in the province, and some there were, who, considering the course pursued by the French in St. Domingo, entertained considerable fears

---

* Martin's History of Louisiana.

as to the security of the tenure of a certain kind of property. Those fears were made more keen by the discovery of a conspiracy among the colored population, at the instigation and under the leadership of an American, named Sopper. This fact is related, and the name thus spelt, in a despatch from Morales, of the 29th of March, to the Spanish government.

"The Louisianians," says Barbé Marbois in his History of Louisiana, "had reason to fear for themselves the calamities which had been, for many years, ruining the other colonies of France. St. Domingo was the most agitated and unfortunate of all. The colonists repeated with horror, at New Orleans, these words which the First Consul had caused to be proclaimed, in his name, in the revolted colony, and which were addressed to all classes. "*Inhabitants of St. Domingo, whatever may be your color or your origin, you are all free; all equal in the eyes of God and the Republic.*" General Leclerc, on his arrival in the colony, had said: "*I promise liberty to all the inhabitants.*" * * * *
* * * * * * *

"Some of the refugee colonists of St. Domingo had brought a part of their negroes to Louisiana, and were therefore, secretly, far from desiring another removal, or participating in the views of those who had lost every thing. They easily made the Louisianians acquainted with the danger that they would incur, in case the French Republic, as the supreme Legislative power, should one day proclaim manumission and freedom in this colony * * * * From all those disasters the Louisianians expected to be preserved, if the sovereignty of the Catholic King was not transferred to the French Republic."

If these facts had been taken into due consideration an eye-witness, speaking of the sentiments which were manifested on the occasion of the arrival and reception of Laussat, would not have been as much surprised as he was. "Every one," said he,* "will be astonished to learn, that a people of French descent have received without emotion and without any apparent interest a French magistrate, who comes to us, accompanied by his young and beautiful family, and preceded by the public esteem. Nothing has been able to diminish the alarms which his mission causes. His proclamations have been heard by some with sadness, and by the greater part of the inhabitants with the same indifference as the beat of the drum is listened to, when it announces the escape of a slave or a sale at auction."

One of Laussat's first cares was to examine the fortifications which, eleven years before, had been erected by the Baron de Carondelet, and this is the description which he gave of them to the minister Decrès: "The fortifications have never been kept up, and are falling into decay; the ditches are filling up; the terraces are crumbling down; the palisades are wanting, or rotten; the bridges have given way, or consist only of one or two beams; the gates are off their hinges, and are lying on the ground. It had lately been proposed to the King of Spain to raze or at least greatly to reduce these works, as being useless and even mischievous, because the fevers which every year carry off the most valuable portion of the population of this city, date from the time when were dug round it those ditches which are always full of stagnating water. The precarious condition in which the Spanish government found itself has alone prevented it from deciding on this matter, which is now left to the consideration of the French Government.

"With regard to public edifices, those which we find

---

* Barbé Marbois's History of Louisiana.

here are the same which had been left by the French. The Spaniards have not made any solid and permanent constructions. They contented themselves with renting, or, when compelled to do so, with erecting wooden edifices, which are of no value. A rich Spaniard, however, (Andres Almonaster) has built up with brick and mortar a charity hospital, a town hall, and a church."

As to the administration of justice under the Spanish Government, Laussat thus expressed his opinion in a despatch of the 24th of May:

"I will now proceed to say how justice is administered here, which is worse than in Turkey.

"All judgments are given in the name of the Governor, except in matters appertaining to the revenue, in which the authority of the Intendant is supreme.

"The Governor signs his name as a mere formality, his signature is a matter of course and entitles him to a fee, and this is one of the branches of the contingent salary allowed to his office.

"But at the elbow of the Governor is what is called an auditor, who is a sort of Lieutenant-Governor, and the Governor cannot decide on any thing, except in military matters, before having taken the advice of this individual, who is, in fact, the sole judge both in civil and criminal cases. Assessors are not even required to act with him as assistants or adjuncts. A power which a justice of the peace in France could not exercise in relation to an amount of twenty dollars, is allowed to the auditor in New Orleans as to any amount. For these reasons, his judgments are not relied on, and command no respect. Whether they be correct or not, they never fail to be the object of the most shameful suspicions.

"At times, it is a capital accusation, the character of which is suddenly changed, or which, after having been permitted to be kept aside and forgotten for months, disappears for ever from the docket. Frequently, there is to be no end to a lawsuit, and it is destined to be eternal, because the auditor has got possession of all the papers, and will never give them up.

"Besides, suits are so expensive, that a good many individuals prefer to sacrifice their interests, however considerable they may be, than to maintain them at law.

"The right of appeal to Cuba and to Madrid, is a slow and ruinous remedy, &c., &c.

Laussat's statement is unfortunately confirmed by a communication from Daniel Clark, the United States' consul at New Orleans, addressed in 1803 to the Department of State at Washington: "The auditor of war," said he, "and the assessors of government and intendancy, have always been corrupt; and to them only may be attributed the mal-administration of justice, as the Governor and other judges, who are unacquainted with law, seldom dare to act contrary to the opinions they give. Hence, when the auditor, or assessor, was bribed, suitors had to complain of delays and infamous decisions. All the officers plunder when the opportunity offers; they are all venal. A bargain can be made with the governor, intendant, judge, or collector, down to the constable; and if ever an officer be displeased at an offer of money, it is not at the offer or offerer, but because imperious circumstances compel him to refuse, and the offerer acquires a degree of favor which encourages him to make a second offer, when a better opportunity is presented." This is a frightful picture. That there were but too many cases of corruption seems to be true, but that it should have been systematically carried to the extent here described by Laussat and Daniel Clark, is somewhat rebutted by other testimony, and not confirmed by living witnesses of great respectability.

Immediately after his arrival, Laussat obtained from

the Intendant, that French vessels, on their coming into the colony and on their going out, be put exactly on the same footing with Spanish vessels.

On the right of deposit which had been granted by the Spaniards to the Americans, Laussat said, in a despatch to his Government: "The consequence of this privilege is, that the Anglo-Americans can keep their goods and effects in deposit at New Orleans, without paying anything else than storage. So far, this deposit has been effected on the single declaration of the owners of the goods when putting them in the stores of individuals, whereby the profits of the storage accrued only to the merchants in whose hands the merchandise was placed. But the Government made nothing by it, because in an open city and in an open province like these, every sort of fraudulent importation may be safely carried on. To remedy this evil, all that is necessary is, that the goods of the Americans be deposited in the stores of the Government, out of which they would not be taken without its knowledge; or, in conformity with the right reserved by Spain to establish the place of deposit elsewhere after the expiration of a certain time, should it be required by her interests, it would be proper to designate, instead of New Orleans, the Balize, or some other untenable spot." It appears by this document that the French Prefect, Laussat, was quite as hostile to the continuation of this privilege in favor of the Americans, as the Spanish Intendant, Morales.

Struck with the necessity of increasing as soon as possible the population of the boundless province he had been sent to govern, Laussat hastened to write to Chaptal, the Minister of the Interior, that it was of the utmost importance to transmit annually to Louisiana, at least from one thousand to twelve hundred families, from the departments contiguous to Switzerland, the Rhine, or the

Low Countries, "because," said he, "the emigrants from the southern provinces are good for nothing."

A few days after his arrival, Laussat had issued a proclamation in the name of the French Republic.

This document begins, says Judge Martin, in his History of Louisiana, "by stating that the separation of Louisiana from France marked in the annals of the latter one of the most shameful eras under a weak and corrupt Government, after an ignominious war and dishonorable peace. With this unnatural abandonment by the mother country, the love, loyalty, and heroic courage of the people of Louisiana formed a noble contrast, with which every heart in France was now moved, and would long preserve the remembrance of. The French still remembered that a portion of the inhabitants of Louisiana were their descendants, with the same blood running in their veins. As soon as France, by a prodigious succession of triumphs in the late revolution, had recovered her own freedom and glory, she turned her eyes towards Louisiana, the retrocession of which signalized her first peace. But the period was not yet arrived—it was necessary that a man, who is a stranger to nothing that is national, great, magnanimous, or just; who, to the most distinguished talent for conquering, adds the rare one of obtaining for his conquests the happiest results, and who, by the ascendency of his character, at once strikes terror into his enemies and inspires his allies with confidence—whose expansive mind discovered at once the true interests of his country, and was bent on restoring to France her pristine grandeur and her lost possessions—should accomplish this important work.

"This man," said the Prefect, "presides over the destinies of France and Louisiana, to insure their felicity. In the latter nothing more is necessary than to improve the advantages of which nature has been so prodigal towards her.

"He observed that it was the intention of the Government, to live in peace and amity with the neighboring Indians, and to protect the commerce of the colony, encourage its agriculture, people its deserts, promote labor and industry, respect property, opinions, and habits, protect public worship, preserve the empire of the laws, amend them slowly and with the light of experience only, maintain a regular police, introduce permanent order and economy in every branch of the administration, and tighten the bonds which a common origin and a similarity of manners had already established between the colony and the mother country.

"After a short eulogy of the two high magistrates with whom he was associated, and of the officers who had hitherto governed the colony under the authority of Spain, whom he said that the French officers would endeavor to imitate, he concluded with the assurance that the devotion of the people of Louisiana to the French Republic, their gratitude for those by whom they were reunited to it, and the spectacle of their prosperity, were the rewards which he aspired to, and should endeavor to deserve by a zeal which would know no limits in the fulfilment of his duties."

These were honied words indeed—promising halcyon days; but not many changes of the moon had happened since they were uttered, when the *magnanimous, just* and *powerful* government of Bonaparte, after *a prodigious succession of triumphs, and after having recovered for France her freedom and glory*, did exactly what had been done by the *shameful, weak* and *corrupt government* of Louis XV., after an *ignominious war* and *dishonorable peace*. Bonaparte had been as anxious to *sell* what he could not keep, as Louis had been to *give* what was an expensive encumbrance to him. There is no doubt that France, when ceding Louisiana to the United States, acted wisely for herself and beneficially for that province. But it is not the less true, that the similarity of the policy which she was compelled to pursue, with that which her representative had so bitterly censured, shows the imprudence of vituperation, particularly in connexion with any thing dependent on the political mutability of human affairs.

A large number of planters, among whom were A. Trouard, De Pain, Manuel Andry, Jacques de la Groue, Noel Perret, P. St. Martin, Louis Foucher, Charles Perret, &c., replied to Laussat's proclamation by a spirited address, in which they declared that their most ardent wish had always been to resume the glorious name of Frenchmen, and that the proclamation which announced to them that their long cherished hope was gratified had *filled their souls with the delirium of extreme felicity.* " But," said they, " we should be unworthy of what is to us a subject of so much pride, if we did not imitate you in the example you have given us by your expressing such generous sentiments, and if we did not acknowledge that we have no cause of complaint against the Spanish Government. We have never groaned under the iron yoke of an oppressive despotism. It is true that the time was, when our unfortunate kinsmen reddened with their blood the soil which they wished to preserve for France. A weak and unfeeling Government aimed at depriving us of that cherished possession. But the calamities which were inflicted upon us were due to the atrocious soul of a foreigner (the Irishman O'Reilly) and to an extreme breach of faith. O plaintive shades, if you still haunt the spot which witnessed your martyrdom, forget your sorrows ! Your descendants, your friends, are called back to the bosom of their beloved mother. Their grateful tears will wash out the traces of the blood you have shed. Long ago, we proved to the Spaniards, in the plains of Baton Rouge, of Mobile and Pensacola, that we did not consider them as the accomplices of those atrocities. We have become bound together by family connexions and by the bonds of friendship. Let them have the untrammelled enjoyment of all the property they may own on the soil which has become the land of freedom, and let us share with them, like brothers, the blessings of our new position."

The inhabitants of New Orleans presented also an address to Laussat. It was signed by M. Fortier, Cavalier Sr., Etienne Boré, Labatut, M. Lefebvre, G. Debuys, J. Livaudais, P. Derbigny, N. Broutin, St. Avid, E. Plauché, L. Chabot, B. Durel, A. Garidel, F. Blache, S. Hiriart, J. B. Verret, R. Ducros, and many others. It read thus:

"Citizen Prefect,—France has done justice to our sentiments, when believing in the unalterable attachment we have preserved for her. Thirty-four years of foreign domination have not weakened in our hearts the sacred love of country, and our joy in returning to our national flag is equal in intensity to the grief we felt when we were forcibly separated from it. Happy are the colonists of Louisiana who have lived long enough to see their reunion to France, which they had never ceased to desire, and which now satisfies their utmost wishes!

"In an age so fruitful in astonishing events, it is unquestionable that some have occurred, which are greater, more imposing and more memorable, but perhaps none offer a spectacle as interesting and as affecting as that of victorious and triumphant France holding out a protecting hand to her children cast away, of old, from her bosom, in consequence of the weakness and prevarication of a pusillanimous government, and calling them to a share in the fruits of a glorious peace, which has terminated in so brilliant a manner the most bloody and terrible revolution.

"You have signalized, Citizen Prefect, the return of the French Government, by strikingly authenticating its beneficent views. Your proclamation, in announcing them to us, has filled us with gratitude for the parental care of France. The blessings of our union with the French Republic begin already to be felt. The fortunate selection of the patriotic chiefs whom she has designated to govern us, and whose honorable reputation has already reached the colony, the choice troops she sends for our protection, are sure pledges of the prosperity which she has in store for us. In return we tender her our zeal, obedience and love, and we swear to prove ourselves ever worthy of being incorporated with her.

"Perhaps France would attach less value to the homage of our fidelity, if she saw us relinquishing without any regret our allegiance to the sovereign who has loaded us with favors, during all the time he has reigned over us. Such culpable indifference is not to be found in our hearts, in which our regret at our separating from him occupies as much space as our joy in securing the nationality we had lost, and it is by keeping up an eternal recollection of his favors, that we intend to show ourselves worthy of the parental attachment and of the benefits which we expect from the French Government."

These two addresses are very remarkable testimonials in favor of the Spanish administration in Louisiana. It is not often that departing power is greeted with such hosannas, and that the incense of public worship is offered to the setting sun.

On the 10th of April, Sebastian de Caso Calvo de la Puerta y O'Farril, Marquis de Casa Calvo, who, it will be recollected, had acted formerly as military governor of Louisiana after the death of Gayoso de Lemos, arrived from Havana, he and Salcedo having been made joint commissioners to deliver the province to France. On the 18th of May, they issued a proclamation,* in which they announced the intention of their sovereign to surrender the province to the French Republic, and declared that his Majesty, retaining as ever the same affection for the inhabitants of Louisiana, and desiring to continue to them the same protection which they had enjoyed, had determined:

"That the cession of the colony and island of New Orleans should be on the same terms as those of the cession made by his most Christian to his Catholic Majesty; and that, consequently, the limits on both sides of the river St. Louis, or Mississippi, should continue as they remained by the 5th article of the definitive treaty of peace concluded at Paris on the 10th of December, 1763, and accordingly, the settlements from the Bayou Manchac to the line of separation between the dominions of Spain and those of the United States, should remain a part of the monarchy of Spain and be annexed to the province of West Florida.

"Every individual, employed in any branch of the King's service, and wishing to remain under his government, might proceed to Havana or any other part of his dominions, unless he preferred entering into the service of the French Republic, which he was permitted to do; but if any just reason prevented his immediate departure, he might urge it in proper time.

"The King's generosity induced him to continue to widows and others their respective provisions, and he would make known in due time, in what manner he wished they should avail themselves of this favor.

* Martin's History of Louisiana, vol. ii., p. 188.

"They declared it to be the expectation of the King, their master, that, from the sincere friendship and alliance which existed between him and the French Republic, orders would be given to the governors and other officers employed by France in Louisiana, to the effect that the clergy and the other religious institutions should be permitted to remain in the discharge of their offices within their respective curacies and missions, and enjoy their former emoluments, privileges and exemptions—that the tribunals established for the administration of justice should be allowed to continue to administer it according to the former laws and usages of the province—the inhabitants maintained in the peaceable possession of their property, and all grants made to them by the former governors confirmed, even when not ratified by the King—and finally, that the French Government should continue to the people of Louisiana the favor and protection they had enjoyed under Spain."

In relation to the effect produced by his arrival and by the news of the cession of Louisiana by Spain to France, Laussat wrote to Decrès, the minister of marine, a confidential despatch, in which he said: "My arrival and my proclamation excited the enthusiasm of the colonists.* On all sides, I received addresses to the First Consul containing the most ardent wishes for the arrival of the coming expedition, and the most energetic expression of devoted attachment to France.† I kept up as much as I could those sentiments, which were of good omen for the future. Unfortunately, everything seems, successively, to have conspired to destroy them.

"Governor Salcedo is an infirm old man who is in his dotage. His son, who is a young officer of infantry, and

---

* Laussat's despatch is not in accordance, on this point, with other reports.
† Lettre confidentielle de Laussat à Decrès en date du 30 Messidor.

whose brains are still very green, is the true governor under his father's name.

"But the soul of the government is a certain Don Andres Lopez de Armesto, a sort of half lettered fellow, who has grown old in the office of secretary of the government, which office is given by the king of Spain. This man has seen in turn a series of governors filing off before him, and knows in all their details the corrupt practices prevalent in the colony for the last twenty years. To a great deal of natural arrogance he joins an inexhaustible fund of ready compliance and suppleness towards his superiors. In every district he has his creatures and tools, who warmly espouse his interests. and who have very good cause for so doing.

"The judge, who is called here the auditor, and who is the governor's right arm in civil matters, is a cunning old dog who sells almost publicly his decisions, and who is the sole authority to pass judgment over the most important civil and criminal cases. After all, venality is a common sin, which is openly committed. The intendant is the only one who is not suspected of it.

"The Marquis de Somoruelos, Captain-General of Cuba, of whose government this province is a dependency, felt, no doubt, that old Salcedo was not presentable to the French, and could not be permitted to act alone in the delivery of the colony to them. But whether the measure originated with him, or whether it emanated from Madrid, the Marquis de Casa Calvo arrived at New Orleans five weeks after me, with the title of royal commissioner, authorized to act jointly with the Governor in delivering over the colony to us. Then it was that the aspect of things changed materially.

"The Marquis de Casa Calvo, who is allied to O'Reilly, and whose niece, besides, has married the son and heir of that general, accompanied him to this place as cadet or page, in 1769, and was eighteen years old when he witnessed the execution of the six Frenchmen whom O'Reilly put to death without necessity and from sheer cruelty, in compliance with an erring policy, and to gratify his personal ambition.

"The same Marquis de Casa Calvo was, in January, 1793, and during the following months, in command of Fort Dauphin at St. Domingo, and was at the head of his troops drawn up in battle array, when the blacks, led by Jean François, massacred seventy-seven defenceless Frenchmen, who were relying on the faith of treaties. The colonists of St. Domingo still speak of this fact with feelings of horror; and the English newspapers, which misspelt the name of the Marquis and called him Caracola, related this event, at the time, with indignation.

"Four years ago, the office of Governor of Louisiana having become vacant by the death of the incumbent, the Captain-General of the Island of Cuba sent to this colony the Marquis de Casa Calvo to take the military command of it *ad interim*. This officer exercised those functions eighteen months, probably on account of the state of war then existing. He left in the province the reputation of a man of violent temper, who hated the French. By what fatality is this very same individual, precisely on an occasion of this kind, intrusted with the mission of offering them the welcome to which they are entitled, of delivering to them a colony which the Spaniards therein living and those in Cuba regret to part with, and of settling with us so many interesting and important questions in which we shall have to doubt his good dispositions.

"Hardly had the Marquis set foot in this province, when he summoned all the military officers (and thanks to the militia system there is scarcely an inhabitant of any consequence whatever, who is not reputed a military officer) to come to his lodging, and declare by *yea* or *nay*, whether they intended to remain in the service of the King of Spain. Please to observe, Citizen Minister, that the fortune and the pensions of many of them depended altogether on the nature of their answer. The Marquis went so far as to exact a declaration in the *affirmative* from two companies of men of color in New Orleans, which were composed of all the mechanics that city possesses. Two of those mulattoes complained to me of their having been detained twenty-four hours in prison, to force them to utter the *fatal yea* which was desired of them.

"To Terre aux Bœufs, where there exists a precious class of small farmers, who were transported thither from the Canary Islands, a priest has been sent, who induced those simple-minded men to promise that they would follow the Spaniards.

"Orders have been given to the commandants at the several posts, to subject the inhabitants and the curates to the same ordeal. The whole clergy had to go through it.

"And the expedition does not arrive! And I see these things without daring to take exception, for fear of making them worse!

"The Spanish authorities have shown themselves exceedingly reserved, more captious, and even almost haughty towards me. Our correspondence gradually became sharp, at first about trifles, and on account of their ill-mannered proceedings, which insensibly acquired a more decided character. In the beginning, the men in office, next the Spaniards, then all their adherents, and at last the vulgar crew of what may be called the *timid part* of the population, have feared to come near me; and now, to do so, would be looked upon almost as a crime. To every one of my demands or applications the Government has an evasive answer ready prepared. It shuns, isolates and watches me. It takes umbrage at the least of my steps or proceedings, and even at my language, however insignificant it may be. It is afraid of complying with my plainest requests. Firmness and dignity are all that I have to oppose to their prejudices and unreasonableness. But, frequently, I am obliged to keep pent up within my breast my feelings of vexation, because the Spanish authorities might take offence at them and revenge themselves, without my being able to prevent it, on the friends of the French.

"The Attakapas are peopled with French families who could not refrain from expressing their joy at our return. A native of Bordeaux, named St. Julien who is an honest planter and much esteemed, had the imprudence to head some of his letters with the word *Citizen*. Thereupon, a great conspiracy was suspected, and the Spanish Government ordered this individual to be made a prisoner and conducted here. In the meantime, whilst he was airing himself on his gallery at night, two shots were fired at him, one of which killed his wife.* He defended himself; and his assailants, breaking six of his ribs, left him lying down apparently dead. What followed? *He was accused of being a rogue and an assassin, who had murdered his own wife, and who had voluntarily put himself in a dying condition.* The commandant of that post, M. De Blanc, a military officer full of honor, and the descendant of St. Denis, the founder of Natchitoches, was in New Orleans when that occurrence took place; but, as he is well known for his devotion to the French, he was deprived of his command and ordered

---

* This affair, with other causes, gave rise to so serious a feud between the influential families of De Clouet, De Blanc, and others, that it almost threatened to produce a civil war in that district, and it became of sufficient importance to compel Governor Claiborne to go and quiet it in person, in 1804.

to remain at New Orleans, until further notice. In his place was put a M. Duralde, a tool of the Secretary of the Government, who makes a great parade of his exclusive and blind zeal for Spain, and who, to prove his sincerity, is the declared persecutor of all those who in his district have any sympathies for the French. People shoot at each other, and civil war has begun. The authorities here conceal these facts with sedulous care, and are anxious to keep me in complete ignorance of what is going on.

"The planters who still preserve their attachment for us, inquired of me secretly, whether they must give it up.

"That wretched Burthe* has, also, too long contributed by his indiscreet and intemperate language to cause the arrival of our troops to be apprehended, and, by his outbreaks against me, has assisted in discrediting the influence of our government.

"The Anglo-Americans have spread the rumor that there will be no cession, or that, should there be one, it would only be as a preliminary to a second cession in favor of the United States. * * *
* * * * * * *

"At all events, it behooves the honor of the French nation to take care that none shall suffer for having shown attachment to France."

The ill-humor displayed in this despatch was the result of the awkward position in which Laussat found himself. The fact is, that he had discovered the ground on which he stood to be beset with difficulties, which seemed to thicken upon him as he attempted to push his way through them. The Spaniards and their adherents had no cause to be disposed to favor him and his Government, and there was a great deal of discontent

---

* Ce misérable Burthe, &c., (one of the French Adjutants-General.)

among the natives of Louisiana, and even among the French, some of whom feared the doctrines of which he was supposed to be the representative, whilst others thought that he was not sufficiently progressive.* Besides, a furious conflict of authority had sprung up between him and the Adjutant-General Burthe, and was carried on with such animosity as to betray both parties into disgraceful acts and expressions. For instance, the Prefect Laussat, having been invited to dinner by the Marquis de Casa Calvo, and finding, on entering the saloon of the Marquis, that Burthe was one of the guests, retired abruptly, much to the astonishment and mortification of the punctilious Spaniard, who even took some offence at the Frenchman's unceremonious retreat. In illustration of General Casa Calvo's habits, turn of mind, and extreme courtesy, it may not be improper to relate here the following anecdote. One day when, in company with his private secretary, he was sauntering in the streets of New Orleans, a negro having bowed to him, he took off his hat with as much respectful courtesy as if he had been saluting an equal. Being under the impression that this had been done from sheer absence of mind, his secretary remarked with a smile; "Your Excellency did not observe that it was a negro."—" On the contrary, Sir," was the reply, " but did you think I

---

* A certain individual, named Fretté, who was notorious for the mad exaltation of his red republicanism, called on Laussat, a short time after the arrival of that functionary in the colony. Fretté burst into the Prefect's apartment with all the confidence derived from his faith in the doctrine that all men are born to fraternize on terms of equality, and addressed him in this familiar tone: "Citizen, I come to tell thee that we, the jacobins of New Orleans, have resolved," &c. &c., —" Who is this fool?" exclaimed Laussat, interrupting the intruder and looking at his secretary Daugerot, to whom he was dictating at the time. Without replying, Daugerot quietly got up from his seat, whispered a few words to some attendants in the next room, and citizen Fretté was much horrified at the expedition with which he was thrust out of the presence of the representative of the French Republic. This gave great offence to the progressists.

would permit myself to be excelled in politeness by a negro!"

On the 28th of July, Laussat wrote to the French Government, that the rumor of a cession of Louisiana to the United States was still gaining ground in the colony, but that he had treated it as a calumnious report. But hardly had his despatch been sealed and sent, when, by the arrival of a vessel from Bordeaux, he discovered that the supposed calumny was an authentic and undeniable truth. On the 6th of June, the First Consul had appointed Laussat Commissioner on the part of France, to receive possession of the province of Louisiana and deliver it to the Commissioners to be appointed on behalf of the United States.

On the 30th of November, in consequence of the orders received, Casa Calvo, Salcedo, and Laussat, accompanied by a large retinue of the clergy and of all the civil and military officers in the employ of France and Spain, and of many other persons of distinction, met in the City Hall, where Laussat exhibited to the Spanish Commissioners an order from the King of Spain for the delivery of the colony, and his credentials from the French Government to receive it. Whereupon, the keys of New Orleans were handed to Laussat; and Salcedo and Casa Calvo declared that from this moment, according to the powers vested in them, they put the French Commissioner in possession of Louisiana and its dependencies, in all their extent, such as they were ceded by France to Spain, and such as they remained under the successive treaties made between his Catholic Majesty and other Powers. They further declared that they absolved from their oath of fidelity and allegiance to the crown of Spain, such of his Catholic Majesty's subjects in Louisiana as might choose to live under the authority of the French Republic. A record was made of these proceedings in

French and Spanish,* and the three commissioners walked to the main balcony, when the Spanish flag was saluted by a discharge of artillery on its descent from a pole erected on the public square in front of the City Hall, and that of the French Republic greeted in the same manner on its ascent. The square was occupied by the Spanish troops and some of the militia of the colony. It was remarked that the militia had mustered up with difficulty, and did not exceed one hundred and fifty men. It was the indication of an unfavorable feeling, which had been daily gaining strength, and which Laussat attributed in his despatches to the intrigues of the Spanish authorities. Although the weather had been tempestuous in the preceding night and in the morning, and continued to be threatening, the crowd round the public square was immense, and filled not only the streets, but also the windows, and even the very tops of the neighboring houses.

On the same day, Laussat issued this proclamation:

"LOUISIANIANS:

"The mission which brought me among you across the sea, through a distance of seven thousand and five hundred miles, that mission on which I had long rested so many fond hopes, and so many ardent wishes for your happiness, is now totally changed; and the one with which I am now charged, less gratifying, but still equally flattering to me, offers me one source of consolation—which springs from the reflection, that it will, in its results, be more advantageous to you.

"The Commissioners of his Catholic Majesty, in conformity with the powers and orders which they and I have respectively received, have just delivered me pos

---

* Martin's History of Louisiana, vol. ii., p. 195.

session of the province. You see the flag of the French Republic now displayed, and you hear the repeated detonations of her guns, announcing to you, to-day, on all sides, the return of French domination. It will be for an instant only, Louisianians, and I am on the eve of transferring the possession of this colony to the Commissioners of the United States. They are near at hand—I expect them soon.

"The approaching struggles of a war begun under the most sanguinary and terrible auspices, and threatening the safety of the four quarters of the world, had induced the French Government to turn its attention towards Louisiana, and to reflect on her destinies. Considerations of prudence and humanity, connecting themselves with those of a more vast and durable policy—worthy, in one word, of the man whose genius weighs, at this very hour, in its scales, the fates of so many great nations, have given a new direction to the beneficent intentions of France towards Louisiana. She has ceded it to the United States of America.

"Preserve thus, Louisianians, the precious pledge of the friendship which cannot fail to grow, from day to day, between the two republics, and which must so powerfully contribute to their common repose and their common prosperity.

"The article 3d, of the treaty of cession, cannot escape your attention. It says: '*that the inhabitants of the ceded territories shall be incorporated into the Union of the United States, and admitted, as soon as possible, according to the principles of the Federal Constitution, to the enjoyment of all the advantages and immunities of citizens of the United States; and that, in the meantime, they shall be maintained and protected in the free enjoyment of their liberties and property, and in the unrestrained exercise of the religion they profess.*'

"Thus are you, Louisianians, suddenly invested with the rights and privileges appertaining to a free Constitution and Government, secured and guaranteed by the force of arms, cemented by treaties, and tested by time and experience.

"You will be incorporated with a nation already numerous and powerful, renowned besides for its industry, its patriotism, and the degree of civilization and knowledge it possesses, and which by its rapid progress seems destined to the most brilliant rank that a people ever enjoyed on the face of the earth.

"It has been happily blessed with such a position, that its successes and its splendor cannot, at least for a long time, interfere with its felicity.

"However benevolent and pure may be the intentions of a mother country, you must be aware that an immense distance between the two secures impunity to oppression and exactions, and prevents the correction of abuses. The facility and the certitude of concealing them have even a frequent tendency to corrupt the man who, at first, looked upon them with aversion and fear.

"From this day forth, you cease to be exposed to this fatal and dangerous disadvantage.

"By the nature of the Government of the United States, and of the privileges upon the enjoyment of which you immediately enter, you will have, even under a provisional government, popular rulers, whose acts you will be at liberty to censure, or to protest against with impunity, and who will be permanently in need of your esteem, your suffrages and your affection.

"The public affairs and interests, far from being interdicted to your consideration, will be your own affairs and interests, on which the opinions of wise and impartial men will be sure to exercise, in the long run, a preponderating influence, and to which you could not even remain indifferent without exposing yourselves to bitter repentance.

"The time will soon come when you will establish for yourselves a form of government, which, although respecting the sacred principles consecrated in the social pact of the Federal Union, will be adapted to your manners, your usages, your climate, your soil and your peculiar localities.

"It will not be long before you shall feel the advantages of an upright, impartial, and incorruptible administration of justice, in which the invariable forms and the publicity of judicial proceedings, together with the restraints carefully imposed over an arbitrary application of the laws, will co-operate with the moral and national character of the Judges and Jurors, in affording to the citizens the most effective security for their persons and property.

"The principles and legislation of the American people, the encouragements which they have given to the interests of agriculture and commerce, and the progress which they have made in those two departments of industry, are well known to you, Louisianians, particularly from the many advantages you have derived from them for some years past.

"There is not and there cannot be a metropolitan Government, which will not establish a more or less exclusive colonial monopoly. On the contrary, from the United States you have to expect a boundless freedom of exportation, and only such duties on your imports as may be required by your public wants and the necessity of protecting your home industry. The result of unlimited competition will be to cause you to buy cheap whilst selling dear, and your country will become an immense warehouse or place of deposit, affording you countless profits. The Nile of America, the Mississippi, which flows, not through parched deserts of sand, but through the most extensive and the most fertile plains of the new world, will soon see its bosom darkened with a thousand ships belonging to all the nations of the earth, and mooring at the quays of another Alexandria.

"Among them your eyes will, I hope, Louisianians, always distinguish with complacency the French flag, and your hearts will never cease to rejoice at the sight of its glorious folds. This we firmly hope. I solemnly profess it here in the name of my country and government.

"Bonaparte, in stipulating by the 7th Article of the treaty of cession, that the French shall be permitted, during twelve years, to trade in this province without paying higher duties than the citizens of the United States, and exactly on the same footing, had, as one of his principal aims, that of giving to the ancient relations existing between the French of Louisiana and the French of Europe sufficient opportunity and time, for renewing, strengthening and perpetuating themselves. A new bond of union will be formed between us from one continent to the other, the more satisfactory and durable from the fact that it will be entirely founded on a constant reciprocity of sentiments, services and advantages. Your children, Louisianians, will be our children, and our children will be yours. You will send yours to perfect their education and their talents among us, and we will send ours to you, to increase your forces, and, by contributing their share to your labors and industry, assist you in wresting from an unsubdued wilderness its reluctant tributes.

"It has been gratifying to me thus to describe, somewhat at length, the advantages which are secured to you, in order to soothe your complaints of being forsaken, and the affectionate regrets which a sincere attachment for the country of your ancestors has caused so many of you to express. France and her Government will hear of it with gratitude and with corresponding love. But you will be convinced ere long, that, by the treaty of cession, she has conferred upon you the most eminent and the most memorable of blessings.

"The French Republic is thus the first to give to modern times the example of voluntarily emancipating a colony, in imitation of the liberal policy pursued towards those colonies, whose existence we love to recall to our memory, as constituting one of the most brilliant periods of the days of antiquity. Thus may, now and for the future, a Frenchman and a Louisianian never meet, in any part of the world, without a mutual feeling of tender emotion, and without exchanging the affectionate appellation of 'brothers!' May this word hereafter be the only one sufficiently expressive to convey an adequate idea of their eternal friendship and reciprocal reliance!"

On that same day (30th November), the Prefect issued several decrees in relation to the organization of the government of the province. M. Garland was appointed, provisionally, Administrator-General and Director of the Custom-house, and Navailles, Treasurer. For the Spanish Cabildo were substituted a Mayor, two Adjuncts, and a Municipal Council composed of ten members. By order, the following list of officers was immediately published: Etienne Boré, Mayor; Pierre Derbigny, Secretary; Destréhan, First Adjunct; Sauvé, Second Adjunct; Livaudais, Petit Cavelier, Villeré, Johns, Fortier, Donaldson, Faurie, Allard, Tureaud, and John Watkins, members of the Municipal Council. Labatut was appointed its Treasurer. To Bellechasse was given, with the grade of Colonel, the command of the militia of New Orleans, including the companies formed by the freemen of color, and all its other officers were re-commissioned. It is true that no alacrity was shown to accept these commissions; but the French Prefect was unjust at the time, when he supposed that it was owing to the intrigues of the Spaniards. On the contrary, several natives, of Spanish descent, consented to be commissioned as officers of the militia, and among others, Charles Anastase Gayarré,* the grandson of the Royal Comptroller, or Contador, who came to the colony with Ulloa in 1766. Although it may be that he was influenced by his father-in-law, Etienne Boré, the new Mayor of New Orleans, nevertheless it is evident that he would not have pursued this course, if it had been contrary to the wishes of the Spanish authorities, as his feelings must have been enlisted on their side, and as he was then in office† under the appointment of the King of Spain.

By a special proclamation, the Black Code given by Louis XV. to the province, excepting such parts of it as were inconsistent with the Constitution and Laws of the United States, was declared to be in force.‡

"Soon after," says Monette, in his History of the Valley of the Mississippi, "the Spanish troops were withdrawn and the military posts were evacuated. In the city and suburbs of New Orleans there were four military posts or forts, relinquished by the Spanish troops, which might be exposed to the depredations, and equally so to the unlawful occupancy of disaffected persons and nocturnal disturbers of the peace. The troops of the United States, designed for the occupation of these forts, not having arrived within the limits of the ceded province, many were apprehensive of outrage and violence from a lawless and disaffected populace, composed of the lowest

---

* The Author's father.   † Official de contadoria.
‡ Martin's History of Louisiana, vol. ii., p. 197.

class of Spaniards, Mexicans, and free persons of color who infested the city, and other disorderly persons and desperadoes of all nations, who, released from the restraint of a standing army, might be prompted by the hope of pillage to fire the city, or to commit other acts of violence.

"To guard against any such attempt, and to preserve order in the city, a number of enterprising young Americans associated themselves into a volunteer battalion, to be placed under the command of Daniel Clark, Jr., the American Consul. Their first muster was at Davis's rope-walk on Canal St., where they were joined by a number of patriotic young Creole Frenchmen, who continued to serve until the battalion was finally discharged. Having organized, they placed themselves under their commander, and proceeded to the head-quarters of the Colonial Prefect, to whom they made a formal tender of their services for the purpose of preserving order in the city, and for the occupancy of the forts until the arrival of the American Commissioners and troops. The battalion* continued to increase by the voluntary enrolment of Americans and French Creoles, until the whole number exceeded three hundred men. The Americans were chiefly captains and mates of vessels, supercargoes, merchants, clerks, and seamen belonging to vessels in port. The French, by their zeal, vigilance, and patriotism during their time of service, proved themselves worthy of American citizenship. Their services were gladly accept-

---

* The battalion of volunteers was formed at the instance of the following gentlemen, then resident in New Orleans: George Martin, since parish judge of St. Landry, Colonel Reuben Kemper, George King, George Newman, Benjamin Morgan, Daniel Clark, American consul, Doctor William Flood, since a distinguished physician of New Orleans, Maunsel White, since a wealthy merchant and planter and a state senator, and Woodson Wren, who subsequently settled in the State of Mississippi, where he was lately postmaster at Natchez.—*Monette's Valley of the Mississippi*, vol. i., p. 561.

ed, and detachments from their numbers were detailed upon regular tours of duty in patrolling the city by day and by night."

The following confidential despatch addressed by Laussat to his Government, on the course he deemed proper to pursue on that occasion, and dated on the 10th of December, will not be read without interest.

"Citizen Minister, I deferred writing to your Excellency by the last mail, in the hope that the commissioners of the United States were to arrive here yesterday, and that the same despatch would have conveyed to you the information of our taking and delivering possession, in the name of the French Republic, without any intervening delays. It seems, however, that the arrival of the Americans is postponed until next week. I cannot, therefore, and will not put off any longer, giving you an account of the actual state of things.   *   *

*   *   *   *   *   *   *

"On the 23rd of November, General Wilkinson, one of the commissioners for the United States, came to my house at six o'clock in the evening. The other commissioner is W. C. C. Claiborne, Governor of the territory of Mississippi.

"Wilkinson was returning from the frontiers of Florida, and was on his way to join his colleague at Fort Adams, near the dividing line between the territory of Mississippi and the district of Baton Rouge. We had just had a conference of two hours in reference to the course to be pursued towards the Spanish commissioners in all possible contingencies, when, on breaking up the interview and stepping out of my room, I met the French officer, citizen Landais, who had been sent to put me in possession of the original documents containing the instructions of our Government for taking possession of Louisiana, and delivering it over to the United States.

"I did not hesitate, and I resolved to accelerate that event; for, you have seen in my preceding despatches that I suspected the good will of the Spaniards, and it was prudent not to give them time to know the system of opposition which the Minister of his Catholic Majesty at Washington had openly and impetuously pursued in protesting against the cession, because it was to be feared that the Spanish commissioners might in their turn be tempted to imitate him.

" On the morning of the next day, I urged General Wilkinson to hasten his departure and to go and wait for further information from me at the head of his troops, whose numbers he might increase or diminish accordingly.

" Moreover, I immediately busied myself with preparing the ground around me.

" In the first place, I secured a chief for the militia, and I was lucky indeed in laying my hands on an officer who had served twenty-four years, who was not personally well disposed towards the Marquis de Casa Calvo, on account of his having been dismissed from active service on unfavorable terms, and who enjoyed an excellent reputation and much popularity in the country. He is, besides, the owner of considerable property in the vicinity of the city, and his name is Deville de Goutin Bellechasse. Once sure of him, I availed myself of his aid in all the principal and subordinate military measures which I had to conceive and execute.

"I thought also of securing, without loss of time, an imposing support in the civil department of the government, and I selected for Mayor of the city, M. Etienne Boré, a native of Louisiana, of a distinguished family, formerly *Mousquetaire** in France, one of the

---

* The "Mousquetaires" were privileged companies in the King's household troops, each private having the rank of Captain, and every Captain the rank of

largest and most skilful planters of the province, and a gentleman renowned for his patriotism and for a character of undeviating independence. I made a powerful appeal to him in the name of his country, whose interests required his services, and I had the satisfaction to win him over.

"As we were in the grinding season for the sugar cane, there could not have been a more unpropitious time to draw the planters away from their fields and the superintendence of their negroes.

"After M. Boré, and through his influence, I secured the services of some of the most distinguished among the colonists. I took every care to join with them in authority some of the most respectable inhabitants of the city, who had a capacity for business, who were used to it, who were known as such, and who had a knowledge of the three languages spoken in the colony— the French, English and Spanish.

"It was with a true feeling of joy that I put in authority M. Villeré, the son of one of the most interesting of O'Reilly's victims, himself much loved in the colony, and held in great repute for his probity, his good conduct and his merit. I thus discharged a second debt on the part of France.

"It was essential for me to have, immediately, a municipality animated with a proper disposition, enlightened, active and respectable. Under the Spanish domination, the municipal council (cabildo) was an insignificant institution—a mere show or parade, lacking real power, generally composed of heterogeneous elements, of devoted tools, of beings mostly disgraced and bespattered with mud.* The Governor, individually,

---

Lieutenant-General. To enter this corps it was necessary to prove gentle birth.

* On the contrary, that body was generally composed of respectable citizens

was the army—the law—the tribunal of justice—the police—the administration of the country.

"It was therefore an indispensable obligation for me, considering the circumstances in which I might be placed and the total want in which I was of every thing, to create immediately a moral power which, as soon as I should assume the reins of the government, might of itself become an irresistible political lever.

"I labored without intermission to obtain that result, on the Saturday, Sunday, and Monday which preceded the cession.*

"I shall always remember with pleasure that, on Tuesday evening, at nine o'clock, I had succeeded in gathering round me what Louisiana possesses of most respectable and distinguished, within thirty miles, in point of reputation, virtue, talent, influence and wealth. The gentlemen thus assembled were the first to whom, according to your despatches, Citizen Minister, and your instructions, I made known the treaty of cession, and the views of the Government in negotiating it. I explained to them the successive changes of domination which would be the sudden result of that cession, and the first of which would take place on the next day. I laid out before them the plan on which I intended to proceed, commented on the difficulties which might be in the way, unfolded what I expected from their co-operation, and discussed the powerful motives which ought to induce them to give me their assistance.

"The day before, I had delivered your letter of introduction to the Spanish Commissioners, and I had declared to them that my intention was to take possession two days after, that is, on Wednesday, 30th of November.

But Laussat was an excitable and prejudiced man, looking at every thing Spanish with the inflamed eye of passion.

* The cession was effected on Wednesday, the 30th of November.

I had communicated to them the procès-verbal, such as it was subsequently signed, and such as I send a copy of to your Excellency.

"In answer, the first thing which was said to me by the Spanish Commissioners was: What are the forces with which you will take possession?—I replied: with the militia and the French who are in New Orleans.—As this is but a mere formality, observed the Spanish Commissioners, our troops might assist you, and might continue in your service until the arrival of the Americans. We shall thus contribute with pleasure to help you, considering the union which exists between the two nations. —This would be contrary to my instructions, and I can do very well without it.—But the officers of the militia are mostly, and especially the Colonel who commands them, commissioned and paid by the King of Spain.—I will recommission them instantly. All that I ask of you is to draw the militia together, and to keep them under arms at the moment when you will deliver the colony to me.—We have received no orders different from the first, and therefore the colony shall be delivered to you.— The Marquis de Somoruellos wrote to me, a few days ago, that he had lately renewed to you the orders to do so.— This evening, one of us will call on you, and we shall come to some final understanding as to the style of the procès-verbal and as to the details of the ceremony.

"At nine o'clock, the Marquis de Casa Calvo called at my house with the Secretary of the Government, Armesto. Some insignificant expressions were altered in the procès-verbal, and we examined the Spanish translation, in which we concurred. We easily came to an agreement as to what was a mere matter of etiquette The Marquis renewed the proposition, or the equivalent of it, which he had made in the morning. I declined it peremptorily, as I had done already. He observed that the Cabildo was composed of officers appointed by his Catholic Majesty, but that, on the eve of passing under the domination of the United States of America, they would willingly, in concert with the Commissioners of their Sovereign, give such assistance as circumstances might require. I answered that I would establish a new municipal body.

"On Tuesday, I understood from various sources that the militia companies had been operated upon, and that they would not answer the call when summoned to the ceremony of the next day.

"For the last few days, I had been on the best footing of intelligence, at the request of the American Government, with Mr. Daniel Clark, their Consul, and a rich planter and merchant, who knows perfectly this country, in which he has resided twenty years, who is extremely zealous in favor of the cession, and whose penetration and talents for intrigue are carried to a rare degree of excellence.

"Whilst I was counteracting, through M. de Bellechasse and some other military gentlemen, the practices which were carried on among the militia, and which were but the continuation of those I had witnessed without being able to check them, Mr. Clark was forming a numerous company of American volunteers, and, through my friends, I caused to be drummed up about a hundred of the Frenchmen who have lately come here; and most of whom had served in our armies during the revolution.

"I undoubtedly knew that there would be no impediment to the execution of the treaty, but it was necessary to prevent its becoming a cause of annoyance for France in a country peopled with Frenchmen, who, in reality, love her passionately. It was necessary to avoid that the Commissioner of the French Government be laughed at, on account of the state of embarrassment and isolation in which he might be placed. It was necessary to prevent the Americans and the Europeans from turning into a joke our manner of taking possession. It was necessary not to run the risk of some disturbances, and not to be compelled perhaps to adjourn the ceremony, and to make an appeal to the troops of the United States.

"This is, Citizen Minister, what was the constant basis of all my steps and acts.

"I will not relate to you the street talk and fibs which were current on Tuesday, during the whole day.

"On Wednesday morning, at 10 o'clock, M. Fortier, who commanded the militia, with the grade of Colonel, who was commissioned and paid as such by the King of Spain, and who, besides, was the intimate friend of the Marquis de Casa Calvo, came on the part of the Marquis, to inform me of the difficulties which were felt in the attempt to draw the militia together, in a number sufficiently large to be respectable. He proposed to me, in the name of the Marquis, to have recourse, either to the Spanish troops, or to the few militia that could be collected, as *auxiliaries*. This was his expression.

"After the militia had been assembled, rather poorly than otherwise, the Marquis had said to them: "We have mustered you up to take possession of the province in the name of the French Republic. It is for you to determine if you wish to serve her for fifteen days.

"My answer to the Marquis's message was short: '*Assure the Marquis,*' said I, '*that if the companies of the militia are not, at 12 o'clock, drawn up under arms, in a respectable number, to obey the orders of the French Republic, the Republic and myself will lay the blame and responsibility where it ought to be; that I have not reached my forty-seventh year to be the dupe of such child's play; that France does not stand in need, on this occasion, of the auxiliaries he offers; that, in the absence of the means which he thinks are the only ones on which I can rely, I have others in readiness, and that my taking possession of the province will be accomplished; and accomplished without delay, with efficacy and with dignity. Please further to inform the Marquis that, as we have already had together an intercourse of six months, I had flattered myself that he had had ample time to know me.'*

"I redoubled, however, my efforts to have, in case of need, a spontaneous armed force that might be ready to show itself simultaneously.

"It was not long before I was informed, that the Spanish officers were earnestly striving to draw together at least two or three companies of militia, and particularly that of the grenadiers.

"At twelve o'clock, I went, with a considerable escort of Frenchmen, to the City Hall, where I found the Spanish Commissioners. They delivered to me the province in the form and manner described in the procès-verbal hereto annexed. * * *
* * * * * * *

"As soon as the French flag had been hoisted up, and the Spanish Commissioners had withdrawn, I placed myself in the centre of the militia companies, and I presented to them M. Bellechasse as their Colonel and Commander. I also caused to be proclaimed in their presence the composition of the staff.

"There were about one hundred and fifty militia-men present, among whom were about sixty grenadiers.

"I returned to the City Hall to establish and organize the Municipal body.

"I have published a proclamation sufficiently moderate not to displease the Spaniards, or the Americans.

"Possession of the province having been taken, it was proper that it should be solemnly authenticated and irrevocably fixed. Hence the multiplicity of my acts.

"From the moment of the cession, Casa Calvo has behaved towards me with *exquisite politeness*."

Such were Laussat's comments on what he had thought and done, and on what he believed he had seen, or had been correctly informed of. But it seems, from his own version of the facts, as related in this despatch, that if there was any indecent display of ill temper, hasty conclusions, undignified and offensive suspicions, as well as of arrogant language, it was not on the side of his adversaries; that if there was, as he complains, a good deal of child's play, he had a handsome share in it; and that his vision must have been singularly dimmed by his apprehensions of the supposed hostile dispositions of the Spaniards, not to have discovered, sooner than after the cession, the uniformity of Casa Calvo's *exquisite politeness*.

Whilst all these mutations had been going on, or had been in the act of preparation, Laussat and Casa Calvo had been vieing in giving splendid entertainments to the inhabitants of New Orleans, and the republican Prefect had struggled not to yield in pomp and display to the proud and wealthy nobleman. It was no doubt with them a matter of policy, as well as of taste or pride. A French author,* who witnessed those festivities, says: "M. Laussat exhibited in brilliant entertainments, embellished by the graces of his affable and beautiful wife, that fascinating elegance which seems to be one of the attributes of the French character. The Louisianian ladies, who looked upon her as a model of taste, appeared at those entertainments with a magnificence which was a just

---

* Voyages dans l'intérieur de la Louisiane par C. C. Robin.

cause of astonishment in such a colony, and which might have been successfully compared with any efforts of that sort even in the principal cities of France. The Louisianian ladies, who may justly be said to be remarkable for their habitual gravity, are generally tall and exquisitely shaped; the alabaster whiteness of their complexion, which was admirably set off by their light dresses, adorned with flowers and rich embroidery, gave a fairy-like appearance to these festivities. The last one, particularly, astonished me by its magnificence. After tea and the concert were over, the dancing was interrupted at midnight, and the guests went down to a saloon—where, on a table laid for sixty to eighty persons, arose, on the top of rocks, the temple of Good Faith surrounded with columns, and surmounted by a dome, under which was placed the allegorical statue of the goddess. But, farther on, beyond that room, one was attracted by the flood of light which burst from an immense pavilion, in the shape of a gallery. There, forty or fifty tables, covered with a variety of dishes, were spread for the accommodation of four or five hundred guests, who grouped themselves round them in small detached parties.

"The tendency of these festivities was, no doubt, to spread the taste for pleasure and luxury in a colony which, being in its nascent state, still needs a great deal of economy and labor; but, nevertheless, these entertainments, under the circumstances in which they were given, were the result of a useful and enlightened policy, because they strengthened the common customs and manners which connected us and the colonists, causing them to cherish what is French, and impressing them with a proper sense of the grandeur of the mother country."

In the meantime, as apprehensions were entertained

by the Government of the United States that difficulties might arise in relation to the cession, in consequence of the disposition manifested a few years before by the Colonial Government of Louisiana to retain possession of the posts situated above the 31st degree, and in consequence of the energetic protests recently made at Washington by the Spanish Minister, in the name of his Catholic Majesty, the President[*] had ordered a part of the militia of the States of Ohio, Kentucky and Tennessee, to be held in readiness to march at a moment's warning. Considerable forces had been assembled at Fort Adams, and five hundred Tennesseans had come as far as Natchez, under the command of Colonel Dogherty. Claiborne, the Governor of Mississippi, had ordered a volunteer company of horse of that territory to be prepared to march with him on the 10th of December.

Claiborne met at Fort Adams, on his way to New Orleans, General Wilkinson, who was coming from that city, where he had had with Laussat the interview I have mentioned. The troops who were at this post were set in motion in company with the volunteers, and, on the 17th of December, the two American commissioners encamped within two miles of New Orleans. On the day following, they despatched an officer to Laussat, to inquire whether he was disposed to receive their visit; Laussat answered in the affirmative, and immediately sent in his carriage an officer named Vinache, with Bellechasse, the Colonel in command of the militia, and a French citizen named Blanque, to meet Claiborne and Wilkinson. The commissioners came to Laussat's house with an escort of thirty of the Mississippi horse volunteers, and, on their approach, were saluted with nineteen guns. The next day, at half past

---

[*] Martin's History of Louisiana, vol. ii., p. 197.

ten in the morning, Laussat went on horseback to their camp with an escort of sixty men, and thus returned officially the formal visit he had received.

On Tuesday, the 20th of December, the Prefect ordered all the militia companies to be drawn up under arms,* on the public square in front of the City Hall. The crowd of spectators was immense, and the finest weather favored the curiosity of the public.

The commissioners of the United States arrived at the gates of the city with their troops, and, before entering, were reconnoitred according to military usages, by a company of the militia grenadiers.

The American troops, on entering the city, were greeted with a salute of twenty-one guns from the forts, and formed on the opposite side of the square, facing the militia.

At the City Hall, the Commissioners of the United States exhibited their powers to Laussat. The credentials were publicly read, next the treaty of cession, the powers of the French Commissioner, and finally the procès-verbal. The Prefect proclaimed the delivery of the province to the United States, handed the keys of the city to Claiborne, and declared that he absolved from their allegiance to the French Republic such of the inhabitants as might choose to pass under the new domination. "Claiborne now rose," says Judge Martin in his History of Louisiana, "and offered to the people his congratulations on the event which irrevocably fixed their political existence, and no longer left it open to the caprices of chance. He assured them that the United States received them as brothers, and would hasten to extend to them a participation in the invaluable rights forming the basis of their own unexampled prosperity, and that, in the meanwhile, the people would be protected in the enjoyment of their liberty, property

* Laussat's despatches.

and religion; that their commerce would be favored, and their agriculture encouraged. He recommended to them to promote political information in the province, and to guide the rising generation in the paths of republican energy and virtue."

The three commissioners then went to one of the balconies of the City Hall. On their making their appearance, the French flag that was floating at the top of a pole in the middle of the square came down, and the American flag went up. When they met half way, a gun was fired as a signal, and immediately the land batteries began their discharges, which were responded to by the armed vessels in the river. "A group of American citizens who stood at a corner of the square," says Judge Martin, "waved their hats, in token of respect for their country's flag, and a few of them greeted it with their voices; no emotion was manifested by any other part of the crowd. The colonists did not appear conscious that they were reaching the *Latium sedes ubi fata quietos ostendunt.*"

Laussat then presented the American commissioners to the militia, and delivered to them the command of that body. Afterwards, Claiborne and Wilkinson proceeded to have all the posts and guardhouses occupied by their troops. Thus ended the French domination, if it can be so called, twenty days after it had begun. The Spanish Government had lasted thirty-four years and a few months.

On this day, when he took possession of the colony (the 20th of December, 1803), Claiborne issued the following proclamation:

" Whereas, by stipulations between the Governments of France and Spain, the latter ceded to the former the Colony and Province of Louisiana, and with the same extent which it had at the date of the above mentioned treaty in the hands of Spain, and that it had when France possessed it, and such as it ought to be after the treaties subsequently entered into between Spain and other States; and whereas the Government of France has ceded the same to the United States by a treaty duly ratified, and bearing date the 30th of April in the present yéar, and the possession of said Colony and Province is now in the United States according to the tenor of the last mentioned treaty; and whereas the Congress of the United States, on the 31st of October, in the present year, did enact that until the expiration of the Session of Congress then sitting (unless provisions for the temporary government of the said territories be sooner made by Congress), all the military, civil, and judicial powers exercised by the then existing government of the same, shall be vested in such person or persons, and shall be exercised in such manner as the President of the United States shall direct, for the maintaining and protecting of the inhabitants of Louisiana in the free enjoyment of their liberty, property, and religion; and the President of the United States has, by his commission bearing date the same 31st of October, invested me with all the powers, and charged me with the several duties heretofore held and exercised by the Governor-General and the Intendant of the Province:

"I have therefore thought fit to issue this my Proclamation:

"Making known the premises, and to declare that the government heretofore exercised over the said Province of Louisiana, as well under the authority of Spain as of the French Republic, has ceased, and that of the United States of America is established over the same; that the inhabitants thereof will be incorporated in the Union of the United States, and admitted as soon as possible, according to the principles of the Federal Constitution, to the enjoyment of all the rights, advantages, and immunities of citizens of the United States; that, in the meantime, they shall be maintained and protected in the free enjoyment of their liberty, property, and the religion which they profess; that all laws and municipal regulations which were in existence at the cessation of the late government, remain in full force; and all civil officers charged with their execution, except those whose powers have been specially vested in me, and except also such officers as have been intrusted with the collection of the revenue, are continued in their functions during the pleasure of the Governor for the time being, or until provision shall otherwise be made.

"And I hereby exhort and enjoin all the Inhabitants and other persons within the said Province to be faithful and true in their allegiance to the United States, and obedient to the laws and authorities of the same, under full assurance that their just rights will be under the guardianship of the United States and will be maintained free from all force and violence from without or within."

The situation in which Louisiana was, when transferred to the United States, is fully described in a document* communicated by the President to Congress on the 14th of November. When O'Reilly took final possession of the colony in 1769, its population was about 13,000 or 14,000 souls, allowing to New Orleans 3190 souls. In 1803, it was estimated at 49,000 or 50,000 souls for the whole province, putting down New Orleans at 8000 or 10,000 souls,† and not including the Indians, who, scattered about on that immense territory, were not supposed to number more than 25.000 or 30,000

---

* American State Papers, vol. i., p. 344. Miscellaneous.

† It is believed that the population was underrated, and that, to set it down at 60,000 souls would be a closer approximation to truth. Some contemporaries who are entitled to much credit even think that the population was considerably larger.

SITUATION OF THE COLONY IN 1803.

souls. The revenues of the city of New Orleans were $19,278, and its expenses hardly amounted to ten thousand dollars. The annual produce of the province was supposed* to consist of 3000 pounds of indigo (rapidly declining)—20,000 bales of cotton of 300 pounds each—5000 hogsheads of sugar of 1000 pounds each—5000 casks of molasses of 50 gallons each. The estimate of the produce shipped from New Orleans in the year 1802, including that of the settlements on the Mississippi, Ohio, &c., did not exceed 40,000 tons. The exports were estimated at $2,158,000, and the imports at $2,500,000. The revenues accruing to the King's Treasury hardly went up, on an average, to $120,000 a year, and the expenditures of the government had gradually risen so high as to exceed $800,000 in the year 1802.

When the Spaniards took possession of the colony, there were in it seven millions of paper money issued by the French Government, then losing 75 per cent. On its retrocession to France, the paper issued and to be redeemed by the Spaniards hardly exceeded six hundred thousand dollars. "It consisted of emissions made in the early part of the Spanish administration, and of a debt due by the Government for supplies furnished to the troops and the King's stores,† and for salaries of officers and workmen, for which *liberanzas*, or certificates, were regularly issued, of which there was afloat, at the time of the cession, a sum of from four hundred and fifty to five hundred thousand dollars. They bore no interest, and were commonly to be bought at a discount of from 25 to 50 per cent. At the change of Government the discount was thirty. This depreciation was not the result of a want of confidence, or of any apprehension that the certificates would not be paid, but the

---

* Martin's History. † Ib., vol. ii., p 211.

consequence of the increased value of money, produced by the scarcity of it in the market."

As far as I have been able to judge, I think I may safely come to the conclusion that the ordinary and extraordinary expenses incurred by Spain in relation to Louisiana, over and *above* the small revenue she derived from that colony, may, without exaggeration, be put down at about fifteen millions of dollars, from the 5th of March, 1766, when Ulloa landed at New Orleans, to the 30th of November, 1803, when the retrocession to France took place.

It will be recollected that, as previously related, the Marquis of Grimaldi, who was a member of the Cabinet of Madrid, had written, on the 11th of May, 1767, to the Count of Fuentes, then Ambassador of Spain at Versailles: "The Duke of Praslin (one of the French Ministers) will remember that there were doubts on our part, as to the acceptation of the donation tendered by his most Christian Majesty. But, as the same reasons which had made France believe in the necessity of the cession, prompted Spain to accept it, the King gave it his assent, although it was well known that we were acquiring nothing but an annual incumbrance of two hundred and fifty to three hundred thousand dollars, in consideration of a distant and negative utility—which is—that of possessing a country to prevent its being possessed by another nation."

Thus Spain had assumed an *incumbrance*, which cost her in the end fifteen millions of dollars, in the vain hope of establishing a barrier between her Mexican Colonies and the danger which she foresaw was to come from the Northern Colonies of England in America. Recent events have proved how futile was the attempt to protect herself against an inevitable evil, and experience has demonstrated that the application of European treasure, blood and industry to the creation, the purchase or the conquest of colonies in America, is not destined to be a profitable investment. Spain therefore acted wisely when she at last determined to part with a possession which was a useless and expensive incumbrance to her, and which was on the eve of being wrested from her by her powerful neighbors, who, by so doing, would have obeyed rather the dictates of a stern necessity, than of an ambition yet dormant in the cradle.

Louisiana, when in its colonial state, has the honor of having produced several distinguished men, among whom the following are the most remarkable :

Aubert Dubayet* was born in Louisiana on the 17th of August, 1759. He was the son of Adjutant-Major Aubert, one of those officers who, in 1769, were sent by Governor Aubry, at the request of General O'Reilly, to arrest the French Commissary Foucault. He entered in early life into the French army, and served in America during the war of Independence between Great Britain and the United States. He was in France at the commencement of the Revolution, and soon began to take an active part in public affairs. In 1789, he published a pamphlet against admitting the Jews to the rights of citizenship. But he afterwards became one of the principal advocates for innovation, and, in 1791, was chosen a member of the Legislative Assembly, in which he acted a conspicuous part. In 1793, he resumed his military profession, and was made Governor of Mayence, which, after an obstinate defence, he was obliged to surrender to the King of Prussia. Aubert Dubayet then commanded as General-in-chief in La Vendée, and, being defeated at Clisson, became the object of denunciations against which he

* Gorton's Biographical Dictionary.

successfully defended himself. Employed again at Cher bourg, he was called by the Directory to the post of Minister of War, which he held only three months, when he was appointed Minister of the Republic at Constantinople, where he closed a life of active service, on the 17th of December, 1797, at the age of thirty-seven.

Etienne Bernard Alexandre Viel, a learned Jesuit, was born in New Orleans, on the 31st of October, 1736, and died on the 16th of December, 1821, at the college of Juilly, in France, where he had been educated, and where, in his turn, he had devoted himself to the education of youth, after having resided many years in Attakapas, where he made himself beloved by all the inhabitants. He is known in the erudite world by a very beautiful translation, in Latin verse, of Fénélon's Telemachus, also by some little poems in Latin verse which he offered to the public, in 1816, under the title of "Miscellanea Latino-Gallica," and by an excellent French translation of the Ars Poetica, and of two of Horace's epistles.

Jean Jacques Audubon, the celebrated naturalist, was born near New Orleans, in 1780, and died in the State of New York, in 1851, bequeathing to posterity those works which have already acquired for him an immortal fame.

Bronier de Clouet, born in Louisiana, about the year 1764, entered the Spanish army in early life, rose to the grade of Brigadier-General, was for some time Governor of the province of Hagua in the island of Cuba, was created Count de la Fernandina de Hagua, and had just been raised to the Senate by Queen Isabella II., when he died in Madrid, lately, in his eighty-fourth year.

Daunoy, or rather D'Aunoy, was born in New Orleans, about the year 1775. Having become a Spanish officer, he rose by degrees to the grade of Lieutenant-General, after having greatly distinguished himself against the

French in the Peninsular war. He died at an age when he was still capable of rendering more services to the Spanish monarchy.

Joseph Villamil, who was born in New Orleans in 1789, took a part in the war of independence waged by the South American provinces, fought his way to celebrity and to the grade of General, and has lately been appointed Chargé d'Affaires by the Republic of Ecuador near the government of the United States.

Many other Louisianians, although having made themselves less conspicuous, rose to honorable distinction in the service of France, Spain and other powers; and the number of those who thus distinguished themselves becomes remarkable, when taken in connexion with the smallness of the colonial population from which they sprang.

In conclusion, I must call the attention of the reader to a singular anomaly—which is—that, with all the foul abuses and tyrannical practices with which it has been so long the general custom to reproach the government of Spain every where, her administration in Louisiana was as popular as any that ever existed in any part of the world; and I am persuaded that I can rely on the unanimous support of my contemporaries when I declare, that they scarcely ever met in Louisiana an individual, old enough to have lived under the Spanish government in the colony and judged of its bearing on the happiness of the people, who did not speak of it with affectionate respect, and describe those days of colonial rule as the golden age, which, with many, was the object of secret, and with others, of open regrets. Such a government would, of course, have been insupportable to us, but it is not hence to be inferred that it did not suit the tastes and feelings, and deserve the gratitude of our ancestors.

Thus ends the Colonial History of Louisiana. I have attempted to write it faithfully, accurately and impartially, with an unabating love for truth, and with an unselfish desire of serving in this way, if not in any other, the country to which I am bound by so many ties—not only by birth, education and habit, but also by so many endearing recollections of the past, and even so many family associations and traditions, which, for me, clothe with the charm almost of private interest the relation of public events in Louisiana.

THE END.

APPENDIX.

(Page 42.)

CERTIFICAT DU GOUVERNEUR AUBRI.

"Nous, Charles Aubri, chevalier de l'ordre royal et militaire de St. Louis, ancien commandant pour sa Majesté très chrétienne de la province de la Louisiane,—certifions que Monsieur Etienne de Gayarré, contador principal de cette province pour sa Majesté Catholique, arrivé dans cette colonie sous l'expédition commandée par M. Antoine de Ulloa, qui était venu pour en prendre possession, laquelle a été différée par divers accidents imprévus depuis le cinq mars mil sept cent soixante-six, jusqu' au dixhuit août dernier, qu'elle a été prise par son Excellence Don Alexandre O'Reilly, s'est toujours maintenu, comporté et représenté suivant l'état et la décence dû à sa place honorable, s'acquittant parfaitement de toutes les charges attachées à son emploi, selon l'expérience que j'en ai eue sous les yeux et les sentiments les plus distingués avec lesquels mon dit sieur de Ulloa a toujours traité avec lui, et, particulièrement depuis son absence de la fin d'octobre de l'année dernière jusqu' à ce jour, sur plusieurs affaires délicates concernant les services de leurs Majestés très Chrétienne et Catholique, en sa qualité de Contador, ayant même fait souvent les fonctions d'Intendant dans plusieurs occasions, en l'absence et longue maladie de M. Jean Joseph de Loyola, et aussi après sa mort ; accomplissant ponctuellement toutes les obligations du service des rois de France et d'Espagne, avec tout le zèle, l'application, et la conduite la plus régulière, qui lui ont attiré l'estime, l'amitié et l'approbation de tous les honnêtes gens ; en foi de quoi, je lui ai donné avec plaisir et toute la satisfaction possible, le présent pour lui servir et valoir partout où besoin sera. Fait double à la Nouvelle Orléans, le 23 novembre, 1769.

"AUBRI."

[TRANSLATION.]

CERTIFICATE OF GOVERNOR AUBRI.

"I, CHARLES AUBRI, knight of the royal and military order of St. Louis, late Governor of the Province of Louisiana for his most Christian Majesty, certify that M. Etienne de Gayarré, Chief Contador of this province for his Catholic Majesty, who came to this colony in the expedition commanded by M. Antoine de Ulloa, which was sent to take possession of it, but which ceremony had been deferred, owing to sundry unforeseen accidents, from March 5, 1766, to the 18th of August last past, when it was accomplished by his Excellency Don Alexander O'Reilly,—has always conducted himself in accordance with the requirements of his honorable station, faithfully discharging all the duties incumbent upon him,—and this I vouch for from my own personal observation, as well as from the exalted opinion which the said Sieur de Ulloa has always expressed concerning him,—and particularly since his absence from the end of last October to the present time upon various delicate affairs connected with the service of their most Christian and Catholic Majesties, in his office as Contador, having even often discharged the functions of Intendant on several occasions, during the absence and protracted sickness of M. Jean Joseph de Loyola, and also after his decease, punctually fulfilling all the requirements of the service of the Kings of France and Spain, with a zeal, application, and punctuality which have won for him the esteem, friendship and approbation of all honorable men. In testimony of which, with the greatest pleasure and satisfaction, I have given him these presents, that they may serve him in case of need. Given in duplicate at New Orleans, November 23, 1769

"AUBRI."

APPENDIX. 631

(Page 99.)

UNZAGA'S PROCLAMATION.

"WE DON LUIS DE UNZAGA, Colonel in the armies of his Majesty, and his Intendant and Governor-General in and for the province of Louisiana :

"Make it known that having, from experience, become acquainted with the different frauds and malpractices which are apt to be committed in all sales, exchanges, permutations, barters, and generally in all alienations concerning negroes, immoveables, and real estates, which are made clandestinely and in violation of the public faith, by a simple deed in writing under private seal, whereby the inhabitants of this province are greatly distressed, their rights put in jeopardy, and the administration of justice reduced to a state of confusion ; and wishing, first, to remedy such pernicious abuses, and next, to establish good order in this commonwealth and to govern it as are all the other possessions of his Majesty :

"We order and decree, that no person, whatever be his or her rank or condition, shall henceforth sell, alienate, buy, or accept as a donation or otherwise, any negroes, plantations, houses and any kind of sea-craft, except it be by a deed executed before a Notary Public ; to which contracts and acts of sale and alienation shall be annexed a certificate of the Registrar of Mortgages; that all other acts made under any other form shall be null and void, and as if they had never been made; that the sellers and buyers shall have no right to the things thus sold, bought or exchanged ; that they cannot acquire any just and legitimate possession thereof ; and that in cases of fraud, all parties therein concerned shall be prosecuted with all the severity of the law ; that the Notary who shall make a bad use of the confidence reposed in him by the public and of the faith put in the fidelity of his archives, and who shall have the audacity to antedate or postdate the deeds executed before him, shall, for this delinquency, be declared unworthy of the office he holds, and shall be condemned to undergo all the penalties provided for such a case ; and said Notary, should he forget to annex to his acts the certificate of the Registrar of Mortgages as aforesaid, shall be proceeded against according to the circumstances of the case ; and that no one shall plead ignorance of this proclamation we order and decree, that it be promulgated with the beat of the drum ; and that copies thereof certified by the Secretary of the Government and by the Secretary of the Cabildo be posted up at the usual places in this town, and sent to all the posts dependent on this Government.

"Given at the Government-House, on the 3rd of November, 1770.

"LUIS DE UNZAGA."

(Page 398.)

REGULATIONS OF INTENDANT MORALES REGARDING GRANTS OF LAND.

" 1. To each newly-arrived family, à chaque famille nouvelle, who are possessed of the necessary qualifications to be admitted among the number of cultivators of these provinces, and who have obtained the permission of the Government to establish themselves on a place which they have chosen, there shall be granted, *for once*, if it is on the bank of the Mississippi, four, six, or eight arpents in front on the river, by the ordinary depth of forty arpents; and if it is at any other place, the quantity which they shall be judged capable to cultivate, and which shall be deemed necessary for pasture for their beasts, in proportion and according to the number of which the family is composed; understanding that the concession is never to exceed eight hundred arpents in superficies.

" 2. To obtain the said concessions, if they are asked for in this city, the permission which has been obtained to establish themselves in the place from the Governor, ought to accompany the petition; and if, in any of the posts, the Commandant at the same time will state that the lands asked for are vacant, and belong to the domain, and that the petitioner has obtained permission of the Government to establish himself; and referring to the date of the letter or advice they have received.

" 3. Those who obtain concessions on the bank of the river, ought to make, in the first year of their possession, levees sufficient to prevent the inundation of the waters, and canals sufficient to drain off the water when the river is high; they shall be held, in addition, to make, and keep in good order, a public highway, which ought to be at least thirty feet wide, and have bridges of fifteen feet over the canals or ditches which the road crosses; which regulations ought to be observed, according to the usages of the respective districts, by all persons to whom lands are granted, in whatever part they are obtained.

"4. The new settlers who have obtained lands shall be equally obliged to clear and put in cultivation, in the precise time of three years, all the front of their concessions, for the depth of at least two arpents, under the penalty of having the lands granted .reunited to the domain, if this condition is not complied with. The Commandants and Syndics will watch that what is enjoined in this and the preceding article, be strictly observed; and occasionally inform the Intendant of what they have remarked, well understanding that in case of default they will be responsible to his Majesty.

"5. If a tract of land belonging to minors remain without being cleared, or as much of it as the regulations require; and that the bank, the road, the ditches, and the bridges are not made, the Commandant or Syndic of the district will certify from whom the fault has arisen; if it is in the guardian, he will urge him to put it in order; and, if he fails, he shall give an account of it; but, if the fault arises from want of means of the minor to defray the expense, the Commandant or Syndic shall address a statement of it to the intendancy, to the end that sale of it may be ordered for the benefit of the minor, to whom alone this privilege is allowed; if, in the space of six months, any purchaser presents himself; if not, it shall be granted gratis to any person asking it, or sold for the benefit of the treasury.

"6. During the said term of three years, no person shall sell or dispose of the land which has been granted to him, nor shall he ever after the term, if he has failed to comply with the conditions contained in the preceding article; and to avoid abuses and surprise in this respect, we declare that all sales made without the consent of the intendancy, in writing, shall be null and of no effect; which consent shall not be granted until they have examined, with scrupulous attention, if the conditions have or have not been fulfilled.

"7. To avoid, for the future, the litigations and confusion of which we have examples every day, we have also judged it very necessary that the Notaries of this city, and the Commandants of posts, shall not take any acknowledgment of conveyances of land obtained by concession; unless the seller (grantor) presents and delivers to the buyer the title which he has obtained, and in addition, being careful to insert in the deed the metes and bounds, and other descriptions, which result from the title, and the *procès-verbal* of the survey which ought to accompany it.

"8. In case that the small depth of the points, upon which the land on the river is generally formed, prevent the granting of forty arpents, according to usage, there shall be given a greater quantity in front to compensate it; or, if no other person asks the concession, or to purchase it, it shall be divided equally between the persons nearest to it, who may repair the banks, roads, and bridges, in the manner before prescribed.

"9. Although the King renounces the possession of the lands sold, distributed, or conceded, in his name, those to whom they are granted or sold ought to be apprised that his Majesty reserves the right of taking from the forests known here under the name of cypress woods, all the wood which may be necessary for his use, and more especially which he may want for the navy, in the same manner and with the same liberty that the undertakers have enjoyed to this time; but this, notwithstanding, they are not to suppose themselves authorized to take more than is necessary, nor to make use of or split those which are cut down and found unsuitable.

"10. In the posts of Opelousas and Attakapas, the greatest quantity of land that can be conceded, shall be one league front by the same quantity in depth; and when forty arpents cannot be obtained in depth, a half league may be granted; and, for a general rule, it is established, that, to obtain, in said posts, a half league in front by the same quantity in depth, the petitioner must be owner of one hundred head of cattle, some horses and sheep, and two slaves, and also in proportion for a larger tract, without the power, however, of exceeding the quantity before mentioned.

"11. As much as it is possible, and the local situation will permit, no interval shall be left between concessions; because it is very advantageous that the establishments touch, as much for the inhabitants, who can lend each other mutual support, as for the more easy administration of justice, and the observance of rules of police, indispensable in all places, but more especially in new establishments.

"12. If, notwithstanding what is before written, marshy lands, or other causes, shall make it necessary to leave some vacant lands, the Commandants and Syndics will take care that the inhabitants of the district alone may take wood enough for their use only, well understanding they shall not take more; or, if any individual of any other post, shall attempt to get wood, or cut fire-wood without having obtained the permission of this intendancy, besides the indemnity which he shall be held to pay the treasury for the damage sustained, he shall be condemned, for the first time, to the payment of a fine of twenty-five dollars; twice that sum for the second offence; and, for the third offence, shall be put in prison, according as the offence may be more or less aggravated; the said fines shall be divided between the treasury, the Judge, and the Informer.

"13. The new settler, to whom land has been granted in one settlement, cannot obtain another concession without having previously proven that he had possessed the first during three years, and fulfilled all the conditions prescribed.

"14. The changes occasioned by the current of the river, are often the cause of one part of a concession becoming useless, so that we have examples of proprietors pretending to abandon and re-unite to the domain a part of the most expensive, for keeping up the banks, the roads, the ditches, &c., and willing to reserve only that which is good; and seeing that, unless some remedy is provided for this abuse, the greatest mischief must result to the neighbours, we declare that the treasury will not admit of an abandonment or re-union to the domain of any part of the land the owner wishes to get rid of, unless the abandonment comprehends the whole limits included in the concession or act in virtue of which he owns the land he wishes to abandon.

"15. All concessions shall be given in the name of the King, by the General-Intendant of this province, who shall order the Surveyor-General, or one particularly named by him, to make the survey and mark the land, by fixing bounds, not only in front, but also in the rear; this (survey) ought to be done in the presence of the Commandant or Syndic of the district and of two of the neighbors; and these four shall sign the *procès-verbal* which shall be drawn up by the Surveyor.

"16. The said *procès-verbal*, with a certified copy of the same, shall be sent by the Surveyor to the Intendant, to the end that, on the original, there be delivered, by the consent of the King's Attorney, the necessary title paper; to this will be annexed the certified copy forwarded by the Surveyor. The original shall be deposited in the office of the Secretary of the Treasury, and care shall be taken to make annually a book of all which have been sent, with an alphabetical list, to be the more useful when it is necessary to have recourse to it, and for greater security, to the end that, at all times, and against all accidents, the documents which shall be wanted, can be found. The Surveyor shall also have another book, numbered, in which the *procès-verbal* of the survey he makes shall be recorded, and, as well on the original, which ought to be deposited on record, as on the copy intended to be annexed to the title, he shall note the folio of the book in which he has enregistered the figurative plat of survey.

"17. In the office of the finances there shall also be a book, numbered, where the titles of concessions shall be recorded; in which, beside the ordinary clauses, mention shall be made of the folio of the book in which they are transcribed. There must also be a note taken in the contadoria (or chamber of accounts) of the army and finances, and that under the penalty of being void. The chamber of accounts shall also have a like book; and, at the time of taking the note, shall cite the folio of the book where it is recorded.

"18. Experience proves that a great number of those who have asked for land think themselves the legal owners of it; those who have obtained the first decree, by which the Surveyor is ordered to measure it, and to put them in possession; others, after the survey has been made, have neglected to ask the title for the property; and, as like abuses, continuing for a longer time, will augment the confusion and disorder which will necessarily result, we declare that no one of those who have obtained the said decrees, notwithstanding, in virtue of them, the survey has taken place, and that they have been put in possession, can be regarded as owners of land until their real titles are delivered, completed with all the formalities before recited.

"19. All those who possess lands in virtue of formal titles given by their Excellencies the Governors of this province, since the epoch when it came under the power of the Spanish; and those who possessed them in the time when it belonged to France, so far from being interrupted, shall, on the contrary, be protected and maintained in their possessions.

"20. Those who, without the title or possession mentioned in the preceding article, are found occupying lands, shall be driven therefrom, as from property belonging to the crown; but, if they have occupied the same more than ten years, a compromise will be admitted to those who are considered as owners, that is to say, they shall not be deprived of their lands. Always that, after information, and summary procedure, and with the intervention of the Procureur of the King, at the board of the treasury, they shall be obliged to pay a just and moderate retribution, calculated according to the extent of the lands, their situation, and other circumstances, and the price of estimation for once paid into the royal treasury. The titles to property will be delivered, on referring to that which has resulted from the proceedings.

APPENDIX. 637

"21. Those who are found in a situation expressed in the 18th article, if they have not cleared nor done any work upon the land they consider themselves proprietors of by virtue of the first decree of the Government, not being of the number of those who have been admitted in the class of new comers, in being deprived or admitted to compromise, in the manner explained in the preceding article : if they are of that class, they shall observe what is ordered in the article following.

"22. In the precise and peremptory term of six months, counting from the day when this regulation shall be published in each post, all those who occupy lands without titles from the Governor, and those who, in having obtained a certain number of arpents, have seized a greater quantity, ought to make it known, either to have their titles made out, if there are any, or to be admitted to a compromise, or to declare that the said lands belong to the domain, if they have not been occupied more than ten years; understanding, if it passes the said term, if they are instructed by other ways, they will not obtain either title or compromise.

"23. Those who give information of lands occupied, after the expiration of the term fixed in the preceding article, shall have for their reward the one-fourth part of the price for which they are sold, or obtained, by way of compromise ; and, if desirable, he shall have the preference, either by compromise, at the price of appraisement, and there shall be made a deduction of one-fourth, as informer.

"24. As it is impossible, considering all the local circumstances, that all the vacant lands belonging to the domain, should be sold by auction, as it is ordained by the law 15th, title 12th, book 4th, of the collection of the laws of these kingdoms, the sale shall be made according as it shall be demanded, with the intervention of the King's Attorney for the board of finances, for the price they shall be taxed, to those who wish to purchase ; understanding, if the purchasers have not ready money to pay, it shall be lawful for them to purchase the said lands at redeemable quit-rent, during which they shall pay the five per cent. yearly.

"25. Besides the moderate price which the land ought to be taxed, the purchasers shall be held to pay down the right of *media annata*, or half-year's, to be remitted to Spain, which, according to the custom of Havana, founded on law, is reduced to two and a half per cent. on the price of estimation, and made 18 per cent. on the sum, by the said two and a half per cent.; they shall also be obliged to pay down the fees of the Surveyor and Notary.

"26. The sales of land shall be made subject to the same condition and charges of banks, roads, ditches and bridges, contained in the preceding article. But the purchasers are not subject to lose their lands, if, in the three first years, they do not fulfil the said conditions. Commandants and Syndics shall oblige them to put themselves within the rule, begin to perform the conditions in a reasonable term, and, if they do not do it, the said work shall be done at the cost of the purchasers.

"27. Care shall be taken to observe in the said sales, that which is recommended in the 11th article, seeing the advantages and utility which result from consolidating the establishments always when it is practicable.

"28. The titles to the property of lands which are sold, or granted by way of compromise, shall be issued by the General-Intendant, who, after the price of estimation is fixed, and of the *media annata* (half-year's) rent, or quit-rent, the said price of estimation shall have been paid into the treasury, shall put it in writing according to the result of the proceeding which has taken place, with the intervention of the King's Attorney.

"29. The said procedure shall be deposited in the office of the finance, and the title be transcribed in another book, intended for the recording of deeds and grants of land, in the same manner as is ordered by the 17th Article, concerning gratuitous concessions. The principal chamber of accounts shall also have a separate book, to take a note of the titles issued for sales and grants under compromise.

"30. The fees of the Surveyor, in every case comprehended in the present regulation, shall be proportionate to the labor and that which it has been customary until this time to pay. Those of the Secretary of Finances, unless there has been extraordinary labor, and where the new settlers are not poor [for in this case he is not to exact any thing of them] shall be five dollars; and this shall include the recording and other formalities prescribed, and those of the Appraisers, and of the Interpreter, if, on any occasion, there is reason to employ him to translate papers, take declarations or other acts, shall be regulated by the provincial tariff.

"31. Indians who possess lands within the limits of the Government, shall not, in any manner, be disturbed; on the contrary, they shall be protected and supported; and to this, the Commandants, Syndics, and Surveyors, ought to pay the greatest attention, to conduct themselves in consequence.

"32. The granting or selling of any lands shall not be proceeded in without formal information having been previously received that they are vacant; and, to avoid injurious mistakes, we premise that, beside the signature of the Commandant or Syndic of the district, this information ought to be joined by that of the Surveyor, and of two of the neighbors well understanding. If, notwithstanding this necessary precaution, it shall be found that the land has another owner besides the claimant, and that there is sufficient reason to restore it to him, the Commandant or Syndic, the Surveyor, and the neighbors who have signed the information, shall indemnify him for the losses he has suffered.

"33. As far as it may be practicable, the inhabitants must endeavor that the petitions presented by them, to ask for lands, be written in the Spanish language; in which ought, also, to be written the advice or information which the Commandants are to give. In the posts where this is not practicable, the ancient usage shall be followed.

"34. All the lots or seats belonging to the domain, which are found vacant, either in this city, or boroughs, or villages, already established, or which may be established, shall be sold for ready money, with all the formalities prescribed in Article the twenty-fourth, and others, which concern the sale of lands.

"35. The owners of lots or places, which have been divided, as well those in front, as towards the N. E. and S. W. extremities, N. E. and S. W. shall, within three months, present to the intendancy the titles which they have obtained; to the end that, in examining the same, if any essential thing is found wanting it may be supplied, and they assured of their property in a legal way.

"36. The same thing must be done before the sub-delegates of Mobile and Pensacola, for those who have obtained grants for lots in these respective establishments; to the end that this intendancy, being instructed thereon, may order what it shall judge most convenient to indemnify the royal treasury, without doing wrong to the owner.

"37. In the office of the comptroller, contadoria of the army, or chambers of accounts of this province, and other boards under the jurisdiction of this intendancy, an account shall be kept of the amount of sales or grants of lands, to instruct his Majesty every year what this branch of the royal revenue produces, according as it is ordered in the thirteenth article of the ordinance of the King, of the 15th of October, 1754.

"38. The Commandants, or Syndics, in their respective districts, are charged with the collection of the amount of the taxes or rents laid on lands; for this purpose the papers and necessary documents are to be sent to them; and they ought to forward annually, to the general treasury, the sums they have collected, to the end that acquittances, clothed with the usual formalities of law, may be delivered to them."

(Page 524.)

No. 1.

TREATY AND CONVENTIONS BETWEEN THE UNITED STATES AND THE FRENCH REPUBLIC.*

" *Treaty between the French Republic and the United States, concerning the Cession of Louisiana, signed at Paris the* 30th *of April,* 1803

" THE President of the United States of America, and the First Consul of the French Republic, in the name of the French people, desiring to remove all source of misunderstanding relative to objects of discussion, mentioned in the second and fifth articles of the convention of the 8th Vendemiaire, an 9 (30th of September, 1800), relative to the rights claimed by the United States, in virtue of the treaty concluded at Madrid the 27th of October, 1795, between his Catholic Majesty and the said United States, and willing to strengthen the union and friendship which at the time of the said convention was happily re-established between the two nations, have respectively named their plenipotentiaries; to wit, the President of the United States of America, by and with the advice and consent of the Senate of the said States, Robert R. Livingston, Minister Plenipotentiary of the United States, and James Monroe, Minister Plenipotentiary and Envoy Extraordinary of the said States, near the government of the French Republic; and the First Consul, in the name of the French people, the French citizen Barbé Marbois

* The treaty and convention are given from the American copies, and the United States are consequently named first in them.—TRANS.

APPENDIX. 641

Minister of the Public Treasury, who, after having respectively exchanged their full powers, have agreed to the following articles:—

"ART. 1st. Whereas, by the article the third of the treaty concluded at St. Ildephonso, the 9th Vendemiaire, an 9 (1st October, 1800), between the First Consul of the French Republic and His Catholic Majesty, it was agreed as follows: 'His Catholic Majesty promises and engages, on his part, to retrocede to the French Republic, six months after the full and entire execution of the conditions and stipulations herein relative to his Royal Highness the Duke of Parma, the colony or province of Louisiana, with the same extent that it now has in the hands of Spain, and that it had when France possessed it; and such as it should be after the treaties subsequently entered into between Spain and other States.' And, whereas, in pursuance of the treaty, and particularly of the third article, the French Republic has an incontestable title to the domain, and to the possession of the said territory: The First Consul of the French Republic, desiring to give to the United States a strong proof of his friendship, doth hereby cede to the said United States, in the name of the French Republic, for ever and in full sovereignty, the said territory, with all its rights and appurtenances, as fully and in the same manner as they had been acquired by the French Republic in virtue of the above-mentioned treaty concluded with his Catholic Majesty.

"ART. 2d. In the cession made by the preceding article are included the adjacent islands belonging to Louisiana, all public lots and squares, vacant lands, and all public buildings, fortifications, barracks, and other edifices which are not private property. The archives, papers, and documents, relative to the domain and sovereignty of Louisiana and its dependencies, will be left in the possession of the commissaries of the United States, and copies will be afterwards given in due form to the magistrates and municipal officers of such of the said papers and documents as may be necessary to them.

"ART. 3d. The inhabitants of the ceded territory shall be incorporated in the Union of the United States, and admitted as soon as possible, according to the principles of the Federal Constitution, to the enjoyment of all the rights, advantages and immunities of citizens of the United States; and in the mean time they shall be maintained and protected in the free enjoyment of their liberty, property, and the religion which they profess.

"ART. 4th. There shall be sent by the government of France a Commissary to Louisiana, to the end that he do every act necessary, as well to receive from the officers of his Catholic Majesty the said country and its dependencies, in the name of the French Republic, if it has not been already done, as to transmit it in the name of the French Republic to the commissary or agent of the United States.

"ART. 5th. Immediately after the ratification of the present treaty by the President of the United States, and in case that of the First Consul shall have been previously obtained, the Commissary of the French Republic shall remit all the military posts of New Orleans and other parts of the ceded territory, to the Commissary or Commissaries named by the President to take possession; the troops, whether of France or Spain, who may be there, shall cease to occupy any military post from the time of taking possession, and shall be embarked as soon as possible, in the course of three months after the ratification of this treaty.

"ART. 6th. The United States promise to execute such treaties and articles as may have been agreed between Spain and the tribes and nations of Indians, until, by mutual consent of the United States and the said tribes or nations, other suitable articles shall have been agreed upon.

"ART. 7th. As it is reciprocally advantageous to the commerce of France and the United States to encourage the communication of both nations for a limited time in the country ceded by the present treaty, until general arrangements relative to the commerce of both nations may be agreed on, it has been agreed between the contracting parties, that the French ships coming directly from France or any of her colonies, loaded only with the produce or manufactures of France or her said colonies; and the ships of Spain coming directly from Spain or any of her colonies, loaded only with the produce or manufactures of Spain or her colonies, shall be admitted during the space of twelve years in the ports of New Orleans, and in all other legal ports of entry within the ceded territory, in the same manner as the ships of the United States coming directly from France or Spain or any of their colonies, without being subject to any other or greater duty on merchandise, or other or greater tonnage than those paid by the citizens of the United States.

"During the space of time above-mentioned, no other nation shall have a right to the same privileges in the ports of the ceded territory: the twelve years shall commence three months after the exchange of ratifications, if it shall take place in France, or three months after it shall have been notified at Paris to the French government, if it shall take place in the United States: it is, however, well understood that the object of the above article is to favor the manufactures, commerce, freight, and navigation of France and of Spain, so far as relates to the importations that the French and Spanish shall make into the said ports of the United States, without in any sort affecting the regulations that the United States may make concerning the exportation of the produce and merchandise of the United States, or any right they may have to make such regulations.

"ART. 8th. In future, and for ever after the expiration of the twelve years, the ships of France shall be treated upon the footing of the most favored nations in the ports above-mentioned.

"ART. 9th. The particular convention, signed this day by the respective Ministers, having for its object to provide for the payment of debts due to the citizens of the United States by the French Republic, prior to the 30th of September, 1800 (8th Vendemiaire, an 9), is approved, and to have its execution in the same manner as if it had been inserted in the present treaty; and it shall be ratified in the same form, and in the same time, so that the one shall not be ratified distinct from the other.

"Another particular convention, signed at the same date as the present treaty, relative to the definitive rule between the contracting parties, is in the like manner approved, and will be ratified in the same form, and in the same time, and jointly.

"ART. 10th. The present treaty shall be ratified in good and due form, and the ratifications shall be exchanged in the space of six months after the date of the signature by the Ministers Plenipotentiary, or sooner if possible.

"In faith whereof, the respective Plenipotentiaries have signed these articles in the French and English languages; declaring, nevertheless, that the present treaty was originally agreed to in the French language; and have thereunto put their seals.

"Done at Paris, the tenth day of Floreal, in the eleventh year of the French Republic, and the 30th of April, 1803.

"ROBERT R. LIVINGSTON
"JAMES MONROE,
"BARBÉ MARBOIS."

No. 2.

"*Convention between the United States of America and the French Republic, of the same date with the preceding Treaty.*"

THE President of the United States of America and the First Consul of the French Republic, in the name of the French people, in consequence of the treaty of cession of Louisiana, which has been signed this day, wishing to regulate definitively every thing which has relation to the said cession, have authorized to this effect the Plenipotentiaries, that is to say, the President of the United States has, by and with the advice and consent of the Senate of the said States, nominated for their Plenipotentiaries, Robert R. Livingston, Minister Plenipotentiary of the United States, and James Monroe, Minister Plenipotentiary and Envoy Extraordinary of the said United States, near the government of the French Republic; and the First Consul of the French Republic, in the name of the French people, has named as Plenipotentiary of the said Republic, the French citizen Barbé Marbois, who, in virtue of their full powers, which have been exchanged this day, have agreed to the following articles:

" ART. 1st. The Government of the United States engages to pay to the French Government, in the manner specified in the following articles, the sum of sixty millions of francs, independent of the sum which shall be fixed by another convention for the payment of debts due by France to citizens of the United States.

" ART. 2d. For the payment of the sum of sixty millions of francs, mentioned in the preceding article, the United States shall create a stock of eleven millions two hundred and fifty thousand dollars, bearing an interest of six per cent. per annum, payable half-yearly in London, Amsterdam, or Paris, amounting by the half-year to three hundred and thirty-seven thousand five hundred dollars, according to the proportions which shall be determined by the French Government, to be paid at either place; the principal of the said stock to be reimbursed at the treasury of the United States, in annual payments of not less than three millions of dollars each; of which the first payment shall commence fifteen years after the date of the exchange of ratifications: this stock shall be transferred to the Government of France, or to such person or persons as shall be authorized to receive it, in three months at most after the exchange of the ratifications of this treaty, and after Louisiana shall be taken possession of in the name of the Government of the United States.

"It is farther agreed, that if the French Government should be desirous of disposing of the said stock to receive the capital in Europe, at shorter terms, that its measures for that purpose shall be taken so as to favor, in the greatest degree possible, the credit of the United States, and to raise to the highest price the said stock.

"ART. 3d. It is agreed that the dollar of the United States, specified in the present convention, shall be fixed at five francs $\frac{3333}{10000}$, or five livres eight sous tournois. The present convention shall be ratified in good and due form, and the ratifications shall be exchanged in the space of six months, to date from this day, or sooner if possible.

"In faith of which, the respective Plenipotentiaries have signed the above articles both in the French and English languages; declaring, nevertheless, that the present treaty has been originally agreed on and written in the French language; to which they have hereunto affixed their seals.

"Done at Paris, the tenth of Floreal, eleventh year of the French Republic (30th April, 1803).

"ROBERT R. LIVINGSTON, (L.S.)
"JAMES MONROE, (L.S.)
"BARBÉ MARBOIS, (L.S.)"

No. 3.

"*Convention between the United States of America and the French Republic, also of the same date with the Louisiana Treaty.*

"THE President of the United States of America and the First Consul of the French Republic, in the name of the French people, having by a treaty of this date terminated all difficulties relative to Louisiana, and established on a solid foundation the friendship which unites the two nations, and being desirous, in compliance with the second and fifth articles of the convention of the 8th Vendemiaire, ninth year of the French Republic (30th September, 1800), to secure the payment of the sum due by France to the citizens of the United States, have respectively nominated as Plenipotentiaries, that is to say: the President of the United States of America, by and with the advice and consent of the Senate, Robert R. Livingston, Minister Plenipotentiary, and James Monroe, Minister Plenipotentiary and Envoy Extraordinary of the said States, near the government of the French Republic, and the First Consul, in the name of the French people, the French citizen Barbé Marbois, Minister of the Public Treasury; who, after having exchanged their full powers, have agreed to the following articles:—

"ART. 1st. The debts due by France to the citizens of the United States, contracted before the 8th Vendemiaire, ninth year of the French Republic (30th September, 1800), shall be paid according to the following regulations, with interest at six per cent., to commence from the period when the accounts and vouchers were presented to the French Government.

"ART. 2d. The debts provided for by the preceding article are those whose result is comprised in the conjectural note annexed to the present convention, and which, with the interest, cannot exceed the sum of twenty millions of francs. The claims comprised in the said note, which fall within the exceptions of the following articles, shall not be admitted to the benefit of this provision.

"ART. 3d. The principal and interest of the said debts shall be discharged by the United States by orders drawn by their Minister Plenipotentiary on their treasury; these orders shall be payable sixty days after the exchange of the ratifications of the treaty and the conventions signed this day, and after possession shall be given of Louisiana by the Commissioners of France to those of the United States.

"ART. 4th. It is expressly agreed, that the preceding articles shall comprehend no debts but such as are due to citizens of the United States, who have been and are yet creditors of France for supplies, embargoes, and for prizes made at sea, in which the appeal has been properly lodged within the time mentioned in the said convention of the 8th Vendemiaire, ninth year (30th September, 1800).

"ART. 5th. The preceding articles shall apply only, 1st, to captures of which the Council of Prizes shall have ordered restitution; it being well understood that the claimant cannot have recourse to the United States otherwise than he might have had to the Government of the French Republic, and only in case of the insufficiency of the captors: 2d, the debts mentioned in the said fifth article of the convention, contracted before the 8th Vendemiaire, an 9 (30th September, 1800), the payment of which has been heretofore claimed of the actual Government of France, and for which the creditors have a right to the protection of the United States; the said fifth article does not comprehend prizes whose condemnation has been or shall be confirmed: it is the express intention of the contracting parties not to extend the benefit of the present convention to reclamations of American citizens, who shall have established houses of commerce in France, England, or other countries than the United States, in partnership with foreigners, and who by that reason and the nature of their commerce ought to be regarded as domiciliated in the places where such houses exist. All agreements and bargains concerning merchandise, which shall not be the property of American citizens, are equally excepted from the benefit of the said convention, saving, however, to such persons their claims in like manner as if this treaty had not been made.

"ART. 6th. And that the different questions which may arise under the preceding article may be fairly investigated, the Ministers Plenipotentiary of the United States shall name three persons, who shall act from the present and provisionally, and who shall have full power to examine, without removing the documents, all the accounts of the different claims already liquidated by the bureau established for this purpose by the French Republic; and to ascertain whether they belong to the classes designated by the present convention and the principles established in it, or if they are not in one of its exceptions, and on their certificate, declaring that the debt is due to an American citizen or his representative, and that it existed before the 8th Vendemiaire, ninth year (30th September, 1800), the creditor shall be entitled to an order on the treasury of the United States, in the manner prescribed by the third article.

"ART. 7th. The same agents shall likewise have power, without removing the documents, to examine the claims which are prepared for verification, and to certify those which ought to be admitted by uniting the necessary qualifications, and not being comprised in the exceptions contained in the present convention.

"ART. 8th. The same agents shall likewise examine the claims which are not prepared for liquidation, and certify in writing those which, in their judgments, ought to be admitted to liquidation.

"ART. 9th. In proportion as the debts mentioned in these articles shall be admitted, they shall be discharged with interest at six per cent., by the treasury of the United States.

"ART. 10th. And that no debt which shall not have the qualifications above-mentioned, and that no unjust or exorbitant demand may be admitted, the commercial agent of the United States at Paris, or such other agent as the Minister Plenipotentiary of the United States shall think proper to nominate, shall assist at the operations of the bureau, and co-operate in the examination of the claims; and if this agent shall be of opinion that any debt is not completely proved, or if he shall judge that it is not comprised in the principles of the fifth article above-mentioned; and if notwithstanding his opinion, the bureau established by the French Government should think that it ought to be liquidated, he shall transmit his observations to the board established by the United States, who, without removing the documents, shall make a complete examination of the debt and vouchers which support it, and report the result to the Minister of the United States. The Minister of the United States shall transmit his observations, in all such cases, to the Minister of the Treasury of the French Republic, on whose report the French Government shall decide definitively in every case.

"The rejection of any claim shall have no other effect than to exempt the United States from the payment of it, the French Government reserving to itself the right to decide definitively on such claim so far as it concerns itself.

"ART. 11th. Every necessary decision shall be made in the course of a year, to commence from the exchange of ratifications, and no reclamation shall be admitted afterwards.

"ART. 12th. In case of claims for debts contracted by the Government of France with citizens of the United States, since the 8th Vendemiaire, ninth year (30th September, 1800), not being comprised in this convention, they may be pursued, and the payment demanded in the same manner as if it had not been made.

"ART. 13th. The present convention shall be ratified in good and due form, and the ratifications shall be exchanged in six months from the date of the signature of the Ministers Plenipotentiary, or sooner if possible.

"In faith of which, the respective Ministers Plenipotentiary have signed the above articles, both in the French and English languages declaring, nevertheless, that the present treaty has been originally agreed on and written in the French language; to which they have hereunto affixed their seals.

"Done at Paris, the tenth day of Floreal, eleventh year of the French Republic (30th April, 1803).

"ROBERT R. LIVINGSTON, (L.S.)
"JAMES MONROE, (L.S.)
"BARBE MARBOIS, (L.S.)"

www.ingramcontent.com/pod-product-compliance
Lightning Source LLC
Chambersburg PA
CBHW022044160426
43198CB00008B/121